Implications of the External Factors on the Organization

The five critical design challenges as mentioned by Kates and Galbraith (2007), based on which they built the STAR Model (Kates & Galbraith, 2007) for the purpose of categorizing the implications have been used to explain the effects in an organization. These five design challenges, viz., strategy, structure, process, rewards, and people, are the most common and most relevant ones in organization designing. I have purportedly used the concepts of organization designing for explaining the implications, as they are well-defined. Challenges imposed on strategy, structure, processes, rewards, and people by the external changes, are my focus area of interest here. In order for organizations to cope effectively and regain control, they need to re-design the organization, and hence the concept of organization design is of importance here. Organization design is defined as "*the deliberate process of configuring structures, processes, reward systems, and people practices to create an effective organization capable of achieving the business strategy*" (Kates & Galbraith, 2007, p. 1). Organization designing is focused on creating a stable structure being in a relatively stable state (Emelah & Enyia, 2018; Waring, 2016), which is also the desired goal here. The STAR Model is one of the most widely used, accepted, and proven model by practitioners across organizations, for effective organization designing, and hence, I have also used its concepts in this paper. In the sub-sections below, I shall discuss the impacts on each factor, in detail, within the context of this paper.

Strategy

Organizations have moved toward building resilience, business continuity and agility in this pandemic situation. Focus has been on maintaining continuity, especially with the economic recession scenario, predicted worse than the 2008 financial crisis, the severest since the World War II levels.[2] Many businesses have been forced to close, with unprecedented disruption of commerce in most industry sectors. Apart from short-term

[2] Retrieved on 4 October 2020 at 1:00 hrs from https://www.worldbank.org/en/news/press-release/2020/06/08/covid-19-to-plunge-global-economy-into-worst-recession-since-world-war-ii.

challenges like health and safety measures, supply-chain, workforce retention/retrenchment, cash flow, sales, and marketing, companies have to face the additional woe of consumers becoming more averse to spending, thanks to the job losses, pay cuts, and uncertain future created due to the economic recession, across nations across the world. This can best be explained by the contingency theory perspective, as organizations are required to adapt and change according to the changed environment. Also, the change itself is a radical change, due to its suddenness and uncertainty involved (Gersick, 1991).

In order to maintain continuity, many organizations opted for, even imposed mandatory work-from-home policies for their employees, at wherever and whichever role possible. Other roles temporarily shut down. In fact, new-age tech stalwarts like Google, Facebook, Amazon have mandated one-year work-from-home mandates, with Twitter going so far as to even provide for life-time work-from-home options, should the employees so desire.[3] In India, too, companies like Citibank, BCG, HUL, KPMG, RPG Group, Cognizant, Infosys, Philips, Pfizer, Pidilite and TCS[4] to name a few, have mandated that only essential workers are required to be physically present in the office premises. 85% of the IT workforce in India is working from home, with MHA (India) extending work-form-home mandated till 31 December 2020 for IT & BPO companies.[5] A survey conducted in July in India (by Lenovo)[6] revealed that the majority of the people also preferred to work-from-home. While such

[3] Retrieved on 4 October 2020 at 00:40 hrs from https://indianexpress.com/article/technology/social/twitter-employees-work-from-home-forever-covid-19-6407724/.

[4] Retrieved on 1 September 2020 at 22:00 hrs from https://economictimes.indiatimes.com/news/company/corporate-trends/playing-it-safe-amidst-covid-19-work-from-homes-working-so-india-inc-wants-it-to-stay/articleshow/77252879.cms?utm_source=contentofinterest&utm_medium=text&utm_campaign=cppst.

[5] Retrieved on 10 September 2020 at 1400 hrs from https://www.india.com/news/india/work-from-home-for-it-companies-till-december-31-what-does-this-mean-4091309/.

[6] Retrieved on 12 April 2020 at 20:00 hrs from https://www.businessnewsdaily.com/15259-working-from-home-more-productive.html#:~:text=Working%20From%20Home%20Increases%20Productivity&text=According%20to%20one%20study%2C%20remote,weeks%20of%20work%20per%20year.&text=One%20of%20the%20most%20effective,taking%20breaks%20throughout%20the%20day.

surveys revealed that remote working increases productivity levels,[7] they also revealed that respondents were more stressed and struggled to maintain work-life balance, due to increased role conflict, inability to manage time, as well as demarcate work and life.

This decision of the organizations, that is, to apply work-from-home, draws support from various organizational theories. As per the transaction cost economics theory (Williamson, 1979, 1986) removing traditional work setup decreases the infrastructural and administrative costs associated with physical offices (overhead costs), while increasing expenditures in supporting technologies (cybersecurity, smooth internet connection, devices, etc.). In addition, the productivity of employees also increases due to such flexible work arrangements (remote, WFH), as substantiated by various studies (Baltes et al., 1999; Bloom, 2014; Mcnall et al., 2009), even during the pandemic, as supported by a study conducted by Lenovo in India.[8] Other benefits include companies having access to a bigger and wider talent pool to hire from, unrestricted from geographic limitations, and more positive image (supportive organization) with more satisfied employees (Baltes et al., 1999; Chen et al., 2018; Mcnall et al., 2009).

Structure

The traditional hierarchical structure is affected due to the work-from-home mandates. Majority of the companies across industries, barring the new-age ones preferred to have their workforce under a traditional office setup, with formal hierarchy and supervision structure in place. While in the context of the STAR Model, the authors spoke about units formed around functions, products, geographies, or customers, and suggested formal hierarchy which enables unhindered management and decision making and communication, the covid19 pandemic situation has changed the scenario quite drastically, and also permanently. The strategic decision to work-from-home, to retain business continuity in the times of

[7] Retrieved on 10 September 2020 at 14:05 hrs from https://timesofindia.indiatimes.com/life-style/relationships/work/work-from-home-survey-66-employees-feel-their-work-productivity-has-gone-up-considerably/articleshow/77649776.cms.

[8] Retrieved on 10 September 2020 at 14:05 hrs from https://timesofindia.indiatimes.com/life-style/relationships/work/work-from-home-survey-66-employees-feel-their-work-productivity-has-gone-up-considerably/articleshow/77649776.cms.

lockdown and social movement restrictions, has opened up avenues for structural changes in the formal hierarchy system itself.

In order to address these issues of communication, management, and decision making in such work arrangements where the physical meeting is absent, the hierarchical structure of the organization needs to be looked at with a different lens. Having an organization that is informational rather than industrial is what is required. A dynamic, non-hierarchical (or flatter hierarchy), technologically advanced organization, while being agile and supple, not only helps in quick adaptation to the dynamic environment, but also reduces costs and maintains business continuity.

Processes

Process, as defined in the context of the STAR Model, is "*a series of connected activities that move information up and down and across the organization*" (Kates & Galbraith, 2007, p. 17). Advances in technology, digitization, and focus on agility have been nudging organizations to change the mediums of information flow since long, the covid19 situation, again, acted as a catalyst to accelerate the changes. While electronic mediums were already present (videoconferencing, teleconferencing, email, skype, zoom, etc.), most organizations had in place a blended system, using a cocktail of physical as well as virtual presence. In fact, a new era of workforce, the jet-setters who traveled all across the world frequently, boomed the aviation and hospitality industry. However, the pandemic situation had restricted travel severely, and hence, these virtual online platforms have come to the aid. Moving away from traditional workplaces and workspaces, the employee is made (forced) to work-from-home, along with the constraints associated. This requires supportive changes from the organization at the technological level (having devices like laptop/desktop, uninterrupted wi-fi connection, issues of cybersecurity) as also the administrative level (challenges of monitoring, smooth unhindered communication across the team, ethical issues, employee well-being, etc.).

Those organizations who lied the positive end of digitization, i.e., were more technologically advanced, flourished, and the others lagged behind—having to race to catch up now. The tech companies, be it in finance, e-commerce, IT/ITES are the ones who have led till now. Manufacturing, automotive industries have been struggling, especially those who required physical workers presence to function. Exploring the

constraints and challenges of those sectors are outside the purview of this paper. Still, needless to say, organizations across industries, across the world, have moved to work-from-home whichever role possible, and this has been aided with technological support and digitization.

One of the key challenges, apart from the infrastructural ones, is that of cybersecurity. The use of technology, in fact, brings with it more issues and threats, in this covid19 pandemic, including DDoS attack, malicious domains, malicious websites, malware, ransomware, spam emails, malicious social media messaging, business email compromise, mobile apps, and browsing apps (Khan et al., 2020).

Rewards

With the economic recession, uncertain situation, and the overall negative outlook, profitability and work continuity for many industries are at stake. There have been many instances of job losses, pay cuts, furloughs, etc. across boards, rewards have admittedly taken a backseat for many. Simultaneously, the importance of skillsets, especially technological knowledge demands have increased commensurate salary expectations. Work-from-home arrangements throw up challenges of monitoring and performance, and this required a changed rewards system. While different organizations follow different compensation and rewards policy, based on a variety of internal and external factors, the impact of all the external uncertainties has shifted the power dynamics by greater emphasis on some roles while reducing/devaluing others. For example, with the rise in cybersecurity concerns, such roles/persons with requisite skillsets are much in demand, while those having traditional job roles are diminished.

People

Within the context of STAR Model, people practices include the human resources policies looking at the selection, staffing, training, and development of the employees, focused on forming the capabilities and mindsets essential to perform the organization's strategy. While it is undeniable that HR practices aid in creating sustained competitive advantage (Collins & Clark, 2003; Delery & Roumpi, 2017), as well as increase organization effectiveness and performance (Belfield & Marsden, 2003), in the covid19 pandemic scenario, the role of HRM is also rapidly evolving, requiring a different approach. Digitization has been onset even in the pre-Covid19

era, with artificial intelligence, machine learning, big data analytics, and the like. E-HRM has been adopted by organizations since the past four decades (Marler & Parry, 2015), with the desired outcomes of cost reduction, service improvements, and reorientation toward strategic HR (Ruël et al., 2007). Within the purview of work-from-home mandate, the issue of monitoring and control of people is of prime importance, along with employee adjustment and well-being, compensation structure, and retaining organizational and work culture (Carnevale & Hatak, 2020).

Factors Influencing Implementation of Work-From-Home

Work-from-home mandates, though on paper may be applicable for all employees of an organization, cannot be practically implemented as a blanket cover for all. There are various factors which are at play here.

Digitization Readiness of the Industry

Each industry functions differently, and are at different stages of digitization. We can only look at the automotive industry and e-commerce—these are very unique and different industries per se, each having their challenges and advantages of operations. Except maybe support functions, which can be done remotely, the job functions which are/can be completed for work-from-home would be different among both. Even within the industry itself, the levels of digitization vary from one organization to the next. For example, the level of digitization in Tata Motors is quite different from, say, Bajaj Auto. While institution theory emphasizes that in the long run, organizations tend to "isomorph" (Dimaggio & Powell, 1983) however, this depends a lot on other factors like the size, strategy (defender/analyser/prospector, reactor) (Miles et al., 1978), etc. In fact, Kotey and Koomson (2019), in their study, observed that organization size affected the relationship between flexible work arrangements and financial performance. Hence, it is proposed that firms can be clustered under three categories, depending upon their digitization readiness—low, medium, and high, based on their size and strategy. Accordingly, It is proposed as:

P_1: Organizations which are high on digitization readiness are the ones who are agile prospectors, who are also already invested more in the digitization process.

Internal Capabilities

By internal capabilities, the employees' readiness, and willingness toward accepting digitization. While there are many studies looking at the positive outcomes of flexible work arrangements (Bloom, 2014), here I am interested in looking at the readiness of the employees as a whole. There are two aspects to internal capabilities—the individual employees' readiness, meaning the specific skillsets, the knowledge required. The second aspect is that of the employees' willingness. In the current situation, with no vaccine yet for the Covid19 virus, people are more prone to accept work-from-home mandates, for safety, security, and health concerns. There are added benefits of increased productivity, performance, and job satisfaction (Baltes et al., 1999). However, there is also the added stress of being confined in one place, decreased social interaction (colleagues, supervisors, subordinates), and stress created due to blurred boundaries between work and life (Kossek et al., 2006; Lapierre & Allen, 2006). Man being a social animal, social isolation creates havoc on the physical and psychological health. Thus, the long-term willingness of employees is something which needs to be addressed, and herein lies the work of the HR manager. Shockley and Allen (2012), observed that individuals were more driven toward flexible work arrangements due to work-related motives than life management motives. Prior research has found that people having higher self-efficacy (Butler et al., 2004) opted for such flexible arrangements, as also those who are need-motivated (Shockley & Allen, 2010). For such employees, monitoring issues will also be lesser. Within this context, in the current scenario, therefore, it is proposed that:

P_2: Employees with technical know-how, who are self-motivated, having higher self-efficacy will be more ready and willing to embrace the digitization process.

Internal Supports

By internal supports, I mean the infrastructural supports required for digitization. Quite a lot of factors are at play here. Organizations already invested in digitization, and having an industry advantage, with a strategic orientation toward digitization will be spending more on infrastructure building for supporting digitization. In the current scenario, with the covid19 situation and mandated work-from-home, organizations are forced to invest more in such associated costs, like hardware and software support for remote work, uninterrupted internet connectivity, cybersecurity, etc. Let me take the example of an IT company, who had implemented work-from-home for its employees till the end of this calendar year. Initially, employees had to manage/arrange for their own internet connection. However, due to the fluctuations of bandwidth, connectivity issues, etc., the company entered into a tie-up with a leading broadband service provider to give discounted internet connection to all its employees across India. Yet another MNC, a corporate bank, which did not even allow USB access or laptop in the office due to security and confidentiality concerns, had to change its policies drastically to implement work-from-home for its employees across the world. To address the data confidentiality issues, the company provided secured devices for each employee covered under work-from-home, and this was a significant overhead cost incurred. Thus, from the above, the research proposal has been constructed as:

P3: Organizations who already have greater internal support (thus incurring lower infrastructure costs and overhead costs), will be more advanced in the digitization process.

Theoretical Model

Based on the above understandings, as discussed in previous sections, I propose the following model, given as Fig. 15.1, for gauging the success or failure of the WFH in the organization. This model will also enable the organization to understand where it stands, that is, which quarter it belongs to, and thus put in necessary interventions for improvement.

The three factors determining the implementation of work-from-home mandates are as stated below:

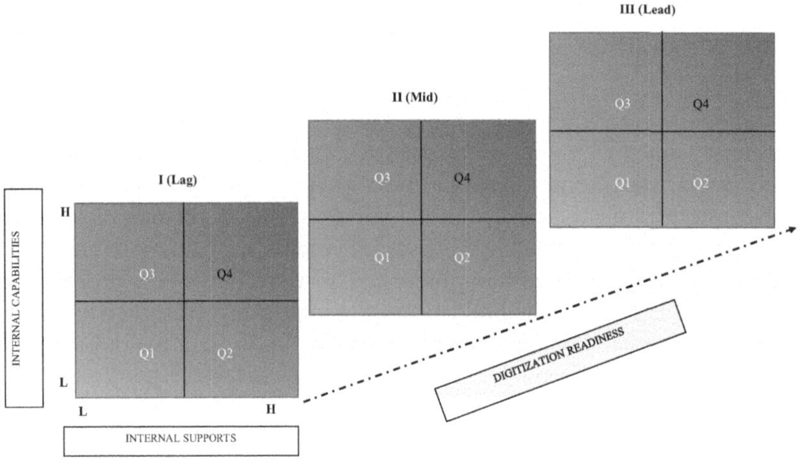

Fig. 15.1 Theoretical model (*Source* Author)

(i) X-axis—Internal Supports (infrastructure costs, overhead costs)
(ii) Y-axis—Internal Capabilities (employee readiness, employee willingness)
(iii) Z-axis—digitization readiness (organization size, organization strategy).

There are 3 levels of digitization readiness of the industry—lag (I), mid (II), and lead (III), these are clusters of organizations within than industry. Low cluster ones are those firms which are more traditional in nature, and not that much digitized, while high cluster ones are those firms which are already on advanced digitization, the pioneers in that industry.

In this XY plane, within the clusters, there are 4 quadrants where a firm can lie, viz., Q1, Q2, Q3, Q4. These are such that firms which are low in both internal capabilities and internal support, lie in Q1, while those firms which are high on both internal capabilities and internal support, lie in Q4. In Q2 lies those firms which are low in internal capabilities but high in internal support, and in Q3 lies those firms which are high in internal capabilities but low in internal support.

Implications

For Researchers

This model is, to the best of my knowledge, the first of any such framework aimed to gauge the implementation of flexible work arrangements (work-from-home), from a macro-level. I hope this would open up further interest into the macro-level analyses of this arena, more so in the current context where flexible work arrangements are gaining importance at a broader level. Researchers interested in the digitization process, as also those of E-HRM, may find this model interesting. Testing the above model, for its reliability and validity, may open up more areas of in-depth research yet not explored.

For Practitioners

This model should enable practitioners to assess the current position of the firm, based on the level and quadrant they fall into, and thus help in identifying improvement areas. The aim of a firm should be to reach Q4 within that level of digitization readiness (I, II or III). Thus, the first step would be in identifying the current quadrant and level for the firm, and then put in necessary interventions to move ahead to the highest quadrant, i.e., Q4. For example, a firm lying in level I of organizational readiness cluster, and Q2 quadrant (low internal capabilities but high internal support), the role of HRM practitioners would be to see whether employee willingness or employee readiness (or both) is lacking, and thence provide necessary interventions (for willingness policy/reward structure changes to increase motivation; for readiness—training or hiring to match the required skillsets). This exercise needs to be done periodically, so as to monitor the progress/regress/change, and it is hoped that such data would allow create knowledge base, aid decision making and contribute to its strategic choices. Especially from the HRM perspective, the role of HR as a strategic partner to the core business is hoped to be strengthened.

Future Research

The first step would be to test the above model with real-world data. For this, identification of testable variables, along with scales of measurement has to be done. I envisage this to be a longitudinal study, so as to assess

the movement of firms across quadrants and levels. Results from such analyses would help in further honing and modifying the above model, so as to make it more useful and applicable, not only for the academicians but also for the practitioners.

References

Balsa-Barreiro, J., Vié, A., Morales, A. J., & Cebrián, M. (2020). Deglobalization in a hyper-connected world. *Palgrave Communications, 6*(1), 1–4.

Baltes, B. B., Briggs, T. E., Huff, J. W., Wright, J. A., & Neuman, G. A. (1999). Flexible and compressed workweek schedules: A meta-analysis of their effects on work-related criteria. *Journal of Applied Psychology, 84*(4), 496–513.

Baral, R., & Bhargava, S. (2011). Examining the moderating influence of gender on the relationships between work–family antecedents and work–family enrichment. *Gender in Management: An International Journal, 26*(2), 122–147. https://doi.org/10.1108/17542411111116545

Belfield, R., & Marsden, D. (2003). Performance pay, monitoring environments, and establishment performance. *International Journal of Manpower, 24*(4), 452–471. https://doi.org/10.1108/01437720310485933

Bloom, N. (2014). Harvard Business Review: *To raise productivity, let more employees work from home*. Retrieved September 4, 2020, from https://hbr.org/2014/01/to-raise-productivity-letmore-employees-work-from-home

Butler, A., Gasser, M., & Smart, L. (2004). A social-cognitive perspective on using family-friendly benefits. *Journal of Vocational Behavior, 65*(1), 57–70.

Byron, K. (2005). A meta-analytic review of work–family interference and its antecedents. *Journal of Vocational Behavior, 67*, 169–198.

Carnevale, J. B., & Hatak, I. (2020). Employee adjustment and well-being in the era of COVID-19: Implications for human resource management. *Journal of Business Research, 116*, 183–187. https://doi.org/10.1016/j.jbusres.2020.05.037

Chen, W., Zhang, Y., Sanders, K., & Xu, S. (2018). Family-friendly work practices and their outcomes in China: The mediating role of work-to-family enrichment and the moderating role of gender. *The International Journal of Human Resource Management, 29*(7), 1307–1329. https://doi.org/10.1080/09585192.2016.1195424

Čiarnienė, R., Vienažindienė, M., & Adamonienė, R. (2018). Implementation of flexible work arrangements for sustainable development. *European Journal of Sustainable Development, 7*(4), 11–21. https://doi.org/10.14207/ejsd.2018.v7n4p11

Collins, C. J., & Clark, K. D. (2003). Strategic human resource practices, top management team social networks, and firm performance: The role of human

resource practices in creating organizational competitive advantage. *Academy of Management Journal, 46*, 740–751. https://doi.org/10.2307/30040665
Craigen, D., Diakun-Thibault, N., & Purse, R. (2014). Defining cybersecurity. *Technology Innovation Management Review, 4*(10), 13–21.
Delery, J. E., & Roumpi, D. (2017). Strategic human resource management, human capital and competitive advantage: Is the field going in circles? *Human Resource Management Journal, 27*, 1–21. https://doi.org/10.1111/1748-8583.12137
DiMaggio, P. J., & Powell, W. W. (1983). The iron cage revisited: Institutional isomorphism and collective rationality in organizational fields. *American Sociological Review, 48*(2), 147–160.
Emelah, G. E., & Enyia, C. D. (2018). Exploring the tensions in organizational theories. *European Scientific Journal, 14*(10), 373–377. https://doi.org/10.19044/esj.2018.v14n10p373
Fisher, L. M. (2010). *Flexible work arrangements in context: How identity, place & process shape approaches to flexibility*. Doctoral dissertation. Available from https://etd.ohiolink.edu/!etd.send_file?accession=ucin1275070770&disposition=inline
Gersick, C. J. G. (1991). Revolutionary change theories: A multilevel exploration of the punctuated equilibrium paradigm. *Academy of Management Review, 16*(1), 10–36.
Hayman, J. R. (2009). Flexible work arrangements: Exploring the linkages between perceived usability of flexible work schedules and work/life balance. *Community, Work and Family, 12*(3), 327–338.
Jain, S., & Nair, S. K. (2017). Work support and family support as predictors of work-to-family enrichment and family-to-work enrichment. *Global Business Review, 18*(5), 1307–1324. https://doi.org/10.1177/0972150917710332
Kates, A., & Galbraith, J. R. (2007). *Designing your organization: Using the star model to solve 5 critical design challenges* (1st ed.). Jossey-Bass.
Khan, N. A., Bohri, S. N., & Zaman, N. (2020). Ten deadly cyber security threats amid COVID-19 pandemic. *TechRxiv. Preprint*. https://doi.org/10.36227/techrxiv.12278792.v1
Kossek, E. E., Lautsch, B. A., & Eaton, S. C. (2006). Telecommuting, control, and boundary management: Correlates of policy use and practice, job control, and work–family effectiveness. *Journal of Vocational Behavior, 68*(2), 347–367.
Kotey, B., & Koomson, I. (2019). Firm size differences in financial returns from flexible work arrangements (FWAs). *Small Business Economics, 56*(1), 65–81. https://doi.org/10.1007/s11187-019-00201-5
Lambert, A. D., Marler, J. H., & Gueutal, H. G. (2008). Individual differences: Factors affecting employee utilization of flexible work arrangements. *Journal of Vocational Behavior, 73*, 107–117.

Lapierre, L. M., & Allen, T. D. (2006). Work-supportive family, family-supportive supervision, use of organizational benefits, and problem-focused coping: Implications for work–family conflict and employee well-being. *Journal of Occupational Health Psychology, 11*(2), 169–181.

Lee, M. D., MacDermid, S. M., & Buck, M. L. (2002). Reduced-load work arrangements: Response to stress or quest for integrity of functioning? In D. L. Nelson & R. J. Burke (Eds.), *Gender, work stress, and health* (pp. 169–190). American Psychological Association.

Lin, Z. J., Zhao, X., Ismail, K. M., & Carley, K. M. (2006). Organizational design and restructuring in response to crises: Lessons from computational modeling and real-world cases. *Organization Science, 17*(5), 598–618. https://doi.org/10.1287/orsc.1060.0210

Litrico, J., & Lee, M. D. (2008). Balancing exploration and exploitation in alternative work arrangements: A multiple case study in the professional and management services industry. *Journal of Organizational Behaviour, 29*, 995–1020. https://doi.org/10.1002/job.553

Marler, J. H., & Parry, E. (2015). Human resource management, strategic involvement and e-HRM technology. *The International Journal of Human Resource Management, 27*, 2233–2253. https://doi.org/10.1080/09585192.2015.1091980

Mazzoleni, S., Turchetti, G., & Ambrosino, N. (2020). The COVID-19 outbreak: From "black swan" to global challenges and opportunities. *Pulmonology*, S2531-0437(20)30075-1. Advance online publication. https://doi.org/10.1016/j.pulmoe.2020.03.002

McNall, L. A., Masuda, A. D., & Nicklin, J. M. (2009). Flexible work arrangements, job satisfaction, and turnover intentions: The mediating role of work-to-family enrichment. *The Journal of Psychology, 144*(1), 61–81. https://doi.org/10.1080/00223980903356073

Mesmer-Magnus, J. R., & Viswesvaran, C. (2006). How family-friendly work environments affect work/family conflict: A meta-analytic examination. *Journal of Labor Research, 4*, 555–574.

Miles, R. E., Snow, C. C., Meyer, A. D., & Coleman, H. J. (1978). Organizational strategy, structure, and process. *Academy of Management Review, 3*(3), 546–562.

Peretz, H., Fried, Y., & Levi, A. (2018). Flexible work arrangements, national culture, organisational characteristics, and organisational outcomes: A study across 21 countries. *Human Resource Management Journal, 28*, 182–200. https://doi.org/10.1111/1748-8583.12172

Platje, J., Harvey, J., & Rayman-Bacchus, L. (2020). COVID-19—Reflections on the surprise of both an expected and unexpected event. *Emerging Issues in Energy, Climate Change and Sustainability Management, 4*(1). https://doi.org/10.29015/cerem.874

Rudolph, C. W., & Baltes, B. B. (2017). Age and health jointly moderate the influence of flexible work arrangements on work engagement: Evidence from two empirical studies. *Journal of Occupational Health Psychology, 22*(1), 40–58. https://doi.org/10.1037/a0040147

Ruël, H. J. M., Bondarouk, T. V., & Van der Velde, M. (2007). The contribution of e-HRM to HRM effectiveness: Results from a quantitative study in a Dutch Ministry. *Employee Relations, 29*(3), 280–291. https://doi.org/10.1108/01425450710741757

Scott, W. R., & Davis, G. F. (2007). *Organizations and organizing: Rational, natural, and open system perspectives*. Prentice Hall.

Shockley, K. M., & Allen, T. D. (2007). When flexibility helps: Another look at the availability of flexible work arrangements and work–family conflict. *Journal of Vocational Behavior, 71*(3), 479–493.

Shockley, K. M., & Allen, T. D. (2010). Investigating the missing link in flexible work arrangement utilization: An individual difference perspective. *Journal of Vocational Behavior, 76*(1), 131–142.

Shockley, K. M., & Allen, T. D. (2012). Motives for flexible work arrangement use. *Community, Work & Family, 15*(2), 217–231.

Stanley, A. (1995). *Mothers and daughters of invention: Notes for a revised history of technology*. Rutgers University Press. ISBN: 9780813521978.

Sweet, S., Pitt-Catsouphes, M., Besen, E., & Golden, L. (2014). Explaining organizational variation in flexible work arrangements: Why the pattern and scale of availability matter. *Community, Work & Family, 17*(2), 115–141. https://doi.org/10.1080/13668803.2014.887553

Taleb, N. N. (2007). *The Black Swan: The impact of the highly improbable*, 2nd ed. Penguin. ISBN 978-0-14103459 1.

Tang, H. (2020). *Globalization in crisis*.

Townsend, K., McDonald, P., & Cathcart, A. (2017). Managing flexible work arrangements in small not-for-profit firms: The influence of organisational size, financial constraints and workforce characteristics. *The International Journal of Human Resource Management, 28*(14), 2085–2107. https://doi.org/10.1080/09585192.2015.1136671

Wadsworth, L. L., & Owens, B. P. (2007). The effects of social support on work-family enhancement and work-family conflict in the public sector. *Public Administration Review, 67*(1), 75–87. https://doi.org/10.1111/j.1540-6210.2006.00698.x

Waring, Stephen P. (2016). *Taylorism transformed: Scientific management theory since 1945*. UNC Press Books.

Williamson, O. E. (1979). Transaction-cost economics: The governance of contractual relations. *The Journal of Law and Economics, 22*(2), 233–261.

Williamson, O. E. (1986). Vertical integration and related variations on a transaction-cost economics theme. In *New developments in the analysis of market structure* (pp. 149–176). London: Palgrave Macmillan.
Wind, T. R., Rijkeboer, M., Andersson, G., & Riper, H. (2020). The COVID-19 pandemic: The 'black swan' for mental health care and a turning point for e-health. *Internet Interventions, 20*, 100317. https://doi.org/10.1016/j.invent.2020.100317
Zhang, L., Lin, Y., & Wan, F. (2015). Social support and job satisfaction: Elaborating the mediating role of work-family interface. *Current Psychology, 34*(4), 781–790. https://doi.org/10.1007/s12144-014-9290-x

CHAPTER 16

Determinants of E-Governance Health Care Services Requirements and Rural Citizen Satisfaction

M. Bhuvana and S. Vasantha

Introduction

The term "E-governance" is defined as the process of providing government services through ICT (Information and Communication Technology). ICT is considered to be a convenient mode for exchanging information among the government and the citizens (Varun Kumar & Venugopal, 2015). The phrase e-governance is referred to as the activity of facilitating government services through Information and Communication Technology (ICT). It is said to be a comfortable platform for

M. Bhuvana · S. Vasantha (✉)
School of Management Studies, Vels Institute of Science, Technology & Advanced Studies (VISTAS), Chennai, India
e-mail: vasantha.sms@velsuniv.ac.in

M. Bhuvana
e-mail: bhuvana.sms@velsuniv.ac.in

Rajagopal and R. Behl (eds.), *Managing Disruptions in Business*, Palgrave Studies in Democracy, Innovation, and Entrepreneurship for Growth, https://doi.org/10.1007/978-3-030-79709-6_16

transferring the information between the government and the citizens in the most productive manner (Varun Kumar & Venugopal, 2015). Experts termed e-governance services as Simple, Moral, Accountable, Responsible, and Transparent Model (SMART) for reaching the government services to all the citizens residing in our country. The preliminary objective of e-governance services is to perform its functions in a smooth, transparent, and effective manner in reaching people. It also acts as a guideline for greater communication and interaction between the government to government, government to citizens, government to employees, and government to businesses (Armstrong & Gandhi, 2012). This system has been already successfully implemented in various countries across the world. But the developing countries like India the usage of Information and Communication Technology seems to be in a growing state. Nearly 70 percentage of the entire population in India resides in rural villages. This shows that it seems to be a greater challenge for the officials in the government department to reach the rural people for delivering its services (GOI, 2020).

The Government of India has taken several initiatives for the development of rural areas in meeting the needs and requirements of the rural citizen. They have made different strategies for conducting awareness programs to create knowledge among the rural people for effectively accessing e-governance services. To meet these objectives the government has set up Common Service Centers at the nearby places of the rural citizen localities for accessing the government services in the field of Agriculture, Education, Health Care Services, Banking, and Insurance Services (Bhuvana & Vasantha, 2020a, b). Hence the research study has strongly focused on examining the rural citizen satisfaction in utilizing the e-governance health care services. Table 16.1 represents the list of Health Care Systems Maintained in the State of Tamil Nadu (Bolton, 2019).

This study aims at identifying the determinants of e-governance health care service requirements and analyzing the effect of e-governance health care services requirements and rural citizen satisfaction.

Determinants of E-Governance Health Care Services on Rural Citizen Satisfaction

The phrase "Citizen Satisfaction" is defined as the collective perception of the citizen toward the quality in the production of the Government in providing their services (Van Ryzin, 2013). Researchers have examined

Table 16.1 List of health care systems maintained in the state of Tamil Nadu, India

S.No.	*Health care management system*	*Services*
1.	Hospital Management System (HMS)	Maintaining information about the patients, doctors, and administrators
2.	Dr. Muthulakshmi Reddy Maternity Benefit Scheme (MRMBS)	Facilitating cash assistance of Rs. 12,000 for pregnant and delivered mothers at rural villages
3.	Health Management Information System (HMIS)	Generating unique identification numbers for hospitals, doctors, and patients for facilitating e-health care services
4.	State Health Data Resource Centre (SHDRC)	It acts as a central repository for gathering data from the Health Management Information System (HMIS) in the state of Tamil Nadu
5.	Pregnancy and Infant Cohort Monitoring and Evaluation (PICME)	Generating PICME number for registering the details of pregnant women. The data can be utilized for monitoring high-risk cases during pregnancies
6.	National Teleconsultation Services	For providing healthcare services at home through structured video calls
7.	Tele Diabetology Services	For screening the diabetic patients and facilitating medical services at rural villages

Source Laura Bolton (2019)

that Information Quality, Usability, and Trust are the three important factors for examining the rural citizen satisfaction on using e-governance services (Bhuvana & Vasantha, 2020b, c). Many academicians have stated that service quality and customer satisfaction seem to be an associated construct even they are distinct (Irfan et al., 2016; Parasuraman et al., 1994; Oliver & Gregg, 2017). Various factors of service quality are considered for analyzing the satisfaction of the customers based on the performance of the institution or an organization (Connolly & Bannister, 2007). Each citizen in our country is considered to be a consumer in the field of receiving e-governance services. The regulations, policies, and decisions are to be executed productively for satisfying the needs of the citizens (Axelsson et al., 2013).

Information Quality

The term information quality is defined as the quality of information facilitated by the system (Madnick et al., 2009). Information quality includes both subjective and objective elements such as reliability, validity, credibility, trust, and transparency of information that is being shared with the users (Diakopoulos & Essa, 2008). It is defined as the high quality of information that is acceptable when a new system is designed. Professionals have stated that believability, interpretability, and accuracy are the important dimensions of Information Quality (Embury et al., 2009). Information consists of actual data and facts that are organized for decision making (Jung, 2004). The issue occurs where the information and data quality are found to be inconsistent and it may result in quality problems (Lyytinen, 2009; Bhuvana & Vasantha, 2020a). Information quality on e-governance websites is considered to be a preliminary and essential requirement for obtaining the benefits by the people (Tayyaba Rasool et al., 2018a, 2018b).

System Quality

A system is defined as the association of several components that perform its functions for a common objective (Hardcastle, 2011). It is also described as the outcome of an information system that concern with reliability, convenience, ease of use, and other various system-associated metrics and components (Bhuvana & Vasantha, 2019; Petter & McLean, 2009). It has the most important features of the Information system such as response time, flexibility, and sophistication (Saxena, 2005). The phrase system quality is also referred to as an efficiency and productivity of e-governance information system for ease of using the systems by the citizens (Shareef et al., 2010). The variable "System Quality Functionality" is referred to as the outcome of the e-governance information system that is strongly associated with the reliability and functionality of the citizens (Kolsaker & Lee-Kelley, 2008). The paper has highlighted that high-quality software improves information system quality (Gabriel & Obara, 2013). By accessing e-governance websites both the government and citizens receive better and convenient services with lesser management and operating cost (Sivaporn et al., 2005).

Service Quality

The phrase "Service" is described as the collection of perishable, intangible, and inseparable performance of the system that satisfies the requirements of the system. Six sigma of ISO, TQM (Total Quality Management) practices, benchmarking, and balance card are the concepts of the service quality dimensions that measure the system of e-governance (Bhuvana & Vasantha, 2020b, d; Gupta et al., 2016). Assurance, Tangibility, Responsiveness, and Empathy are the various components of service quality in banking, tourism, and transport industries (Parasuraman et al., 1988). Attitude, Behavior, credibility, recovery, and trust are the preliminary factors that measure the service quality of an organization (Gronroos, 1984). To analyze the overall satisfaction of the customer that dimensions of service quality such as responsiveness, quality, reliability, and personalization are to be considered and measured (Lee & Lin, 2005).

Behavioral Intention

The term "Behavioral Intention is referred to as the likelihood of the person who adopts an application to improve his/her performance" (Davis et al., 1989). Zeithaml et al. (1996) has structured the model of intentions that represents the repurchase intentions, loyalty, behavior, word of mouth, and price sensitivity. High service quality results in favorable behavior intention among the consumers for adopting technology-based services (Bhuvana & Vasantha, 2017; Chen & Chen, 2010). Burton et al. (2003) has stated that customer experiences are highly related to their intentions for buying products or services. Furthermore, the loyal consumer recommends their friends and relatives to buy the product or service by performing as an advertising agent (Shoemaker & Lewis, 1999). Nzaramyimana and Susanto (2019) have done an investigation of the dimensions affecting the behavioral intention of the people in using e-governance services. The authors have measured behavioral intention with four different variables namely Social Influence, Trust, Propensity, and the Internet. The study strongly supported that the dimension of trust was found to be highly significant with the factor loading of 0.584.

Research Gap

Several research studies have focused on the challenges faced by rural people for using e-governance services. Various authors have theoretically explained the initiatives taken by the government toward e-governance services. Very few researchers have examined rural citizen satisfaction toward e-health care services. Our Indian Government has taken huge initiatives and spent lakhs and lakhs of money for redesigning the process of facilitating its services to the rural citizens through ICT (Information and Communication Technology). But still accessing ICT-based services are found to be lacking in rural villages particularly in acquiring health care services. Hence this research study has focused on the rural citizens' satisfaction toward accessing e-governance health care services. The study has found the most predominant gap from the previous literature reviews on measuring the rural citizen satisfaction on e-governance health care services. The present research study has also analyzed the dimensions of e-health care service requirements for measuring the behavioral intention of rural citizens for accessing e-governance health care services.

Theoretical Motivation

The study has adopted DeLone and McLean (2003) Information System Model for analyzing rural citizen satisfaction by identifying the determinants of e-governance health care service requirements. The authors have considered Information Quality, Service Quality, and System Quality as the dimensions of e-governance health care services requirements which has an impact on behavioral intention to use e-health care services. Through analyzing the behavioral intention to use e-health care services, the outcome variable Rural Citizen Satisfaction has been measured Fig. 16.1 represents the Determinants of e-governance on health care services requirements and Rural Citizen Satisfaction.

Methodology

The research has structured a questionnaire to analyze the rural citizen satisfaction for accessing e-governance health care services in villages of Kancheepuram District. The survey questionnaire framed for the research study has 31 questions with two different sections. Section "Introduction" analyzes the demographic profile of the respondents and

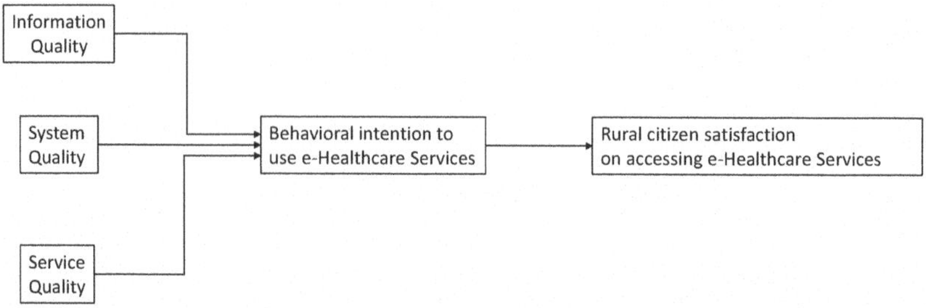

Fig. 16.1 Determinants of e-governance on health care services requirements and rural citizen satisfaction (*Source* Authors)

Table 16.2 Displays the number of items for the variables used in the study and its sources

S.No	*Variable name*	*Number of items*	*Sources*
1.	Information quality	5	Ibrahim et al. (2014), Karunasena and Deng (2012)
2.	System quality	5	Ibrahim et al. (2014), Nabafu and Maiga (2012)
3.	Service quality	5	Barnes and Richard (2006), Ibrahim et al. (2014)
4.	Behavioral intention	5	Delone and McLean (2003), Davis et al. (1989)
5.	Rural citizen satisfaction	5	Mohammed et al. (2016), Malik et al. (2016)

section "Determinants of E-Governance Health Care Services on Rural Citizen Satisfaction" measures the study variables (Information Quality, System Quality, Service Quality, Behavioral Intention to use e-governance health care services, and Rural Citizen Satisfaction). Descriptive research design is adopted for the study. Table 16.2 displays the number of items for the variables used in the study and its sources.

Data Collection

A Descriptive research design is adopted for the study. The primary data for the study has been collected from randomly selected 500 respondents residing in the villages of Kancheepuram district through the purposive

sampling technique since the rural literacy rate of Kancheepuram district is found to be 75.9 percentage that is lesser than the average literacy rate of Tamil Nadu (80.33%).

Hypothesis Framed for the Study

H_1: e-health Care Services Requirements is positively associated with Behavioral Intention

Sub Hypothesis

- H_a: Information Quality influences the e-health Care Services Requirements
- H_b: System Quality influences the e-health Care Services Requirements
- H_c: Service Quality influences the e-health Care Services Requirements

H_2: Behavioral Intention positively associated with the Rural Citizen Satisfaction

Analysis and Findings

SPSS 21 (Statistical Package of Social Sciences) has been used for data analysis and AMOS 22 has been used for generating the factor loadings, measuring Construct Reliability, Discriminant validity, and Model fit for the proposed conceptual framework. Table 16.3 displays the demographic profile of rural respondents.

Factor Loadings, Construct Reliability and Average Variance Extracted Values for All the Variables Used in the Study

Through the generated factor loading, the construct reliability and AVE (Average Variance Extracted) values of all the variables used in the study are computed. Table 16.4 highlights the calculated CR and AVE values for all the variables used in the study. From the table, it is clear that the factor loadings are greater than 0.5 for all the variables. The extracted CR for all the variables is greater than 0.7 and AVE values are found to be

Table 16.3 Demographic profile of the respondents

Variable	*Description*	*Frequency*	*Percentage*
Gender	Male	246	49.0
	Female	254	51.0
Age (years)	18–25 years	151	30.0
	26–35	150	30.0
	36–45	112	22.0
	46–55	60	11.0
	Above 55	27	5.0
Marital status	Married	460	91.8
	Unmarried	40	8.2
Occupation	Farmer	141	28.2
	Employed	265	53.0
	Business	75	15.0
	Student	19	3.8
Education	Below 10th Std.	111	22.2
	Passed 10th Std.	127	25.4
	Passed 12th Std.	144	28.8
	Graduate	118	23.6
Income	Rs. 25k to Rs. 50k	278	55.6
	Rs. 51k to 1 Lakh	186	37.2
	Above Rs. 1 Lakh	36	7.2

Source Authors

higher than 0.5. This shows that the construct validity for all the variables used in the study is found to be reliable (Fornell & Larcker, 1981).

Discriminant Validity

Discriminant Validity represents the interdependence of the variables used in the research study. It also evaluates the extent to which items of the variable differ from the items used in the other variables in the study (Bagozzi, 2007). According to Fornell and Larcker (1981), discriminant validity can be measured by comparing the range of variance extracted by the variable and the amount of variance shared by the other variables. Table 16.5 displays the discriminant validity of all the constructs used in

Table 16.4 Factor loadings, construct reliability and average variance extracted values for all the Variables used in the study

Construct name	*Item name*	*Factor loadings*	*CR value*	*AVE value*
Information quality	IQ1	0.845	0.712	0.901
	IQ2	0.834		
	IQ3	0.883		
	IQ4	0.852		
	IQ5	0.841		
System quality	SQ1	0.852	0.708	0.898
	SQ2	0.791		
	SQ3	0.830		
	SQ4	0.825		
	SQ5	0.814		
Service quality	SEQ1	0.795	0.748	0.852
	SEQ2	0.869		
	SEQ3	0.842		
	SEQ4	0.811		
	SEQ5	0.823		
Behavioral intention	SEQ1	0.846	0.702	0.921
	SEQ2	0.823		
	SEQ3	0.878		
	SEQ4	0.832		
	SEQ5	0.889		
Rural citizen satisfaction	RCS1	0.828	0.708	0.932
	RCS2	0.834		
	RCS3	0.872		
	RCS4	0.838		
	RCS5	0.815		

Source Authors' data analysis

Table 16.5 Discriminant validity

Construct	*IQ*	*SQ*	*SEQ*	*BI*	*RCS*
IQ	0.901				
SQ	0.351	0.898			
SEQ	0.473	0.231	0.852		
BI	0.521	0.170	0.421	0.921	
RCS	0.531	0.430	0.321	0.621	0.932

Source Authors

Table 16.6 Variables of structural equation model (SEM)

Variables			*S.E*	*Standardized coefficient*	*t value*	*P value*	*Result of hypothesis*
Behavioral intention	<--	e-health care services requirements	0.505	0.20	4.367	0.000	H_1 is supported
Rural citizen satisfaction	<--	Behavioral intention	0.038	0.20	5.865	0.000	H_2 is supported
Information quality	<--	e-health care services requirements	0.321	0.841	4.261	0.000	H_a is supported
System quality	<--	e-health care requirements	0.254	0.788	3.432	0.000	H_b is supported
Service quality	<--	e-health care requirements	0.395	0.751	4.358	0.000	H_c is supported

Source Author's data analysis

the study. This shows that the variance extracted for all the variables is higher than the square of the correlation values of all the variables.

Hypothesis Validation

For examining the gathered primary data from the respondents and analyzing the relationship between the study variables Structural Equation Modeling (SEM) is utilized. Table 16.6 displays the relationship that exists between the variables. It is proved that the *p*-value is found to be less than 0.05. Hence the hypothesis framed for the study is accepted and remains a significant relationship between the constructs.

Assessment of Model Fit

Table 16.7 represents the model fit assessment of the conceptual model framed for the study. It shows that the P-value is greater than 0.05 this shows that the model is said to be a complete fit model. The values of GFI, CFI, NFI, and AGFI are found to be greater than 0.9. The value of RMSEA is found to be lesser than 0.08. This represents the conceptual model framed for the research study is a completely fit model (Hu & Bentler, 1999; Hair et al., 2006).

Table 16.7 Model fit summary for structural equation model

Goodness of fit statistics	*Value*
Chi square value (CMIN)	93.860
P value	0.07
Chi square/Df (CMIN/Df)	2.890
Goodness of fit index (GFI)	0.978
Root mean square error of approximation (RMSEA)	0.072
Adjusted good of fit index (AGFI)	0.961
Comparative fit index (CFI)	0.978
Normed fit index (NFI)	0.902

Source Authors' data analysis

General Discussion

It is found that out of 500 rural respondents 246 are male and the remaining 254 are female respondents. The majority of the respondents belong to 18–25 years of age category. Out of 500 respondents, 460 respondents are married and 265 respondents are employed and 144 respondents have passed 12th Std. 278 respondents belong to the income group between INR 25,000 to 50,000.

It is proved that there exists a positive relationship between the e-health Care Requirements and Behavioral Intention to use e-governance health care services. This research findings have been coincided with the findings of Verma et al. (2019). They have examined that behavior intention found to be an important dimension for analyzing the acceptance of e-health Care services among the citizen. It is verified that there exists a significant relationship between the variables Behavioral Intention and Rural Citizen Satisfaction.

The study has found that there exists a significant relationship between behavioral intention to access e-governance health care services and rural citizen satisfaction. This research findings have been coincided with the findings of Wayan Ardani et al. (2019), they have highlighted that the relationship that exists between the satisfaction of the customer and their behavioral intention for accessing any services has drawn a most significant observation in the market space of any kind of industry. DeLone and McLean (2003) have measured the net benefits attained by the users toward accessing an information system. The authors have developed the conceptual model by considering System Quality, Information Quality,

and Service Quality as the dimensions for measuring behavioral Intention. The present research study has tested the model and it has derived the outcome, out of these three dimensions (Information Quality, System Quality, and Service Quality), the dimension "Information Quality" is found to be a highly significant factor of e-health care requirement with the standardized coefficient value of 0.841 for measuring the Behavioral Intention of rural citizens for using e-health care services. Table 16.3 represents the model fit of the conceptual framework.

Implications

The research study has explored the maximum information related to rural citizen satisfaction in e-governance health care services. The findings of the study can be effectively utilized by the government institutions, policymakers, financial institutions, medical practitioners, Website developers, and many funding agencies for analyzing the needs and requirements of the rural citizens for accessing e-governance health care services. The information about e-governance health care services acts can be used as guidance for supporting the general public in understanding the importance of e-governance health care services.

The study has highlighted the association that exists between the variables "Information Quality", "System Quality", Service Quality", "Behavioral Intention to Use e-governance service" and "Rural Citizen Satisfaction". From the research findings, it has been evaluated that the dimension "Information Quality" highly significant with the behavioral intention of the rural citizen for attaining satisfaction in accessing e-governance health care services. This finding helps the regulators and implementers of e-governance services for achieving maximum satisfaction among rural citizens for frequently accessing e-health care services.

Conclusion

Health care services under e-governance initiatives are said to be an originating field toward transferring medical informatics, public health, delivering information, and providing health care services with innovative technologies Rushender et al. (2016). It remains a greater challenge in developed countries in India for facilitating its services to the rural villages, make them adopt the services through ICT, and meet their needs and requirements. The present study has made a contribution to

the existing literature on measuring the rural citizen satisfaction on using e-governance health care services. Hence the researchers conclude that to satisfy the requirements of the health care services, the Information Quality of the system has to be given more importance for developing the applications.

References

Ardani, W., et al. (2019). Customer satisfaction and behavioral intentions in tourism: A literature review. *International Journal of Applied Business & International Management, 4*(3), 85–93.

Armstrong, L., & Gandhi, N. (2012). Factors influencing the use of information and communication technology (ICT) tools by the rural famers in Ratnagiri District of Maharashtra, India. In *Proceedings of the Third National Conference on Agro-Informatics and Precision Agriculture 2012* (pp. 58–63).

Axelsson, K., Melin, U., & Lindgren, I. (2013). Public e-services for agency efficiency and citizen benefit—Findings from a stakeholder centered analysis. *Government Information Quarterly, 30*(1), 10–22.

Bagozzi, P. (2007). The legacy of the technology acceptance model and a proposal for a paradigm shift. *Journal of the Association for Information Systems, 8*(4), 244–254.

Barnes, J., & Vidgen, R. T. (2006). An integrative approach to the assessment of e-commerce quality. *Journal of Electronic Commerce Research, 3*, 114–127.

Bhuvana, M., & Vasantha, S. (2017). A structural equation modeling (SEM) approach for mobile banking adoption—A strategy for achieving financial inclusion. *Indian Journal of Public Health Research and Development, 8*(2), 175–182.

Bhuvana, M., & Vasantha, S. (2019). An outlook of financial inclusion with mediating effect of direct benefit transfer in LPG subsidy towards actual usage of banking technology. *International Journal of Engineering and Advanced Technology (IJEAT), 8*(6S), 804–811.

Bhuvana, M., & Vasanth, S. (2020a). Determinants of behavioral intention to access e-governance services by rural people with the mediating effect of information and communication (ICT) literacy. *Journal of Advanced Research in Dynamical & Control Systems, 12*(2), 176–187.

Bhuvana, M., & Vasantha, S. (2020b). Assessment of rural citizens satisfaction on the service quality of common service centers (CSCS) of e-governance. *Journal of Critical Reviews, 7*(5), 302–305.

Bhuvana, M., & Vasantha, S. (2020c). Role of information and communication technology (ICT) for rural development through e-governance initiatives. *International Journal of Psychosocial Rehabilitation, 24*(8), 2705–2713.

Bhuvana, M., & Vasantha, S. (2020d). Neural network machine learning techniques using R studio for predicting the attitude of rural people for accessing e-governance services. *Journal of Advanced Research in Dynamical & Control Systems, 12*(2), 2552–2562.

Bolton, L. (2019). *E-governance innovations in India, K4D*. Institute of Development Studies.

Burton, S., Sheather, S., & Roberts, J. (2003). Reality or perception? The effect of actual and perceived performance on satisfaction and behavioral intention. *Journal of Service Research, 5*(4), 292–302.

Chen, C.-F., & Chen, F.-S. (2010). Experience quality, perceived value, satisfaction and behavioral intentions for heritage tourists. *Tourism Management, 31*(1), 29–35.

Connolly, R., & Bannister, F. (2007). Consumer trust in Internet shopping in Ireland: Towards the development of a more effective trust measurement instrument. *Journal of Information Technology, 22*(2), 102–118.

Davis, F. D., et al. (1989). User acceptance of computer technology: A comparison of two theoretical models. *Management Science, 35*(8), 982–1003.

DeLone, W. H., & McLean, E. R. (2003). The DeLone and McLean model of information systems success: A ten-year update. *Journal of Management Information Systems, 19*(4), 9–30.

Embury, M., Missier, P., Sampaio, S., Mark Greenwood, R., & Preece, D. (2009). Incorporating domain-specific information quality constraints into database queries. *Journal of Data and Information Quality, 1*(2), 1–3.

Fornell, C., & Larcker, D. F. (1981). Structural equation models with unobservable variables and measurement error: Algebra and statistics. *Journal of Marketing Research, 18*(3), 382–388.

Gabriel, J., & Obara, L. C. (2013). Management information systems and corporate decision-making: A literature review. *The International Journal of Management, 2*(3), 78–82.

Gronroos, C. (1984). A service quality model and its marketing implications. *European Journal of Marketing, 18*, 36–44.

Gupta, K. P., Bhaskar, P., & Singh, S. (2016). Critical factors influencing e-government adoption in India: An investigation of the citizens' perspectives. *Journal of Information Technology Research, 9*(4), 28–44.

Hair, J. F., Black, W. C., Babin, B. J., Anderson, R. E., & Tatham, R. L. (2006). *Multivariate data analysis* (6th ed.). Pearson University Press.

Hardcastle, E. (2011). *Business information systems*. Ventus Publishing ApS.

Hu, L., & Bentler, P. M. (1999). Cutoff criteria for fit indexes in covariance structure analysis: Conventional criteria versus new alternatives. *Structural Equation Modeling: A Multidisciplinary Journal, 6*(1), 1–55.

Ibrahim, M., Rahman, M. A., & Yasin, R. (2014). Determining factors of students' satisfaction with Malaysian skills training institutes. *International Education Studies, 7*(6), 9–24.

Irfan, M., Shamsudin, M. F., & Hadi, N. U. (2016). How important is customer satisfaction? Quantitative evidence from mobile telecommunication market. *International Journal of Business and Management, 11*(6), 57–69.

Jung, W. (2004). A review of research: An investigation of the impact of data quality on decision performance. *Proceedings of the 2004 international symposium on Information and communication technologies, 90*, 16–171. ACM International Conference Proceeding Series.

Karunasena, K., & Deng, H. (2012). Critical factors for evaluating the public value of e-government in Sri Lanka. *Government Information Quarterly, 29*(1), 76–84.

Kolsaker, A., & Lee-Kelley, L. (2008). Citizens' attitudes towards egovernment and e-governance: A UK study. *International Journal of Public Sector Management, 21*(7), 723–738.

Lee, G.-G., & Lin, H.-F. (2005). Customer perceptions of e-service quality in on-line shopping. *International Journal of Retail & Distribution Management, 33*(2), 161–176.

Lyytinen, K. (2009). Data matters in IS theory building. *Journal of the Association for Information Systems, 10*(10), 715–720.

Madnick, S. E., Lee, Y. W., Wang, R. Y., & Zhu, H. (2009). Overview and framework for data and information quality research. *Journal of Data and Information Quality, 1*(1), 1–22.

Malik, B. H., Shuqin, C., Shuqin, C., Mastoi, A. G., Mastoi, A. G., Gul, N., Gul, N., Gul, H., & Gul, H. (2016). Evaluating citizen e satisfaction from e-government services: A case of Pakistan. E*uropean Scientific Journal, ESJ, 12*(5), 346.

Mohammed, M. A., Aboobaider, B. M., Ibrahim, H., Abdullah, H. A., Ali, M. H., Jaber, M. M., & Shawkat, A. (2016). Egovernment and its challenges in developing countries: Case study Iraqi e-government. *The Social Sciences, 11*(17), 4310–4319.

Nabafu, R., & Maiga, G. (2012). E-government principles: Implementation, advantages and challenges. *International Journal of Electronic Business, 9*(3), 255–270.

Nicholas, D., & Essa, I. (2008, November 28–30). An annotation model for making sense of information quality in online video. In *Proceedings of the 3rd International Conference on Pragmatic Web, ICPW 2008* (pp. 31–34).

Nzaramyimana, L., & Susanto, T. D. (2019). Analysis of factors affecting behavioural intention to use e-government services in Rwanda. *Procedia Computer Science, 161*, 350–358.

Oliver, J., & Gregg, G. (2017). Motivated reasoning about public performance: An experimental study of how citizens judge the affordable care act. *Journal of Public Administration Research and Theory, 27*(1), 197–209.

Parasuraman, A., Zeithaml, V. A., & Berry, L. L. (1988). SERVQUAL: A multiple-item scale for measuring consumer perceptions of service quality. *Journal of Retailing, 64*(1), 12–40.

Parasuraman, A., Zeithaml, V., & Berry, L. (1994). Reassessment of expectations as a comparison standard in measuring service quality: Implications for further research. *Journal of Marketing, 58*, 111–124.

Petter, S., & McLean, E. R. (2009). A meta-analytic assessment of the DeLone and McLean IS success model: An examination of IS success at the individual level. *Information & Management, 46*(3), 159–166.

Prachi, V., et al. (2019). Understanding the factors affecting consumer's acceptance of e-healthcare services. *International Journal of Recent Technology and Engineering (IJRTE), 8*(2S10), 468–473.

Rushender, R., Balaji, R., & Parasuraman, G. (2016). A study on effective utilization of health care services provided by primary health centre and sub-centres in rural Tamil Nadu, India. *International Journal of Community Medicine and Public Health, 3*(5), 1054–1060.

Saxena, K. B. C. (2005). Towards excellence in e-governance. *International Journal of Public Sector Management, 18*(6), 498–513.

Shareef, M. A., et al. (2010). E-Government implementation perspective: Setting objective and strategy. *International Journal of Electronic Government Research, 6*(1), 59–77.

Shoemaker, S., & Lewis, R. (1999). Customer loyalty: The future of hospitality marketing. *Hospitality Management, 18*, 345–370.

Tayyaba Rasool, N., et al. (2018a). A study of the information quality of e-government websites in Pakistan. In *Proceedings of the 11th International Conference on Theory and Practice of Electronic Governance* (pp. 433–442).

Tayyaba Rasool, N., et al. (2018b). Information quality of e-government websites as perceived by university students in Pakistan. *Journal of Political Studies, 25*(2), 181–195.

Van Ryzin, G. (2013). An experimental test of the expectancy-disconfirmation theory of citizen satisfaction. *Journal of Policy Analysis and Management, 32*(3), 597–614.

Varun Kumar, M., & Venugopal, P. (2015). E-Governance and rural development (A study specially focused on villages of Katpadi Taluk, Vellore District of Tamil Nadu). *International Journal of Applied Engineering Research, 10*(92), 319–324.

Wangpipatwong, S., et al. (2005, November 19–20). Factors influencing the adoption of Thai eGovernment websites: Information quality and system

quality approach. In *Proceedings of the Fourth International Conference on eBusiness* (pp. 14.1–14.7).

Zeithaml, V. A., Berry, L. L., & Parasuraman, A. (1996). The behavioral consequences of service quality. *Journal of Marketing, 60*(2), 31–46.

Website

Government of India. (2020). [Online]. Available: https://www.mygov.in/aarogya-setu-app/

CHAPTER 17

Framework for Crowdfunding Adoption Across Countries

Chandresh Baid and Devesh Baid

Introduction

The crowdfunding industry has grown at a fast pace since its inception after the global financial crisis in 2008 (Pierrakis & Collins, 2013) but it has remained concentrated in few parts of the world, mainly USA and Europe (Kshetri, 2015). According to an industry report, the USA and Europe account for 95% of the total market (www.massolution.com, 2013). Despite the economic and technical strength of some of the countries in Asia like India, China, Japan and South Korea, adoption of crowdfunding as an alternate source of finance has been low and it can be

C. Baid
Seidman College of Business, Grand Valley State University,
Grand Rapids, MI, USA
e-mail: baidc@gvsu.edu

D. Baid (✉)
International Management Institute, Bhubaneswar, Odisha, India
e-mail: devesh@imibh.edu.in

Rajagopal and R. Behl (eds.), *Managing Disruptions in Business*,
Palgrave Studies in Democracy, Innovation, and Entrepreneurship for Growth, https://doi.org/10.1007/978-3-030-79709-6_17

attributed to the institutional barriers in these countries (Kshetri, 2015). The difference in adoption rate of crowdfunding across various countries can be explained by the difference in institutions such as national laws, national culture and business norms across countries.

Individuals and firms are embedded in institutional settings and these settings impact the behavior of both individuals and firms in subtle but permanent way. In this paper, I focus on the institutional differences across countries to analyze variation in adoption rate of crowdfunding. I specifically focus on the question: How do formal and informal institutions impact the adoption of crowdfunding in a global context?

Theoretical Foundation

Institutional theory has been widely used in the management literature. Institutional role has long been recognized in shaping the organizations. Different theorists at different points in time have suggested different views of institutional impact on organization. Institutions can be broadly classified into three categories: regulatory, normative and cognitive (Scott, 1995). Regulatory elements include the rules and laws that regulate the behavior of individuals and organizations. Normative elements provide a moral framework of values and behaviors to be exhibited by individuals and organizations and cognitive elements provide the shared meaning that develops among individuals and organizations through social interaction. Variation in crowdfunding adoption across countries can be understood by analyzing the variations in configurations of regulatory, normative and cognitive institutions (Bruton et al., 2005; Scott & Davis, 2007).

Hypothesis Development

In crowdfunding context, Entrepreneurs suffer from the paradox of disclosure (Gans & Stern, 2003). They need to share the idea with potential funder but then once they share the idea, it's in the public domain and known to everyone and not in their control. Incumbent firms with ample resources and economies of scale can learn about the product ideas and beat the entrepreneur in time to market and price by shear strength of existing resource capabilities. In such scenario entrepreneurs will not be willing to share their product on CFPs as they will fear imitation and appropriation of rent by other people and firms from their product idea

in the absence of well-defined intellectual property regulations (Schwienbacher & Larralde, 2010). It can be derived from above discussion that having well-defined IP Laws and administrative mechanisms by which entrepreneurs can acquire IP rights for their invention is an important factor in the selection of crowdfunding as mechanism to source fund for his venture.

Hypothesis 1 IP law strength will be positively related to technologically innovative crowdfunding campaign creation

Having explicit IP law is necessary but what is equally important are the enforcement practices related to a particular law (Ostergard, 2000; Porta et al., 1997). Many countries have well-defined laws but they do not have well-oiled machinery backing the laws resulting in a random enforcement of laws (Bruton et al., 2005; Kshetri, 2015). These random enforcement leads to opportunistic behavior by self-interested firms and individuals (Roy & Oliver, 2009) and creates a feeling of uncertainty in the society with respect to law enforcement. Such an environment will discourage entrepreneur to share his invention on the crowdfunding platform because even if invention is protected by IP laws, it can be imitated by incumbent organizations in absence of effective enforcement of IP protection by relevant authorities.

Hypothesis 2 IP law enforcement will be positively related to technologically innovative crowdfunding campaign creation

Society plays a critical role in promotion of entrepreneurial activities in a region. Some societies have high regard for entrepreneurial activities where as others do not. Some societies perceive it as vehicle for growth where as others societies perceive at it as vehicle for exploitation. Societies that have positive attitude toward entrepreneurship may develop social systems such as status and recognition for entrepreneurs to encourage people to start new business (Gnyawali & Fogel, 1994). Thus societies play a role in establishing the legitimacy of entrepreneurship in a region. In crowdfunding context, the entrepreneur reaches out to the society directly with his funding request. An entrepreneur will be encouraged to use crowdfunding as mechanism to source fund in societies which have high regard for entrepreneurs as such societies will value his work and will also provide him with support, encouragement and wisdom to carry out entrepreneurial activities effectively (Krueger & Brazeal, 1994).

Hypothesis 3 Attitude toward entrepreneurs will be positively associated with crowdfunding campaign creation

In certain societies failure is considered bad. It is observed as a characteristic of the individual rather than an interaction of individual and context. Some other societies consider failure as a stepping stone to success and take failure as an event and not as a characteristic of an individual. Entrepreneurs operate in an uncertain environment. More entrepreneurial ventures fail than succeed. That is the nature of the game in entrepreneurship. Societies which look down on failure will discourage entrepreneurship in general (Hindle & Klyver, 2011). Those who chose to become entrepreneurs in such society will restrain themselves from taking risky action as they will fear that society will look down upon them in event of failure. In the context of crowdfunding, an entrepreneur creates a funding request on a public platform where the success or failure of the campaign will be visible to all. If an entrepreneur fails to secure fund on crowdfunding platform, he will be looked down by the society which considers failures as bad. In such a society an entrepreneur will be discouraged to use crowdfunding platform as he would not like society to build a negative perception about him (Simmons et al., 2014).

Hypothesis 4 Fear of failure will be negatively associated with crowdfunding campaign creation

Crowdfunding as a funding mechanism has philanthropic element embedded into it. Donation-based crowdfunding is a complete philanthropic act but backers on other crowdfunding platforms such as reward based or lending based also showcase philanthropic reasons alongside or above monetary reasons (Kshetri, 2015). As per industry report, social causes is the most popular category in crowdfunding and accounts for 30% of total funding activity (www.massolution.com, 2013) leading to the conclusion that crowdfunding is a viable channel to fund projects that have social elements. For-profit projects can use the same instruments during their early phases when they are startups and when they have characteristics, such as innovative technology, which can attract altruistic supporters (Hemer, 2011). Under such circumstances supporters may be motivated by non-pecuniary returns such as desire to be part of a philanthropic cause (Agrawal et al., 2011). Desire to help others varies by societies. Some societies have high propensity to support social causes or engage in philanthropic activities than others. Legal systems like tax incentives also contribute to the development of charitable culture in a region

(Kshetri, 2015). An entrepreneur will be encouraged to use crowdfunding platform to raise fund for his venture in a society which has a higher tendency to allocate resources for social cause.

Hypothesis 5 Charitable culture will be positively associated with crowdfunding campaign creation

Uncertainty avoidance is defined as the degree to which members of a society feel uncomfortable with uncertainty and ambiguity (Hofstede, 1983). Societies with high uncertainty avoidance levels have lower tolerance for uncertainty and high need for structures and institutions. People in high uncertainty avoidance culture also show high resistance to change, presumably because change often involves uncertainties (Lim et al., 2004). Uncertainty avoidance is shown to manifest a wide variety of behavior from the type of beverage consumed to choice of insurance policy to online shopping (Vishwanath, 2003). Entrepreneurial ventures, as discussed above, are risky by nature. There is high degree of uncertainty around an entrepreneurial venture during its nascent stage. The use of online-based crowdfunding platform adds another layer of uncertainty to entrepreneurial venture as investors do not have the benefit of physical access to entrepreneur and his venture. Under such a scenario entrepreneur will be discouraged to use crowdfunding platform to raise fund for his venture (Fig. 17.1).

Hypothesis 6 Uncertainty avoidance culture will be negatively associated with crowdfunding campaign creation

Variables

Dependent Variable

Crowdfunding Adoption: For hypotheses 1 and 2 where I explore the impact of intellectual property right on adoption for technologically innovative campaign, I will measure the number of campaigns created under technology category on global crowdfunding platform—indiegogo.com across all countries for a given year. Indiegogo is one of the world's leading crowdfunding platform and operates in 223 countries ("About Us|Indiegogo," n.d.).

For all other hypotheses, I define crowdfunding adoption as the number of crowdfunding platforms operating in a country for a given

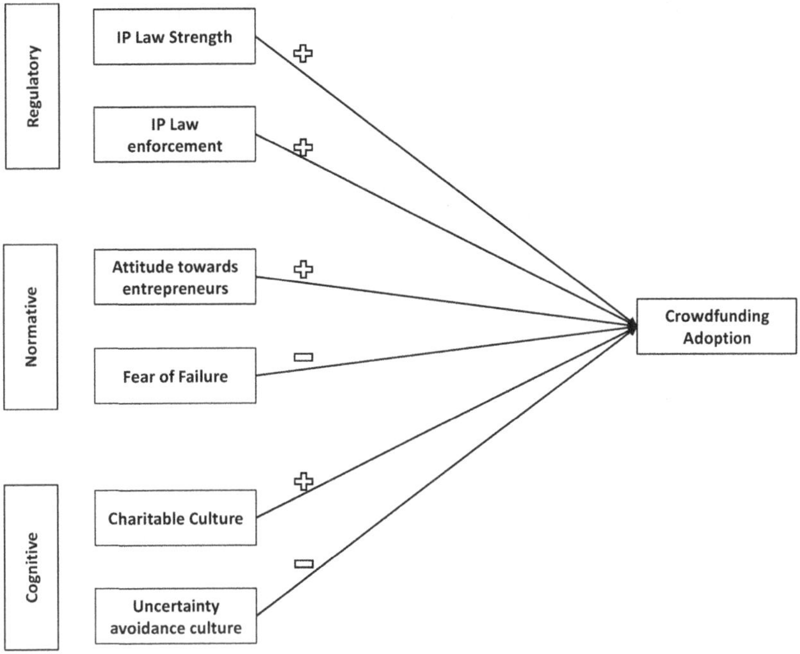

Fig. 17.1 Overall model (*Source* Authors)

year. I adopt this measure from research done by world bank on crowdfunding potential in developing world (infoDev, 2013).

Independent Variables

IP Law Strength: I define IP Law Strength as the strength of a country's patent law based on five criteria: coverage, membership in international treaties, restrictions on patent rights, enforcement and duration of protection as defined in International Property Rights Index (IPRI) (Carciente, 2016). IPRI consists of three core components: legal and political environment (LP), physical property rights (PPR) and intellectual property rights (IPR) ("International Property Rights Index," n.d.). Intellectual property rights (IPR) further consist of three components: protection of intellectual property rights, patent protection and copyright piracy. I use patent protection component as measure of IP Law strength. The patent

protection component uses data from Ginarte-Park Index (Park, 2008). It was published for the first time in 1997, is updated every 5 years, and has been widely used in patent and IPR related research.

IP Law Enforcement: I define IP Law enforcement as perceived effectiveness of IP Laws by experts in the country as defined in International Property Rights Index (IPRI) (Carciente, 2016). IPRI uses Global Competitive Index from the world economic forum as dataset to arrive at this measure. World economic forum conducts executive opinion survey to gather data. Apart from calculating Global Competitive Index, the executive opinion dataset has been used to compute many other indexes such as enabling trade index and human capital index. The global competitiveness index has 12 categories called pillars of competitiveness and I am using the "intellectual property protection" element of the institutions pillar. This element is measured by asking the question "In your country, to what extent is intellectual property protected? [1 = not at all; 7 = to a great extent]."

Attitude Toward Entrepreneurs: I define this variable as the attitude of society toward entrepreneurship measured as the "Entrepreneurship as good career choice" from the entrepreneurial behavior and attitude dataset of GEM Adult Population Survey (APS). APS includes measures for social values toward entrepreneurship and individual attributes of entrepreneurs and is administered to 2000 people in each participating country. This variable—Entrepreneurship as good career choice—indicates the percentage of 18–64 age population who agree that in their country most people consider starting a business a desirable career choice.

Fear of Failure: I define this variable as the fear of failure an entrepreneur has and which inhibits him from starting a business and measured as "Fear of Failure Rate" from the entrepreneurial behavior and attitude dataset of GEM Adult Population Survey. This variable indicates the percentage of 18–64 age population who perceives good opportunities to start a business but indicates that a fear of failure would prevent them from setting up a business. This variable is the only available measure of fear of failure at country level and has been used widely in previous research (Wyrwich et al., 2016). It has also been used in the context of stigma due to business failure in extant literature (Simmons et al., 2014).

Charitable Culture: I define charitable culture as helping behavior in terms of time and money by members of the society to an unknown individual or charitable organization measured as "World Giving Index" from

Charity Aid Foundation. Charity Aid Foundation is a leading charity organization in the United Kingdom ("About CAF—Motivating Society to Give More Effectively," n.d.). They are serving mankind for over 90 years. They also have a very active research program with numerous publications which focuses on understanding determinants of charitable giving. World Giving Index consists of average of response received on 3 questions pertaining to help provided to a stranger, money to a charity or time to an organization. World Giving Index has been used as a measure of charitable culture in studies on print media coverage about philanthropy and shaping of national character (McDonald & Scaife, 2011). It has also been used as a measure of charitable giving in study that focused on ways to increase the charitable pie (List & Price, 2012). A study on determinants of social entrepreneurship has also used it as a measure of philanthropic support (Griffiths et al., 2013).

Uncertainty Avoidance Culture: I define uncertainty avoidance as the degree to which the members of the society feel uncomfortable with uncertainty and ambiguity and measure it using Uncertainty Avoidance Index (UAI) from Hofstede's national culture dimensions (Hofstede, 1983). UAI is a widely used measure of tolerance for ambiguity in life and has been used in studies pertaining to risk-taking and entrepreneurship orientation (Kreiser et al., 2010), and organization of financial systems (Kwok & Tadesse, 2006). A meta-analysis done on the use of UAI in international research identified 118 articles in the *Journal of International Business Studies* that have used this index, of which 30 have used UAI as independent or control variable (Rapp et al., 2010).
Control variables:

I use *education* (World Bank—Education Statistics), *Internet penetration* (www.internetworldstats.com), *Population* (World Bank data) and *GDP* (World Bank data) as control variable in study. Internet penetration level in a country will have impact on the adoption of CFPs as internet is a prerequisite for participation in crowdfunding. Education can also impact the growth of crowdfunding adoption in a country. Education is positively associated with entrepreneurship in general (infoDev, 2013). Education is a salient variable for crowdfunding adoption due to the fact that an individual must have basic skillset of reading and writing to be able to participate in crowdfunding phenomenon. The population of a country can confound the research as countries with large population like India and China host about 30% of the world's population

between them (infoDev, 2013). The probability of having more crowdfunding platforms in India and China on account of its population size (1.3 billion each roughly) is higher than in a country like Switzerland (8 million). Similarly GDP of a country is measure of economic activity in a region and should be used to control for country-level variations in economic activities (infoDev, 2013).

Data Collection

Data collection will be done via secondary sources. For number of crowdfunding platforms internet search will be used as primary tool. A list of crowdfunding platforms operating in each country will be identified by making a targeted search for a given country. Any relevant governmental or industry association website containing information on crowdfunding platforms for a given country, if found, will also be used for data collection. Once the list of websites is collected, domain registration details or company registration details will be used to arrive at the launch year of crowdfunding platform. With the availability of web portal suite customization offerings, it's very quick to launch a new platform and any delay between website registration and/or company registration and platform launch is going to be minimal. For all independent variables, I will use the sources discussed in the variables section, namely, IPRI ("IPRI 2016," n.d.), GEM ("GEM Global Entrepreneurship Monitor," n.d.), World Giving Index ("Charities Aid Foundation (CAF)—Charity Giving Made Simple," n.d.) and National Culture ("Geert Hofstede—Geert Hofstede," n.d.). For control variables, data will be used from World Bank data sources ("DataBank|The World Bank," n.d.) and Internet World Stats ("Internet World Stats—Usage and Population Statistics," n.d.).

The data collection strategy employed in this research is feasible for all dependent and control variables as they are adopted measures from authentic sources. Independent variable will require primary data collection as there is no established measure or source for number of crowdfunding platforms across the world. Reports from infoDev/World Bank, Massolutions and Nesta show a general trend in the growth of crowdfunding platforms but do not offer a complete list. In this research, I plan to use them as a starting point and build on them using the method outlined above. One challenge in using internet search will be language barrier. Since the search will be conducted in English language, it is possible to miss some crowdfunding platforms conducting business

operations in native languages only. With the global nature of crowdfunding industry and involvement of diaspora in funding, it is less likely that platform will not support English as an alternate language.

Methods

Since the dependent variable in my analysis is a count data and since it will contain zero as a value for many countries for many years, I will use Poisson or negative binomial regression (special case of Poisson) depending on whether assumption for variance equal to mean is satisfied or not. Poisson regression will ensure that the zero values in dependent variable are not dropped from the model as in case of regular OLS regression (Katila & Ahuja, 2002).

Discussion

If the hypothesis is confirmed, it would mean that institutions in a country should focus on improving the law and enforcement for intellectual property as a prerequisite to promoting crowdfunding as additional source of funding. This would also mean that institutions should establish activities which improve the image of entrepreneurs in the society by highlighting the contribution that entrepreneurial activities make to society at large in terms of employment, innovation and social welfare, leading to change in society's attitude toward entrepreneurs and entrepreneurial activities. This will lead to acceptance of entrepreneur and will enable support from society for entrepreneurial activities and will encourage entrepreneurs to use crowdfunding to connect with society. Institutions should also create an environment of trust and transparency to reduce feeling of uncertainty in society and to enable acceptance of crowdfunding as a medium of financial support. Institutions should define and enforce regulations pertaining to crowdfunding and online financial transactions, bring in transparency by making entrepreneurs and intermediaries (like CFPs) accountable for any wrongdoing and crack down any fraudulent activity swiftly.

If the hypothesis is not confirmed, it would be mean that institutions may not play a role in adoptions of crowdfunding in a country. Based on the extant research done on the role of institutions in general and entrepreneurial finance in particular, I would consider this as anomaly and would relook at the theoretical foundations to find missing elements. It might be possible that constructs and operational variables used in this

study were not an accurate reflection of the on ground phenomenon and more in-depth observation and analysis is required to unearth the right constructs or operational variables.

Future Research

Future research should try to test the impact of cyber laws on adoption of crowdfunding platforms. The use of online integrated payment systems makes an interesting case for the study of cyber law strength in a country with respect to adoption of e-commerce platforms in general and crowdfunding in particular where you cannot have Cash on Delivery model devised by e-commerce platforms as an alternate to online payment.

Future research should also try to improve on the measure of crowdfunding adoption used in this study. Instead of using a count of crowdfunding platforms, future research should try to use utilization measures of crowdfunding platforms such as number of campaigns created or amount of funding sought/received. Such a measure will be more representative of crowdfunding adoption in a country.

This research has focused only on the patent's aspect of intellectual property protection. Future research may expand on this work and try to look at the strength of IP laws using a composite index of patents, copyrights and trademarks.

References

About CAF—Motivating Society to Give More Effectively. (n.d.). Retrieved April 14, 2017, from https://www.cafonline.org/about-us

About Us|Indiegogo. (n.d.). Retrieved April 13, 2017, from https://www.indiegogo.com/about/our-story

Agrawal, A. K., Catalini, C., & Goldfarb, A. (2011). *The geography of crowdfunding*. National Bureau of Economic Research. Retrieved from http://www.nber.org/papers/w16820

Bruton, G. D., Fried, V. H., & Manigart, S. (2005). Institutional influences on the worldwide expansion of venture capital. *Entrepreneurship Theory and Practice, 29*(6), 737–760.

Carciente, S. L. (2016). *International property rights index 2016*. Retrieved from http://s3.amazonaws.com/ipri2016/IPRI+2016+Full+Report.pdf

Charities Aid Foundation (CAF)—Charity Giving Made Simple. (n.d.). Retrieved April 19, 2017, from https://www.cafonline.org/

DataBank|The World Bank. (n.d.). Retrieved April 19, 2017, from http://databank.worldbank.org/data/home.aspx

Gans, J. S., & Stern, S. (2003). The product market and the market for "ideas": Commercialization strategies for technology entrepreneurs. *Research Policy, 32*(2), 333–350.

Geert Hofstede—Geert Hofstede. (n.d.). Retrieved April 19, 2017, from https://geert-hofstede.com/

GEM Global Entrepreneurship Monitor. (n.d.). Retrieved April 19, 2017, from http://www.gemconsortium.org/

Gnyawali, D. R., & Fogel, D. S. (1994). Environments for entrepreneurship development: Key dimensions and research implications. *Entrepreneurship Theory and Practice, 18*, 43–43.

Griffiths, M. D., Gundry, L. K., & Kickul, J. R. (2013). The socio-political, economic, and cultural determinants of social entrepreneurship activity: An empirical examination. *Journal of Small Business and Enterprise Development, 20*(2), 341–357. https://doi.org/10.1108/14626001311326761

Hemer, J. (2011). *A snapshot on crowdfunding* (Working papers firms and region). Retrieved from https://www.econstor.eu/handle/10419/52302

Hindle, K., & Klyver, K. (Eds.). (2011). *Handbook of research on new venture creation*. Edward Elgar.

Hofstede, G. (1983). National cultures in four dimensions: A research-based theory of cultural differences among nations. *International Studies of Management & Organization, 13*(1–2), 46–74.

infoDev. (2013). *Crowdfunding's potential for the developing world*. Retrieved from http://www.infodev.org/infodev-files/wb_crowdfundingreport-v12.pdf

International Property Rights Index. (n.d.). Retrieved March 22, 2017, from http://internationalpropertyrightsindex.org/

Internet World Stats—Usage and Population Statistics. (n.d.). Retrieved April 19, 2017, from http://www.internetworldstats.com/

IPRI 2016. (n.d.). Retrieved April 19, 2017, from http://internationalpropertyrightsindex.org/

Katila, R., & Ahuja, G. (2002). Something old, something new: A longitudinal study of search behavior and new product introduction. *Academy of Management Journal, 45*(6), 1183–1194. https://doi.org/10.2307/3069433

Kreiser, P. M., Marino, L. D., Dickson, P., & Weaver, K. M. (2010). Cultural influences on entrepreneurial orientation: The impact of national culture on risk taking and proactiveness in SMEs. *Entrepreneurship Theory and Practice, 34*(5), 959–983. https://doi.org/10.1111/j.1540-6520.2010.00396.x

Krueger, N. F., & Brazeal, D. V. (1994). Entrepreneurial potential and potential entrepreneurs. *Entrepreneurship Theory and Practice, 18*, 91–91.

Kshetri, N. (2015). Success of crowd-based online technology in fundraising: An institutional perspective. *Journal of International Management, 21*(2), 100–116. https://doi.org/10.1016/j.intman.2015.03.004

Kwok, C. C. Y., & Tadesse, S. (2006). National culture and financial systems. *Journal of International Business Studies, 37*(2), 227–247. https://doi.org/10.1057/palgrave.jibs.8400188

Lim, K. H., Leung, K., Sia, C. L., & Lee, M. K. (2004). Is eCommerce boundary-less? Effects of individualism–collectivism and uncertainty avoidance on Internet shopping. *Journal of International Business Studies, 35*(6), 545–559.

List, J. A., & Price, M. K. (2012). Charitable giving around the world: Thoughts on how to expand the pie. *Cesifo Economic Studies, 58*(1), 1–30. https://doi.org/10.1093/cesifo/ifr023

McDonald, K., & Scaife, W. (2011). Print media portrayals of giving: Exploring national "cultures of philanthropy": Print media portrayals of giving. *International Journal of Nonprofit and Voluntary Sector Marketing, 16*(4), 311–324. https://doi.org/10.1002/nvsm.430

Ostergard, R. L. (2000). The measurement of intellectual property rights protection. *Journal of International Business Studies, 31*(2), 349–360. https://doi.org/10.1057/palgrave.jibs.8490911

Park, W. G. (2008). International patent protection: 1960–2005. *Research Policy, 37*(4), 761–766. https://doi.org/10.1016/j.respol.2008.01.006

Pierrakis, Y., & Collins, L. (2013). *Banking on each other: Peer-to-peer lending to business: Evidence from funding circle*. Retrieved from http://eprints.kingston.ac.uk/29078/

Porta, R. L., Lopez-De-Silanes, F., Shleifer, A., & Vishny, R. W. (1997). Legal determinants of external finance. *The Journal of Finance, 52*(3), 1131. https://doi.org/10.2307/2329518

Rapp, J. K., Bernardi, R. A., & Bosco, S. M. (2010). Examining the use of Hofstede's uncertainty avoidance construct in international research: A 25-year review. *International Business Research, 4*(1), 3.

Roy, J.-P., & Oliver, C. (2009). International joint venture partner selection: The role of the host-country legal environment. *Journal of International Business Studies, 40*(5), 779–801. https://doi.org/10.1057/jibs.2008.110

Schwienbacher, A., & Larralde, B. (2010, forthcoming). Crowdfunding of small entrepreneurial ventures. In *Handbook of entrepreneurial finance*. Oxford University Press. Retrieved from http://papers.ssrn.com/sol3/papers.cfm?abstract_id=1699183

Scott, W. R. (1995). *Institutions and organizations* (Vol. 2). Sage.

Scott, W. R., & Davis, G. F. (2007). *Organizations and organizing: Rational, natural and open systems perspectives*. Pearson Prentice Hall.

Simmons, S. A., Wiklund, J., & Levie, J. (2014). Stigma and business failure: Implications for entrepreneurs' career choices. *Small Business Economics, 42*(3), 485–505. https://doi.org/10.1007/s11187-013-9519-3
Vishwanath, A. (2003). Comparing online information effects: A cross-cultural comparison of online information and uncertainty avoidance. *Communication Research, 30*(6), 579–598. https://doi.org/10.1177/0093650203257838
www.massolution.com. (2013). *Massolution 2013CF full report*. www.massolution.com. Retrieved from www.massolution.com
Wyrwich, M., Stuetzer, M., & Sternberg, R. (2016). Entrepreneurial role models, fear of failure, and institutional approval of entrepreneurship: A tale of two regions. *Small Business Economics, 46*(3), 467–492. https://doi.org/10.1007/s11187-015-9695-4

PART V

Health Sector and COVID-19

CHAPTER 18

Towards an Empathetic HRM in Industrial Relations: Need of the Hour in Disruptive Times

Abhipsa Satpathy, Lalatendu Kesari Jena, and Kalpana Sahoo

Introduction

The first quarter of the year 2020 concluded with the beginning of uncertainty, apprehension, and confusion in the whole world due to the COVID-19 pandemic. Industries ended up loaded with unforeseen challenges, at a time when they could not summon the human resources to come up with the know-how to deal with it. HR managers were invested with the dirty job of firing their employees for no fault of theirs. Ratan

A. Satpathy (✉) · L. K. Jena · K. Sahoo
School of Human Resource Management, XIM University, Bhubaneswar, India
e-mail: abhipsa@xustudent.edu.in

L. K. Jena
e-mail: lkjena@xim.edu.in

K. Sahoo
e-mail: kalpana@xim.edu.in

Rajagopal and R. Behl (eds.), *Managing Disruptions in Business*, Palgrave Studies in Democracy, Innovation, and Entrepreneurship for Growth, https://doi.org/10.1007/978-3-030-79709-6_18

Tata, the noted industrialist and chairman of TATA group, denounced the practice of mass layoffs adding that the companies need to understand their employees' position, the action of hastening layoffs has shown lack of empathy by the companies (The Wire, 2020). Understanding someone's position or keeping oneself in the other person's shoes requires *empathy*. Emotional aspects such as empathy are the grey areas in human resource management and industrial relations which are usually perceived as a non-rational part of the system. The quality of an organization to let its employees have a thorough knowledge of and access to organization-related information sets the stage for *transparency*. It gives them the environment to learn about the organization in a clear and unobstructed manner (Parris et al., 2016). The organization's intentions are lucidly conveyed to the employees in companies which incorporate transparency in their systems. With the spread of the COVID-19 pandemic, a large number of countries went into a locked down phase putting the industries in disarray and the stakeholders at a loss of agency. Some companies have relieved the employees of their jobs without being open about compensations and future prospects (Ranipeta, 2020). Disclosing facts related to downsizing, compensations, and aftercare is the need of the hour to respect the *trust* vested by the employees in the company.

The foundation of employer–employee relationship, just like any other, needs to be accorded by *trust*. However, studies have shown that the trust of employees in their companies has been seeing a downward slope (Bingham, 2017). The current pandemic has taken this distrust to new heights because employees have been abandoned helplessly by many organizations. Apart from monetary assurance, employees also need an emotional outreach by the employers to feel assured that their contribution to the organization is valued. Trust in the organization implies the employees' belief in the organization that it will not take advantage of its vulnerability (Martins, 2000). Trust also talks about the employees' intent to put their confidence in the organization that it will take decisions which is beneficial to both the parties (Berg & Martins, 2013). Trust cannot be built in a day or by calculated acts of benevolence. Trust has a psychological aspect to it which could be nurtured especially by understanding each other in challenging times. Employee counselling has proven to build trust in the organization (Personneltoday.com, 2014). Counselling is a steady process whereby the client builds trust in the counsellor and vice versa. When the counsellor becomes a permanent part of the organization, it will help extend the trust to an organizational level.

Empathy as an ingrained part of the organizational culture can be beneficial to productivity as well as wellbeing (Moreno, 2017). Especially, during the pandemic times, empathy needs to be incorporated in communication; this will help in keeping the employees' trust in the organization alive (Kumaran, 2020). Empathy is a learnable skill and hence leaders and employees can be trained to be more empathetic (Cclinnovation, 2020). Although empathy can be simply described as understanding how the other person might be feeling, in practice it is not as simple as it sounds. The definition of empathy for our model is an emotional response to another person or groups' distress with a recognition that the distress may or may not be have a source in the workplace (Cuff et al., 2014). Empathy is an essential skill of any psychological counsellor. A counsellor is equipped with how to express empathy and how to train people in empathetic behaviour. Many companies have started training their HR professionals in counselling skills but those are not enough to provide therapy or emotional support as and when required (Hughes, 2014). Thus, a culture of empathetic HRM can be installed by employing counsellors in the system that will not be on part-time basis but as an integral part of the organization.

Need for Employee Counselling During and Post COVID-19

The declaration of the coronavirus disease as a pandemic ensued reorganization of workplaces, changes in terms of working, and relying hugely on working from home. These changes are too much to take at a single time, creating stress, burnouts, and low productivity among the employers and employees (Birla, 2020). That is why, some companies like *Mpower* have started providing counselling solutions to organizations so that the employees get the psychosocial support they need in this disruptive times (Birla, 2020). Business giants like Microsoft, Deloitte, and P&G have roped in professional assistance to help the employees cope up with the challenges arising out of social distancing, remote working, increased screen exposure, etc. (Dave, 2020) Providing employees an increased access to wellness programmes is one way in which The Bank of Ireland has reached out to its employees (Jll, 2020). Dedicated helplines connecting with psychologists, counsellors, and mental health professionals are being used by some big corporations (Ghosh, 2020).

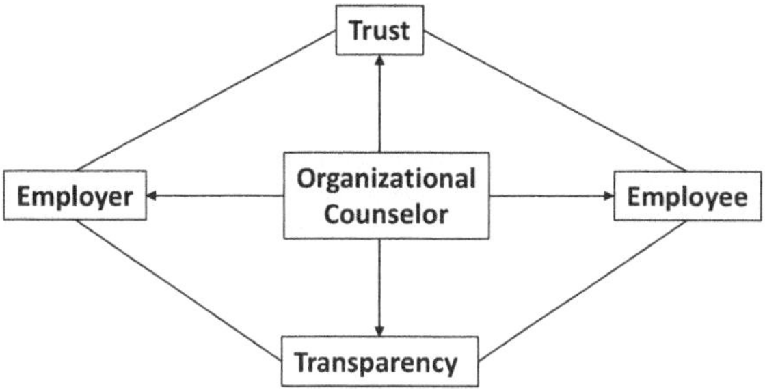

Fig. 18.1 Research model (*Source* Authors)

Looking at the need in the current times, it can be predicted that the need for constant psychological support is here to stay even after the pandemic is over, or else have normalized. In the "*new normal*" scenario, we propose a model which considers a solution of the emotional gap among employees, employers, and employees and among employers. Employee counselling needs to move beyond Employee Assistance Programs, in which the psychological service provider is not an integral part of the organization. Rather, they operate as extra services given to the employees as a pro bono act of employee wellbeing. An integrated model is proposed (see Fig. 18.1) keeping in view the above discussed needs.

The Preventive Approach

The preventive approach to counselling is based on the view that the members of an organization could be trained in empathy, transparency, and trust with the help of an organizational counsellor. Prevention orientation to helping is useful in empowering client and systems (Conyne, 2004). Prevention averts maladjustment in individuals with a risk of negative outcomes (Hage et al., 2007). The organization as a system has traditionally looked at employee redressal as a bottom-up approach whereby the employees seek help from the HR personnel, and they in turn, helped the employees with the rules, regulations, laws, and code of conduct (Contributor, 2020). This model seeks to bridge the emotional gap which is not addressed in the organization through regular HR problem-solving. Employees and even employers might not always be

facing a problem which has a solution in the rational part of the system. Lately, organizations have been connecting the employees to outsourced counselling service providers to take care of their emotional needs. This is the curative approach, where a person in distress is empowered through counselling and enabled to be back on a healthier state of being. Preventive approach tries to set an environment, which is positive, conducive to work in, minimizes the stressors, and ensures wellbeing of the members of the organization. Therefore, we propose,

P_1: Preventive model of employee counselling will help build a positive environment.

Stressful environment leads to various mental health concerns sooner or later. It adversely affects the productivity and health of the employees, strains relationship with the employer, and leads to dissatisfaction and frustration. Stressors in an organizational setting can crop up from difficult employer–employee interactions, which include lack of transparency and trust in the communications. Here, empathy can help fill the emotional gaps by fostering better understanding. Thus, prevention includes workshops, meetings, role plays, events in the annual functions, and training in approaches which will promote empathy among organization members. The organizational counsellor will play a major role in the dissemination of knowledge, development of content for meetings and practices, and delivery of counselling services. The organizational counsellor will be the agent of creating a positive empathetic work culture where every member tries to be empathetic towards the other, is transparent, and trusts the organization and its members. This will enhance the teamwork and give a sense of belonging which is a great motivator. The preventive approach will also look at eliminating the stigma around mental health in the organization. It is a fact that even the educated masses find it difficult to consult a counsellor or therapist due to the fear of being branded unfit for their job. So, through various discourses and desensitization programmes, the employees and employers can be educated about the importance of mental health and how as a part of the same organization, they can respect each other's emotional needs. This will strengthen the relationship between the employers and the employees.

P2: Transparency, Trust, and Empathy between employer and employee will help cope up with the crisis.

An important pretext of building strong employer–employee relationships is how comfortable the employees are in the presence of the employer. It matters whether the employees feel encouraged or threatened to put forth ideas or grievances amid a group of senior employees or the employer. If the relationship compels any of the members of the organization to hold back opinions, problems, or exchange of ideas, there is a need for transparency in the industrial relationships. Lack of transparency could range from a simple denial of feedback to someone's work and can go up to hiding important organizational intentions from the employee. In a time of crisis, such as the COVID-19 pandemic, the withholding of information about further information on layoffs, compensations, and employee assistance programs can lead to lack of trust of the employee in the organization. Here, transparency can play a great role in saving the trust that the employees vest in their employers.

Organizational trust in the time of crisis can be fostered with the help of empathy. The act of empathy in organizations could be practised with the intervention of an organizational counsellor. The role of the OC will be to provide *psychoeducation* to all the members of the organization through one to one as well as group counselling. Without breaking the confidentiality of any employee or employer, the OC will enlighten the employer of the probable consequences of various interactions in the organization. This will help the employers understand the employees' *mental status* and interact in a manner which will not hurt the dignity of the employees. Likewise, the employees could be *desensitized* about the process of furloughing, appraisals, payrolls, and compensations so that they do not feel abandoned in the middle of a crisis. Trust in an organization can be developed by empathy (Feng et al., 2004). Trust is an important predictor of cooperative behaviour (Zalabak et al., 2000). An important concern to be considered in this context is the employees' reluctance to seek one on counselling with an organization. The stigma attached to seeking mental help can be addressed through a *systematic desensitization* of all the members of the organization which will lead to a better understanding and acceptance of around the idea of mental health assistance. The whole process of desensitization is based on the idea of empathy as we need to understand that providing counselling assistance

is not enough unless the employees who are in need are willing to seek the help or understand their peers who need help.

P3: Counselling will help reduce the stress and emotional problems of the employees.

Employee assistance programs have been put in place by many companies to look after the emotional needs of employees. Still, many employees hesitate to utilize this facility for the fear of being judged. A counsellor is trained in providing non-judgemental assistance, but the help seekers are nevertheless exposed to a largely judgemental organizational environment which makes them refuse to go for counselling even when they need it. Counselling in this paper refers to changing and extending the boundaries of work assigned to an organizational counsellor. Here, the counsellor needs to make his/her presence visible to all the members as a wellness coach, a contributor to learning and development in the organization, and a promoter of inclusion and diversity. These roles will help increase acceptance among employees of individual limitations, strengths, and weaknesses and give better insight into making teamwork more productive. The counsellor will be equipped with the legal knowledge of the employees' rights and duties to help them deal overcome *cognitive dissonance* arising out of faulty employer–employee communications.

Emotional problems at workplace can also emerge from various errors in thought processes such as *self-fulfilling prophecy*, *Pygmalion effect*, *self-defeating social comparisons*, and *halo effect*. If an employee is under confident about a task and ends up faring poorly in it, this could be caused because the employee had prior notions about his performance. This is the self-fulfilling prophecy which needs to be countered with rationality. Likewise, the employer's negative expectations from an employee can lead to the employee ending up faring badly in an assignment, as explained by the Pygmalion effect. This can also be related to the stigma attached to mental health. A negative expectation of the employer from an employee, for example, expecting the employee to not be productive because of seeking mental help, can lead the employee being less productive. Social comparisons in a negative way such as demeaning oneself before a peer having a better growth or pay raise can lead to curbing of individual creativity and unique strengths. An employee who gets furloughed is in no way a lesser individual than a counterpart who is not given an out. Halo

effect in organizations obstructs mutual understanding by generalization of one's overall personality. Clichéd phrases like "*the boss is always right*" have social undertones which affect employer–employee relationships. An employer or employee cannot be termed as good or bad in every situation. These changes in perspectives can foster mutual respect and deal better even in a crisis. Thus, a change in perspective can help counter the faulty pattern of thoughts and nurture understanding of self and others. Now, to bring about these changes, certain skills and knowledge are required which are better understood by a counsellor. So, the organizational counsellor can be an agent of transformation in organizational settings, as proposed next.

P4: Preventive model of employee counselling will bring about a transformation in the way industrial relations is perceived.

Organizations seek transformational changes when the existing situation fail to provide a solution to emerging problems (Schalock et al., 2018). The existing nature of employee counselling is not enough to boost an organizational culture based on transparency, trust, and empathy in industrial relations. Thus, the proposed model provides a change in the perception and practice of employee counselling which will lead to transformation in organizations. The components of this transformation will be a transformation in *work culture and employer–employee interactions*, *leadership*, *policy*, and *wellbeing*. Transformational leadership is closely related to leaders with empathetic skills of the leadership is closely related to empathy towards the employees. Transformation in leadership style will be one component of the transformation proposed in the model. The organizational counsellor will be a proactive member of the organization who will promote empathetic approaches in employer–employee interactions. At the same time, he will take care that transparency and trust are not violated in due process.

Work culture is the sum of an organization's ideologies and principles as well as employee's beliefs, thought processes, and attitudes. Work culture can be largely influenced by the type of interaction among employees, and between employer and employee. Freedom to be creative, expressive, sociable, and proactive can all be affected by the way industrial relations are perceived by the employees. Peers' belief of each other as equal partners in growth rather than competition, can be a source of

emotional support during the crisis. Bringing empathy into the picture as a rational and actively practised behaviour can improve industrial relations to a great extent. Employees will find a more accepting culture and employers will have a happier and more enthusiastic workforce.

Change in the present state of the organizational culture can be strengthened with the help of policy level amendments. The roles and responsibilities of the counsellor need to clearly charted. The new policy will mandate the counsellor to carry out activities within the organization to consolidate the ideas of transparency, trust, and empathy. Without a legit framework, the validity of the proposed model could be questioned by others whereas a policy level change will substantiate the authenticity of the position held by the counsellor. This is the way whereby the organizational counsellor's emotional reach out programmes can be seen as a rational part of the industrial relations.

The presence of an organizational counsellor as an agent of transformation will affect many areas of the human resource management practices, wellbeing of members being the most important one. Wellbeing of employees has been found to be strongly related to organizational productivity. Thus, investing in wellbeing of all the members with the help of a counsellor is a secure way of achieving organizational goals. Empathetic practices lead to a better employer–employee relationship which in turn ensures wellbeing. Emotional grievances can be addressed by the organizational counsellor with a genuine concern for the emotional health of the help seeker.

Implications of the Proposed Model

Our aim in developing the model was to introduce an integrated system of employee counselling in organizations so that the emotional requirements such as transparency, trust, and empathy, of all the organizational members, could be taken care of during and post COVID-19 disruption. We have developed the model as an exploratory research, whose implications can be put to test by organizations who are willing to develop a robust work culture to enhance industrial relations. For practice, our model can serve as a ground for better industrial relations, it goes a step further from employee assistance programs and mandates an organizational counsellor to proactively work in fostering relationships and understanding in the organization. It can create opportunities for counsellors and therapists to specialize in an organizational setting

and come up with novel approaches to cater to the psychosocial and emotional needs of employees and employers. This will further lead to better environment to work in, boost creativity, individual growth, utilize the talents in the organization, and enhance productivity. It can actuate better communication between employer and employee as well as among employees. It gives an overview of how an organizational counsellor can be an agent of transformation in the organization. This idea can be taken forward to develop flexible programmes to propagate empathetic HRM practices in organizations.

The model serves as a potent one for future research. The variables emphasized in the model are transparency, trust, and empathy. Other variables such as type of leadership, personality, errors in thought processes could be explored in which the organizational counsellor can intervene to strengthen industrial relations. Research can be undertaken to frame and structure the roles and responsibilities of an organizational counsellor in consonance with transparency, trust, empathy, and ethics. Research can be carried out to specify the difference between counselling through employee assistance programs and the proposed model. Structural changes in organizational policies can be brought about to build a strong and rational foundation for empathetic HRM. After all, the need for more humane practices in HRM is going to increase soon (Mishra & Kar, 2020). The model can be taken as a reference point for furthering research in better human resource management practices.

Limitations and Conclusion

The model introduces a novel combination of employer–employee and the organizational counsellor due to which, any previous attempt to this model has not been cited. Although the model caters to the need of the hour, that is catering to emotional gaps in human resource practices, it is new idea and thus, it requires strong marketing to be recognized by organizations. Employing an organizational counsellor as a proactive part of the organization, surpassing the existing passive roles is liable to questions because, it will require a restricting of roles and responsibilities to ensure it does not overlap with that of the HR professionals. Organizations need to have genuine concern for better human resource practices to incorporate this model. Organizations have need to be convinced that the organizational counsellor can work as an agent of promoting positive environment in a way any other professional cannot.

In this paper, we presented a model which promotes empathetic HRM in industrial relations by using transparency, trust, and empathy. We have put the organizational counsellor at the heart of the model who will establish and maintain an emotionally fulfilling environment in organizations by interacting with the employers and employees and cementing their relationships. The COVID-19 pandemic has created a dire need for transparency, trust, and empathy in industrial relations and thus we have emphasized on these elements to cultivate a more humane HRM practices in organizations.

References

Berg, Y. V. D., & Martins, N. (2013). The relationship between organisational trust and quality of work life. *SA Journal of Human Resource Management, 11*(1). https://doi.org/10.4102/sajhrm.v11i1.392

Bingham, S. (2017, May 3). If employees don't trust you, it's up to you to fix it. *Harvard Business Review*. https://hbr.org/2017/01/if-employees-dont-trust-you-its-up-to-you-to-fix-it

Conyne, R. K. (2004). *Preventive counseling*. https://doi.org/10.4324/9780203336052

Cuff, B. M., Brown, S. J., Taylor, L., & Howat, D. J. (2014). Empathy: A review of the concept. *Emotion Review, 8*(2), 144–153. https://doi.org/10.1177/1754073914558466

Feng, J., Lazar, J., & Preece, J. (2004). Empathy and online interpersonal trust: A fragile relationship. *Journal of Behavior & Information Technology, 23*(2), 97–106.

Hage, S. M., Romano, J. L., Conyne, R. K., Kenny, M., Matthews, C., Schwartz, J. P., & Waldo, M. (2007). Best practice guidelines on prevention practice, research, training, and social advocacy for psychologists. *The Counseling Psychologist, 35*(4), 493–566. https://doi.org/10.1177/0011000006291411

Martins, N. (2000). Developing a trust model for assisting management during change. *SA Journal of Industrial Psychology, 26*(3). https://doi.org/10.4102/sajip.v26i3.716

Parris, D. L., Dapko, J. L., Arnold, R. W., & Arnold, D. (2016, February 8). *Exploring transparency: A new framework for responsible business management*. https://www.emerald.com/insight/content/doi/10.1108/MD-07-2015-0279/full/html

Schalock, R. L., Verdugo, M. A., & Loon, J. V. (2018). Understanding organization transformation in evaluation and program planning. *Evaluation and Program Planning, 67*, 53–60. https://doi.org/10.1016/j.evalprogplan.2017.11.003

Zalabak, P. S., Ellis, K., & Winograd, G. (2000). Organizational trust: What it means, why it matters. *Organization Developmental Journal, 18*(4), 35–49.

Web References

Birla, N. (2020, June 13). How companies can maintain employee mental health in the time of Covid-19. *Business Standard*. https://www.business-standard.com/article/economy-policy/how-companies-can-maintain-employee-mental-health-in-the-time-of-covid-19-120061300423_1.html

Contributor, C. (2020, August 25). *How do human resources managers benefit employees in an organization?* Small Business—Chron.com. https://smallbusiness.chron.com/human-resources-managers-benefit-employees-organization-10431.html

Dave, S. (2020, March 25). Covid-19: Companies rope in psychiatrists, experts for emotional counselling of work from home employees. *The Economic Times*. https://economictimes.indiatimes.com/news/company/corporate-trends/covid-19-companies-rope-in-psychiatrists-experts-for-emotional-counselling-of-work-from-home-employees/articleshow/74819122.cms

*Empathy in the workplace a tool for effective leadership**. (2020). https://cclinnovation.org/wp-content/uploads/2020/03/empathyintheworkplace.pdf

Ghosh, S. (2020). *Importance & ways to manage emotional well-being of employees amid COVID-19*. TCS. https://www.tcs.com/perspectives/articles/why-the-emotional-well-being-of-your-employees-should-be-a-top-priority-during-covid-19

Hughes, R. (2014, November 21). How workplace counselling helps employees and employers. *Personnel Today*. https://www.personneltoday.com/hr/workplace-counselling-helps-employees-employers/

Jll. (2020, May 5). *How companies are supporting employees during COVID-19*. Commercial real estate. https://www.us.jll.com/en/trends-and-insights/workplace/how-companies-are-supporting-employees-during-covid-19

Kumaran, D. (2020, April). Ensuring the mental wellness of employees at the time of COVID-19. *BW People*. http://bwpeople.businessworld.in/article/Ensuring-The-Mental-Wellness-Of-Employees-At-The-Time-Of-COVID-19/22-04-2020-189966/

Layoffs during pandemic shows India Inc's lack of empathy: Ratan Tata. (2020). The Wire. https://thewire.in/business/ratan-tata-layoffs-covid-19

Mishra, A. K., & Kar, A. K. (2020, June 19). *Role of human resource in the post-COVID environment*. Retrieved October, from http://bwpeople.businessworld.in/article/Role-of-Human-Resource-in-the-Post-COVID-Environment/19-06-2020-289219/

Moreno, D. (2017, June 2). *7 Benefits of empathy in the workplace*. https://www.civcom.com/blog/7benefits

Ranipeta, S. S. (2020, May 28). COVID-19 impact: A list of companies that have laid off employees amid the pandemic. *The News Minute*. https://www.thenewsminute.com/article/covid-19-impact-list-companies-have-laid-employees-amid-pandemic-125473

CHAPTER 19

Training Need Identification of Nursing Professional's Competencies During Pandemic and Scale Development

Sharanika Dhal and Snigdha Mohapatra

Introduction

The Healthcare Sector is one of the largest employer in the world and Nurses are the biggest part of it. According to World Health Organization (WHO), it is estimated that there are 42 million health workers in the world and 19.7 million are nurses and midwives. In a Published Report "Nursing and Midwifery in the History of the world health organization" (1948–2017) by the World Health Organization (WHO); it is projected that by 2030 the health workforce needs to grow to 71.8 million of which 37.2 million will be nurses and midwives. For doing excellence in this

S. Dhal (✉) · S. Mohapatra
Birla School of Management, Birla Global University, Bhubaneswar, India
e-mail: Sdhal.scholar18@bgu.ac.in

S. Mohapatra
e-mail: snigdha.mohapatra@bgu.ac.in

Rajagopal and R. Behl (eds.), *Managing Disruptions in Business*, Palgrave Studies in Democracy, Innovation, and Entrepreneurship for Growth, https://doi.org/10.1007/978-3-030-79709-6_19

sector; this large workforce needs proper planning, guidance, theoretical and practical knowledge and also a proper policy set up which can be done by systematic competency mapping. Nurses should be best in their clinical and nonclinical practice by proper competency gap identification. The concept of competence (Bowden & Masters, 1993; Sternberg & Kolligian, 1990) and competency model development (Boyatzis, 2008) are earlier introduced by several researchers to assess competencies starting from 1970s till now to measure the job performances. Identification and development of competencies (Lindholm & Rothwell, 1999) will help them to deliver better service to the patients. That's why there should be proper competency assessment done to improve their skills which will strengthen the performance in the respective workplace (Boxall et al., 2011) and a competency assessment scale is having a great role in this whole process. Competency mapping, assessment and scale development are the subject of research required to upgrade skill or to develop competencies nowadays in each sector. Competency mapping is the process of identifying the knowledge, skill and abilities required to fulfill the job role and responsibilities (Priyadarshini & Dave, 2012). A competency assessment tool is necessary to evaluate the psychometric properties for each level of the nursing sector (Hwang and Jo 2020).

As per the global perspective and pandemic situation, there are lot of challenges now related to working environment (Letourneau et al., 2020) (Ex: Most of the work is done in virtual environment), job responsibilities, chronic illnesses availability of physical resources, etc. For handling COVID-19 situation; nurses are developing some special competencies, i.e., personal resilience (Eby et al., 2019; Mc. Donald et al., 2013), Disaster handling competencies, stress management by some creative therapies, Online working or e-learning (Cronenwett et al., 2009; Eby et al., 2017; Mercurio, 2015; Noe et al., 2014), change management, personal resilience, technological skills (Campbell & Wiernik, 2015; Clardy, 2007; Flood et al., 2019), Psychological counseling, social consciousness and nursing research, etc. This study will put emphasis on identifying competencies which will help to train them in current demanding situations and it will also facilitate the construction of a competency-based assessment scale for the nursing sector.

Literature Review

The present dynamic environment in the healthcare industry needs more competent nursing staffs who will accept the challenges and issues with a positive attitude. To develop competent and well-trained staffs, competency mapping or competence-based assessment is the important tool in the area of training and development (Garavan 2011). Professional competencies can be increased by acquiring proper knowledge and skill after measuring the performance by using dimensions/factors/scale, etc. There should be always an upgradation of the scale or process of competency mapping as per the requirement. As per the self-assessment, they may be trained accordingly to improve themselves. A learning organization culture always helps them in a positive way by customized training.

Nursing Sector as an Important Subcomponent of Indian Healthcare Industry

As per Indian Nursing Council, nurses are the most important part of the industry as there are around 1.79 million registered nurses and 786,796 auxiliary nurses-cum-midwives are in India and this area needs great attention as the whole hospital industry depends upon it. Due to the heterogeneous structure of nursing curriculum in India, it is necessary to do competency mapping during service.

In India, four types of nurses provide care to the patients.

There are several issues in the nursing sector (Tiwari et al., 2012) in India related to its educational curriculum and professional development. Competency mapping is necessary in service as there is improper streamlining of education and non-uniform syllabus in the basic level of courses of A.N.M., G.N.M. and B.S.c. Nursing. Area of focus for improvements in the nursing sector in India (Tiwari et al., 2012) as follows: Streamlining nursing education, enriching the curriculum, strengthening nursing faculty development and Increase use of innovative teaching and learning techniques.

Concept of Competency

Competency is the specified skills, knowledge, attitudes and behavior necessary to fulfill a task. As many of the researchers stated that employees are the intellectual capital or tangible asset of the organization; it is necessary to invest in it and make the employees more competent. According to Rothwell and Lindholm (1999), "Job competency is the motive, trait, skill and aspects of one's self image in an organization and organizational core competency depends upon collective learning, diverse production skills and multiple streams of technologies." According to Clardy (2008) core competencies are the competitive advantages of an organization. Competency is the characteristic of an individual that helps to perform well in any type of situation. Windsor et al. (2011) mentioned that there should be some policies to make the individuals more competent to deliver good services in healthcare sector. Competencies help to show proper behavior where as its misuse leads to errors. According to O'Connor et al. (2019), competence is a central tenet of nursing practice, with the underlying premise that "patients have a right to receive quality care by competent nurse and midwives who practice in a safe environment." Competency is described as serving an individual or a community through the habitual and judicious use of knowledge, technical skills, clinical reasoning, emotional intelligence, values and reflection in daily practice (Bam et al., 2019). Competencies should concentrate on self-assessment, Ethical practices, cost control and delivery of high-quality services. Studies are shown that proper learning culture should be embedded to the organization strategies to improve the competencies of the nurses (Dias et al., 2018). Weiss et al. (2018) summarized the relevant training and availability of guidelines that required improving competencies of nurses. Nursing depends upon some of the human factors like knowledge, experience and skill for good professional practices. Baxter and Edvardsson (2018) explore the impact of critical care postgraduate certificate course on nurses self-competence and confidence. To develop a particular competence one should continue the learning process. Learning culture helps to improve the competencies of the nurses (Dias et al., 2018). Kumar et al. (2018) studied the association between the variables related to organizational cultural competence and the teamwork climate in a health system. For Ex: Teamwork process may

depend on different variables like leadership, collaboration of management with operations, communication process, service delivery, support system, workforce diversity training, data collection, public accountability and quality improvement.

Training Needs Identification of Nurses

Training and development help the organization to produce competent staffs that are considered as an asset. Aguinis and Kraiger (2008) studied the benefits of training and development for individuals, teams, organizations and society and different aspects of training and competence-based training need assessment and its effectiveness. Competency mapping and development helps in career development. Boxall et al. (2011) described that training and career development is an important practice of HR in every sector and there are various ways of assessment. Rao et al. (2011) described about the motivational factors in healthcare sector in India, i.e., monetary incentives, educational incentives or training, workforce policies and public private partnership, subordination, supervision and leadership which enhance the nursing sector. There is National Health Policy to improve healthcare in India and more and more research should be done to improve condition or to change policies in India (Redmond et al. 2011). There are many researchers suggest to study comparative analysis of training need assessment or competency mapping of nurses for public or private sector hospitals as the culture and clients/patients are different (Franco & Tavares, 2013). There are several factors affecting professional development (Breckelmans, 2013) are as follows: Availability of resources, fund and time, Organizational strategy, Commitment of key decision-makers, Infrastructure, Support of employers and employees, Learning Culture or workplace learning, Organization culture, Teamwork and Attitude. Competency-based training assessment scale is a validated decision tool, correlated to a specific group of activities that describes key knowledge, skills and abilities for performing various activities. Aragon et al. (2014) studied the effectiveness of training that includes organizational training, managerial training, leadership training, error management training and team training. Before training, it is necessary to assess competencies by conducting job task analysis. Competency identification process is exhibited in Table 19.1 illustrating the research studies that identified various variables contextual to competencies.

Table 19.1 Identification of various competencies of nurses

Sl. No.	*Different competencies (KSAs)*	*Authors*
1	Interpersonal relationship skill	Schwirian (1978), Spruill et al. (2004), Riggio and Lee (2007), Franco and Tavares (2013), McDonald et al. (2013), Wan et al. (2015), Hicks et al. (2017), Karimi et al. (2019), Skarsater et al. (2018), Boyle et al. (2019), Santo et al. (2020)
2	Building professional identity/Occupational identity	Schwirian (1978), Kirpal (2004), Kaslow et al. (2005), Franco and Tavares (2013), Brekelmans et al. (2013), Felton and Royal (2015), Kol et al. (2017), Hicks et al. (2017), Dias et al. (2018), Karimi et al. (2019), Tuomikoski et al. (2019)
3	Emotional intelligence/Emotional competence	Akerjordet and Severinsson (2008), Riggio and Lee (2007), McDonald et al. (2013), O'Boyle et al. (2011), Kozub et al. (2016), Oysy et al. (2016), Crowne et al. (2017), Santo et al. (2020)
4	Leadership development	Schwirian (1978), Davies et al. (2002), Jennings et al. (2007), Akerjordet and Severinsson (2008), Felton and Royal (2015), Campbell and Wiernik (2015), Kozub et al. (2016), Hicks et al. (2017), Crowne et al. (2017), Kumra et al. (2018), Kim et al. (2019), Tuomikoski et al. (2019)
5	Teaching and collaboration	Schwirian (1978), Davies et al. (2002), Cronenwett et al. (2009), McDonald et al. (2013), Nagel et al. (2016), Skarsater et al. (2018), Kim et al. (2019), Boyle et al. (2019), Immonen et al. (2019)
6	Planning and evaluation	Schwirian (1978)
7	Critical care management	Schwirian (1978)

(continued)

Table 19.1 (continued)

Sl. No.	*Different competencies (KSAs)*	*Authors*
8	Communication skill	Schwirian (1978), Davies et al. (2002), Aguinis and Kraiger (2008), Kozub et al. (2016), Oysy et al. (2016), Campbell and Wiernik (2015), Felton and Royal (2015), Felton and Royal (2015), Kumra et al. (2018), Weiss et al. (2018), Tuomikoski et al. (2019), Kim et al. (2019), Boyle et al. (2019), Wan et al. (2019), Immonen et al. (2019), Chen et al. (2020)
9	Learning skill	Rothwell and Lindholm (1999), Dooley et al. (2004), Clardy (2007), Noe et al. (2014), Guzman et al. (2015), Hicks et al. (2017), Dias et al. (2018), Immonen et al. (2019), Chen et al. (2020), Santo et al. (2020), Salas et al. (2020)
10	Decision-making skill	Davies et al. (2002), Felton and Royal (2015), Campbell and Wiernik (2015), Karimi et al. (2019), Carter et al. (2016), Kim et al. (2019), Labrague et al. (2019), Santo et al. (2020)
11	Team management	Aguinis (2008), Kailash and Lee (2009), Cronenwett et al. (2009), Redmond et al. (2011), Salas et al. (2012), Noe et al. (2014), Campbell and Wiernik (2015), Oysy et al. (2016), Smollan (2017), Barton et al. (2017), Carter et al. (2016), Kumra et al.(2018), Brunner et al. (2018), Boyle et al. (2019), Salas et al. (2020)
12	Ethical practices	Spruill et al. (2004), Kaslow et al. (2005), Felton and Royal (2015), Boyle et al. (2019), Bam et al. (2019), Immonen et al. (2019)

(continued)

Table 19.1 (continued)

Sl. No.	*Different competencies (KSAs)*	*Authors*
13	Nursing research	Sheer and Wong (2008), Redmond et al. (2011), Davies et al. (2002), Noe et al. (2014), Campbell and Wiernik (2015), Adamson and Prion (2015), Oermann et al. (2017)
14	Mentoring	Dooley et al. (2004), Anatole et al. (2012), Noe et al. (2014), Smollan (2017), Guerrero and Brenner (2016), Brunner et al. (2018), Chlan et al. (2019), Tuomikoski et al. (2019), Immonen et al. (2019)
15	General management	Davies et al. (2002), Salas et al. (2012), Noe et al. (2014), Oysy et al. (2016), Felton and Royal (2015), Kol et al. (2017), Kumra et al. (2018), Brunner et al. (2018)
16	Writing skill	Brunner et al. (2018), Carter et al. (2016)
17	Online program learning/E-Learning/Informatics	Cronenwett et al. (2009), Noe et al. (2014), Cannifold et al. (2014), Smythe et al. (2016), Eby et al. (2017)
18	Clinical assessment	Godkin and Godkin (2004), Felton and Royal (2015), Lee et al. (2016), Barton et al. (2017), Weiss et al. (2018), Bam et al. (2019)
19	Organization cultural competence	Spruill et al. (2004), Clardy (2007), Aguinis and Kraiger (2008), Bazarko et al. (2013), Hicks et al. (2017), Kumra et al. (2018), Chen et al. (2020)
20	Workforce diversity management	Rothwell and Lindholm (1999), Kaslow et al. (2005), McDonald et al. (2013), Kumra et al. (2018),
21	Social consciousness/Community engagement	Kumra et al. (2018)
22	Quality improvement	Clardy (2007), Barton et al. (2009), Cronenwett et al. (2009), Felton and Royal (2015), Hicks et al. (2017), Kumra et al. (2018)

(continued)

Table 19.1 (continued)

Sl. No.	*Different competencies (KSAs)*	*Authors*
23	Knowledge management	Clardy (2007), Aguinis and Kraiger (2008), Guzman et al. (2015), Carter et al. (2016), Hicks et al. (2017), Tuomikoski et al. (2019)
24	Strategic adaptation/Flexibility	Kumar et al. (2002), Aguinis and Kraiger (2008), McDonald et al. (2013), Kozub et al. (2016), Santo et al. (2020)
25	Innovative thinking (New ideas generation)	Kumar et al. (2002), Aguinis and Kraiger (2008), McDonald et al. (2013), Cashin (2014), Felton and Royal (2015), Campbell and Wiernik (2015)
26	Stress management	Bazarko et al. (2013), Bazarko et al. (2013), Regina et al. (2013), Smollan (2017), Kol et al. (2017), Eby et al. (2017), Hicks et al. (2017), Skarsater et al. (2018), Karimi et al. (2019)
27	Psychological intervention and assessment	Krishnamurthy et al. (2004), Kaslow et al. (2004), Kaslow et al. (2005), Ranue and Kthyaani B. (2019)
28	Evidence-based practices	Spruill et al. (2004), Cronenwett et al. (2009), Labrague et al. (2017), Tuomikoski et al. (2019), Zhanming et al. (2018), Immonen et al. (2019)
29	Critical thinking	Davies et al. (2002), Spruill et al. (2004), Noe et al. (2014), Smollan (2017), Carter et al. (2016), Bam et al. (2019), Immonen et al. (2019)
30	Self-consciousness or care/Self Confidence	Spruill et al. (2004), McDonald et al. (2013), Baxter and Edvardsson (2018)
31	Self-evaluation or appraisal or self-assessment	Spruill et al. (2004), Noe et al. (2014), Cannifold et al. (2014), Campbell and Wiernik (2015), Markoulli et al. (2017), Bam et al. (2019)
32	Resilience	McDonald et al. (2013), Folke (2016), Eby et al. (2017), Hicks et al. (2017)

(continued)

Table 19.1 (continued)

Sl. No.	*Different competencies (KSAs)*	*Authors*
33	Psychological counseling	Weiss et al. (2018), Skarsater et al. (2018), Salas et al. (2020)
34	Clinical support or Supervision skill	Noe et al. (2014), Campbell and Wiernik (2015), Smollan (2017), Kol et al. (2017), Hicks et al. (2017), Tuomikoski et al. (2019), Harvey et al. (2020)
35	Chronic disease management or prevention practices	Hicks et al. (2017)
36	Change management	Smollan (2017), Bam et al. (2019)
37	Empathy	Smollan (2017), Wan et al. (2019)
38	Clinical management	Sheer and Wong (2008), Felton and Royal (2015), Oysy et al. (2016), Kozub et al. (2016), Labrague et al. (2019), Tuomikoski et al. (2019), Immonen et al. (2019)
39	Administrative practices/Documentation	Dooley et al. (2004), Clardy (2007), Noe et al. (2014), Campbell and Wiernik (2015)
40	Technological skill	Dooley et al. (2004), Clardy (2007), Campbell and Wiernik (2015)
41	Reflective practices	Canniford et al. (2014), Carter et al. (2016), Santo et al. (2020)
42	Conflict management/Problem-solving skill	Davies et al. (2002), Felton and Royal (2015)
43	Safety management	Cronenwett et al. (2009), Barton et al. (2009), Felton and Royal (2015), Salas et al. (2020)
44	Time management	Noe et al. (2014)

Source Authors' analysis

Need of Identification of Competencies in Strengthening Improvement of Performances of Nurses

Training need identification helps to build up proper professional and personal identity by updating knowledge and skill which will help to enhance the job performance. It provides a vision to develop a good career path and present a proper identity in the service sector as person's identity depends upon interest, role, attitude, value and orientation.

Schwirian (1978) conceptualized nursing performances in six dimensions as stated below:

- Teaching and collaboration,
- Planning and evaluation,
- Critical care,
- Interpersonal care and communication,
- Leadership and
- Professional development

Maximum performance is believed to occur when the person's ability is congruent with the need of job and organization (Boyatzis, 1982). According to Theory of Action and Job performance or Basic Competency theory, there are three components as stated below, which are congruent for effective actions or behavior:

1. The individual Competencies
2. The Job Demands
3. The Organizational Environment

It studied core competencies to analyze management work. Core competencies based on superior organization routines and processes provide an ideal source for competitive advantages. Competency model helps in increasing performances by training and development (Rothwell & Lindholm, 1999). Competency gap analysis helps in psychological assessment which leads to enhance the job performances (Kaslow et al., 2004; Krishnamurthy et al., 2004). Assessment of core competencies also helps in designing customized training programs which will help in performance improvement.

Career of nurses is needed to be better developed and systematized for delivery of best care in clinical practices which can be done by proper competency gap analysis (Kirpal, 2004). According to Clardy (2008), individual performance is depending upon workflow process, cultural value and belief, technological competencies and administrative practices. According to Aguinis and Kraiger (2008), Organization performance depends upon effectiveness, profitability and sales and job performance depends upon tactic skills, innovation and communication. Competency model helps to train professionals in the required skill sets. In India there

should be an increase in the training institutions to perform better in the respective sector or it will produce competent staffs (Rao et al., 2011).

Monetary incentives, educational incentives, workforce policies, new talent acquisitions and public–private partnership will be the motivations for the nursing sector. In India subordination, supervision and leadership skills will be important for the clinical and public health dept. for nurses. Stevens (2013) gives importance to competency model builds up as it will help in the process of selection, training and development, promotions, job assignments and compensation. Personal resilience also affects job performance. It enhanced to adopt/change Vulnerable environment, to enhance work, impact interpersonal relationship, enhance group behavior, critical situation handling, etc. (Mc. Donald & Jackson, 2013). Hurst and Patterson (2014) discussed the issues relating to getting the right health and social care staff with the right skills in the right place at the right time and at the right time and in the right place. Skilled workforces always perform better in service delivery. Learning also helps to enhance performances in individual, group level organization level, etc. (Noe et al., 2014). It is seen as one of the important competencies, i.e., Patient-centered care consists of Theories or science, Self-development knowledge, Art transformative nursing, Ethical practices, social justices to understand vulnerability (Felton & Royal, 2015) required to deliver quality service as per patient's satisfaction.

Several competencies are evolved in nurses during pandemic situation like technological competencies, leadership, coordination, mentoring, stress management, personal resilience, emotional intelligence, etc. They love to work as a team and called as COVID-19 warriors. They provide psychological support and counseling during treatment of affected patients and their families. Technological competency enhances the job performance like e-health, online working, data recording, documentation by different software, etc. It helps on patient-centric system that reduces complexity (Meier et al., 2015). Campbell and Wiernik (2015) suggested competency models help in assessment of performance in a work role. There are certain skills are evolved due to the dynamic situations which will help in doing job in a better way. Ex: Clinical reasoning is a skill is required for handling critical situations. There is always a need of designing a program which can identify nurse's accurate and appropriate reasoning skills (Lee et al., 2016). Job performance will be increased by proper training need identification and that will be done by proper competency gap analysis. Professional competence is increased

by proper skill and knowledge (Kol et al., 2017). Stress management helps in increase resiliency and enhance the task performance (Eby et al., 2017) which is required to handle COVID-19 situation. HRD programs should develop more and more skills to supervise support and mentor the programs that mitigate stressful change within the context of a supportive organization culture (Smollan, 2017). The Job Characteristics Theory (JCT) developed by Hackman and Oldham, is widely used as a framework to study how particular job characteristics affect job outcomes, including job satisfaction.

The five job characteristics are skill variety, task variety, task significance, autonomy and feedback (Asiamah et al., 2019; Mayrowetz et al., 2007). Empowerment is possible by increasing communication, displaying support and providing necessary support which is seen during pandemic. To identify and characterize the core curriculum outcomes among training programs for nurse practitioners is important to enhance the performance (Hicks et al., 2019).

Some of the competencies having its own effect on the individual performance; like Emotional intelligence (Karimi et al., 2019), Stress management, Teamwork management, organization culture competence, knowledge management, etc. Adequate training, availability of resources, continuing education, use of technology, proper documentation, IT infrastructure, patient-centered care, focus on leveraging the roles of each team member, mutual respect, relationship building and communication will help in effective job performance (Boyle et al., 2019). As per the AMO Theory (Ability, Motivation and Opportunities), increase training programs are act as motivational factors to enhance job performance as it increases skill variety and job knowledge (Asiahmah et al., 2019). Salas et al. (2020) suggested that teamwork and safety are required for effective job performance and identified team level criteria that enable teamwork, i.e., psychological safety, team trust, collective efficacy, shared mental models and situation awareness. Chen et al. (2020) explored nursing cultural competence which enhances job performance consists of Cultural awareness, Sensitivity, Appropriateness Humility, etc. It is an important issue as related to culture, race, gender and sexual orientation. Leininger's theory of cultural diversity focused on nursing theories, competent care and studied patient's treatment within a culturally dynamic setting. In-depth study should be done on learning of new skills in the healthcare to improve the performance. Clinical supervision is important to support development programs and better task performance (Harvey et al., 2020).

Methods

Participants and Design

The standard Hennessy-Hicks questionnaire is modified as per the requirement of the training needs after doing a pilot study of 170 nurses who is working in the particular hospital. In-depth interview is done with the nursing staffs which includes interns, staff nurse, senior staff nurse, senior sister in charge, senior nursing supervisor, Assistant Nursing Superintendent, Clinical instructor. To develop the modified questionnaire; different sources are used in the research procedure like some of the current practices and relevant studies obtained from the literature review, points from the appraisal process in the given organization and also from the interactions with the nursing staffs and some suggestions from the experts in the respective field. It may be described as non-probabilistic sampling method with convenient sampling is used to collect the feedbacks from the participants. The research method is analytical or empirical study.

The Instrument (Hennessy-Hicks Assessment of Training Needs)

In order to identify the training needs of nursing staffs, a structured questionnaire is designed from a validated questionnaire called as Hennessy-Hicks assessment of training needs. This instrument is developed in 1996 and it consists of a core set of 30 items and can be modified as per the requirement of the research. It is highly popular to do training need assessment for allied health professional, cross-cultural studies of health care practitioners and to identify specialist continuing development needs. It is used to collect feedback to do training need assessment without compromising its psychometric properties (Hennessy et al., 2006). It is invented in UK but widely used in the countries like Greece, Indonesia, USA and Australia (Carlisle et al., 2011).

Research Instrument

It consists of 40 items showing different areas and there is a five point rating scale used to collect the feedback and rating is given by the respondents as per their preference in training needs. It is administered to 502 nurses and 330 feedbacks are collected successfully. Then the whole data is analyzed by SPSS using factor analysis method.

Ethical Consideration

Before data collection, an approval has obtained from the head of the departments of the three hospitals of Bhubaneswar. All the nursing professionals are informed about the objectives of the study. The data should be kept confidential is assured to the participants.

Data Analysis

Validation of the Data

To check the validity of the instrument's structure and its reliability, an Exploratory Factor Analysis is done by using SPSS s/w. Using a Varimax rotation and Cronbach's Alpha assessment data reliability is checked. Cronbach's Alpha is 0.819 (Table 19.3) for all 40 standardized items which show data is reliable; KMO (Kaiser–Meyer–Olkin) became measures the sample adequacy and Bartlett's test of sphericity, $p = 0.000$ showing data is significant (Table 19.4). The factor analysis yielded six factors with components are having Eigenvalues of >1.0 (Presented in Table 19.2).

Table 19.2 Sample characteristics (Demographics)

Variables	*Category*	*Frequency (%)*	*Mean (SD)*
Age	20–30	170 (51.5)	110 (94.9)
	31–40	159 (48.2)	33.3 (28.6)
	41–50	1 (0.3)	
Educational qualification	Diploma	218 (66.1)	165 (74.9)
	BSc. Nursing	112 (34.0)	50.05 (22.698)
Job position	Junior Nurse	170 (51.5)	110 (94.5)
	Senior Nurse	159 (48.1)	33.3 (28.6)
	Nursing Superintendent	1 (0.3)	
Experience	Less than equal to 5	150 (45.5)	110(35.5)
	5–10 Years	81 (23.6)	33 (11.2)
	11–25 years	99 (30)	

Source Authors' data analysis

Table 19.3 Item analysis and retrieved components:

Dimensions	*Nomenclature*	*Construct validity (Cronbach's Alpha)*	*Cumulative variance (%)*
A1	Interpersonal skill	0.919	17.6
A2	Technological skill	0.312	28.1
A3	Research and analytical skill	0.863	37.54
A4	Professional development	0.785	45.15
A5	Clinical skill	0.809	51.54
A6	Mentoring	0.530	57.3
A7	Emotional intelligence	0.094	63
A8	Personal resilience	0.562	63.02
A9	Ethical skill	0.621	73.3

Source Authors' data analysis

Discussion

The aim and objective of the study are to identify particular training needs for the registered nurses of few hospitals of Bhubaneswar as per the requirement of the present demanding situation. Data collections, instrument selection, design and discussions regarding the training need identification have been done as per the expert advices of the selected organizations and some of the evidences from the past literatures of similar situations. Before data analysis, data reliability and adequacy checked by using the calculated value of Cronbach's Alpha and Kaiser–Meyer–Olkin Measure of Sampling Adequacy which is 0.819 and 0.621, respectively, as shown in (Table 19.3) and (Table 19.4). Data is significant as the value of Bartlett's Test of Sphericity is 0.00 (Table 19.4). As shown in Table 19.2, the nurses mean age is 28.6 years (range 20–30 years). Regarding educational qualification; 66.1% of total participants are having Diploma in Nursing and 34% are having B.Sc. in Nursing and they are educated from various private and Govt. institutions. During interviewing it is explored that theoretically may be the course curriculums are same but they need to be updated with practical knowledge about the current nursing practices. New techniques of various Dept. of the organization should be learned as per many of the senior nurses. During COVID-19 situation, training was required about the treatment of the related patients as it involved various complications. For handling COVID-19 patients, separate ward is constructed and training is given batch by batch with

Table 19.4 Factor loading and item statements ($n = 330$)

Item No	*Description*	*Cronbach's Alpha*
Factor-1	Interpersonal skill (A1)	
22	Acceptance of other's suggestions in a constructive way	0.885
15	Co-operation with others and patient's needs	0.822
21	Adjustment in working with others	0.800
14	Identifying other's strengths and weaknesses and motivates them to do work	0.795
25	Promotes teamwork and team coordination	0.789
12	Sharing of workload with others	0.756
3	Communicating with others along with patients and their families	0.755
4	Building trust in the workplace	0.740
7	Help others to learn new things	0.594
1	Establishing relationship with patients	0.544
Factor-2	Technological Skill (A2)	
13	Writing communication skill for reporting	0.813
2	Data Recording and Data Input both clinical and nonclinical	0.759
9	Using various tools and techniques in daily activities	0.735
11	Adaptation of new technologies	0.707
24	Analyzing clinical data accurately or comprehensively	0.637
18	Use of advanced technology in clinical activities	0.617
Factor-3	Research and Analytical Skill (A3)	
34	Integration of new research findings to the nursing practice	0.917
26	Designing a clinical research study or new learning method to study new things	0.902
39	Reading books and use different techniques to learn new things in nursing practice	0.897
27	Introduction of new ideas	0.631
28	Accessing research sources (Time, money, Information and equipment)	0.607
40	Decision-making using scientific principles	0.562
Factor-4	Professional Development (A4)	
20	Identifying own learning needs	0.866
6	Self-appraisal or personal assessment	0.725
19	Use of new techniques for personal assessment	0.677
5	Use learning opportunities for personal and professional growth	0.673

(continued)

Table 19.4 (continued)

Item No	*Description*	*Cronbach's Alpha*
10	Always searching for new opportunities for professional development	0.655
Factor-5	Clinical Skill (A5)	
36	Clinical assessment, planning a treatment plan and recording of data	0.897
38	Psychological counseling of patients and their family	0.865
Factor-6	Mentoring Skill (A6)	
8	Coaching to juniors and colleagues	0.914
17	Support and supervision to other staffs	0.558
Factor-7	Emotional Intelligence (A7)	
30	Conflict management	0.858
33	Manage emotions to accept changes in the environment easily	0.697
29	Beware of own and other's emotions	0.544
Factor-8	Personal Resilience (A8)	
37	Showing positive attitude	0.877
32	Adopt any critical situations easily, flexible attitude and motivating others to overcome a negative situation	0.681
Factor-9	Ethical Skill (A9)	
35	Obeying all the ethical consideration of the organization	0.911
31	Respect patient's right to choice and self-determination in nursing and healthcare	0.663

Source Authors' data analysis

isolation period of 14 days if any of them had contaminated during treatment. About 48.1% of senior nurses are active participants of the survey and as per them they needed more and more training about sanitization, medication, biomedical wastage treatment, psychological counseling and stress management along with the traditional knowledge Training should be done about donning and doffing of PPE kit during sample collection for testing for the junior nursing staffs. As per experiences, 30% of participants having 11–25 years of experiences and 45.5% are having less than or equal to 5 years.

As per the Exploratory Factor Analysis, it can be derived that nine constructs are derived as shown in Table 19.3. From the nine constructs, seven are consistent and two of them are not considered for study as Cronbach's Alpha are 0.312 (A2) and 0.094 (A7), respectively. So the

final identified areas of training can be; interpersonal skill, research and analytical skill, professional development, clinical skill, mentoring skill, Personal resilience and ethical skill. A2 and A7 can be studied again by taking a large no. of sample as technological skill and emotional intelligence are the important areas to be considered as per the areas of training according to some of the participants.

From Table 19.4, it is seen that 73.3% cumulative variance explained about ethical skills which are all about obeying all the organizational rules and regulations related to clinical and nonclinical practice. 63.02% of variance explained about the factor personal resilience. 63% of total variance is explaining about emotional intelligence. Communication skill, being empathetic, emotional resilience, good judgment, leadership skill, teamwork, interpersonal relationship, etc., required for patient's care (Maria & Rania, 2017). As the data is inconsistent about the factor A7; it can be further studied elaborately with new sample collection. A6 is the mentoring skill explaining about the supervision of staffs and colleagues. There is a study done at Rwanda examining that mentorship is having a great role in quality improvement in nursing sector by assessing the competencies of nurses. It describes about the positive outcomes of the implementation of a healthcare program called The Mentoring and Enhanced Supervision at Health centers (MESH) by mentorship. This study mentioned that mentors assess the presence of necessary health equipment, medication and trained staffs during their visit to the working site of nurses. Mentorship program is necessary for the competency-based assessment for any organization and also for skill development (Brenner et al., 2016). There should be a formal review done for implementing the mentorship program and a survey tool can be created to measure the gap that how well the mentors can be addressed. So it can be suggested that proper mentorship can enhance the skills in the nursing sector. 360-degree competency-based management is developed for healthcare staffs but tested for midlevel managers to identify low and top performers. Mentoring competence is required for professional development and performance improvement (Tuomikioski et al., 2019). Proper mentoring requires clinical practice, knowledge about proper patient care and feedback.

According to Hennessy et al. (2006) there are six areas identified as the areas of training described as, Clinical care and service management, managing change and the application of knowledge, case management and networking, nursing care and leadership, making decisions and

extending care provisions. It is important to identify the variables which affect patient satisfactions and healthcare quality in a hospital to build positive reputation. That can be; physical skill and expertise, physician and nurse courtesy, diet for patients, general hospital evaluation, recommendations by hospitals, core services, professional credibility, competence, communication, etc. (Naidu, 2009). The present study showed that 51.54% of total variance explained about clinical management or clinical skills (A5) of patients. An increasing demand of quality nurses in clinical and nonclinical services leads to proper training need assessment and identification process. There are other factors that are also reviewed which will help in providing proper training as follows (Tsang et al., 2017). So that it is important to maintain the expertise of the nurses by designing and implementing special education programs in particular intervals. Every sector nowaday is concentrating on how to improve the skill sets or competencies of manpower. Work-related experience and organizational commitment are necessary to motivate identity construction in an organization (Collin, 2009). Training helps in performance improvement as it is helping in reskilling and upskilling.

Professional development (A4) is necessary for nurses explained by 45.15%. As the nursing staffs are the important part of the hospital industry, they need to be improved in every aspect starting from patients care, administrative duties, managerial and supervisory skills, clinical skills, planning and organizing skills, team working, etc. (Devi & Rao, 2012). Shah and Gopal (2012) use assessment centers, individual interviewing methods and psychological tests to identify the training needs for an organization. Breckelmans et al. (2012) studied that availability of resources, fund, time and infrastructure; organizational strategy, commitment of key decision-makers, internal support, attitude and teamwork are necessary for professional development of nurses. Nurses should be perfect in assessment, planning, implementation and evaluation of healthcare. There is a positive relationship between the nurses training and building up professional identity which helps in quality service delivery. Training facilitates change management and includes proper value to the career and profession. The identity of nurses is influenced by sharing of own experiences and adoptability of the organization's culture. As much as training program implemented successfully, the knowledge, skill and ability improved (Franco & Tavares, 2013). Psychological assessment skill, critical thinking skill is necessary in clinical nursing practice (Donovan et al., 2013).

Research and analytical skill (A3) is explained 37.5% of total variance and having consistency of 0.863 as Cronbach's Alpha. The dimension is consisting of two types of competencies that is clinical research skill and analytical skill. Clinical research is necessary for upskilling as different methods and techniques are used in various organizations to handle various difficult situations in organizations; for example: in RMRC, Bhubaneswar they have used a new machine called COBAS for testing numerous COVID-19 samples at a time for investigation. Analytical is required to think, plan and execute new ideas to the nursing practice in daily activities. Training programs are helping to update knowledge and skills about modern technologies about pandemic situations. Interpersonal skill or behavioral competencies (A1) are necessary to build up trust and develop positive relationship between patients and themselves according to maximum participants. 17.6% variance is shown as per Table 19.3 about the need of training in the area of interpersonal skill development.

Implications

This study may contribute to developing one fundamental instrument for the measurement of the quality and management skills of nurses in hospitals. In further, the developed instrument can be implemented and evaluated as per requirement. It is very much important that the quality of the healthcare professionals should be monitored and improved. This can be helpful to update the policies protocol about the nurses. To validate the instrument and for better result another round of study can be done soon with larger sample size and can be taken from different hospitals of different cultures. This paper is helpful for identifying new constructs in the area of training in nursing area.

References

Aguinis, H., & Kraiger, K. (2008). Benefits of training and development for individuals and teams, organizations, and society. *Annual Review of Psychology, 60*, 451–474. https://doi.org/10.1146/annurev.psych.60.110707.163505

Akerjordet, K., & Severinsson, E. (2008, July). Emotionally intelligent nurse leadership: A literature review study. *Journal of Nursing Management, 16*(5), 565–577. https://doi.org/10.1111/j.1365-2834.2008.00893.x. PMID: 18558927

Anatole, M., Magge, H., Redditt, V., Karamaga, A., Niyonzima, S., Drobac, P., Mukherjee, J., Ntaganira, J., Nyirazinyoye, L., & Hirschhorn, L. (2012). Nurse mentorship to improve the quality of health care delivery in rural Rwanda. *Nursing Outlook*, 61. https://doi.org/10.1016/j.outlook.2012.10.003

Baxter, R., & Edvardsson, D. (2018, June). Impact of a critical care postgraduate certificate course on nurses' self-reported competence and confidence: A quasi-experimental study. *Nurse Education Today, 65*, 156–161. https://doi.org/10.1016/j.nedt.2018.03.004. Epub 2018 Mar 13. PMID: 29579568

Boxall, P., Ang, S. H., & Bartram, T. (2011). Analysing the 'Black Box' of HRM: Uncovering HR goals, mediators, and outcomes in a standardized service environment. *Journal of Management Studies*, 48. https://doi.org/10.1111/j.1467-6486.2010.00973.x

Bowden, J. A., & Masters, G. N. (1993). *Implications for higher education of a competency-based approach to education and training*. Department of Employment.

Boyatzis, R. E. (2008). Competencies in the 21st century. *Journal of Management Development*, *27*(1), 5–12. Yale University. https://doi.org/10.1108/02621710810840730Press

Brekelmans, G., Poell, R., & Wijk, K. (2013). Factors influencing continuing professional development: A Delphi study among nursing experts. *European Journal of Training and Development*. 37. https://doi.org/10.1108/03090591311312769

Brunner et al. (2018), M., McGregor, D., Keep, M., Janssen, A., Spallek, H., Quinn, D., Jones, A., Tseris, E., Yeung, W., Togher, L., Solman, A., & Shaw, T. (2018). An Ehealth capabilities framework for graduates and health professionals: Mixed-methods study. *Journal of Medical Internet Research, 20*(5), e10229. https://doi.org/10.2196/10229

Campbell, J., & Wiernik, B. (2015). The modeling and assessment of work performance. *Annual Review of Organizational Psychology and Organizational Behavior, 2*, 47–74. https://doi.org/10.1146/annurev-orgpsych-032414-111427

Carter, W., Nesbit, P., Badham, R., Parker, S., & Sung, L.-K. (2016). The effects of employee engagement and self-efficacy on job performance: A longitudinal field study. *The International Journal of Human Resource Management,* 1–20. https://doi.org/10.1080/09585192.2016.1244096

Chen, S.-C., Lai, Y.-H., & Tsay, S.-L. (2020, June). Nursing perspectives on the impacts of COVID-19. *Journal of Nursing Research*, *28*(3), p e85. https://doi.org/10.1097/NRJ.0000000000000389

Clardy, A. (2008). Human resource development and the resource-based model of core competencies: Methods for diagnosis and assessment. *Human Resource*

Development Review., *7*, 387–407. https://doi.org/10.1177/1534484308324144

Cronenwett, L., Sherwood, G., Pohl, J., Barnsteiner, J., Moore, S., Sullivan, D. T., Ward, D., & Warren, J. (2009, November–December). Quality and safety education for advanced nursing practice. *Nurse Outlook, 57*(6): 338–348. https://doi.org/10.1016/j.outlook.2009.07.009. PMID: 19942035.

Crowne, K., Young, T., Goldman, B., Patterson, B., Krouse, A., & Proenca, J. (2017). Leading nurses: Emotional intelligence and leadership development effectiveness. *Leadership in Health Services,* 30. https://doi.org/10.1108/LHS-12-2015-0055

Donovan, R. O., Doody, O., & Lyons, R. (2013 September 12–25). The effect of stress on health and its implications for nursing. *The British Journal of Nursing, 22*(16), 969–970, 972–973. https://doi.org/10.12968/bjon.2013.22.16.969. PMID: 24037402.

Eby, L., Allen, T., Conley, K., Smith, R., Henderson, T., & Mancini, V. (2019). Mindfulness-based training interventions for employees: A qualitative review of the literature. *Human Resource Management Review, 29*, 156–178. https://doi.org/10.1016/j.hrmr.2017.03.004

Flood, B., Smythe, L., Hocking, C., et al. (2019). Interprofessional practice: Beyond competence. *Advances in Health Science Education, 24*, 489–501. https://doi.org/10.1007/s10459-019-09879-4

Folke, C. (2016). Resilience (republished). *Ecology and Society, 21*(4), 44. https://doi.org/10.5751/ES-09088-210444

Franco, M., & Tavares, P. J. (2013). The influence of professional identity on the process of nurses' training: An empirical study. *Leadership in Health Services, 26*, 118–134.

Garavan, T. (2011). *Fundamentals of human resource development.*

Godkin, J., & Godkin, L. (2004). Caring behaviors among nurses. *Health Care Management Review, 29*, 258–267. https://doi.org/10.1097/00004010-200407000-00011

Guerrero, A. P. S., & Brenner, A. M. (2016). Mentorship: A return to basics. *Academic Psychiatry, 40*, 422–423. https://doi.org/10.1007/s40596-016-0516-0

Hennessy, D., Hicks, C., Hilan, A., & Kawonal, Y. (2006). A methodology for assessing the professional development needs of nurses and midwives in Indonesia: Paper 1 of 3. *Human Resources for Health, 4*, 8. https://doi.org/10.1186/1478-4491-4-8

Hurst, K., & Kelley Patterson, D. (2014). Health and social care workforce planning and development—An overview. *International Journal of Health Care Quality Assurance, 27*(7), 562–572. https://doi.org/10.1108/IJHCQA-05-2014-0062

Hwang, W. J., & Jo, H. H. (2020). Development and application of a program for reinforcing global health competencies in university nursing students. *Frontiers in Public Health, 8*, 263. https://doi.org/10.3389/fpubh.2020.00263

Immonen, K., Oikarainen, A., Tomietto, M., Kääriäinen, M., Tuomikoski, A. M., Kaučič, B. M., Filej, B., Riklikiene, O., Flores, V.-M. M, Perez-Cañaveras, R. M., De Raeve, P., & Mikkonen, K. (2019, December). Assessment of nursing students' competence in clinical practice: A systematic review of reviews. *International Journal of Nursing Studies, 100*, 103414. https://doi.org/10.1016/j.ijnurstu.2019.103414. Epub 2019 Aug 31. PMID: 31655385

Junior, R., Guedes dos Santos, J., Copelli, F., & Balsanelli, A. (2020). Enterprising tendency and interpersonal communication of nursing students. *Revista da Escola de Enfermagem da USP, 54*, 3615. https://doi.org/10.1590/S1980-220X2018056603615

Karimi, A., Teimouri, H., Shahin, A., & Shaemi Barzoki, A. (2019). Competency-based recruitment and managerial succession. *Human Systems Management,* 37, 411–423. https://doi.org/10.3233/HSM-17184

Kaslow, N., Celano, M., & Stanton, M. (2005). Training in family psychology: A competencies-based approach. *Family Process, 44*, 337–353. https://doi.org/10.1111/j.1545-5300.2005.00063.x

Kirpal, S. (2004). Work identities of nurses: Between caring and efficiency demands. *Career Development International, 9*(3), 274–304. https://doi.org/10.1108/13620430410535850

Krishnamurthy, R., VandeCreek, L., Kaslow, N., Tazeau, Y., Miville, M., Kerns, R., Stegman, R., Suzuki, L., & Benton, S. (2004). Achieving competency in psychological assessment: Directions for education and training. *Journal of Clinical Psychology, 60*, 725–739. https://doi.org/10.1002/jclp.20010

Labrague, L., McEnroe-Petitte, D., Papathanasiou, I., Edet, O., Tsaras, K., Leocadio, M., Colet, P., Kleisiaris, C., Fradelos, E., Rosales, R., Santos-Lucas, K., & Velacaria, P. (2017). Stress and coping strategies among nursing students: An international study. *Journal of Mental Health, 27*, 1–7. https://doi.org/10.1080/09638237.2017.1417552

Lee, H., Kim, M., Kiang, P., & Shi, L., Tan, K., Chea, P., Peou, S., Grigg-Saito, D. (2016). *Public health nursing*.

Markoulli, M., Lee, C., Byington, E., & Felps, W. (2017). Mapping human resource management: Reviewing the field and charting future directions. *Human Resource Management Review, 27*, 367–396. https://doi.org/10.1016/j.hrmr.2016.10.001

McDonald, M., Kazemi, E., & Kavanagh, S. (2013). Core practices and pedagogies of teacher education. *Journal of Teacher Education, 64*, 378–386.

Mercurio, Z. A. (2015). Affective commitment as a core essence of organizational commitment: An integrative literature review. *Human Resource Development Review, 14*(4), 389–414. https://doi.org/10.1177/1534484315603612

Nagel, Y., Towell, A., Nel, E., & Foxall, F. (2016). The emotional intelligence of registered nurses commencing critical care nursing. *Curationis, 39*(1), e1–e7. https://doi.org/10.4102/curationis.v39i1.1606

Noe, R., Clarke, A., & Klein, H. (2014). Learning in the twenty-first-century workplace. *Annual Review of Organizational Psychology and Organizational Behavior, 1*, 245–275. https://doi.org/10.1146/annurev-orgpsych-031413-091321

O'Boyle, E., Humphrey, R., Pollack, J., & Hawver, Story, P. (2011). Emotional intelligence and job performance: A meta-analysis. *Journal of Organizational Behavior, 32*, 788–818. https://doi.org/10.1002/job.714

O'Connor, P., Hill, A., Kaya, M., & Martin, B. (2019). The measurement of emotional intelligence: A critical review of the literature and recommendations for researchers and practitioners. *Frontiers in Psychology*, 10. https://doi.org/10.3389/fpsyg.2019.01116

Oermann, M., Nicoll, L., Chinn, P., Ashton, K., Conklin, J., Edie, A., Amarasekara, S., & Williams, B. (2017). Quality of articles published in predatory nursing journals. *Nursing Outlook*, 66. https://doi.org/10.1016/j.outlook.2017.05.005

Priyadarshini, R. R. G., & Dave, D. (2012). Competency-based training needs assessment model. *Management and Labour Studies, 37*(3), 195–207. https://doi.org/10.1177/0258042X13484834

Rao, M., Rao, K. D., Kumar, A. K., Chatterjee, M., & Sundararaman, T. (2011, February 12). Human resources for health in India. *Lancet, 377*(9765), 587–598. https://doi.org/10.1016/S0140-6736(10)61888-0. Epub 2011 Jan 10. PMID: 21227499.

Redmond, A. D., O'Dempsey, T. J., & Taithe, B. (2011, March). Disasters and a register for foreign medical teams. *Lancet, 26*; 377 (9771), 1054–1055. https://doi.org/10.1016/S0140-6736(11)60319-X. PMID: 21440794

Regina, O., Doody, O., & Lyons, R. (2013). The effect of stress on health and its implications for nursing. *British Journal of Nursing., 22*, 969–973.

Riggio, R., & Lee, J. (2007). Emotional and interpersonal competencies and leader development. *Human Resource Management Review, 17*, 418–426. https://doi.org/10.1016/j.hrmr.2007.08.008

Schwirian, P. M. (1978). Evaluating the performance of nurses: A multidimensional approach. *Nurse Researcher, 27*, 347–351.

Shah, H., & Gopal, R. (2012). Training needs analysis for bus depot managers at GSRTC. *European Journal of Training and Development, 36*, 527–543. https://doi.org/10.1108/03090591211232084

Sheer, B., & Wong, F. (2008). The development of advanced nursing practice globally. *Journal of Nursing Scholarship: An Official Publication of Sigma Theta Tau International Honor Society of Nursing / Sigma Theta Tau, 40*, 204–211. https://doi.org/10.1111/j.1547-5069.2008.00242.x

Skärsäter, I., Keogh, B., Doyle, L., Ellilä, H., Jormfeldt, H., Lahti, M., Higgins, A., Meade, O., Sitvast, J., Stickley, T., & Kilkku, N. (2018, September). Advancing the knowledge, skills and attitudes of mental health nurses working with families and caregivers: A critical review of the literature. *Nurse Education in Practice, 32*, 138–146. https://doi.org/10.1016/j.nepr.2018.07.002. Epub 2018 Jul 7. PMID: 30007849

Smollan, R. (2017). Supporting staff through stressful organizational change. *Human Resource Development International, 20*, 1–23. https://doi.org/10.1080/13678868.2017.1288028

Spruill, J., Rozensky, R., Stigall, T., Vasquez, M., Bingham, R., & Olvey, C. (2004). Becoming a competent clinician: Basic competencies in intervention. *Journal of Clinical Psychology, 60*, 741–754. https://doi.org/10.1002/jclp.20011

Sternberg, R. J., & Kolligian, J., Jr. (Eds.). (1990). *Competence considered.*

Stevens, K. R. (2013, May 31). The impact of evidence-based practice in nursing and the next big ideas. *Online Journal of Issues in Nursing, 18*(2), 4. PMID: 23758422.

Tiwari, R., Sharma, K., & Zodpey, S. (2012). Situational analysis of nursing education and work force in India. *Nursing Outlook,* 61. https://doi.org/10.1016/j.outlook.2012.07.012

Tuomikoski, A. M., Ruotsalainen, H., Mikkonen, K., & Kääriäinen, M. (2019). Nurses' experiences of their competence at mentoring nursing students during clinical practice: A systematic review of qualitative studies. *Nurse Education Today, 85,* 104258. https://doi.org/10.1016/j.nedt.2019.104258

Victoria Bam, A. K.-A. D., Ernest Asante, A. Y. L., & Pearl Adade, B. A. A. (2020). Self-assessed competencies of nurses at an emergency department in Ghana, *African Journal of Emergency Medicine, 10*(1), 8–12. ISSN 2211-419X, https://doi.org/10.1016/j.afjem.2019.09.002 (http://www.sciencedirect.com/science/article/pii/S2211419X1930148X)

Weiss, S., & Bongartz, H., Boll, S., & Heuten, W. (2018). *Applications of immersive virtual reality in nursing education—A review.*

Zhanming, L., Felicity C. B., Peter F. H., David S. B., Sandra G. L., Dennis, W., David E., & Aziz, R. (2018). An evidence-based approach to understanding the competency development needs of the health service management workforce in Australia, *BMC Health Services Research, 18*(1). https://doi.org/10.1186/s12913-018-3760-z

PART VI

Case Studies

CHAPTER 20

Valuation of Mass Shoe Last Company Limited

Devesh Baid

Background

Mr. Neeraj Aggarwal worked with Shoe Last Pvt Ltd (SLPT) for more than two decades and retired as the Director of operations. He was a mechanical engineering graduate and had completed post-graduation in industrial and Production engineering before heading manufacturing operations at SLPT. His key role at SLPT was design of indigenous machines for manufacturing shoe last and was responsible for smooth functioning of all plants of SLPT. SLPT was India's first and currently the largest manufacturer of plastic shoe lasts. Currently, SLPT operates two state-of-the-art production facilities in Agra and Vellore, two model development centres in Chennai and Kanpur with corporate office in Mumbai—making them the only last maker with a pan-India presence.

D. Baid (✉)
International Management Institute, Bhubaneswar, India
e-mail: devesh@imibh.edu.in

Rajagopal and R. Behl (eds.), *Managing Disruptions in Business*, Palgrave Studies in Democracy, Innovation, and Entrepreneurship for Growth, https://doi.org/10.1007/978-3-030-79709-6_20

Earlier they also had a plant at Vadodara, Gujarat which was closed in 2014. Mr. Neeraj was stationed at Vadodara and visited other units whenever required.

The Beginning

After his retirement in September 2013 from SLPT, Mr. Neeraj thought of setting up a manufacturing unit of shoe last. Every time a shoe company prepares a new design, they needed shoe last according to the design and size. Mr. Neeraj made an estimate of investment required to set up a plant. Total cost of machinery and other fixed assets was INR[1] 15.08 million and working capital requirement was assessed at INR 13.33 million for 400 pairs of shoes last to be produced in one shift per day. Including incidental expenses of setting up the company and making it operational, total project was estimated to cost around INR 30 million.

As the investment was big for Mr. Neeraj alone, he approached his two of his colleagues at SLPT—Mr. Rajesh Biyani and Mr. Kamal Shah. Both were working at Agra and Kanpur plant of SLPT. Both readily agreed to join hands. It was also decided to set up unit at Agra as the location was suitable for such a company. Agra and Kanpur are hubs of shoe manufacturing in India. Once a new design is given by a shoe company, shoe last must be prepared and supplied quickly so that the company can manufacture and market shoes at the earliest. Time from design-to-market is very critical for any shoe company. Agra has a leather park, where major shoe manufacturers are located. Mr. Neeraj shifted to Agra to set up the unit.

MASS Shoe Last Company (MAS) was incorporated in May 2013 with an initial capital of INR 10 million. In June 2014, a land of 2000 square metres (sq.mt.) with shed of app 1000 sq.mt. was taken on lease at rent of INR 150 thousand per month located at a village in Agra. The rent was high, but many shoe manufacturers were in the vicinity and Leather Park was also close by so the location was most appropriate for getting order.

Mr. Neeraj had designs of all the machines required for manufacturing shoe last. While few machines were imported from China, He got rest of the machines manufactured in Vadodara and shipped them to Agra. He anticipated to start production in October 2014 but due to various

[1] INR currency is Indian Rupee.

operational issues, the production could commence only from May 2015. Mr. Pradeep, son of Mr. Neeraj, after the commencement of production at MAS, joined his father in this business. He was a mechanical engineer working as a maintenance engineer in a firm at Vadodara. Initially he was responsible for maintenance of the plant at MAS but gradually he had taken over the responsibility of entire production.

Industry Scenario

Apart from numerous small players, there were two major players in the industry—Sanghavi Shoe Accessories Pvt Ltd and Chemrow India Pvt Ltd. There were no listed companies under this segment. Even the other major players were micro and small enterprises so the information about sales, profitability, and growth for shoe last segment of industry was not available. The demand for shoe lasts was a derived demand and depended upon introduction of new designs by the shoe manufacturers. Sales and performance of shoe last Industry were, therefore, based on performance of the footwear industry.

Globally India stood second after China in footwear production. It produced 2.1 billion pair accounting for 13% of total annual global production of 22 billion pair which is much below China's share of 60%. 90% of the production was consumed domestically while the remaining 10% was exported primarily to European markets. In value terms, the export was estimated at Rs 18,000 Crores and the total market size was INR 500 billion. Of the footwear market, leather footwear market accounted for 20% and the balance was accounted for by synthetic footwear. The footwear exports from India had grown at a compound annual growth rate (CAGR) of 20% in Indian rupee terms during the five-year period ending March 2015. India's share was 1.9% in the global export market of US$120 billion, which was much lower than the China's share of 40%.

The average footwear consumption in India stood at 1.66 pair per annum which was very low as compared to the developed countries' average of 6–7 pair per annum and the Global average of 3 pairs per annum. This gap coupled with increasing disposable incomes, rising middle class, and changing consumer preferences provides a tremendous opportunity for the Indian footwear market to grow at a rapid pace going forward. According to the forecasts KPMG Report (2016), it was expected to grow from the current market size of 10 billion USD in 2016

to 25 billion USD by 2020, 50 billion USD by 2025, and 80 billion USD by 2030. Shoe last industry was expected to follow same growth trends as share of rubber and leather industry in value terms was same. It was one of the 25 top priority sectors for Make in India programme launched by the Government of India 2014. Generally, the industry was considered green with no real burden on country's natural resources. It was also considered environment friendly as it did not produce significant effluents, liquid or water waste, and noise pollution. Effluents, if any, could be dealt with relatively easily. Land requirements and electricity consumption were low as compared to large industries such automotive, refining, etc., and it was quite labour intensive relative to other industries. It was also easy to skill labour and start operations in the footwear industry.

Both organised and unorganised sector had equal share in value terms in domestic market. There were almost 15,000 SMEs operating largely in the unorganised sector with relatively few entities operating in the organised sector. The primary reason for the unorganised and small scale set up of Indian footwear industry was historical restrictions of licensing and SME reservation of the sector, which continued till 2001. Since then, the government had permitted 100% foreign direct investment through the automatic route for the footwear sector. The government of India was also setting up dedicated footwear complex and footwear components parts where footwear clusters were located. There had been active interest in collaborating with Indian footwear companies from some of the European countries like Italy, Spain, and Portugal.

Manufacturing Process at Shoe Last

The basic raw material for manufacturing shoe last is High-Density Polyethylene (HDPE) and Linear Low-Density Polyethylene (LLDPE). LLDPE is used to reduce hardness. HDPE and LLDPE are used in the ratio of 5:1. Many companies like Reliance Industries, Indian Oil Corporation Ltd (IOCL), Gas Authority of India Ltd manufacture and supply HDPE and LLDPE granules and it is readily available. MAS normally bought these two raw materials from IOCL, Kanpur. Even reprocessed granules were also added for preparing the shoe last. This reduced the cost without compromising much on the quality. MAS prepared reprocessed granules from its rejections and purchased the used shoe lasts from shoe companies. Every company differentiated its shoe last by adding a master colour. MAS used light blue as its master colour. The step-in

manufacturing process was passing the mixture (HDPE, LLDPE, reprocessed granules, and master colour) through injection moulding machine for preparation of moulds. The mixture was then heated at the high temperature and later poured in the moulds of required size. Once the rough blocks (shoe mould) were ready, it was passed through water and were put in the wooden boxes for cooling. It took six to eight hours for the rough blocks to cool. They were 'made to stock' based on forecasted demand. On confirmed order for shoe lasts, these rough blocks were then finished as per the requirement. This helped to meet the order supply in a short time, which was crucial in the industry.

The shoe last is a die which helped in making the shoes. Shoes cannot be made without the use of a shoe last. Initially, the sample of the shoe last (model last) is developed by hand filling with the help of highly skilled person. This model is then used to make a shoe last (YouTube video of shoe last manufacturing is available at https://www.youtube.com/watch?v=Cb_e5h2Ac90). When the model last is received for production, rough blocks of appropriate size are converted as per the order specification. Machines at the heart of the manufacturing process are CNC machines for rough turning and fine turning. These machines had been imported from China. Rough turning is done after end cutting and centring the rough block. Other processes include drilling holes in the rough block, cutting the block into two parts with a particular profile, slotting it, and then fixing the hinge and link plates with pins. Thereafter fine turning operation is carried out. Further, toe dog and heel dog which are formed during rough turning, drilling, and fine turning operations are cut and toe shaping is done using toe dog cutting machine and toe shaping machine. Then sleeve hole and sleeve fixing are done and plate as per customer requirement is fixed at bottom of the last. Finally, finishing and inspection are carried out before packing and dispatch. A brief of shoe last manufacturing process is given in Fig. 20.1.

Financing Through Bank

A term loan of INR 10 million was sanctioned by The Oriental Bank of Commerce in January 2015 which was later transferred to the Axis Bank in May 2016. The Bank was changed to avail benefit under Credit Guarantee Fund Trust Scheme for Micro and Small Enterprises.[2] The tenure

[2] The Credit Guarantee Fund Scheme for Micro and Small Enterprises (CGS) was launched by the Government of India (GoI) to make available collateral-free credit to the

of the term loan was seven years with a moratorium period of eighteen months with first instalment of INR 215,172 due from July 2016. The term loan was hypothecated against plant, machinery, and other fixed assets of the firm worth INR 15.8 million. Also, a cash credit limit of INR 10 million, which was earlier sanctioned by the Oriental Bank of Commerce for working capital (WC) was transferred to a bank in May 2016. The working capital loan was against hypothecation of raw material, stock in process, finished goods, stores and spares, receivables, and other current assets. Collateral security of INR 15.6 million was given for securing cash credit limit in the form of residential properties and LIC policies by the promoters. In April 2016, MAS was rated as OBC SME5

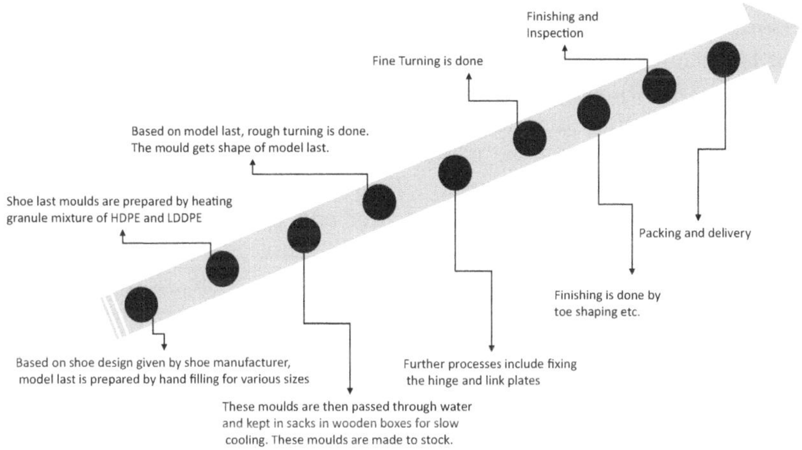

Fig. 20.1 Manufacturing process of Shoe Last (*Source* Author)

micro and small enterprise sector. Both the existing and the new enterprises are eligible to be covered under the scheme. The guarantee cover available under the scheme is to the extent of maximum 85% of the sanctioned amount of the credit facility. The guarantee cover provided is up to 75% of the credit facility up to INR 5 million (85% for loans up to INR 500 thousand provided to micro enterprises, 80% for MSEs owned/operated by women and all loans to NER including Sikkim) with a uniform guarantee at 50% for the entire amount if the credit exposure is above INR 5 million and up to INR 10 million.

and the working capital loan was renewed by the bank at an interest rate of MCLR[3] plus 3%. The same rate was charged for both the loans.

Financials

The sales by the firm both in terms of quantity and revenue had grown over the two years of operations. This trend was evident if one were to compare on quarter-to-quarter basis (Exhibit 20.1). However, due to low-capacity utilisation and high fixed operating and financial cost, the firm's entire capital had been wiped out (Exhibits 20.2 and 20.3). Although looking at the industry scenario, it was expected that the sales would increase over the next few years and the firm should report profit as a consequence. The cost of direct material for one pair of the shoe last was INR 122.52 (Exhibit 20.4). Other manufacturing costs and administrative expenses at different level of production were estimated as given in Exhibits 20.5 and 20.6. Cost structure and profit at different level of sales were estimated as given in Exhibit 20.7. However, MAS did not have sufficient funds to meet its working capital requirement. As the debt was out of question and promoters were also not in a position to provide further equity, additional equity from new shareholders (private equity) seemed to be the only way out. This necessitated valuation of the firm so that the price of new equity to be issued can be fairly determined.

Valuation of MAS

MAS approached a consultant for raising equity through private investors. Before investors could be approached it was necessary to value the firm and determine the price at which stock could be issued. The consultant thought of using the two prominent methods—the discounted cash flow technique and the relative valuation based on market multiples—for valuation. These methods are most suitable for conventional manufacturing industries. For doing valuation through the discounted cash flow technique, the cash flows, and the cost of capital (both debt and equity) had to be estimated. Cost of debt can be computed rather easily as the debt was only from the bank and the promoters (Exhibit 20.3). As MAS was a private limited firm and as there were no shoe last firms listed on any exchange, estimating the cost of equity was not easy as CAPM-based cost of equity estimate required estimation of beta (sensitivity to the

[3] MCLR stood for marginal cost-based lending rate and referred to the minimum interest rate of a bank below which it normally cannot lend.

market). For estimating beta and the cost of equity, firms in footwear industry were looked. BSE had 10 firms listed under footwear industry. Footwear industry itself was divided into leather based and non-leather based (rubber, PVC etc.). Since a shoe last is used only by manufacturers of leather shoes, sandals, etc., firms dealing in leather-based products were chosen. Out of these 10 firms, based on Reuter's database,[4] three firms Bata India Ltd, Liberty Shoes Ltd, and Mirza International Ltd were identified for computation of beta. Market capitalisation and beta values of these firms were estimated as given in the Exhibit 20.8. Beta of these firms varied from a low of 1.08 to a high of 1.82. Footwear industry beta and cyclical consumer goods and services sector beta values, respectively, are 0.84 and 1.31.

Risk-free rate was measured as the yield on the 10-year Indian government bond which was 6.81% as of April 2017. Risk premium was measured based on a survey study of 41 countries Fernandez et al. (2015). Median risk premium for India stood at 8.3% while mean was 8.4%. Difference in mean risk premium was found at −0.1% compared to figures reported in a similar survey done in 2013. Relative measures of valuation include various multiples such as P/E ratio, price to sales ratio, price to book value ratio, and price to cash flow ratio. Values as per Reuters for footwear industry and cyclical consumer goods and services sector are given in Exhibit 20.9. Exhibit 20.10 gives a snapshot of three major players of footwear industry in leather segment.

Meeting with Consultant

Based on the above information, consultant set down with Mr. Neeraj and Mr. Pradeep to discuss the certain issues relating to firm and valuation. First issue was about depreciation charged during last two years which has significantly reduced the book value, resulted in reporting heavy losses, and eroded entire capital base. This happened as depreciation was charged in accounting books as per income tax laws for ease of calculation. Assets were highly underutilized. Revaluation of balance sheet was considered as it will reflect true situation. In that case 10% depreciation on straight line

[4] The Thomson Reuters Business Classification (TRBC) is an industry classification of global companies; it is owned and operated by Thomson Reuters and is also the basis for Thomson Reuters Indices. Each company is allocated an Industry, which falls under an Industry group, then Business Sector, which is then part of an overall economic sector. TRBC consists of 10 economic sectors, 28 business sectors, 54 industry groups, 143 industries, and 837 activities.

method was considered appropriate. However, for income tax purposes depreciation will be charged at 25%. Also, allotment of shares was done for application money received earlier form promoters and other investors.

Another issue was about the investment in capex required to maintain the current capacity. Based on the experience of Mr. Neeraj an amount equal to depreciation over five years was thought appropriate for capex investment in fifth year. Last issue was about working capital. This industry is a working capital-intensive industry. Working capital will increase with increase in sales as per operating cycle of four months (fifteen days of raw material, fifteen days of WIP, and another three months for finished goods and debtors). Since Mass Shoe Last is new firm with excess capacity, sales of the firm were expected to grow at double the growth rate till 2020, one and half time of growth rate till 2015 and same till 2030 of expected growth for footwear industry and thereafter a modest Hindu growth rate of 5% was thought appropriate. Based on the above information consultant agreed to determine the value of the firm and appraise Mr. Pradeep about the same within a weeks' time.

Appendices

See Exhibits 20.1, 20.2, 20.3, 20.4, 20.5, 20.6, 20.7, 20.8, 20.9, and 20.10.

Exhibit 20.1 Sales for last six quarters at MASS (in INR)

Month	*Sales units*	*Revenues (Rs)*	*Average S.P per unit (Rs)*
July 15–Sept 15	5975	3,201,099	536
Oct 15–Dec 15	7123	3,799,506	533
Jan 16–Mar 16	7313	3,874,935	530
April 16–June 16	9332	5,011,284	537
July 16–Sept 16	9154	4,805,085	525
Oct 16–Dec 16	7675	4,051,104	528

Note Drawn from internal company records of monthly sales

Exhibit 20.2 Trading and profit and loss account (in INR)

Trading and profit and loss account

Particulars	*Dec-16(Prov)*	*Mar-16*	*Mar-15*	*Particulars*	*Dec-16*	*Mar-16*	*Mar-15*
Opening stock	2,658,374	0	0	Sales Account	25,158,638	11,501,363	0
Purchase	16,104,207	5,704,153	0	Closing Stock	6,669,582	2,658,374	0
Direct expenses (Ele, Mfg, Freight, Loading, Sanit	5,476,093	2,358,381	0				
Gross profit	7,589,546	6,097,203	0				
	31,828,220	14,159,737	0		31,828,220	14,159,737	0
Accounting and audit charges	14,000	212,650	47,000	Gross Profit	7,589,546	6,097,203	0
Bank charges & comm (Inc loan expin 1st year)	163,697	10,830	269,866	Income Tax Refund	1580	0	0
Bank interest	1,678,434	2,239,462	229,899	Other Income - Scrap Sale	458,600	0	0
Building renovation and maintenance	3679	152,711	753,327	Rebate & Discount	0	0	139
Computer repair and maintenance	10,915	0	0	Exchange Rate Difference	0	0	5129
Consumables stores (1nd year Mat Trial Prod)	274,503	40,404	123,004				
Conveyance expenses	235,325	286,348	121,141				
Exchange rate difference	4657	2993	0				
Custom duty and cess	13,137	0	0				
Depreciation	0	2,811,594	2,473,282				
Electric repair and maintenance	31,361	69,085	2100				
EPF and ESI contribution	59,677	52,996	0				

Trading and profit and loss account

Particulars	*Dec-16(Prov)*	*Mar-16*	*Mar-15*	*Particulars*	*Dec-16*	*Mar-16*	*Mar-15*
Exhibition Exp and guest house Exp	0	162,062	74,420				
Factory Exp	31,918	61,212	0				
Factory lease rent	1,565,316	1,834,000	1,530,000				
Factory license fee (Val in 1 & 2 Year)	2500	5600	16,004				
Festival Exp	178,659	89,014	1800				
General Exp	12,480	17,796	54,059				
Generator fuel and maintenance	64,107	468,971	52,986				
Insurance Exp	0	87,997	91,351				
Job contract Exp	0	841,455	0				
Legal and provisional charges	22,000	3000	0				
Machine repair and maintenance	493,308	600,127	20,380				
Miss Exp	5643	0	17,096				
Packing material and printing Exp	12,713	23,001	4100				
Postage and courier charges	361	5433	5935				
Printing and stationary Exp	76,347	144,128	12,393				
Production incentive	45,267	0	0				
Rebate and discount	126,846	36,055	0				
ROC Expenses	62,000	1000	227,494				

(continued)

Exhibit 20.2 (continued)

Trading and profit and loss account

Particulars	*Dec-16(Prov)*	*Mar-16*	*Mar-15*	*Particulars*	*Dec-16*	*Mar-16*	*Mar-15*
Sales promotion Exp	2250	4785	0				
Service tax (Inc Penalty in 2nd Yr Rs 7362)	9199	24,912	0				
Staff salary and guard	1,459,557	1,936,249	121,876				
Staff welfare Exp	228,759	238,588	7349				
Telephone bill Exp	52,304	64,493	15,537				
Tour and travelling Exp	78,566	75,828	104,448				
Tax (Deferred)		−344,397					
Net profit	1,030,241	−6,163,179	-6,371,579				
	8,049,726	**6,097,203**	**5268**		**8,049,726**	**6,097,203**	**5268**

Note Financial for period April 2016 to Dec 2016 are provisional as per books of accounts. No depreciation has been provided for the period. Financial for period ending March 2015 and March 2016 is as per audited financial statements submitted for tax return

Exhibit 20.3 Balance sheet from 2015 to 2017 (in INR)

Particulars		*31-Mar-15*	*31-Mar-16*	*31-Mar-17*
A	*Equity and liabilities*			
1	Shareholders' funds			
	(a) Share capital (Issued and paid up)	300,000	300,000	300,000
	(b) Reserves and surplus	−6,739,187	−12,902,366	−11,872,125
		−6,439,187	**−12,602,366**	**−11,572,125**
2	Share application money	**10,600,000**	**11,775,000**	**14,775,000**
3	Non-current liabilities			
	(a) Long-term borrowings (**Term loan from bank**)	9,620,453	10,104,394	9,869,077
	(b) Deferred tax liabilities	0	0	0
		9,620,453	**10,104,394**	**9,869,077**
4	Current liabilities			
	(a) Short-term borrowings **(Cash credit limit from bank)**	3,317,594	9,610,275	9,611,372
	(b) Trade payables	1,054,798	1,931,045	3,136,198
	(c) Other current liabilities	154,243	1,685,144	1,163,701
	(d) Short-term provisions	0	0	129,281.00
		4,526,635	**13,226,464**	**14,040,552**
	TOTAL LIABILITIES	**18,307,901**	**22,503,492**	**27,112,504**
B	*Assets*			
1	Non-current assets			
	(a) Fixed assets			
	(i) Tangible assets	10,907,013	12,356,111	12,551,058
		10,907,013	**12,356,111**	**12,551,058**
	(b) Long-term loans and advances	0	0	0
	(c) Other non-current assets	650,000	633,550	633,550

(continued)

Exhibit 20.3 (continued)

Particulars		*31-Mar-15*	*31-Mar-16*	*31-Mar-17*
	(d) Deferred tax assets (net)	0	344,397	0
		650,000	**977,947**	**633,550**
2	Current assets			
	(a) Inventories	0	2,658,374	6,669,582
	(b) Trade receivables	14,000	5,117,485	6,997,526
	(c) Cash and cash equivalent	2,737,093	472,370	81,523
	(d) Short-term loans and advances	3,999,795	921,205	179,265
	(e) Other current assets	0	0	0
		6,750,888	**9,169,434**	**13,927,896**
	TOTAL ASSETS	**18,307,901**	**22,503,492**	**27,112,504**

Note Reserves and Surplus for March 2015 includes loss of 367,068 for previous financial year ending March 2014

Exhibit 20.4 Material cost per unit of Shoe Last

Particulars	*Quantity/Unit*	*Rate (Rs)*	*Amount (Rs)*
Basic material			
HDPE (kg)	0.250	91.00	22.75
LLDPE (kg)	0.050	92.70	4.64
Reprocess granules (kg)	0.700	68.00	47.60
Mater batch (kg)	0.003	154.92	0.46
			75.45
Hardware			
Heel plate (kg)	0.075	54.84	4.11
Buttress nails (Nos)	12	0.06	0.72
Filler (Nos)	2	0.40	0.80
Slidomatic hinge (Nos)	2	6.55	13.10
Link plate big (Nos)	2	4.95	9.90
Pin (Nos)	6	1.84	11.04
Sleeve (Nos)	2	2.80	5.60
Colour code (Nos)	2	0.90	1.80
			47.07
TOTAL MATERIAL COST			**Rs. 122.52**

Exhibit 20.5 Other Mfg. Cost at different levels of capacity utilisation (in INR)

Other manufacturing cost	*200 pairs/day*	*250 pairs/day*	*300 pairs/day*	*350 pairs/day*
Electricity cost	30.77	30.77	30.77	30.77
Wages	86.54	86.54	86.54	86.54
Fuel	14.42	14.42	14.42	14.42
Indirect consumables	4.81	6.01	7.22	8.42
AMC (compressor and DG)	0.35	0.35	0.35	0.35
Maintenance spares	9.62	9.62	9.62	9.62
Job work for recycling	4.48	5.6	6.72	7.84
Job work grading	2.63	2.63	2.63	2.63
TOTAL	**Rs. 153.62**	**Rs. 155.94**	**Rs. 158.27**	**Rs. 160.59**

Exhibit 20.6 Administrative expenses at different levels of capacity utilisation (in INR)

Administrative expenses	*200 pairs/day*	*250 pairs/day*	*300 pairs/day*	*350 pairs/day*
Rent of factory (Agra and Kanpur)	36.92	29.54	24.61	21.1
Security services	1.54	1.23	1.2	0.88
Consultation expenses	2.08	1.66	1.39	1.19
Freight Expenses	3	3.75	4.5	5
Conveyance and travelling expenses	9.5	10.5	11.5	12
Advertisement ETC. Exp	2.4	2.4	2.4	2.4
Misc. and other expenses	3	3.5	4	4
Telephone and other exp	0.4	0.6	0.8	1
Stationary exp	2.3	2.5	2.75	3
Packing exp	1	1.25	1.5	1.5
P.F and ESI	8	8	8	8
Total cost of sales	**Rs. 70.14**	**Rs. 64.93**	**Rs. 62.65**	**Rs. 60.07**

Exhibit 20.7 Profit per unit at different levels of capacity utilisation (in INR)

Capacity utilisation	*200 pairs/day*	*250 pairs/day*	*300 pairs/day*	*350 pairs/day*
Average S.P	525	525	525	525
Total cost of sales	399.05	396.17	396.04	395.96
Finance cost	99.89	79.91	66.59	57.08
Total cost of sales per pair	498.94	476.08	462.63	453.04
PROFIT PER PAIR	**Rs. 26.06**	**Rs. 48.92**	**Rs. 62.37**	**Rs. 71.96**

Exhibit 20.8 Footwear companies beta values

No	*Name*	*Beta (Company, Industry—Footwear, Sector—Cyclical consumer goods and services)*
1	BATA INDIA LTD	1.08, 0.84, 1.31
2	LIBERTY SHOES LTD	1.53, 0.84, 1.31
3	MIRZA INTERNATIONAL LTD	1.82, 0.84, 1.31

Note Beta values taken from www.in.reuters.com on 12.04.2017

Exhibit 20.9 Relative ratios

	Industry	*Sector*
P/E ratio (TTM)	22.48	24.77
P/E high—Last 5 Yrs	26.2	33.27
P/E low—Last 5 Yrs	8.2	14.88
Price to sales (TTM)	1.74	4,676.82
Price to book (MRQ)	1.7	2.74
Price to tangible book (MRQ)	2.31	3.1
Price to cash flow (TTM)	14.86	523,108.86
TTM stands for trailing twelve months and MRQ stands for most recent quarter		

Note Ratios taken from www.in.reuters.com on 12.04.2017

Exhibit 20.10 Comparative financials of major footwear players

	Bata	*Liberty*	*Mirza*
LTP (In INR)	570.95	169	86.1
52 W high (In INR)	613.55	209	110.5
52 W low (In INR)	400	129.15	69
Results (in Cr.)	Dec-16	Dec-16	Dec-16
Sales	640.81	126.91	228.05
PAT	37.71	1.15	17.17
Equity	64.26	17.04	24.06
Face value	5	10	2
Ratios			
OPM %	11.39	7.56	17.42
NPM %	5.89	0.91	7.53
EPS (In Rs)	2.93	–	1.43
CEPS (In Rs)	4.19	2.7	2.05
PE	49.34	–	12.19
Ownership	Mar-17	Dec-16	Mar-17
Promoter & promoter Grp	6,80,65,514	1,05,20,146	88,755,981
Indian	–	10,520,146	88,755,981
Foreign	6,80,65,514	–	–
Public	60,462,026	6,519,854	31,550,019
Institution	36,096,704	30,912	699,416
FII	–	–	–
DII	36,096,704	30,912	699,416
Non-institution	24,365,322	6,488,942	30,850,603
Bodies corporate	–	–	–

Note Data taken from www.in.reuters.com on 12.04.2017

References

Fernandez, P., Ortiz, A., & Acin, I. F. (2015). *Discount rate (risk-free rate and market risk premium) used for 41 countries in 2015: A survey*. IESE Business School. Downloaded from https://papers.ssrn.com/sol3/papers.cfm?abstract_id=2598104&download=yes

KPMG Report. (2016). *Indian footwear, leather and accessories*. Downloaded from http://cfla.co.in/wp-content/uploads/2016/08/Footwear-Leather-Accessories-in-India-06.2016-1-KPMG.pdf

CHAPTER 21

Do Women Directors Add Value? A Study of India Inc.

Supriti Mishra and Pitabas Mohanty

Boards have been found to be largely male dominated across countries. Women are found to be under-represented in the top management of companies all across the globe. A report by Catalyst (2008) suggests that currently only 4.2% of CEOs' positions in Fortune 500 list of companies are held by women. According to a study by Deloitte, percentage of women in the boards across the globe varies from as low as 1.4% in Japan to as high as 39.7% in Norway. Following enough debates and discussions about lack of representation of women in the board of directors, governments have come up with regulations to ensure the inclusion of women on the board.

S. Mishra (✉)
International Management Institute, Bhubaneswar, India
e-mail: mishrasupriti@imibh.edu.in

P. Mohanty
XLRI School of Management, Jamshedpur, India
e-mail: pitabasm@xlri.ac.in

Rajagopal and R. Behl (eds.), *Managing Disruptions in Business*, Palgrave Studies in Democracy, Innovation, and Entrepreneurship for Growth, https://doi.org/10.1007/978-3-030-79709-6_21

Section 149 (1) of Companies Act of 2013 and Clause 49 of Securities Exchange Board of India (SEBI) made it mandatory for all the listed companies in India to have at least one woman director from 31 March 2015. In May 2018, SEBI further stipulated that the large companies in India must have at least one woman independent director by March 2020. These regulatory mandates raise questions about the actual benefits of such measures for Indian companies. However, India is not alone in taking such initiatives (Afsharipour, 2015). Governments in both Norway and Spain have gone a step ahead and made it mandatory for the companies to have at least 40% women on the board (Catalyst, 2008). Spain, France, and Belgium have similar laws with compliance deadlines in three phases-2015 (Spain Equality Law, 2007), 2017, and 2018 (Catalyst, 2011). Germany and Sweden have adopted a "comply or explain" approach (Catalyst, 2011).

There has been often debate about whether it is really useful to have more women on the Board (Erhardt et al., 2003). Various studies have enumerated the benefits of having women in boards (Erhardt et al., 2003; Liu et al., 2014; Lückerath-Rovers, 2013). A report from Credit Suisse, conducted between 2005 and 2011, shows that companies across the world with at least some female representation performed much better than those with no women on the board. Similar studies by McKinsey and Thomson Reuters in different time periods find positive correlation between board diversity and firm performance. Investors also react positively to the appointment of women directors (Kang et al., 2010). Other studies, however, report mixed results. While the presence of women directors affects the accounting performance positively, they are not related to market-based performance measures (Post & Byron, 2014).

With this background, this paper makes an attempt to (i) briefly review the academic literature to see why companies may not appoint more women directors and what benefits companies obtain by having women directors and (ii) examine Indian data to see if companies with more women on the Board have are indeed more profitable.

Literature Review

Board diversity as a research agenda has risen into prominence recently. Female representation on corporate boards has also become the focus of policy agendas. Women on the board increase organizational creativity

and innovation, produce more effective problem-solving, promote corporate monitoring, decrease the private benefits of managerial control, enhance the effectiveness of corporate leadership, and encourage a better understanding of the complexities of the business environment (Carter et al., 2010; Richard et al., 2007; Robinson & Dechant, 1997). As a result, women directors have a positive effect on the organizational integration of knowledge that increases corporate governance efficiency (Adams & Ferreira, 2009; Francoeur et al., 2008; Milliken & Martins, 1996). Studies establish a positive relationship between performance (Tobin's Q) and diverse boards (Carter et al., 2003). Apesteguia et al., (2012) establish that diversity is related to corporate performance. Changing the gender composition of Boards has long-lasting impacts on firm performance (Adams & Funk, 2012).

Though there are many research establishing a business case for women board members, few other researchers are skeptical about such a stance (Ferreira, 2015). Companies having more women on the board are not necessarily more profitable nor do they generate higher stock returns for their shareholders. In fact, it has also been found that companies that are well-governed, suffer when they hire women directors for the Board. Research studies in the context of countries such as USA and Australia do not establish any significant relation between firm performance and board diversity (Carter et al., 2010; Chapple & Humphrey, 2014). Few studies (Adams & Ferreira, 2009) even establish a negative relation between gender diversity and company performance. Studies document decrease in the firm value with the introduction of 40% gender quota for directors in Norway (Ahern & Dittmar, 2012; Matsa & Miller, 2011).

There could be various reasons for women directors negatively impacting a firm's performance. First, despite being equally qualified as their male counterparts (Burke, 1997), women directors usually lack experience when they join a board (Singh et al., 2008). Women executives often face breaks in their careers and do not undertake challenging assignments in the early stages of their careers compared to their male counterparts. Second, women directors do not receive adequate mentoring thereby losing chances to serve on multiple boards (McDonald & Westphal, 2012). Watson and McNaughton (2007) suggest that women are more conservative and risk averse than men and exhibit less risky behavior in personal financial decisions. Past research documents that firms run by female CEOs make less risky financing and investment decisions (Faccio et al., 2016; Srinidhi et al., 2011) which might adversely impact a firm's profitability.

Data and Method

We conduct an exploratory research to find out whether the boards of directors of Indian companies are well represented with women directors and whether their presence adds to firm value. To measure gender diversity on corporate boards, studies often use the percentage of women holding board membership in corporates and the percentage of companies with at least one woman on their board. We studied data of all companies listed in either the Bombay Stock Exchange (BSE) or National Stock Exchange (NSE) in India for which the relevant data were available in the Prowess database of Centre for Monitoring Indian Economy (CMIE). We looked at the composition of the board for the fiscal year ending 2015 for 2870 companies and 20,999 directors.

Subsequently, we examined the profitability data of these companies to see if companies having women board members are more profitable. Extant research on corporate governance uses mostly accounting-based measures such as ROA, ROE, net margin or the capital market-based measures such as the stock returns or capital market-based measures (Bhagat & Bolton, 2008; Rob et al., 2004). We looked at the ROE data for the 3-year period of 2013, 2014, and 2015 to examine the profitability of these companies. We computed the ROE by dividing the average return on equity over the 3 years period of study. As the ROE in a particular year may get affected by some unusual situations, it is always better to look at a longer time period. Hence, we considered 3 years for the study.

Analysis and Discussion

This study examines whether Indian corporate boards are well represented by women directors. Further, this study finds out if the presence of women directors adds to the profitability of Indian firms. Our initial examination of the presence of women directors in 2870 Indian companies showed that out of 20,999 directors in the corporate boards, there were nearly 1806 or about 8.6% women directors. In as many as 2017 companies, there were no women directors (Fig. 21.1).

In 760 companies, there was only a woman director on the board. In the remaining 72 companies, there were two or more women directors on the board. We find similar trends in the corporate boards in the USA

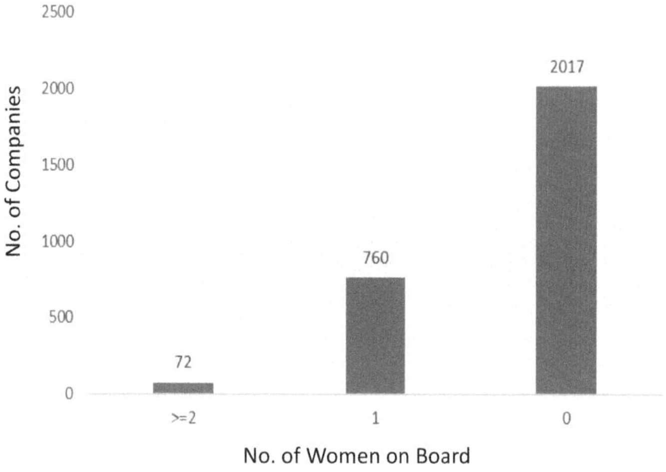

Fig. 21.1 Women in Indian corporate boards (*Source* Authors)

that we find in India. As US companies are not the focus of this study, we do not mention it in detail.

We also find better attendance records in boards having women members in India. We also find another interesting result while analyzing the board membership data. Attendance of male directors in board meetings increases if the board has at least one woman director. Boards having male CEOs, have one-and-half times more women on the board than boards having women CEOs. One of the reasons for this could be that women lighten up the atmosphere in board rooms (Huse & Solberg, 2006), thereby increasing board attendance of members from other genders (Fig. 21.2).

As far as firm profitability is concerned, we find two interesting trends in India. First, companies having women directors on the board are less profitable compared to companies having no woman on the board. We also find that this difference is more severe for women independent directors. These findings are consistent with past research. It is similar to what other researchers have found out in the context of developed economies such as the USA, Australia, Canada, and UK (Carter et al., 2010; Chapple & Humphrey, 2014).

As can be seen in Table 21.1, there is no significant difference with respect to profitability in companies having male and female executive

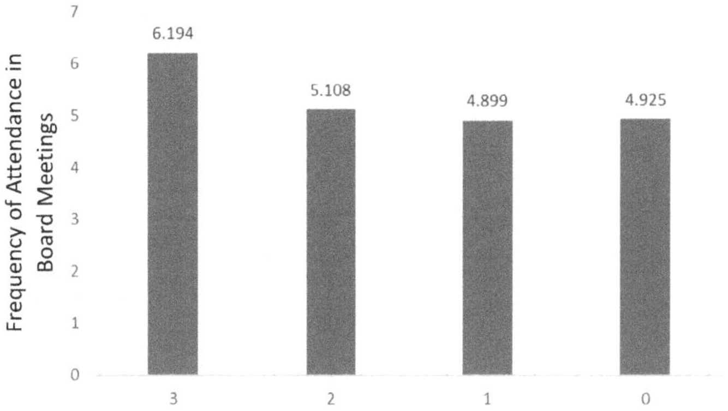

Fig. 21.2 Attendance in board meetings (*Source* Authors)

Table 21.1 ROE during 2013–2015 with different criteria for board membership

Criteria for board membership	*ROE-2013 (%)*	*ROE-2014 (%)*	*ROE-2015 (%)*
At least one female board member	5.31	4.17	4.35
All male board members	7.03	5.86	5.76
Companies having all male executive directors	6.67	5.61	5.54
Companies having at least one female executive director	6.76	5.58	5.49
Companies having all male independent directors	6.69	5.63	5.60
Companies having at least one female independent director	4.77	3.84	3.94

Source Authors

directors. However, companies that are less profitable have some women directors on the board. Particularly, companies with female independent directors are less profitable compared to those with male independent directors. Of course, these results do not imply any causal relationship between women board members and company profitability. It might be possible that poorly performing companies get pressurized by their shareholders to have more diversified boards. In such a scenario, we would

get an inverse relationship between profitability and diversified boards, at least in the short run.

Our results are consistent with findings from past research (Carter et al., 2010; Chapple & Humphrey, 2014). Though mandatory provisions to include women in corporate boards to ensure board diversity is being practiced across the globe, researchers point out that any regulation that forces firms to do things beyond their current practice, will impose some costs. When firms are forced to recruit female directors so that they can comply with the law without ensuring parity in the qualification and related criteria, it can reduce profitability. As women traditionally make fewer investments in their education and work experience (Tharenou et al., 1994), it is difficult to find more qualified women for senior roles including board membership.

Dearth of qualified women directors may indicate two things. First, CEOs like to be surrounded by people having similar experience, background, perspective, value, and gender. Hence lack of qualified women directors may discourage them to meet board diversity at any cost by appointing less qualified women board members. Second, most of the boards across world have only one woman member in the board. This suggests that such appointments are probably made more as a compliance and image building exercise than for any strategic considerations.

Conclusion

Using board membership data for all the listed companies for which we could get data from the Prowess database of CMIE for the fiscal year 2015, we find that most of the boards in India do not have any women directors and a few boards have only a token membership of women directors on the board. We also surprisingly find that boards having a woman CEO have fewer women members on the board than in boards having male CEOs. Also, companies that have more independent women directors are less profitable compared to companies with boards having no women directors.

Study findings may change as time progresses. A three-year study may not be adequate to establish anything. With only 8.6% of the total board members in India being women, there is tremendous shortage of qualified women personnel to serve the corporate boards. India Inc. must gear up to welcome more women to the Board whereas women must warm up to boost the performance of companies by bringing diversity

and quality decision-making to the board room. However, simply looking at the relationship between appointment of women directors and profitability, without taking into consideration other important factors such as socio-cultural, political, or behavioral factors into consideration, could be misleading. Women generally face the glass-ceiling effect. Even if they succeed in breaking through that they face the challenges from gender-stereotyping during the appointment of directors into the board. Though mandatory norms for inducting women director into boards address this concern to some extent, but the influence of traditional socio-cultural factors in predominantly male-dominated managements, act as a deterrent. Future research must include the mediating or moderating role of such factors while studying the efficacy of women directors in adding to firm values.

Recent surveys show encouraging trends in India. According to a recent study on "Women on Board 2020" by MyHiringClub.com and Sarkari-Naukri.info, India's global rank is 12th regarding the presence of women members on board. The survey finds out that 55% of 628 listed companies in India have women directors, which is 14% higher than the previous year (Mint, 2020). However, to make these increasing number of women directors more value adding, there must be systematic efforts toward mentoring and training them, and free them from gender-stereo biases. This will lead to more inclusive corporate boards across countries including India.

References

Adams, R. B., & Ferreira, D. (2009). Women in the boardroom and their impact on governance and performance. *Journal of Financial Economics, 94*(2), 291–309.

Adams, R. B., & Funk, P. (2012). Beyond the glass ceiling: Does gender matter? *Management Science, 58*(2), 219–235.

Afsharipour, A. (2015). The one woman director mandate: History and trajectory. *CORPORATE GOVERNANCE IN INDIA: CHANGE AND CONTINUITY* (Ed. Indian Institute of Corporate Affairs). (Oxford University Press, Forthcoming).

Ahern, K. R., & Dittmar, A. K. (2012). The changing of the boards: The impact on firm valuation of mandated female board representation. *The Quarterly Journal of Economics, 127*(1), 137–197.

Apesteguia, J., Azmat, G., & Iriberri, N. (2012). The impact of gender composition on team performance and decision making: Evidence from the field. *Management Science, 58*(1), 78–93.

Bhagat, S., & Bolton, B. (2008). Corporate governance and firm performance. *Journal of Corporate Finance, 14*(3), 257–273.

Burke, R. J. (1997). Women on Corporate Boards of Directors: A needed resource. In R. J. Burke (Ed.), *Women in corporate management* (pp. 37–43). Springer Netherlands. https://doi.org/10.1007/978-94-011-5610-3_5

Carter, D. A., D'Souza, F., Simkins, B. J., & Simpson, W. G. (2010). The gender and ethnic diversity of US boards and board committees and firm financial performance. *Corporate Governance: An International Review, 18*(5), 396–414.

Carter, D. A., Simkins, B. J., & Simpson, W. G. (2003). Corporate governance, board diversity, and firm value. *Financial Review, 38*(1), 33–53.

Catalyst. (2008). *Catalyst census of women board directors of the Fortune 500.* Catalyst.

Catalyst. (2011). *Increasing gender diversity on boards: Current index of formal approaches.* Catalyst.

Chapple, L., & Humphrey, J. E. (2014). Does board gender diversity have a financial impact? Evidence using stock portfolio performance. *Journal of Business Ethics, 122*(4), 709–723.

Erhardt, N. L., Werbel, J. D., & Shrader, C. B. (2003). Board of director diversity and firm financial performance. *Corporate Governance: An International Review, 11*(2), 102–111.

Faccio, M., Marchica, M.-T., & Mura, R. (2016). CEO gender, corporate risk-taking, and the efficiency of capital allocation. *Journal of Corporate Finance, 39*, 193–209.

Ferreira, D. (2015). Board diversity: Should we trust research to inform policy? *Corporate Governance: An International Review, 23*(2), 108–111.

Francoeur, C., Labelle, R., & Sinclair-Desgagné, B. (2008). Gender diversity in corporate governance and top management. *Journal of Business Ethics, 81*(1), 83–95.

Huse, M., & Solberg, A. G. (2006). Gender-related boardroom dynamics: How Scandinavian women make and can make contributions on corporate boards. *Women in Management Review, 21*(2), 113–130.

Kang, E., Ding, D. K., & Charoenwong, C. (2010). Investor reaction to women directors. *Journal of Business Research, 63*(8), 888–894. https://doi.org/10.1016/j.jbusres.2009.06.008

Liu, Y., Wei, Z., & Xie, F. (2014). Do women directors improve firm performance in China? *Journal of Corporate Finance, 28*, 169–184.

Lückerath-Rovers, M. (2013). Women on boards and firm performance. *Journal of Management & Governance, 17*(2), 491–509. https://doi.org/10.1007/s10997-011-9186-1

Matsa, D. A., & Miller, A. R. (2011). Chipping away at the glass ceiling: Gender spillovers in corporate leadership. *American Economic Review, 101*(3), 635–639.

McDonald, M. L., & Westphal, J. D. (2012). Access denied: Low mentoring of women and minority first-time directors and its negative effects on appointments to additional boards. *Academy of Management Journal, 56*(4), 1169–1198. https://doi.org/10.5465/amj.2011.0230

Milliken, F. J., & Martins, L. L. (1996). Searching for common threads: Understanding the multiple effects of diversity in organizational groups. *Academy of Management Review, 21*(2), 402–433.

Mint, 2020. India ranked 12th in women member presence on companies' board globally. https://www.livemint.com/news/india/india-ranked-12th-in-women-member-presence-on-companiesboard-globally-11583674190248.html. Accessed on December 8, 2020.

Post, C., & Byron, K. (2014). Women on boards and firm financial performance: A meta-analysis. *Academy of Management Journal, 58*(5), 1546–1571. https://doi.org/10.5465/amj.2013.0319

Richard, O. C., Murthi, B. S., & Ismail, K. (2007). The impact of racial diversity on intermediate and long-term performance: The moderating role of environmental context. *Strategic Management Journal, 28*(12), 1213–1233.

Rob, B., Nadja, G., & Roger, O. (2004). Empirical evidence on corporate governance in Europe: The effect on stock returns, firm value and performance. *Journal of Asset Management, 5*(2), 91–104.

Robinson, G., & Dechant, K. (1997). Building a business case for diversity. *Academy of Management Perspectives, 11*(3), 21–31.

Singh, V., Terjesen, S., & Vinnicombe, S. (2008). Newly appointed directors in the boardroom: How do women and men differ? *European Management Journal, 26*(1), 48–58. https://doi.org/10.1016/j.emj.2007.10.002

Spain Equality Law. (2007). *Ley Orga'nica de Igualdad. Ley Organica 3/2007, de 22 de marzo, para la igualdad efectiva de mujeres yhombres*. BOE no 71 de 23/3/2007.

Srinidhi, B. I. N., Gul, F. A., & Tsui, J. (2011). Female directors and earnings quality. *Contemporary Accounting Research, 28*(5), 1610–1644.

Tharenou, P., Latimer, S., & Conroy, D. (1994). How do you make it to the top? An examination of influences on women's and men's managerial advancement. *Academy of Management Journal, 37*(4), 899–931.

Watson, J., & McNaughton, M. (2007). Gender differences in risk aversion and expected retirement benefits. *Financial Analysts Journal, 63*(4), 52–62.

CHAPTER 22

Role of Technology Business Incubator (TBI) in Sustaining Start-Ups: The Case of Startup Incubation and Business Innovation Lab (SIBIL)

Rajeev Verma, Jyoti Verma, and Ranjani Kumari

Introduction

India is progressing fast on the track of development, with relentless efforts being made toward strengthening infrastructure and promoting industrial growth. In these lines, the Government of India launched Startup Policy, 2016 to boost entrepreneurship and encourage start-ups with job creation at micro level. Action plan of this initiative is largely focusing on three areas namely, business handholding; funding support; industry-academia partnership and incubation. The key features of this

R. Verma (✉) · J. Verma · R. Kumari
Chandragupt Institute of Management Patna (CIMP), Patna, India
e-mail: rajeev.verma@cimp.ac.in

J. Verma
e-mail: jyoti@cimp.ac.in

Rajagopal and R. Behl (eds.), *Managing Disruptions in Business*, Palgrave Studies in Democracy, Innovation, and Entrepreneurship for Growth, https://doi.org/10.1007/978-3-030-79709-6_22

policy include funding support to the start-ups like seed grant up to 1 million, free of cost valuation for start-ups, success fee @2% of investment for mobilizing investment from state-registered angel investors and zero cost for filing patents. Any manufacturing and service led firm working toward innovation, new product development or improvisation of products, processes or services is considered under this scheme. Scalable business models with a high potential of employment generation are also being considered under this scheme. In continuation of this, we are discussing a case of incubation center situated in the state of Bihar in India working for the implementation of startup scheme.

To make incubation happen, government has selected resourceful higher academic institutions in the state as host institutes. Startup Incubation and Business Innovation Lab (SIBIL) is one such initiative supporting this cause in the state of Bihar. Chandragupta Institute of Management Patna (CIMP) is a host institution for SIBIL. Incubation center provides facilities like mentoring, plug and play office, co-working space, etc., to start-ups (Exhibit 22.1). The objectives of SIBIL include, creating physical infrastructure and support systems necessary for business incubation activities; facilitating networking with professional resources including mentoring, expert consultation, business advisory; facilitating knowledge creation, innovation and entrepreneurial activities. Each incubation center commands certain competencies and on similar lines SIBIL majorly focuses on E-commerce-based services, Health-tech, Fin-tech and Edu-tech services.

Based on the general guidelines of Startup Policy 2016 of Government of Bihar, SIBIL has also been planning to get engaged in providing specialized services to existing MSMEs in the region in terms of facilitating technology commercialization and transfer, new product development, patent filing and commercialization. Till March 2021, SIBIL has received more than 450 applications from the Department of Industries, Government of Bihar for mentoring and incubation under the Bihar Startup Policy 2017. Apart from the Government-sponsored projects, this start-up center is also facilitating nationwide students to start their own venture under Startup India.

The CEO of SIBIL, Mr. Nair strongly believes in the need of redefining the Indian version of Innovation by educating new entrepreneurs on what exactly is Innovation and how it can be scaled up. In the new age of innovation, technology led start-ups such as data and analytics are one among the most preferred by the entrepreneurs

followed by health, educations, renewable energy, agriculture and manufacturing. The startup landscape for India looks promising due to the rising confidence of angel investors, improvement of technological penetration and promising schemes launched by government. He believes that with right guidance incubate, investors and incubators will further enrich the startup ecosystem. But with the advent of Novel Coronavirus 2019 (Covid-19), the whole landscape of startup seems to be vulnerable, they are facing several formidable challenges both, from a business as well as from an operations' perspective. Most of the start-ups have witnessed a decline in demand, except for start-ups dealing with essential services. Further, Moody highlights that in the Q2-3, FY 20-21, several investors have pulled back from closing current funding rounds. Thus, one of the major challenges faced by the start-ups has now become fund sourcing[1]. This post-COVID business landscape has also put a case on sustenance of incubation centers as many of the start-ups have failed to sustain. In this situation what should an incubator like SIBIL do to support these start-ups and maintain its own sustenance?

Rationale of the Case Study

The incubation process led by SIBIL is over 5 years old. Since then, it has incubated 125 start-ups (as of March 2021). In Bihar, the formal incubation process is only over a decade old with handful of incubation centers. It is only with the advent of Bihar Startup policy 2016, 19 technology business incubators (TBIs) have been set up in different locations. In the process of strengthening incubation process, firms have been given a focused approach to understand their unique requirement. These institutes integrate various components associated with the system of innovation. However, to fulfill this case study, we have identified SIBIL as our core organization.

The guided rationale behind the selection of SIBIL comprises various indicators and attributes such as active engagement in knowledge creation, collaborative research at the incubation center, market research and extent of commercialization of products. SIBIL is the only incubation center in East India that has combined facility to manufacture project prototypes in its respective incubation center. However, along with this,

[1] SS Rana & Co, Impact of COVID-19 on Start-ups, https://www.lexology.com/library/detail.aspx?g=43b26766-1842-4db8-b360-80e55d2090fe, 2 June 2020.

the legal status of SIBIL is also different from the entire country. While almost all TBIs either have company or society acts as their legal status, the SIBIL incubation center is a part of its parent institute, CIMP.

Methodology

The firm level data was collected from SIBIL and research organizations monitoring incubation process in the country, i.e., Invest India. The data from incubation center has been collected from November 2020 to March 2021. The secondary data has been collected from the annual reports, registrar of companies apart from collecting primary data from entrepreneurs and incubatee. In addition, data analysis has been carried out using IBM SPSS.

It has been observed that the concept of incubation has shifted merely from progress sharing to handholding into new product development and marketing research. As of demand of the incubates the task of incubation centers extends from knowledge creation, safeguarding and transfer of knowledge. The type of support firm needs from an incubation center includes knowledge creation and transfer, commercialization, marketing research, handholding in new product development and informed decision-making. However, the earlier studies on incubation process were focused more on providing physical facilities such as combined office space, logistics and management support. With the changing times, these requirements have seen a major shift and companies are more and more looking for accelerators to expand in their business operations. Our current case studies are also talking about two such firms that are engaged into the active incubation processes and seek guidance in marketing research, which is being supported by SIBIL.

Case 1: the first case originates from the interaction of Mr. Nair, CEO of SIBIL with Mr. Kumar, MD and CEO of Hanuman Inc. The preliminary discussions were held way back in January 2020. Hanuman Inc. is a medical service provider startup incorporated in the year 2016 as health-tech startup. They are mainly into the business of medical diagnostics, pathology lab testing, 24×7 home delivery of medicines and emergency ambulance services. It works through a mobile application which is very popular amount city locals in Patna, Bihar. Its main competition comes from apps like 1mg, *Pharmeasy* and *Netmeds* that largely operate at national level. Importantly, Hanuman being confined to a single city limits offers services at much faster rate. In one of the winter afternoons in

January 2020, Mr. Kumar shared a thought of expanding their customer base by offering various sales promotion and discounts to its prospective customers. This seems commonsensical to him as for ages people consider discount as a means of increasing consumer base. Nair being a marketing professional, understood discounts do not built a brand, it kills. Nair shared that for short-term goals do not jump into sales promotion or discounts. With more than 0.1 M downloads, the app has been in the reach of 5 percent of the city population. To further expand the business, Nair suggested to make a strong consumer base using loyalty program so as it rewards and encourages all who are dedicated app customers. Mobile application-based start-ups face largest difficulty in terms of consumer churning. The average churn rate of the industry is around 38 percent and it varies based on the type of service. Kumar was clueless about research techniques used for prediction of loyal customers.

Nair explained that prediction analytics is required to understand the underlying phenomenon. Based on the customer relationship database, Nair's research team has been able to identify a set of loyal customers and their innate attributes. His approach is to develop a discriminant function that can predict the future behavior of any prospective customer. However, he understands such models are not free from errors and hence model precision is of much importance. The exercise of model prediction got completed by June 2020. However, due to COVID protocol and subsequent lockdown in the country, it has been observed a surge into the mobile application-based home delivery business. New customers joined at the rate of 18 percent and their retention rate increased to 80 percent. Company also launched a dedicated loyalty card with minimum cashback of 20 percent. Company witnessed an increased footfall of 32 percent and increase in number of loyal customers by 11 percent within first 2 quarters of FY 2020–21. Trend continued till Q4 of FY 2020–21 and company witnessed an increase of revenue by 45 percent. It is a phenomenal milestone in the journey of small startup. Kumar understands that prediction analytics-based discriminant model had a role to play into it. However, we also cannot negate the impact of COVID into the online consumer surge. To reflect, he thought of underpinning the success factors. The support information is attached into Appendix 1.

Case 2: Kartkio India Pvt. Ltd. is an online e-commerce platform targeting young Indian consumers. Company primarily deals in the trendy and fashionable dresses targeting consumers from tier-2 and tier-3 cities.

Company started its operation in the year 2017 and till date having a dedicated consumer base of around 1500 unique consumers covering around 400 postal pin codes in the country. However, the scale of operation of the firm remains small and even today total of 2650 SKUs are only sold on the platform. Revenue just met company's day-to-day operation and even today breakeven has not been achieved. Vikram, CEO being a management graduate desires to segment its customer base to develop a targeted marketing approach. They desire to segment their potential customers based on their attitudes and perceptions. Vikram shared his intentions with Mr. Nair regarding conducting a suitable marketing research. Incubation team initially carried a preliminary research and the variables that could have some impact on consumer preferences were identified. These variables were converted into a questionnaire in the form of statements. Respondents were asked to provide their responses to each statement on a 5-point Likert scale. The purpose of this study was to find out the right target segment for the prospective customers. With this, company is not only able to minimize its marketing expenditure but also able to reduce its marketing efforts. Appendix 2 shares tables of the cluster analysis outcome.

These case studies highlight that how SIBIL support and lend its expertise into the firm's journey of growth and sustainability. Technology incubators like SIBIL play a very significant role in the growth and sustenance of start-up in the country. In all the above cases, companies may replicate their learning and witness better growth and opportunities.

Impact of COVID-19 on Start-Ups

Overall whole investment sector has been adversely impacted due to the Novel Coronavirus 2019. Among all the business sectors, start-ups are the most vulnerable and are facing huge challenges. The value of investment in India fell off nearly 81.1%, from $1.73 billion in March 2019 to $ 0.33 billion in March 2020. Therefore, the major challenge the new start-ups are facing is sourcing funds, resulting cash flow issues for many start-ups[2]. There was a dip of 50 percent in overall funding during the lockdown versus pre-COVID-19 levels; around 40 percent start-ups were negatively

[2] SS Rana & Co, Impact of COVID-19 on Start-ups, https://www.lexology.com/library/detail.aspx?g=43b26766-1842-4db8-b360-80e55d2090fe, 2 June 2020.

impacted and 15 percent of the Indian start-ups were forced to discontinue operations due to COVID-19.[3] The lockdown implemented across the nation and in various states not only impacted the daily business operations, but it made many start-ups to prepare contingency plans to limit workforce and to decrease employee salaries. Various start-up founders have also taken pay-cuts to limit the losses faced.

Opportunities and Challenges for Incubators in Post-COVID Era

Opportunity

Although COVID-19 has brought tragedy of massive proportion, it has also acted as a breeding ground for new problems requiring new innovations. This is a big drive for action from start-ups to innovate and incubators to help and support them in a way which can be sustainable. In this type of tough situations, the incubators like SIBIL and its advisors are found to adopt very different approach to add value to start-ups and they play a very crucial role in shaping the future of innovation-oriented start-ups. In contemporary world there is huge uncertainty and recession is more frequent so there is a constant need of support of these advisors for the new start-ups. More information technology-based innovation ideas are required for the post-COVID business ground due to Coronavirus guidelines.

Challenge

This pandemic has changed the way the incubators operate, incubators need to reflect and re-strategize if they want to remain relevant in the new post-COVID world. Policymakers and grant-making organizations are concerned about the high incubators mortality rates and low success rates of their graduating start-ups. These advisors and institutions do not have much financial success in comparison to other entities in the value chain of the incubation process, and as public funds are becoming scarce,

[3] Covid impact: 40% of Indian start-ups hit, but recovery is strong, says report, https://www.thehindubusinessline.com/news/covid-impact-40-of-indian-start-ups-hit-but-recovery-is-strong-says-report/article32854724.ece, 14 October 2020. Note: All the names used in the study are fictitious in nature.

these incubators are being asked to re-evaluate their business models to help generate revenues and become self-sustainable organizations. With the changing business landscape of post-COVID, the incubators need to be more technological oriented to adapt to the new requirements of the start-ups.

What Should Be the SIBIL's Future Action Plan?

SIBIL plays a very important role in supporting and providing expertise to the innovative start-up, as we can see in the described cases and they are also very good in their expertise like market research, which is helping the start-ups to flourish. But there is not much financial success being the incubator. On the other hand, side there is huge opportunity of new innovations with the start-ups in the post-COVID era. Along with this there is huge threat also for the incubation centers due to the changed way of market operations, which needs to be re-worked for mentoring the start-ups in the post-COVID era. After analyzing the situations with all the opportunities and challenges, what should be the future action plan by SIBIL? What should SIBIL do to make themselves sustainable in the new post-COVID business world? How should they re-evaluate their business models to help generate revenues and become self-sustainable organization?

Conclusion

The main purpose of these case studies is to highlight the learning trajectory in and around companies in the incubation centers. With the help of existing empirical evidence, we would like to highlight the learning associated with each of the case. It also highlights the efforts related to seed funding, research support and commercializing technologies. This case poses a challenging question to the budding entrepreneur and businessman to understand the present situation and how these organizations should work to remain self-sustainable. With time, it requires the mapping of the incubation center for the collective learning so as firms across states learn from the past set examples and with the ongoing condition they need to modify and rework their strategies to sustain.

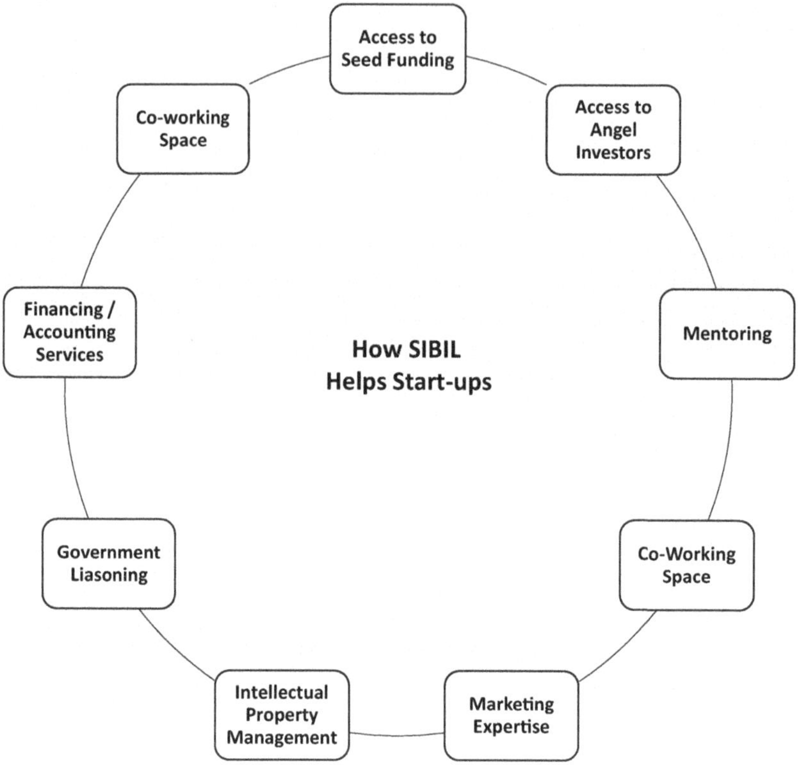

Exhibit 22.1 SIBIL's core functions (*Source* Author's developed)

Exhibit

See Exhibit 22.1

Appendix 1. Summary of canonical function (Hanuman Inc)

See Tables 22.1, 22.2, 22.3, 22.4

Appendix 2. Summary of K-means clustering (Kartkio India Pvt. Ltd.)

See Tables 22.5, 22.6, and 22.7

Table 22.1 Eigenvalues

Function	*Eigenvalue*	*% of Variance*	*Cumulative %*	*Canonical correlation*
1	1.811[a]	100.0	100.0	.803

[a]Model 1 eigen value

Table 22.2 Standardized canonical discriminant function coefficients

	Function 1
Age[a]	.907
Income	.924
Yrs. Married	.285

[a]Factors studied

Table 22.3 Canonical discriminant function coefficients

	Function 1
Age	.194
Income	.000
Yrs. Married	.160
(Constant)	−9.076

Table 22.4 Functions at group centroids

Risk	*Function 1*
High	– 1.269
Low	1.269

Note Classification accuracy is 80 percent

Table 22.5 Final cluster centers

	Cluster			
	1	*2*	*3*	*4*
Email[a]	1.60	3.50	2.80	2.75
quality_pr	2.40	3.33	2.20	2.50
think_tw	3.60	2.17	3.20	3.75
TV	3.00	3.33	2.60	3.00
car	3.60	3.83	2.60	2.50
fastfood	4.40	3.50	3.40	4.00
hlth_cons	2.20	4.00	1.40	3.50
forgn_cos	2.40	1.83	4.60	2.75
women	3.20	2.00	1.80	4.50
politics	2.80	4.00	3.00	3.25
movies	3.00	3.50	4.20	4.00
settle_abr	1.60	3.17	3.60	4.00
brded_pdts	2.00	3.83	2.40	4.00
week_out	2.00	3.83	2.40	4.00
ccard	4.20	2.50	1.80	3.75

[a]Items covered for clustering

Table 22.6 ANOVA

	Cluster		*Error*		*F*	*Sig.*
	Mean square	*df*	*Mean square*	*df*		
email	3.317	3	1.266	16	2.621	.086
quality_pr	1.406	3	1.396	16	1.007	.415
think_tw	2.739	3	1.599	16	1.713	.205
TV	.489	3	1.158	16	.422	.740
car	2.322	3	1.640	16	1.416	.275
fastfood	1.100	3	1.619	16	.680	.577
hlth_cons	7.400	3	.812	16	9.108	.001
forgn_cos	7.522	3	.874	16	8.607	.001
women	7.050	3	.787	16	8.952	.001
politics	1.550	3	1.472	16	1.053	.396
movies	1.417	3	1.269	16	1.117	.372
settle_abr	5.239	3	1.077	16	4.864	.014
brded_pdts	4.972	3	1.252	16	3.971	.027
week_out	4.972	3	1.252	16	3.971	.027
ccard	6.050	3	.866	16	6.989	.003

Notes The *F* tests should be used only for descriptive purposes because the clusters have been chosen to maximize the differences among cases in different clusters. The observed significance levels are not corrected for this and thus cannot be interpreted as tests of the hypothesis that the cluster means are equal

Table 22.7 Number of cases in each cluster

Cluster	1	5.000
	2	6.000
	3	5.000
	4	4.000
Valid		20.000
Missing		.000

Index

Rajagopal and R. Behl (eds.), *Managing Disruptions in Business*, Palgrave Studies in Democracy, Innovation, and Entrepreneurship for Growth, https://doi.org/10.1007/978-3-030-79709-6

U

V

W

The manufacturer's authorised representative in the EU is Springer
Nature Customer Service Centre GmbH, Europaplatz 3, 69115 Heidelberg,
Germany. If you have any concerns regarding our products, please
contact ProductSafety@springernature.com

Printed and bound by CPI Group (UK) Ltd, Croydon, CR0 4YY
30/09/2026
02225443-0011

Work-Life Interface

Toyin Ajibade Adisa · Gbolahan Gbadamosi
Editors

Work-Life Interface

Non-Western Perspectives

palgrave
macmillan

Editors
Toyin Ajibade Adisa
HRM & Organisational Behaviour
Royal Docks School of Business and Law
London, UK

Gbolahan Gbadamosi
Organisational Behaviour and HRM at the Business School
Bournemouth University
Bournemouth, UK

ISBN 978-3-030-66647-7 ISBN 978-3-030-66648-4 (eBook)
https://doi.org/10.1007/978-3-030-66648-4

This Palgrave Macmillan imprint is published by the registered company Springer Nature Switzerland AG
The registered company address is: Gewerbestrasse 11, 6330 Cham, Switzerland

To my parents, family, colleagues, and all my students.

—Toyin Ajibade Adisa

To all the lovely students I have had the pleasure of teaching and/or supervising

—Gbolahan Gbadamosi

Contents

Notes on Contributors

Olatunji David Adekoya is a Doctoral Researcher in Human Resource Management at the University of East London, United Kingdom. He studied at the University of Wales, Trinity Saint David, United Kingdom, where he obtained his master in Business Administration, while his first degree in Economics was obtained from the University of Lagos, Nigeria. His key research examines HRM in African countries, with a strong focus on work-life balance, organisational flexibility and employment relations in SMEs and large firms. As a young and adept researcher, he has published in peer-reviewed journals with interests of Human Resource Management, Business Management, International Business and Economics.

Toyin Ajibade Adisa is a Senior Lecturer at the Royal Docks School of Business and Law, University of East London, UK. He holds masters and Ph.D. degrees in international business management and human resource management from UEL and Brunel University London, respectively. He has taught and research issues in human resource management, organisational behaviour, employment relations, organisational culture, gender and inequality, flexibility and work-life balance, and reforms in emerging and developing economies. He is a fellow of Higher Education Academy, a fellow of Chartered Management Institute (CMI) and a member of chartered institute of personnel development (CIPD). He has published articles in journals such as *Personnel Review*, *Employee Relations*, *Gender in Management*, *Journal of Managerial Psychology* and *Career Development International*. In addition, one of his articles was awarded the Emerald Literati Network Award: highly commended for best paper award 2017 Emerald Literati Network Awards for excellence. He is passionate about teaching and researching in HRM/OB subject area. He is currently the course leader for the HRM undergraduate Programme at the University of East London.

Kwame Adom is Senior Lecturer in the Department of Marketing and Entrepreneurship, University of Ghana Business School. He holds a Ph.D. in Management (Entrepreneurship focus), M.B.A. (Finance) from the University of Sheffield and University of Leicester in the UK, respectively, as well as B.Sc. Planning from Kwame Nkrumah University of Science and Technology, Kumasi—Ghana. His research interests draw on experiences from Africa, specifically Ghana, to inform theoretical developments in entrepreneurship, future of work, gender/culture and entrepreneurship, motives of informal workers and the relationship between formal and the informal economy and socio-economic development. He has consulted for individuals and institutions for over ten years in the area of entrepreneurship and marketing.

Wee Chan Au is a Lecturer in the Department of Management, Monash University. Her research interest lies in work and well-being (work-life balance specifically), organisational and HR practices in facilitating work and well-being. She has published her research work in international journals and presented at international conferences. She has been involved in several empirical studies about work and well-being of working adults, migrant domestic workers, women entrepreneurs and academics. She has received funding from the British Council and Academy of Science Malaysia (2018), and most recently, the Ministry of Higher education (2019) to investigate work, health and well-being issues in Malaysia. She has also been actively involved in regional, national and industry-related projects commissioned by Economic Planning Unit (under the Prime Minister's Office) Malaysia (2014–2016), Malaysian Plastics and Machinery Association (MPMA) (2016, 2020), Certified Practising Accountants (CPA) Australia (2016–2020) and The Asia-Pacific Economic Cooperation (APEC) (2018).

Camila Botero is Ph.D. candidate in psychology at Pontifical Catholic University of Argentina (UCA) with research grant from the National Scientific and Technical Research Council (CONICET). Her research interests are on work performance, emotional intelligence and psychological well-being.

Nasima M. H. Carrim is an Associate Professor in the Department of Human Resource Management at the University of Pretoria, South Africa. Her research focuses on gender in management, culture, religion and minorities in the workplace from an intersectionality and identity perspective. Her research strategy is based on qualitative research mainly using life story interviews. She has authored many articles in international journals related to the challenges that minorities face in the workplace. She has also authored chapters in international books and published articles related to diversity management. She was the recipient of the Emerald African Management Research Fund Award in 2014 for her study related to Indian male managers' upward mobility in corporate South Africa. In 2014, she also received the certificate of merit for teaching excellence and innovation at the University of Pretoria for her undergraduate course in diversity management. In 2017, she received the 2016 Best Junior Researcher in Management Sciences in the Economic and Management Sciences Faculty at the University of Pretoria.

Xi Wen Chan is a Lecturer in Organisational Psychology at the School of Applied Psychology, Griffith University, in Brisbane, Australia. She graduated with B.Com. (Hons)'13 and Ph.D. (Organisational Behaviour & Human Resources)'18 from The Australian National University. She conducts research on the work-life interface of various occupations (e.g. nurses, social workers, flexible knowledge workers and public servants) with a focus on flexible/remote working, work-life boundary management and self-efficacy to regulate work and life. Her work has been published in the *International Journal of Human Resource Management*, *British Journal of Social Work*, *Stress and Health*, *Personnel Review*, *International Journal of Manpower* and *Frontiers in Psychology*.

V. Chandra is a Professor of Communication and HR and OB at International Management Institute, New Delhi, India. A social anthropologist by qualification and training, she has over two decades of experience in teaching, training and research in organisational communication, cross-cultural issues in management and international human resource management. She has authored three books and has published several research papers in both national and international journals. Her current research interests include cross-cultural and career issues at workplace.

Gisela Delfino (Ph.D., University of Buenos Aires) is Professor at Pontifical Catholic University of Argentina (UCA), Associate Researcher at National Scientific and Technical Research Council (CONICET) and Visiting Professor at Universidad Andres Bello (Doctorado en Educacion y Sociedad), Chile. Her research interests are on psychological and social well-being and citizen participation.

Masthan Devalapalli is currently Professor at Deanship of Quality and Academic Accreditation, Imam Abdurrahman Bin Faisal University, Saudi Arabia. Formerly, he was with King Saud University (KSU), Saudi Arabia and Al Dar University College, Khawarizmi International College, United Arab Emirates (UAE), leading educational institutions in Middle East Region, as Full Professor of Organizational Behaviour & Human Resource Management in College of Business Administration. He published two books: *Strengthening Leadership- Best Practices for Urban Cooperative Banks* and *Leadership Development in Public Sector Banks*. He was the founder of the Centre for Leadership Research and Development (CLRD), Hyderabad, India (research, consulting and training organisation in management).

Ghada El-Kot is a Professor of Human Resources and Organisational Behaviour, and Deputy President for Strategic Affairs at the Arab Academy for Science, Technology and Maritime Transport (AAST-MT). She has served in numerous senior leadership roles since 2004 and has worked for decades as an international consultant, researcher, trainer and reviewer in the HR and OB field in Egypt, the Arab region and Europe. Her main research interests have encompassed Human Resources Management practices and their effects on organisational performance, employees' effectiveness and well-being. Her current research revolves around women's empowerment and work-life balance in leadership and management positions in Egypt. As a professor, she has supervised and externally examined a number of successful masters and Ph.D. students (13 as supervisor; 18 as external examiner), and she has published over 40 international peer-reviewed papers and book chapters. Her awards include: The Women Leadership and Excellence Awards (WLEA) Exemplary Woman Mentor Award 2020; 2011 Outstanding Paper Award from Emerald for her research on "Work engagement among managers and professionals in Egypt: potential antecedents and consequences". She is listed in Who's Who in the World from 2006. The Best Ph.D. thesis in 2001 on Teamwork Effectiveness in Egypt from the University of Plymouth, UK and The Best Master thesis in 1997 on evaluating simulation training techniques in Egypt from Alexandria University, Egypt.

Sarah Fahmy, M.A. is a Theatre and Performance Studies Ph.D. Student, an applied theatre facilitator and a member of the child language learning lab in the Speech and Language Hearing Sciences Department at the University of Colorado, Boulder. Her research focuses on voice, emotion and identity formation of young bilingual Middle Eastern youth. She is interested in the intersection of theatre and speech science to assess the cultural, socio-economic and educational impacts on vocal and linguistic development. She is one of the founders of the Middle Eastern Theatre Focus Group at the Association for Theatre in Higher Education conference, and an education advisor with the Egyptian Ministry of Expatriate Affairs' "Egypt Can" committee, working on various national educational initiatives. She is also the recipient of the 2019 North American Arab Women of Excellence Award. At CU she has served as the President of the Graduate and Professional Student Government, the Lead Graduate Instructor for the Theatre Department, is a member of interdisciplinary performance groups: Inside the Greenhouse, Performers Without Borders, CU Playback, and is the Co-founder of CU EnActs.

Gbolahan Gbadamosi is an Associate Professor on Organisational Behaviour and Human Resource Management at the Business School, Bournemouth University, UK and holds a Ph.D. in organisational behaviour. As a researcher, he uses a multi-method research approach having used both quantitative and qualitative methods in his over 100 academic publications, most in high impact scholarly academic journals. He teaches research methods, organisational behaviour and people resourcing and development. He has supervised 4 PhDs and has examined 18 PhDs across organisational behaviour and HRM. He has also completed several funded research projects including for UNAIDS/UNDP and the British Academy. Some of his recent publication has appeared in *Personnel Review*, *Employee Relations*, *British Educational Research Journal*, *Journal of Education and Work*, *International Journal of Production Economics*, among others. His current research interest focuses on: employee health, well-being, and work-life interface; managing unethical work practices; employee engagement; and careers.

Eileen Koekemoer is an Associate Professor in the Human Resource Management Department from the Faculty of Economic and Management Sciences at the University of Pretoria in South Africa. She is a registered industrial psychologist with the Health Profession Council of South Africa (HPCSA). The areas of her research include work-life interaction, career success and the well-being of employees. She is involved in various research projects that investigate the interaction between employees' work and family life and how it influences their career success and/or well-being. She is the mother of three daughters and constantly juggles her own work-life balance between her children and her career as academic and researcher.

Mike Leat is now an Honorary Research Fellow at the University of Plymouth Business School having recently retired from his positions as Director of Undergraduate Programmes, Deputy Director and Acting Head of School. He fulfilled a number of Senior Management roles in the Business School over the last decade but before that was an active academic and researcher and published a number of books and peer-reviewed journal articles. His primary research interests were in International and Comparative Human Resource Management, HR Issues in the European Union, Employee Relations and more latterly Supply Chain Management. He published in all these fields, including a number of articles with Professor El Kot on HRM in Egypt. He acted as Director of Studies for a number of successful Ph.D. students and has examined externally at that level.

Xuchu Liu is a Lecturer in the School of Management, Henan University of Chinese Medicine, in Henan, China. She is also a visiting scholar at the University of Waikato's Management School in New Zealand. She graduated with Bachelor of Counselling and Master of Science in Psychology from Henan University in China. Her research interests are in employees' emotions, resilience and well-being, as well as their work-life experiences. Currently, she is also conducting research on moral leadership, servant leadership and how different leadership styles affect employees' work-life balance.

Gladys Muasya obtained her Ph.D. from Arizona State University ASU. She is a Senior Lecturer at St. Paul's University Kenya in the Faculty of Business, Computer Science and Communication Studies where she teaches business and communication courses. One of her major research interests is the intersection of work and family—which encompasses work and life balance/conflict. She has published various articles and book chapters in work-life balance related topics in *Sage Open*, *South Africa Journal of Education*, *South African Journal of Labour Relations*, and *Howard Journal of Communications*, among others. While at ASU, she was the 2013 Recipient of Lind Herberger Fellowship Award for contribution to work-life balance and conflict.

Ibrahim Noorani is a Lecturer at the Department of Public Administration, Benazir Bhutto Shaheed University, Karachi. He holds a masters degree in Public Administration and Master of Science in Management Sciences. He is currently pursuing Ph.D. in Public Administration at the University of Karachi. His areas of interest include organisational psychology, training and development, moral philosophy and employee ethics.

Daniel Nzengya obtained his Ph.D. in Sustainability from Arizona State University (ASU). He is a Senior Lecturer and Director of Research and Innovations, at St. Paul's University, Kenya. He is also the Programme leader, Doctoral Programme in Development Studies at SPU. He teaches courses in Research Methodology, Statistics, Environmental Management and Innovations for Sustainability. His research interests largely focus on water, environment and sustainability, but also likes to explore the intersections of gender and work-life balance conflict particularly on community-managed water and sanitation interventions settings in the sub-Saharan Africa.

Sivasankar Prabaharan did his doctoral degree in Physiotherapy and presently works as Lecturer at Quality Measurement and Evaluation Department, Deanship of Quality and Academic Accreditation (DQAA), Imam Abdulrahman Bin Faisal University (IAU), Dammam, Kingdom of Saudi Arabia (KSA). He completed his Master's Degree in Business Administration (MBA) in Hospital Management. He completed the Six Sigma Black Belt from Indian Statistical Institute, Coimbatore, and a Lean & Six Sigma Master Black Belt certification from Anexas, Europe. His research interest is to enhance the Quality in Higher Education and Healthcare using Six Sigma methods. He possesses extensive clinical and academic experience in the field of Physiotherapy and has completed various research projects.

Khurram Shakir is Assistant Professor at the Benazir School of Business, Benazir Bhutto Shaheed University, Karachi. He holds a Ph.D. in Management Sciences from Iqra University, Karachi. His areas of expertise include organisational development, human resource development and employee quality management.

Sudong Shang is a Lecturer at the Griffith Business School, Griffith University in Gold Coast, Australia. He graduated with a Ph.D. in Organisational Psychology from the University of Waikato in 2017. His research interests are in work–family conflict, specifically investigating Chinese immigrants' work–family experiences from the perspective of acculturation. He is also working on research projects on the relationship between the usage of electronic devices and work–family conflict among millennials. His work has been published in *Human Resource Management*, *Frontiers in Psychology*, *Stress and Health* and *Leadership & Organization Development Journal*.

Arun Vijay Subbarayalu is currently Assistant Professor and Chairman of Quality Measurement and Evaluation, Department of Deanship of Quality and Academic Accreditation, Imam Abdulrahman Bin Faisal University, Saudi Arabia. He obtained both Bachelor's (BPT) and Master's (MPT) degrees from the Tamilnadu Dr. MGR Medical University, Chennai, India, and a Ph.D. in Physiotherapy from Ramakrishna Mission Vivekananda University, Coimbatore, India. He also obtained a Master of Business Administration degree (M.B.A.) from the University of Madras, India, and a Ph.D. in Business Administration with a specific focus on Total Quality Management from Madurai Kamaraj University, India. Moreover, he is a recipient of "Six Sigma Black Belt" certification from the Indian Statistical Institute (ISI), Coimbatore, and a Lean & Six Sigma Master Black Belt certification from Anexas, Europe. His research areas include higher education and healthcare quality management, focusing on developing continuous quality improvement strategies. He has published two textbooks and more than 40 publications in highly indexed journals. He is a recipient of the best teacher award from the Tamilnadu Dr. MGR Medical University for his exceptional teaching contributions in the year 2010. He has also received the best researcher award from the Indian Association of Physiotherapists for this scientific research contributions during the year 2018.

List of Figures

List of Tables

Part I

Introduction and Theory

1

Introduction

Gbolahan Gbadamosi and Toyin Ajibade Adisa

Work-life Interface: Definition, Theory and Measurement

The challenges of work-life constructs including work-life interface (WLI), work-family conflict (WFC), work-family enrichment (WFE), work-life balance (WLB), is global and without geographical location preferences, yet much of what we know from the empirical and theoretical work-life literature is dominated by the Global North coming mainly from Europe and North America. Although, the literature from

G. Gbadamosi (✉)
People and Organisation Department, Bournemouth University Business School, Bournemouth, UK
e-mail: ggbadamosi@bournemouth.ac.uk

T. A. Adisa
Royal Docks School of Business and Law, University of East London, London, UK
e-mail: t.adisa@uel.ac.uk

T. A. Adisa and G. Gbadamosi (eds.), *Work-Life Interface*,
https://doi.org/10.1007/978-3-030-66648-4_1

the Global South are rapidly evolving and being documented across a range of scholarly outlets yet much more work is required as the yawning gap is unsettling.

While the very idea of a work-life balance (WLB) probably goes as far back as the existence of paid work, its emergence in scholarly circles probably dates back to the late 1970s and early 1980s when the term WLB has been used to depict the coexistence and lack of opposition between one's life and their other non-work life roles.

Definition

The seminal work defining work-family conflict (WFC) and its dimensions can be traced to the work of Greenhaus and Beutell (1985). Yet, some of the earliest works on work and family lives were dominated by a conflict perspective (Barling & Sorensen, 1997; Greenhaus & Parasuraman, 1999) and the earliest theoretical models include work/family border theory (Clark, 2000), work-family enrichment (Greenhaus & Powell 2006), and a comprehensive guide for future research directions on theoretical models (Wayne, Grzywacz, Carlson, & Kacmar, 2007).

A popular seminal definition of work-life balance states that it is "the extent to which an individual is equally engaged in—and equally satisfied with—his or her work and family role" (Greenhaus, Collins, & Shaw, 2003, p. 513). Another good landmark point for the definition of work-life dates to the work of Wayne et al. (2007, p. 64) who defined work-family facilitation as: "the extent to which an individual's engagement in one life domain (i.e., work/family) provides gains (i.e., developmental, affective, capital, or efficiency) which contribute to enhanced functioning of another life domain (i.e., family/work)". Yet, the concept remains unclear (Fleetwood 2007). Furthermore, both Özbilgin, Beauregard, Tatli, and Bell (2011) and Gatrell, Burnett, Cooper, and Sparrow (2013) who were both credited with early comprehensive literature reviews also provides good start points for the collection of literatures on the definitions for WLB.

Some of the earliest and most credible literature reviews are attributed to the work of Özbilgin et al. (2011) who used the lens of diversity to identify blind spots in WLB research focusing on both positivists and critical scholarships. Gatrell et al. (2013) also did a comprehensive investigation on the problems of definition and inequity on WLB within the fields of sociology, psychology and management studies demonstrating how the early narrow definitions have led to inequities within research also shows how the definitions had been problematic rather than enriching.

More recently is the comprehensive review of Bansal and Agarwal (2020) which reviewed different conceptualisations of WLC, WLE and WLB but also how they relate to each other. On the basis of their recent review, they provided four propositions to guide future research about the relationship among the various work-life constructs: (1) work-life conflict (WLC) reduces WLB; (2) work-life enrichment (WLE) enhances WLB; (3) work-life conflict and enrichment influence individual attitudes and behaviours; (4) WFC and WLE influence individual attitudes and behaviours through WLB.

Employers and academic writers are beginning to replace the word balance in work-life balance with interface, integration, and more recently harmony. One of the main arguments being that work-life harmony allows your work to be part of your life such that work and life are in sync and fun in both the home and work terrain.

However, the term work-life harmony has been more commonly used outside of scholarly works in blogs, commercial writings, consulting and other popular social media. Yet, the term work-life harmony has appeared in scholarly works such as McMillan, Morris, and Atchley (2011), Small, Harris, Wilson, and Ateljevic, (2011), Ong and Jeyaraj (2014), and Lloyd and McAchran (2019). As researchers continue to revisit the conceptualisation of the terms work-life balance (WLB), work-life interface (WLI) and work-life harmony (WLH) in the literature not much differences have been evidenced to validate any differences until Ong and Jeyaraj (2014) provided empirical support that participants in WLB condition elicit higher levels of cognitive dissonance compared with participants in the WLH condition. Notwithstanding, much of what we know about the concept is exploratory and in early days. Work-life harmony is defined as: "an individually pleasing, congruent arrangement of work and life roles that is interwoven into a single narrative of life" (McMillan et al., 2011).

As future research continues to validate and examine the details of how we can measure the concept and evidence its clear distinction and discriminatory values from what we currently know about WLB, the concept—WLH—would still require cautious use and application.

Theory

On the theoretical front, a recent special topic forum of the Academy of Management Review (volume 44, number 1) produced several groundbreaking contemporary positions. As new academic work begin to emerge going forward, these new theories would continue to be tested and validated. Powell, Greenhaus, Allen, and Johnson (2019), the editors of the special forum, argued that work-life theory has not kept up with the explosion in research in the area. The special topic forum produced six articles (each proposing a new theory) and seeking to offer corrective course by developing new theory which will make sense of the research to date and guide future research. Four of the articles focus on work-life perspective (Bear, 2019; Bourdeau, Ollier-Malaterre, & Houlfort, 2019; Crawford, Thompson, & Ashforth, 2019; Leslie, King, & Clair, 2019) while two focus on work-family perspective (Hirschi, Hirschi, Shockley, & Zacher 2019; Ladge & Little, 2019).

Two examples from the work-life theory perspectives include Crawford et al. (2019) who proposed a model of dual-earner couples' and partners' sensemaking of work-life shock events and couples' resource investment decisions. Leslie et al. (2019) similarly proposed the construct of work-life ideologies, three independent types of work-life ideologies, and a model of their antecedents and consequences. On the other hand, from the work-family perspective Hirshi, Shockley and Zacher (2019) proposed a theoretical model that explains how people can jointly attain work and family goals by using four action strategies: allocating resources, changing resources and barriers, sequencing goals, and revising goals.

It is interesting that while these six theoretical propositions set us on the part of a new horizon as far as theoretical underpinning for work-life research in the future, it remains muddy waters as researchers continue to seek convergence of theory in the work-life research domain. Moreover, several research gaps remain uncovered by these new theories, for example, there are still gaps from careers perspective, societal or national culture perspective, the diversity perspective, and all others that go with the dichotomous "work-life" interface (Powell et al., 2019). What seems clear and incontrovertible is that work-life researchers have only just navigated into another maze of what we do not yet know rather than into a field of what we now know. The empirical validation of these new propositions through testing would be an appropriate way to engage in any new research in the work-life area. Future research will certainly become richer with the guidance provided by these new propositions yet new questions would only begin to emerge as these theories are tested in empirical investigations.

Measurement

Measurement of the construct WLB has also received considerable attention of scholars. Unlike many behavioural constructs, scale development in the work-life literature has not attracted much research attention in sociology, psychology or management studies. Yet, it is critical to be able to scientifically measure the WLB / WLI / WLH constructs since many early works adopted the positivist approach in their research. Perhaps the earliest credible measuring scale was attributed to Carlson, Kacmar, Wayne, and Grzywacz (2006) who developed an 18-item multidimensional measure of work-family enrichment. Other measures widely documented include those of Greenhaus et al. (2003), Hill, Hawkins, Ferris, and Weitzman (2001), and Dex and Bond (2005). In addition to widely used and popular Carlson et al. (2006) scale, Bansal and Agarwal (2020) in their review organised other scales used to measure WFC, WLE and WLB into those mostly used (e.g. Carlson, Kacmar, & Wiliams, 2000; Grzywacz & Marks, 2000; Netemeyer, Boles, & McMurrian, 1996); those sparsely used (e.g. Brough et al., 2014; Fisher,

Bulger, & Smith, 2009; Haar, 2013; Hill, 2005) and those hardly used (e.g. Carlson, Grzywacz, & Zivnuska, 2009; Kacmar, Crawford, Carlson, Ferguson, & Whitten, 2014; Voydanoff 2004).

The Future of Work-Life Interface Research

There are massive qualitative and quantitative outputs on WLB / WLI, there are also significant numbers of theoretical and conceptual papers. There are important ways we should advance WLI studies, including introducing greater diversity early on in the research process from operationalization, to sampling and analysis (Özbilgin et al., 2011; Gatrell et al., 2013). More varying levels of analysis from individual, group, societal, institutional, relationships and contextual are all key to the future success of work-life research. Methodological pluralism which includes historical analysis would enable deeper and more reflective investigation than purist approaches embedded in the positivist or interpretivist tradition (Özbilgin et al., 2011). Transdisciplinarity as a means of addressing troubling themes of class, gender, difference and enrichment (Gatrell et al., 2013) comes handy. Very little progress has been made with regard to these specific and important aspects that could advance our knowledge and certainly much less so from the non-western outputs. It would, therefore, seem a lot more care needs to go into research design in these areas such that every little added research begins to matter.

Richert-Kaźmierska and Stankiewicz (2016) provided evidence in a survey in the Scandinavian that age does matter in WLB as older age groups are more likely to indicate the maintenance of WLB and more frequently do not agree that all workers have equal opportunities. Similarly, Sav (2019) investigated the role of religion in WLI. The findings support the proposition that religiosity can be beneficial for WLB, rather than competing with work and other non-work roles for time and energy. Religion can be important for WLB and needs to be included more in WLI research (Sav, 2019).

While these two studies pointed to the value to age and religion in WLB research, we could ask similarly whether the following also matter: gender, race, sexual orientation and sexuality, disability, belief systems including superstitions, urban versus rural residence, full versus part-time work, paid versus self-employment, mothers versus fathers, use of technology, employers' commitment to corporate social responsibility, workplace flexibility, labour legislation, social class, among others. More recent studies suggest focusing on multiple time-period measurements in data collection and long-term cost-benefit analyses of work-life initiatives (Ong & Jeyaraj, 2014).

McNall, Nicklin, and Masuda (2010) advanced the value of important outcome variables such as burnout, alcohol/drug abuse, job stress as well as important moderator variables such as family characteristics, work hours, organisational tenure in future research. They also advocated multisource data to minimise the limiting impact of cross-sectional and self-report data. Future studies would also benefit from more cross-cultural studies, particularly using multiple countries in the West and other parts such as Asia, Africa or South America to allow more evidence-based comparisons (Le, Newman, Menzies, Zheng, & Fermelis, 2020), as well as deeper investigations into why economic, institutional and cultural differences may account for differences (Le et al., 2020). Cultural beliefs may specifically be and area whose impact on WLB may have been self-evident (Kelliher, Richardson, & Boiarintseva 2019). Furthermore, Kelliher et al. (2019) propose that we need to extend the concepts of both work and life to incorporate different life worlds and social groups and different working arrangements and employment relationships. They argue that "some employees, "life" involves things other than childcare responsibilities including activities that are important to them, such as hobbies, education, exercise, religious or community activities, and other types of caring" (Kelliher et al., 2019, p. 107).

These aforementioned enumerated areas continue to attract much less investigation and this is particularly more evident in non-western contexts. There are important decision researchers in work-life research have to make which would affect both their output and especially their contribution or indeed if they will be able to make a contribution. It is about the research design and process, sampling and data, outcome, predictor and moderating variables selection, context and culture. It is also about a more holistic and more nuanced appreciation and incorporation of these issues in future research.

Why Is the Non-Western Perspectives Important and How Does the Book Improve the Boundary of Knowledge?

Work-life balance is harmonious reconciliation of employees' work and private lives. Its importance whether implicit or explicit, to organisations and employees cannot therefore be ignored. Yet, the preponderance of work-life balance studies which have appeared in books and journal articles were undertaken and focus on western context. Much fewer authors have reported studies on the non-western perspectives of work-life balance in an ever-changing globalised world economy.

There have been a number of books that have focused on work-life balance (Clutterbuck, 2003; Crane & Hill, 2009; Poelmans, 2005); and more recently tangentially in a quality of life and well-being (Michalos, 2014). The pioneering books on the subject are all produced through the lens of the West. Very few books have been focused specifically on Africa (Mokomane, 2013) and Asia (Lu, & Cooper, 2015).

The book titled, "Work-family interface in Sub-Saharan Africa", edited by Z. Makomane in 2013 was a trailblazer on the subject in Africa. However, the book is constrained by two points. First, it focuses only on work-family balance, an aspect of work-life balance which represents a small aspect of a much bigger debate on work-life balance. Secondly, it is restricted to the African continent—indeed, sub-Saharan Africa. More recently, Lu and Cooper (2015) produced another book that focused on Asia titled "Handbook of Research on Work-Life Balance in Asia".

There is no book to date on work-life balance that focuses more broadly on the Global South, especially the three non-western continents. There are remarkable similarities in the way of life and levels of development across these continents and a synergy of a more global book might bring together a more coherent and holistic perspective. The current book therefore uniquely encompasses three continents (Africa, Asia and South America). The book thus fills this gap and gives a broader view of the concept. The book therefore adds to the growing literature from the Global South and non-western countries.

The book also offers a critical perspective and understanding of work-life balance, interface. It focuses on how employees in the non-western environments achieve balance between their work and private lives with a huge dissimilarity from western nations in terms of culture and institutional framework. Thereby improves our understanding of the impact of cultural and institutional framework on employees' ability to achieve balance and harmony between their work and private lives. Much of the extant studies from western literature may not be applicable in similar ways to these employees. Several studies have argued and evidenced that context always does matters in these organisational behaviour and management research (Bamberger, 2008; Johns, 2001; Le et al., 2020; Michailova, 2011).

The book also contributes to the academic debate by offering a non-western perspective providing a strong basis of comparative analysis of WLB/WLI more globally. It showcases a collection of conceptual and theoretical papers as well as rich set of global empirical studies that draws on qualitative and mixed methodologies. There is clearly room for more quantitative studies in work-life research in non-western contexts. Furthermore, the book is expected to be of significant value to academics, international and domestic business organisations, policy makers, and undergraduate and postgraduate students and researchers generally.

This Book and Its Structure: A Brief Overview of the Chapter Content

As a book of readings, this book will appeal to undergraduate and Masters students who require a comprehensive yet coherent and integrated coverage of debates on work-family conflict, work-life balance, and work-life interface from a non-western perspective. It includes both empirical and theoretical perspectives and current developments from various parts of the world. Doctoral students and other researchers will equally find this research book a good literature to cite providing a sound introduction to studies in the different countries covered in the book. While the academic underpinning is strong throughout, yet many of the chapters are very much applied in their findings and implications. It also calls attentions to a lot of new research opportunities. Consequently, the book will be found accessible for practitioners looking for solutions to work-life balance challenges and international human resource management discourse from a non-western tilt.

There are several pillars and frameworks presented in many of the chapters that serve as useful guides in managing people. The aim of the book is to bring together for the first time a number of contributions from leading authorities around the world in a cooperative and cohesive manner to shed light on multiple views of work-life research in their domain as a way of extending knowledge within the human resource management context. We also hope readers will gain insight into some of the divergent viewpoints and controversies within selected countries.

Our intention is to contribute to both the wider HRM debate as well as the critical management literature and therefrom provoke more focused research and debate on the areas where gaps have been identified especially in non-western contexts. This would potentially create opportunities for more carefully designed future research that would guide work-life research, management thinking, research and probably some application in practice. We hope that you will enjoy reading this book as we look forward to increasing the global coverage and country focus in subsequent editions.

There were four chapters based on an empirical investigation (Ghana, South Africa, Malaysia and Pakistan). Another six chapters were conceptual or based on some form of literature review (Kenya, Nigeria, Egypt, China, India and Argentina). The chapters on Nigeria and Saudi Arabia utilise some additional secondary data and extracts from extant empirical works. Another five chapters were focused on women or emphasises gender difference as it relates to women (Ghana, South Africa, Egypt, Pakistan and Argentina). The chapter on Saudi Arabia provides case study that focuses on higher education institutes and healthcare sector. While all the country based chapters touched on aspects of culture, the chapters on China, South Africa, India and Pakistan places a lot more emphasis and depth on aspects of culture especially the Chinese and Pakistani cultures.

The book is divided into four parts. In Part 1, "Introduction and Theory", there are two chapters that address the basic overview and foundation of field. It also addresses a rethinking of the border theory presenting an implementable and control model that helps underpin future research. In Part 2, "Africa and the Arab world", there are six chapters covering, Ghana, Kenya, Nigeria, South Africa, Egypt and Saudi Arabia. These are three strategic countries in Africa (Nigeria, South Africa and Kenya); and two key countries in the Arab world (Egypt and Saudi Arabia) with Egypt being of dual value being a dominant country in Africa yet a key player in the Arab world. We turn the questions in each country to how work-life research has progressed and what are the current practices. We explore the differences in these domains and showcase management implications as well as future research directions. In Part 3, "Asia", presented over four chapters we discuss four strategic countries of Asia: China, India, Malaysia and Pakistan. These were undertaken using both critical engagement and empirical data from these countries. Finally, in Part 4, "Latin America", we showcase recent research from Argentina and provides some insight from a much less discussed country in anglophone publications albeit important country in South America. Together the thirteen chapters provide a good spread across the world of the state of the arts regarding work-life research and practice.

Part1: Introduction and Theory

In Chapter 1, *Gbolahan Gbadamosi* and *Toyin Ajibade Adisa* in the Introduction provides an academic overview and background of the scholarly journey of work-life research. This chapter provides snapshots of various narratives regarding the conceptual definition through time identifying the key landmarks and contributions to the present time evolving from work-family conflict, work-life balance, work-life enrichment to the emerging work-life harmony. It also summarises the various key measurements of the construct, from the widely used and popular ones to the sparsely used ones and the rarely used measures. The chapter then examines current research as a prelude to proposing future research direction of work-life interface research. Furthermore, the chapter identify current research gaps and rationalises the need for more outputs from a non-western perspectives. Thereafter, it evidences how the book pushes the boundary of knowledge by attempting to bridge the knowledge gap. In the final subsection, the book's structure is described; brief overview of each chapter content is also highlighted.

In Chapter 2, *Toyin Ajibade Adisa* and *Gbolahan Gbadamosi* outline a re-evaluation of the border model and border control with the presentation of the border theory. The border theory is mainly a work-family balance theory. The chapter draws on a critical review of the literature and contemporary research to present a work-life border control model which furthers our understanding of employees' movement across the border from the work to the non-work domain. This model provides a comprehensive and coherent theoretical framework to understand employees' movements from work to non-work domains, thus border flexibility and permeability. The chapter shows how the border theory is similar and yet distinct from other theories such as spill-over model (Staines, 1980), the conservation of resource model (Hobfoll, 1989), the compensation model (Lambert, 1990), the segmentation model (Young & Kleiner, 1992). The chapter makes five propositions to guide future research directions, drawing managerial applications that will inform decision making and policies. The chapter calls attention to new theoretical models. The border theory provides a theoretical basis for contemporary and future studies.

Part 2: Africa and the Arab World

In Chapter 3, *Kwame Adom*, in an empirical investigation using institutional theory examines the role of culture in the work-life border management. It provides an insight from the formal sector focusing on Ghanaian married female workers. The study found that married female employees in Ghana experienced role conflicts that were culturally embedded. The study adopted a qualitative approach with 15 in-depth interviews with Ghanaian women. The study finds that the Ghanaian culture has contributed to women's role-conflicts and that managing WLB is challenging for married working-class females as a result of lack of flexible work schedules and the exploitative nature of some employers.

Women therefore rely on support from family, hiring the services of non-family, and effective planning for success in balancing their work with their life roles. The role of culture in managing WLB in this context is therefore significant, not symbolic. The author offers important policy implications and future research direction.

In Chapter 4, *Gladys Muasya* and *Daniel Nzengya* conducted a systematic review of WLB related studies from Kenya during the period 2008 to 2020 presenting the current state of research. From an initial 65 hits on relevant materials, after clean up they ended up with 20 relevant and usable materials that formed the basis of the chapter. They argued that much of the publications were western leaning both in conceptualisation and operationalisation. However, some progress has been made in the formal sector but very little or no coverage of the informal sector. They identified significant research areas gaps and directed researchers and practitioners at valuable research opportunities for future research contribution.

In Chapter 5, *Toyin Ajibade Adisa, Gbolahan Gbadamosi* and *Olatunji David Adekoya* focus on the "Myth and the Reality of Work-life Balance in Nigeria". They provide a conceptual overview of work-life literature in Nigeria. The chapter extracts empirical evidence from almost exclusively Nigeria based studies. The chapter starts with a comprehensive synthesis of a more global and academic WLB conceptualisation of work, life and balance as it is situated within HRM practices. Some overarching factors such as individual/organisational differences and expectations, cultural attributes and the institutional forces regulate work-life patterns working time were identified. The chapter also outlines and discusses key factors relating to WLB in Nigeria to include: working conditions (broken down as work intensification, physical presence at work, and lack of supportive culture), gender complexities, and institutional policies and initiatives as they affect the WLB experiences. The contribution of each of these factors to enhancing WLB was discussed including broad-ranging future research ideas and managerial implications. In Nigeria, long working hours, irregular work schedules, and general lack of WLB policies such as flexi-time options characterised the culture of many organisations and as such many employees working under poor conditions, are less likely to achieve WLB. The chapter concludes by pointing in the direction of recent global influences and consequent changes thus the need to adopt new and evolving business realities during the COVID-19 pandemic. The authors point to a massive opportunity for researchers to tap into the yawning gap of how business activities have changed in the management of WLB policies and initiatives and how all stakeholders have responded.

In Chapter 6, *Nasima M.H. Carrim* and *Eileen Koekemoer* focus on WLB of younger and older Indian women managers South Africa. They adopt a qualitative approach using the cultural identity theory as underpinning theory. They focused on the following research question: Do younger and older Indian women managers experience the same challenges in balancing their work and home lives? They found differences in how younger and older South African Indian women achieve WLB and the extent to which they engage in cultural identity work. Moreover, younger women managers are better able to achieve WLB and engage in lower levels of cultural identity work compared to their older counterparts mainly due to the changing social roles within the Indian community. Also, family size did not make a difference to how participants balanced work-family life and engaged in identity work. Another key finding is that workplaces do not do enough to ensure that women who are mothers can achieve high productivity levels by providing them with flexible work arrangements. They discussed policy implications as well as made useful recommendations for future research.

In Chapter 7, *Ghada El-Kot, Mike Leat* and *Sarah Fahmy*, provided another gender-based chapter which zero-in on women and focused on the connections between WLB and gender roles within the context of the Egyptian government strategy for sustainable development. First, they discussed the contextual influences on gender roles and WLB; then they reviewed the determinants, nature and consequences of WLB while identifying potential benefits for Egyptian women and organisations. Finally, they drew conclusions on the challenges and opportunities, as well as areas for further research to inform future policies and initiatives for achieving WLB in Egypt.

In Chapter 8, *Arun Vijay Subbarayalu, Sivasankar Prabaharan* and *Devalapalli Masthan* in a literature review discuss WLB in Saudi Arabia using extant studies and secondary data from higher education institutes and healthcare organisations in the country. They examined work-to-family conflict and family-to-work conflict within the context of work-life debate. This chapter reports the challenges faced by higher education and health sector employees in Saudi Arabia in managing WLB and how it varies with different age groups, gender, ethnicity, marital status, organisation culture, job security, work autonomy and supportive work culture. The chapter is significantly policy focused and advances several recommendations for the improvement of both WLB both in the higher education and healthcare sectors. Some suggestions were also made for future research.

Part 3: Asia

In Chapter 9, *Sudong Shang*, *Xi Wen Chan* and *Xuchu Liu* analyse the role of culture in the work-life discourse focusing on work-life conflict (WLC) from a Confucian cultural perspective. The chapter is very detailed in providing information about the Chinese context and Confucian values. It holistically investigates the individual-, organisational- and societal-level factors that may influence employees' WLC in China from a Confucian cultural perspective. They traced the narrative of inconsistencies in recent literature between the evidence and the cultural values that are considered. They argued that work- and non-work-related values (culture) likely leads to some unique cultural occurrences of work-life conflict, and the strengths of the relationships vary between unique and universal occurrences (in other cultures) of work-life conflict. They provided a comprehensive review and synthesis of previous work-life research conducted within the context of the Confucian culture and inspect the unique and universal antecedents and outcomes of work-life conflict. The chapter also extends the discussion to "work–family" to "work-life" to acknowledge other non-work aspects such as community, education and after-work entertainment. Finally, they discuss why WLC has unique antecedents and outcomes in a Confucian culture and their relationships with universal antecedents and outcomes of WLC. The authors provided recommendations for future research that helps contextualise WLC research in specific Chinese cultural context.

In Chapter 10, *V. Chandra* discusses WLB policies and practices in India as well as look into the future of research in this area. This literature review chapter also utilises secondary data from Indian work practices. The chapter explores the WLB policies and practices within the changing institutional contexts while attempting to identify gaps between policies and practices, what causes such gaps and the consequences therefrom. The author discusses the causes and consequences of work-life imbalance along with the coping strategies. The chapter finally throws some light on how the gendered norms predominating the national culture interferes at the operational level thus often creating gaps between stated policy and actual practice. Significant policy recommendations were made.

In Chapter 11, Wee Chan Au examined the implicit and explicit influence of WLB in Malaysia. Using a qualitative approach, the author interviewed 25 Malaysian working adults exploring institutional factors at the national- and organisational-level shaping experience of WLB. The chapter reported that lack of WLB practices at the organisational level and passive role of employers in WLB (meso-environment) is evidenced by the lack of policies and legislation at the national level (macro-environment). There are no legislated policies that enforce employers to offer WLB benefits, consequently self-initiated WLB practices at the organisational level remain rare. The author concluded that the lack of government legislation contributes to slow adoption of WLB facilities in organisations. Moreover, Malaysian employees perceive MNCs much more favourably than local companies when selecting an employer, especially if WLB is a priority for the individual. A large number of Malaysian middle-class households depend on domestic help for household chores and childcare support, with the collectivist nature of Malaysian society also facilitating support from immediate families. The chapter further argues that there is a growing gap between employees' increasing awareness of the importance of WLB and the availability of work-life support from employers and government in Malaysia. Practical and theoretical implications were further discussed.

In Chapter 12, Ibrahim Noorani and Khurram Shakir focused on the role of Pakistani women and traditional values in WLB. The chapter provides a very comprehensive Pakistani contextual background exploring the impact of culture on the achievement of WLB among

Pakistani women. The empirical research found that culture plays a significant role in shaping the lives of Pakistani women thus influencing their ability to achieve WLB. The social caste system was also found to be a strong predictor of WLB within the confines of the Pakistani culture. The Pakistani caste system generates some contradictory outcomes among the working women across the three dominant social classes (upper, middle and lower). The chapter also reported that the inevitable need for women (particularly low-income earners) to combine work and home duties triggers a variety of coping skills and creativity which end up being useful in the workplace. Some policy implications and future research directions were highlighted.

Part 4: South America

In Chapter 13, Gisela Delfino and Camila Botero examine the challenges of finding a balance between work and private life among Argentine Workers. The authors argue that it is important, to analyse WLB based on gender because there are still significant differences and preferences in the job opportunities that men and women are exposed to. The chapter provides some detailed contextual background for the Argentine environment especially with respect to structural inequalities. The chapter provides useful narratives and discussion around some important issues within the Argentine work environment including: work-private life balance, teleworking, unemployment, and women and household work. They also discussed the psychosocial disturbances at work especially workaholism and burnout. The authors argue that a lack of balance between private life and work tend to be associated with people who have jobs and family obligations especially with young children. Education also plays a very positive role in this state of affairs.

References

Bamberger, P. (2008). From the editors beyond contextualization: Using context theories to narrow the micro-macro gap in management research. *Academy of Management Journal, 51*(5), 839–846.

Bansal, N., & Agarwal, U. A. (2020). Examining the Relationships among work-life constructs: A review. *Business Perspectives and Research, 8*(2), 257–271.

Barling, J., & Sorensen, D. (1997). Work and family: In search of a relevant research agenda. In C. L. Cooper & S. E. Jackson (Eds.), *Creating tomorrow's organizations* (pp. 157–169). New York: Wiley.

Bear, J. B. (2019). The caregiving ambition framework. *Academy of Management Review, 44*(1), 99–125.

Bourdeau, S., Ollier-Malaterre, A., & Houlfort, N. (2019). Not all work-life policies are created equal: Career consequences of using enabling versus enclosing work-life policies. *Academy of Management Review, 44*(1), 172–193.

Brough, P., Timms, C., O'Driscoll, M. P., Kalliath, T., Siu, O. L., Sit, C., & Lo, D. (2014). Work–life balance: A longitudinal evaluation of a new measure across Australia and New Zealand workers. *The International Journal of Human Resource Management, 25*(19), 2724–2744.

Carlson, D. S., Grzywacz, J. G., & Zivnuska, S. (2009). Is work-family balance more than conflict and enrichment? *Human Relations, 62*(10), 1459–1486.

Carlson, D. S., Kacmar, K. M., Wayne, J. H., & Grzywacz, J. G. (2006). Measuring the positive side of the work–family interface: Development and validation of a work–family enrichment scale. *Journal of Vocational Behavior, 68*(1), 131–164.

Carlson, D. S., Kacmar, K. M., & Williams, L. J. (2000). Construction and initial validation of a multidimensional measure of work–family conflict. *Journal of Vocational Behavior, 56,* 249–276.

Clark, S. C. (2000). Work/family border theory: A new theory of work/family balance. *Human Relations, 53*(6), 747–770.

Clutterbuck, D. (2003). *Managing work-life balance: a guide for HR in achieving organisational and individual change.* London: CIPD Publishing.

Crane, D. R., & Hill, J. E. (Eds.). (2009). *Handbook of families and work: Interdisciplinary perspectives.* University Press of America.

Crawford, W. S., Thompson, M. J., & Ashforth, B. E. (2019). Work-life events theory: Making sense of shock events in dual earner couples. *Academy of Management Review, 44*(1), 194–212.

Dex, S., & Bond, S. (2005). Measuring work–life balance and its covariates. *Work, Employment and Society, 19,* 627–637.

Fleetwood, S. (2007). Why work–life balance now? *International Journal of Human Resource Management, 18,* 387–400.

Fisher, G. G., Bulger, C. A., & Smith, C. S. (2009). Beyond work and family: A measure of work/nonwork interference and enhancement. *Journal of Occupational Health Psychology, 14*(4), 441–456.

Gatrell, C. J., Burnett, S. B., Cooper, C. L., & Sparrow, P. (2013). Work–life balance and parenthood: A comparative review of definitions, equity and enrichment. *International Journal of Management Reviews, 15*(3), 300–316.

Greenhaus, J. H., & Beutell, N. J. (1985). Sources of conflict between work and family roles. *Academy of Management Review, 10,* 76–88.

Greenhaus, J. H., Collins, K. M., & Shaw, J. D. (2003). The relation between work–family balance and quality of life. *Journal of Vocational Behavior, 63,* 510–531.

Greenhaus, J. H., & Parasuraman, S. (1999). Research on work, family, and gender: Current status and future directions. In G. N. Powell (Ed.), *Handbook of gender and work* (pp. 391–412). Newbury Park, CA: Sage.

Greenhaus, J. H., & Powell, G. N. (2006). When work and family are allies: A theory of work-family enrichment. *Academy of Management Review, 31*(1), 72–92.

Grzywacz, J. G., & Marks, N. F. (2000). Reconceptualizing the work family interface: An ecological perspective on the correlates of positive and negative spillover between work and family. *Journal of Occupational Health Psychology, 5*(1), 111–126.

Haar, J. M. (2013). Testing a new measure of work–life balance: A study of parent and non-parent employees from New Zealand. *The International Journal of Human Resource Management, 24*(17), 3305–3324.

Hill, E. J. (2005). Work–family facilitation and conflict, working fathers and mothers, work–family stressors and support. *Journal of Family Issues, 26*(6), 793–819.

Hill, E. J., Hawkins, A. J., Ferris, M., & Weitzman, M. (2001). Finding an extra day a week: The positive influence of perceived job flexibility on work and family life balance. *Family Relations, 50*(1), 49–58.

Hirschi, A., Shockley, K. M., & Zacher, H. (2019). Achieving work-family balance: An action regulation model. *Academy of Management Review, 44*(1), 150–171.

Hobfoll, S. E. (1989). Conservation of resources: A new attempt at conceptualizing stress. *American Psychologist, 44*(3), 513.

Johns, G. (2001). In praise of context. *Journal of Organizational Behavior, 22*(1), 31–42.

Kacmar, K. M., Crawford, W. S., Carlson, D. S., Ferguson, M., & Whitten, D. (2014). A short and valid measure of work-family enrichment. *Journal of Occupational Health Psychology, 19*(1), 32.

Kelliher, C., Richardson, J., & Boiarintseva, G. (2019). All of work? All of life? Reconceptualising work-life balance for the 21st century. *Human Resource Management Journal, 29*(2), 97–112.

Ladge, J. J., & Little, L. M. (2019). When expectations become reality: Work-family image management and identity adaptation. *Academy of Management Review, 44*(1), 126–149.

Lambert, S. J. (1990). Processes linking work and family: A critical review and research agenda. *Human Relations, 43*(3), 239–257.

Le, H., Newman, A., Menzies, J., Zheng, C., & Fermelis, J. (2020). Work–life balance in Asia: A systematic review. *Human Resource Management Review*, 100766.

Leslie, L. M., King, E. B., & Clair, J. A. (2019). Work-life ideologies: The contextual basis and consequences of beliefs about work and life. *Academy of Management Review, 44*(1), 72–98.

Lloyd, G. L., & McAchran, S. E. (2019). Burnout, happiness, and work–life harmony. In *Navigating Organized Urology* (pp. 123–134). Cham: Springer.

Lu, L., & Cooper, C. L. (Eds.). (2015). *Handbook of research on work-life balance in Asia*. Cheltenham, UK: Edward Elgar.

McMillan, H. S., Morris, M. L., & Atchley, E. K. (2011). Constructs of the work/life interface: A synthesis of the literature and introduction of the concept of work/life harmony. *Human Resource Development Review, 10*(1), 6–25.

McNall, L. A., Nicklin, J. M., & Masuda, A. D. (2010). A meta-analytic review of the consequences associated with work–family enrichment. *Journal of Business and Psychology, 25*(3), 381–396.

Michalos, A. C. (Ed.). (2014). *Encyclopedia of quality of life and well-being research*. Dordrecht, Netherlands: Springer.

Michailova, S. (2011). Contextualizing in international business research: Why do we need more of it and how can we be better at it? *Scandinavian Journal of Management, 27*(1), 129–139.

Mokomane, Z. (Ed.). (2013). *Work–family Interface in sub-Saharan Africa: Challenges and responses*. Cham: Springer Science & Business Media.

Netemeyer, R. G., Boles, J. S., & McMurrian, R. (1996). Development and validation of work–family conflict and family–work conflict scales. *Journal of Applied Psychology, 81*(4), 400.

Ong, H. L. C., & Jeyaraj, S. (2014). Work–life interventions: Differences between work–life balance and work–life harmony and its impact on creativity at work. *Sage Open, 4*(3), 2158244014544289.

Özbilgin, M. F., Beauregard, T. A., Tatli, A., & Bell, M. P. (2011). Work–life, diversity and intersectionality: A critical review and research agenda. *International Journal of Management Reviews, 13*(2), 177–198.

Poelmans, S. A. (Ed.). (2005). *Work and family: An international research perspective*. London: Psychology Press.

Powell, G. N., Greenhaus, J. H., Allen, T. D., & Johnson, R. E. (2019). Introduction to special topic forum: Advancing and expanding work-life theory from multiple perspectives. *Academy of Management Review, 44*(1), 54–71.

Richert-Kaźmierska, A., & Stankiewicz, K. (2016). Work–life balance: Does age matter? *Work, 55*(3), 679–688.

Sav, A. (2019). The role of religion in work-life interface. *The International Journal of Human Resource Management, 30*(22), 3223–3244.

Small, J., Harris, C., Wilson, E., & Ateljevic, I. (2011). Voices of women: A memory work reflection on work-life dis/harmony in tourism academia. *Journal of Hospitality, Leisure, Sport & Tourism Education, 10*(1), 23–36.

Staines, G. (1980). Spillover versus compensation: A review of the literature on the relationship between work and nonwork. *Human Relations, 33*(2), 111–129.

Voydanoff, P. (2004). The effects of work demands and resources on work-to-family conflict and facilitation. *Journal of Marriage and Family, 66*(2), 398–412.

Wayne, J. H., Grzywacz, J. G., Carlson, D. S., & Kacmar, K. M. (2007). Work–family facilitation: A theoretical explanation and model of primary antecedents and consequences. *Human Resource Development Review, 17*(1), 63–76.

Young, L., & Kleiner, B. H. (1992). Work and family: Issues for the 1990s. *Women in Management Review, 7*(5), 24–28.

2

Work-Life Border Control Model: A Re-think of Border Theory

Toyin Ajibade Adisa and Gbolahan Gbadamosi

Introduction

Organisation restructuring of the twenty-first century has compelled many organisations to alter their internal and external operations (Sarfo, 2002). The burning desire of Generation X (workers born after 1963) for work-life balance (WLB) (Chao, 2005), the need for most organisations stay operational at all times (Tan & Klaasen, 2007; Torrington, Hall, & Taylor, 2008), the prevalence of dual-earner families and the rise of older employees in the workforce (Galinsky, Aumann, & Bond,

T. A. Adisa (✉)
Royal Docks School of Business and Law, University of East London, London, UK
e-mail: t.adisa@uel.ac.uk

G. Gbadamosi
Organisational Behaviour and Human Resource Management
At the Business School, Bournemouth University, Bournemouth, UK
e-mail: ggbadamosi@bournemouth.ac.uk

T. A. Adisa and G. Gbadamosi (eds.), *Work-Life Interface*,
https://doi.org/10.1007/978-3-030-66648-4_2

2009; Raley, Mattingly, & Bianchi, 2006), demographic and social changes (Sharma & Mishra, 2013) that have resulted in an influx of women entering the labour force (Jones, Burke, & Westman, 2006), and the economic uncertainties (Hughes & Bozionelos, 2007) leading to the global economic downturn in 2008 (United Nations, 2011). These factors have collectively affected employees' movements from work domain to the non-work domain, consequently, creating a shift in the construct and application of border theory. These changes have driven many organisations to change their functions, strategies, and human resources management (HRM) policies to include policies that facilitate employees' unrestricted movement from work domain to non-work domain. Thus, it is necessary to re-think border theory in terms of its components and application.

Border theory is a work-family balance theory. It explains employees' movements from work domain to home/family domain. According to Clark (2000), employees are border crossers who travel between work and home domains. This article, however, takes Clark's study further by introducing the work-life border control model. This model describes employees as border crossers who journey between work and non-work domains. It draws a distinction from the spill-over model (Staines, 1980), the conservation of resource model (Hobfoll, 1989), the compensation model (Lambert, 1990), the segmentation model (Young & Kleiner, 1992), Clark's (2000) work/family border theory, and other studies on border theory (Ashforth, Kreiner, & Fugate, 2000; Edwards & Rothbard, 2000; Nippert-Eng, 1996a, 1996b; Zerubavel, 1993), which only dealt with how employees construct, maintain, negotiate and cross the borders between work domain and home/family domain and ignored employees' other non-familial activities. This article also aims to build upon the aforementioned theories, especially border theory, in order to accommodate what has previously been omitted in these early studies.

In other words, the work-life border control model is not just about work and family/home but rather work and life domain domains. It is imperative to have a model that consider 'life' as an enclave for employees' non-work general activities. According to Osoian, Lazar, and Ratiu (2011), there are many other activities in the non-work domain that are equally as important as family responsibilities, depending on each employee's status. For example, single employees who have no familial responsibilities to cater for may choose going to the gym, attending religious, social, or community activities, etc. as their non-work duties as opposed home/familial duties. Home or family is by no means the only activity in the 'life' domain that matter to employees. Rantanen, Kinnunen, Mauno, and Tillemann (2011) called for a WLB model that would capture that whole gamut of activities in 'life' domain. Furthermore, there is a need for a model that will explain factors that determine employees' movements across the border. This will illuminate our understanding of how employees' movements between work and life domains are bordered. Although Clark (2000) have argued that employees' movements depend on borders' strength and permeability. However, aside that Clark's (2000) border theory portrayed home/family as the only 'life' domain activity, the factors that determine the strength and weakness of the borders are also limited to spatial, temporal and psychological. This model attempts to expand work-family theory by discussing in-depth the five main factors that determine the strength or weakness of the borders. Ransome's (2007, p. 374) argued that 'it is rather important to use an established theory and concepts as a basis to develop a new one'. The current study is expected to broaden the scope of discussions on work-life border theory and enrich the literature in that aspect of study.

Historical Evolution of Border Theory

Boundary theory grew from a miscellany of studies about cognitive organisation of roles (Berg & Piszczek, 2012). Its development can be traced back to Zerubavel's (1993, 1996) lumping and splitting heuristic classification of organisational frames and Nippert-Eng's (1996a, 1996b) work on 'Home and Work: Negotiating Boundaries through Everyday Life'. According to Zerubavel (1993, 1996), people use heuristic methods of classification to organise physical and mental constructs by either 'lumping' several categories into a single one or by 'splitting' one mental category into distinct, separate entities. Zerubavel argues that lumping and splitting classifications are socially constructed and based on individual identification process. Berg and Piszczek (2012, p. 3) concluded that 'the mental categorisations at the heart of boundary theory are influenced by broader social factors, which cause individuals in the same social structures to create similar classification schemas'. Zerubavel (1993, 1996) posits that individual fashion 'islands of meaning' out of reality and potentially separate chunks of reality from the world and occurrences around them. 'The islands of meaning are not part of the nature; rather they are cluster of things which are similar to one another within their circle of classification' (Zerubavel 1991, pp. 70–80). Zerubavel, from a cognitive sociological perspective, further suggests that islands are outcomes of active construction, which complement the processes of lumping and splitting. These processes are at the heart of border theory and deal with cognitive processes that are neither personal nor logical (Zerubavel, 1997). He further identified the need for a comparative approach in social classification in order to clarify different classification schemas across thoughts communities (Zerubavel, 1996).

However, Nippert-Eng (1996a, 1996b) broadened the discussion by applying the notion of cognitive sociological classification to the work-family interface. Initially, she developed the concept of individual segmentation and integration of work and home mental categorisation into a theoretical cline. In 'boundary work', she classified employees as segmentors or integrators (Nippert-Eng, 1996a). Segmentation happens 'when the border between work and home is impregnable, while integration occurs when work and home are the same' (Nippert-Eng, 1996c, pp. 567–568). Warhurst, Eikhof, and Haunschild (2008, p. 10) stated that 'segmentors have two key rings, one for work, the other for the house and integrators affix all keys to one key ring'. However, despite the fact that integrating roles brings about less difficulties in role transition, yet it has been argued that less integrated roles lead to clearer and more easily maintained borders (Desrochers & Sergent, 2004). Literature is somewhat contradictory on this issue.

Nippert-Eng interpreted border theory beyond heuristic to include a strategic choice (Berg & Piszczek, 2012) in which employees' boundary management plans include those principles that they use to organise and separate role demands and expectations into particular spheres (Kossek,

Noe, & DeMarr, 1999). For Nippert-Eng (1996a, 1996b), employees who prefer and engage themselves in high overlapping between work and home domains are integrators while those who opt to keep work and home domain distinct are separators. Employees differ in their preferences, which often influence them in their decisions as to whether to separate or integrate work and family domains (Kossek et al., 1999). It is imperative to understand that the notion of strategy was incorporated into border theory by Nippert-Eng (1996c) in her conceptualisation of the border negotiation, in which she focused on employees as active role players. Consistent with Nippert-Eng's (1996c) position, mental categories of work and home can be managed by using three tools: internalised cultural images, socio-structural constraints, and personal practices within situational constraints. However, research has neglected the first two tools and embraced only the third one which consequently narrows the potential for understanding how and why employees segment or integrate their mental categorisation (Berg & Piszczek, 2012).

Nippert-Eng (1996c) underscored the importance of Zerubavel's social classification scheme in developing boundary theory. She argued that socio-structural forces act as constraints in boundary negotiation and influence the extent to which an employee is a separator or an integrator. Although she believes that employees cognitively construct the work and home domains, she maintained that individual thinking is nothing less than the embodiment of group thinking (Nippert-Eng, 1996c). She also posited that boundaries can be different in terms of the size of their conceptual territory and that their size can change from time to time as employees change in their thinking and behaviour. She identified permeability as an 'essential ease of transition from one mental category to another and part of boundary's structure profile' (Nippert-Eng, 1996c, p. 280). Undoubtedly, Nippert-Eng's (1996c) work made a significant contribution to border theory; however, she did not deal with 'how socio-structural forces are shaped by domestic institutions at higher and theoretical levels' (Berg & Piszczek, 2012, p. 5). Furthermore, Nippert-Eng's work focuses mainly on 'home' as the only aspect of employees' life, whereas, 'life' (or non-work domain) involves more than just family/home (Osoian, Ratiu, & Lazar, 2011; Warhurst et al., 2008). It is, however, essential to note that the term 'boundary theory' is often attributed to Nippert-Eng (1996c). Even though her work was not the first theoretical examination of work and home boundaries, she was one of the first to examine them in a systematic and broad fashion (Berg & Piszczek, 2012).

The insightful work of Perry-Jenkins, Repetti, and Crouter (2000) and Bianchi and Milkie (2010) showed the interrelationship between work and home domains. They identified the structural factors that facilitate and impede employees' efforts to integrate their different responsibilities, but their studies ignored the boundaries that exist between these two domains (Desrochers, Sargent, & Hostetler, 2012). In the same vein, Ashforth et al. (2000) developed their study on the conceptualisation of the characteristics of boundaries, while Clark (2000) propounded work/family theory. Clark (2000) developed on the previous border theories based on the premise that they did not sufficiently explain, predict or solve the problems confronted by employees when balancing work and family responsibilities. However, Poelmans, O'Driscoll and Beham (2005) argued that previous border theories did not operate on the assumption that they are universally valid in all environments.

Clark's Work/Family Border Theory

Clark (2000) described the work and family domains as two asymmetric spheres with a penetrable or permeable boundary between them. She describes employees as border-crossers who make numerous trips across these two domains on a daily basis. The transition between the two domains may be easy or difficult, depending on the similarity of the variables within the two spheres. For example, in the domains in which the language and culture are similar, the transition is easier. However, in the domain in which language, culture and the expected behaviour are significantly different, transition is difficult (Kinnunen et al., 2005). According to Clark (2000, p. 747), 'border theory' addresses how domain integration and segmentation, border creation and management, border-crosser participation, and the relationship between border-crossers (employees) and others at work and home influence work/family balance. Clark (2000) argued that the boundaries between work and family domains are temporally, spatially and psychologically permeable. Clark (2000) recognised changes which blur boundaries that separate work and family domains and the two domains interact.

The activities in the two domains occur at different time and in different places (Clark, 2001). The theory posits that the primary relationship between work and family systems is not emotional as previous theories claimed, it is human. The theory further posits that employees can shape their environment just as the environment can also shape them and 'it is these contradictions of determining and being determined by the two domains that make work/family balance a very challenging concept' (Clark, 2000, p. 748). According to Clark, an individual employee manages and negotiates between the two spheres. However, striking a balance between these two settings is somewhat varied among employees. It depends on the differences between their purposes, statuses and cultures. Border-crossers often 'modify their focus, goals and interpersonal style to fit the unique demands of each domain' (Clark, 2000, p. 751). As earlier mentioned, this article aims to expand on Clark's (2000) work/family border theory by developing a work-life border control model.

Characteristics of Borders

Clark (2000) argues that borders are demarcations between work and family domains and define benchmarks for acceptable behaviour. Ashforth (2001, p. 262) defined boundaries as 'mental fences used to simplify the environment'. Boundaries have been referred to as 'the physical, emotional, temporal, cognitive and/or relational limit that define entities as separate from one another' (Ashforth, et al., 2000, p. 474). It is 'a gateway into the functions of domains' (Mathews & Barnes-Farell, 2010, p. 330). The boundary separates domains from each other yet promotes and/or constrains how domains are connected and related (Kreiner, Hollensbe, & Sheep, 2006). Boundaries define the perimeter and the range of any domain (Kreiner, Hollensbe, & Sheep, 2009) and they become institutionalised to the extent that they are hard to alter once they are socially shared (Zerubavel, 1991). Arguably, once employee activities are ritualised, it becomes difficult to change. Boundaries could be physical (seen or felt), temporal (scheduled work and family commitments) or psychological (thoughts and emotions) (Clark, 2000, p. 756). While weak boundaries allow a great deal of permeability and flexibility, strong boundaries are impermeable and highly inflexible (Clark, 2000; Kinnunen et al., 2005). Nippert-Eng (1996c) and Clark (2000) argue that flexibility and permeability are the two main characteristics of the boundaries.

Border Flexibility and Permeability

Border flexibility is the capacity of the border to be shifted (Berg & Piszczek, 2012). Flexibility can also be defined as the malleability of the border between two or more roles (Desrochers & Sargent, 2004) or the ability of the border to expand or contrast to accommodate the demands of another domain (e.g. an employee working from home takes the opportunity to pick children from school) (Desrochers et al., 2012). In fact, flexibility answers the question of when and where a role can be enacted (Sundaramurthy & Kreiner, 2008). Border permeability, however, refers to the extent to which a domain's border is easily penetrated by the thoughts or behaviour connected with another domain. For Ashforth et al. (2000, p. 474), 'permeability is the degree to which a role allows an employee to be physically located in the role's domain but psychologically and/or behaviourally involved in another role'. The permeability of any border determines the extent of integration or segmentation of the content of the bounded domains (Kreiner et al., 2009). For example, an employee who can switch easily from non-work-related responsibilities to deal with work related issues and vice-versa is said to have a highly permeable border (Glavin & Schieman, 2011). Permeability, according to Nipert-Eng (1996c, p. 280), is part of a boundary's 'structural profile'. Pleck (1984) refers permeability as the ability of one pre-defined role to encroach upon the physical and temporal territory of another. Flexibility and permeability are, thus, central to employees' movements across the border.

Development of Work-Border Control Model

Practically, all of the studies undertaken on border theory centred on work and family/home domains (Ashforth et al., 2000; Clark, 2000; Nipper-Eng, 1996c; Zerubavel, 1993, 1996). However, globalisation and organisational restructuring means non-work-related activities are no longer confined to home/family duties. This has necessitated the replacement of the term 'work-family balance' with 'work-life balance'. Furthermore, scholars have recognised the fact that work-life balance issues are not restricted to women and family issues alone (Chan, 2008; Osoian et al., 2011). There are many other activities in the non-work domain that are equally important to employees as familial duties, depending on the individual employees' personal circumstances (Osoian et al., 2011) (Fig. 2.1).

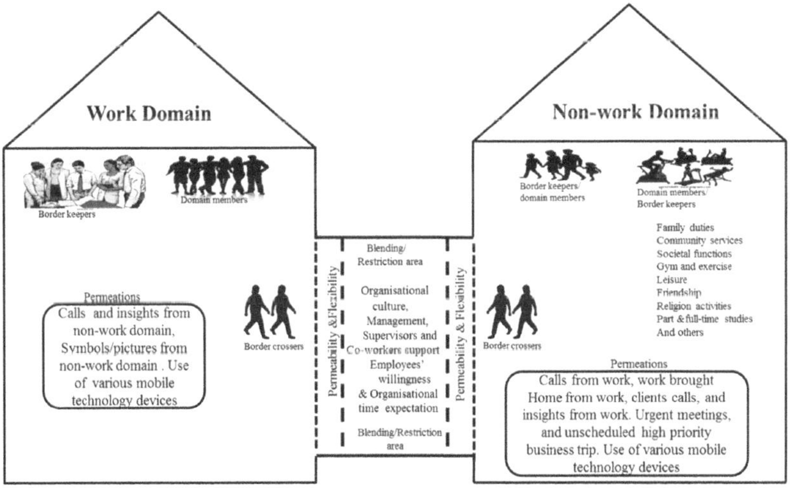

Fig. 2.1 Pictorial Representation of Work–Life Border Control Model

This model is a theoretical extension which seeks to identify essential constituents of border theory to offer a fresh perspective on work-life balance. The work-life border control model is divided into two domains. The work domain (daily work activities) provides an employee with income and a sense of accomplishment (Clark & Farmer, 1998) and the non-work domain which provides an employee with fulfilment and personal happiness (Clark & Farmer, 1998). Work activities fully engage domain members throughout their working hours. Non-work-related activities include but not limited to family duties, community services, societal functions, gym/exercise, leisure, friendship, religious activities, part-time or full-time studies. The main crust of this model is that employees' movement between work and non-work domains are determined by organisational culture, management support, supervisors' support, co-workers' support, employees' willingness to cross the border and organisational time expectation. Clark (2000, p. 757) stated that 'when a great deal of permeability and flexibility occurs around the border, blending occurs'. However, the work-life border control model proposes that restriction occurs in the border area when all or any of these forces are present.

Determinant Factors

Organisational Culture

Organisational culture is one of the factors in the work-life border control model which determines employees' movements across the border. In an organisation, culture represents the written and the unwritten rules and norms about the organisation. The spoken and unspoken widely shared assumptions unobtrusively manipulate organisational members (Schein, 1992). Most of the time, culture is invisible (Stinchcomb & Ordaz, 2007). Schein (2010) explains the three levels of culture, which range from the visible and tangible manifestations to the deeply embedded, unconscious and basic assumptions which is 'the essence of culture' (Schein, 2010, p. 23).

According to Schein, the basic underlying assumptions are the core of an organisation's culture with espoused beliefs and values forming the next level and artefacts forming the surface aspect of the organisational culture (Schein, 1985). In Schein's model of culture, there is a hierarchy between these levels which distinguishes between observable and unobservable elements of culture (Dauber, Fink, & Yolles, 2012). The mere existence of WLB policies in an organisation without duly implementation may be considered as organisational artefacts. Ramachandran, Chong and Ismail (2011) observe that artefacts are easy to recognise but related meanings are often ambiguous to people outside the organisation. Only members of the organisation would know whether WLB policies actually are available or not. A firm parading itself to the public as WLB supportive organisation may not be in practice. The employees may understand this paradox, but would not openly discuss the issue with outsiders. To support Schein's (1985) model of culture, Thompson, Beauvais, and Lyness (1999, p. 394) define work-family culture as 'the shared assumptions, beliefs, and values regarding the extent to which an organisation supports and value the integration of employees work and private lives'. Employees will view a supportive organisational culture as one that takes care of the well-being of its employees and a non-supportive culture as one that cares less about the well-being of its employees (Peeters, Wattez, Demerouti, & de Regt, 2009). However, there are organisations whose culture and system of operations such as commitments to effectiveness and efficiency may restrict employees from using WLB policies. For example, the medical profession has a culture that prevents employees (especially doctors) from using WLB policies and practices (see Adisa, Mordi, & Osabutey, 2017). This profession has a culture of visibility (required physical presence in the hospital at all time of the doctors' shifts) which is equal to productivity (Adisa et al., 2017). Furthermore, the culture of long hours and shift work patterns is prominent among doctors and nurses in order to monitor safety and promote continuity of patient care (Wise, Smith, Valsecchi, Mueller, & Gabe, 2007). Unfortunately, this culture restricts the employees' movements between work and non-work domains, which affects their WLB (Timmins, 2002). Organisational culture, therefore, is a critical factor in determining employees' movements across the border area. This is because a supportive work-life organisational culture will facilitate easy and frequent movements of employees across the border while an unsupportive culture will restrict employees' movement which may lead to work-life conflict (WLC) (Burke, 2006).

Proposition 1: *An organisational culture supportive of work-life balance would enhance frequency and ease of employees' movements across the border, while an unsupportive culture would tighten border and restrict employees' movements across the border.*

Management or Supervisor Support

Management and supervisor play a prominent role in whether an employee uses WLB policies or not. The work-life border control model proposes that, if management is unsupportive of work-life balance policies employees' movements across the border will be restricted. Management support is the degree to which employees believe their organisation cares about their well-being and values their contributions (Rhoades & Eisenberger, 2002). Formal and informal management support is required for achieving WLB (Allen, 2001; Thompson et al., 1999). In this context, supportiveness refers to the extent to which an organisation's management and its supervisors at all levels support and allow employees to use of WLB policies. Thompson et al. (1999) assert that management support is critical for the success of WLB practices because of power they wield. Management support promotes positive outcomes, facilitates employees' general well-being, and enhances a positive spill-over from work to family which is particularly useful in promoting employees' confidence (Ayman & Antani, 2008; Hammer, Kossek, Yragui, Bodner, & Hanson, 2009). The work-life border control model perceives that the responsibility of formulating WLB policies lies in the hands of the organisation's management. Therefore, an organisation whose leadership or management are unsupportive of WLB policies and practices will tighten the border that exists between its employees' work and non-work domains thus making movements between the domains almost impossible.

Support from supervisors is the extent to which employees perceive that their supervisors care about them and values their contributions (Eisenberger, Singlhamber, Vandenberghe, Sucharski, & Rhoades, 2002; Simosi, 2012). It is essential to note that support from supervisors is not the same as management support. Supervisors represent management by overseeing and directing employees' performance and general behaviour (Eisenberger et al., 2002). Supervisors are, often, responsible for operational decisions at work and they are responsible for the decisions about who uses what policies at what time (Maxwell & McDougall, 2004) and their decisions are regarded by employees as reflective of an organisation's views (Simosi, 2012). The work-life border control model proposes that supervisors can make the border weak or strong by allowing or preventing employees' use of WLB policies. The model argues that support from supervisors remains a strong determinant of employees' movement across the border. This is because even if management provides WLB policies for its workforce, supervisors may still prevent the use of those policies. Supervisors can restrict or prevent employees from using the policies (De Cieri, Holmes, Abbott, & Pettit, 2005). The disinclination of supervisors to sanction the use of WLB policies could be personal or a reflection of the organisation's embedded culture. Sakazume (2009) argued that some supervisors reject WLB initiatives because they assume that allowing WLB policies and practices would negatively influence employee morale and efficiency. It is important to note that the management/supervisor actions are often guided by unwritten rules deeply ingrained in organisational culture, thus making employees' movement across the border easy or difficult.

Proposition 2: *The more supportive an organisation's management/supervisors are towards allowing employees use work-life balance policies, the weaker the borders between work and non-work domains and vice versa.*

Co-Workers' Support

Support from co-workers determines employees' movements across the border. Co-workers' support is the extent to which employees perceive that their colleagues respect their contributions and care about their well-being (Eisenberger et al., 2002; Simosi, 2012). Adisa (2015) highlighted the importance of co-workers' support to achieving employees' WLB. Adisa et al. (2017) found that co-workers sometimes complain and pass insinuations on employees who often use WLB policies. This often dissuades employees from using them or makes the organisation or supervisors to altogether stop employees from using them. Therefore, the support an employee receives from his/her colleagues to use WLB policies has an impact on border flexibility and permeability such that it determines movements across the border. In other words, co-workers could determine how strong or weak a border would be. This assertion is supported by Marks' (1977) argument that having supportive colleagues can lead to positive results. Additionally, research has revealed that support from co-workers is a potential predictor of good WLB and its absence could lead to WLC (Ferguson, Carlson, Zivnuska, & Whitten, 2012; Lu, Siu, Spector, & Shi, 2009; Ng & Sorensen, 2008). The work-life border control model thus postulates that lack of support from co-workers will restrict employees from using WLB policies, which will then prevent or slow down employees' movements across the border. White, Hill, McGovern, Mills, and Smeaton (2003) expounded that fear of alienation and resentment from co-workers often forms a significant concern for many workers. Kirby and Krone (2002) argued that resentment from co-workers often discourages employees from using WLB policies. The work-life border control model proposes that support from co-workers determine employees' movements across the border and vice-versa.

Proposition 3: *The more employees support each other in using WLB policies, the more flexible and permeable the border becomes and the more freely and frequently employees move across the border.*

Employees' Willingness to Cross the Border

It is one thing to be supported by management, supervisors, and colleagues to use WLB policies and practices and quite another for an individual employee to be willing to use the policies. Employees' willingness to cross the border means their willingness to use the various WLB available to them. Employees' willingness to use WLB policies often hangs on some overarching factors such as marital status, non-work responsibilities, perceived impact of using WLB policies on career, and support from the organisation and supervisors (Adisa, 2015). For example, an unmarried employee with no care responsibilities will make less or no use of WLB policies. Studies have shown that single employees who have no care responsibilities often perceive colleagues with family and care responsibilities as lazy and less committed (Beauregard & Henry, 2009; CIPD, 2007; Eikhof et al., 2007). Consequently, employees who need to use WLB policies may be reluctant or unwilling to them (McDonald, Townsend, & Wharton, 2013). In the same vein, some employers consider employees who make use of WLB policies as less productive (Osoian et al., 2011) and uncommitted (Wharton, Chivers, & Blair-Loy, 2008). Furthermore, employees' willingness to use WLB policies could be determined by fear of lack of career progression (Beauregard & Henry, 2009). Some professions (such as the medical profession) place serious importance on employees' physical presence at work. For medical doctors, a requirement of physical presence at work at all times of the shift is a core tenet of medical profession (Adisa, 2015). This is required to care for and monitor the patients and also for doctors' career advancement (Adisa et al., 2017). McDonald, Bradley, and Brown (2008) and Wu, Uen, Wu, and Chang (2011) argued that employees' willingness to use WLB policies will be limited dramatically if using the policies will have negative consequences on their career. Similarly, a report of the American Bar Association stipulated that 95% of law firms in the US offer WLB policies but only 3% of lawyers subscribe to them due to the fear of the negative consequences it will have on their career advancement (Cunningham, 2001). Hence, work-life border control model posits that a greater unwillingness to cross the border prevails in a situation in which there is a circulated perception among the employees that crossing the border would have damaging consequences on their career progression or their images and reputations. In other words, employees' perceived negative consequences of using WLB policies on their career progression could mitigate its use.

Proposition 4: *The greater the employees' preparedness and willingness to cross the border, the more flexible and permeable the border and the more frequent the employees' movements and vice-versa.*

Organisational Time Expectations

The issue of organisational time expectations (OTE) is concerned with the number of hours which employees are required to devote to work-related activities (Bailyn, 1997; Lobel & Kossek, 1996). This invariably influences employees' movements from the work domain to non-work domain. For instance, if an organisation link long working hours to commitment, loyalty, productivity, and promotion then its employees will be inclined to put in longer hour at work, which is antithetical to the principle of WLB (Bailyn, 1997; Joyce, Pabayo, Critchley, & Bambra, 2010; Pocock, Van Wanrooy, Strazzari, & Bridge, 2001). In such organisation, employees who often use WLB policies and eschew working for long hours are perceived as lazy and less committed (Lewis, 1997). For example, Adisa (2015) found that medical profession (in Nigerian context) have a high OTE. This is because in medicine, long working hours is attached to patients' care and doctors' training. This consistently keeps doctors in the hospital for unbelievably longer hours. Based on this, work-life border control model suggests that organisations in which OTE is high, employees' movements from work domain to non-work domain would be greatly restricted. This is because the number of hours worked will be high and this will invariably affect employees' activities in the non-work domain.

Proposition 5: *The lower the OTE, the flexible and permeable the border that exists between work and non-work domains, and the frequent the employees' movements across the border, and vice-versa.*

Implications

The work-life border control model is essential in the contemporary application and understanding of the border theory. It is important for WLB researchers because it provides a comprehensive and coherent understanding of a framework within which employees' movements from work to non-work domains (border flexibility and permeability) can be studied. The work-life border control model provides the theoretical framework which has been missing in WLB studies. In order to embrace and absorb WLB as a leverage point for practice, organisations should make informed decisions about, and alter their culture, attitudes and policies to accommodate WLB policies and practices, which will enhance the border flexibility and permeability, and facilitate employees' free movement from work domain to non-work domain. In this way, organisations will be able to keep their skilled and talented employees (Sholarios & Marks, 2004). Furthermore, employees flourish when their organisations and their various entities help them on what matter most at work and in the non-work aspects of their lives (Whittington, Maellaro, & Galpin, 2011). This contribution is theoretically appealing particularly now that the study of WLB is attracting serious attention. It also provides a theoretical basis for the contemporary and future studies.

Discussion and Conclusions

This study presented work-life border control model. A model that extend our thinking and understanding on work-life border theory. This model builds on previous studies on border theory (Ashforth et al., 2000; Clark, 2000; Edwards & Rothbard, 2000; Nippert-Eng, 1996c; Zerubavel, 1993, etc.) that describe home/family as the only non-work activities. Work-life border control model has two important elemental divisions.

Firstly, this model recognises other life activities, which are equally important to employee in the non-work domain as opposed to just home/family proposed by previous studies border theory. According to Osoian et al. (2011) and Chan (2008), WLB issues are not restricted to women and/or family matters alone. The model incorporates familial duties, community services, societal functions, gym/exercise, leisure, friendship, religious activities, part-time or full-time studies in the non-work domain's activities. Boyar, Maertz, and Keough (2003) highlighted the importance of achieving a balance between social and work life. Dean (2007) also averred that achieving a balance between religious/spiritual life and work-life is increasingly becoming important among employees. These studies further attest that non-work activities go beyond the family/home duties. We posit that whatever is important to an employee (depending on employee's status, taste, needs/wants and preferences) besides work-related activities becomes his/her non-work activities. This means that what constitutes non-work domain's activities differ from one employee to another.

Secondly, the model outlined factors that determine the flexibility and permeability of the border (employees' movement across the border). The work-life border control model, based on Adisa's (2015) and Adisa et al.'s (2017) identified five factors that determine how strong or weak the border: organisational culture, management/supervisors' support, co-workers' support, employees' willingness to cross the border, and organisational time expectations. These factors determine the flexibility and permeability of the border. The model proposes that a WLB supportive organisational culture will enhance employees' easy and frequent movements across the border and vice-versa. For example, Adisa et al. (2017) found that medical organisational culture (in Nigerian context) is unsupportive of WLB policies, which then make achievement of WLB for the Nigeria doctors difficult. Unsupportive organisational culture allows for little or no flexibility and permeability in the border area. However, as stated in Proposition 1, organisational culture must be supportive of WLB policies and practices in order for employees to be able to move freely and frequently across the border.

In addition, management and supervisors' support play a prominent role in border flexibility and permeability. The management creates WLB policies and supervisors may enhance or prevent their usage. For example, Rodgers and Rodgers (1989) argued that the well-being of American families primarily lies in the hands of first-line supervisors. Clark (2000) argues that supervisors can bend the rules to accommodate employees' family commitments or they can choose to be less-flexible. In recognition of the importance of supervisors' support in border flexibility and permeability, some organisations require their supervisors to undergo employees' WLB training programmes (Galinsky & Stein, 1990). This would help the supervisors to be able to recognise the need for WLB and help their employees to achieve it. Proposition 2 thus state that the more supportive the management of an organisation and its supervisors are towards allowing employees to use WLB policies, the more flexible and permeable the borders between work and non-work domains and vice versa.

The work-life border control model's third proposition bothers on co-workers' support. This is the support that employees receive from their co-workers in using WLB policies and practices. According to Marks (1977), having supportive colleagues can be very helpful and often lead to positive results. This assertion is also supported by Kirby and Krone (2002). Resentment from co-workers towards a particular employee or group of employees for using WLB policies can compel the management or supervisors to prevent employees from using WLB policies. Additionally, employees' preparedness to use WLB policies and OTE were also identified as determinants of employees' movement across the border. The perceived consequences of using WLB policies and practices on employees' image and career progression often dissuade from using the policies (Cunningham, 2001). While OTE (the number of hours an employee is required to devote to work related activities) keeps employees at work for longer hours, which is anti-WLB. Adisa et al. (2017) found that medical organisations (in Nigeria) have a high OTE, which keep medical doctors in the hospital for longer hours, thereby negatively impacting the flexibility and permeability of the border between the work domain and non-work domain.

It is important to note that border must not be too flexible and too permeable. This is because if either of the extremities occurs, it may affect employees' performance and organisational success. However, organisations must find a balance between the two extremist. As mentioned, the development of the work-life border control model is in strict acquiescence with Ransome's (2007, p. 374) argument that 'it is rather important to use an established theory and concepts as a basis to develop a new one'.

The need for more carefully contrived scholarly guidance to theory building especially in work-life studies has recently dominated sociology, psychology and management studies. Powell, Greenhaus, Allen, and Johnson (2019) argues that the explosion in work-life research stems from several social trends, such as the changing nature of gender roles, families, work, and careers. A special issue of the Academy of Management Review was recently devoted to theory building and development in work-life literature. There were six papers in all, each proposing a new theoretical argument. While four of the articles focused on a work-life perspective (Bear, 2019; Bourdeau, Ollier-Malaterre, & Houlfort, 2019; Crawford, Thompson, & Ashforth, 2019; Leslie, King, & Clair, 2019), it is the two papers that focus on the work-family perspective (Hirschi, Shockley, & Zacher, 2019; Ladge & Little, 2019) that are of preeminent interest to this chapter.

In the first paper, Ladge & Little (2019) suggest that work-family images influence the assessment of individuals both at work and their personal lives which can invariably have important consequences for working parents' identities. They introduced a work-family image construct suggesting that individuals are often evaluated on their competence in both their family and work roles. From a psychology background work, they linked the debate of work-family to impression management (Gardner & Martinko, 1988). The theory they present captures the dynamic interplay between image and identity. It illuminates on how work-family norms influence work-family image discrepancies and impression management strategies and lead to identity adaptation.

In the second paper, Hirschi et al.'s (2019) theoretical model was interested in how people can attain work-family balance that are useful for designing practical interventions. They presented a novel theoretical model that showcases a sound understanding of the work-family interface. They proposed the types of action strategies that could be used and under which circumstances to proactively achieve goals in both work and family domains.

Powell et al. (2019), the editors of the special forum, provided a rationale for the development of these new theories arguing that work-life theory has not kept up with the explosion in research in the area, thus a need for a re-evaluation of the theoretical advancement, theory testing and practice implications. Essentially, they argue that such new theories will advance the course of future research by provided deeper reflection of research design and contribution.

This chapter essentially joins these recent contributions to work-life theory by offering yet another novel guidance for future research. We thus offer guidance for employees, couples, HR practitioners and all supervisors/managers, organisations and policy makers. The work-life border control model recasts contemporary understanding by bringing to light a new idea in the application of the border theory. It is hoped that the model will be useful to academics, WLB researchers, and organisational practitioners in theorising their works. The model can be used descriptively and prescriptively, and it can be used in all environments. Future studies can develop propositions from the model before data collection in order to eliminate the use of theory post-hoc.

References

Adisa, T. A. (2015). *The inter-relationship between work life balance and Organisational Culture: An empirical study of Nigerian health sector*. A Thesis Submitted for the Degree of Doctor of Philosophy at College of Business, Arts and Social Sciences, Brunel University London.

Adisa, T. A., Mordi, C., & Osabutey, E. (2017). Exploring the implications of the influence of organisational culture on work-life balance practices: Evidence from Nigerian medical doctors. *Personnel Review, 46*(3), 454–473.

Allen, T. D. (2001). Family supportive work environments: The role of organizational perceptions. *Journal of Vocational Behavior, 58*(3), 414–435.

Ashforth, B. E. (2001). *Role transitions in organisational life: An identity-based perspective*. Mahwah, NJ: Lawrence Erlbaum Associates.

Ashforth, B. E., Kreiner, G. E., & Fugate, M. (2000). All in a day's work: Boundaries and micro role transitions. *Academy of Management Review, 25*(3), 472–491.

Ayman, R., & Antani, A. (2008). Social support and work family conflict. In K. Korabik, D. S. Lero, & D. L. Whitehead (Eds.), *Handbook of work-family integration* (pp. 287–304). Academic Press: London.

Bailyn, L. (1997). The impact of corporate culture on work-family integration. In S. Parasuraman & H. Greenhaus (Eds.), *Integrating work and family: Challenges and choices for a changing world* (pp. 209–219). Westport, CT: Quorum Books.

Bear, J. B. (2019). The caregiving ambition framework. *Academy of Management Review, 44*(1), 99–125.

Beauregard, T. A., & Henry, L. C. (2009). Making the link between work-life balance practices and organisational performance. *Human Resource Management Review, 19*, 9–12.

Berg, P., & Piszczek, M. M. (2012, June). *The role of institutions in work-family boundary management*. A Paper Presented to the Work-Family Researchers Network Conference, New York, NY.

Bianchi, S. M., & Milkie, M. A. (2010). Work and family research in the first decade of the 21st century. *Journal of Marriage and the Family, 72*(3), 705–725.

Bourdeau, S., Ollier-Malaterre, A., & Houlfort, N. (2019). Not all work-life policies are created equal: Career consequences of using enabling versus enclosing work-life policies. *Academy of Management Review, 44*(1), 172–193.

Boyar, G. S., Maertz, A. P., & Keough, S. (2003). Work-family conflict: A model of linkage between work and family domain variables and turn-over intention. *Journal of Managerial Issue, 40*(2), 175–190.

Burke, R. J. (2006). *Research companion to working time and work addiction.* Cheltenham: Edward Elgar.

Chan, C. K. Y. (2008). Border crossing: Work-life balance issues with Chinese entrepreneurs in New Zealand. A thesis submitted to Auckland University of Technology in partial fulfilment of the requirement for the degree of Master of Business (MBus).

Chao, L. (2005, November 29). For Gen Xers, its work to live: allowing employees to strike balance between job and life can lead to better retention rates. *Wall Street Journal*, Eastern edition, p. B6.

Chartered Institute for Personnel and Development (CIPD) (2007). *Extending the right to flexible working could boost business and reduce chances of a divided workforce*. Available at www.cipd.co.uk/publicsites/cScape.CIPD.PressOffice/Templates/PressRelease.

Clark, S. C. (2000). Work/family border theory: A new theory of work/family balance. *Human Relations, 53*(6), 747–770.
Clark, S. C. (2001). Work cultures and work/family balance. *Journal of Vocational Behavior, 58*(3), 348–365.
Clark, S. C., & Farmer, P. M. K. (1998, October). Living in two different worlds: Measuring cultural and value differences between work and home, and their effects on border crossing. Paper presented at the Institute of Behavioural and Applied Management Annual Conference, Orlando, FL.
Crawford, W. S., Thompson, M. J., & Ashforth, B. E. (2019). Work-life events theory: Making sense of shock events in dual earner couples. *Academy of Management Review, 44*(1), 194–212.
Cunningham, K. (2001). Father time: Flexible work arrangements and the law firm's failure of the family. *Stanford Law Review, 53*(4), 967–1008.
Dean, H. (2007). Tipping the balance: The problematic nature of work-life balance in a low-income neighbourhood. *Journal of Social Politics, 36*(4), 519–537.
Dauber, D., Fink, G., & Yolles, M. (2012, March). A configuration model of organisational culture. *Sage Open.*
De Cieri, H., Holmes, B., Abbott, J., & Pettit, T. (2005). Achievements and challenges of work-life balance strategies in Australian organisations. *The International Journal of Human Resource Management, 16*(1), 90–103.
Desrochers, S., & Sargent, L. D. (2004). Boundary/Border theory and work-family integration. *Organisation Management Journal, 1*(1), 40–48.
Desrochers, S., Sargent, L. D., & Hostetler, A. J. (2012). Boundary-spanning demands, personal mastery, and family satisfaction: Individual and crossover effect among dual-earner parents. *Marriage and Family Review, 48*(5), 443–464.
Edwards, J. R., & Rothbard, N. P. (2000). Mechanisms linking work and family: Clarifying the relationship between work and family constructs. *The Academy of Management Review, 25*(1), 178–199.
Eikhof, D. R., Warhust, C., & Haunschild, A. (2007). Introduction: What Work? What Balance? Critical reflections on work-life balance debate. *Employee Relations, 29*(4), 325–333.
Eisenberger, R., Singlhamber, F., Vandenberghe, C., Sucharski, I., & Rhoades, L. (2002). Perceived supervisor support: Contributions to perceived support and employee retention. *Journal of Applied Psychology, 87*(3), 565–573.
Ferguson, M., Carlson, D., Zivnuska, S., & Whitten, D. (2012). Support at work and home: The path to satisfaction through balance. *Journal of Vocational Behaviour, 80*(2), 299–307.

Galinsky, E., Aumann, K., & Bond, J. T. (2009). *Times are changing: Gender and generation at work and at home* (pp. 1–24). New York: Families and Work Institute.

Galinsky, E., & Stein, P. J. (1990). The impact of human resource policies on employees: Balancing work/family life. *Journal of Family Issues, 11*(4), 368–383.

Gardner, W. L., & Martinko, M. J. (1988). Impression management in organizations. *Journal of Management, 14*(2), 321–338.

Glavin, S., & Schieman, P. (2011). Education and work-family conflict: Explanations, contingencies and mental health consequences. *Social Forces, 89*(4), 1341–1362.

Hammer, L. B., Kossek, E. E., Yragui, N. L., Bodner, T. E., & Hanson, G. C. (2009). Development and validation of a multidimensional measure of family supportive supervisor behaviours (FSSB). *Journal of Management, 35*(4), 837–856.

Hirschi, A., Shockley, K. M., & Zacher, H. (2019). Achieving work-family balance: An action regulation model. *Academy of Management Review, 44*(1), 150–171.

Hobfoll, S. E. (1989). Conservation of resources: A new attempt at conceptualizing stress. *American Psychologist, 44*(3), 513–524.

Hughes, J., & Bozionelos, N. (2007). Work-life balance as source of job dissatisfaction and withdrawal attitude: An Exploratory Study on the Views of Male Workers. *Personnel Review, 36*(1), 145–154.

Jones, F., Burke, R. J., & Westman, M. (2006). *Work-life balance: A psychological perspective*. Hove and New York: Psychology Press.

Joyce, K., Pabayo, R., Critchley, J. A., & Bambra, C. (2010). Flexible working conditions and their effects on employee health and wellbeing. *Cochrane Database Systematic. Reviews, 17*(2), 1–89.

Kinnunen, U., Mauno, S., Geurts, S., & Dikkers, J. (2005). Work-family culture in organizations: Theoretical and empirical approaches. In S. A. Y. Poelmans (Ed.), Series in applied psychology. *Work and family: An international research perspective* (pp. 87–120). Lawrence Erlbaum Associates Publishers.

Kirby, E., & Krone, E. (2002). 'The policy exists but you can't really use it': Communication and the structuration of work-family policies. *Journal of Applied Communication Research, 30*(1), 50–77.

Kossek, E. E., Noe, R., & DeMarr, B. (1999). Work-family role synthesis: Individual, family and organisational determinants. *International Journal of Conflict Resolution, 10*(2), 102–129.

Kreiner, G. E., Hollensbe, E. C., & Sheep, M. L. (2009). Balancing borders and bridges: Negotiating the work-home interface via boundary work tactics. *Academy of Management Journal, 52*(4), 704–730.

Kreiner, G. E., Hollensbe, E. C., & Sheep, M. L. (2006). Where is the "Me" among the "We"? Identity work and the search for optimal balance. *Academy of Management Journal, 49*(5), 1031–1057.

Ladge, J. J., & Little, L. M. (2019). When expectations become reality: Work-family image management and identity adaptation. *Academy of Management Review, 44*(1), 126–149.

Lambert, S. J. (1990). Processes linking work and family: A critical review and research agenda. *Human Relations, 43*(2), 239–257.

Leslie, L. M., King, E. B., & Clair, J. A. (2019). Work-life ideologies: The contextual basis and consequences of beliefs about work and life. *Academy of Management Review, 44*(1), 72–98.

Lewis, S. (1997). 'Family Friendly' employment policies: A route to changing organizational culture or playing about at the margins? *Gender, Work and Organization, 4*(1), 13–24.

Lobel, S. A., & Kossek, E. E. (1996). Human resource strategies to support diversity in work and personal lifestyles: Beyond the 'family friendly' organization. In E. E. Kossek & S. A. Lobel (Eds.), Managing diversity: Human resource strategies for transforming the workplace (pp. 221–243). Cambridge, MA: Blackwell.

Lu, J. F., Siu, O. L., Spector, P. E., & Shi, K. (2009). Antecedents and outcomes of a fourfold taxonomy of work-family balance in Chinese employed parents. *Journal of Occupational Health Psychology, 14*(2), 182–192.

Marks, S. R. (1977). Multiple roles and role strain: Some notes on human energy, time, and commitment. *American Sociological Review, 42*(6), 921–936.

Mathews, R. A., & Barnes-Farell, J. L. (2010). Development and initial evaluation of an enhanced measure of boundary flexibility for work and family domains, *Journal of Occupational Health Psychology, 15*(3), 330–346.

McDonald, P., Townsend, K., & Wharton, A. (2013). The legitimation and reproduction of discourse-practise gap in work-life balance. *Personnel Review, 42*(2), 205–222.

McDonald, P., Bradley, L., & Brown, K. (2008). Visibility in the workplace: Still an ingredient for career success. *International Journal of Human Resource Management, 19*(12), 2198–2215.

Maxwell, G. A., & McDougall, M. (2004). Work-life balance: Exploring the connections between levels of influence in the UK public sector. *Public Management Review, 6*(3), 377–393.

Ng, T. W., & Sorensen, K. L. (2008). Toward a further understanding of the relationships between perceptions of support and work attitudes: A meta-analysis. *Group Organization and Management, 33*(3), 243–268.

Nippert-Eng, C. (1996a). Calendars and keys: The classification of 'home' and 'work.' *Sociology Forum, 11*(3), 563–582.

Nippert-Eng, C. (1996b). *Home and work.* Chicago: University of Chicago Press.

Nipper-Eng, C. (1996c). *Home and work: Negotiating the boundaries of everyday life*. Chicago: University of Chicago Press.

Osoian, C., Lazar, L., & Ratiu, P. (2011). *The benefits of implementing and supporting work-life balance policies in organisations.* Investing in people! Project co-financed by the European Social Fund, Sectoral Operational Programme Human Resources Development 2007–2013, Babes-Bolyai University, Cluj-Napoca, Romania.

Peeters, M., Wattez, C., Demerouti, E., & de Regt, W. (2009). Work-family culture, work-family interference and well-being at work: Is it possible to distinguish between a positive and a negative process. *Career Development International, 14*(7), 700–713.

Perry-Jenkins, M., Repetti, R. L., & Crouter, A. C. (2000). Work and family in the 1990s. *Journal of Marriage and Family, 62*(4), 981–998.

Pleck, J. (1984). The work-family role system. In P. Voydanoff (Ed.), *Work and family: Changing roles of men and women* (pp. 8–19). Palo Alto, CA: Mayfield.

Pocock, B., Van Wanrooy, B., Strazzari, S., & Bridge, K. (2001). *'Fifty families: What unreasonable hours are doing to Australians, their families and their communities'?* Available at www.arts.adelaide.edu.au/. Accessed February 10, 2014.

Poelmans, S., O'Driscoll, M., & Beham, B. (2005). An overview of international research on the work-family interface. In S. A. Y. Poelmans (Ed.), Series in applied psychology. *Work and family: An international research perspective* (pp. 3–46). Lawrence Erlbaum Associates Publishers.

Powell, G. N., Greenhaus, J. H., Allen, T. D., & Johnson, R. E. (2019). Introduction to special topic forum: Advancing and expanding work-life theory from multiple perspectives. *Academy of Management Review, 44*(1), 54–71.

Raley, S. B., Mattingly, M. J., & Bianchi, S. M. (2006). How dual are dual income couples? Documenting change from 1970 to 2001. *Journal of Marriage and Family, 68*(1), 11–28.

Ramachandran, D., Chong, C. S., & Ismail, H. (2011). Organisational culture: An exploratory study comparing faculties' perspectives within public and private universities in Malaysia. *International Journal of Educational Management, 25*(6), 615–634.

Ransome, P. (2007). Conceptualizing boundaries between 'life' and 'work.' *International Journal of Human Resource Management, 18*(3), 374–386.

Rantanen, J., Kinnunen, U., Mauno, S., & Tillemann, K. (2011). Introducing theoretical approaches to work-life balance and testing a new typology among professionals. In S. Kaiser, M. Ringlstetter, D. R. Eikhof, & M. Pina e Cunha (Eds.), *Creating balance?* (pp. 27–46). Berlin, Heidelberg: Springer.

Rhoades, L., & Eisenberger, R. (2002). Perceived organizational support: A review of the literature. *Journal of Applied Psychology, 87*(4), 698–714.

Rodgers, F. S., & Rodgers, C. (1989). Business and the facts of family life. *Harvard Business Review, 67*, 121–129.

Sakazume, H. (2009). The effect of front-line manager's perception of work-life balance practice on leadership behaviours (in Japanese). *Japanese Journal of Administrative Science, 22*(3), 205–221.

Sarfo, M. P. (2002), *A multi-dimensional view on employee attitudes towards change in the public sector*. A dissertation submitted in partial fulfilment of the requirements for the degree of Masters of business administration in the University of Hull.

Schein, E. H. (2010). *Organisational culture and leadership*. San Francisco: Wiley.

Schein, E. H. (1992). The role of CEO in the management of change. In T. A. Kochan & M. Useem (Eds.), *Transforming organisation* (pp. 80–96). New York: Oxford University Press.

Schein, E. H. (1985). *Organisational culture and leadership*. San Francisco, CA: Jossey-Bass.

Scholarios, D., & Marks, A. (2004). Work-life balance and software worker. *Human Resource Management Journal, 14*(2), 54–74.

Sharma, T., & Mishra, K. K. (2013). Devising tools and Techniques for improving work-life balance of marketing field force in oil and gas sector in India. *The Business and Management Review, 3*(3), 115–127.

Simosi, M. (2012). Disentangling organisational support construct: The role of different sources of support to newcomers' training transfer and organisational commitment. *Personnel Review, 41*(3), 301–320.

Staines, G. L. (1980). Spillover versus compensation: A review of the literature on the relationship between work and non-work. *Human Relations, 33*(2), 111–129.

Stinchcomb, J. B., & Ordaz, F. (2007). The integration of two "brotherhood" into one organisational culture: A psycho-social perspective on merging police and fire services. *Public Organisation Review, 7*(2), 143–161.

Sundaramurthy, C., & Kreiner, G. (2008). Governing by managing identity boundaries: The case of family businesses. *Entrepreneurship: Theory and Practice, 32*(3), 415–436.

Tan, W., & Klaasen, I. (2007, September 12–14). *24/7 Environments: A theoretical and empirical exploration from an urban planners perspective paper for European Urban Research Association (EURA).* 10th Anniversary Conference, University of Glasgow, Scotland.

Timmins, N. (2002, April 26). Long-hours culture "stalls better work-life balance": (London Edition). *Financial Times*: 05 (London, UK).

Thompson, C., Beauvais, L., & Lyness, K. (1999). When work-family benefits are not enough: The influence of work-family culture on benefit utilisation, organisational attachment, and work-family conflict. *Journal of Vocational Behaviour, 54*(3), 329–415.

Torrington, D., Hall, L., & Taylor, S. (2008). *Human resource management.* London, UK: FT / Prentice Hall.

United Nations. (2011). *The global social crisis.* Report on the world social situation. Economic and Social Affairs. New York. Available at https://www.un.org/esa/socdev/rwss/docs/2011/rwss2011.pdf.

Warhurst, C., Eikhof, D. R., & Haunschild, A. (2008). Out of balance or just out of bounds? Analysing the relationship between work and life. In C. Warhurst, D. R. Eikhof, & A. Haunschild (Eds.), *Work less, live more? Critical analysis of the work-life boundary.* Basingstoke: Palgrave Macmillan.

Wharton, A., Chivers, S., & Blair-Loy, M. (2008). Use of formal and informal work-family policies on the digital assembly line. *Work and Occupations, 35*(3), 327–350.

White, M., Hill, S., McGovern, P., Mills, C., & Smeaton, D. (2003). High performance management practices, working hours and work-life balance. *British Journal of Industrial Relations, 41*(2), 175–195.

Whittington, J. L., Maellaro, R., & Galpin, T. (2011), Redefining success: The foundation for creating work-life balance. In S. Kaiser, M. Ringlstetter, D. R. Eikhof, & M. P. e Cunha (Eds.), *Creating Balance? International perspectives on the work-life integration of professionals* (pp. 65–77); Berlin, Heidelberg: Springer.

Wise, S., Smith, C., Valsecchi, R., Mueller, F., & Gabe, J. (2007). Controlling working time in the ward and on the line. *Employee Relations, 29*(4), 352–366.

Wu, T., Uen, J., Wu, S., & Chang, T. (2011). Family supportive culture, work-life segmentation and employee's organisational attachment: The case of high-tech industry in Taiwan. *Frontiers of Business Research in China, 5*(1), 79–95.

Young, L., & Kleiner, B. H. (1992). Work and family: Issues for the 1990s. *Women in Management Review, 7*(5), 24–28.

Zerubavel, E. (1991). *The fine line: Making distinctions in everyday life*. New York: Free Press.

Zerubavel, E. (1993). Horizons: On the socio-mental foundations of relevance. *Social Research: An International Quarterly, 60*(2), 397–413.

Zerubavel, E. (1996). Lumping and splitting: Notes on social classification. *Sociological Forum, 11*(3), 421–423.

Zerubavel, E. (1997). *Social mindscapes: An invitation to cognitive sociology*. Boston, MA: Harvard University Press.

Part II

Africa and the Arab World

3

The Role of Culture in the Work-Life Border Management: An Insight from Ghanaian Married Female Workers in the Formal Sector

Kwame Adom

Introduction

The need for dual-income families has increased significantly in recent times due to economic pressures. In recent times, families, considering the economic pressures, require more than one breadwinner to meet rising cost of living (Carrim, 2017; Munn & Chaudhuri, 2016; White & Rogers, 2000). There have also been some structural changes that have made discourse on work-life balance relevant. These include the shift from full-time jobs to part time, contract, and casual jobs, a rise in more irregular and unstable working hours, more females taking up paid jobs, among others (Feldman & Bolino, 2000; Yamaguchi, 2018). One thing that has characterized the lives of several working-class people, especially females, is "role conflict". "Role conflict" arises mainly due

K. Adom (✉)
Department of Marketing and Entrepreneurship, University of Ghana Business School, Accra, Ghana
e-mail: kadom@ug.edu.gh

T. A. Adisa and G. Gbadamosi (eds.), *Work-Life Interface*,
https://doi.org/10.1007/978-3-030-66648-4_3

to the combination of personal, domestic, and societal demands and expectations (Nambisan & Baron, 2019; Posig & Kickul, 2004). The participation in work roles has the potential to make it cumbersome for females to partake in projected family roles. Likewise, the carrying out of family roles can make it difficult for females to participate in work roles (Hundera, Duijsters, & Naudé, 2019; James-Hawkins, Qutteina, & Yount, 2017). This communicates an interplay of work and family roles, requiring the effective management of these varying roles, hence work-life balance. Work-life balance is considered as one of the tough issues families in contemporary times face. In this study, work-life balance is about the "satisfaction and good functioning at work and at home, with a minimum of role conflict" (Clark, 2000, p. 751).

The participation of females in paid workforce is one of the most momentous social changes of the twenty-first century (Glauber & Day, 2018; Straub, 2007). Scholars postulate that work-life balance is a herculean task for women than men due to cultural and societal norms which expect women to concentrate on providing care for the family, whilst men focus on career (Biggs & Brough, 2005; Buttner & Moore, 1997; Haar & O'Driscoll, 2005). This expectation is not different in Ghana and other African countries.

Despite the widespread attention given to the study of work-life balance, the subject is still at an incipient stage in developing countries (Mushfiqur et al., 2018). As such, work-life balance in the Ghanaian context has been understudied. According to Adisa, Mordi, and Osabutey (2017, p. 454), countries in the sub-Saharan African region constitute "a neglected and little understood area of inquiry". This presents a research gap considering the differences in the institutional systems that have probable effect on careers and work-life balance (Ituma, Simpson, Ovadje, Cornelius, & Mordi, 2011). Again, scholars have made calls for "country-specific career studies" as termed by Ituma et al. (2011, p. 3639) in non-Western nations and Africa. The essence of this is to broaden perspectives regarding the issues employees face when it comes to balancing work and non-work-related matters (Perrons, 2003). Going by this call, researchers are likely to contribute or provide guidelines to the "development of career management theory and practice in these regions" (Ituma et al., 2011, p. 3638), as well as provide different conceptualizations of work-life balance that is different from the Anglo-Saxon perspective(s) (Mushfiqur et al., 2018). A study by Darko-Asumadu, Sika-Bright, and Osei-Tutu (2018) conducted in the Ghanaian context finds that married employees have a harder time balancing work-life, and most importantly, women employees experience more role conflicts than their male counterparts. Edwards and Oteng (2019) state that one of the causes of role conflicts among females in Ghana is cultural or gendered assumptions and societal expectations. One thing these studies failed to espouse is how these females try to manage work-life balance considering the cultural setting they find themselves. Goel (2017), as an editor of the International Journal of Manpower, calls for studies on work-life balance that focus on females. These gaps identified in the literature provide justification for this study. Therefore, the key aim of this study is to fill the prevailing research gaps by exploring the impact of culture on the work-life balance management of married women in the formal work setting, framed by the unique institutional structures in Ghana. This study employs the institutional theory (IT) which deals with several frameworks within which societal and work-related issues occur with respect to cultural, societal, and regulatory factors (Mayrhofer et al., 2004). Drawing on the cultural aspect of the institutional theory, this study examines how the Ghanaian culture impacts on females in their effort to manage their work-life. Hence, the research question the study seeks to answer is:

> RQ1. How is the Ghanaian culture shaping the work-life balance management of married female employees in the formal sector of Ghana?

To answer the above research question, the study assumes an institutional theory approach in examining the role of institutional dynamics (specifically, culture) on the work-life balance management of married females in Ghana. The study adopts abductive reasoning to create meaning that entailed the researcher going back and forth data and theory to make sense out of the study (Robson, 2002). The study also uses interpretivist and phenomenologist approaches.

The rest of the chapter is structured as follows: extant literature is reviewed with focus on work-life balance and the context of Ghana;

explaining culture; an overview of the Ghanaian culture and the institutional theory. Next, the methodology of the research is highlighted by reconnoitring data source, method, and analytical tools adopted. This is successively followed by the findings of the study and discussions. The final part of the study presents the conclusions made from the study, the implications, and future research directions.

Understanding Work-Life Balance and the Ghanaian Context

Generally, females in sub-Saharan Africa and hence, Ghana have a protracted history in the participation in income-generating activities albeit in the informal sector (Aryee, 2005; Asongu & Odhiambo, 2019). But in recent times, the involvement of females in the formal sector has witnessed a surcharge due to better education and economic opportunities, and urbanization and industrialization (Aryee, 2005; Bay, 2019). The increasing participation of females in the Ghanaian labour force, in recent times, cannot be overemphasized. The remarkable progress of females in the Ghanaian labour space can be linked to improved access to education, equity legislations, and the resilient propagation of feminist perspectives (Abraham, Ohemeng, & Ohemeng, 2017). Irrespective of this, the advancement with respect to gender transformation and equity in the Ghanaian workplace is still unsatisfactory (Asongu & Odhiambo, 2019).

The challenges females encounter in efforts to successfully enter and persevere in working environments originate from traditional gender hierarchies and norms that prevail in the family and society. Despite gender equality and empowerment, the household unit had a traditional structure—and still has—that makes males the dominant gender (Hegewisch, Liepmann, Hayes, & Hartmann, 2010). These traditional stereotyped role expectations (Adom & Anambane, 2019) spill over to organizational policies and practices to maintain women's marginalized work roles (Bobbitt-Zeher, 2011) and become entrenched in a gender-biased organizational culture (Prescott & Bogg, 2011), making work-life balance to become an issue of interest in the context.

The concept of work-life balance, although modern (Edwards & Oteng, 2019), represents a rather old notion (Chandra, 2012). Scholars like Felstead, Gallie, and Green (2002) state that there is no definite definition for work-life balance. According to Greenhaus, Collins, and Shaw (2003), work-life balance describes the extent to which individuals are satisfied with work and family roles, without neglecting the other. Clark (2000) expresses similar view on the relatedness of work-life balance and satisfaction by defining it as the state at which people gain the desired satisfaction from functioning well at both workplace and home, without facing enormous role conflicts. The idea of work-life balance emerged to mitigate role conflict (Agarwal & Lenka, 2015; Sirgy & Lee, 2016). Work-life balance has been posited as a choice that employees have the freedom to make (Clutterbuck, 2003). This assertion is not applicable in all contexts as studies show there are usually paradoxes to the idea about "choice" (Karatepe, 2010).

Several decades ago, work-life balance was perceived as a Western idea (Lewis, Gambles, & Rapport, 2007). However, in recent times, the concept has witnessed integration into the African context as several African females are constantly getting involved in paid jobs for economic empowerment and the ability to contribute to family needs. In line with this, Mushfiqur et al. (2018) basing on the Nigerian context conceptualized work-life balance as the "interface of work and family and the consequences of these two variables on commitment to work, job satisfaction, family roles and social related themes" (p. 870).

Typical traditional African societies and institutions make it difficult for females engaged in paid employment to cater for family and work at the same time, given the persisting patriarchal and cultural dynamics (Anambane & Adom, 2018; Ituma et al., 2011). Patriarchy in the Ghanaian society places women in a situation where their roles in family conflict their occupational lives. This has made work-life balance a herculean task for females (Darko-Asumadu et al., 2018). In traditional Ghanaian society, and in common practice, the division of labour is firm in homes. Whereas males are expected to be breadwinners, females are saddled with the duties of taking care of the home (Waterhouse, Hill, & Hinde, 2017). In other words, economic responsibility is the jurisdiction of males, and domestic chores and childcare are the preserve of females. This presents a challenge to females in dual-career relationships especially. The Ghanaian society, however, in recent times is changing. Whereas some sections subscribe to feminist perspectives, making gender roles blur (Frempong, 2019), others still hold onto perspectives that are rooted in traditions, thereby still holding unto gender demarcated roles (Adom & Anambane, 2019). The truth, however, is that, no matter the liberations in the Ghanaian society that promote the blurring of gender-specific roles, females are still viewed as the ones responsible for childcare and domestic duties; just that males that subscribe to feminist perspectives decide to offer some "help" unlike their counterparts who would watch females do their "duties". In the midst of these prevailing issues in the Ghanaian society, females are increasingly picking up paid jobs, advancing in their careers, and may need to work for extended periods or travel out of town for work purposes (Ahmed & Carrim, 2016). Discussions on work-life balance become complicated when it involves females in traditional societies (Ahmed, Saleem, & Kaneez, 2019) such as Ghana. In such societies, time management, family responsibilities, mental and physical issues, care for dependents, multiple roles, among others, have been the major factors affecting the work-life balance of females (ibid.).

In effort to support work-life balance in the Ghanaian working environment, some companies or businesses have developed work-life balance policies, albeit most of these policies do not enhance employee commitment (Darko-Asumadu et al., 2018; Markwei, Kubi, Quao, & Attiogbe, 2019). Obimpeh (2018) opines that the work-life balance policies in organizations in Ghana are often too general and hence, do not suit the needs of female employees. Darko-Asumadu et al. (2018) suggest that study leave, paternity leave, and part-time working schedules are incentives that could enhance work-life balance in the Ghanaian banking sector. Aryeetey, Yeboah, and Sanda (2012) reveal that role conflict, the imbalance between work roles and home roles, is a source of stress to females and has the potential to push professional female employees to vacate jobs. The most preferred initiatives that can enhance women work-life balance are telecommuting and compressed work-weeks. Although several women employees are aware of work flexible initiatives like work arrangements that enhance work-life balance, these initiatives are hardly practised in organizations in Ghana (ibid.). This suggests that work-life balance is a critical issue in the Ghanaian working environment, especially in the private sector where employers burden employees with longer working hours without concern for the other aspects of their lives (family) (Asiedu-Appiah, Dufie-Marfo, & Frempong, 2016). Adom, Asare-Yeboa, Quaye, and Ampomah (2018) find that although work-life balance is desired by female entrepreneurs in Ghana, most of them consider family life as the utmost and can sacrifice work life for family life. The rising rate of unemployment is not making the situation any better as employers tend to take advantage of employees (Sarpong, 2019). Over the years, female employees have adopted strategies such as asking for family support and hiring nannies to perform home tasks, with family support being the most effective (Obimpeh, 2018).

Explaining Culture

The definition of culture is a herculean task considering that culture is a complex phenomenon (Hofstede, 2015). As such, Yaganeh (2013) maintains that the idea of culture cannot be fully comprehended on the surface. Despite these notions, several scholars have presented diverse definitions of culture. One of the earliest definitions of culture is given by Tylor (1871). According to the author, culture is the multifarious and interrelated sets of elements, encompassing beliefs, arts, values, knowledge, beliefs, manners and morals, and all other kinds of skills and habits learned by a human as a member of a particular society. Whereas Tylor (1871) links culture to the learning of certain skills and habits by human beings in society, Kluckhohn (1951) views culture to be more of emotions than learning by relating it to thinking, feeling, and reacting. Kluckhohn (1951) avers that culture is the patterned way of thinking, feeling, and reacting which is obtained and predominantly transferred via symbols. The definition of culture by Kroeber and Parsons (1958) seems to be an amalgamation of the previous definitions. The authors define culture as the transmission and creation of content and patterns of values, ideas, and other symbolic-meaningful systems that shape human behaviour and the artefacts produced through behaviour.

In the 2010s, other scholars defined culture. These definitions are not so variant from the aforementioned ones. For instance, Beugelsdijk and Maseland (2010) state that culture is the collective identity of communities. Duman, Beduk, Koyluoglu, and Ay (2015) delineate culture as the common features of a group of people that is transferred from generation to generation. Hofstede (2015) maintains that culture means shared and transferable perceptions, values, or practices. Last but not the least, Woodside, Bernal, and Coduras (2016) aver that culture signifies a complex whole of attitudes, beliefs, values, and behaviour. An analysis of the various definitions of culture suggests that there is a unified ideology of what culture is; it is the way a group of people behave; and it is learned and transferred—hence, lingers within a particular society over a period of time.

Although a complex concept, culture can be observed using language, values, religions, country, ethics, among others as points of reference (Hofstede, 2015). Similarly, Usunier and Lee (2005) present several sources of culture: language, education, gender, religion, family, profession, nationality, and social class. These views embody the ideology of sub-cultures. Whereas there could be a national culture for people in a certain country, females in that same country, people from an ethnic group, people of same profession, among others, could have their own way of life (culture). In Ghana, for instance, although the nation has a culture, the different ethnic groups have unique cultures; but these together define the national culture. An analysis of the sources of culture as opined by Hofstede (2015) and Usunier and Lee (2005) suggests that every aspect of human life constitutes culture and is influenced by culture. The influence of culture on human life, however, could be direct or indirect and/or lasting or temporary (Craig & Douglas, 2005). Culture is very much interwoven in all spheres of human life to an extent that it is usually challenging to determine the level at which it affects human life (ibid.). For this reason, Barber and Badre (1998) describe culture as a complex and problematic phenomenon. Aside these, culture is labelled as an abstract notion which is not static but changes over time and its influences also vary with time (Usunier, Lee & Lee, 2005), signifying the dynamism of culture. The changing nature of culture is, however, not an event that occurs overnight but is enduring

(Braidford, Stone, & Tesfaye, 2013). This change in culture or cultural dynamism is often caused by cultural contamination; cultural hybridization; and cultural pluralism, that is, the penetration of elements from other cultures. This has contributed to culture being a more difficult issue to examine (Craig & Douglas, 2005).

As an all-encompassing concept, culture influences on the working lives of humans (Steers, & Sánchez-Runde, 2017). It plays a role in what is expected of individuals both at the formal working environment and at the home. It can be argued that work (paid work) in itself is part of culture. An individual's disposition towards taking up a paid work is highly influenced by culture. Culture also determines who is engaged in paid work. Whereas some cultures consider paid work as the preserve of men, others consider it as an activity that should not be based on gender. As such, examining culture's role in the work-life balance of females is imperative.

An Overview of the Ghanaian Culture

The Ghanaian culture is considered to be rich and vibrant with diverse positive rudiments like respect and consideration for others regardless of age and status, diversity, and a disposition towards cooperation than conflict (Anambane, 2017; Salm & Falola, 2002). These positive rudiments, however, do not include gender dynamics. The Ghanaian national culture rates 80% on power distance, 70% on indulgence, 65% on uncertainty avoidance, 40% on masculinity, 15% on individualism, and 4% on long-term orientation, in line with Hofstede's (1980, 1984) dimensions of national culture. Even though, originally, Ghana was not captured in Hofstede's (1980, 1984) study, rankings were developed for Ghana based on the rankings of similar countries. This was done through the 6D model of national culture (Hofstede, n.d.).

The Ghanaian culture is generally patriarchal (see Adom & Anambane, 2019; Fenrich & Higgins, 2001). This patriarchy is exhibited in the gender stereotyping (Adom & Anambane, 2019) and in the distribution of resources in society (Anambane, 2017; Fenrich & Higgins, 2002). As indicated by Fenrich and Higgins (2002), the cultural setting of Ghana makes it difficult for females to own lands and have control over them, as well as enjoy from the proceeds of the land. Anambane (2017) confirms this by echoing the difficulty females within the Nabdam district face in land inheritance due to cultural issues. This struggle of females to own and manage land is evident in Ewe (an ethnic group in Ghana) saying that "Palm fruits in the land of a woman can never ripen". This is because of the ideology that the land should not be hers, and thus, she cannot keep others away from the palm tree nor benefit from the proceeds of the land alone.

There is also a clear demarcation of gender roles within the Ghanaian culture. Whereas females are responsible for childcare, homecare, and all other nurturing duties, males are to provide for the family (Clark, 1999; Tolhurst & Nyonator, 2006). However, the rising levels of formal education and feminist perspectives, which is blurring gender roles globally, have only placed extra duties on females as they are now expected to contribute to the economic well-being of their families, pushing more females into paid work.

Theoretical Underpinning: The Institutional Theory

The tenets of the institutional theory are that in every society, there are codified rules and regulations that delineate what is acceptable (North, 1990; Webb, Ireland, & Ketchen, 2014). The theory avers that institutions, in other words, long-term systems, shape the actions of individuals and firms (Clemens & Cook, 1999). Conventionally, the institutional theory is used to demonstrate how groups and organizations are able to maintain positions of legitimacy in society or within certain contexts, by adhering to the rules and norms of the environment where they find themselves (Meyer & Rowan, 1991; Scott, 2007). Roy (1997) positions that the institutional theory is concerned with the regulatory, social, and cultural effects that promote the survival and legitimacy of an organization rather than exclusively concentrating on efficiency-seeking behaviour.

The institutional theory hinges on the conceptualization of "institutions". According to North (1990, p. 3), institutions are "the humanly devised constraints that structure human interaction". Kostova and Roth (2002) describe institutions as the instruments that allow economic players in society to engage in efficient interactions and exchanges. Institutions are also the less prescribed shared interaction systems (Jepperson, 1991) and ex ante agreements (Bonchek & Shepsle, 1996) that organizations and individuals in specified environments have to follow. North (1990) proposes that institutions are in two forms: formal and informal institutions. Formal institutions refer to laws, regulations, and their supporting tools such as law enforcement agencies and regulatory bodies that guide behaviour in a context (North 1990; Webb et al., 2014). Also, informal institutions signify the norms, values, and beliefs which determine socially acceptable behaviour within specific contexts (North, 1990). In summary, institutions can then be defined as the formal and informal instruments that govern environmental, social, and economic exchanges (North, 1990).

The focus of this study is on informal institutions; specifically, how norms, values, and beliefs (which form culture) impact the work-life balance efforts of married working females in Ghana. In traditional African society like Ghana, informal institutions make it perplexing for females in paid working environments to double as caretakers of the family, in line with the region's patriarchal issues that emanate from culture (Ituma et al., 2011), hence the application of this theory. Patriarchy in Ghana positions females such that their roles in occupational life conflict with that of family life. Further, there is increasing pressure for Ghanaian females to support their families economically given the economic situations in the country. They have since taken up paid jobs that have impact on roles at home. The job demands of these females conflict with the expected demands at home, and vice versa. These are issues relating to the informal institutions. The usage of the institutional theory in this study is thereby justified.

Over the years, several studies have applied the institutional theory in examining work-life balance of women. To begin with, Mushfiqur et al. (2018), apply it to examine the challenges female doctors in Nigeria encounter in work-life balance efforts and its impact on social sustainability. Stavrou and Ierodiakonou (2018) advance the discourse of work-life balance to lesbian, gay, bisexual, and transgender (LGBT) employees through the lens of the institutional theory. The institutional theory was again used by Cuéllar-Molina, García-Cabrera, and Lucia-Casademunt, (2018) to study the well-being of female managers in Europe. No study was found to have applied this theory in the area of culture and work-life balance of females.

Methodology

Work-life balance has been underexplored in the Ghanaian context. For this reason, the study adopts a qualitative approach to collecting and analysing data. One strength of the qualitative research approach is its ability to provide deeper insights into research phenomena (Cassell Bishop, Symon, Johnson, & Buehring, 2009). The qualitative approach also enhances interaction between literature and evidence; this is useful in understanding the representativeness across a broader range of issues (Ciao, 2011). The study further draws on the interpretivist and phenomenologist traditions which focus on individual experiences (Guba & Lincoln, 1994), to make its argument. This methodological locus gave the researcher an in-depth understanding of the phenomenon under scrutiny (Creswell, 2008). It finally led to the unearthing of opulent detailed accounts of individual experiences (Fassinger, 2001). The interpretivist and phenomenologist tradition to qualitative enquiry has been embraced by different scholars in different environments (Ituma et al., 2011). Additionally, the case study approach was adopted by this study. It gave the researcher the opportunity to explore the daily live activities, experiences, and views on the issue under enquiry (Creswell, 2008).

Primary data were collected from fifteen (15) female employees in private and public organizations. The age of the respondents ranged from twenty-eight (28) to fifty-four (54) years. The data collection was done through semi-structured interviews, with the aid of an interview guide. Semi-structured interviews were preferred because of its forte in disinterring relevant and hidden facts regarding organizational behaviour and human life (Qu & Dumay, 2011). Participants were solicited through administrators or managers of various organizations. Convenience sampling technique was then used in selecting the respondents; that is, working married females who were available and willing to participate in the study were interviewed. The respondents were asked the same questions although the interviews were done on individual basis at different times and locations to reduce the chance of bias. All the respondents met the criteria for selection, married and working class. Specifically, some of the questions asked were: What is work-life balance? How do you manage your work life and family? How does the Ghanaian culture affect your working and family life? How do you manage your working life considering how the Ghanaian culture views females with respect to being career oriented? These questions are, however, not exhaustive as follow-up questions were asked based on the responses of the participants.

Pseudonyms have been used in place of the original names of the respondents to satisfy the promise of confidentiality made to the participants. At the start of each interview, participants were presented consent forms which indicated the purpose of the study. Participants were also educated about their right to partake in the study or withdraw from the study at any stage of the interview process. All interview sessions were conducted in the English language as it is the official language of Ghana and used in the workplace. Interview sessions lasted between twenty (20) minutes to thirty-two (32) minutes. The interview sessions were recorded electronically with the permission of the respondents. This was to enable the study to capture the words of the participants verbatim in order to arrive at nuanced and logical findings (Bryman & Becker, 2012). The essence of the recording was to also aid identify if any relevant issues had been missed during the interview so that supplemental interviews could be carried out afterwards. After interviewing 12 respondents, it was noticed that the themes that emerged were recurrent, meaning the data had reached a point of saturation. It was therefore unlikely that further data collection would yield new themes. However, to enhance data reliability and ensure that relevant themes had not been relegated, three (3) more interviews were conducted, bringing the total number of interviews to fifteen (15). The additional three (3) interviews confirmed the previous emerging themes. At this point, the data collection had reached a "theoretical saturation" as illustrated by Glaser and Strauss (1967, p. 61).

The collected data were transcribed verbatim. After the data were transcribed, the researcher meticulously went through all the recordings to ensure that the transcribed data exactly matched the recorded version. After the transcription, open coding was done. The purpose of the coding was to identify the key points that were significant in the data (Boeije, 2005). At this juncture, the focus was on the ability of the researcher to interrogate the meaning of certain words or phrases and carefully think about what they mean (Corbin & Strauss, 2014). The first set of codes was grouped according to common codes. Afterwards, the codes that had similar underlying ideas were combined. Three dominant themes and eight sub-themes emerged. The coding categories were not preconceived by the researcher. The researcher was open-minded and allowed the themes or categories to emerge from the data so that important themes will not be missed. The labelling of the categories are considered precise and reflect the meaning of the feelings of the respondents regarding their work-life balance, albeit the researcher is aware that it is an inherently subjective issue, considering that one "cannot escape background preconceptions embedded in the language and life of their authors" (Gill & Johnson, 2010, p. 144).

The coding categories were marked with different colours for easy identification to expedite data analysis. The key categories were fine-tuned through recurrent assessments until a full picture was created. Thematic textual analysis (TTA) was adopted based on the recommendation of Corbin and Strauss (2014) and done based on the guide proposed by Braun and Clarke (2006). TTA is "a research strategy for identifying and reporting patterns (themes) within a data set or text corpus" (Mushfiqur et al., 2018, p. 875). The themes that emerged were the categories for the analysis and the researcher applied investigator triangulation (Polit & Beck, 2004). The study is situated in Accra (the capital of Ghana). Data were collected in December 2019 and lasted for three (3) weeks. The data were collected by the researcher.

Data Analysis and Discussion of Findings

The data were analysed using thematic textual analysis as indicated earlier. The emerging themes of the study and some illustrative extracts are presented in Table 3.3. Role conflict among married females in Ghana, work-life balance in the face of the Ghanaian culture, and mitigating the impact of culture on work-life balance management are the three main themes that emerged from the data.

The study, however, presents the profile of the respondents before diving to discuss the main issues of the study. This enhances the reliability of the study and also provides better understanding of the lived experiences of the respondents.

Profile of Respondents

A total of fifteen (15) respondents were covered by the study. All respondents were working-class females and married. Married females were the interest of the study since they have multiple families to take care of (nuclear family, family of birth, and family of marriage), increasing their roles in families. The profile of the respondents the study took interest in is age, occupation, educational level, number of years in paid employment, and number of children the respondents had. With respect to age, majority of the respondents (46.7%) fall within the age group of 25–34 years. The youngest participant was aged twenty-eight (28) and the oldest was fifty-four (54) years. This age group distribution is a good representation of married working-class women. A greater portion of the respondents (73.3%) worked with privately-owned institutions. This has some implications for the study as several private institutions either do not have or do not adhere to human resource policies that seek to enhance the work-life balance of females in the workplace. The participants generally worked in corporate bodies. As such, the study had no representation of nurses, teachers, and security services. The respondents came from several sectors such as hospitality, insurance, financial services, consultancy, and education, among others. This enabled the study to present a broader perspective on the subject. Over 86.7% of

Table 3.1 Profile of respondents

Profile	Measurement	Frequency (%)
Age	25–34	46.7
	35–44	33.3
	45–54	20.0
Occupation	Government employee	26.7
	Private employee	73.3
Level of education	Tertiary	86.7
	Secondary	13.3
Number of years as an employee	1–5	26.7
	6–10	40.0
	11–15	20.0
	16–20	13.3

Source Researcher's Findings (2020)

the participants had tertiary education. In Ghana, tertiary education refers to any educational level beyond secondary school education, that is, polytechnic, training colleges, and universities. With respect to the number of years the respondents had been in paid employment, majority (40%) had worked between six (6) and ten (10) years. This implies that the participants were experienced and knowledgeable enough to participate in this study. No participant had worked beyond twenty (20) years. All except one respondent was mother with the least and highest number of children being one (1) and four (4) respectively. Information on the number of children the respondent had helped understand their experiences (Table 3.1).

The chapter also presents details of the respondents using pseudonyms. This is to enhance transparency of the research. The details are presented in Table 3.2.

A summary of the major and sub-themes as well as some illustrative extracts is presented in the Table 3.3.

Role Conflicts Among Women in Ghana

An emerging theme of the study was factors contributing to role conflicts among women in Ghana. All the respondents had an understanding of the meaning of "role conflicts" and work-life balance. There was a

Table 3.2 Details of respondents

Name	Age	Occupation	Sector	No of children
Susan	35	Finance Officer	Port Management	1
Muniratu	30	Administrative Assistant	Consultancy	2
Abena	42	Secretary	Education	4
Linda	33	Customer Service Personnel	Financial Services	2
Marayam	37	Gender Activist	Civil Service	3
Karen	29	Administrator	Education	1
Lamisi	54	Manager	Consultancy	3
Kumiwaa	34	Marketer	Food and Beverage	2
Gifty	49	Underwriter	Insurance	3
Cindy	36	Accounts Clerk	Automobile	1
Adelaide	33	Accountant	Health and Beauty	3
Ayorkor	33	Trainer	Oil and Gas	3
Senam	38	Banker	Financial Services	2
Nasara	28	Receptionist	Hospitality	None
Vivian	50	Manager	Hospitality	4

Source Researcher's Findings (2020)

general consensus that females, especially the married ones, experience staid levels of role conflicts (Darko-Asumadu et al., 2018). Often the role one has to play at the workplace is affected by family duties (Waterhouse et al., 2017). The reverse is also true. There are times that working married females had to attend to unscheduled family duties that crop up at periods when one was at one. The respondents agree that role conflict is a prevalent issue among working-class married females in Ghana (Asiedu-Appiah et al., 2016). As expressed by Suzan, a thirty-five (35)-year-old finance officer in government-owned establishment:

> Role conflicts is an issue that affects us a lot. Most at times, we do not even know how and when to separate work from family duties. Because sometimes, while at work, they call you that your child at school is sick, meaning you have to seek permission and leave to take care of that.

Table 3.3 Emerging themes and illustrative extracts

Main theme	Sub-theme	Excerpts
Role conflicts among women in Ghana	Societal expectations	*"Now, women are expected to bring money home and at the same time care for the home. That has been a positive change though but has an impact on women."*—**Abena**
	Lack of good employment policies	*"Some workplaces are hell. You work with them without any proper contract. They do not even state what you are entitled to. Even going on annual leave is a problem."*—**Kumiwaa**
	Lack of planning	*"I think it is all about planning. If you plan your daily activities well that this is what I am going to do at his time errrr, I do not think something should take you off schedule."*—**Karen**
Work-life balance in the face of the Ghanaian culture	Lack of flexible working schedules	*"Our situation is like we have rigid schedules everywhere, especially at work. Yes! The work timing is not flexible for us. It is just one. No variety you can pick from to ease things up for you."*—**Linda**

Main theme	Sub-theme	Excerpts
	Exploitative nature of some employers	*"My work makes it difficult for me to balance both duties well. My work starts as early as 7:30am and I can never close before 8:00 pm. Meanwhile, I have three kids, boys. But I need to work."*—**Adelaide**
Ghanaian women and work-life Balance management	Family and spousal support	*"I get support from my family. Sometimes when work is taking me out of town, I take my kids to my sister. She has been of great support."*—**Ayorkor**
	Help away from the family	*"I have hired a house-help. I have a son of three years. I can't leave work to take him from school. I don't also like him hanging around at school till after 5:00 pm. So, the help does that."*—**Karen**
	Effective Planning	*"Like I said earlier on, it is mostly about planning and sticking to it. I for one, I plan what I am to do at each hour of the day. […]."*—**Lamisi**

Source Researcher's Findings (2020)

However, it is not only the duties at the workplace that suffer when role conflicts arise. The roles one has to play at home sometimes do also suffer. For instance, Muniratu, a thirty (30)-year-old administrative officer with a private entity, avers that "*[…] It is not always that our official duties suffer because of the duties we owe our families. It is a two-sided issue*". When probed further about the reasoning behind such a comment, she added "*My work is such that you could be called upon even on a weekend. Sometimes, depending on the projects at hand, I need to come to work on Saturdays; a day I could use to do my work at home and also bond with my family*". The severity of the issue of role conflicts is declared by Senam, a 38-year-old banker in a private institution as she opines thus:

> It is never easy taking care of your kids, work, family, and husband. Each of them want attention from you, but no one gives it to you. Women are like captain planet. Hahahahaaaa. We just have to make everything happen…. In fact, it is stress 'ankasa' (indeed). May God give us strength.

At this point, the study ascertains that role conflict is a dominant issue affecting married working-class females in Ghana. This validates the need for work-life management for these women.

Moving forward to the causes of role conflicts in the lives of working-class women, three sub-themes emerged: societal expectations; lack of good employment policies; and lack of planning. It must be highlighted that some respondents mentioned more than one factor. As such, the frequency of each factor is against the total sample size of fifteen (15).

To begin with, societal expectations of women which emanate from culture have been a key cause of role conflicts in the Ghanaian context as highlighted by 86.7 of the respondents. A lot is expected of a woman in the Ghanaian society: from childcare, caring for other adults in the family, and having to be involved in the economic contribution for the family. As culture is dynamic, women in the contemporary Ghanaian society are expected to take up paid work unlike women in past generations. No longer are women expected to play only the role of caregivers at home but contribute to the economic situations of families by engaging in paid work. This means that in contemporary times, women are expected to carry out paid work duties and family duties. They are expected to combine these perfectly without failing in any as women who have failed to raise responsible children or keep a "good" home because of their focus on career goals are criticized severely. In the times of old where culturally, financial contributions to families were not expected of women, the topic of role conflicts and work-life balance was irrelevant in such societies. With the change in the Ghanaian national culture where females have been fairly educated at the same levels as males and expected to engage in paid work, the duties of women in society have increased. In support of the forgone discussion, Abena, a forty-two (42)-year-old secretary in a government-owned organization, says "*Now, women are expected to bring money home and at the same time care for the home. That has been a positive change though but has an impact on women*". Similarly, Linda, a 33-year-old customer service person with a private company, said "*Times have really changed when it comes to the role of women in economic issues. But when it comes to the role of women in homes, that one 'diiier'* (in particular) *it has not changed*".

It is evident that irrespective of changes in the Ghanaian culture creating the space and the chance for women to be engaged in paid work, women are still the sole caretakers of the home, which worsens the role conflicts that women face. An illustration of this assertion, excerpt from the interview with Maryam, a 37-year-old gender activist within a government organization, is presented below:

> How society managed to make women the sole owners of care work still perplexes me. I recently was admitted at the hospital at Tema (a suburb in Accra, the capital of Ghana). While there, I witnessed a young woman cry because she had exhausted her leave days and her child was still on admission. My question was: where is the father of the child? Busy, I guess. Meanwhile, he has leave days as well ooooo.

Additionally, lack of planning on the part of the women involved was found as a cause of role conflict in the lives of women. A little over 26% of the respondents maintained that women faced role conflicts because they do not plan their activities well. They hold that having a detailed plan of how one was going to go about her daily activities was helpful and could eliminate role conflicts. The proponents of this idea were, however, quick to add that this only worked in situations where one worked in a well-organized firm. Even with that, it was indicated that there were times impromptu family duties come up during working hours, but it is still helpful to have a well laid own plan of daily activities. In support of this, Karen, a 29-year-old administrator of a senior high school, states "*I think it is all about planning. If you plan your daily activities well that this is what I am going to do at his time errrr, I do not think something should take you off schedule*". Muniratu contributes to this by saying:

> To me, planning counts. You can plan your duties well. This is perfect when you work in a good organization where if they say you are closing at 5pm, you are closing at 5pm. No, stay back because of another thing. That way, you are able to manage your life well. But it is not so with some of us.

In an indication of the idea of impromptu activities being a bane to effective planning, Lamisi, a 54-year-old manager of a small and medium-scale enterprise, avows:

> What I do is that I plan. So, I know I am doing this at this time and I try to stick to it. But the truth is that there could be impromptu family duties coming up at the time you are at work. But for me...., my children are grown. So, I don't have issues of one is sick at school so come pick him; this one has swallowed a coin ...hahahahahaaha... so come pick him. So, when I plan, it works sometimes. Sometimes too it doesn't, I must be frank. So, I am not totally free from role conflicts, just that I think it is better for me than the younger ones we have around here.

A third cause of role conflicts that emerged is the lack of well-written work contracts as stated by 40% of the participants. In recent times where finding jobs has become a herculean task, some employers have taken advantage of employees (Sarpong, 2019) by even employing staff without giving out well-written job contract that speculates the expectation of the employee as well as benefits due to the employee. This has caused a lot of role conflicts for the women involved. Some women have had to work without having the opportunity to paid annual leave and maternity leave. In the study context, there have been reports in the media circles about women that are seeking legal actions against firms they worked with that had dismissed them from work because they needed maternity leave. The culprits have mainly been privately-owned firms that tend to disobey the country's labour laws. Working in such environments is stressful for women, increased their role conflicts, and decreased their ability to manage their work and personal life. This is illustrated by Kumiwaa, a 34-year-old marketer with a private firm assert:

> "Some workplaces are hell. You work with them without any proper contract. They do not even state what you are entitled to. Even going on annual leave is a problem". *When asked why women subscribe to such jobs, she states* "The unemployment situation in this country is glaring. And we need to work. So, in the absence of a proper work, you take what is offered whilst praying for the best".

A similar view is raised by Linda:

> Unless you have a government work or work with a well-established business, there are a lot of things that would go on to make your duties at work and home crisscross. Imagine, due to a lack of well laid down human resource policies, your boss can call to work even on holidays and weekdays. Some too annual leave is denied. It is a very difficult situation.

From the abovementioned discussion, it can be deduced that it is increasingly becoming a norm and a culture for individuals in Ghana to work without explicit contracts. This is rather an unfortunate situation and suggests that unemployment in Ghana has reached a crisis level. Without the improvement of the unemployment situation in Ghana, role conflicts for women are not likely to reduce, and thus, the work-life balance for women would be a near non-existent phenomenon.

In this section, culture has been identified as a strong root cause of role conflicts among married working-class females in Ghana. It is therefore imperative for the researcher to consider how culture plays a role in the work-life balance management of married working women in Ghana. This is discussed in the next section.

Work-Life Balance in the Face of the Ghanaian Culture

Deeper insights gained about issues surrounding the work-life balance of married working women in the Ghanaian cultural context are espoused under this section. The study firstly explores the understanding of culture by the respondents. There was a general understanding that culture was the way of life of a group of people (Dumanet al., 2015). It is manifested in norms, values, traditions, taboos, language, and others. For instance, Lamisi says "*I know culture to be the way we do things in this country or in our various hometowns*". Similarly, Gifty maintains that "*Culture relates to our norms, traditions, and the likes among people in a wider country or ethnic groups; or even work culture*". It is clear that the respondents understand what culture is and the existence of national culture and sub-cultures. It was necessary to know what culture meant to them as it would be the basis for answering subsequent questions.

The study ascertained that work-life balance management is not an easy thing to do in Ghana though possible. The study found that the Ghanaian culture and therefore the culture with which several organizations in Ghana operate make the ideology of work-life balance for females very difficult. There was a general consensus among the respondents. Suzan answers thus "*very difficult*" when asked how work-life balance was to her as a Ghanaian married working-class female.

It was evident that the lack of flexible working arrangements and the exploitative nature of some Ghanaian employers, especially private ones, have contributed to worsening effective work-life balance among women.

About 60% of the respondents held that the Ghanaian corporate working environment did not have flexible working hours that allow women to sometimes schedule work shifts that favour them (Aryeetey et al., 2012). The work culture in the corporate world in Ghana is that individuals work from 8:00 am to 5:00 pm; the work schedules are rigid. Therefore, people and in this case married females do not have the chance to select work schedules that suit their needs. For instance, a woman may need to attend to some critical childcare duties during the daytime on a particular day. By so doing, she could opt for another shift within that day that suits her. Gifty, forty-nine (49) years old, who works as an underwriter in a government-owned insurance firm, denotes "*Our work schedules are kind of rigid. There are no even shifts whereby you can sometimes lobby for a particular shift because you need to attend to something critical*". To buttress the preceding notion, Linda asserts "*Our situation is like we have rigid schedules everywhere, especially at work. Yes! The work timing is not flexible for us. It is just one. No variety you can pick from to ease things up for you*". Also, in modern times, emerging flexible work schedules have emerged. For example, due to technological advancement, some employees are able to work from home. This changing trend has, however, failed to be effective or yet to be effective in Ghana (Ayeerty et al., 2012). A reason for this could be that the Ghanaian culture is highly risk avoiding (see Hofstede, 1984). Hence, subscribing to new trends such as these could take a very long time. The inculcation of these modern working practices would be beneficial to Ghanaian females and support them balance their work lives and personal lives. This ideology is expressed by Cindy, a 36-year-old accounts clerk in an automobile company:

> In this country, we have to be physically present at the workplace to show we are working. But times are changing elsewhere. People are beginning to work from home and it doesn't spoil anything. But we are different, still depending on same working methods which make it difficult for women……I know men also have their personal stuff to do though, but it is always worse for the married women.

Again, 46.7% of the respondents indicate that one's ability to balance her working life and personal life is challenging considering that several of the organizations in Ghana, especially the privately held ones, exploit their workers. A similar view was expressed in previous sections as the cause of role conflicts. It is therefore not surprising that it arises in this section as a bane to the efforts married females make to balance their work and personal lives. One factor that has encouraged such practices of most privately-owned entities is the culture of not complaining because "half a loaf is better than none". The Ghanaian would rather work under exploitative conditions than be without work. Also, the Ghanaian national culture which does not encourage people to complain or stand up for better treatment has been a contributing factor. Ranking low on long-term orientation as a dimension of culture (Hofstede, n.d.), the Ghanaian culture focuses more on the present and past than the future. Hence, employees in bad situations resolve to making do with what they have than considering the future effects of their present situation. Somehow, the ideology of the existence of a supreme being that would later deal with the people that treat others bad is also lingering. With the belief that the employers who mistreat employees would "reap what they sow", most Ghanaians would rather not complain or demand a better treatment. These acts have made it possible for some private businesses to hire people and flaunt the Ghanaian labour laws that seek to aid females to manage their work and personal lives like maternity leave and annual leave. If these situations are not curbed and if the right authorities do not ensure that the labour laws of the country are adhered to, it would soon become a Ghanaian culture for one to work a whole year without an annual leave, or to be delivered of a child without enjoying the compulsory three (3)-month paid leave since the private sector dominates the economy. In view of these, Suzan mentions:

> I had worked with a private firm before getting this my current job. It was hell for me. Can you imagine I had no annual leave? Eiiiiiiiii. What broke the camel's back was that I was due for delivery and my supervisors wanted me to return to work after two weeks of delivery. So, after I delivered, I spent time to nurse my baby and forget of them. That was like in 2013.

Muniratu echoes the views of Suzan by saying "*I know people, I mean women who work without annual leave. No rest, nothing. Always on the run*".

Another way employers exploit employees in Ghana is overburdening them with tasks and extending the working hours beyond the normal 8:00am to 5:00 pm working time. Some employers, especially privately-owned firms, demand that their employees work more than eight (8) hours a day (Asiedu-Appiah et al., 2016). Aside this, some are still required to show up at work during weekends. This is so stressful and makes it difficult for women to achieve work-life balance. Adelaide, a thirty-three (33)-year-old accountant in privately-owned spa avers "*My work makes it difficult for me to balance both duties well. My work starts as early as 7:30am and I can never close before 8:00pm. Meanwhile, I have three kids, boys. But I need to work*".

The researcher again probed further why women picked up such exploitative jobs or continued to work there and why they did not fight for what was right. The respondents revealed that the increasing unemployment in Ghana does not give one the luxury to quit a job you have been fortunate to secure. If one left such a job, there are a thousand people who will be willing to fill that post. Hence, the employers feel they do not lose in anyway. The respondents also failed to request for the right thing to be done for fear of being laid off and also for the belief that the employers will one day pay for every wrong done. Adelaide says "*well, I haven't complained because one, I need to keep this job, and two, even if I leave another person will take it so the right thing will never be done*". Muniratu also states "*Where are you going to if you leave? You may have to still spend years looking for one work. But what goes around comes around. 'e go beee'* (it shall be well) *one day*".

It is therefore evident that the Ghanaian culture makes work-life balance management very difficult for married females who are in paid employment.

Ghanaian Women and Work-Life Balance Management

It was imperative to ascertain how Ghanaian working-class married females managed their working lives and personal lives. This helps to understand the role of informal institutions (culture) in work-life management of women in the study context. Three emerging sub themes emerged under this discussion. They are: getting family support, getting external help, and proper planning.

To begin with, 53.3% of the respondents affirm that with support from family, they are making progress when it comes to work-life balance (Obimpeh, 2018). Over the years, married females in the Ghanaian context have relied on family members for support when it comes to managing their duties at home. This has been made possible because of the reverence for the extended family system as Ghana ranks high on collectivism (Hofstede, n.d.). Thus, most people have large families and are able to draw support from them. The situation is even better for married females; they have their own families to rely on, as well as that of their husbands. Some married women therefore make arrangements for some family members to stay with them in order to help them out with home duties. The thoughts of Susan reflect this as she professes:

> To keep off all the stress of my work life and personal one, I depend on family for support. Like when I gave birth, my mom, ...well not my real mom but my aunty who brought me up......came to help me out for like two months. She was really helpful. After she left, I brought my husband's niece to stay with me. Now, with her presence, I stay peaceful at work knowing that when my children close form school, there is an older person at home to take care of home till I get back.

Ayorkor, thirty-three (33) years old, who works with a private oil and gas firm, adds that "*I get support from my family. Sometimes when work is taking me out of town, I take my kids to my sister. She has been of great support*".

However, this act is fast becoming a difficult thing to do as it is not easy living with extended family members, especially younger ones due to family interferences. Family support also comes from spouses. In recent times, a lot of husbands are beginning to have a different perspective on how they were raised. They are beginning to see household chores as a duty for all. They therefore participate in undertaking some of these duties to relieve wives of some of them. This is depicted in the assertions of Adelaide: "*My husband helps at home sometimes. By the time I get home, he feeds the kids and supervise their bathing. I then do the remaining chores*". This comment suggests that even with the involvement of the men, there are still duties to be carried out by wives as it appears the men cannot or do not do it all.

Further, 40% of the participants also depend on getting help away from the family. Some hire house-helps to carry out some home or family duties on their behalf (Obimpeh, 2018). As a result, there has been an upspring of businesses that train house-helps and nannies and outsource them to homes who seek these services. These house-helps mostly undertake the household chores so that their employers can concentrate on work duties. Linked to the help rendered by family members, house-helps are usually home to attend to the children of the employers whilst they are away at work. This enhances full concentration at work knowing that one's dependents are safe at home. To this, Karen states "*I have hired a house-help. I have a son of three years. I can't leave work to take him from school. I don't also like him hanging around at school till after 5:00pm. So, the help does that*". This is echoed by Senam when she says:

> Over the years, I have depended on house-helps. But that one too is another issue on its own as finding a good one is a challenge. That is why some mothers keep changing them every now and then. Others think you don't have character, but it is not so. Now, I have resorted to getting them from agencies, so that our relationship become strictly formal.

Lastly, 20% of the respondents indicate that balancing work and personal life is being made possible by proper planning. These respondents believe that if one is able to plan her activities well, roles conflict will reduce and hence, work-life balance will be achieved. However, it is not just about planning, but also being disciplined enough to go by the plans made. Lamisi who holds this view utters:

> Like I said earlier on, it is mostly about planning and sticking to it. I for one, I plan what I am to do at each hour of the day. I plan I am cooking at 6:00 pm and going to bed by 9:00pm and that is that. No matter the movie they are showing on TV, I will never watch but go to bed so that I can wake up at the planned time the next day to begin my day.

From the above discourse, it is apparent that several married working-class females in Ghana depend on the help of either family or non-family. The act of receiving this help is rooted in the Ghanaian culture where large extended families are considered as one and people within families are ready to offer support to one another (collectivism). It is based on these strong family ties that the idea of people from different families servicing others in the capacity of house-helps emerged. Traditionally, house-helps were not paid. Their hosts only ensured they catered for their current and future needs. In recent times, however, the phenomenon that is rooted in culture and traditions has been commercialized due to the rising need for females to have a balanced working and family life.

Discussion of Findings

This chapter sought to explore how married working-class females in Ghana manage their work life and personal life in view of the prevailing cultural issues in Ghana. Focusing on fifteen (15) married women who worked in corporate organizations, some relevant findings emerged. Basing on thematic textual analysis (TTA), meanings were deduced from the interviews with the respondents. At the end of the analysis of the collected data, the study finds that the Ghanaian culture and therefore informal institutions have been a fertile ground for role conflicts among married working females in Ghana. The position of women in society as caretakers of the home and at the same time the expectation of society that women contribute economically to the well-being of families placed extra burdens and duties on them. Fulfilling all these duties is stressful as duties of the home keep obstructing that of the workplace and vice versa. Also, Ghanaians in general, rooted in culture and traditions, are not confrontational and do not protest when being exploited at the workplace. This has given several operators of private enterprises the chance to place extra demands on employees, knowing that they will not be confronted nor taken on. These actions have made role conflicts common among females in Ghana. It can thence be said in short that culture is a root cause of role conflicts. This finding echoes the findings of Edwards and Oteng (2019) which opine that one of the causes of role conflicts among females in Ghana is culture, which breeds gendered assumptions and societal expectations. However, this current study moves forward to indicate how culture causes role conflicts among women; this Edwards and Oteng (2019) do not present.

Further, married Ghanaian females find work-life balance difficult to attain. This confirms the findings of Darko-Asumadu et al. (2018). This is because of the lack of flexible working arrangement as Aryeetey et al.

(2012) find and the exploitative nature of some organizations, especially privately-owned ones. The work schedule in corporate Ghana is rigid and that limits females in fixing work schedules that suit their needs. Further, the nature of work in the Ghanaian private sector especially is mostly exploitative which makes it extra difficult for married females to have a balanced working and personal life. The issue of having to work extra hours and denial of annual and maternity leave depict the exploitative nature of such jobs. This features in the works of Asiedu-Appiah et al. (2016). The Ghanaian labour laws require that all employees receive paid annual leave and maternity leave (GIPC, n.d.). However, these rules are not adhered to by several enterprises. These issues have so far been a bane to effective work-life balance of married women in Ghana.

Again, the study reveals that married Ghanaian females work towards having a balanced work and family life by gaining support from others as well as effective planning. The former corroborates Obimpeh (2018). In the Ghanaian cultural setting, the extended family system has always been a system of support. The veneration for the extended family system has offered females the opportunity to have people to rely on in times where work and family roles become overwhelming. Women have therefore used this support system to help reduce the overwhelming duties that are expected of them. Aside this, support is also obtained from hiring the services of house-helps and nannies, creating a new and booming business sector. The ideology of house-help which finds itself in the Ghanaian traditions has witnessed commercialization in the effort of women to achieve a balanced working and family life balance.

From the above discussions of the findings of the research, it is shown that in relation to work-life balance management of married women in Ghana, culture is seen to be playing a tripartite role—that is, culture as a breeding grounds for role conflicts, culture as a bane to work-life balance, and culture as a tool for mitigating the effects of work-life balance. This study thus terms this scenario as the "tripartite role of culture in work-life balance of women".

Conclusions, Implications, and Future Research

Work has become part of life and culture. Recent decades have witnessed a surge in the participation of women in paid employment. Despite the increasing numbers of this participation, studies that explore the role of culture in the work-life border management of females are scant, necessitating this study. This study hence explores the work-life balance of married working-class females in the Ghanaian cultural context through the lens of the institutional theory. The study focused on married females due to the assertions of scholars like Darko-Asumadu et al. (2018) that work-life balance is difficult for married females than all others. A qualitative research methodology was adopted since the phenomenon has been underexplored in the Ghanaian context. Specifically, the interpretivist and phenomenologist research approaches were used to examine the research issue from the lived experiences of the study participants.

Basing on thematic contextual analysis from in-depth interviews with fifteen (15) married females, the study finds that the Ghanaian culture has largely contributed to role conflicts in the lives of married females. The study also reveals that work-life balance management is challenging for married working-class females in the study context as a result of the lack of flexible work schedules and the exploitative nature of some employers. Females in the corporate environment in Ghana make efforts to balance their work and personal lives through gaining support from family, hiring the services of non-family, and effective planning. The study thus concludes that culture has a tripartite role on the work-life balance of married females in Ghana. The study contributes new knowledge to the research phenomenon of work-life border management of married females.

The findings of this study have some policy implications. Firstly, the findings of the study are a wake-up call for authorities to ensure that the Ghanaian labour laws are adhered to irrespective of the firm involved: whether privately-owned or government-owned. Annual leave, maternity leave, and uninterrupted time of one hour each working period for nursing mothers to nurse their babies as stipulated by the Labour Act 2003 should be strictly implemented. The adherence of these laws would to a larger extent aid females to have a better working and personal/family life. Secondly, collective agreements could be reached and firms, especially the larger ones, provide conducive places where nursing mothers could nurse their children within the one-hour nursing break they are entitled to during the day. This study is, however, limited. In view of the methodological framework of the study, generalizing the findings to Africa, developing countries, or Ghana is unachievable. There is therefore the need for a study of such nature that can permit generalizability. As such, the study recommends that future research works can adopt quantitative research methods to make generalizability possible.

References

Abraham, A. Y., Ohemeng, F. N. A., & Ohemeng, W. (2017). Female labour force participation: Evidence from Ghana. *International Journal of Social Economics, 44*(11), 1489–1505.

Adisa, T. A., Mordi, C., & Osabutey, E. L. (2017). Exploring the implications of the influence of organisational culture on work-life balance practices. *Personnel Review, 46*(3), 454–473.

Adom, K., & Anambane, G. (2019). Understanding the role of culture and gender stereotypes in women entrepreneurship through the lens of the stereotype threat theory. *Journal of Entrepreneurship in Emerging Economies, 12*(1), 100–124.

Adom, K., Asare-Yeboa, I. T., Quaye, D. M., & Ampomah, A. O. (2018). A critical assessment of work and family life of female entrepreneurs in Sub-Saharan Africa. *Journal of Small Business and Enterprise Development, 25*(3).

Agarwal, S., & Lenka, U. (2015). Study on work-life balance of women entrepreneurs–review and research agenda. *Industrial and Commercial Training, 47*(7), 356–362.

Ahmed, J., Saleem, N., & Kaneez, F. (2019). Factors influencing work life balance of women entrepreneurs: A case of Quetta (Pakistan). *Dialogue (1819–6462), 14*(3).

Ahmed, S. F., & Carrim, N. M. (2016). Indian husbands' support of their wives' upward mobility in corporate South Africa: Wives' perspectives. *SA Journal of Industrial Psychology, 42*(1), 1–13.

Anambane, G. (2017). *Culture and women entrepreneurship: A case study of Nabdam District* (Doctoral dissertation, University of Ghana).

Anambane, G., & Adom, K. (2018). Assessing the role of culture in female entrepreneurship in contemporary sub-Saharan society: Insights from The Nabdam District of Ghana. *Journal of Developmental Entrepreneurship, 23*(03), 1850017.

Aryee, S. (2005). The work-family interface in urban Sub-Saharan Africa: A theoretical analysis. *Work and family: An international research perspective*, 261–286.

Aryeetey, M., Yeboah, F. Y., & Sanda, M. A. (2012). Learning towards enabling work-family life balance for female professionals in Ghanaian organizations. *Business and Management Quarterly Review, 2*(4), 1–13.

Asiedu-Appiah, F., Dufie-Marfo, I., & Frempong, E. (2016). Work-Life Balance as a tool for stress management in selected banking institutions in Ghana. *Global Advanced Research Journal of Management and Business Studies, 2*(5), 291–311.

Asongu, S., & Odhiambo, N. (2019). Inequality and the economic participation of women in sub-Saharan Africa. *African Journal of Economic and Management Studies, 11*(2).

Barber, W., & Badre, A. (1998, June). Culturability: The merging of culture and usability. *Proceedings of the 4th Conference on Human Factors and the Web, 7*(4), 1–10.

Bay, E. G. (2019). *Women and work in Africa*. London: Routledge.

Beugelsdijk, S., & Maseland, R. (2010). *Culture in economics: History, methodological reflections and contemporary applications*. Cambridge: Cambridge University Press.

Biggs, A., & Brough, P. (2005). Investigating the moderating influences of gender upon role salience and work-family conflict. *Equal Opportunities International, 24*(5), 30–41.

Bobbitt-Zeher, D. (2011). Gender discrimination at work: Connecting gender stereotypes, institutional policies, and gender composition of workplace. *Gender & Society, 25*(6), 764–786.

Boeije, H. (2005). *Analysing in qualitative research*. The Hague, The Netherlands: Boom Lemma.

Bonchek, M. S., & Shepsle, K. A. (1996). *Analyzing politics: Rationality, behavior and institutions*. New York: W. W. Norton.

Braidford, P., Stone, I., & Tesfaye, B. (2013). Gender, disadvantage and enterprise support–lessons from women's business centres in North America and Europe. *Journal of Small Business and Enterprise Development, 20*(1).

Braun, V., & Clarke, V. (2006). Using thematic analysis in psychology. *Qualitative research in psychology, 3*(2), 77–101.

Bryman, A., & Becker, S. (2012). *Qualitative research.* In S. Becker, A. Bryman, & H. Ferguson (Eds.), Understanding research for social policy and social work: Themes, methods and approaches (2nd ed., pp. 274–278). Understanding Welfare: Social Issues, Policy and Practice Series. Bristol: Policy Press.

Buttner, E. H., & Moore, D. P. (1997). Women's organizational exodus to entrepreneurship: Self-reported motivations and correlates with success. *Journal of Small Business Management, 35,* 34–46.

Carrim, N. (2017). Muslim identity in corporate South Africa: A reflexive approach. In J. Mahadevan & M. Claude-Hélène (Eds.), *Muslim minorities, workplace diversity and reflexive HRM* (pp. 77–94). Abingdon: Routledge.

Cassell, C., Bishop, V., Symon, G., Johnson, P., & Buehring, A. (2009). Learning to be a qualitative management researcher. *Management Learning, 40*(5), 513–533.

Chandra, V. (2012). Work–life balance: Eastern and western perspectives. *The International Journal of Human Resource Management, 23*(5), 1040–1056.

Ciao, B. (2011). Management studies through qualitative analyses: Epistemological justification, verification of originality, and efforts of conceptualization. *GSTF Business Review (GBR), 1*(1), 106.

Clark, G. (1999). Mothering, work, and gender in urban Asante ideology and practice. *American Anthropologist, 101*(4), 717–729.

Clark, S. C. (2000). Work/family border theory: A new theory of work/family balance. *Human Relations, 53,* 747–770.

Clemens, E. S., & Cook, J. M. (1999). Politics and institutionalism: Explaining durability and change. *Annual Review of Sociology, 25*(1), 441–466.

Clutterbuck, D. (2003). *Managing work-life balance: A guide for HR in achieving organisational and individual change.* London: CIPD Publishing.

Corbin, J., & Strauss, A. (2014). *Basics of qualitative research: Techniques and procedures for developing grounded theory.* Thousand Oaks: Sage.

Craig, C. S., & Douglas, S. P. (2005). *International marketing research.* Chichester: Wiley.

Creswell, J. W. (2008). *Research design, qualitative and mixed methods approaches.* Thousand Oaks, CA: Sage.

Cuéllar-Molina, D., García-Cabrera, A. M., & Lucia-Casademunt, A. M. (2018). Is the institutional environment a challenge for the well-being of female managers in Europe? The mediating effect of work-life balance and role clarity practices in the workplace. *International Journal of Environmental Research and Public Health, 15*(9), 1813.

Darko-Asumadu, D. A., Sika-Bright, S., & Osei-Tutu, B. (2018). The influence of work-life balance on employees' commitment among bankers in Accra, Ghana. *African Journal of Social Work, 8*(1), 47–55.

Duman, L., Bedük, A., Köylüoğlu, A. S., & Ay, K. (2015). Entrepreneurship culture at SMEs: A case study in Konya. *Procedia-Social and Behavioral Sciences, 207,* 492–501.

Edwards, A. K., & Oteng, R. (2019). Attaining work-life balance as in modeling the way among female teachers in Ghana. *International Journal of Education Policy and Leadership, 15*(7).

Fassinger, R. E. (2001). Diversity at work: Research issues in vocational development. *The intersection of race, class, and gender in multicultural counseling,* 267–288.

Feldman, D. C., & Bolino, M. C. (2000). Career Patterns of the Self-Employed: Career Motivations and Career Outcomes. *Journal of Small Business Management, 38*(3), 53–68.

Felstead, A., Gallie, D., & Green, F. (2002). *Work skills in Britain 1986–2001.* Nottingham: DfES Publications.

Fenrich, J., & Higgins, T. E. (2001). Promise unfulfilled: Law, culture, and women's inheritance rights in Ghana. *Fordham International Law Journal, 25,* 259.

Frempong, F. (2019). Gender and Ethical conduct of hotel employees in Kumasi Metropolis, Ghana. *Journal of Business Ethics, 154*(3), 721–731.

Gill, J., & Johnson, P. (2010). *Research methods for managers.* London: Sage.

Glaser, B., & Strauss, A. (1967). *The discovery of grounded theory* (pp. 1–19). London: Weidenfield & Nicolson.

Glauber, R., & Day, M. D. (2018). Gender, spousal caregiving, and depression: Does paid work matter? *Journal of Marriage and Family, 80*(2), 537–554.

Goel, A. (2017). Handling work-family conflicts: Future agenda. *International Journal of Manpower, 38*(8), 1058–1064.

Greenhaus, J. H., Collins, K. M., & Shaw, J. D. (2003). The relation between work–family balance and quality of life. *Journal of Vocational Behavior, 63*(3), 510–531.

Guba, E. G., & Lincoln, Y. S. (1994). Competing paradigms in qualitative research. *Handbook of Qualitative Research, 2*(163–194), 105.

Haar, J. M., & O'Driscoll, M. P. (2005). Exploring gender differences in employee attitudes towards work-family practices and use of work-family practices. *Equal Opportunities International.*

Hegewisch, A., Liepmann, H., Hayes, J., & Hartmann, H. (2010). Separate and not equal? Gender segregation in the labor market and the gender wage gap. *IWPR Briefing Paper, 377,* 1–16.
Hofstede, G. (1980). Motivation, leadership, and organization: Do American theories apply abroad? *Organizational Dynamics, 9*(1), 42–63.
Hofstede, G. (1984). Cultural dimensions in management and planning. *Asia Pacific journal of management, 1*(2), 81–99.
Hofstede, G. J. (2015). Culture's causes: The next challenge. *Cross Cultural Management, 22*(4), 545–569.
Hundera, M. B., Duijsters, G. M., & Naudé, W. A. (2019). How do female entrepreneurs experience and cope with role conflict in Sub-Saharan Africa: Case study from Ethiopia. *International Journal of Entrepreneurship and Small Business, 38*(1–2), 177–209.
Ituma, A., Simpson, R., Ovadje, F., Cornelius, N., & Mordi, C. (2011). Four domains of careers success: How managers in Nigeria evaluate career outcomes. *International Journal of Human Resource Management, 22*(17), 3638–3660.
James-Hawkins, L., Qutteina, Y., & Yount, K. M. (2017). The patriarchal bargain in a context of rapid changes to normative gender roles: Young Arab women's role conflict in Qatar. *Sex Roles, 77*(3–4), 155–168.
Jepperson, R. (1991). Institutions, institutional effects, and institutionalism. *The new institutionalism in organizational analysis*, 143–163.
Karatepe, O. M. (2010). The effect of positive and negative work-family interaction on exhaustion. *International Journal of Contemporary Hospitality Management, 22*(6), 836–856.
Kluckhohn, C. (1951). *The study of culture. The policy sciences* (pp. 86–101). Stanford: Stanford University Press.
Kostova, T., & Roth, K. (2002). Adoption of an organizational practice by subsidiaries of multinational corporations: Institutional and relational effects. *Academy of Management Journal, 45*(1), 215–233.
Kroeber, A. L., & Parsons, T. (1958). The concepts of culture and of social system. *American Sociological Review, 23*(5), 582–583.
Lewis, S., Gambles, R., & Rapoport, R. (2007). The constraints of a 'work–life balance' approach: An international perspective. *The International Journal of Human Resource Management, 18*(3), 360–373.
Markwei, U., Kubi, M., Quao, B., & Attiogbe, E. J. (2019). Work-family balance of female parliamentarians in Ghana. *Gender in Management: An International Journal, 34*(1), 1754–2413.

Mayrhofer, W., Iellatchitch, A., Meyer, M., Steyrer, J., Schiffinger, M., & Strunk, G. (2004). Going beyond the individual: Some potential contributions from a career field and habitus perspective for global career research and practice. *Journal of Management Development, 23*(9), 870–884.
Meyer, J. W., & Rowan, B. (1991). Institutionalized organizations: Formal structure as myth and ceremony (Chap. 2). *The New Institutionalism in Organizational Analysis*, 41–62.
Munn, S. L., & Chaudhuri, S. (2016). Work–life balance: A cross-cultural review of dual-earner couples in India and the United States. *Advances in Developing Human Resources, 18*(1), 54–68.
Mushfiqur, R., Mordi, C., Oruh, E. S., Nwagbara, U., Mordi, T., & Turner, I. M. (2018). The impacts of work-life-balance (WLB) challenges on social sustainability. *Employee Relations, 40*(5), 868–888.
Nambisan, S., & Baron, R. A. (2019). On the costs of digital entrepreneurship: Role conflict, stress, and venture performance in digital platform-based ecosystems. *Journal of Business Research.*
North, D. C. (1990). A transaction cost theory of politics. *Journal of Theoretical Politics, 2*(4), 355–367.
Obimpeh, M. O. (2018). *Work-life balance among female administrators in public universities in Ghana* (Doctoral dissertation, University of Ghana).
Perrons, D. (2003). The new economy and the work–life balance: Conceptual explorations and a case study of new media. *Gender, Work & Organization, 10*(1), 65–93.
Polit, D. F., & Beck, C. T. (2004). *Nursing research: Principles and methods.* Philadelphia: Lippincott Williams & Wilkins.
Posig, M., & Kickul, J. (2004). Work-role expectations and work family conflict: Gender differences in emotional exhaustion. *Women in Management Review, 19*(7).
Prescott, J., & Bogg, J. (2011). Segregation in a male-dominated industry: Women working in the computer games industry. *International Journal of Gender, Science and Technology, 3*(1), 205–227.
Qu, S. Q., & Dumay, J. (2011). The qualitative research interview. *Qualitative Research in Accounting & Management, 8*(3), 238–264.
Robson, C. (2002). *Real world research.* Oxford: Blackwell.
Roy, W. G. (1997). *Socializing capital. The rise of the large industrial corporation in America.* Princeton, NJ: Princeton University Press.
Salm, S. J., & Falola, T. (2002). *Culture and customs of Ghana.* Westport, CT: Greenwood Publishing Group.

Sarpong, S. (2019). The challenges of job hunting and recruitment in Ghana: Opportunity for improvement. *Global Business and Organizational Excellence, 38*(3), 35–42.

Scott, D. H. (2007). *Strengthening the governance and performance of state-owned financial institutions.* The World Bank.

Sirgy, M. J., & Lee, D. J. (2016). Work-life balance: A quality-of-life model. *Applied Research in Quality of Life, 11*(4), 1059–1082.

Stavrou, E., & Ierodiakonou, C. (2018). Expanding the work–life balance discourse to LGBT employees: Proposed research framework and organizational responses. *Human Resource Management, 57*(6), 1355–1370.

Steers, R. M., & Sánchez-Runde, C. J. (2017). Culture, motivation, and work behavior. *The Blackwell Handbook of Cross-Cultural Management*, 190–216.

Straub, C. (2007). A comparative analysis of the use of work-life balance practices in Europe. *Gender in Management, 22*(4), 289.

Tolhurst, R., & Nyonator, F. K. (2006). Looking within the household: Gender roles and responses to malaria in Ghana. *Transactions of the Royal Society of Tropical Medicine and Hygiene, 100*(4), 321–326.

Tylor, E. B. (1871). *Primitive culture: Researches into the development of mythology, philosophy, religion, art, and custom* (Vol. 2). J. Murray.

Usunier, J. C., Lee, J. A., & Lee, J. (2005). *Marketing across cultures.* New Delhi: Pearson Education.

Waterhouse, P., Hill, A. G., & Hinde, A. (2017). Combining work and child care: The experiences of mothers in Accra, Ghana. *Development Southern Africa, 34*(6), 771–786.

Webb, J. W., Ireland, R. D., & Ketchen, D. J., Jr. (2014). Toward a greater understanding of entrepreneurship and strategy in the informal economy. *Strategic Entrepreneurship Journal, 8*(1), 1–15.

White, L., & Rogers, S. J. (2000). Economic circumstances and family outcomes: A review of the 1990s. *Journal of Marriage and Family, 62*(4), 1035–1051.

Woodside, A. G., Bernal, P. M., & Coduras, A. (2016). The general theory of culture, entrepreneurship, innovation, and quality-of-life: Comparing nurturing versus thwarting enterprise start-ups in BRIC, Denmark, Germany, and the United States. *Industrial Marketing Management, 53,* 136–159.

Yamaguchi, S. (2018). *Effects of parental leave policies on female career and fertility choices.* Available at SSRN 2498212.

Yeganeh, H. (2013). A compound index of cultural dimensions: Implications and applications. *International Journal of Organizational Analysis., 21*(1), 53–65.

4

Work-Life Balance in Kenya: A Systematic Review of Literature

Gladys Muasya and Daniel Nzengya

Introduction

Background to the Study

Worldwide, work-life balance has continued to gain prominence as a topical issue today. This has been attributed to the changing nature of the working landscape that most families have found themselves in. There is an increase in dual-career families implying that mothers are taking full-time demanding jobs (Abele & Volmer, 2011). The cost of living in most sub-Saharan Africa towns and cities is among the highest in the world (Adegoke, 2018). Also, the region has continued to experience one of the world's highest trends in rural-urban migration, attributed to hardships in the rural livelihoods due to prevalent droughts and climate change (Nickanor, Crush & Pendleton, 2016). Urban life and associated economic costs exert strain on traditional childcare systems, with

G. Muasya (✉) · D. Nzengya
St. Paul's University, Limuru 00217 Private Bag, Kenya

T. A. Adisa and G. Gbadamosi (eds.), *Work-Life Interface*,
https://doi.org/10.1007/978-3-030-66648-4_4

many families switching to the market for childcare services (Mokomane, 2014). Compared to life in the rural areas, the schedules in both informal urban work and formal employment tend to be overwhelmingly quite demanding and intense. A recently completed research by one of the authors has examined issues related to parenting guilt due to less time devoted to parenting children (Muasya, in press). There is a growing body of scholars advocating for work-life balance.

Kenya's economy has not been spared by the rising work-life balance challenges confronting employees and employers. There is increasing advocacy that organizations consider the work-life balance (WLB) issues encountered by their employees. Work-life balance is defined as "the individual perception that works and non-work activities are compatible and promote growth in accordance with an individual's current life priorities" (Kalliath & Brough, 2008, p. 326). Another closely related term is the work-life conflict which is defined as, "the degree to which participation in the non-work or life role is made more difficult by participation in the work role (work-to-life conflict) and the degree to which participation in the work role is made more difficult by participation in the non-work or life role (life-to-work conflict)" (Michel, Clark, & May, 2013, p. 59). Several studies have looked at the different aspects of WLB issues in Kenya such as WLB on employee performance (Mwangi, Boinett, Tumwet, & Bowen, 2016), turnover (Chemirmir, Musebe, & Nassimua, 2018), work-life balance practices (Muindi, Nzulwa, & Muinde Anne, 2015), and childcare centres (Clark, De Almada, Kabiru, Muthuri, & Wanjohi, 2018). However, no study has sought to systematically review the state of WLB research in Kenya and give perspectives and gaps in the Kenyan literature. This necessitated this study. This chapter is organized as follows: first, it gives a historical background to the history of work-life balance in Kenya. Second, the methodology; third the results; fourth, the discussion; and finally, a conclusion.

Historical Background of Work-Life Balance in Kenya

Kenya was colonized by Britain and attained her independence in 1963. Before independence, many of the workers were absorbed in the blue economy (artisans) and worked in white farms. Most of the people who worked in towns or white farms left their families in the village. The education system of the colonial government aimed to equip the Africans with artisan skills and religious skills, while managerial leadership was for the Europeans (Bagonko 1992; Otiende, Wamahiu, & Karuga, 1992). After independence, the Kenyan government sought to develop a worker force to fill the positions originally occupied by the white managers (Bagonko, 1992; Godia, 1987). Efforts to fill up vacant positions targeted males predominantly positions within the public sector. Many of these government offices were in urban centres. This implies that immediately after independence many of the formal workers were men. Consequently, the working-class experienced none or very marginal forms of work-balance challenges because their spouses were largely still in the rural homes managing and taking care of the family. During the 1970s, there was increased advocacy of girl-child education to increase women's participation in the economy. This resulted in increased enrolment of women in schools, thus more women joining the formal sector. By 2009, there were 83,025 females (42%) and 115,094 males (58%) at the university level (Kenya Bureau of Statistics, 2009). Most of these graduates seek employment in the formal sector mostly found in urban settings. Consequently, more women now work far from home and away from their extended families.

In Kenya, formal employment in the public and private sector is predominantly office-related work. This sector mirrors the Western models of organizing work schedules, 8 am–5 pm. The informal sector may allow a level of flexibility in working hours and schedules. Most low-income workers and artisan-related workers are found in the informal sector. In 2016, the percentage of the informal sector workers were 83% (Institute of Economic Affairs, 2016). A high percentage of women work in the informal sector—92.8% of women and 74.8% of men work in the informal sector (Donovan & Zhu, 2020). In the informal sector, women may go with their children to work. Thus, it is not a surprise to see women selling their wares in the market along with their young children.

The first seminal work in work-life balance in Kenya and sub-Saharan Africa started with the works of scholars such as Poelmans, O'Driscoll, and Behan (2005) who questioned whether the work-life balance studies carried in the Western contexts had validity to be generalized in other cultures and contexts where cultures differ. One scholar who followed this line of argument is Aryee (2005), who argued that since most sub-Saharan countries are collectivistic in nature, they may have different theorizing of what family and work means compared to that in the West. According to Aryee, in the West, working middle-class women with young children could be regarded as working for selfish reasons. Women, especially from the middle class who sought work outside their homes faced the criticism of sacrificing the family for personal gains. This discourse has led to the mommy wars between working women and stay-at-home mothers (Williams, 1999). However, Aryee (2005) asserts that in sub-Saharan Africa, work is *for* the family, and this could make it easy for women to seek work outside their homes.

Another seminal work around work and life is that of Mokomane and Chilwane (2014). Their review study of sub-Saharan Africa found that there was a paucity of research on work-life/family balance. Within the same time frame, Strathmore School of Business as cited by Muasya (2014), found that there were very few firms in Kenya which had family-friendly practices. This was against the backdrop of declining extended family support. Due to the high cost of living, many families in the urban tend to stay with fewer extended family members, with the majority of the people in formal employment relying on house-helps (Muasya, 2014). Most workers in towns, especially Nairobi, take long hours to commute to and from work. These workers leave home early and return extremely late due to traffic congestions, implying there must be someone to look after the children when the parents are away. However, not all employees can afford domestic help as they must be paid a minimum salary which many families cannot afford (ILO, 2011: Muasya, 2014).

It is not just women who aspire to experience a balance in their work and life dimensions, increasing scholarly work confirms that men share the same aspirations. Because of the increasing intensification of work, it appears workers spend more time at work, especially those at higher levels of management. The lack of a work-life balance is often cited as one of the disincentives why the majority of women shy away from ascending to high managerial positions in Kenya (Ombati 2003; Wangui, 2012). In addition, there is a concern of poor parenting in Kenya where both parents are absent from their children and children are being raised by nannies. The fathers are absent to mentor their sons as well (Muasya, in press). To respond to the need for work-life balance, after 2014, there has been a surge in the number of studies that focus on work-life balance and related issues in Kenya, necessitating the need for a systematic review of the literature to explore new trends in research and how work-life balance issue have been addressed.

Methodology

Research Design

Design: This is a systematic review of literature which incorporates all types of studies on work-life balance—qualitative and quantitative sources.

Search Method

The team searched for all studies that have been published between 2008 and 2020 using English database found in the library: AJOL, Google Scholar, Sage, Emerald, ISI Web of Science, Wiley Online, and JSTOR and added some sources manually through searching the references to increase the breadth of the papers. The very first work-life balance research in Kenya began around 2008 with the study of Wang, Lawler, Shi, Walumbwa, and Piao (2008) who did a comparative study of work and family-friendly practices among banks in Kenya, India, and China. The team specifically sought work-life balance articles that specifically had Kenya as their focus or included Kenya as one of the study areas. The study used these keywords: work-life balance, work-family balance, work-family conflict, work-life conflict, work-life balance practices, work-family friendly, among others, which the team combined with the word Kenya.

Search Outcome

After narrowing the search and eliminating the irrelevant journals, the team had 65 articles. The team removed: ten duplicates of the same paper; 16 dissertations and theses of masters and Ph.D. work; 15 papers which sparingly discussed work-life balance issues but did not measure any work-life balance related constructs; and four papers that the authors did not focus on Kenya and it remained with 20 articles (see Table 4.1). The team used the literature review matrix to synthesize the papers. The next section is the results section.

Table 4.1 Sector/organizations of studied populations

Sector/Organization	Tally	Percentage
Sub-Saharan general	2	10
Slums	1	5
General: women related	2	10
Institutions of learning: school and colleges	4	20
Banks	4	20
Health sector—e.g. public hospitals, health NGOs	1	5
Power Utility	1	5
Farming—e.g. horticulture farms	2	10
Police force	1	5
Media	1	5
Gig economy	1	5
Total	**20**	**100**

Source Authors 2020

Results

The results section is organized as follows: first, the chapter gives an overview of the nature of journals selected; second, the methodologies and sample sizes used; third, the conceptualization of work-life balance and work-life balance practices; fourth, the conceptualization of work-life balance in the Kenyan media; fifth, work-life balance and job turnover; sixth, work-life balance practices and supervisor support; seventh, work-life balance practices and organizational performance; eighth, work-life balance practices and employee job satisfaction; ninth, work-life balance practices and employee commitment; tenth, family-oriented work-life balance practices; eleventh, work-life balance practices of women in the informal sector; and twelfth, work-life balance practices in the horticultural farms.

The Nature of the Journal Articles Selected

The most studied areas were institutions such as for learning, banks, hospitals, power utility, and police force (see Table 4.1).

Most studies' independent variables were centred on work-life balance practices, choices, or policies. One study focused on supervisor support, two examined the role of domestic help as a strategy from the family side. Five studies focused on the general work-life balance issues such as childcare and drivers of work-family conflict (see Table 4.2).

Table 4.2 Independent variables studied

Category	Tally	%
Work-life balance practices/choices; family-friendly programmes/policies	11	55
Domestic help	2	10
Stressors/work/childcare	5	25
General work-life balance issues	1	5
Supervisor Support	1	5
Total	**20**	**100**

Source Authors 2020

Table 4.3 Dependent variables studied

Category	Tally	%
Turnover, intent to quit, retention	3	15
Theoretical/general papers	4	20
Job performance/organizational performance/job satisfaction	5	25
Work-life/family balance issues Work-family conflict	8	40
Total	**20**	**100**

Source Authors 2020

Most studies' dependent variables focused on the work side of work-life balance, and how work-life balance practices influenced work outcomes: job performance, organizational performance, job satisfaction, how to reduce staff turnover, and general work-life balance issues within the organization. Very few papers focused on the family side, that is, how work affected the family at home (see Table 4.3). Only three studies were from non-business perspective: two from sociology and one from communication, and 17 from the human resource perspective.

Methodologies and Sample Size Used

Most Kenyan studies were cross-sectional studies that used mainly descriptive study designs and self-reported questionnaires with Likert type of questions; to measure the extent to which work-life balance issues were experienced in the organizations. A number of authors triangulated the questionnaires with interviews. The samples were drawn using stratified sampling and census sampling methods. Many of the studies used descriptive statistics, frequency distributions, mean, standard deviation, and correlation. The multivariate analysis was predominantly regression analysis (enter method) to test the regression models/ and, a few studies used chi-square. Very few studies controlled for socio-economic status (SES) or examined the mediating or moderating factors in their analysis. Two studies examined work-life balance issues in sub-Saharan Africa, and only one study (Wang, Lawler, & Shi, 2011) was a comparative study between India, China, and Kenya. Most studies covered one organization, e.g. Kenya Power and Lighting Company, or a sector such as banking. The lack of multi-sectorial studies leads to an organization or sector-specific work-life balance recommendations. Several studies were from students' Masters' dissertations and a few from students' doctoral theses. Few studies used qualitative analyses, and none of the studies sampled used critical analysis. Several theories were used to study work-life balance practices. These are: Abraham Maslow hierarchy of needs, role theory, the theory of work-family enrichment, component theory, job characteristics model, border theory, the spillover theory, and conservation of resources theory, among others. These theories were developed in the Western context; there is a need to develop a work-life balance theory from a Kenyan/ sub-Saharan perspective.

Conceptualization and Operationalization of Work-Life Balance and Work-Life Balance Practices

Many studies were concerned with measures to mitigate work-life balance effects—through work-life balance practices, rather than exploring the antecedents of the work-life balance. Moreover, there was no consensus on the operationalization of WLB balance and WLB practices. Though studies quoted definition of work-life balance to be the ability to have time for family, work, and non-work activities, different authors used different measures for WLB (agreed on the concept but not how it was operationalized).

For instance, the measures for work-life balance practices varied with the study and the organization being studied. For some authors, work-life balance practices included: employee welfare support (health facilities, transport, housing, and recreation facilities), employee dependent support (flexibility, infant, or site services,), employee leave programmes (annual leave, maternal, and sick leave), and flexible working arrangements (part-time, flexitime, job sharing) (Munyiva & Wainaina, 2018). The study by Chemirmir, Musebe, and Nassiuma (2018) conceptualized the WLB practices in flower farms to include a conducive work environment which included: protective clothing, e.g. protection from chemicals.

In another horticulture sector-oriented study (Muindi et al., 2015), the authors incorporated work-life balance practices to do with the place (teleworking), practices relating to the job (orientation, job sharing, work autonomy, protective clothing, training in the use of equipment, performance feedback), and practices related to benefits (staff-leave, day-care facilities, family fun day, low-interest loans, tuition for staff and their children, work canteen, transport to work, employee assistance programmes, and subsidized meals).

Kegoro, Otieno, and Akoyo (2020) study on WLB and performance of national police service in Kenya: operationalized WLB practices as permission to attend family issues, being able to delegate duties to others when the officer was overwhelmed, able to consult counsellors, control on ways to manage leisure, time to relax after work with family, visit family upcountry, use leave days effectively, ways to manage stress, being motivated when assigned duties outside their workplace, and feeling relaxed after completing their leave days. Why is this so? The Kenyan Police force tends to be posted in remote stations away from their home-towns and areas. Furthermore, the police leave their families behind and work in difficult conditions and poor pay. The police force is known of high suicidal cases and one of the cause is work-related stress (Otieno, 2019).

In the health sector, Kinyili (2019) conceptualized work-life balance practices to include: leaves, flexible time and work arrangements, child-care services, mental relaxation programmes, and medical and education schemes for self and family. This implies work-life balance practices were understood to include other human resource benefits that employees expect in an organization. For example, the participants even requested things such as support for children's education, volunteer work, and phased retirement.

Conceptualization of Work-Life Balance in the Kenyan Media

The media is a key player in addressing work-life balance issues that Kenyans face. Muasya (in press) did a study using the framing theory to explore how the media framed and defined the causes and solutions for work-life balance issues. The study focused on two print media: The *Daily Nation* and The *Standard Media.* The media narratives were gendered, with men 22.3% of all the 114 stories. The study period was from 2009 to 2016. In the media, work-life balance was considered a myth or an illusion something difficult for professionals to attain. The causes of work-life balance were: nature of work which had fixed reporting time, employers preference of employees working within the work premises—face time than in remote locations, traffic jams in the big cities, the technology—tethered life that most professional found themselves in, and for women, they were blamed for the desire to "have it all in life"—a successful career and being fully engaged at home. Anne-Marie Slaughter's article, "Why *women can't have it all*" circulated in the *Atlantic* magazine in 2012, fuelled a heated discussion in the local media whether women could have it all.

These authors reported media reframing of work-life balance discourse. While being a stay at home mother is cherished among middle-class women in the West, in Kenya women who chose to stay at home and be full-time mothers were regarded to have wasted their brains. The professional women resisted the notion that good parenting necessarily entailed the quantity of hours parents spent with the children, and instead reframed the idea of good parenting to entail the quality of time mothers spent with their children. The media too seemed to reframe traditional role of women as full-time mothers and wives: that women may always not be at home, so the husbands were expected to step in and make their own food and take care of children when the wives were away at work. The media further seemed to reframe a good husband as someone who assisted in household chores and childcare. The media tended to carry the position of middle-class women and their work-life balance struggles. The media articulated domestic help to be a work-life balance strategy but failed to highlight the work-life balance issues that house-helps encounter. Childcare was framed as an individual family issue and not a societal issue. According to the sample of media stories analysed, the author noted that mothers largely relied on hired house-helps for childcare and house chores, exhibiting limited or no reliance on extended family as hypothesized by Aryee (2005).

Work-Life Balance and Job Turnover

Several studies reviewed hypothesized a relationship between work-life balance and job turnover. To start with, Chemirmir et al. (2018) sought to investigate the role of WLB on employee turnover in flower farms in Kenya. The researchers indeed found that workers experienced work-life balance challenges. Most participants agreed that they were relaxed when they felt stable and secure at their workplace. In addition, more than half of the workers felt relaxed and stable in their lives when their work hours fitted in well with their personal lives. For the participants, their work conditions mattered, and they raised the need for protective clothing as they worked with chemicals which to them was an aspect of a conducive environment. A significant number of workers experienced a conflict between work and family life and felt stressed due to challenges of child-care which affected their performance. Other causes of the disagreement noted included the long daily and working hours, role conflict, and demands of working in a flower farm. Flower firms typically do not offer facilities to work from home due to the nature of their work. The main concerns of the participants were: exposure to chemicals and lack of adequate maternity leave. In this study, the work-life balance had a weak correlation with all the indices of turnover (attribution, resignation, and dismissal). According to the authors, the participants rated themselves as more stable and there was a weak negative correlation between WLB and employee turnover, implying WLB could not be the only factor that determined employee turnover.

The work of Kinyili (2019) explored work-life balance practices and staff retention in public health institutions in Machakos County. The author used mixed research design, with a sample size of 227 healthcare practitioners from 156 public health institutions. The author reported a positive relationship between work-life balance practices and staff retention. Only 7% of turnover could be explained through work-life balance practices. The health sector in Kenya has witnessed a high staff turnover due to many factors including the brain-drain. Most of work practices' scales focused on the work side but not the family side. The work-life balance practices included practices to do with time management, leaves, work benefits such as medical cover, and children's education services. In the public health sector, the critical WLB concerns were related to a lack of childcare facility on-site, flexible work schedules, and time for social and family ties. The health sector offered leaves (maternity, paternity, sick offs, annual leaves, and compassion leaves).

The researcher reported that employees requested for comprehensive medical cover to be allowed to access free medical services, childcare services, maternity leave to be extended to six months to encourage breastfeeding, increase paternity leave, increase in the number of off days, provide flexitime, flex week, time to go for mourning in case they lost a loved one, mental and relaxation programmes. In addition, another study by Muasya (2017) explored the relationship between work-family conflict, support, and intention to quit among female teachers working in public schools. The author sampled 375 female teachers with young children from Nairobi city and three other urban towns. The study reported that there was a higher *intent to quit* among teachers in secondary schools compared to primary schools. Similarly, there was a high intent to quit of teachers in Nairobi city compared to teachers working in smaller towns. The study further reported a positive relationship between work-family conflicts with intent to quit. In addition, the authors reported a statistically insignificant relationship between support from co-workers and work-family conflict the teachers experienced. However, there was a negative relationship between the supervisor's support and intent to quit. The study found that supervisor support did not moderate the relationship between work-family conflict and intent to quit. Kenya is among the countries in the world with high turnover among teachers and high levels of stress following the introduction of free primary education in 2000. The workload for many schoolteachers particularly in public schools is overwhelming. To add on, apart from staff-leave which is a statutory requirement, the Ministry of Education does not provide schoolteachers with other forms of work-life/family support; teachers have to rely largely on individual arrangements between the supervisor and the teacher.

Work-Life Balance Practices, and Supervisor Support

Several studies reviewed contend that the immediate supervisor support is required to enable employees to balance work and life demands. To add on the study of Muasya (2017), already discussed in the preceding section, Karani and Paul (2018) did study on how project supervisors enabled employees to achieve work-life balance in Kenya Power and Lighting Co. a public company. The authors hypothesized on aspects of supervisor support to include technical, conceptual, and interpersonal skills. Karani and Paul conceptualized technical skills to include the technical knowhow, conceptual skills to include strategizing skills, and managerial skills, and lastly interpersonal to include people skills.

The authors noted that despite the company having work-life balance policies, employees still worked long hours more than 16 hours a day. These employees had a backlog of leave days left which they had not consumed, and some of the employees had up to 60% of their salaries from overtime work. This led to low productivity and less time for family. The author found a significant relationship between interpersonal skills and WLB policies, conceptual skills, and WLB policies; however, the authors did not report a significant relationship between technical skills and WLB policies. The authors suggested the need to interrogate whether economic hardships were the motivation behind employees working for long hours. The authors opined that managers need more training in interpersonal and conceptual skills because they were responsible for ensuring compliance with the implementation of organizations' policies aimed to achieve work-life balance. This study shows the presence of work-life balance policies does not imply the employees are using them, thus the need to sensitize the immediate supervisors.

Work-Life Balance Practices and Organizational Performance

Several studies have explored the relationship between work-life balance practices and organizational performance. Interestingly, the Kenyan banking sector is the most studied sector, and employees in the banking sector are perceived to work for long hours. This made the banking sector to be ranked 3/24 (ILO, 2010) among the most affected by work-life imbalance. For instance, Mungania, Waiganjo, and Kihoro (2016) did a study on the influence of wellness programmes on organizational performance, among 43 different registered banks in the Nairobi metropolitan area. Mungania et al. conceptualized wellness to constitute: the need to promote preventive care, train, and educate workers on the importance of good health practices, and have supportive managers who support health-related programmes in the organization.

Mungania and colleagues used a questionnaire that sought ratings on items such as subsidized gymnasium membership fees, subsidized balanced meals at work, regular employee health and counselling programmes, and rest between work sessions. Organizational performance was conceptualized to include customer satisfaction, employee satisfaction, and the company meeting its target standards. The results showed that a small per cent—3.2%—of the variation in the regression model in organizational performance could be attributed to wellness programmes. This study enforces the need for preventive health programmes which could increase employee satisfaction and productivity. This would further reduce the medical costs that employers face. Due to working for long hours, employees in the banking sector would require programmes that enable them to relax. Similarly, Mokaya and Gitari (2012) in their survey study found that recreation services in Utalii College—a hospitality institution—enabled the staff to relax and lower their stress levels, improve concentration, and improve confidence and self-esteem. Recreation services at the workplace have a positive impact on employee performance. The author noted that recreation increased employee commitment, bonding, job satisfaction, customer satisfaction, and productivity.

Work-Life Balance Practices and Employee Job Satisfaction

Besides studies focusing on organizational performance, other studies just focused on employee job satisfaction. Muema, Nzioki, and Kinyili

(2018) sought to find out whether there was a relationship between time-related work-life balance practices and employee job satisfaction among employees in commercial banks in Machakos County. The study conceptualized work-life balance practices relating to time to consist of: flexitime, part-time working arrangements, and job sharing; 134 participants filled a survey. Flexitime was operationalized to include: enough time for family and personal issues, part-time work arrangements for employees on the study, time to relax, among others. Flexible working time would enable the employees to manage their schedules, engage in family activities, and improve their output. The study reported that banks had not adopted part-time work staff arrangements.

Overall, the study found that most of the workers were satisfied with the bank's work-life balance practices. There was a positive correlation between work-life balance practices with employee job satisfaction. Thus, the presence of work-life practices could increase employee job satisfaction.

Work-Life Balance Practices and Employee Commitment

Employee commitment was another organizational aspect studied. Wang et al. (2011) did a comparative study on the effects of perceived availability of childcare and work flexibility family-friendly programmes/policies, and their effects on organizational commitment and work-family conflict. The authors studied 36 domestic banks in four cities in collectivistic countries Nairobi, Kenya (13); New Delhi, India (7); Beijing, China (7); and Bang Kong, Thailand (9). Wang et al. sought to investigate the influence of family-friendly programmes on employee behaviours and attitudes in a developing economy context. In Kenya and Thailand, there was a positive relationship between childcare-related family-friendly programmes and organizational commitment and a negative relationship with work-family conflict.

The authors hypothesized that the perceived importance of childcare programmes and work flexible programmes would moderate the effects of perceived availability of family-friendly programmes (childcare and work flexible programme) with organizational commitment and work-family conflict. The "authors" report found that childcare-related family-friendly policy had a differentiated effect on employees with a different perception of the policy importance. Employees who highly regarded the childcare policy also showed more organizational commitment and lower work-family conflict. This is unlike those who had low regard for the policy which was true for Kenya and Thailand. The study concluded that the more employees perceived that the work environment supported them by providing family-friendly policies, the more they would be committed to the organization, which would further lower their perception of work-family conflict. This study indicates that the importance employees attach to work and family-friendly policies can eventually influence their perception of the level of balance they have between work and non-work life. The next two sections will focus on work-life practices from the family side.

Family-Oriented Work-Life Practices—Family Practices

A few studies have attempted to explore family-based work-life balance practices. Most women in formal employment in Kenya and with young children tend to hire domestic help (Muasya 2014). However, this strategy comes with its own challenges. Muasya and Martin (2016) sought to find the extent to which professional women used domestic workers as a work-life balance strategy and the conflicts that arose among the employer-employee relationships within the home sphere. The authors sought to look at work-life balance issues from an organizational communication perspective. The study focused on professional women working in private and public universities and their domestic workers using both interviews and in-depth interviews. Most of these women sought domestic workers to assist with house chores and childcare.

Most of the work-related conflicts came from the unsatisfying work, integrity concerns of the domestic workers, and outside or interpersonal influence on the working relationship between professional women and their employees. The most common strategy to resolve employer-employee conflicts was terminating their employees' contracts while seeking assistance from third parties to resolve conflicts. The use of dialogue, threats, and reprimands, were moderately used as a conflict resolution strategy. A few employers opted to do nothing, and a handful of employees sought to improve how they supervised domestic tasks. Though professional women use domestic helps, this strategy comes with its own set of challenges, especially in interpersonal communication challenges. This observation agrees with Muasya (2020) where the female teachers cited unreliable domestic help as one of their major stressors.

Work-Life Balance Practices of Women in the Informal Sector

Childcare Centres

A second work-life balance strategy that this study explored is the use of centre-based childcare. Clark et al. (2018) investigated the gendered economic strategies employed and unemployed mothers use to combine work and childcare. The authors focused on childcare centres in a Nairobi slum. Clark et al. used a mixed study design where 1200 women filled a survey and 13 of the women further participated in in-depth interviews. These centres are early learning centres where pre-schoolers can attend at age of 3 years. These centres offer some form of learning at a fee, and they are either subsidized by donor organizations, some are faith-based institutions, and the government operates only a few. The women in slum areas tend to have three options for childcare: (1) combine work and childcare roles, (2) rely on kin and neighbours, and (3) use centre-based childcare. In the villages, children accompany their mothers to agricultural activities, but this may not be possible if the mother is working in a more dangerous worksite such as collecting metals for recycling.

Moreover, some employers may not encourage their workers to come with the baby to work as it will lead to divided attention and poor quality of work performed. So, these women must seek some form of childcare. Culturally, women left their children in the hands of other women folk in the family, especially grandmothers. However, as people move to town, they leave their relatives in the village, or it is too expensive to stay with them. In addition, relying on relatives for childcare can lead to strained relations. In this sample, only 7% reported using grandmothers and 3% using other relatives. This implies the use of relatives is limited. Neighbours can assist but to a limited degree. A good number of slum women earn meagre income mostly from vending, cleaning, and washing jobs and cannot afford domestic help so they result in using centre-based childcare centres for a fee. This mode of childcare can be more prevalent in informal settlements if the costs of the centres are subsidized. However, the study does not shed light on what happens if you have a much younger child who is not yet ready to join the centre-based care.

Work-Life Balance Practices and Choices of Women in the Gig Economy

Besides, women from the urban slums who work predominantly in the informal sector, there are the gig workers. Workers in the gig economy get their work through digital platforms that connect them with the market. Services such as cleaning and domestic work can be arranged through these platforms.

Workers in the informal sector may experience financial insecurity and thus engage in a patchwork of income activities to make ends meet. Hunt et al. (2019) carried out a longitudinal study to explore the gendered experiences of women working in the gig economy; to understand the nature of their work and how they managed to combine it with domestic work and care responsibilities in Kenya and South Africa. Gig work may offer some flexibility to when to work. However, job opportunities may not come at the time and quantity to enable these workers to have a decent wage. Workers in these platforms are not privileged to collective action. Due to the low incomes, the women in the gig economy face challenges of taking care of children and the elderly. Women tend to carry a big portion of care work, and they must search for ways to take care of their children. Childcare was their biggest obstacle to their economic opportunities and work-life balance. These women relied on informal childcare, such as using family members, neighbours, and friends; when this option failed, they could leave the children alone or in the care of slightly older children.

The gig platforms can develop supporting modalities such as training, certification, enabling workers to access more social protection and develop partnerships with other service providers such as financial institutions, transport, and childcare services. There is also the need for the government to provide infrastructure for childcare for workers in the informal sector. From this discussion, it is apparent a person's financial standing may influence the type of work-life balance options that they may enjoy.

Work-Life Balance Practices in Horticultural Farms

Horticultural farms tend to be located away from towns, and the assumption is that employees predominantly come from neighbourhoods situated adjacent to horticulture firms. Muindi et al. (2015) investigated the work-life practices employed in flower farms in Kenya. The horticulture sector contributes significantly to the livelihoods of people living along the Lake Naivasha region. The region has up to 55 flower farms that employ close to 55,000 workers. Earlier studies by Dwasi (2006) and Tsimbiri, Moturi Sawe, Henry, and Bend (2015) had indicated that the horticultural sector had challenges of poor labour practices and non-environmentally friendly production processes. There were allegations some work-life balance practices were not extended to causal workers, for instance, maternity leave, dependent care provision, and transport. To add on, workers worked for long hours, with low pay, and there was a challenge of adhering to safe work practices. Moreover, there was a high prevalence of respiratory, skin, nervous, joints, and bone sicknesses among the employees working in flower farms. This was attributed to poor work and safety measures in these farms, and exposure to pesticides. The study of Muindi et al (2015) used a cross-sectional survey with a sample of 22 farms. The authors had the human resource managers of these farms fill a survey on the nature and level of work-life practices that their organizations practised. The authors reported that the sampled farm managers acknowledged their organizations had a work-life balance policy and asked several questions regarding work-life balance practices. Muindi et al. reported these programmes were minimally enforced: practices to do with flexible reporting time and flexible working hours, teleworking, teleworking resources, flexible work pay, study leave, paid tuition for children and staff education, day-care centres, family fun day, low-interest loans, no-interest loans, free company products, workplace transport, employee assistance programmes, and free subsidized meals. These programmes were moderately enforced: exchange of working shifts, job sharing, and performance feedback practices. On the other hand, these programmes were more entrenched in the horticulture sector: flexible working days, days off for overtime, restricted overtime, time off to meet family emergencies, optional weekend, and job rotation. Furthermore, statutory leaves were also provided such as maternity, paternity, and compassionate leave. The sector also provided regular plant maintenance, regular training on the use of equipment, and protective clothing. This study differs from that of Tsimbiri et al. (2015) which alleged poor health and work safety standards. Besides statutory leaves, the sector provided health programmes and workplace shops.

The nature of work-life balance practices that workers enjoyed depended on the nature of work and industry, which differed from sector to sector, or even the calibre of workers whether permanent or temporal. For example, free meals or subsidized meals, could cater to the low income bracket—blue collar workers. The perspective of the employees themselves on the work-life practices was also lacking.

Discussion

Study Implications

First, a recap of the main findings reveals that in most studies, they tended to use definitions and theories already used before in Western scholarship. This is apart from Aryee (2005) who sought to theorize that work-life/family balance may show some collectivistic tendencies. To Aryee, work should not be framed as a choice, especially for the middle-class women as it is perceived in some Western literature, but a necessity for family survival. This conceptualization of work will result in different opinions; people will attach to work—work will be *for* the family.

Second, the conceptualization of work-life balance from the academic studies showed that work-life balance is something that can be attained and measured. However, the print media portrayed work-life balance as something that was not easy to be attained, a myth, and an illusion. In both media and academia, the two spheres of work and non-work life remain bifurcated, though some media stories suggested the need for weaving work and life together.

Third, the 20 work-life balance journals reviewed that focus on Kenya tended to focus on the effects of work-life balance or work-life/family conflict, rather than on the antecedents of work-life balance itself. This shows the area of antecedents of work-life balance is not yet explored in detail. Moreover, most studies from the human resource perspective tended to look at work-life balance from the work perspective, i.e., organization performance, job commitment, job satisfaction, and job turnover. There is a need to explore how work-life balance affects the family side as well such as in marriage satisfaction and parenting. Since Kenya is a collectivistic country, the bigger extended family can also be explored. In addition, how work-life balance affects health and well-being.

The conceptualization of work-life practices tended to differ from sector to sector or across different organizations. Leaves such as maternity leave, paternity leave, sick leave, and compassionate leave are well established across the formal sector. However, from the study, it cannot be ascertained whether all employees such as casual workers and contract workers in the organizations enjoyed these leaves. Likewise, it cannot be established if workers in the informal economy enjoy these leaves. Leaves such as study leave are not yet widely practised, maybe with some exceptions of those in the university sector, where training is highly encouraged. Flexible reporting time and leaving time deferred from sector to sector. Flexible working days were a practice in the horticultural sector (Muindi et al., 2015); working from home was not well entrenched in the flower industry due to the nature of work. The practice of part-time working and flexible payday was not entrenched in the organizations studied. Very few organizations reported the provision of day-care centres at their work place. Generally, very few organizations have day-care centres for their workers. The findings also revealed that though organizations could have enacted work-life balance policies, they could not have been enforced and supervisor support was necessary to enforce these policies (Karani & Paul, 2018).

Finally, the informal sector seems to experience work-life balance differently, from the formal sector. The women with low income in gig economy (Hunt et al., 2019) and slums (Clark et al., 2018) may not afford domestic help, or enjoy the work-life balance benefits given at the workplace. The nature of their work makes them more adversely affected by work-life balance challenges. Thus, sectorial solutions may not suffice for all working employees facing work-life balance challenges, and this may require government policy to resolve it. Below is the section of suggestions for further research.

Suggestion for Further Studies

Indeed, firms in Kenya experience work-life conflict and some effort has been put in place to address work-life balance issues that differ from firm to firm. Among the 20 Kenyan studies reviewed, most studies treated the Kenyan employees as a homogeneous group and failed to control for social economic and demographic factors, with the exception of Wang et al. (2011), and those that studied one gender such as Clark et al. (2018), and Muasya(2016, 2017, 2020). This implies there could be gendered differences on the level of work-life balance experienced and the work-life practices that mattered to them the most. Furthermore, these Kenyan results could differ according to age, marital status, income, years of experience, number of children and their ages, and level of supervisor support as suggested in work-life/family meta-analyses such as that done in the West (Anderson, Coffey, & Byerly, 2002); in addition, the perceived importance of work-life balance and their availability could vary with someone's seniority in the organization, if they could appropriate it, or able to negotiate about it as other non-Kenyan studies have established (Lambert & Waxman, 2005).

Along the same lines, there is a need for longitudinal studies, with larger samples and which crosscut the different Kenyan sectors, using a variety of methods of analyses (e.g., such as structural equation modelling), and methods of inquiry (e.g., critical theory). There are also Kenyan populations not yet studied (e.g., students, different classes of people working in the informal sector—taxi and truck drivers, quarry workers, and religious organizations). There is a need in Kenya to study work-life balance from other perspectives too, e.g. health, development, sustainability, etc., to get a more nuanced position as most of the current studies are from a human resource perspective. Finally, there is a need for theory building from a Kenyan perspective.

In addition, the majority of Kenya's population resides in rural settings, where their main sources of livelihood is small-scale subsistence agriculture and informal mining activities. The majority of the labourers in these settings are women; thus, WLB experienced in a rural context is needed. Also, close to 70% of Kenya is arid- and semi-arid land and hosts huge populations of nomadic pastoral communities. Further research is needed to shed light on WLB experienced by pastoral nomadic communities. Most work on WLB in Kenya has been informed by Eurocentric theoretical perspectives; future work would need to tease out the relevance of afro-centric theories in understanding WLB in Kenya. The work-from-home arrangements necessitated by the COVD-19 government lockdowns are likely to persist during the post-COVID-19 era; thus, there is an opportunity for further research related to WLB challenges and opportunities associated with the work-from-home arrangements, particularly for young women with dependents.

Such research will be critical for exploring previous hypotheses related to questions of flexibility offered by work-from-home arrangements.

Conclusion

Research on work-life balance is in the nascent stage in Kenya. This is shown by the level of conceptualization already carried out. The studies seem to concentrate on the work sphere and less on the non-work sphere, and more attention should be directed to the non-studied areas. Kenyan firms have made some progress in enacting work-life balance practices, especially those that are statutory in nature, though more can still be achieved to make their employees able to balance the demands of work and life and remain healthy and productive.

References

Abele, A. E., & Volmer, J. (2011). Dual-career couples: Specific challenges for work-life integration. In *Creating balance?* (pp. 173–189). Berlin and Heidelberg: Springer.

Adegoke, Y. (2018, November 11). *It's really expensive for Africans to live in their own cities*. Retrieved from https://qz.com/africa/1459482/african-cities-are too-expensive-for-ordinary-africans/.

Anderson, S. E., Coffey, B. E., & Byerly, R. T. (2002). Formal organisational initiatives and informal workplace practices: Links to work-family conflict and job-related outcomes. *Journal of Management, 28*(6), 787–810.

Aryee, S. (2005). The work-family interface in urban Sub-Saharan Africa: A theoretical analysis. In S. A. Y. Poelmans (Ed.), *Work and family: An international perspective* (pp. 261–285). Mahwah: Lawrence Erlbaum Associates Inc.

Bogonko, S. N (1992). *A history of modern education in Kenya (1895–1991).* Nairobi: Evan's Brother Ltd

Chemirmir, M. J., Musebe, R., & Nassiuma, B. K. (2018). The role of work-life balance on employee turnover in the flower industry in the North Rift

Kenya. *International Journal of Research in Social Sciences and Humanities, 7*(1), 50–62.

Clark, S., De Almada, M., Kabiru, C. W., Muthuri, S., & Wanjohi, M. (2018). Balancing paid work and childcare in a slum of Nairobi, Kenya: The case for centre-based childcare. *Journal of Family Studies, 27*, 1–19.

Donovan, L., & Zhu, A. (2020, April 10). *Kenya Labour market wasn't made for a pandemic*. https://foreignpolicy.com/2020/04/10/kenya-labor-corona virus-pandemic-informal-workers-economic-crisis/.

Dwasi, J. (2006). Kenya: A study in international labor standards and their effect on working women in developing countries: The case for integration of enforcement of World Bank policies, Wisconsin. *International Law Journal, 17*, 347–462.

Godia, G. (1987). Education and the unemployment problem in Kenya. *The Journal of Negro Education, 56*(3), 356–367.

Hunt, A., Samman, E., Tapfuma, S., Mwaura, G., Omenya, R., Kim, K., ... Roumer, A. (2019). *Women in the gig economy: Paid work, care, and flexibility in Kenya and South Africa*. Retrieved from https://www.odi.org/sites/odi.org.uk/files/resource-documents/women_in_the_gig_economy_final_digital.pdf.

Institute of Economic Affairs. (2016, December 7). *Economic burden of the informal sector*. Retrieved from https://www.ieakenya.or.ke/number_of_the_week/economic-burden-of-the-informal-sector.

International Labour Office. (2010). *World of work report 2010: From one crisis to the next?* Geneva: International Institute of Labour Studies.

International Labour Organisation. (2011). *C189: Domestic workers convention, 2011* (No. 189). Retrieved from https://www.ilo.org/dyn/normlex/en/f?p=NORMLEXPUB:12100:0::NO::P12100_INSTRUMENT_ID:2551460.

Kalliath, T., & Brough, P. (2008). Work-life balance: A review of the meaning of the balance construct. *Journal of Management & Organization, 14*(3), 323–327.

Karani, M. H., & Paul, S. N. (2018). Effect of project supervision on work-life balance on state corporations in Kenya. A case of Kenya Power. *International Journal of Social Sciences and Information Technology, IV*(II), 2767–2784.

Kegoro, H. O., Otieno, D. A., & Akoyo, S. I. (2020). Work-life balance and performance of National Police Service in Kenya. *Journal of Human Resource & Leadership, 4*(1), 10–18.

Kenya National Bureau of Statistics. (2009). *Kenya census 2009*. Retrieved from https://www.knbs.or.ke/Census%20Results/KNBS%20Brochure.pdf.

Kinyili, J. M. (2019). Work-life balance practices and staff retention: A case of public health institution in Machakos County, Kenya. *International Journal of Advanced Research in Management and Social Sciences, 8*(1), 1–19.

Lambert, S. J., & Waxman, E. (2005). *Organizational stratification: Distributing opportunities for balancing work and personal life*. Mahwah: Lawrence Erlbaum Associates Publishers.

Michel, J. S., Clark, M. A., & Beiler, A. A. (2013). Work-life conflict and its effects. In *Handbook of work-life integration among professionals*. Cheltenham: Edward Elgar Publishing.

Mokaya, S., & Gitari, J. W. (2012). Effects of workplace recreation on employee performance: The case of Kenya Utalii College. *International Journal of Humanities and Social Science, 2*(3), 176–183.

Mokomane, Z. (2014). Introduction. In Z. Mokomane (Ed.), *Work-family interface in Sub-Saharan Africa* (pp. 3–16). New York, NY: Springer.

Mokomane, Z., & Chilwane, D. (2014). A review of work-family research in Sub-Saharan Africa. In Z. Mokomane (Ed.), *Work-family interface in Sub-Saharan Africa* (pp. 195–205). New York, NY: Springer.

Muasya, G. M. (2014). The role of house helps in the work-family balance of women employed in the formal sector in Kenya. In Z. Mokomane (Ed.), *Work-family interface in Sub-Saharan Africa* (pp. 149–159). New York, NY: Springer.

Muasya, G. (2016). Is Work-family balance a possibility? The case of Kenyan female teachers in Urban Public Schools. *International Journal of Educational Administration and Policy Studies, 8*(5), 37–47.

Muasya, G. (2017). Work-family conflict, support, and intention to quit among Kenyan female teachers in urban public schools. *South African Journal of Labour Relations, 41*(1), 33–45.

Muasya, G. (2020). Stressors and work-family conflict among female teachers in urban public schools in Kenya. *South African Journal of Education, 40*(2), Art# 1769, 11 pp. https://www.sajournalofeducation.co.za.

Muasya, G. (in press). Print media framing of the definitions causes and solutions to work-life balance issues in Kenya. *Communicatio*. https://doi.org/10.1080/02500167.2020:1854806.

Muasya, G., & Martin, J. N. (2016). Conflict in Kenyan households: An exploratory study of professional women and domestic workers. *Howard Journal of Communications, 27*(4), 385–402.

Muema, F. N., Nzioki, S., & Kinyili, J. (2018). Time-related work-life balance practices influencing employee job satisfaction in Machakos County commercial banks, Kenya. *International Journal of Economics Commerce and Management, VI*(10), 229–315.

Muindi, F., Nzulwa, J., & Muinde Anne, N. W. (2015). Work-life balance practices adopted in horticultural farms in Kenya. *DBA Africa Management Review, 5*(2), 101–123.

Mungania, A. K., Waiganjo, E. W., & Kihoro, J. M. (2016). Influence of wellness programs on organizational performance in the banking industry in Kenya. *International Journal of Academic Research in Business and Social Sciences, 6*(7), 179–185. ISSN: 2222-6990.

Munyiva, M. J., & Wainaina, L. (2018). Work life balance and employee performance at the kenya ports authority in Mombasa County, Kenya. *Journal of Human Resource and Leadership, 3*(4), 16–42.

Mwangi, L., Boinett, C. C., Tumwet, E., & Bowen, D. (2016). Effects of work-life balance on employees' performance in institutions of higher learning. A case study of Kabarak University. *Kabarak Journal of Research & Innovation, 4*(2), 60–69.

Nickanor, N., Crush, J., & Pendleton, W. (2016). Migration, rural-urban linkages, and food insecurity. In *Rapid urbanisation, urban food deserts and food security in Africa* (pp. 127–142). Cham: Springer.

Ombati, O. F. V. (2003). *Women's participation in educational leadership in Kenya: The case of Nairobi and Thika municipal primary schools* (ProQuest Dissertations and Theses, 133 pp.). State University of New York at Buffalo. Retrieved from https://login.ezproxy1.lib.asu.edu/login?url=https://search.proquest.com/.

Otiende, J. E., Wamahiu, S. P., & Karugu, A. M. (1992). *Education and development in Kenya*. Nairobi, Kenya: Oxford University Press.

Otieno, S. (2019, June 10). *Police boss lists 8 reasons behind officers' rampant suicide*. Retrieved from https://www.kenyans.co.ke/news/40511-police-boss-lists-9-reasons-behind-officers-rampant-suicides.

Poelmans, S., O'Driscoll, M., & Beham, B. (2005). An overview of international research on the work-family interface. *In Work and family: An international research perspective* (pp. 3–46). Mahwah, NJ: Lawrence Erlbaum Associates.

Slaughter, A. (2012, July–August). Why women can't have it all. *The Atlantic*. https://www.Theatlantic.com.

Tsimbiri, P. F., Moturi, W. N., Sawe, J., Henley, P., & Bend, J. R. (2015). Health impact of pesticides on residents and horticultural workers in the Lake Naivasha Region, Kenya. *Occupational Diseases and Environmental Medicine, 3*(02), 24.

Wang, P., Lawler, J. J., Shi, K., Walumbwa, F., & Piao, M. (2008). Family-friendly employment practices: Importance and effects in India, Kenya, and China. In *The global diffusion of human resource practices: Institutional and cultural limits*. Emerald Group Publishing Limited.

Wang, P., Lawler, J. J., & Shi, K. (2011). Implementing family-friendly employment practices in banking industry: Evidence from some African and Asian countries. *Journal of Occupational and Organizational Psychology, 84*(3), 493–517.

Wangui, P. M. (2012). *The lived experiences of female headteachers in rural primary schools in Kenya* (Doctoral dissertation). University of South Africa.

Williams, J. (1999). *Unbending gender: Why family and work conflict and what to do about it*. Oxford: Oxford University Press.

5

The Myth and the Reality of Work-Life Balance in Nigeria

Toyin Ajibade Adisa, Gbolahan Gbadamosi, and Olatunji David Adekoya

Introduction

As with most emerging and industrialised economies, Nigeria is confronted with the changing nature of paid work, and the realities of managing work with other non-work responsibilities persist with looming consequences (Amazue & Onyishi, 2016). The ability to balance work demand and non-work responsibilities, commonly referred to as work-life balance (WLB) (see Adisa et al., 2017; Beauregard & Henry, 2009; Bird, 2006), continues to stimulate research and trigger

T. A. Adisa (✉) · O. D. Adekoya
Royal Docks School of Business and Law, University of East London, London, UK
e-mail: t.adisa@uel.ac.uk

G. Gbadamosi
Organisational Behaviour and Human Resource Management at the Business School, Bournemouth University, Bournemouth, UK
e-mail: ggbadamosi@bournemouth.ac.uk

T. A. Adisa and G. Gbadamosi (eds.), *Work-Life Interface*,
https://doi.org/10.1007/978-3-030-66648-4_5

debate among academics and policymakers for implementable WLB policies that will improve employees' well-being. The clear need for workplace flexibility (i.e. employee's ability to decide when, how, and where work is to be undertaken) has propelled many organisations to initiate various WLB policies, which is beneficial to both the employer and the employees (Guest, 2002).

This chapter articulates some conceptual issues associated with the relationship between work and non-work life, specifically in Nigeria. At first, we explore the concepts around work-life, to establish a foundation in the context of WLB. The chapter examines the realities and experiences of WLB in Nigeria. In order to achieve these objectives, we analyse the working time among Nigerian employees; second and the working conditions prevalent in Nigeria. We also analyse the issue of gender as it affects WLB and, lastly, we consider the influence of the WLB policies and initiatives in Nigeria. The chapter surveys a variety of materials for the review of the realities of work-life balance in Nigeria and presents data in the form of interview extracts and data sets used in the analysis. We then draw conclusion based on our analysis.

A Brief Outlook of WLB

The concept of WLB is not novel. The issue of WLB has been around for many decades and still continue to attract attention and generate debate till date. This may be due to an increase in interest in how employees manage to balance work-related obligations and non-work-related responsibilities (Wheatley, 2012); especially, in the present time when the value of work is changing and there continues to be room for personal interests, environment and family obligations aside from work commitments. Furthermore, many organisations, due to economic uncertainty and organisational restructuring, now demand unalloyed commitment and higher productivity from their employees (Hughes & Bozionelos, 2007; Naithani, 2010a, 2010b). Consequently, many people now feel more pressured in their jobs and at home—making work and non-work aspects of their lives to collide and become difficult to maintain.

The concept of WLB is problematic. However, it is crucial to understand the fundamental elements that constitute the term 'WLB' in order to have a clear understanding of the concept. Over the years, researchers have come up with various subjective and objective interpretations of what 'work', 'life', and 'balance' mean. For example, Warhurst, Eikhof, and Haunschild (2008, p. 2) define work as 'a sphere of physical and mental demands that steals time and energy from employees' real lives. This definition of work draws an argument that employees engage in multiple roles that uses their time, effort, and energy for paid and unpaid work (Drew & Daverth, 2007). Paid work is when an individual is compensated through remuneration for a particular job or series of tasks undertaken over a period of time (Mitsakis & Talampekos, 2014). While unpaid work comprises of work that does not attract any form of monetary or contractual payments, such as voluntary and unpaid domestic work (Rapoport Bailyn, Fletcher, & Pruitt, 2002).

Conversely, 'life' means employees' non-work duties and responsibilities, which promote self-fulfilment, love, and social belongingness (Neequaye, 2016). Depending on several demographic factors (such as age, marital status, gender, and social, political and religious affiliations); 'life' can also be divided into personal life and family life (Greenhaus & Beutell, 1985). Personal life refers to an individual's dedicated time and energy to self-development, happiness and leisure. This could include activities such as education, hobbies, cultural interests and social or religious activities that contribute to personal identity. While family life refers to an individual's roles and responsibilities that contribute to familial interests, including embracing house chores and caring duties (Warhurst et al., 2008).

There is a mythical connotation associated with the meaning of balance (Guest, 2002) given that the 'balance' in WLB is almost impossible. The common definition of 'balance' refers to an equal allotment of time, efforts, and energy towards an individual's work and personal lives (Ranjan & Prasad, 2013). However, Clark (2000, p. 751) disagrees by defining 'balance' as 'satisfaction and good functioning at work and home, with a minimum of role conflict'. Balance, therefore, does not mean a total absence of conflict between an individual's work and non-work roles; rather it means the degree to which such conflicts are managed to produce desirable outcomes in both work and personal life. More so, the concept of balance arises from the notion that work and life are inseparable domains (Guest, 2002). However, this is contrary to the assumption of the segmentation theory of WLB (see Young & Kleiner, 1992). The theory assumes that an individual's work and personal lives are two separate segments; hence, they act independently of each other (Warhurst et al.,2008). Many other theories of WLB have critiqued the segmentation theory by attempting to emphasise the relationship between the work-related and non-work-related roles of an employee. Some of these theories include the border theory (Clark, 2000), compensation theory (Zedeck & Mosier, 1990), boundary theory (Nippert-Eng, 1996), spillover theory (Staines, 1980), and enrichment theory (Greenhaus & Powell, 2006).

The concept of WLB is broad. It recognises employees' multiple roles, which often affect each other (Kalliath & Brough, 2008). WLB means an employee's ability to successfully negotiate work-related and family commitments, as well as other non-work responsibilities and activities (Kesting and Harris, 2009; Parkes & Langford, 2008; Wheatley, 2012). It means an effective management of the interaction between an individual's work demand and non-work obligations (Mishra, Boynton, & Mishra, 2014). WLB is 'associated with numerous aligned socio-cultural goals and organisational programs such as the provision of flexible work arrangements, equity and diversity policies and health and well-being outcomes' (McDonald, Townsend, & Wharton, 2013, p. 207). Contrastingly, Fleetwood (2007) argues that despite the various policies implemented by the government and organisations, the social consensus of WLB is disconnected with the realities and experiences of employees. We, therefore, argue that the numerous existing WLB initiatives neither sufficiently reflect its goals in achieving work-life integration nor drastically reduce the occurrence of work-life conflict (WLC), which is the opposite of WLB.

Nizam and Kam (2018) opined that WLB is rooted in five critical elements, which include working hours, workload, leave policies, work arrangements and reward schemes. An effective WLB is expected to benefit both employees and employers, family members, and the community at large (Mishra et al., 2014). Employees are motivated and tend to perform better when they are able to exercise some degree of control over when and where their work is undertaken. Research has also confirmed that creating a balance between work and personal life enhances factors surrounding an individual's functionality outside of work and improves work productivity and organisational performance (Pradhan, 2016; Rao, 2017). Oktosatrio (2018) supports this argument and aver that WLB ensures job satisfaction and acts as a catalyst for improving employees' motivation. Findings from various studies (Muchiti & Gachunga, 2015; Okpara & Wynn, 2007) also indicate that work flexibility and job satisfaction could not be undermined in pursuit of organisation performance. This brief outlook evinces the concept of WLB as an important area of human resource management (HRM).

Realities of WLB in Nigeria

Nigeria is a West African country with a population of over 200 million people and more than 250 ethnic groups across its six geo-political zones (Central Intelligence World Factbook, 2019; Worldometer, 2020). Nigeria is the largest economy in Africa and the twenty-seventh largest in the world (World Population Review, 2020) with oil as its major revenue source (Central Intelligence World Factbook, 2019). Nigeria workforce is estimated at about 60 million people with an unemployment estimated rate of 16.5% (Central Intelligence World Factbook, 2019). Nigeria, as a developing nation, has its peculiarities which makes it an interesting context for research in WLB. In the last ten years, WLB has gained a significant academic attention in Nigeria with studies examining WLB of different categories of workers (Adisa, 2015; Adisa et al., 2016; Adisa, Mordi, & Mordi, 2014; Akanji, 2012; Mordi et al., 2013; Ojo Salau, & Falola, 2014). However, more research is still needed in order to capture the realities of WLB in Nigeria and to increase not just the quantity but the quality and reach of WLB research undertaken in the country. Therefore, the reality of WLB in Nigeria is presumed to hinge on some overarching factors such as individual/organisational differences and expectations, cultural attributes and the institutional forces that regulate work-life patterns. While considering these factors, we consider working time, working conditions, gender complexities, and institutional policies as they affect the WLB experiences of the Nigerian workforce in determining the myth and reality of WLB in Nigeria.

Working Time

Issues associated with the number of working hours are similar across nations, regardless of their levels of economic growth and development (International Labour Organization—ILO, 2005). According to Lee, McCann, and Messenger (2007), working time around the world has often been regulated by the ILO to ensure that organisations prioritise the well-being of their workers. This is because the number of hours worked is one of the determinants of employee WLB (see Adisa, Abdulraheem, & Osabutey, 2016). The ILO has proposed a standard working time of 8 hours a day or 40 hours per week in order to enhance the employees' standard of living (ILO, 2020). However, in reality, a significant number of employees work beyond the standard working time globally (ILO, 2019; Messenger, 2018).

In Nigeria, the reality of working time is bedevilled predominantly by the long working hours culture prevalent in many organisations (Adisa, Mordi, & Osabutey, 2017; Mmakwe & Ojiabo, 2018). The vagueness in the usage and implementation of flexible working options among Nigerian workers and employers respectively is undoubtedly the primary impediment to the achievement of WLB (Adisa et al., 2014; Akinyele, Peters, & Akinyele, 2016; Epie & Ituma, 2014). Over time, studies have revealed that while no sector of the Nigerian economy is expunged from long working hours, there are marginal differences across the diverse sectors (Epie & Ituma, 2014). The medical profession is one of the many professions burdened with long working hours considering the shortage of doctors and other medical practitioners across the country (Adisa et al., 2017; Mushfiqur et al., 2018). The shortage, consequently, engenders the medical staff to work beyond their regular working hours and embrace anti-social working hours, which often leads to a high rate of staff turnover and occupational migration (Adisa et al., 2017). Adisa et al.'s study establishes that a culture of long working hours is inherent in the medical profession (medical doctor) in Nigeria—exacerbating work-life imbalance among medical doctors in Nigeria.

Similarly, the Nigerian banking, telecommunications and insurance industries present another reflection of long working hours coupled with the use of overtime, which is deemed as a norm within these industries (Akanji, 2012; Ugwu, Amazue, & Onyedire, 2017). Furthermore, Ukaegbu (2000) revealed the precarious working condition in the Nigerian manufacturing industry subject employees to work beyond the standard hours. In the same vein, Adekoya, Ajonbadi, and Mordi (2019) reveal an excessive working hours culture in the Nigerian Army, which is detrimental to their achieving WLB.

The informal sector is no exception, it also presents working time challenges to the workers who struggle to achieve WLB. The fact that the informal sector is unregulated, and consist of workers who are predominantly unskilled, exposes the labour force within it to unregulated working hours (Tamunomiebi & Ukachukwu, 2018). This sector is characterised by low level of pay (often below the national minimum wage), which subjects the workers to take up more hours at work or look for a second job to meet their basic needs (Fajana, 2008).

Although many Nigerian workers may not work beyond the standard closing time, however, many take work home, which interferes with the limited time available to attend to other non-work roles (Olaoye, 2012). Nevertheless, employees have different reasons for working longer hours. A central assumption is that employees working for longer hours are either workaholics that have taken their jobs as their 'first love' and prioritise their careers over their personal lives; or they work longer hours to show their level of commitment and loyalty to their employers in favour of personal gains; or do so to earn more money (Adisa et al., 2017; Epie & Ituma, 2014). It is evident from the above studies that many employees in Nigeria find it challenging to balance their work-life and non-work work life, despite the various coping strategies available to them (see Adisa, Gbadamosi, and Osabutey [2016] for the review of the coping strategies available to the Nigerian workers). We, therefore, argue that the inability of the Nigerian workers to achieve WLB is an active stressor for WLC. This is because their experiences of long working hours generate a negative spillover from their work domain to non-work domain (see Adisa, Gbadamosi, & Osabutey, 2016). Undoubtedly, long working hours have arduous implications on the Nigerian workers' lives and pose a huge barrier to their achieving WLB.

Working Conditions

Working conditions are presumably one of the determinants of WLB (McGinnity & Russell, 2015). Working conditions comprise a variety of factors which are critical to employee wellbeing and WLB (Nordenmark, Vinberg, & Strandh, 2012; Wilkinson, 1999). Employees tend to perform better in an enabling atmosphere where they are able to make independent and collective decisions regarding their choice of work engagement and participation (McGinnity & Russell, 2015). According to Akinyele (2010), the Nigerian working environment is less supportive. This may be attributed to poverty, corruption, and bad leadership (Nzewi, Augustine, Mohammed, & Godson, 2018). The working conditions of the Nigerian workers have been negatively affected by work intensification, required physical presence at work, and a lack of supportive culture.

Work Intensification

Work intensification, also known as work overload, remains one of the widespread issues associated with working conditions globally (Lewis Gambles, & Rapoport, 2007; Skinner & Pocock, 2008). The increase in organisational efforts to meet set targets resulting from demand and supply pressures and the effort to balance the books subject employees to the danger of work overload, which breeds stress, burnout and has debilitating effects on employees' general well-being (Fein, Skinner, & Machin, 2017; Yu, 2014). Work-overload has been identified as one of the strongest predictors of work-life imbalance in that employees exerted extra energy or time (long working hours) to achieve organisational objectives (Boxall & Macky, 2014).

As reported by Epie and Ituma (2014), the presence of work intensification in the Nigerian labour market coupled with institutional failures has resulted in WLC for the Nigerian workers. Similarly, Adisa, Osabutey, and Gbadamosi (2016) found work pressure/overload to be one of the primary sources of WLC, hence, affirming the presence of negative spillover from work domain to non-work domain. In a similar study, work pressure is mirrored as a dominant factor that impedes the achievement of WLB among Nigerian employees (Mushfiqur et al., 2018). This study aligns with the empirical evidence on the impact of work intensification on WLB achievement among Nigerian workers. We suggest that organisational expectations through work intensifications often engender a negative spillover from work domain to the non-work domain of many employees across the country.

Required Physical Presence at Work

Research has also suggested that the prevailing requirement of physical presence at work in the Nigerian work environment mirrors the low level or lack of usage of WLB policies such as telework and other flexible work arrangements across the country (Adekoya et al., 2019; Adisa et al., 2017). While accepting that not all jobs can be undertaken offsite, we however argue that jobs that require employee's physical presence at work at all times may lead to strict supervision, which could distract employees and lead to underperformance or errors. Such performance reports could demoralise employees who are likely to transfer their emotions to their non-work domain. More so, there is a dichotomy that a manager's close supervision, which is obtainable in the workplace, induces improved performance (Andrade, Westover, & Kupka, 2019). However, we argue that employees are likely to perform better when offered flexible working options, which include getting work done outside the confines of the workplace. The absence of adequate flexibility options in Nigeria deprives workers the ability to balance their work demands and non-work responsibilities.

It is evident from the literature that many workers in Nigeria find it challenging to manage their work and personal lives due to the culture of required physical presence at work (see Adekoya et al., 2019; Adisa, Mordy, et al., 2017). For some professions, physical presence at work is an obligation and not a choice on the premise that it bespeaks the level of the employee's commitment and seriousness on the job (Adisa, Mordy, et al., 2017). Having employees present at work at all times is found to encroach into their personal space and time—thus causing work-life imbalance (Adekoya et al., 2019). Just like in many other countries, the time taken to travel to places of work, particularly in Nigerian cities, exposes employees to prolonged traffic stress, which may result in fatigue and other associated medical issues—thus affecting productivity (Mushfiqur et al., 2018). The risks associated with plying Nigerian roads and the employees' aspirations to achieve WLB makes sufficient business case for employers to reduce the need for the regular onsite presence of employees and embrace WLB policies such as telework and other flexible work arrangements.

Supportive Culture

The degree of support received by employees is critical to their achievement of WLB (Allen, 2001). According to Abendroth and den Dulk (2011), the supportive roles of organisations, family, and government are essential to the attainment of WLB among workers worldwide. The study further discusses the impact of emotional and instrumental support both in the workplace and within the family as a crucial tool for reducing work stress and burnout. Within the Nigerian context, we also found evidence that reinforces the claim that organisational and family support are predictors of WLB (Amazue & Onyishi, 2016). On the one hand, organisational support is represented mainly by support from supervisors and colleagues (Adisa et al. 2017); on the other hand, support from spouse, parents and other close relatives are regarded as family support (Agba, Nwosu, & Innah, 2015).

Adisa, Mordi, and Osabutey (2017) found that unsupportive culture resulting from a lack of support from managers, supervisors and colleagues are prevalent in Nigerian organisations. This thus exacerbates the challenges that the Nigerian workers face in coping with work demands and non-work-related responsibilities. Even though the Nigerian family system, which comprises of spouses and close relatives (mostly grandparents, uncles, aunties and cousins) play an important role in providing support to one another; many organisations in Nigeria do not have WLB policies in place to support their employees in their efforts to achieve WLB. Family support is important, but it is not enough. Employees need all the support (organisational, supervisor, colleagues and government supports) to achieve desired WLB.

Gender Complexities

Until recently, gender issues in the WLB debate have been ignored as concentration was mainly on the physical, political, social and cultural factors as they affect employees' work and non-work life (Emslie & Hunt, 2009). However, the incessant influx and participation of women in paid employment have increased interests in how work and life are managed among men and women (Lewis et al., 2007). In today's work environment, the role of gender in WLB cannot be overemphasised due to various factors associated with the differences between men and women. The issue of gender is central to the discussion of WLB. This is because the level of involvement in work and non-work roles (e.g. family role) is different across borders, and it depends on traditional gender role expectations. For instance, women's involvement in family roles in patriarchal societies in SSA (such as Nigeria) is high compared to the situation in relatively egalitarian countries such as the UK and the US (Adisa, Osabutey, & Gbadamosi, 2017). This, arguably, means that Nigerian women will experience more work-family conflict than their counterparts in the UK and the US (Adisa et al., 2014).

Typically, Nigeria is a less egalitarian society ingrained in a patriarchal hegemonic social system, in which women are subordinated and dominated by men both at work and home (Adisa, Abdulraheem, & Isiaka, 2019). This dichotomic-gendered nature of the Nigerian society has institutionalised the roles of men and women. Men are meant to be 'breadwinners' and not participate in domestic duties, and women are supposed to be 'homemakers' and shoulder all domestic duties, even if that woman is engaged in a full-time paid job. These belief, culture and norms often make it difficult for women to find dignifying jobs but are instead engaged in low paid jobs or dirty work (Aderinto, 2001). As the Nigerian society struggles to detach itself from patriarchal hegemonic culture, which breeds gender inequality, women, influenced by the feminist movements and the need to become independent, are increasingly taking up more jobs both in the private and public sectors (Makama, 2013). This increase participation of the women in the labour force is continually pushing forward a case for WLB and family-friendly policies in the country (Nigeria) where women constitute about half of the 200 million population (Makama, 2013). Additionally, the huge task of combining work demands and non-work responsibilities continues to burden employed women (Aderinto, 2001). This may be the reason why women in this part of the world are unable to achieve socially sustainable work as they find it difficult to cope with their multiple roles (Mushfiqur et al., 2018).

Akanji, Mordi, Simpson, Adisa, and Oruh (2020) argued that the concept of WLB to many childless single employees, which is also gendered, is worth researching. This is because many employers categorise unmarried employees as individuals without familial responsibilities based on the presumption that they have no childcare responsibilities. These assumptions clearly disregard their obligations to other family members. This stereotypical prejudice engenders an increase in the workload of unmarried employees—thus making balancing their work and non-work demands difficult. Undoubtedly, a gendered WLB is challenging for both genders. However, women find it more challenging to cope with their multiple roles as a result of prevalent patriarchy in Nigeria. The Nigerian society portrays a family-collectivistic orientation that offers more informal support as couples or single parents can solicit the help of close relatives to fulfil some domestic and caring responsibilities as a mechanism for improving WLB. However, this form of support given its peculiarities and limitations also present some challenges within the WLB debate; one of such is the lack of parental care experienced by the children affected (Aderinto, 2001). Nevertheless, as the Nigerian employees continue their struggles to achieve WLB, it is essential to understand the institutional roles of organisations and the government in alleviating the current deplorable situation.

WLB Policies and Initiatives in Nigeria

Even though WLB policies and initiatives are similar in countries and organisations around the world, implementations and uptakes are different. The pursuit of improving employee well-being has since propelled organisations, government and labour unions to initiate policies that facilitate labour flexibility. Contextually, one of the challenges facing the Nigerian organisations is the sustained deficiency in formulating and implementing policies that promote employee well-being (Bolaji, Gray, & Campbell-Evans, 2015). The government as the primary economic regulator has not lived up to its responsibilities in terms of WLB campaign. The Nigerian government has also not been able to protect employees from labour market exploitation. This is evident in the 'Decent Work Country Programme II' report presented by the International Labour Organization (ILO, 2018). The report mirrors the undue complacency of the Nigerian government regarding the prevailing labour market conditions which has further exacerbated the poor living and wellbeing conditions of employees in the country. The report further revealed that the Nigerian government has failed to alleviate the deficits in the labour market through its negligence to the labour standards proposed by the ILO. The Nigerian Labour Act was introduced in 1979 and reviewed in 2004 (ILO, 2018). Apparently, there have been several positive developmental changes in the workplace over the years since the Labour Act was last reviewed. Furthermore, the complex nature of work and the need for WLB policies such as flexible working arrangement evince the urgent need for a new Labour Act in Nigeria (KPMG, 2019).

The Nigerian Labour Act (2004) states that the daily working hours are to be fixed by mutual agreement or collective bargaining. This loophole is often exploited by employers to increase an employee's working hours, which often leads to work-life conflict (WLC). The few WLB policies contained in the Act are maternity leave, sick leave, and annual leave; most of which are outdated and inconsistent with the current practices and realities of work and working conditions. Organisational roles in facilitating WLB policies are crucial to the well-being of employees. Despite the many existing WLB practices and initiatives introduced in recent years globally, Nigerian employees are still not enjoying the full benefits of various WLB policies. Flexible working initiatives that are provided by Nigerian organisations are often limited to 'adjusted working hours, shortened workweek, job sharing and casual leave allowance' (Akanji et al., 2020). The availability and awareness of WLB initiatives across the country have been deemed to be worrisome, given that the Nigerian employees are either ignorant or lack the institutional support to use these initiatives (Adisa et al., 2014). Table 5.1 mirrors the level of awareness, availability and usage of WLB initiatives among a section of Nigerian employees.

As shown in Table 5.1, the availability of WLB policies in the Nigerian medical profession is minimal, likewise its awareness among the professionals. The data reveals that the commonly used WLB policy is the maternity leave and study leave, while casual leave is sparsely used. The data also suggests that employees are not aware of many WLB policies such as school holiday cover, nanny share, reduced and compressed working hours, annualised hours, teleworking, shift swapping, and staggered working hours. Unsurprisingly, 100% of the medical professionals engaged in full-time employment with an almost zero availability and usage of part-time employment. This could be a result of the shortage of medical personnel in the industry (see Adebulu, 2019). Similarly, another study undertaken by Ojo et al. (2014) in three different sectors (Banking, education, and power—see Table 5.2) revealed the availability and usage of WLB initiatives in these sectors.

Tables 5.1 and 5.2 reveal the WLB initiatives in four different sectors (medical, banking, educational and power) of the Nigerian economy. It is evident in these studies that Nigerian employees, besides the limited availability of WLB initiatives and policies, are very reluctant to use those initiatives. Ojo et al. (2014, p. 12) argued that long working hours, work intensification, unsupportive managerial and organisational culture, ineffective implementation strategy, lack of communication and failure to evaluate the impact of the initiatives are some of the barriers that stand

Table 5.1 Work-life balance policies awareness, availability, and uptake among nigerian female doctors and nurses

WLB policies	Awareness among doctors		Awareness among nurses		Availability among doctors		Availability among nurses		Uptake among d doctors		Uptake among n nurses	
	Yes (%)	No (%)	Yes (%)	No (%)	Yes (%)	No (%)	Yes (%)	No (%)	Yes (%)	No (%)	Yes (%)	No (%)
Full-time	100	–	100	–	100	–	100	–	100	–	100	–
Part time	80.0	20.0	76.4	23.6	1.9	98.1	2.2	97.8	–	100	–	100
Family medical leave	–	95	–	98.4	–	100	–	100	–	–	–	–
Maternity leave	100	–	100	–	100	–	100	–	100	–	100	–
Paternity leave	–	100	–	100	–	100	–	100	–	100	–	100
Casual leave	98.2	–	94.0	–	23.0	77.0	21.8	78.2	15.0	85.0	17.0	83.0
On-site childcare	45	55	58.2	41.8	–	100	–	100	–	100	–	100
Emergency childcare	–	100	–	100	–	100	–	100	–	100	–	100
Backup adult & eldercare	–	100	–	100	–	100	–	100	–	100	–	100
School holiday cover	–	100	–	100	–	100	–	100	–	100	–	100
On-site WLB expert	–	100	–	100	–	100	–	100	–	100	–	100
Nanny share	–	100	–	100	–	100	–	100	–	100	–	100
Reduced working hours	–	100	–	100	–	100	–	100	–	100	–	100
Compressed working hrs	–	100	–	100	–	100	–	100	–	100	–	100

(continued)

Table 5.1 (continued)

WLB policies	Awareness among doctors		Awareness among nurses		Availability among doctors		Availability among nurses		Uptake among d doctors		Uptake among n nurses	
	Yes (%)	No (%)	Yes (%)	No (%)	Yes (%)	No (%)	Yes (%)	No (%)	Yes (%)	No (%)	Yes (%)	No (%)
Annualised hours	–	100	–	100	–	100	–	100	–	100	–	100
Teleworking	–	100	–	100	–	100	–	100	–	100	–	100
Crèche	88.0	12.0	97.0	3.0	–	100	–	100	–	100	–	100
Career break	82.0	18.0	85.5	14.5	–	100	–	100	–	100	–	100
Term time working	–	100	–	100	–	100	–	100	–	100	–	100
Sabbatical leave	–	100	–	100	–	100	–	100	–	100	–	100
Flexi-time schemes	–	100	–	100	–	100	–	100	–	100	–	100
Study leave	97.1	2.9	95.7	4.3	68.5	31.5	47.0	53.0	58	42	39	61
Shift swapping	–	100	–	100	–	100	–	100	–	100	–	100
Self-rostering	–	100	–	100	–	100	–	100	–	100	–	100
Working from home	–	100	–	100	–	100	–	100	–	100	–	100
Cultural/religious leave	–	100	–	100	–	100	–	100	–	100	–	100
Staggered working hours	–	100	–	100	–	100	–	100	–	100	–	100

Source Adapted from Adisa et al. (2014, p. 29)

Table 5.2 WLB initiatives availability and usage across three sectors in Nigeria

WLB Initiatives	Banking sector (availability)	Banking sector (usage %)	Educational sector (availability)	Educational sector (usage %)	Power sector (availability)	Power sector (usage %)
Full time	✓	100	✓	91	✓	93
Part time	X	0	✓	9	✓	7
Flexitime	✓	6	✓	35	X	0
Term time	X	0	✓	37	X	0
Home working	✓	4	✓	17	X	0
Study leave	✓	31	✓	59	✓	26
Parental leave	✓	41	✓	32	✓	29
Maternity leave	✓	27	✓	26	✓	19
Paternity leave	✓	2	X	0	X	0
Childcare arrangements	✓	42	✓	34	✓	42

Source Adapted from Ojo et al. (2014, p. 10)

between the Nigerian workers and WLB initiatives. As noted by Bond (2004), an employee's reluctance to use WLB initiatives is largely dependent on a lack of supportive culture within the organisation. Adisa et al. (2017) argued that a supportive culture is an important factor in employees' ability to function well both at work and as good members of their families.

The role of the labour and trade unions as advocates for employees is crucial to facilitating employee well-being across the world (Webster & Forrest, 2019). However, the weak bargaining power of labour and trade union has been negatively affecting the implementation of welfare policies (including WLB policies) in public and private companies, both in the industrialised and developing countries (Visser, 2019). Like in many other societies, the Nigerian labour and trade unions are plagued with a deficient bargaining power, which has resulted in the deplorable state of employees' welfare (Ngwama, 2016). The Nigerian labour market faces several labour challenges as a result of the weakened power of autonomy among its unions. Consequently, members of the unions remain despondent in the exploitative hands of their employers. The lingering issues in these unions thus have negative implications for WLB policies formulation and implementation. We argue that WLB in Nigeria will have to be supported by human resource management (HRM) policies and practices, supportive organisational, cultural and institutional forces to be effective.

Discussion and Conclusions

Reconciling work demands and non-work responsibilities, like every other worker around the world, matters to the Nigeria workers. However, there has been little or no effort from the Nigerian government, private and public organisations and other institutions to make WLB a reality for the teeming Nigerian workers. In examining the myth and reality of WLB in Nigeria, we explored the interpretations of the perception of work, life and balance. We also disentangled the concept of allotting equal amount of time, energy, and effort to work and non-work domains as the meaning of WLB is generally misconstrued by some people. This chapter supports defining WLB as a satisfactory balance between work and non-work domains with a minimum role conflict. This definition means that WLB does not mean a total absence of conflict; rather, the ability to manage foreseeable conflicts to promote desirable outcomes in both work and life spheres (see Clark, 2000).

This chapter identifies the realities of working time as it affects WLB in Nigeria. We ascertained that the prevailing working hours across the country was fundamental to achieving WLB. Long working hours prevailed as the main predictor of work-life imbalance given that employees directly or indirectly allocated more working time, which interfered with their non-work-related roles and obligations. In Nigeria, long working hours, irregular work schedules, and general lack of WLB policies such as flexi-time options characterised the culture of many organisations. It is, therefore, safe to say that unregulated working time is a major barrier to achieving WLB for many Nigeria workers. Working conditions were also recognised as another factor responsible for work-life imbalance among Nigeria workers. The working condition, influenced by work intensification, required physical presence at work, and supportive culture plays a significant role in the attainment of WLB. We postulate that work intensification or work overload, among others, have a compelling influence on the achievement of WLB. The Nigerian workers typically are overloaded with work, which often results in lack of energy to function well in the non-work domain. The intensification of work often results in negative spillover from work to non-work domain—thus causing displeasure and conflict. More recent studies, Nwagbara (2020) confirms not much progress has been made regarding working conditions and policies as the study confirms entrenched work inflexibility, normalised unequal engagement, unsupportive workplace, and legitimised instrumentalist workload. The study underscores how national institutions shape and legitimise managerialist employment relations, resulting in WLB challenges for employees. The chapter also identified the required physical presence at work at all time as a barrier to achieving WLB. We thus argue that the more employees are exposed to poor working conditions, the less likely they will achieve WLB.

Although WLB affects both men and women, however, gender complexities portrayed a significant relationship within the WLB debate. The chapter emphasises the impact of gender on the achievement of WLB. More so, the prevailing patriarchal hegemonic Nigerian culture enervates women's efforts to WLB (see Adisa et al., 2019). The chapter establishes that the institutional bodies (government, organisations and labour/trade unions) have failed in their respective responsibilities to boost the welfare of employees across the country. This is mirrored by the insignificant level of the availability, awareness, and usage of WLB initiatives in Nigerian organisations and industries. In conclusion, it is vivid from the review conducted in this chapter that WLB is still miles away in Nigeria when compared to WLB initiatives and implementation in the western-developed world. As a matter of pertinence, employees must be supported through the implementation of adequate WLB initiatives to reduce the occurrence of role conflicts and enhance individual well-being, organisational productivity and societal gratification. Furthermore, there should be a re-think of patriarchal hegemonic culture that heaps bulky domestic duties on women. This will enable them to have time and energy to non-work activities that matter to them. There is also a need for government and organisations to take the issue of WLB seriously by initiating practicable WLB policies, which will enhance employees' well-being, productivity and societal gratification.

Recent business growth and developments within the formal sector on the Nigerian economy especially as it relates to financial services industries, oil and gas sector, and aspects of manufacturing and telecommunications sectors have all recently witnessed influx of mergers and takeovers, and some foreign direct investments. These changes have brought about international and expatriate staff as well as the transfer of managerial practices from western countries. Consequently, many such businesses have had to effectively adopt several global best practices that already exist in their home offices/global headquarters which includes but not limited to home and teleworking, and other flexible work practices in their Nigerian offices. Nigeria is a very dynamic business environment and open to new technology uptakes. There is, therefore, need for more updated and well-guided research to update recent practices in Nigeria the business environment. Mainstream publications on WLB in Nigeria have been dominated by qualitative studies, there is room for more positivist quantitative approaches to be adopted in future research. This will reduce the overreliance on extant studies that may be reporting pre-2019 realities and HRM business practices outside of the fast pace developments in bigger cities in Nigeria's business environment. This is, particularly, important given the impact COVID-19 has had on the work culture and how many Nigerian businesses have responded with adjustments. There is a massive opportunity for researchers to tap into these yawning gap.

References

Abendroth, A., & den Dulk, L. (2011). Support for the work-life balance in Europe: The impact of state, workplace and family support on work-life balance satisfaction. *Work, Employment and Society, 25*, 234–256.

Adebulu, T. (2019). *NMA president: It will take 25 years to reduce shortage of doctors in Nigeria*. Available at https://www.thecable.ng/nma-it-will-take-25-years-to-reduce-shortage-of-doctors-in-nigeria. Accessed 02/04/2020.

Adekoya, O. D., Ajonbadi, H. A., & Mordi, C. (2019). Whenever the clarion call, whatever the time, you shall work: Work-life balance in the Nigerian army. *Economic Insights-Trends and Challenges, 8*(2), 27–42.

Aderinto, A. A. (2001). Patriarchy and culture: The position of women in a rural Yoruba community, Nigeria. *The Anthropologist, 3*(4), 225–230.

Adisa, T. A. (2015). *The inter-relationship between work life balance and organisational culture: An empirical study of Nigerian health sector*. A Thesis Submitted for the Degree of Doctor of Philosophy to College of Business, Arts and Social Sciences, Brunel University London. Available at https://bura.brunel.ac.uk/handle/2438/11561.

Adisa, T. A., Abdulraheem, I. & Osabutey, E. L. C. (2016). *Long working hours and the challenges of work-life balance: The case of nigerian medical doctors*. A paper presented at the British Academy of Management Conference, 6–8 September, Newcastle, UK.

Adisa, T. A., Abdulraheem, I., & Isiaka, S. B. (2019). Patriarchal hegemony: Investigating the impact of patriarchy on women's work-life balance. *Gender in Management: An International Journal, 34*(1), 19–33.

Adisa, T. A., Gbadamosi, G. & Osabutey, E. L. C. (2016). Work-family balance: A case analysis of coping strategies adopted by Nigerian and British working mothers. *Gender in Management: An International Journal, 31*(7), 414–433.

Adisa, T. A., Mordi, C., & Mordi, T. (2014). The challenges and realities of work-family balance among Nigerian female doctors and nurses. *Economic Insights-Trends and Challenges, 3*(3), 23–37.

Adisa, T. A., Mordi, C., & Osabutey, E. L. C. (2017). Exploring the implications of the influence of organisational culture on work-life balance practices: Evidence from Nigerian medical doctors. *Personnel Review, 46*(3), 454–473.

Adisa, T. A., Osabutey, E. L. C., & Gbadamosi, G. (2016). Understanding the causes and consequences of work-family conflict: An exploratory study of Nigerian employees. *Employee Relations, 38*(5), 770–788.

Adisa, T. A., Osabutey, E. L. C., & Gbadamosi, G. (2017). The implications of work-family balance among dual-earner couples: The case of medical practitioners in Nigeria. *Career Development International, 22*(4), 351–371.

Agba, A. M., Nwosu, U. W., & Innah, D. E. (2015). Correlates between family and employees' work life in Nigeria: The need for proper integration. *International Journal of Capacity Building in Education and Management, 2*(3), 25–42.

Akanji, B. (2012). Realities of work life balance in Nigeria: Perceptions of role conflict and coping beliefs. *Business, Management and Education, 10*(2), 248–263.

Akanji, B., Mordi, C., Simpson, R., Adisa, A. A., & Oruh, E. S. (2020). Time biases: Exploring the work–life balance of single Nigerian managers and professionals. *Journal of Managerial Psychology, 35*(2), 57–70.

Akinyele, F. T., Peters, M. C., & Akinyele, F. E. (2016). Work-life balance practices as panacea for employee performance: Empirical evidence from River state television, Nigeria. *Arabian Journal of Business and Management Review, 6*(5), 34–47.

Akinyele, S. T. (2010). A critical assessment of environmental impact on workers productivity in Nigeria. *Research Journal of Business Management, 4*(1), 61–72.

Allen, T. D. (2001). Family supportive work environments: The role of organizational perceptions. *Journal of Vocational Behavior, 58*(3), 414–435.

Amazue, L. O., & Onyishi, I. E. (2016). Stress coping strategies, perceived organizational support and marital status as predictors of work–life balance among Nigerian bank employees. *Social Indicators Research, 128*, 147–159.

Andrade, M. S., Westover, J. H., & Kupka, B. A. (2019). The role of work-life balance and worker scheduling flexibility in predicting global comparative job satisfaction. *International Journal of Human Resource Studies, 9*(2), 80–115.

Beauregard, T. A., & Henry, L. C. (2009). Making the link between work-life balance practices and organizational performance. *Human Resource Management Review, 19*(9), 9–22.

Bird, J. (2006). Work-life balance doing it right and avoiding the pitfalls. *Employment Relations Today, 33*(3), 21–30.

Bolaji, S. D., Gray, J. R., & Campbell-Evans, G. (2015). Why do policies fail in Nigeria? *Journal of Education & Social Policy, 2*(5), 57–66.

Bond, S. (2004). Organisational culture and work-life conflict in the UK. *International Journal of Sociology and Social Policy, 24*(12), 1–24.

Boxall, P., & Macky, K. (2014). High-involvement work processes, work intensification and employee well-being. *Work, Employment & Society, 28*(6), 963–984.

Central Intelligence World Factbook. (2019). *Nigeria economy*. Available at: https://www.cia.gov/library/publications/resources/the-world-factbook/geos/ni.html.

Clark, S. C. (2000). Work/family border theory: A new theory of work/family balance. *Human Relations, 53*(6), 747–770.

Drew, E., & Daverth, G. (2007). Negotiating work/life balance: The experience of fathers and mothers in Ireland. *Recherches Sociologiques et Anthropologiques, 38*(2), 65–81.

Emslie, C., & Hunt, K. (2009). 'Live to work' or 'work to live'? A qualitative study of work-life balance among men and women in mid-life. *Gender, Work and Organization, 16*(1), 151–172.

Epie, C., & Ituma, A. (2014). Working hours and work-family conflict in the international context of Nigeria. In Z. Mokomane (Ed.), *Work–family interface in Sub-Saharan Africa, international perspectives on social policy, administration, and practice* (pp. 57–74). Cham, Switzerland: Springer International Publishing.

Fajana, S. (2008). The Nigerian informal economy: Instigating decent work and pay, and national development through unionisation. *Employee Relations, 30*(4), 372–390.

Fein, E. C., Skinner, N., & Machin, M. A. (2017). Work intensification, work–life interference, stress, and well-being in Australian workers. *International Studies of Management & Organization, 47*(4), 360–371.

Fleetwood, S. (2007). Why work-life balance now? *International Journal of Human Resource Management, 18,* 387–400.

Greenhaus, J., & Beutell, N. (1985). Sources of conflict between work and family roles. *The Academy of Management Review, 10*(1), 77–92.

Greenhaus, J. H., & Powell, G. N. (2006). When work and family are allies: A theory of work-family enrichment. *The Academy of Management Review, 31*(1), 72–92.

Guest, D. E. (2002). Perspectives on the study of work-life balance. *Social Science Information, 41*(2), 255–279.

Hughes, J., & Bozionelos, N. (2007). Work-life balance as source of job dissatisfaction and withdrawal attitude: An exploratory study on the views of male workers. *Personnel Review, 36*(1), 145–154.

International Labour Organisation. (2018). *Decent work country programme II (2015–2018).* Available at: https://www.ilo.org/wcmsp5/groups/public/---africa/---ro-abidjan/---ilo-abuja/documents/publication/wcms_458263.pdf.

International Labour Organization. (2005). *Hours of work: From fixed to flexible?* Available at: https://www.ilo.org/public/english/standards/relm/ilc/ilc93/pdf/rep-iii-1b.pdf.

International Labour Organization. (2019). *Guide to developing balanced working time arrangements.* Geneva: International Labour Office.

International Labour Organization. (2020). *Working time.* Available at: https://www.ilo.org/global/topics/working-time/lang--en/index.htm.

Kalliath, T., & Brough, P. (2008). Achieving work-life balance. *Journal of Management & Organisation, 14*(3), 224–226.

Kesting, S., & Harris, C. (2009). Providing a theoretical foundation for work-life balance—Sen's capability approach. *New Zealand Journal of Employment Relations, 34*(1), 47–61.

KPMG. (2019). *The labour act for review*. Available at: https://home.kpmg/ng/en/home/insights/2019/11/the-labour-act-for-review-.html.

Lee, S., McCann, D., & Messenger, J. C. (2007). *Working time around the world: Trends in working hours, laws and policies in a global comparative perspective*. London: Routledge.

Lewis, J., Gambles, R., & Rapoport, R. (2007). The constraints of a work-life balance approach: International perspectives. *International Journal of Human Resource Management, 18*(3), 360–373.

Makama, G. A. (2013). Patriarchy and gender inequality in Nigeria: The way forward. *European Scientific Journal, 9*(17), 115–144.

McDonald, P., Townsend, K., & Wharton, A. (2013). The legitimation and reproduction of discourse-practice gaps in work-life balance. *Personnel Review, 42*(2), 205–222.

McGinnity, F., & Russell, H. (2015). Work-life balance, working conditions and the great recession. In S.Ó. Riain, F. Behling, R. Ciccia, & E. Flaherty E. (Eds.), The *changing worlds and workplaces of capitalism.* International Political Economy Series. London: Palgrave Macmillan.

Messenger, J. (2018). *Working time and the future of work*. Geneva: International Labour Office.

Mishra, K., Boynton, L., & Mishra, A. (2014). Driving employee engagement: The expanded role of internal communications. *International Journal of Business Communication, 51*(2), 183–202.

Mitsakis, F. V., & Talampekos, G. (2014). Work life balance (WLB) and flexibility in paid work (FPW) for "generation y": A discussion. *Business and Management Horizons, 2*(1), 34–46.

Mmakwe, J. A., & Ojiabo, K. (2018). Work-life balance and employee performance in Nigerian banks, Port Harcourt. *International Journal of Advanced Academic Research, 4*(1), 107–119.

Mordi, C., Mmieh, F., & Ojo, S. I. (2013). An exploratory study of managers' perspective of work-life balance in Nigeria: A case analysis of the Nigerian banking sector. *Thunderbird International Business Review, 55*(1), 55–75.

Muchiti, E., & Gachunga, H. (2015). Influence of work life balance on employee productivity in Kenya: A Case of Milimani Law Courts Nairobi. *The Strategic Journal of Business and Change Management, 2*(48), 1–20.

Mushfiqur, R., Mordi, C., Oruh, E., Nwagbara, U., Mordi, T., & Turner, I. (2018). The impacts of work-life-balance (WLB) challenges on social sustainability: The experience of Nigerian female medical doctors. *Employee Relations, 40*(5), 868–888.

Naithani, P. (2010a). Overview of work-life balance discourse and its relevance in current economic scenario. *Asian Social Science, 6*(6), 148–155.

Naithani, P. (2010b). Recession and work-life balance initiatives. *Romanian Economic Journal, 37,* 55–68.

Neequaye, S. (2016). Off balance: Getting beyond the work-life balance myth to personal and professional satisfaction by Matthew Kelly. *European Journal of Training and Development, 40*(5), 366–368.

Ngwama, J. C. (2016). Framework for occupational health and safety in Nigeria: The implication for the trade union movement. *Journal of Economics and Sustainable Development, 7*(11), 98–109.

Nippert-Eng, C. E. (1996). *Home and work.* Chicago, IL: The University of Chicago Press.

Nizam, I., & Kam, C. (2018). The determinants of work-life balance in the event industry of Malaysia. *International Journal of Management, Accounting and Economics, 5*(3), 141–168.

Nordenmark, M., Vinberg, S., & Strandh, M. (2012). Job control and demands, work-life balance and wellbeing among self-employed men and women in Europe. *Vulnerable Groups & Inclusion, 3*(1), 188–196.

Nwagbara, U. (2020). Exploring how institutions shape managerialist employment relations and work-life balance (WLB) challenges in Nigeria. *Employee Relations: The International Journal.* https://www.emerald.com/insight/0142-5455.htm.

Nzewi, H. N., Augustine, A., Mohammed, I., & Godson, O. (2018). Physical work environment and employee performance in selected brewing firms in Anambra State, Nigeria. *Journal of Good Governance and Sustainable Development in Africa, 4*(2), 131–145.

Ojo, I. S., Salau, O. P., & Falola, H. O. (2014). Work-life balance practices in Nigeria: A comparison of three sectors. *Journal of Competitiveness, 6*(2), 3–14.

Okpara, J. O., & Wynn, P. (2007). The impact of ethical climate on job satisfaction, and commitment in Nigeria: Implications for management development. *Journal of Management Development, 27*(9), 935–950.

Oktosatrio, S. (2018). Investigating the relationship between work-life-balance and motivation of the employees: Evidences from the local government of

Jakarta. *International Journal of Academic Research in Business and Social Sciences, 8*(2), 205–221.

Olaoye, I. (2012). *Work-life balancing and job performance of workers in private universities in South-Western Nigeria*. Munich: GRIN Verlag. Available at: https://www.grin.com/document/267275.

Parkes, L. P., & Langford, P. H. (2008). Work-life balance or work-life alignment? A test of the importance of work-life balance for employee engagement and intention to stay in organisations. *Journal of Management and Organization, 14*(3), 267–284.

Pradhan, G. (2016). *Conceptualising work-life balance* (Working Paper). Bangalore: The Institute for Social and Economic Change.

Ranjan, R., & Prasad, T. (2013). Literature review report on work-life balance of loco-pilots (railway drivers) in India. *European Journal of Business Management, 5*(19), 17–27.

Rao, I. (2017). Work-life balance for sustainable human development: Cultural intelligence as enabler. *Journal of Human Behavior in the Social Environment, 27*(7), 706–713.

Rapoport, R., Bailyn, L., Fletcher, K. J., & Pruitt, H. B. (2002). *Beyond work-family balance: Advancing gender equity and workplace performance*. San Francisco: Jossey-Bass.

Skinner, C., & Pocock, B. (2008). Work-life conflict: Is work time or work overload more important? *Asia Pacific Journal of Human Resources, 46*(3), 303–315.

Staines, G. (1980). Spillover versus compensation: A review of the literature on the relationship between work and nonwork. *Human Relations, 33*(2), 111–129.

Tamunomiebi, C. C., & Ukachukwu, M. D. (2018). Indecent work and workers in the informal sector in Nigeria. *International Journal of Scientific & Engineering Research, 9*(3), 630–643.

Ugwu, F. O., Amazue, L. O., & Onyedire, N. G. (2017). Work-family life balance in a Nigerian banking sector setting. *Cogent Psychology, 4*(1), 1–9.

Ukaegbu, C. (2000). Working conditions and employee commitment in indigenous private manufacturing firms in Nigeria: Managing business organisations for industrial development. *The Journal of Modern African Studies, 38*(2), 295–324.

Visser, J. (2019). Can unions revitalize themselves? In *The future of work: Trade unions in transformation* (pp. 17–48). Geneva: International Journal of Labour Research – International Labour Office.

Warhurst, C., Eikhof, D. R., & Haunschild, A. (2008). Out of balance or just out of bounds? Analysing the relationship between work and life. In C. Warhurst, D. R. Eikhof, & A. Haunschild (Eds.), *Work less, live more? Critical analysis of the work-life boundary* (pp. 1–21). New York: Palgrave Macmillan.

Webster, E., & Forrest, K. (2019). Precarious work: Experimenting with new forms of representation: South African labour responds. In: *The future of work: Trade unions in transformation* (pp. 49–72). Geneva: International Journal of Labour Research – International Labour Office.

Wheatley, D. (2012). Work-life balance, travel-to-work, and the dual career household. *Personnel Review, 41*(6), 813–831.

Wilkinson, A. (1999). Employment relations in SMEs. *Employee Relations, 21*(3), 206–217.

Worldometer. (2020). *Countries in the world by population.* Available at: https://www.worldometers.info/world-population/population-by-country/.

World Population Review. (2020). *GDP ranked by country 2020.* Available at: https://worldpopulationreview.com/countries/countries-by-gdp/.

Young, L., & Kleiner, B. H. (1992). Work and family: Issues for the 1990s. *Women in Management Review, 7*(5), 24–28.

Yu, S. (2014). Work–life balance—Work intensification and job insecurity as job stressors. *Labour & Industry: A Journal of the Social and Economic Relations of Work, 24*(3), 203–216.

Zedeck, S., & Mosier, K. L. (1990). Work in the family and employing organization. *American Psychologist, 45*(2), 240–251.

6

The Work-Life Balance of Younger and Older Indian Women Managers in Corporate South Africa

Nasima M. H. Carrim and Eileen Koekemoer

Introduction

A considerable amount of literature has been published on how individuals attempt to combine work and family responsibilities and how employees attempt to obtain some degree of balance between these domains (commonly referred to as work-life balance [WLB] or work-family balance). From the outset, studies of WLB have focused on the challenges faced by parents, particularly mothers, and more recently by dual-career couples with dependent children (Kelliher, Richardson, & Boiarintseva, 2018). Although various researchers agree that contemporary societal changes necessitate a more encompassing and dynamic understanding of how individuals experience WLB, research on the subject has been mostly restricted to how employees pursue WLB and the various strategies that work for a specific group of people (in most cases

N. M. H. Carrim (✉) · E. Koekemoer
University of Pretoria, Pretoria, South Africa
e-mail: nasima.carrim@up.ac.za

T. A. Adisa and G. Gbadamosi (eds.), *Work-Life Interface*,
https://doi.org/10.1007/978-3-030-66648-4_6

this excludes minority groups). Already in 2008, work-life research had been criticised for only focusing on the experiences of middle and upper class, younger, white, western and heterosexual women (Aycan, 2008). According to Gatrell, Burnett, Cooper, and Sparrow (2013), WLB is often viewed as a problem for middle-class dual-earner parents, which would mean that extant research and theory only provide a partial view of the work-life needs and experiences of the workforce. This chapter therefore aims to examine how younger and older Indian women (a minority group in South Africa) managers balance their work and home lives and how they succeed in reaching senior and top management posts in the process.

Kelliher et al. (2018) suggested that existing knowledge is mainly concerned with life (meaning caring for dependent children) and work which is based on a traditional model of full-time, permanent employment. However, recently Ryan and Briggs (2019) observed that work-life literature is expanding to incorporate samples that are more diverse and research is increasingly documenting the unique experiences of multiply marginalised individuals. Furthermore, they advocate that by focusing on various identities would mean bringing attention to unidentified needs, respecting ignored values, increasing awareness of unacknowledged conflicts and providing more supportive advice. This can provide a more explicit recognition of the social structures that contribute to challenging contexts for work-life integration and balance for those who are multiply stigmatised (Ryan & Briggs, 2019).

Concerning minority groups, investigating WLB is a continuing concern for researchers and organisations in Africa. According to Ugwu, Orjiakor, Enwereuzor, Onyedibe, and Ugwu (2016), intensifying research in Africa is crucial especially given the unique social system, the culture, and the lifestyle which is distinct from the Western form (where most work-life research originate). WLB research from the African continent include mostly studies among South African Indian women (Bharathi & Mala, 2016; Carrim, 2017; Jaga & Bagraim, 2017; Saxena & Bhatnagar, 2018; Shanmugam, 2017; Valk, Van der Velde, Van Engen, & Godbole, 2014), women working in African contexts (Ajayi, Ojo, & Mordi, 2015; Bahiru & Mengistu, 2018; Carrim, 2017; Jaga, Arabandi, Bagraim, & Mdlongwa, 2018; Mkhize & Msomi, 2016; Muasya, 2016) or women of colour (Dillard, 2018; Hamidullah & Riccucci, 2017; Kachchaf, Ko, Hodari, & Ong, 2015). Overall, these studies provide important insights into the challenges and struggles minority women in Africa experience during their attempt to balance work and family life.

Remarkably, Jean (2007) argues that as the number of women increases in the workforce and in leadership roles, it is important to understand gender and leadership identities. Although women's leadership significantly contributes to building high-performing organisations, Bahiru and Mengistu (2018) are of the opinion that the challenges that these women in leadership positions experience with regard to balancing work and family responsibilities are inhibiting them from exerting their fullest potential towards either their career or home life. According to Beckwith, Carter, and Peters (2016), although African American women have overcome challenges such as race and gender bias in the workplace, barriers to promotion and obstacles for career growth; these women are still very much underrepresented in executive leadership positions. In addition, the study of Bhirugnath-Bhookhun and Kitada (2017) highlights that to be successful in their careers, women managers tend to live a work-led life rather than one that is work-life balanced.

On the other hand, Bobat, Mshololo, and Reuben (2012) found in their study (a study exploring women managers' WLB over the life course), that generally, women experienced the positive impact of WLB. However, they do acknowledge that there are challenges to WLB in all occupations, but that these challenges should be considered in relation to their contexts and perhaps differences according to class, age and race. They advocate that these differences need to be recognised in any search of a holistic in-depth understanding of WLB.

Given the rise of interest in South African Indian women in leadership positions (Carrim, 2017), the goal of this chapter is to illustrate how Indian women (as a minority group in South Africa) managers balance their work and home lives and how they succeed in reaching senior and top management posts in the process. The examination of the WLB of Indian Women in South Africa is relevant because despite operating in western organisational contexts these women still hold on to certain cultural values, especially related to taking care of their families and homes. The next section focuses on the literature related to work-life balance of women managers, followed by the theoretical perspective. The methodology, analysis and discussion sections follow and the chapter ends with a conclusion and recommendations for future studies.

Literature Review

WLB research topics from the African continent cover a variety of work-family aspects, most of which are related to challenges women from diverse cultural or minority groups face.

WLB Among African Women

In terms of understanding the WLB as experienced for African women, some insightful studies are available. For example, the study of Mkhize and Msomi (2016) explains how African single mothers are confronted with systemic issues, such as under-employment, poverty, and economic marginalisation. Furthermore, the study explains how the traditional model of the family (i.e. comprising a mother, a father, siblings, and a supportive extended family) is declining, and how that makes it more difficult for these women to find the time to balance their family, work or career aspirations.

In addition, for black women professionals, negotiating gender, race, work and family in post-apartheid South Africa, remains challenging (Jaga et al., 2018). Jaga et al. (2018), found that for black professional women, the persistence of gender and racial discrimination are remaining, despite their education and skill set. Consequently, the perception of discrimination leads to preoccupation and loss of energy hindering women's performance in the family domain. Similarly, women leaders in Ethiopia, are experiencing workplace challenges such as work overload, cultural and social norms, family responsibilities, and upbringing related behaviours, which all hinder their WLB (Bahiru & Mengistu, 2018). The struggle of balancing work and family life remains prominent for Ethiopian women leaders as it seems that organisations in their country are demanding more outcomes than the resources they provide, and demand extra hours of work (Bahiru & Mengistu, 2018).

A different WLB aspect often being examined is the use of domestic workers to alleviate the pressure in balancing work and family. In the study of Muasya (2016), it was found that due to the increase in costs of domestic workers, Kenyan women are shifting their work–family practices by only using domestic workers as-needed or only on weekends and taking their older children to day-care centres (although such facilities are not always present in Kenyan organisations).

Interestingly, Ajayi et al. (2015) found a negative relationship with the ability to balance work-family roles and those women falling in the age brackets between 30–39 and 40–49. Furthermore, the results show that the majority of the women in this study, marital status notwithstanding, across all the work categories experience a level of work-family imbalance.

Overall, these African-based studies seem to point to various contributing organisational, societal, and individual factors that inhibit the contribution that African women can make in building high performing organisations and how these women struggle with their work-family needs.

WLB Among Indian Women

Investigating WLB among Indian women working in IT has recently been on the increase. In the study of Bharati and Mala (2016), specific challenges and enhancers as determinants of WLB were identified. For those women working in IT organisations in India, personal challenges included inadequate self-attention, insufficient time spent on elders and children, feelings of depression or suffering with hypertension alongside the professional challenge of extended or odd working time. According to Shanmugam (2017) although women in India seem to have embraced the benefits and availability of employment, they are continuously caught between the growing pressure to pursue a career and the primacy of motherhood over other life roles. This reflects the notion of familial roles over professional roles for Indian women.

This is also evident in the study among Hindu mothers in South Africa (Jaga & Bagraim, 2017), where the findings suggest that despite the mothers having careers, in most instances they prioritised their family role over their work role. This is in line with the cultural norms of Indian mothers, and the importance of family and maintaining such strong relationships, (Agarwal, 2007; Carrim, 2017).

On the other hand, in the recent study of Saxena and Bhatnagar (2018), findings indicate that this same traditional society, (which at times restrains the professional growth of women through its heavily gendered expectations to take care of the family first), also acts as facilitator for these Indian women to pursue further studies which require them to stay away from their families for a substantial period of time. Motives for these women to take career breaks and pursue further rigorous educational programs are mostly related to the dissatisfaction with their work situation, their need for skill enhancement, and an urge to develop their own identity. This is in line with the study of Valk et al. (2014), who found that in their contemporary careers, Indian women wanted to fulfil their potential and have a deeper sense of meaningfulness for themselves and for others by contributing to issues that are of economic and social concern.

Rising against the underrepresentation of African women in leadership positions (Beckwith et al., 2016), the findings of Das (2006) suggests that work-life practices can have a positive impact on women's representation in management. Her study highlights the important role of context in impacting work-life practices on women's progress into management.

Even though the concept of WLB has attracted extensive research in a local, industry and national settings, there is limited evidence of minority groupings of migrants operating in Western settings, in particular (Ali, Malik, Pereira, & Ariss, 2017). The challenge of WLB is further compounded in the case of minority migrant groups such as Asian Indian women living and working in Western contexts. Asian Indian migrant workers might face additional challenges owing to their strong patriarchal cultural, economic, familial and WLB pressures as well as due to ethnic discrimination at work in Western nations. For example, Ali and Kramar (2015) describe how in Pakistan (an Asian Indian majority country), women are being restricted to the 'inside' space of home and household. This restricts these women's access to education, employment, training opportunities and social services. Thus, when such Asian Indian women migrate to Western countries and choose to work, they experience WLB issues due to the strong expectations of their households to focus on family needs.

Furthermore, Asian Indian migrant workers have been noted to lack confidence and skills needed in several Western settings. However, Ali et al. (2017) argue that through higher education Asian Indian migrant women can acquire new skills, competence and confidence that will allow them to develop their social networks and consequently develop a better cultural understanding of their work domain. Understanding how minority groups experience WLB is significant as this has specific implications for people who face multiple disadvantages due to two or more layers of identities even more so as research suggests that culture and ethnicity influence WLB.

According to Syed (2015), many issues stemming from intersecting and multiple identities are being ignored within WLB policies. This results in many workers not fully benefitting from the governmental and organisational WLB initiatives. Furthermore, Syed (2015) argue that while Asian Indian female modesty occurs as a value in many cultures, it is particularly explicit and the influence of such cultural practices is huge on working women's lives. Particularly when Asian Indian women are working in western countries, the practice of modesty and inhibition may lead to discomfort and uneasiness of both Asian Indian women and their colleagues. For instance, the lack of socialising due to religious reasons may hinder the process of networking at the workplace, which leads to other consequences affecting performance and career development (Ali & Kramar, 2015).

Cultural Identity Work

According to Hall (1990), there are two ways of defining cultural identity. First, cultural identity is regarded as representing a shared culture that is entrenched in a shared ancestry and history that one has in common with other people. Thus, an individual's cultural identity is a demonstration of the cultural codes and shared historical experiences that provide an individual a fixed, established and uninterrupted frame of orientation underpinned by the fluctuating partitions of one's authentic history. Second, cultural identity comprises numerous points of similarity as well as difference, reproducing what we have become due to the intervention of history. Hence, cultural identity belongs both to the past and the future. Cultural identities have a history but are also constantly transformed and are therefore fluid (Hall, 1990). A person's family, community, peers and religious institutions play a role in the development of one's cultural identity (Erikson, 1968). Thus, a person's cultural identity develops based on the beliefs, values, attitudes and norms of one's cultural group (Campbell, 2000).

Nevertheless, this socially constructed definition of cultural identity does not include the likelihood that people may identify with their cultures to different intensities, especially when these are communicated across generations or when political and socio-economic contexts change (Grossman & Charmaraman, 2009) as these two aspects may affect social arrangements within homes. People also follow group customs and aspects that mirror their own prototypical personalities, thereby bolstering the group's practices, prestige and values. Thus, Indian women will adopt traditional cultural roles as long as others enforce these in their environment; the reason being that within Indian society, sociocultural influences play a vital role and social acceptance is regarded above individual decision-making as individuals want to feel protected and recognised within society (Banerjee, 2008).

Thus, the question of 'who are we?' takes primacy over the question 'who am I?' Nevertheless, when traditional gender roles begin to change or weaken due to outside influences the result is that members of that society start to work and rework their cultural identities to acclimatise to new identities and roles, resulting in cultural identity work. Hence, cultural identity work concerns the extent to which group members from traditional cultures work and rework their identities to decrease the anxiety they feel in negating prescribed social gender norms (Carrim, 2018).

Studies conducted in India show that the number of dual-career households has increased but that men in these households still adhere to their traditional cultural values and identities. For instance, Saraff and Srivastava's (2010) study in India found that husbands were anxious when wives worked outside the home as it went against their cultural identities of being the sole breadwinners. Husbands achieved cultural identity congruence by taking unilateral decisions in their homes and not providing wives with support in household chores in their homes. In patriarchal and hierarchical societies, such as the Indian community, cultural identities of individuals are rigid (Coltrane, 2000). Men's cultural identities are centred on their roles as breadwinners, their participation in pursuits outside the home and their absence of involvement in household chores. Within such societies, men's status is higher, they are accorded more privileges compared to women, and are less involved than women in household chores and childcare (Saraff & Srivastava, 2010). Considering gender roles are rigid in such societies, men provide limited social support to wives (Carrim, 2016), and therefore wives engage in minimal cultural identity work.

Gender norms within the Indian society are traditional and men have power. In this type of cultural setting, where traditional gender roles do not enable professional women to have any bargaining power regardless of their earnings. Thus, wives cannot negotiate household chores with spouses (Schneider, 2011) as men take decisions and wives are responsible for childcare and domestic labour (Saraff & Srivastava, 2010). Hence, traditionally Indian women engage in minimal cultural identity work as they adhere to prescribed roles. For example, Rajadhyaksha and Velgach (2009) discovered in their study of 160 dual-earner couples in India that wives wanted their spouses to assist them in household chores and childcare. But wives in the study were unable to sway husbands from traditional cultural roles as these are slow to change in India as husbands hold on to traditional cultural identities.

Carrim (2017) posits that, furthermore to cultural prescripts, norms and values within the macro-environment influences the mindsets of individuals towards gender roles and the division of domestic labour and childcare. Studies reveal that men's share of domestic labour and participation vary across nations (Kan, Sullivan, & Gershuny, 2011;

Ruppanner, 2010). These differences are ascribed to varying social policies related to women's labour force participation and childcare (Cooke, 2007). Men who live in countries that have liberal social policies shoulder a larger portion of domestic duties compared to men who live in countries that have traditionalist policies. Conservative policies promote traditional gender roles and follow the model of the male being the breadwinner and the female being the caregiver (Cooke, 2007; Kan et al., 2011; Ruppanner, 2010). However, a drawback of studies such as these is that they cannot account for all variables, such as the cultures of individuals.

Next, the attention turns to the South African context related to gender roles.

The South African Context Regarding Gender Roles

During the colonial and apartheid eras, men held power in South African society and this status quo has not changed during the post-apartheid era (Carrim & Senne, 2019). In the past, whites had the most power and Africans the least, whereas Indians had somewhat more power than the latter group (Vangarajaloo, 2011). In the democratic era, Indians have less power compared to whites and Africans (Carrim, 2016). In the past, South Africa was based on a patriarchal system where men dominated in the workplace and the home and these arrangements still persist in homes where traditional cultures are practised (Carrim, 2019).

In Indian homes, men were the breadwinners as women were not allowed to enter the job market due to a lack of job opportunities during the apartheid era and they were expected to uphold the respectability of their families (Vangarajaloo, 2011). These days South African Indian women do indeed work but men remain the head of households (Carrim, 2017, 2018). This type of home arrangements has resulted in Indians strictly following traditional gender roles where sons and daughters are raised and socialised to regard appropriate gender roles as vitally important to upholding cultural beliefs and values (Vangarajaloo, 2011).

The 1994 elections ushered in a democratic era that allowed Indian women to enter the workplace, which resulted in an increase in dual-career couples (Vangarajaloo, 2011). Within the South African workplace, Indian women face discrimination and stereotyping as a result of their racial and gender identities (Carrim & Nkomo, 2016). During the apartheid era, Indian women were relegated to lower-level posts, while white males dominated management posts. However, after democracy an increasing number of Indian women entered corporate South Africa and were promoted to management posts as a result of labour legislation promulgated to promote previously disadvantaged groups (one such group being Indians) in the workplace (Carrim, 2019). However, Indian women within the workplace face many challenges such as their work being challenged by white male colleagues, facing micro-aggressive behaviour from white colleagues, experiencing overt and subtle forms of racism and patriarchy (Carrim, 2018).

Within the workplace, Indian women have the skills required to reach higher-level positions but due to high levels of racism and discrimination, they face many challenges to their upward mobility (Carrim & Nkomo, 2016). Patriarchy is also practised in Indian homes where parents maintain Indian cultural norms and values related to gender roles (Carrim, 2018). However, the study by Carrim (2017) indicates that some Indian women managers who live in nuclear family units have managed to negotiate egalitarian relationships with husbands as far as household chores and childcare are concerned, but that others have not been able to do so. Nevertheless, Carrim's study does not focus on whether there are differences in how younger and older Indian women managers negotiate their gender roles related to housework and childcare within their respective homes.

It is against this backdrop that this chapter aims to examine how younger and older Indian women (a minority group in South Africa) managers balance their work and home lives and how they succeed in reaching senior and top management posts in the process. With this aim in mind, the following research question emerged:

Do younger and older Indian women managers experience the same challenges in balancing their work and home lives?

Methodology

Research Participants

In order to gain an in-depth understanding of how the participants progressed towards senior and top managerial positions, a qualitative, interpretivist approach was used that allowed the participating women to share their life experiences (Ritchie & Lewis, 2003). Also, considering that much is not known about the WLB of Indian women within the South African context we opted for a qualitative approach. One of the researchers interviewed 13 older women, ages ranging from 35 to 60 years old and 11 younger[1] women ages ranging from 25 to 34 years old in middle, senior and top managerial positions in various South African organisations. Participants were selected using a combination of purposive and snowball sampling (Ritchie & Lewis, 2003). The participants were all provided with pseudonyms to maintain confidentiality.

With purposive sampling, the aim was to only target younger and older Indian women who occupied management positions. Snowball sampling was achieved by asking participants to recommend peers and family members and friends who would be interested in participating in the study. After interviewing 11 older participants and 8 younger participants, we realised that we had reached data saturation. We therefore interviewed two additional older and three younger participants to ensure no new data emerged from the interviews. Considering new information emerged from the data we concluded our interviews. The outcome was that 13 older and 11 younger participants were interviewed.

The participants were in managerial positions across various functional titles, ranging from operations manager to human resource director. They all completed first (three-year) degrees (Bachelor's degrees), and 18 of them had postgraduate degrees. Older participants were born and raised in the apartheid era and grew up in demarcated Indian townships where they were educated in designated Indian schools. Indian

[1]The National Youth Commission Act of 1996 defines younger employees being between the ages of 17–35 years (South Africa, 1996).

schools were not as well equipped as white schools and had a narrow choice of subjects (Carrim, 2012). Indian townships were situated in racially segregated suburbs that were located on the outskirts of the city, where the Indian community resided and were schooled, and from where they would operate their businesses. Municipal offices, banks and cinemas were also erected in these townships so that Indians did not have any need to venture outside these areas (Bhana, 2008). Most of the contact they had with other race groups were with African house helps and gardeners in their homes or with African and white customers in their family businesses. The participants lived in environments that were socially isolated and insulated from other race groups and they were prevented from establishing lasting relationships across racial barriers due to structural segregation (Carrim, 2012).

Younger participants on the other hand lived in multiracial and multicultural communities where they had contact with people from other race groups.

For older participants, the segregation of amenities was enforced by the Reservation of Separate Amenities Act, No. 49 of 1953, which aimed at reducing contact between white and black people, as beaches and public utilities were racially segregated (Marais, 2011). Older participants were educated in designated Indian universities, which were located in KwaZulu-Natal, the province with the highest Indian population in South Africa. Five attended white universities, while four studied through the University of South Africa (UNISA), a correspondence university. Younger participants attended multiracial universities. At the time of the interviews, nineteen of the women were married, one was divorced and four were single (Table 6.1).

Interview Procedure

Interviews were chosen as a method of obtaining information from participants. The reason interviews were chosen was because we wanted to gain an in-depth understanding of the participants' WLB issues. This type of data would not have been adequately captured with other methods. One of the researchers conducted in-depth, semi-structured

Table 6.1 Biographical data of participants

Pseudonym	Age range	Educational level	Position	No of children/marital status
Shamila Rumi	44	Postgraduate	Business Application Manager	2-married
Saira Rahman	36	Postgraduate	Chief Financial Officer	0-single
Waheeda Banu	37	Postgraduate	Senior Public Prosecutor	4-married
Shabana Mahal	46	Postgraduate	Chief Financial Officer	2-married
Firdous Azmi	47	Postgraduate	Executive Director Operations	4-married
Zeenat Khan	42	Postgraduate	Chief Communications Officer	3-married
Bipasha Chaudry	37	Postgraduate	Operations Manager	3-married
Mahima Basu	38	Postgraduate	Legal Manager	0-single
Preity Sen	36	Undergraduate	Project Manager	0-single
Sushmita Zinta	49	Postgraduate	Human Resource Director	1-married
Rani Kapoor	36	Postgraduate	Human Resource Director	2-married
Karina Mukerjee	45	Undergraduate	Senior Marketing Manager	3-married
Shilpa Chopra	43	Postgraduate	Human Resource Director	0-divorced
Deepika Sharma	25	Undergraduate	IT manager	2-married
Anushka Sinha	33	Postgraduate	Finance Manager	2-married
Alia Kapoor	27	Undergraduate	IT Manager	1-married
Sonam Bhatt	32	Postgraduate	Engineering Manager	2-married
Kangana Dixit	30	Postgraduate	Human Resource Manager	4-married

(continued)

Table 6.1 (continued)

Pseudonym	Age range	Educational level	Position	No of children/marital status
Karishma Balan	31	Postgraduate	Manager (Industrial Psychologist)	0-single
Madhuri Kolhapuri	29	Postgraduate	Marketing Manager	3-married
Vidya Dutt	32	Undergraduate	Project Manager	4-married
Malaika Fakhri	25	Undergraduate	IT Manager	2-married
Sonakshi Chawla	32	Postgraduate	Finance Manager	3-married
Nargis Tagore	26	Postgraduate	Finance Manager	2-married

interviews with the participants. Her semi-structured interview protocol probed the work-life balance of Indian women managers in the South African context. The questions invited the women to reflect on their experiences in their current situations. Examples of questions included 'Tell me, how did you manage with children, a home and your career?'; 'What are your support structures?'; 'What made you successful compared to other women managers?'.

One of the author's used probing in order to obtain clarity and to gain a deeper understanding of important aspects relating to the participants' work-life balance (Lincoln & Guba, 1985). This study formed a part of a larger study. The interviews were audiotaped so that it was easy to retrieve and review information and to sustain the validity of the study. Follow-up interviews were conducted with each participant in order to probe deeper and to clarify themes extracted from the data collected in the first round of interviews.

Analysis of Stories

The data obtained from the interviews were analysed in an iterative manner. Specific focus was given to understanding whether there were differences in how younger and older participants achieved work-life balance. Such an analysis requires a close, line-by-line reading of the text compiled based on the interviews. Our analysis moved from first-order coding of statements relating to specific categories to identification of theoretical categories and dimensions and ultimately to relationships among these dimensions (Pratt, 2009). Our goal was to derive a collection of themes that had enough particularity to be grounded and enough abstraction to be conceptualised. Our discussion and analysis of the findings are anchored on the identity tensions experienced by participants. We ensured that we were thoroughly conversant with each participant's life story. In analysing the stories, we used Social Identity theory, specifically cultural identity work and analysed the data in terms of the participants' experiences in corporate South Africa.

Research Findings

Balancing Life During Early Career

The majority of older participants were raised in nuclear homes and some in joint family structures. Younger participants were raised in nuclear homes. The majority of participants indicated that their mothers were housewives, and before marriage they would not be expected to go home, cook and get involved in housework. Participants from joint family structures pointed out that there were many women in the family to handle the chores and they were expected to assist minimally. A few younger and older participants did however indicate that their mothers worked full time and they were expected to assist with cooking and housework. In the latter case, participants indicated that living in homes where moms worked was not a major challenge to participants as they were still able to focus on their careers as household chores were distributed among siblings and parents, thus decreasing workloads. Shamila, an older Business Applications Manager indicated:

> My mom was working as a teacher. She would come home after school and prepare the food and clean the kitchen. She was a super woman. Between my brother and me, we would clean up after supper. During

> weekends my brother and I would clean the house on Saturday mornings and then we would be free for the rest of the weekend with just the kitchen to clean up after meals. We had a three-bedroom house so the household chores could be completed fairly quickly. Since there were only adults living in the house, we did not have a major mess as we all cleaned up after ourselves. So, I had time for my career as well.

Nargis, a younger Finance Manager was on the other hand, raised with a stay-at-home mom commented as follows:

> Before I was married, my mom did everything for me. I didn't lift a finger. At that time, I had lots of free time and did not even worry about balancing work and family.

The majority of older and younger participants indicated that they flourished in their careers during their early years. Not being married and in most cases having the support of their mothers assisted them to focus and build their careers. Shilpa, an older Human Resource Director mentioned that growing up in a joint family structure gave her time to build her career:

> I was very blessed growing up in a joint family. As an aspiring manager, the older females in our family took care of the household and they gave me plenty of time to build my career.

Sonakshi echoed the same sentiments:

> I didn't even think about managing work commitments before marriage. I was able to handle my work responsibilities and lead a full life- going out with friends, completing my studies, doing my job. There was no rush and hurry for anything.

Balancing Lives After Marriage

The majority of older and younger participants indicated that after marriage life became taxing. Although the majority of participants lived in nuclear homes, older participants and some younger women indicated that they could not escape the responsibilities towards their in-laws. The reasons participants provided were that the responsibility of taking care of in-laws within the Indian cultural traditions falls on daughters-in-law. Daughters-in-law are expected to take part in family functions and to take care of in-laws when the need arises. In some cases, in-laws came from large families and tend to entertain regularly and the onus falls on the daughter-in-law to be part of the social functions and to lend a helping hand. Waheeda, an older Senior Public Prosecutor indicated that life became challenging after she got married:

> After marriage I have to cook every day, not only for my husband and children but for his parents as well. Once a month during weekends there are functions as my in-laws have a large extended family. So, I have to cook and take food to these function. Life becomes hectic as I find it difficult to cope with work demands and in-law demands.

According to many younger participants, the roles of daughters-in-law in the Indian community are changing, especially for those who are pursuing careers. Younger participants indicated that they do not take on the responsibilities of taking care of their in-laws. They further indicated that their involvement in social functions is to a minimal extent. Alia, like the younger participants commented that it in families that are more traditional, that younger daughters-in-law tend to carry a major burden of the work. Alia, a younger IT manager like some of the younger participants pointed out that:

> I made it clear to my husband that I will not be able to cope with seeing to my in-laws and my own family, as I'm a career 'woman'. My friends too do not have time for taking care of in-laws- they assist occasionally when there is a wedding in the family. Even when I attend family functions I will prepare a dessert or bake a cake or make some salads but I refused to take on the majority responsibility of the function- I leave all the major work for my sisters-in-law (husband's sisters).

Older participants and some of the younger participants pointed out that their challenges within their homes increased when they started having children. Sonam, a younger Engineering Manager indicated that her life became even more demanding after having children:

> In the Indian culture, the responsibility of taking care of the home and children falls on the mother. It was difficult for me to juggle the various roles in my life, especially after I had children. This was especially difficult for me when the children were dependent on me- I would say in at least the first six years of my children's lives I was very actively involved in nurturing them.

Overcoming Challenges

Participants were asked how they overcame some of the challenges they experienced in balancing their work and careers. We were also interested in exploring how these women advanced in their careers and reached middle, senior and top management posts. The majority of participants indicated that they used various methods of balancing their work and home lives. These ranged from obtaining the assistance of au pairs, household help, and assistance from extended family members and husbands and in a few cases, participants also outsourced cooking. Participants indicated that au pairs and household help are abundant in South Africa. Some participants indicated that they could not afford the services of au pairs and household help. In some cases, participants were reluctant to hire such assistance. The reasons provided by some participants were the high cost of such assistance and the high crime rates resulting from such arrangements. Karina, an older Senior Marketing Manager remarked on hiring au pairs and household assistance:

> I get up at 4 am every morning and prepare food for the day. My husband and children assist with the breakfast and making lunch packages for us to take to work and school. Fortunately, the school is across the street from our house. After school my children see to themselves for lunch and clean up the kitchen. My husband and I do not hire any household help as there have been quite a number of incidences in our area where they were involved in crime, to the extent that they have killed their employers just for money. We cannot therefore compromise our safety. Besides, the

> kids are teenagers now, they are responsible and we have raised them to clean up after themselves. When the children were younger, we had sent them to a full-time day-care centre. We used to fetch them every evening.

Younger participants indicated that they received more assistance from husbands compared to older participants. For example, younger participants indicated that their husbands assisted them in changing diapers, cooking, washing laundry as well as mopping floors and cleaning windows. In the case of older participants, very few obtained assistance around the home from husbands. The results indicate that participants who obtained assistance from husbands in the home and with children made much more strides in moving up the career ladder than those who did not. Firdous, an older Executive Director for operations revealed how she reached a top management post:

> I was criticised by my in-laws, especially by my mother-in-law who feels that I'm not paying enough attention to my children, husband and home. Since marriage, my husband, children and I have not done a stitch of housework or cooking. I have outsourced these chores as we don't have the time to focus on the house.

Madhuri, a younger Marketing Manager obtained the assistance of her husband:

> My husband and I take turns in cooking, taking care of the children and if need be the housework. We have a full-time house help and au pair. When the au pair and house help are not around, he even changes the baby's diapers. My husband is also a great cook and when I'm studying, he takes over the responsibility of childcare and cooking. In this way I can focus on my job and studies without any worries.

Rani, an older Human Resource Director says she got ahead in her career through having good time management:

> In my family, I would never outsource the cooking. I usually cook in the weekend for the entire week and freeze the food. In the mornings, I ensure I pack my children's lunch for school. The au pair warms the meal

> that I had cooked for the children during the afternoons. In the evenings, I warm food for supper for my family which gives me some bonding time with my children.

Anushka, a younger Finance Manager revealed how she got ahead in her career and achieved work-life balance:

> I got the assistance of my aunts and even my mother. I arranged for my children to be fetched from school, fed and taken care of by my aunt. When my aunt is ill, then my mom and sometimes my mother-in-law takes care of the children. In the evenings, my husband and I are very busy with our careers and we leave the children to take care of their own homework. I must say this type of arrangement has made my children become very independent and they really do well at school.

Unmarried participants indicated that they focused on their work and for them it was much easier to achieve work-life balance, as they were only responsible for their own needs. Saira, an older Chief Financial Officer mentioned that she had reached her position quickly as she had a lot of time on her hands:

> All I do is focus on my career, sleep till late over the weekends and visit my friends. Being single has an added advantage as I can work till late at the office and I have time to rest over the weekends as well. It helps when you are building your career.

Married participants were asked if they felt guilty for not being able to pay more attention to their homes and children. In the majority of cases, both younger and older participants indicated that from a young age they were more inclined towards their studies and working and becoming wives and mothers was not their primary aim in life. A few participants with a more traditional outlook indicated that they did indeed feel guilty for not spending more time at home with their children and families. Malaika, a younger an IT manager who was born and raised in a traditional family commented:

> I grew up in a home where my mom was always at home and we would come home from school and get hot food. We would eat elaborate meals every day. Unfortunately, I am unable to provide the same attention for my children as I got when I was a child and I feel so sorry for my kids.

Sushmita, an older Human Resource Director was not inclined towards housework and childcare:

> The reason I only have one child is that I was never one for housework and taking care of children. I came from an extended family setup and my mother and aunts did everything for me. When I got married, I found it difficult to cook and clean. I got my aunt to cook for me and to take care of my home while I pursued my career. My aunt raised my daughter while I focused on my career.

Workplace Support

Younger and older participants indicated that they realised during their upward career mobility that organisations do not want to promote women who are not working till late in the evenings and placing their families ahead of their careers. Organisations according to the participants focus on productivity and there are no concessions for those who want to achieve work-life balance. Shabana, an older Chief Financial Officer commented as follows:

> When you give birth to your first child, the males raise their eyebrows. When you have your second child, they do not see you as management material as they feel you will be more focused on your family. Women find it difficult to achieve a balance between their personal lives and their professional lives. They are so afraid of not being promoted that they cut their maternity leaves short just so that they can be back at work and not be negatively impacted.

Participants indicated that maternity, paternity and family responsibility leave is not enough to achieve work-life balance. Vidya, a younger Project

Manager finds limited support from her organisation in achieving work-life balance:

> I find that although we have all these pieces of legislation to assist us in achieving some balance between our work and personal lives, it's just not enough. My husband and I are so busy building our careers that we cannot even utilise our 'special' leave days adequately. So, our companies try very hard but the culture of work is such that one cannot afford to be away from the office.

Discussion, Conclusion and Recommendations for Future Research

The current chapter focuses on the experiences of younger and older women managers achieving work-life balance in their careers and how they engage in cultural identity work. The results of the study indicate that younger women managers are better able to achieve work-life balance and engage in lower levels of cultural identity work compared to their older counterparts. One of the major factors that resulted in younger participants achieving work-life balance and engaging in lower levels of identity work was due to the changing social roles within the Indian community. With more women from traditional societies entering the workforce and being exposed to western cultural values, younger males and females are also adopting egalitarian values within such societies, an observation which is also highlighted by Carrim (2017) and Vangarajaloo (2011). Older participants are however more steeped in patriarchal relationships with husbands as their generational values are based on traditional norms as indicated in the current study (Adisa, Abdulraheem, & Isiaka, 2019). The result is that more cultural identity work on the part of older participants in balancing their work and home lives occurs. Egalitarian roles within homes for the majority of participants has resulted in women having more time to pursue their careers and studies as indicated in the current study.

Furthermore, the results of the study indicate that family size did not make a difference to how participants balanced work-family life and engaged in identity work. This finding is in contrast to the study conducted by Ajayi et al. (2015) based on women in Nigerian banks where the authors concluded that those who had bigger families found it more difficult to balance their work and home lives.

Also, in the majority of cases participants did not feel guilty nor did they work and rework their cultural identities to reach a sense of coherence for not being able to fulfil their gender roles within their respective homes. This stemmed from their inclination from a tender age in becoming successful in their studies and careers and not paying much attention to household chores even when growing up. This type of mindset manifested in their marriages, where they manifested behaviour which was not prototypical of women who are raised and socialised in traditional homes and communities. This finding is in contrast to the outcome of Bahiru and Mengistu's (2018) study where they found that women leaders in Ethiopia who come from traditional home settings feel guilty for not being able to fulfil their duties towards their families.

Unlike in other western countries where Indian women take time off to take care of their young children (Reitz, Phan, & Banerjee, 2015) within the South African context, the participants did not have to engage in such arrangements. The reason being that household assistance in the form of au pairs and domestic labour are in abundance. Where such assistance was not sought, various strategies such as day-care centre help, extended family member assistance and husbands assisting women with household chores and childcare were opted for by participants. Akhtar (2014) indicates that Indian women within western countries do not make use of formal childcare and this results in them leaving work in order to take care of their families.

Organisational expectations have however not changed over the years. Women are still expected to work longer hours and to prove themselves. The results of this study indicate that not enough is done by the workplaces to ensure that women who are mothers can achieve high productivity levels by having flexible work arrangements. Burke (2009) opines that women would prefer working shorter hours so that they can achieve some level of work-life balance. The results of the current study further indicate that there are not enough policies within organisations in assisting women in achieving work-life balance. In instances where participants are unable to negate their cultural duties towards their families, such arrangements make it difficult to fulfil their traditional roles. The result is a conflict between their organisational and cultural commitments leading to greater levels of negotiating and renegotiating their cultural identities.

In conclusion, if women managers are to make a significant contribution to their careers then government, the family, the workplace and women themselves have to actively engage in changing their approach in assisting working women to achieve work-life balance. Government and workplaces can co-create even more policies to enable women greater flexibility and shorter working hours in the workplace without compromising their future career prospects. Organisations can obtain the input of women employees in structuring policies geared towards them achieving a more balanced work-life arrangement.

Traditional societies should also raise their sons with more egalitarian values as more women are entering the workforce. Society can make arrangement within communities to establish affordable day-care centres where working mothers can leave their children and, in this way, also create jobs for unemployed women in the community.

Women themselves can become more assertive and insist that husbands and sons assist in household chores. Women managers can also employ strategies in their homes to decrease their workloads by investing in smart devices.

Future research can focus on the attitudes of younger and older Indian males related to household chores and childcare. Future research can also focus on the use of digital technology and how this aspect can assist women in achieving work-life balance. Future research can focus on the role of government in developing economies in assisting women to achieve work-life balance.

References

Adisa, T. A., Abdulraheem, I., & Isiaka, S. B. (2019). Patriarchal hegemony: Investigating the impact of patriarchy on women's work-life balance. *Gender in Management: An International Journal, 34*(1), 19–33.

Agarwal, J. (2007). *Hindu Tenets: The founding doctrines of Vedic Hindu Dharma*. New Delhi: Hindoology Books.

Ajayi, F., Ojo, I. S., & Mordi, C. (2015). Work-family balance and coping strategies among women: Evidence from commercial banks in Nigeria. *European Journal of Business and Management, 7*(2), 152–160.

Akhtar, P. (2014). 'We were Muslims but we didn't know Islam': Migration, Pakistani Muslim women and changing religious practices in the UK. *Women's Studies International Forum, 47*, 232–238.

Ali, F., & Kramar, R. (2015). An exploratory study of sexual harassment in Pakistani organizations. *Asia Pacific Journal of Management, 32*, 229–249.

Ali, F., Malik, A., Pereira, V., & Ariss, A. A. (2017). A relational understanding of work-life balance of Muslim migrant women in the west: Future research agenda. *The International Journal of Human Resource Management, 28*(8), 1163–1181.

Aycan, Z. (2008). Cross-cultural approaches to work–family conflict. In K. Korabik, D. S. Lero, & D. L. Whitehead (Eds.), *Handbook of work–family integration: Research, theory, and best practices* (pp. 353–370). San Diego, CA: Academic Press.

Bahiru, B., & Mengistu, A. B. (2018). The challenges of women leaders of business organizations in Addis Ababa, Ethiopia, in balancing work-family responsibilities. *Journal of International Women's Studies, 19*(2), 140–158.

Banerjee, S. (2008). Dimensions of Indian culture, core cultural values and marketing implications: An analysis. *Cross Cultural Management: An International Journal, 15*(4), 367–378.

Beckwith, L., Carter, D. R., & Peters, T. (2016). The underrepresentation of African American women in executive leadership: What's getting in the way. *Journal of Business Studies Quarterly, 7*(4), 115–134.

Bhana, N. (2008). *South African Indians: The past, the present and the future*. Available at: https://scnc.ukzn.ac.za/doc/INDIAN/topicsindex.htm.

Bharathi, S. V., & Mala, E. P. (2016). A study on the determinants of work–life balance of women employees in information technology companies in India. *Global Business Review, 17*(3), 665–683.

Bhirugnath-Bhookhun, M., & Kitada, M. (2017). Lost in success: Women's maritime careers in Eastern and Southern Africa. *Palgrave Communications, 3,* 17023.

Bobat, S., Msholo1o, N., & Reuben, S. (2012). A qualitative exploration of women's work—Life balance over the life course: A case study of retail managers. *Journal of Psychology in Africa, 22*(2), 227–232.

Burke, R. J. (2009). Working to live or living to work: Should individuals and organizations care? *Journal of Business Ethics, 84*(2), 167–172.

Campbell, A. (2000). Cultural identity as a social construct. *Intercultural Education, 11*(1), 31–39.

Carrim, N. M. H. (2012). *"Who am I?"—South African Indian women managers' struggle for identity: Escaping the ubiquitous cage* (Unpublished PhD dissertation). University of Pretoria, Pretoria, South Africa.

Carrim, N. M. H. (2016). Gender and cultural identity work of unmarried Indian breadwinner daughters in South Africa. *Journal of Comparative Family Studies, 47*(4), 441–462.

Carrim, N. M. H. (2017). 'New' men and 'new' women: Cultural identity work of husbands and wives related to housework and childcare. *Asian Social Studies, 13*(11), 1–12.

Carrim, N. M. H. (2018). Behind the mask: Hybrid identity work of Indian women managers in corporate South Africa. *African and Asian Studies Journal, 17*(4), 371–393.

Carrim, N. M. H. (2019). The in-betweeners: Racioethnic and masculine identity work of Indian male managers in the South African private sector. *The Journal of Men's Studies., 27*(1), 3–23.

Carrim, N. M. H., & Nkomo, S. (2016). Wedding intersectionality theory and identity work in organizations: South African Indian women negotiating managerial identity. *Gender, Work and Organization, 23*(3), 261–277.

Carrim, N. M. H., & Senne, Y. (2019). Life context model, intersectionality, and Black feminist epistemology: Women managers in Africa. In E. T. Pereira & P. Paoloni (Eds.), *Handbook of research on women in management and the global labor market* (pp. 136–155). Hershey, PA: IGI Global Publishers.

Coltrane, S. (2000). Research on household labor: Modeling and measuring the social embeddedness of routine family work. *Journal of Marriage and Family, 62*(4), 1208–1233.

Cooke, L. P. (2007). Persistent policy effects on the division of domestic tasks in reunified Germany. *Journal of Marriage and Family, 69*(4), 930–950.

Das, A. (2006). *Asian Indian immigrant women in the San Francisco-Oakland Bay area: Work, home, and the construction of the self* (Unpublished PhD dissertation). University of California, San Diego, CA.

Dillard, N. (2018). Narratives of women at work: Exploring a more inclusive understanding of women of color and the implications for women and leadership. *Journal of Leadership Studies, 12*(1), 49–55.

Erikson, E. (1968). *Identity, youth and crisis.* New York: Norton.

Gatrell, C. J., Burnett, S. B., Cooper, C. L., & Sparrow, P. (2013). Work-life balance and parenthood: A comparative review of definitions, equity and enrichment. *International Journal of Management Reviews, 15*(3), 300–316.

Grossman, J. M., & Charmaraman, L. (2009). Race, context and privilege: White adolescents' explanations of racial-ethnic centrality. *Journal of Youth Adolescents, 38*(2), 139–152.

Hall, S. (1990). Cultural identity and diaspora. In J. Rutherford (Ed.), *Identity: Community, culture and difference* (pp. 224–237). London, UK: Lawrence and Wishart.

Hamidullah, M. F., & Riccucci, N. M. (2017). Intersectionality and family-friendly policies in the federal government: Perceptions of women of color. *Administration & Society, 49*(1), 105–120.

Jaga, A., Arabandi, B., Bagraim, J., & Mdlongwa, S. (2018). Doing the 'gender dance': Black women professionals negotiating gender, race, work and family in post-apartheid South Africa. *Community, Work & Family, 21*(4), 429–444.

Jaga, A., & Bagraim, J. (2017). Work-family conflict among Hindu mothers in South Africa. *International Journal of Manpower, 38*(8), 1086–1101.

Jean, L C. (2007). *Women and leadership: Transforming visions and diverse voices.* Oxford: Blackwell.

Kachchaf, R., Ko, L., Hodari, A., & Ong, M. (2015). Career–life balance for women of color: Experiences in science and engineering academia. *Journal of Diversity in Higher Education, 8*(3), 175–181.

Kan, M. Y., Sullivan, O., & Gershuny, J. (2011). Gender convergence in domestic work: Discerning the effects of interactional and institutional barriers from large-scale data. *Sociology, 45*(2), 234–251.

Kelliher, C., Richardson, J., & Boiarintseva, G. (2018). All of work? All of life? Reconceptualising work-life balance for the 21st century. *Human Resource Management Journal, 29*(2), 97–112.

Lincoln, Y. S., & Guba, E. G. (1985). *Naturalistic inquiry*. Newbury Park, CA: Sage.

Marais, H. (2011). *South Africa pushed to the limit. The political economy of change*. Available at: https://sds.ukzn.ac.za.

Mkhize, N., & Msomi, R. (2016). African single mothers' experiences of work and career in South Africa. *Journal of Comparative Family Studies, 47*(3), 323–342.

Muasya, G. (2016). Work–family balance choices of women working in Kenyan Universities. *SAGE Open, 6*(1), 2158244016630772.

Pratt, M. (2009). For the lack of a boilerplate: Tips on writing up (and reviewing) qualitative research. *Academy of Management Journal, 52*(5), 856–862.

Rajadhyaksha, U., & Velgach, S. (2009, August 5–9). *Gender, gender-role ideology and work-family conflict in India*. Paper presented at the Academy of Management Annual Meeting, University of Chicago, Chicago. Retrieved from https://www.workfamilyconflict.ca/cms/documents/38/GRI_paper-AOM2009.pdf.

Reitz, J. G., Phan, M. B., & Banerjee, R. (2015). Gender equity in Canada's newly growing religious minorities. *Ethnic and Racial Studies, 38*, 681–699.

Ritchie, J., & Lewis, J. (2003). *Qualitative research practice. A guide for social science students and researchers*. London, UK: Sage.

Ruppanner, L. E. (2010). Cross-national reports of housework: An investigation of the gender empowerment measure. *Social Science Research, 39*, 963–975.

Ryan, A. M., & Briggs, C. Q. (2019). Improving work-life policy and practice with an intersectionality lens. *Equality, Diversity and Inclusion: An International Journal, 39*, 533–547.

Saraff, A., & Srivastava, H. C. (2010). Pattern and determinants of paternal involvement in childcare: An empirical investigation in a metropolis of India. *Population Research and Policy Review, 29*(2), 249–273.

Saxena, R., & Bhatnagar, D. (2018). Does distance matter? A study of married Indian women professionals staying away from families to pursue higher studies. *Journal of Education and Work, 31*(2), 159–174.

Schneider, D. (2011). Market earnings and household work: New tests of gender performance theory. *Journal of Marriage and Family, 73*(4), 845–860.

Shanmugam, M. M. (2017). Impact of parenthood on women's careers in the IT sector—A study in the Indian context. *Gender in Management: An International Journal, 32*(5), 352–368.

South Africa. (1996). *National Youth Commission Act, No 19 of 1996*. Available at: https://www.gov.za/sites/default/files/a19-96.pdf.

Syed, J. (2015). Work-life balance. In J. Syed & M. Özbilgin (Eds.), *Managing diversity and inclusion: An international perspective* (pp. 291–314). London: Sage.

Ugwu, D. I., Orjiakor, C. T., Enwereuzor, I. K., Onyedibe, C. C., & Ugwu, L. I. (2016). Business-life balance and wellbeing: Exploring the lived experiences of women in a low-to-middle income country. *International Journal of Qualitative Studies on Health and Well-Being, 11*(1), 304–312.

Valk, R., Van der Velde, M., Van Engen, M., & Godbole, R. (2014). International career motives, repatriation and career success of Indian women in Science & Technology. *Journal of Global Mobility, 2*(2), 203–233.

Vangarajaloo, M. (2011). *Factors influencing the willingness of South African Indian parents to consent to their daughters pursuing tertiary education and careers* (Unpublished master's thesis). University of Pretoria, Pretoria, South Africa.

7

The Nexus Between Work-Life Balance and Gender Role in Egypt

Ghada El-Kot, Mike Leat, and Sarah Fahmy

Introduction

The Egyptian government's 2030 Vision and Sustainable Development Strategy aims to build a just society emphasises the country's need for increased women's empowerment and their active participation in all aspects of national work. The strategy is comprised of four pillars: women's political empowerment and leadership; women's economic empowerment; women's social empowerment; and women's protection

G. El-Kot (✉)
Arab Academy for Science, Technology and Maritime Transport, Alexandria, Egypt
e-mail: gelkot@aast.edu

M. Leat
University of Plymouth Business School, Plymouth, UK

S. Fahmy
University of Colorado Boulder, Boulder, CO, USA

T. A. Adisa and G. Gbadamosi (eds.), *Work-Life Interface*,
https://doi.org/10.1007/978-3-030-66648-4_7

(National Council for Women, 2017). This plan indicates the government's newfound focus on women's education and work opportunities and the intention is to increase rates of female participation in the workforce to reach 35% by 2030 (National Council for Women, 2017). Achieving this objective would have significant beneficial effects for Egypt's sustainable economic development and in the plan there is reference (p. 35) to estimate that raising female rates of engagement in the workforce to that of men would yield an increase in GDP of 34%.

The 2030 Strategic Plan is consistent with the aims of the 2030 UN Agenda for Sustainable Development as expressed by the International Labour Organization (ILO) "*to achieve full and productive employment and decent work for all women and men, including for young people and persons with disabilities, and equal pay for work of equal value*" and "*to achieve gender equality and empower all women and girls*" (ILO, 2018, p. 5). To achieve the UN agenda, it is vital to guarantee the quality of jobs for women; reduce gender stereotypes and discrimination in both the educational systems and the workplace; and redistribute the family responsibilities between men and women in the society (ILO, 2018).

Currently; Egypt ranks low in gender equity compared to other countries worldwide on a range of indices; for example, the World Economic Forum (WEF) 2020, Gender Gap Index (WEF, 2020) ranks Egypt at 134 out of 153 countries worldwide and the United Nations Development Programme (UNDP) Gender Development Index 2019 (UNDP, 2019); which measures gender gaps in human development achievements by accounting for disparities between women and men in three basic dimensions of human development—health, knowledge and living standards, ranks Egypt in the lowest group. As we discuss later, Egypt is a patriarchal society and women are expected to prioritise their family and caring roles and achieving the circumstances for sustainable development is likely to require a transformation of Egyptian work-life culture.

In order for the Egyptian Government to achieve the 2030 strategic plan for sustainable development, more women need to be encouraged and able to participate in the paid for work labour market and in order to enable them to do this; it is important that they are able to achieve Work-Life Balance (WLB) including their family responsibilities. Effective WLB programmes should enable more women to find appropriate work opportunities, they will not need to compromise their pursuit of a career for their family life and children and they will achieve greater economic empowerment and financial independence and be able to contribute more effectively to society.

It is also necessary to focus on vocally empowering women from a young age in order to facilitate their sense of agency, self-authorship and vocal efficacy necessary for taking their place in the labour market and for economic and political empowerment. One of the pillars of the 2030 Strategic Plan is women's political empowerment and both voice and participation in the formal economy (paid workforce) should contribute to this. The more women are able to secure their own economic empowerment and financial independence, the more likely they are to be able to run for political office.

This chapter highlights the critical need to address work-life balance issues for women in Egypt in order to facilitate the achievement of a sustainable economy and the economic and social empowerment of women in a country where gender roles are clearly differentiated, there is a gendered imbalance of power, and gender segregation and discrimination exists in society and in the workplace. The chapter is divided into three parts. In the first part, we highlight elements of the social, religious, cultural, legal, economic, labour market and educational context in Egypt in order to understand current gender roles and identify issues that need to be addressed. In the second part, we examine literature on WLB in order to establish determinants, the potential benefits for organisations and individuals, the obstacles to achievement, the consequences of not doing so and how WLB for women may be enhanced. In the third part, we present our conclusions on gender roles and WLB for women in Egypt. We outline the nature of the prescribed gender roles and then focus on the initiatives that seem appropriate to enabling a more satisfactory WLB for women and the benefits that may accrue. In this final part, we also comment on the need for research to inform future policies and initiatives. There is unfortunately very little published evidence available on the issues of gender roles, WLB and management approaches in Egyptian organisations, and this has inevitably limited our ability to address some of the issues.

Egyptian National Context

Work, family and life domains in Egypt, as in any country, exist and operate within an environment that can be subdivided into a number of areas that influence the role expectations and demands, the stereotypes, and the opportunities for individuals in the society, at work, in their families and their other life domains. Research on gender, work and WLB in the Middle East (ME) region has variously identified the significance of religious, patriarchal, socio-cultural, socio-economic, demographic, institutional, labour market and legal elements of national contexts (Karam & Afiouni, 2014; Karam, Afiouni, & Nasr, 2013; Metcalfe, 2008; Mehdizadeh, 2011; Offenhauer, 2005; Sidani & Thornberry, 2009). In the following sections, we discuss the relevance of these elements of the environment for women and work and for their WLB in Egypt. We start with the elements of that context that arguably have the greatest influence in determining prescribed gender roles.

Determinants of Gender Role

Religion and culture are intertwined in Egyptian society. The patriarchal system that enforces gender-based discrimination has, due to centuries of stereotypical media representation, been associated with Islam, the predominate religion in Egypt (El- Safty, 2004). Within Islam, women have significant legal rights for money and inheritance, equal education opportunities in comparison with men, and they are encouraged to work. There are no constraints against women holding positions of power, and leadership within the workforce; however, patriarchal interpretations of Islam, as noted by Karam and Afiouni (2014) are what create limitation and prohibits choice for women. As Sidani and Thornberry (2009) suggest, Islam has been used by patriarchal society to legitimise discrimination against women. Women are assumed to be the "weaker sex" and thus are socialised to be homemakers, and mothers first. They are assumed to be incapable of handing money or being the primary breadwinners (El-Safty, 2004). These patriarchal binaries, exasperated in low income and impoverished communities, debilitate women's advancement, desire to engage in the workforce, and ability to speak up. Inadequate representation of women in politics, economics and the workforce result in economic and educational inequalities that reduce women's bargaining power in their private and public lives (OECD, 2018).

Patriarchal societal expectations assert that men are the head of the household and must be respected and prioritised in economic, political and private matters. Metcalfe (2008) notes that the QURAN is explicit in identifying the different but complementary roles of men and women and this is reflected in a recurring theme that men and women have equal but different identities. Metcalfe (2008) also notes the ongoing debate among feminist and Islamic scholars about the empowering and disempowering effects of the Islamic philosophy for women. Burke and El-Kot (2011) confirmed that in Egypt there are definitive and separate gender roles, work being perceived as a male activity undertaken in order to perform his role as the breadwinner, whereas women's responsibility is primarily for the home and the family.

There is no doubt that Islam, as the dominant religion in Egypt, has a strong influence on day-to-day lives and the family domain. It is also clear that it has implications for work-related values, the expectations of employees, the behaviour and approach of management (Leat and El-Kot, 2008) and by implication on the achievement of WLB. El-Kot and Burke (2014) argue that the "Islamic Work Ethic" (IWE) emphasises and encourages hard work, engagement in economic activity and is perceived as an obligation. It stresses honesty and justice, an equitable and fair distribution of wealth in society, and it encourages the acquisition of skills and technology. The IWE also emphasises cooperation in work and consultation, the latter being seen as a way of overcoming obstacles or avoiding mistakes. Social relations are important at work to create healthy relationships with both equals and superiors.

It is difficult to separate religion and culture and as Tayeb (1997) suggested religion is one of the many factors that can contribute to the formation of national culture. Leat and El-Kot (2007) in their review of the Egyptian cultural and religious context noted that Arab countries demonstrated moderate masculinity according to Hofstede (1980). However, he concluded that the segregated nature of the labour market and low participation rates of women commonly associated with masculine values was more a product of religion in the Arab Middle East than of Masculine values. Mousa (2018) also notes that in Egyptian society the Masculinity stems to a certain extent from Islamic religious values. Hofstede also characterised Arab countries as demonstrating a preference towards the feminine continuum which focuses on relationships, working conditions and a "work to live" culture.

The GLOBE study (House, Hanges, Javidan, Dorfman, & Gupta, 2004) identified a Middle Eastern cluster which showed high scores on in-group collectivism with low scores on future orientation, gender egalitarianism and uncertainty avoidance. This combination reflects societies that are fatalistic, believing in the will of Allah (God), and in which the family forms insurance against the future and male members of society are looked to for protection and support.

Lyness and Judiesch (2014) undertook a cross-national study of gender egalitarianism and its effect upon self-rating of WLB. Egypt was one of the countries included in the study and along with others in the Middle East was categorised as a low gender egalitarian society. In this context, gender egalitarianism is the dimension of national culture that reflects the degree of differentiation in the prescribed gender roles for men and women and which shapes behaviours, stereotypes of male and female attributes and men and women's abilities to achieve WLB. In low gender-egalitarian cultures, men are expected to prioritise work over family whereas women are expected to do the opposite. For men, high involvement with work and long work hours are congruent with their responsibilities as breadwinners, and it is argued that it is easier for men to balance the requirements of their work and family roles. Women in low egalitarian cultures are expected to focus on family responsibilities and not work and the achievement of WLB therefore becomes more difficult.

Khedr (2017) confirmed the importance of cultural values and norms embedded in Egyptian society as contextual explanations for the perceptions of both genders and for their extension into definitive and separate work roles. Women are expected to marry early, have children early, not work after marriage, respect their husband as the breadwinner and authority in the family. Therefore, women who do not marry do not have children and pursue a career and women who do marry have children, work and pursue a career are not conforming to the stereotype. Because of the prescribed gender roles, workplaces tend to be male dominated, institutionally male and employers and managers may find it difficult to think in terms of, and apply, gender equal policies and to accommodate the needs of women in regard to fulfilling and managing their family and childcare responsibilities and achieving a satisfactory WLB. The Egyptian 2030 Vision and Sustainable Development Strategy recognises the importance of social culture and norms as limiting influences on women's participation and acknowledges the need to change them.

Demographic Context

Population

According to the official data source Egypt in Figures (March 2020); at the beginning of 2020 the total population of Egypt was 99.85 million. The annual growth rate has averaged 2% over the last 20 years and fertility rates have remained steady between 3.0 and 3.5 since 2000. Of the total population 48.5% were female and 51.5% male. Egypt has a young and rapidly growing population, 51.5% are in the age group 0–24 years and of these 34% are in the 0–14-year category whereas the proportion over 64-year olds is 4.6%. This translates into a high age dependency ratio of 63% (young, 0–14, and old, 65 and over, as the proportion of total aged 15–64). This dependency on a relatively small proportion of the population of working age (61.4%) is exacerbated by the low female labour participation rates.

Egyptian Labour Market and Education

Labour Market

Empowering women and integrating them as active participants in the economy is essential to promoting economic growth in Egypt. We noted earlier the government's intentions regarding raising female participation rates. Data for 2019 (World Bank 2020) indicates that while there has been relative stability in the labour force participation rates since 2000, the rate for women in the 15–64 age group has increased from 21.6% in 2000 to 23.8% in 2019. However, there are significant gender differentials, these have narrowed but not significantly, the 15–64 female participation rate at 23.8% is less than a third that for males of 74.7%. For the 15–24 age group, the participation rates for females and males were 18.9 and 38.6%, respectively, in 2019. Since 2000, the gender differential for the 15–64 age group has narrowed from 54.3 to 51% and in the 15–24 age group the differential has narrowed from 24.5 to 19.7%, largely due to a decline in the male participation rate from 43.6 to 38.6%. Unemployment in 2019 was high among the young aged 15–24 at 31.1%, comprised of 41% for females and 26.4% for males.

The low female participation rates would appear to be consistent with and a product of religious and cultural influences on gender roles and the appropriateness of work Mehdizadeh (2011) and Hofstede (1980). Though Offenhauer (2005) contrasts low female participation rates in oil-rich economies in MENA countries with those in some other Muslim states that were pursuing a development strategy based on labour-intensive industrial production and suggests an economies development strategy also plays a role.

The sectoral distribution of those in employment in Egypt also varies by gender. The majority of female employment is in agriculture (35.5%) and the service sector (57.5%) and only a small percentage (7%) work in industry. Male employment respectively is 20.8 and 46.2% with 20.8% in industry (World Bank 2020).

Karam and Afiouni (2014) noted that labour markets in the ME region tend to demonstrate both horizontal and vertical segregation on the basis of gender. Women work in particular sectors that are deemed appropriate in the context of stereotypical male and female traits, which are themselves a product of cultural and religious contexts, as Marinakou and Giousmpasoglou (Marinakou and Giousmpasoglou 2017) asserted that men and women are concentrated in different occupations that ascribe to their gender. Metcalfe (2008) suggests that the segregation within the labour market is often interpreted as respecting the different but not lesser skills and characteristics of women. Traditionally, women work in the public sector (e.g. health, education and social care), and they tend to be occupied in lower-level roles with leadership positions normally reserved for men. Barsoum (2016) has noted that in Egypt while the public service is attractive to both genders, women are attracted by the more family-friendly working conditions. Marinakou and Giousmpasoglou (2017, p. 208) noted that "in the Arab context women are blocked from leadership roles because of the predominant view that leadership is a male's quality".

Education

Egypt has made considerable progress in implementing equal opportunities for girls and boys in the public educational system and this has had a positive impact on enrolment and literacy rates. Enrolment rates in 2017 for girls and boys were almost equal at all levels of education with girls just marginally higher for all levels, and completion rates at primary level being equal at 95% with a greater percentage of girls completing the lower secondary stage, 87.5% compared with 81.7% for boys at the same level (UNESCO, 2020; WEF, 2020).

In 2018, Egypt's Ministry of Local Development announced its intention to eliminate illiteracy in Egypt in the next three years. The adult (15 plus) literacy rates show a significant gender differential and in 2017 the rate for males was 76.5% but only 65.5% for women. Nevertheless, at the lower age groups the improvements in participation are demonstrating improved literacy outcomes and significant reduction of the gender differentials. The literacy rates for the 15–24 age group in 2017 were 89.5% for boys and 87% for girls compared with rates in 2006 of 88 and 82% respectively up from 1986 when the rates were 71 and 54% (UNESCO, 2020).

Egypt is focusing on providing an inclusive and quality education for anyone who seeks it, regardless of gender. The reform focuses on primary and secondary schooling and the focus is to be on teaching real-world knowledge and self-understanding and the development of important life skills such as critical thinking, problem-solving abilities and self-reflection. The reforms address some of the criticisms made of the educational systems in Patriarchal and Islamic societies (Sidani & Thornberry, 2009), acknowledged the need to ensure that the knowledge and skills required in the labour market are provided by the education system and are a reflection of the belief that investing in women's education will promote greater participation of women in the labour force and thereby rapid development in Egypt (USAID, 2020). Khedr (2017) noted that in Egypt education is a strong determinant of labour force participation by women. However, there is also evidence of high levels of female educational attainment being associated with unemployment, which may reflect a lack of congruence between expectations and job opportunities available, inappropriate guidance in what is still a segregated labour market, and the difficulties of achieving satisfactory WLB. It may be as Kemp and Madsen (2014) suggested for Oman that colleges and universities should develop partnerships and programmes which facilitate the exposure of women to workplaces and the working environment and the potential challenges and opportunities in various types of companies and outside the public sector.

Legal Framework in Egypt

The legal framework in any country is likely to play an important role in either supporting or undermining women's access to and participation in employment, their treatment in employment and their ability to manage their respective work and family responsibilities and achieve a satisfactory WLB. Where there is a supportive legal framework effort needs to be exerted in order to ensure that the law is applied otherwise it will not be effective.

The Egyptian labour law No. 12 of 2003 gives women the right to work and prohibits discrimination in wages on the basis of gender but there is no provision for equal pay for work of equal value. The Labour law also prohibits employers from dismissing a woman because of her pregnancy and also offers women up to 90 days of paid maternity leave in the private sector and 120 days of paid maternity leave in the public sector. However, the Labour Code does not apply to domestic workers or to women in agriculture, a sector in which some 35% of women in employment are occupied. Ministerial decrees also restrict women from working in certain occupations, including construction and mining, some types of night work, and roles deemed morally inappropriate.

The 2014 Constitution (Egyptian Constitution, 2014) includes more than 20 articles addressing the rights of women in order to ensure; equal opportunities and prevent discrimination, protection against all forms of violence, and women's empowerment. Article 11 commits the State to ensuring that women are able to reconcile work and family obligations. There are paid Maternity leave provisions, 90 days paid leave for each of up to 3 children for women working in the private sector providing that the women have worked for the employer for more than 10 months. Social security funds 75% of the payments with additional amounts paid by the employer. A woman preserves all her rights and benefits upon return to workplace from maternity leave. Moreover, women employed in establishments with more than 50 employees are entitled to up to two years of unpaid childbearing leave per child. Women are also entitled to two half-hour nursing breaks per day, or alternatively one combined an hour-long break, for 24 months after the date of birth of each child. For establishments employing 100 employees or more, the employer is obliged to provide for an in-house nursery, or alternatively, to take charge of placing employee's children (until the age of schooling is reached) in adequate nurseries. Some of these provisions are enhanced for women working in the Public sector. The Law does not provide provisions for paternity leave and does not mandate employers to allow employees with dependents to care for to work flexible hours.

OECD (2017) noted that there are various ways in which employers may frustrate the intentions of the legal provisions, this may, for example, be due to the costs of the maternity or childcare provisions or because of ingrained stereotypes and organisational cultures and the OECD report asserts this is often not applied. The OECD (2018) reported also encourages the government to adopt a number of ILO conventions in the field of employment and social security that would assist the process of economic empowerment of women.

We conclude that there are a number of issues arising from this contextual analysis which need to be addressed in order to further the opportunity for women to achieve WLB and participate in the labour force. It is clear that Egypt is a patriarchal, low egalitarian society with definitive and separate gender roles. It is a male-dominated society with an imbalance of power and women are expected to give priority to their family responsibilities. Egypt has a rapidly growing and young population with high age dependency ratios, low female labour force participation rates and large gender-based inequalities. The labour market is segregated both horizontally and vertically. In combination, these place critical importance on increasing female labour force participation but also make it difficult to do so.

Equality has been largely achieved in terms of student enrolment and completion rates in the public education system, but the curriculum needs to be refocused in order to prepare students, and particularly to empower women, for the world of work. The legal framework offers some protections to women in terms of discrimination and harassment, and some provisions facilitating women continuing to work after childbirth; however, there are apparent issues relating to implementation and enforcement, a large percentage of the female labour force would appear to not be covered by the legislation and there is room for further initiatives to guarantee equal pay for work of equal value and to mandate organisations to implement flexibilities to support women in work.

WLB—The Concept

Put very simply WLB refers to the "balance between work and the rest of life" (Guest 2002, p. 263). Guest also referred to it as the ability to allow "sufficient time to meet commitments at both work and home". Lyness and Judiesch (2014) used a measure which defines WLB as the balance between work priorities and personal life so that neither is neglected. Initially, the focus was work and the family or work and home but, more recently there has been recognition that individuals have other non-work roles and responsibilities and that as indicated by Lyness and Judiesch the individuals' personal life needs to be incorporated. WLB is the more inclusive term which encompasses work, family and personal roles and responsibilities. However, it must be recognised that the terms WLB and Work-Family Balance (WFB) are used interchangeably, in this chapter we use the term WLB.

WLB has also been defined in terms of an absence of conflict; Clark (2000, p. 751) defining it as "satisfaction and good functioning at work and at home with a minimum of role conflict". This definition also introduces the notion that people occupy multiple roles and that the demands of and in one may conflict with those in another. Emslie and Hunt (2009) point out that much of the research in the field has focused on role conflict and role strain. The most common forms of conflict researched have been family-work and work-family (see the definitions of Guest and Clark above). Adame, Caplliure, and Miquel (2016) note while there is potential for conflict for both genders, the potential for work-family/family-work conflicts are greater for women than men because of the greater number of roles they are expected to perform, wife, mother, daughter and the majority of the research has focused on women and their experiences in trying to balance work and family roles and responsibilities.

Another concept commonly used in the literature is that of domains, with, for example, work being one domain and family another. Eshak et al. (2018) point out that work-family conflict refers to the expectations and demands associated with one domain affecting the other and the term conflict implying that the two domains compete for a person's time and energy in an inverse relationship, so that, for example, work-family conflict arises where fulfilling the demands of the work domain interferes with family life and the opportunities to fulfil obligations as parent or spouse.

In this context, Clark (2000) developed a border theory in which domains are characterised as having borders which can be strong or weak and which people cross as they move between domains, for example, work and family. It is also suggested that domains may have different cultures and values. Emslie and Hunt (2009) note that this theory while useful for conceptualising work-life balance is largely gender blind and in this respect is like many contemporary studies of work-life balance that either ignore gender or take it for granted. Greenhaus et al. (2003,

p. 513) viewed "work-family balance as a matter of degree, a continuum anchored at one end by extensive imbalance in favour of a particular role (e.g. family) through some relatively balanced state to extensive imbalance in favour of the other role (e.g. work) as the other anchor point".

Greenhaus and Allen (2011) noted three common conceptualisations of work-family balance which are equally appropriate for WLB and these were: (1) the absence of work-family conflict, (2) high involvement across multiple roles and (3) high effectiveness and satisfaction across multiple roles. The authors developed an encompassing and overall conceptualisation of WFB as "an overall appraisal of the extent to which individuals' effectiveness and satisfaction in work and family roles are consistent with their life values at a given point in time" Greenhaus and Allen (2011, p. 174). The overall appraisal approach focusses on assessing the general feelings of the individual in balancing between work issues and life/family issues, but also alludes to objective measures of effectiveness.

Greenhaus and Allen's (2011) definition encompasses another of the debates that has been ongoing concerning whether WLB is a subjective and psychological construct (satisfaction and perceived effectiveness and fulfilment) and/or whether it is also a social construct with balance shaped by contextual factors and perhaps particularly the socio-cultural context, and for the purposes of this chapter in particular the gendered nature of social and family roles and the labour market. Individual perceptions of balance take place within the framework of gendered work, social and family role expectations, demands and power relationships, educational and labour market opportunities and experiences, and a legislative context.

Another issue that has been the subject of debate relates to the measurement of WLB or Imbalance. A distinction can be drawn between objective and subjective indicators or measures of balance. Guest (2002) identified a number of possible objective indicators including working hours, the amount of free time available to individuals, the allocation of family roles, behaviour and performance at work and at home, and also assessments of impact on others, again both at work and home. Subjective indicators include individual perceptions of balance between work, home, and life, perceptions of spillover and interference one with the other, assessments of job, career and life satisfaction, mental and physical health and wellbeing and stress.

As noted, the majority of research has been on work-family conflict/balance and another useful development by Carlson et al. (2000) has been the development of a measure encompassing different forms or dimensions of conflict or balance. These have been popular among researchers as a means of analysing and measuring degrees and types of conflict. In particular, three forms have been identified: these being time, strain and behaviour. Time-based imbalance or conflict occurs when the time requirements of one role make it more difficult to participate in the other. Strain-based imbalance refers to the extent to which stress may result from the person's attempts to reconcile the demands of the various roles, and behaviour-based imbalance is where there is an incompatibility between the behavioural expectations and demands in the respective roles.

Determinants, Consequences, Opportunities, Cost and Benefits

Interest in WLB is primarily the product of the impact it can have on personal, organisational, and national, social and economic outcomes. Research initially focused on personal outcomes and performance but more recently the impact on organisational performance has become more widely researched and acknowledged. In terms of national social and economic outcomes, the focus of this chapter is on the part that WLB can have in facilitating the empowerment of women, female participation in the labour force, and thereby, for the economic development and sustainability of the nation. We noted in the introduction the importance the Egyptian government has placed on these national outcomes. In the remainder of this section, we focus on WLB for both individuals and organisations.

WLB and the Individual

Determinants

Guest's (2002) model of the Determinants, Nature and Consequences of WLB included a number of individual factors that were thought might influence an individual's WLB. These include work orientation and commitment to work or life outside work, personality, energy, personal control, gender, age and career stage. Additionally, the individuals' personal family and home life arrangements and demands will have a bearing on WLB and this includes the presence of children and extent and nature of the help and support available.

Emslie and Hunt (2009) reviewed studies on gender and levels of WLB and found the results mixed, but also concluded that although the presence of children in the family was associated with a lack of WLB for both genders the effects were longer lasting for women. Lyness and Judiesch (2014) concluded that men and women tend to report similar levels of WLB, but in low egalitarian countries (Egypt) women did report lower levels of WLB. Burke and El-Kot (2011) found among a sample of Egyptian managers and professionals that women did report higher levels of work-family behaviour-based conflict.

Burke and El-Kot (2010) in their study of Egyptian managers found weak relationships between personal characteristics and Work-Family Conflict (WFC) but stable personality characteristics such as the need for achievement and workaholic job behaviours both increased levels of WFC. In their study of Egyptian Women; El-Kot et al. (2019) found a number of personal demographic characteristics had significant relationships with higher levels of work-family conflict, and these included educational attainment level, more and longer career breaks, working full time, and women at higher organisational levels. Family-Work Conflict (FWC) was positively associated with organisational tenure and educational attainment level. Kargwell (2008); Uppalury and Bhaskar (2014); Metcalfe (2007) and Abalkhail (2019) have identified the significance of the extended family, family support and networks in facilitating childcare and enabling women to pursue careers and to cope with the traditional role demands of Arab Middle Eastern (AME) societies and achieve WLB.

Consequences

The consequences of WLB imbalance for the individuals concerned, and this applies to both genders, can be many in terms of both psychological and work well-being, work outcomes (Lyness and Judiesch, 2014) and performance (Adame-Sánchez, González-Cruz, & Martínez-Fuentes, 2016) who note that these may include: family and life satisfaction, stress, depression, and excessive alcohol consumption. Eshak et al. (2018) noted a positive relationship between WL conflict and poor health and Uppalury and Bhaskar (2014) noted the high emotional costs when careers are not compatible with family and child-rearing and identifies working mothers' feelings of guilt in relationship to the performance of their family responsibilities. Adame et al. (2016) noted research has found support for WLB having implications for personal stress, marital satisfaction, healthier family relationships, higher self-esteem and greater career satisfaction. Uppalury and Bhaskar (2014) also cite research confirming that WLB or imbalance can result in decisions to work or not to work, or to work part time or more flexibly, or to work in a less demanding role. Adame-Sánchez et al. (2016) and Mousa (2018) referred to research confirming WLB can also have significant consequences for an individual's job satisfaction, commitment, intention to remain in the organisation and their performance in their work role. Burke and El-Kot (2010) found that WFC generally had negative relationships with indicators of psychological wellbeing and work outcomes, the latter including job and career satisfaction, job stress and intent to quit.

Coping Strategies and Opportunities

Much of the work that has addressed the coping strategies adopted by women in AME countries has focused on career and career success. However, it is likely that these strategies are also relevant to dealing with Work-Family (WF) and Work-Life (WL) conflict. Central to the issue of individual coping strategies is the capacity for exercising individual choice and agency, Chandra (2012) argued that WLB is a choice and it is a personal responsibility to manage the fulfilment of personal, family and work roles. Abalkhail (2019) identified the significant role that self-empowerment and resistance might play as strategies for women in enabling their career advancement in an AME (including Egypt) context where the institutionally mandated stereotype is that woman will give primacy to the role of wife and mother and give up work after marriage. Women who do not conform to this stereotype, who do not marry and have children, or who do but also work and pursue a career are to some extent exercising their agency and modifying their role. They are exercising choice and taking control, what Abalkhail (2019) referred to as self-empowerment, and central to this is the ability to affirm their own voice and power.

Vocal empowerment can be defined as the belief that what you say is worthwhile, your voice belongs to you, and that you have the right for self-authorship (Osnes and Hackett, 2017) and they argued that it is essential for young women's education. Fahmy (2019) reporting on studies with young women in Egypt argues that instilling this sense of empowerment in women from a young age, increases their likelihood of effectively participating in the workforce when they're older, becoming successful women in leading managerial and professional positions, and capable of advocating for their WLB and actively pursuing WLB initiatives. In male-dominated societies such as Egypt achieving WLB may depend upon women developing and exercising this self-empowerment, the ability to exercise their agency and to use their voice to advocate for their WLB and appropriate WLB initiatives. Karam et al. (2013) and Tlaiss (2015) also noted that individuals can and do through their individual choices and actions conform to and fulfil, moderate or reject the role demands and responsibilities that are mandated by the institutional environment.

Uppalury and Bhaskar (2014) caution that cultures differ in the importance given to individuals and groups and thereby to the importance given to individual choice and agency and as noted in the section on the cultural context in Egypt Arab Middle Eastern cultures tend to focus more on the importance of the family and collectivism. D'Enbeau, Villamil, and Helens-Hart (2015) contrast the prescribed role of women in the Middle East with those in the West, which they suggest are informed by assumptions favouring individual rights, personal responsibility and gender equality. Uppalury (2014) noted research that the pressures and stresses associated with climbing the career ladder, work-life conflict and organisational insensitivity to their problems has led to many women opting out and taking less demanding positions. Other coping strategies include stress relief, time management and the development and use of support networks.

WLB and the Organisation

Determinants

We need to bear in mind that organisations work within national contexts and cultures and as we have already noted these will influence employer attitudes, organisational culture, and the policies and practices pursued as well as employee values, expectations and role requirements. The attitudes, policies and practices of the organisation will impact the individual's ability to manage the work and non-work domains and limit the potential for conflict between their respective demands and achieve WLB.

In his model, Guest (2002) identified two sets of organisational factors as determinants of WLB, the demands and culture of work. Demands he identifies as encompassing working hours, and the intensity of work, and culture and climate he suggests encompass issues of temporal and operational flexibility and capacity for control, along with supportive supervision. Burke and El-Kot (2009) and (2010) found that Egyptian managers working longer hours and in more intense jobs indicated higher levels of WFC and the relationship between hours and intensity and WFC was both strong and consistent, but with intensity being the stronger. Doble (2010) cautions about the potential impact on working hours and intensity of technological developments such as the Internet, e-mail and mobile phones all of which enable organisations to be in contact with employees at any time and which can further the intensification of work demands.

Adame-Sánchez et al. (2016) in their discussion of barriers, drivers and enablers of the implementation of WLB policies note that organisational culture is the internal element that scholars most commonly study. They identify cultural change, hostile work environments, attitudes of managers, poor support services, and a lack of education and training in WLB strategies as negative influences on implementation and highlight managers attitudes as seemingly the most important.

Consequences, Benefits and Costs

For the organisation, there are many potential benefits and costs of facilitating or not WLB for their employees. Adame et al. (2016) and Adame-Sánchez et al. (2016) noted that benefits which may facilitate improving financial performance have been found to include; enhanced ability to attract and retain talent within the firm, improved employee satisfaction, engagement, commitment and motivation, and both lower levels of absenteeism and lower levels of desire to leave. Research conducted by Kim (2014) suggested that affective commitment increases as a result of the positive WLB experience of an employee, which in turn, has a positive influence on his/her in-role performance. This finding affirms the mediating role of affective commitment in the relationship between WLB and organisational performance. Burke and El-Kot (2010) found that higher levels of WFC were associated with less favourable individual wellbeing and work outcomes.

Talukder et al. (2018) developed this theme and suggest that research supports organisational efforts to invest in improving positive links between work and life domains, in helping employees balance the domains of work and life, as it will result in positive work attitudes which will benefit organisational performance. Adame-Sánchez, Gonzalez-Cruz and Martinez-Fuentes (2016) emphasises that the outcome of their research stresses the importance of perceived market-based outcomes as the main factor determining whether firms implement employment and HR policies and practices which facilitate their employees' achievement of WLB.

Opportunities

If there is this potential for benefits to organisations the question, then arises as to how this might be achieved. Prior research has identified a number of policies, practices and approaches that would appear to have potential for enabling women to achieve a more satisfactory balance between their work and non-work roles and responsibilities. At the organisational and pragmatic level, D'Enbeau et al. (2015) emphasises the need in Middle Eastern countries to develop work-life policies that are culturally specific, which recognise the importance of family and religion and the underpinning belief in gender complementarity, a different but equal mentality. Metcalfe (2008); Karam and Afiouni (2014); Afiouni et al. (2013); Marmenout and Liriob (2014) and D'Enbeau et al. (2015) have all emphasised the importance of developing HR models which are indigenously and culturally relevant, which take account of the importance of religion and family and which put women, their needs for flexibility, opportunity and empowerment at centre stage.

Adame et al. (2016) in reviewing the literature have identified the crucial role played by organisational support in the form of management commitment to achieving WLB for their workers, a theme noted repeatedly in research studies, and that managers play a crucial role in putting family-friendly policies into practice. There needs to be a culture of commitment to WLB and responsibility to families and they also suggest that driving and delivering these policies should be the responsibility of the Human Resource department. Karam and Afiouni (2014) also identified the pivotal role HR practitioners can play in mainstreaming gender equality and determining how HR policies respect the different but equal rationale. Interestingly, Adame et al. (2016) research did not support the hypothesis that the presence of women in the labour force would determine the level of implementation of WLB policies; however, the absence of women does seem to determine the absence of such policies.

The crucial role played by organisational culture and supervisory support and commitment, identified as determinants of WLB by Guest (2002) in his model, is also acknowledged by Talukdar et al. (2018). Lapierre and Allen (2006) noted a number of ways in which supervisors can signal support, they can inquire about employees' family needs and circumstances, they can express support, they can be flexible in terms of work schedules and enabling employees deal with non-work commitments and emergencies. Talukder et al.'s research specifically examined the role of supervisory support on employees WLB, job satisfaction, organisational commitment, life satisfaction and performance and reports that supervisory support can enhance all of these. El-Kot et al. (2019) also noted that supervisor employee empowerment behaviours can reduce work-family conflict and they refer to behaviours and approaches including greater delegation, facilitating employee participation in decision making, coaching and mentoring. Marmenout and Liriob (2014) advocated a holistic approach encompassing flexible approaches towards the needs of women, empowering them through mentoring, social support systems and training and further education.

The forms of flexibility identified by Guest as potentially important to perceptions of WLB are reaffirmed as relevant to enabling women achieve WLB, enter and remain in the labour force. Temporal flexibility in terms of support for flexible working hours or part-time working have been advocated by many including (Doble & Supria, 2010; Kemp and Madsen, 2014; Khedr, 2017; Metcalfe, 2007; Marmenout and Liriob, 2014) and we have noted above support for the potential of operational flexibility via delegation and participation in decision making and the flexibility enabled through supportive supervision.

Other suggestions in the literature for policies and practices that are advocated as enabling a better WLB for women include teleworking, and work at home interventions (Doble & Supria, 2010; Kemp and Madsen, 2014) the provision of childcare facilities in the workplace (Doble & Supria, 2010; Marmenout and Liriob, 2014) and maternity leave and pay and parental leave (Khedr, 2017; Metcalfe, 2007). Another focus is on ensuring that gender diversity and equality of opportunity help to frame policies on recruitment and talent retention and on training, development and promotion (Karam and Afiouni, 2014; Kemp and Madsen, 2014).

While WLB may be influenced by a range of personal and family characteristics and circumstances including self-empowerment and orientation to work, it seems feasible that organisations can promote a more satisfactory WLB for women through commitment to WLB culture, enabling the crucial supportive role of supervisors, and adopting more flexible and gender equal approaches to their employment. The potential benefits for women employees are that they will be less likely to suffer from stress, depression and other forms of psychological and physical ill health and more likely to be satisfied with work, marriage, family and life. Organisations should be able to gain from more motivated, committed, productive employees who are less likely to be absent and leave and they are likely to find it easier to attract and retain talented employees and their financial performance should benefit.

Conclusions and Further Research

The purpose of this section is to present our emergent conclusions on gender roles and WLB for women in Egypt. Our focus is on the initiatives that seem appropriate to enabling a more satisfactory WLB for women and the benefits that may accrue from them. It is important to note that the Egyptian government has accepted the need to change, they support full female empowerment and participation in the social and work spheres and this provides a framework conducive to the adoption of initiatives that lead to genuine improvement and empowerment. It is difficult to envisage significant improvement in female empowerment, their participation in society and the labour force without government, religious leaders, business leaders and women's groups in Egypt all agreeing on the need to transform the social and cultural norms that currently prescribe gender roles.

Government and educational leaders must encourage, facilitate and implement developments in the public education sector facilitating the acquisition by women of relevant workplace skills, greater awareness of a wider range of employment opportunities and the empowerment of women through the development of their own voice. Government, political and religious leaders also need to provide a more proactive legislative framework promoting the effective implementation of gender equal policies in employment, recruitment, promotion and development, and flexibility to enable women manage their work and family responsibilities.

Egyptian women have an important role to play in these developments, they will need to advocate change, they need to acquire and use their self-empowerment, their voice, to argue for their rights and aspirations, argue for the changes to workplace culture and flexibilities that will enable them to achieve a satisfactory WLB and manage both work and family responsibilities.

Business leaders, HR practitioners and managers must secure change in the institutionally male workplace culture. They must implement more proactive, flexible and supportive approaches and policies, paying explicit attention to the needs, interests and development of Egyptian women in work, and thereby enabling them to manage effectively their work and non-work responsibilities and make a significant contribution to organisational performance.

Finally, we need to address the importance of further research; as there is a marked lack of a research base of evidence to inform the development of national policy agendas on promoting and enabling cultural change, gender equality, satisfactory WLB for women, and developing an appropriate HRM model for organisations in Egypt that is culturally relevant as well as facilitating the achievement of a sustainable economy. There is clearly a need for further research to be commissioned into a range of issues and relationships.

We know little about current practice in Egyptian organisations regarding a culture of commitment to WLB and gender equality and opportunity, temporal and operational flexibilities and supportive supervision, attitudes of management towards the implementation of appropriate policies and practices and their motivations and expectations in terms of work outcomes and performance. There is also a need for much more evidence on the expectations, aspirations and needs of Egyptian women who want to work and those at work in relation both to work and family responsibilities and roles. Evidence is needed on their experiences of direct discrimination and in the application of policies on recruitment, development, and promotion. What are the work-based policies that would enable more satisfactory WLB, and how do they feel the education system prepares them for work and the advocacy of their interests?

References

Abalkhail Jouharah, M. (2019). Women's career development in an Arab Middle Eastern context. *Human Resource Development International, 22*(2), 177–199.

Adame, C., Caplliure, E. M., & Miquel, M.-J. (2016). Work–life balance and firms: A matter of women? *Journal of Business Research, 69,* 1379–1383.

Adame-Sánchez, C., González-Cruz, T. F., & Martínez-Fuentes, C. (2016). Do firms implement work–life balance policies to benefit their workers or themselves? *Journal of Business Research, 69,* 5519–5523.

Afiouni, F., Karam, C. M., & El-Hajj, H. (2013). The HR value proposition model in the Arab Middle East: Identifying the contours of an Arab Middle Eastern HR Model. *The International Journal of Human Resource Management, 24*(10), 1895–1932.

Barsoum, Ghada. (2016). The public sector as the employer of choice among youth in Egypt: The relevance of public service motivation theory. *International Journal of Public Administration, 39*(3), 205–215.

Burke, R., & El-Kot, G. (2009). Work intensity, work hours, satisfactions and psychological well-being among Egyptian managers. *Education, Business and Society: Contemporary Middle Eastern Issue, 2*(3), 218–231.

Burke, R. J., & El-Kot, G. (2010). Correlates of work-family conflicts among managers in Egypt. *International Journal of Islamic and Middle Eastern Finance and Management, 3*(2), pp. 113–131.

Burke, R. J., & El-Kot, G. (2011). Gender similarities in work and well-being outcomes among managers and professionals in Egypt. *International Journal of Gender and Entrepreneurship, 3*(1), 56–74.

Carlson, D. S., Kacmar, J., & Williams, L. (2000). Construction and initial validation of a multi-dimensional measure of work-family conflict. *Journal of Vocational Behavior, 56,* 249–278.

Chandra, V. (2012). Work–life balance: Eastern and western perspectives. *The International Journal of Human Resource Management, 23*(5), 1040–1056.

Clark, S. C. (2000). Work/family border theory: A new theory of work/family balance. *Human Relations, 53,* 747–770.

D'Enbeau, S., Villamil, A., & Helens-Hart, R. (2015). Transcending work-life tensions: A transnational feminist analysis of work and gender in the Middle East, North Africa, and India. *Women's Studies in Communication, 38,* 273–294.

Doble, N., & Supria, M. V. (2010). Gender differences in the perception of work-life balance. *Management, 5*(4), 331–342.

Egypt Constitution. (2014). https://www.constituteproject.org/constitution/Egypt_2014.pdf.

Egypt in Figures. (2020, March). *Central agency for public mobilization and statistics.*

EL-Kot, G. (2016). Human resource management in Egypt. In P. Budhwar & K. Mellahi (Eds.), *Handbook of human resource management in the Middle East* (pp. 205–225). Cheltenham, UK: Edward Elgar publishing.

El-Kot, G., & Burke, R. (2014). The Islamic work ethic among employees in Egypt. *International Journal of Islamic and Middle Eastern Finance and Management, 7*(2), 228–235.

El-Kot, G., Burke, R. J., & Fiksenbaum, L. M. (2019). Egyptian women supervisory empowerment behaviors on well-being outcomes. *Gender in Management: An International Journal, 34*(5), 350–365.

El-Safty, M. (2004, September). Women in Egypt: Islamic rights versus cultural practice. *Sex Roles, 51*(5/6).

Emslie, C., & Hunt, K. (2009). Live to work' or 'work to live'? A qualitative study of gender and work–life balance among men and women in mid-life. *Gender, Work and Organization, 16*(1), 151–172.

Eshak, E. S., Kamal, N. N., Seedhom, A. E., & Kamal, N. N. (2018). Work-family conflict and self-rated health among dwellers in Minia, Egypt: Financial strain vs social support. *Public Health, 157*, 69–76.

Fahmy, S. (2019). *Vocal empowerment for young Egyptian women: Increasing contributions to sustainable development.* Unpublished Master Thesis, University of Colorado Boulder, USA.

Greenhaus, J. H., & Allen, T. D. (2011). Work–family balance: A review and extension of the literature. In J. C. Quick & L. E. Tetrick (Eds.), *Handbook of occupational health psychology* (2nd ed., pp. 165–183). Washington, DC: American Psychological Association.

Greenhaus, J. H., Collins, K. M., & Shaw, J. D. (2003). The relation between work—Family balance and quality of life. *Journal of Vocational Behavior, 63*, 510–531.

Guest, D. E. (2002). Perspectives on the study of work–life balance. *Social Science Information, 41*, 255–279.

Hofstede, G. (1980). *Culture's consequences: International differences in work-related values* (Vol. 5). Newbury Park, CA: Sage.

House, R. J., Hanges, P. J., Javidan, M., Dorfman, P. W., & Gupta, V. (Eds.). (2004). *Culture, leadership, and organizations: The GLOBE study of 62 societies*. Thousand Oaks, CA: Sage.

International Labour Organisation (ILO). (2018). *World employment social outlook: Trends for women 2018*. Geneva: Global snapshot.

Karam, C. M., & Afiouni, F. (2014). Localizing women's experiences in academia: Multilevel factors at play in the Arab Middle East and North Africa. *The International Journal of Human Resource Management, 25*(4), 500–538.

Karam, C. M., Afiouni, F., & Nasr, N. (2013). Walking a tightrope or navigating a web: Parameters of balance within perceived institutional realities. *Women's Studies International Forum, 40*, 87–101.

Kargwell, S. (2008). Is the glass ceiling kept in place in Sudan? Gendered dilemma of the work-life balance. *Gender in Management: An International Journal, 23*(3), 209–224.

Kemp, L. J., & Madsen, S. R. (2014). Oman's labour force: An analysis of gender in management. *Equality, Diversity and Inclusion: An International Journal, 33*(8), 789–805.

Khedr, W. (2017). Gendered beliefs about glass ceiling in Egypt. *Gender in Management: An International Journal, 32*(6), 404–419.

Kim, H. K. (2014). Work-life balance and employees' performance: The mediating role of affective commitment. *Global Business and Management Research: An International Journal, 6*(1), 37–51.

Lapierre, L. M., & Allen, T. D. (2006). Work-supportive family, family-supportive supervision, use of organisational benefits, and problem-focused coping: Implications for work-family conflict and employee well-being. *Journal of Occupational Health Psychology, 11*(2), 169–181.

Leat, M., & El-Kot, G. (2007). HRM practices in Egypt: The influence of national context? *International Journal of Human Resource Management, 18*(1), 147–158.

Leat, M., & El-Kot, G. (2008). A survey of recruitment and selection practices in Egypt. *Education, Business and Society: Contemporary Middle Eastern Issues, 1*(3), 200–212.

Lyness, K. S., & Judiesch, M. K. (2014). Gender egalitarianism and work-life balance for managers: Multisource perspectives in 36 countries. *Applied Psychology: An International Review, 63*(1), 96–129.

Marinakou, E., & Giousmpasoglou, C. (2017). Gendered leadership as a key to business success: Evidence from the Middle East. In P. Ordoñez de Pablos

& R. Tennyson (Eds.), *Handbook of research on human resources strategies for the new millennial workforce* (pp. 200–230). Hershey, PA: IGI Global.
Marmenouta, K., & Liriob, P. (2014). Local female talent retention in the Gulf: Emirati women bending with the wind. *The International Journal of Human Resource Management, 25*(2), 144–166.
Mehdizadeh, I. N. (2011). Gender and reconciliation of work and family in Iran. *International Labour Review, 150*(3–4), 405–417.
Metcalfe, B. D. (2007). Gender and human resource management in the Middle East. *The International Journal of Human Resource Management, 18*(1), 54–74.
Metcalfe, B. D. (2008). Women, management and globalization in the Middle East. *Journal of Business Ethics, 83,* 85–100.
Mousa, M. (2018). Inspiring a work-life balance: Responsible leadership among female pharmacists in the Egyptian health sector. *Entrepreneurial Business and Economics Review, 6*(1), 71–90.
National Council for Women. (2017). *National strategy for the empowerment of Egyptian women 2030 vision and pillars.*
OECD. (2017). *Women's economic empowerment in selected MENA Countries.*
OECD. (2018, July). *Women's political participation in Egypt barriers, opportunities and gender sensitivity of select political institutions.*
Offenhauer, P. (2005). *Women in Islamic societies: A selected review of social scientific Literature*. The library of Congress.
Osnes, B., & Hackett, C. (2017). *SPEAK: Young women's vocal empowerment curriculum.*
Sidani, Y. M., & Thornberry, J. (2009). The current Arab work ethic: Antecedents, implications, and potential remedies. *Journal of Business Ethics, 91,* 35–49.
Tayeb, M. (1997). Islamic revival in Asia and human resource management. *Employee Relations, 19*(4), 352–364.
Tlaiss, H. (2015). Neither-nor: Career success of women in an Arab Middle Eastern context. *Employee Relations, 37*(5), 525–546.
UNESCO Institute for Statistics. (2020). (http://uis.unesco.org/).
United Nations Development Programme (UNDP). (2019). Human development reports. Gender Development Index.
Uppalury, S., & Bhaskar, R. K. (2014). Social production in a collectivist culture exploring structure and agency in the work-life balance of Indian women executives. *Gender in Management: An International Journal, 29*(6), 352–374.

USAID. (2020). https://www.usaid.gov/egypt/gender-equality-and-womens-empowerment.

Talukder A. K. M., Vickers, M., & Khan, A. (2018). Supervisor support and work-life balance: Impacts on job performance in the Australian financial sector. *Personnel Review, 47*(3), 727–744.

World Economic Forum (WEF). (2020). *Global gender gap report* 2020.

Worldbank. (2020). https://databank.worldbank.org/source/world-development-indicators.

8

Work-Life Balance Outlook in Saudi Arabia

Arun Vijay Subbarayalu, Sivasankar Prabaharan, and Masthan Devalapalli

Introduction

Work-life balance (WLB) reflects the degree to which people can exert control over when, where, and how they work, with an unsaid motive to attain physical and mental harmony along with career success (Collier, 2016). It is a term usually used to describe the balance that a working employee needs between time allocated for work and other aspects of life. It is one of the major problems faced by human resource development (HRD) since work and family domains are mutually dependent and actively impact each other (Odle-dusseau, Britt, & Bobko, 2012). Moreover, the emotions, behaviours, and actions from one domain would be moved to the other domain (Staines, 1980). Maintaining optimal WLB is the essential aspect of a healthy work environment, and it helps to

A. V. Subbarayalu (✉) · S. Prabaharan · M. Devalapalli
Deanship of Quality and Academic Accreditation, Imam Abdulrahman Bin Faisal University (IAU), Dammam, Saudi Arabia
e-mail: ausubbarayalu@iau.edu.sa

T. A. Adisa and G. Gbadamosi (eds.), *Work-Life Interface*,
https://doi.org/10.1007/978-3-030-66648-4_8

reduce stress and prevents burnout in the workplace (Kohll, 2018). It is about creating and maintaining supportive and healthy work environments that enable employees to have a balance between work and personal responsibilities in such a way to strengthen employee loyalty and productivity (Dhas, 2015). WLB is concerned with all aspects of the work and private life of an individual, irrespective of family responsibilities, care, and dependency. It demands both physical (e.g. temporal, and spatial commitment, family size) and cognitive (job/life contentment, pressures, general health, and well-being) involvement (Greenblatt, 2002).

Globalisation, along with the expansion of the service industry and technological advancement, has contributed to the changing nature of work, and its repercussions lead to the higher permeability of work into the family domain, thereby affects WLB (Major & Germano, 2006). Due to globalisation and the changing nature of work, modern-day employees have several competing responsibilities to balance work and other familial responsibilities such as housework, volunteering, taking care of children, spouse, and elderly parental care. All these dual responsibilities place more stress on individuals, families, and the communities in which they live, leading to the work-life conflict (WLC), which is a severe problem that impacts workers, their employers, and communities (Mungania, 2016).

Overview of Workforce in Saudi Arabia

In Saudi Arabia, the total number of employees was reported as 12.928 million, of whom about 10.596 million were male, and 2.332 million were female. Out of this total, 3.101 million were Saudi, and 9.827 million were Non-Saudis or expatriates. It is understood that 76% of expatriates occupied the jobs in the Saudi labour market (General Authority for Statistics, 2019). Besides, Saudi Vision 2030 aimed to raise the participation of Saudi Women in the labour market from 22 to 30%, thereby this would aid in reducing the unemployment rate by 33% among Saudi women (Al-Ghalayini, 2018). Accordingly, the percentage of Saudi women working in the public sector has increased from 39 to 40.3% during the past two years (Saudi Gazette Report, 2019). As of 2017, the private sector showed a 130% rise in the count of Saudi women in the workplace (Al-Ghalayini, 2018).

Though the workforce has expanded across various sectors in Saudi Arabia, this chapter focused explicitly on the workforce in the higher education and healthcare sector. Here, the higher education sector gained its importance since it aimed to meet the world-class standards of education by developing quality, innovative programmes, and initiatives that confirm the students' success and create them as a successful individual in the society (Shafai, 2018). Higher education institutions (HEIs) are essential to prepare a highly skilled workforce and also aid in creating new ideas and businesses (Almahdi, 2019). The Saudi government also established the King Abdullah Scholarship Program, which aimed to aid the students in studying abroad, thereby fulfil the needs of the labour market (Taylor & Albarsi, 2014). Besides, Saudi Vision 2030 focused on aligning the higher education outputs with the needs of the labour market. It also directed the Saudi government to work together with the private sector to guarantee higher education outcomes are in accord with the needs of the labour market (Patalong, 2016).

Another workforce focused in this chapter is the healthcare sector since it plays a vital role in meeting the demands of the growing population, altering demographics, and raising the burden of chronic diseases in Saudi Arabia (Bell, 2018a). In Saudi Arabia, there is a need for a significant rise in the supply of the healthcare workforce to meet the rising demand for its growing and ageing population. By 2030, it is roughly estimated that the Saudi government will require 710,000 healthcare professionals (HCPs) that exert an additional demand of 360,000 HCPs to what it has currently employed. At the same time, a large number of Saudi nationals have to be recruited in the healthcare sector to fulfil the objectives of Saudi Vision 2030 and the national transformation programme (NTP) 2020 (Al-Hanawi, Khan, & Al-Borie, 2019).

Hence, this chapter focused on these two sectors of Saudi Arabia though they differ in their working environment. As the role of the workforce is found to be important in these sectors, this chapter addresses the challenges faced by the higher education and health sector employees in managing their WLB and how it varies with regard to different age groups, gender, ethnicity, marital status, organisation culture, job security, the autonomy of work, and supportive work culture.

Higher Education Sector

In Saudi Arabia, thirty-five universities with a network of 770 affiliated institutions are offering various academic programmes in twenty-six disciplines (Muramalla & Alotaibi, 2019). Further, 1.7 million students are studying in various Saudi universities as of 2016 (ICEF Monitor, 2018). The data indicate that not only the number of Saudi universities is increasing, but the challenges for optimal functioning of these universities are also growing to combat the requirements of the large volume of students. However, the number of faculty members at universities increased to become 73,817 in the year 2014. Due to the rapid increase in students' enrolment in HEIs, there has been a substantial increase in the workload of the faculty members employed at these universities, thus compromising their WLB (Al Kuwaiti & Subbarayalu, 2019).

To add fuel this issue, a substantial drift of the nation's best academics to high paying industry positions because of inadequate incentive and reward systems within the Saudi universities (Al Ankari, 2013). As a result, Saudi universities are challenged by the shortage of highly skilled faculty members to perform the teaching roles (Groccia, Alsudairi, & Buskist, 2012).

The above scenario necessitates the HEIs to implement 'Saudization' policies and replace expatriate faculty members with Saudis (Saudi Gazette, 2016). As a measure to combat this, the Saudi government is heavily investing in education for establishing more universities and colleges and improving the quality of education, thereby improving the skills and employability of Saudi nationals. (Kono, 2013). In conformance with the facts reports, an earlier empirical study conducted by Al-Munajjed (2010) stated that 85% of Saudi working women are observed in the education sector. Another recent survey by Subbarayalu and Al Kuwaiti (2019) found that most of the faculty members (65%) expressed their opinion that they could able to maintain a healthy WLB.

Healthcare Sector

Saudi Arabia owns 487 total hospitals offering 72,981 beds, indicating 22.42 beds per 1000 population in the country. The total count of physicians (including the dentists) was 98074, in which 29.5% were Saudis (i.e. 28896). The dentists alone were counted as 15694. The total number of nurses was 185693, in which 36.7% were Saudis. The pharmacists were observed as 28312 in total, including 22.2% of Saudis. The total count of allied health professionals was 1,11861, in which 74.7% were Saudis (MOH, 2017). Besides, the Saudi population is estimated to be 34.81 million by 2020, from 34.14 million in 2019 (Global Media Insight, 2020). Due to the expansion of the Saudi population, there would be a need for 20,000 additional hospital beds by 2035 (Bell, 2018b).

Moreover, the Saudi government requires a substantial rise in the supply of HCPs to face the rising demands of its population. At the same time, it has to meet the objectives of Vision 2030 and the NTP 2020 by focusing on Saudization in the healthcare sector. However, the strength of Saudi healthcare graduates is insufficient to replace the HCPs who are leaving their jobs. Besides, the Saudi government needs to recruit a high number of nurses by 2030. This accounts for a net average of 6000–7000 new nurses to join the workforce yearly (Al-Hanawi et al., 2019). The nature of work of HCPs such as work in shifts, overtime, working at odd hours affects their physical as well as mental well-being, and balancing their work and life becomes a daunting task for them (Shaikh & Dange, 2017). In the Saudi Arabian context, AlGhamdi. (2014) revealed that female Saudi doctors perceived a poor WLB, and their work adversely affected their family relations. Besides physicians, it was found that 58% (n = 295) of PHC nurses in Saudi Arabia were unable to balance their work and family demands (Almalki, Fitzgerald, & Clark, 2012).

Challenges Facing Academics to Manage the WLB in Saudi Arabia

Demographic Factors: Gender

The profile of academic staff in Saudi universities constitutes 59% male staff and 41% female staff, in which Saudi nationals are comprising of 60% of the workforce and 40% expatriates (Muramalla & Alotaibi, 2019). With the rise in female participation in the Saudi workforce (Al-Ghalayini, 2018), female employees are expected to perform the matriarchal functions in their homes in addition to their employment commitments. This condition leads to occupational stress suffered by these women as they are now committed to perfecting a WLB (Rodrigo, 2016).

A recent study by Al Mousa, Alzuwaed, and Binsaeed (2020) concluded that female faculty members working at a Saudi university are struggling to manage WLB since they play a vital role in performing household tasks and caring children. As a result, they experience stress, which leads to poor job performance. The most significant factor influencing their WLB was observed as a job demands more long working hours after work at home in the evenings or at weekends. They agreed that employers should recognise their personal as well as family responsibilities, and the employers should aid them in balancing their work and life.

Organisational Culture

Work-family culture is defined as "the shared assumptions, beliefs, and values regarding the extent to which an organisation supports and values the integration of employees' work and family lives" (Thompson, Beauvais, & Lyness, 1999, p. 394). It is the extent to which an organisation's culture recognises and respects the family responsibilities of its employees and encourages management and employees to work together to meet their personal and work needs (Dhas & Karthikeyan, 2015). The factors such as the degree of flexibility in working hours, and working conditions, the scope for the employee to influence these matters, expectations of employee behaviour, and the level of consideration given by employers to employees' other-domain commitments can all facilitate or constrain the achievement of WLB (Aldhobaib, 2017). A previous study also indicated that WLB practices need to be supported and encouraged in workplace culture (Arif & Farooqi, 2014). A more recent study indicated that a periodic evaluation is required to reveal the needs of employees and revise the existing WLB policies in Saudi Arabia (Al Mousa et al., 2020). A recent Saudi-based study indicated that only 65% of academics could achieve a healthy balance between their work and home life (Subbarayalu & Al Kuwaiti, 2019). As such, Saudi universities have to offer effective WLB practices to enhance recruitment and retention and reduce work-life conflict among employees.

Increased Workload Load Among Saudi Academics

In Saudi Arabia, the maximum teaching workload of faculty members in the universities is observed between ten to eighteen teaching units per week during a semester, which would differ between faculties, and between public and private universities. It also varied with the academic title (HEC, 1998). In Saudi Arabia, the number of students enrolled has increased to 1,680,913 (2016–2017) from 636,445 (2005–2006). On the other hand, the Saudi government has adapted some mechanisms, including the introduction of paid educational programmes, more scientific chairs, and a rise in charities of universities to organise additional funds. Also, Saudi universities are trying to enhance their funds by delivering consultancy services for both the public and private sectors. These universities are encouraging partnerships and networks for scientific research and utilise the faculty's skills in specialised research and professional consultations (Khayati, Selim, Chan, 2019). This increased workload poses a serious problem to the faculty members, and it interferes with WLB. As a result, 60% of professors and 70% of lecturers employed at Saudi Universities expressed their view that they can able to balance their work and home life in a healthy manner (Subbarayalu & Al Kuwaiti, 2019).

However, Kamel (2013) found that Saudi faculty members perceived the quality of work-life dimensions, including WLB, as above average. Thus, there is a need for developing initiatives to improve the faculty's quality of work-life that includes decreasing workload, improving the sense of job security, and enhancing salary packages. Recently, Muramalla and Alotaibi (2019) reported that faculty members working in Saudi universities have positively perceived equitable workload in terms of teaching, research, and academic administration. Faculty members of public universities are more positive concerning the workload in teaching, academic administration, and research than those working in private universities.

Impact of Job Satisfaction

Brough et al. (2014) indicated that WLB is found to be negatively associated with work demands, turnover intentions and psychological strain, and positively associated with both family and job satisfaction. Recently, Kuwaiti, Bicak and Wahass (2019) have observed a high level of job satisfaction among faculty members of health sciences programmes at a Saudi university towards all domains of job satisfaction except salary, which is observed as the medium. Moreover, there is a significant positive relationship between employees' job satisfaction and their perception of WLB (Walga, 2018). To be precise, the lesser the job satisfaction, the lower the control the employee has to balance his or her work-life (Subbarayalu & Al Kuwaiti, 2019). Thus, there is a need for administrators to improve employees' job satisfaction and satisfaction with WLB to warrant organisational success irrespective of the context of the organisation (Walga, 2018).

Organisation Policies and Practices for WLB

In general, several arrangements are applied by organisations to help employees in balancing between work and their personal lives. Some of these organisational policies include suitable ways of adjusting work hours, through sharing of work between two employees, or part-time working, designing flexible working arrangements such as flexi-time where employees start and finish work at a time of their choice according to their personal needs, but work certain core hours (Bahudhailah, 2019).

A survey conducted by Arab news indicated that nearly 50 per cent of the Saudi workforce believes they can work efficiently from home rather than from an office (Arab News, 2014). Even though the employees prefer to have flexible working hours, such arrangements may not be possible in educational sectors as the teachers have to adhere to their class schedule, which is mostly student dependent, and the students are attending the university in a stipulated time. Saudi universities have a standard working time usually begins at 7.30 am and ends by 2.30 pm every day, and five working days per week is in practice.

Job Crafting

Job crafting necessitates balancing both the demands and resources of the job in which the employee engaged in. Higher job demand means having too much to do in a short time and may result in increased fatigue, pain, and functional limitation (Lundberg, 2002). It involves the social, organisational, and physical aspects of a job that require prolonged personal effort from employees. Time pressure and work intensification are frequent cases of job demands, whereas typical examples of job resources are work-type, job flexibility feedback, and social support (Bakker, Demerouti, & Sanz-Vergel, 2014). In the higher education sector, the role of faculty members in a university is to perform academic tasks, and also to involve actively in research activities, community services, workshops, seminars, and conferences. Involvement in research with a specific focus to publish the research work in the Web of Science

(WoS) database augments the stress level of contracted faculty members. Moreover, research publications are considered as one of the mandatory requirements to get their job contracts renewed on a yearly basis. As a result, workloads have enhanced and faculty felt more burden to "publish or perish" (Winefield, 2003). Furthermore, the nature of the work in higher education sector is monotonous and requires staff to adjust to unanticipated work variations. Faculty members who have the least control over their job have the highest demands imposed on them and receive the least amount of support from the workplace. Such individuals are at the highest risk for developing occupational health problems (Subbarayalu & Al Kuwaiti, 2019). A study by Praveen (2013) observed that the faculty members of a Saudi government university perceived the interference of job demands with their personal activities (home, recreation, and other interest) with the mean score of 2.488. It is suggested that a proper WLB should be preserved and priority should be given to schedule their work to prevent work-life imbalance.

Lack of Job Security

Faculty members in Saudi universities are more or less even mix of Saudis and expatriates, and the administrative positions are held mostly by Saudi nationals. Presently, the Saudi government is attempting to reduce reliance on expatriates through the 'Saudization' programme (Ramady, 2013). Saudi universities continue to recruit and retain non-Saudi academics until a qualified Saudi national is available to take up the higher-level teaching and research roles in the university (Ahmed, 2016). To be precise, public universities in Saudi Arabia can use expatriate workforce as being temporary and they would be offered one-year renewable contracts, and they are allowed to continue their work until Saudi university graduates are able to take up the roles (Havergal, 2017). Such a situation throws uncertainty among expatriate faculty members, which in turn has an impact on their family life, ultimately disturbing WLB.

Compensation and Rewards

An earlier study indicated that adequate and fair compensation showed a strong positive relationship with job satisfaction among faculty members (Tabassum, Rahman, & Jahan, 2012). A satisfied faculty member would positively perceive and balance their WLB (Brough et al., 2014). In Saudi Arabia, WLB of the faculty members was mainly influenced by rewards and compensation (Kamel, 2013). A study of Al-Smadi and Qblan (2015) observed a moderate level of satisfaction towards the salaries and financial support among the faculty members of Najran University, Saudi Arabia. A recent study indicated that only 65% of academics employed at a Saudi university felt they are fairly compensated for their work and can achieve a healthy balance between their work and home life (Subbarayalu & Al Kuwaiti, 2019).

Supportive Relationships

An earlier study indicated that social support from supervisors and colleagues showed a significant positive correlation with WLB among faculty members of a Malaysian public university (Shahid, Amdan, Alwi, Syazreena, & Hassan, 2016). Notably, support from co-workers is essential since it could reduce the stress perceived by faculty members due to the broader responsibilities and heavy workload demand. The policy-makers should focus on providing a conducive work environment that teamwork within and across departments to deliver faculty members with access to support from co-workers in coping with job demands (Shahid et al., 2016). Besides, family support is a significant factor influencing the WLB of female employees (Padma & Reddy, 2013). Unsupportive relationships at work and not getting proper recognition for the job done are leading to an unproductive work environment that makes an employee feel isolated. Similarly, at home, where no one helps each other or considers other people's pressures creates frustration and unhappiness (Jansen, 2016). An earlier study indicated that social support from supervisors and colleagues showed a significant positive correlation with WLB among faculty members of a Malaysian public university (Shahid et al., 2016). In Saudi Arabia, support network at home or work is identified as one of the significant factors influencing WLB of female faculty members of a public university at Riyadh (Al Mousa, Alzuwaed, & Binsaeed, 2020). A recent survey conducted among Saudi academics also revealed that 70% expressed their opinion that they are getting support from their colleagues, and their colleagues are helping them in resolving work-related problems (Subbarayalu & Al Kuwaiti, 2019).

Challenges Faced by Healthcare Sector Employees in Saudi Arabia to Manage Their WLB

Marital Status

Marital status is one of the significant predictors of WLC since young married employees described that they have a high level of work-life conflict than others (Lajtman, 2016). In the healthcare sector, nursing professionals are the most commonly affected people since they have to take care of their families during non-working hours and perform clinical care while working in shifts. Such a scenario forced them to find a suitable method to balance both work and family life (Varma, Kelling, & Goswami, 2016). In the Saudi Arabian context, female Saudi nurses are facing problems such as too long working hours and night shifts, which prevents the Saudi community from agreeing with nursing as a profession, particularly for married women with home and children responsibilities (Aldossary, While, & Barriball, 2008). Altakroni et al. (2019) recently found that some features of married life, such as the number of children, living with or without dependents and having disabled children at home, and age would cause work-life imbalance. However, those features have no statistically significant effect on the productivity of Saudi female nurses. Another most prominent category in the healthcare sector, which is prone to work-life imbalance are doctors, and a recent study indicated that 43% of married female Saudi doctors were unsatisfied in balancing career and family life (AlGhamdi, 2014). However, marital status showed no significant association with the satisfaction of balancing career and family life among doctors.

Long Working Hours

Employees working more than the stipulated time frame failed to meet their family needs (Rajan, 2017). In Saudi Arabia, the life of female Saudi nurses is hard since their working hours are too long when compared to Saudi working women in other fields. Also, shift and night work is another major issue facing those nurses. These problems lead to the female nurse turnover rate being higher than that of male nurses (Aldossary et al., 2008). Moreover, Almalki et al. (2012) revealed that the majority of Saudi nurses (i.e. 80% of 409 participants) felt unhappy with their working hours, which failed to suit their daily life as they have no energy left following work. In that study, it is also stated that 80% of Saudi nurses agreed that the system of working hours adversely influenced their work-life.

Recently, Almazan, Albougami, and Alamri (2019) found that working hours per week were a significant factor influencing the stress levels of Saudi nurses. It is clear that the working hours of Saudi nurses are not in match with their family life, and it leads to stress as well as negatively impact their work-life. A recent study also reported that clinical pharmacists in Saudi hospitals criticised the heavy workload, and the majority of female pharmacists were not satisfied with the working hours (Slimane, 2017). These issues exert a negative impact on pharmacists' ability to handle their work and family obligations.

Like nurses and pharmacists, Saudi residents also reported long working hours and had a high level of burnout. However, residents' burnout failed to show a strong relationship with long working hours. There is a prerequisite for framing national-wide working hour regulations in Saudi Arabia to protect residents' rights and ensure patient safety (Hameed, Masuadi, Al Asmary, Al-Anzi, & Al Dubayee, 2018). Non-Saudi doctors also perceived that working hours, pay, and benefits are unequal for both gender as compared with Saudis (Baqi et al.,

2017). Further, AlGhamdi (2014) explored the balance between career and family life among female doctors in a Saudi Medical City. Out of 174 female doctors, 43.1% perceived a poor balance between work and family, and 51.7% perceived that their work negatively affected. There is a need for developing national-wide working hour regulations in Saudi Arabia to protect residents' rights and ensure patient safety influenced their family affairs.

Working in Shifts

Most HCPs are in need to work for long hours and night shifts, which leads to an imbalance between their work and family life (Shivakumar & Pujar, 2016). Most of the HCPs (i.e. 66% of physicians and nurses) in Saudi Arabia reported the average number of night shifts per month as 6–9. However, it was not significantly associated with high emotional exhaustion and burnout among HCPs. Only a few HCPs reported on-call duties (Alqahtani et al., 2019). A positive association was found between the irregular shift work and employees' work-life imbalance (Greenhaus & Beutell, 1985). Predominantly, women are poorly satisfied with the WLB as a result of the night shift and less time to spend with families. For nurses, the condition is worse since they have to play dual roles to take of family responsibilities during non-working hours and to perform their duties during work shifts. Such a working environment forced nurses to balance these roles effectively (Ross, Rideout, & Carson, 1993).

In Saudi Arabia, 60% of registered nurses (RNs) are female with a high turnover rate than males. Married female RNs having children tend to leave their jobs since they are working 12 hours shifts (Aldossary et al., 2008). A recent study by Alsayed and West (2019) revealed that those Saudi female RNs who worked in 12 hours shift systems shared their experiences towards the organisation of shifts, and they pointed out inflexible working arrangements were a vital issue for Saudi female nurses. Since there was no chance to demand preferred changes in shift work, many of them felt stressful during their efforts to balance work demands and family-related problems. Those RNs with complicated family situations also felt issues in organising shift schedules to accommodate their specific requirements. The most recent empirical study also reported that 50.8% of Saudi female nurses in the Qassim region disliked night shifts (Altakroni et al., 2019).

Work Stress

Previous studies stated that employees' role stress might influence their WLB and further reduce their performance (Al Kahtani, Nawab, & Allam, 2016b). Recently, Nurumal et al. (2017) found that stress as one of the health factors that influence the WLB among teaching hospital nurses in Malaysia. Moreover, Kamal, Al-Dhshan, Abu-Salameh, Abuadas, and Hassan (2012) reported that Saudi nurses in a Taif governmental hospital were exposed to various job-related stressors such as patient's demands, their families' complaints, and nurse's workload. In a Saudi acute hospital setting, Almazan et al. (2019) recently stated that working hours per week and nationality were found to be a significant predictor of nurses' stress levels. It is revealed that the higher the working hours per week, the greater the stress level of nurses.

Further, nurses with Indian nationality perceived higher stress levels than nurses of other nationalities. As they are family-oriented, they might feel homesickness due to the abrupt shifts in their family environments. This situation could lead to diminished concentration and make them return to their familiar atmosphere (Chadda & Deb, 2013). Another recent study by Batayneh, Ali, and Nashwan (2019) in Saudi Arabia reported that the key external sources of stress among multinational nurses are workload, lack of workforce, and conflict with physicians. The extremely stressful situations perceived by those nurses are fear of making a mistake and making decisions in the absence of physicians during medical emergencies.

Workload

The workload is termed as the amount of work that an individual has to complete within a stipulated time (Chen & Spector, 1992). Vogel (2012) stated that employees often get scared about the work-life imbalance if they are overloaded with work. In the healthcare sector, the most critical profession to be affected due to heavy workload is nursing, and it affects nurses' satisfaction with WLB (Holland, Tham, Sheehan & Cooper, 2019). This condition results in when there is a lack of proper organisational support to replenish the individuals' lost resources (Schaufeli & Bakker, 2004). In the Saudi Arabian context, Saudi nurses having higher burnout levels reported high-stress, mainly due to their workload and uncertainty on treatment (Alsaqri, 2014).

Recently, Batayneh et al. (2019) stated that multinational nurses in Saudi Arabia perceived burnout due to workload and work-related stress. The majority of Saudi nurses felt dissatisfaction with the work-life due to those factors comprising family needs, duty hours, and energy left after work. Nurses experienced heavy workload and little energy left after work as they spent more time at work. As a result, the nurses were not able to balance their work and family (Almalki et al., 2012). Alharthi and Damanhouri (2018) also observed that the majority (82.3%) of Saudi nurses were strongly agreed that the work negatively affected their family responsibilities physically and psychologically. These nurses are prone to both physical and psychological fatigue due to the workload that prevents them from enjoying their time out of work. Also, those nurses expressed their opinion that they often abstain from family responsibilities to fulfil their work duties. About the workload of physicians in Saudi Arabia, Altaf et al. (2019) observed that specialists tended to be less satisfied than consultants. As per the recent empirical evidence, 68% of the Saudi consultants slept for $\leq$ 6 hours per day, and those consultants perceived a stressful work environment and a high workload (Alosaimi et al., 2018). A study by Al-Shuhail, Al-Saleh, Al-saleh, Elhassan, and Wajid (2017) stated that many physicians in the Saudi healthcare setting were expatriates, and the prevalence of burnout among them was observed to be moderately high. Many of them perceived that the rise in frequency of work obstructing with family obligations was linked to their exhaustion. Hence, it is essential to address the issues related to workload, working environment, working hours, and mental health, which might reduce the risk of burnout among Saudi physicians.

Organisational Culture

Organisational culture is described as the shared basic assumptions, values, and beliefs that represent a working environment and are adopted and educated to beginners (Schneider, Ehrhart, & Macey, 2013). All organisations have their policies and benefits for their employees that represent the overall organisational culture. Those organisations with properly developed policies and benefits provide a healthy WLB among employees. Some of these organisation-wide policies focus on annual vacation, maternity leave, flexible hours/schedules, sick leave, and communication (Groner, 2018). As such, employees experience a strong WLB if their organisations have family-supportive policies (Lapierre et al., 2008). Nevertheless, employees must sense comfortable in utilising these family-supportive policies that are influenced by the organisational culture and leadership style (Groner, 2018). A recent study indicated that female Saudi RNs concerned with unfair vacation policies by allowing expatriate nurses to organise their vacations as per their needs (Alsayed & West, 2019).

Furthermore, Anderson et al. (2002) stated that several factors associated with organisational cultures such as flexible schedules and job autonomy had improved the work-life imbalance among employees in hospitals. Inflexible working schedules were a key concern for female Saudi RNs working in acute care settings of a Saudi public hospital. The majority of those nurses were not satisfied with the organisation of shift schedules made by nursing managers (Alsayed & West, 2019). Furthermore, Almalki et al. (2012) reported that some primary healthcare nurses (38%) felt as they did not have the required autonomy to make patient care decisions. A recent study by Batayneh et al. (2019) found that multinational nurses felt a highly stressful situation while making decisions in the absence of doctors and are scared of making a mistake during emergencies. Nursing professionals also felt inadequate nursing policies and procedures, inferior respect from top-level management, especially on those policies governing vacations, were unsuitable neither for them nor for their families (Almalki et al., 2012). Most of the female Saudi RNs felt that several structures and policies related to the workplace had been framed to meet the needs of expatriate nurses. This situation makes it hard for Saudi nurses to accommodate work environments. There is an urgent need for the organisation to reframe policies and regulations to acknowledge their obligations to aid them in continuing their profession (Alsayed & West, 2019).

Supportive Work Relations

Recently, Shaikh and Dange (2017) identified that supportive work culture that includes support from superiors, peers, and subordinate is one among the factors which influence the WLB of HCPs. Nurumal et al. (2017) found that supervisor support is one of the influencing factors of WLB among Malaysian nurses working in a teaching hospital. Moreover, lack of social support from colleagues and superiors is recognised as one of the factors causing health problems among Saudi nurses (Al Hosis, Mersal, & Keshk, 2013). A recent study by Alharthi and Damanhouri (2018) found that the majority of Saudi nurses (60%) intended to quit their job due to the issues in their job as well as family and social facets. The most important reasons for leaving their job are lack of support from nursing managers, job dissatisfaction, conflicts between work and family commitments, poor appreciation from society for their profession. Besides, female Saudi RNs experienced an issue concerning the presence of expatriate nursing managers, which develop a power inequity within their working environment. They described their stressed relationships with expatriate co-workers (Alsayed &West, 2019). Further, Alsayed and West (2019) also identified four specific factors that create workplace conflict affecting the interpersonal relationships among nurses and these include: (i) attempts to exclude Saudi nurses from the workplace by expatriate nurses (ii) fear of expatriate nurses about the 'Saudization' programmes (iii) the intention of Saudi nurses to progress towards senior positions, and (iv) lack of interest among expatriate nurses to return to their home.

Aldubai et al. (2019) have also identified that the lack of support from superiors as one of the significant forecasters of burnout among Saudi family medicine residents. Those residents perceiving unfair assessments and lack of support from supervisors were significantly linked with emotional burnout. In contrast, half of the Saudi doctors, regardless of gender and nationality, felt that they experienced informational and instrumental support from their department and supervisors. Nevertheless, mixed responses (neither agree nor disagree) were observed towards their experience on emotional support from supervisors during times of stress or unhappiness. The majority of non-Saudi doctors perceived that their supervisors offered emotional support when required, as compared to Saudi doctors (Baqi et al., 2017). Based on the thorough exploration of the empirical literature as stated above, it is understood that inadequate support from co-workers and supervisors would enhance the stress and work-life imbalance. Further, stress from patient interactions might denote the requirement of peers to discuss the emotional facets of nursing jobs. Interventions addressing stress and work-life imbalance should aid nurses in achieving job satisfaction, retention, and wellness. Such attempts should develop a supportive working environment to augment nurses' well-being and WLB; thus, a satisfied and productive workforce is created (Varma et al., 2016).

Lack of Job Security

WLB is associated with the feeling of job insecurity (Roberts, 2007). Moreover, nurses might experience job insecurity due to the cost-saving nature of hospitals in the nursing workforce. This feeling of job insecurity could lead to stress and work-life imbalance (Chan, Tam, Lung, Wong, & Chau, 2013). Currently, the nursing profession has significantly involved in 'Saudization' to replace expatriate nurses with the local workforce. Training programmes related to 'Saudization' have been established for nurses to face the lack of local Saudi nurses and to boost the replacement of expatriate RNs with trained local RNs (Alsayed & West, 2019). The rise in the number of Saudi RNs would enhance employment among Saudis and provide openings for qualified Saudi RNs to hold the senior rank in their profession, which are commonly occupied by expatriate nurses (Maben, Al-Thowini, West, & Rafferty, 2010). Saudi RNs acknowledged that expatriate nurses were scared about their job insecurity due to the execution of the 'Saudization' programme. They also experienced poor professional relationships with several expatriate nurses due to their fear of 'Saudization', and it leads to workplace conflict. Such conflict occurs between Saudi nurses who were progressing towards their promotion and expatriate nurses who were not interested in losing their current job and returning to their home country. Reasonably, these contradictory aims of both groups were influencing the professional and friendly relations in their working environment (Alsayed & West, 2019).

Moreover, expatriate nurses are employed in Saudi Arabia on an annual contract basis. When their contract is not renewed, their residence permit that is connected with employment is also not renewed. Therefore, they have to return to their own country, and there are few possible chances to transfer visa sponsorship to another employer without exiting Saudi Arabia and starting a new visa application process. The employer also can terminate the contract earlier with a 30-day notice to employees. The limited duration would set a feel of uncertainty among employees regarding their job security. Also, the 'Saudization' programme contributes to the sense of job insecurity among expatriate nurses. It is observed that job insecurity is significantly associated with severe stress, anxiety, and depression among foreign nurses (Saquib et al., 2019). Hence, the 'Saudization' programme and uncertain work situation lead to job insecurity and stress among non-Saudi nurses, which might influence their WLB.

Family Domain

Malik, Saif, Gomez, Khan, and Hussain (2010) stated that social support from family aid employees to reduce their stress and manage their work and home effectively. Concerning the nursing profession, family support is a vital one, and the family should provide its full support by considering the work pressure prevailing in that profession—such family support aid nurses to manage their work-life efficiently (Satpathy, Patnaik, & Jena, 2014). In the Saudi Arabian context, long working hours have impacted the energy level of Saudi nurses, and they find it hard to spend time with their families (Almalki et al., 2012). Moreover, there is a direct association between family affairs and Saudi nurses' turnover when more family responsibilities overlap the work duties (Alharthi & Damanhouri, 2018). The main reasons for avoiding the nursing profession among Saudi women are cultural norms, family disagreement, gender integration, and poor image of working shifts (Al-Mahmoud, Mullen, & Spurgeon, 2012). Thus, it is usually perceived as an unsuitable profession for Saudi women.

On the other hand, female physicians are in need to care for their family responsibilities to develop WLB (Addagabottu & Battu, 2015). Saudi female doctors who were working more than 60 hours per week were unsatisfied with managing their WLB. They felt that their work had negatively affected their relationship with their spouse and children and also the performance of their children at school (AlGhamdi, 2014). However, Baqi et al. (2017) stated that Saudi female doctors spent significantly more hours on home activities and caring for the family than their male counterparts. They observed a gap in their professional life due to family responsibilities other than maternity leave. Besides, the rise in frequency of work interfering with family obligations was associated with burnout among Saudi physicians. There is a need to pay attention to attaining a WLB for healthcare staff (Al-Shuhail et al., 2017). Mone, Ashrafi and Sarker (2019) recommended the hospital administrators to develop more work-family friendly policies for their female physicians to manage the WLB.

Conclusion

WLB among employees is a state of achieving the balance between their work and family needs. On exploring the workforce pattern that exists in Saudi Arabia, a multicultural working environment is witnessed. This chapter gives an overview of the Saudi workforce in both higher education and healthcare industries. In the higher education sector, faculty members felt hard to manage their WLB since their job demands additional long working hours to be carried out at home. The policymakers should recognise the faculty's personal and family responsibilities and assist them in achieving WLB. Though WLB policies are existing, periodic evaluation is needed to reveal the current needs and update the existing systems. Saudi universities should be cautious while involving its faculty members to take additional tasks such as consultancy and other revenue-generating activities as it imposes extra workload on the faculty members, which would affect their work-life balance. Academics also felt job pressure in their working environment and received support from their colleagues; thereby, these factors influence their WLB. Moreover, a high level of faculty's satisfaction with their job and WLB is essential for the success of the organisation. Several empirical evidence indicated job insecurity among non-Saudi academics, and it has negatively influenced their WLB.

In the healthcare sector, the most common professionals face challenges in managing WLB are physicians and nurses. Factors such as job stress, heavy workload, lack of autonomy in making decisions, inflexible working schedules, and poor organisation of shift schedules, inadequate vacation planning, and reduced professional relationships between expatriate and Saudi nurses are directly impacting the WLB of the nursing professionals. Studies also pointed out that nurses tend to quit their jobs due to long working hours, job dissatisfaction, lack of support from superiors, and poor appreciation from the community concerning their profession. Notably, the Saudization programme and uncertain work situation lead to job insecurity and stress among non-Saudi nurses, which affect their WLB. Nurses also felt that hospital administrators should consider reframing policies and regulations to recognise their needs and assist them in continuing their profession.

Moreover, the main reasons for avoiding the nursing profession among Saudi women are cultural norms, family disagreement, working with men, long working hours, and night shifts. Like nursing professionals, female Saudi doctors also perceived that their work adversely affects their family lives. Saudi physicians perceived that raised obstruction of work with family affairs was linked to their burnout. There is a need to address workload, working conditions, working hours, and mental health, which might reduce the risk of burnout among Saudi physicians. Even though Saudi physicians get enough support from their supervisors, Saudi residents feeling unfair assessments and lack of support from supervisors and were significantly associated with emotional burnout. Based on these challenges, the authorities belonging to both the higher education and healthcare sectors should take appropriate measures to overcome those challenges. There is a need for healthcare organisations to frame or revise the WLB policies and practices that support their employees in achieving WLB without hindering their performance.

References

Addagabottu, R. S., & Battu, N. (2015). A study on the variables that influence work-life balance of women doctors and nurses with special reference to government and private hospitals of Guntur district. *International Journal of Research in Management & Business Studies, 2*(3), 33–39.

Ahmed, M. A. (2016). The effects of Saudization on the universities: Localization in Saudi Arabia. *International Higher Education, 86*(2016), 25–27.

Al Ankari, K. M. (2013). *Higher education in Saudi Arabia: Achievements, challenges, and opportunities*. New York and London: Springer, Dordrecht and Heidelberg.

Al Hosis, K. F., Mersal, F. A., & Keshk, L. I. (2013). Effects of job stress on health of Saudi nurses working in ministry of health hospitals in Qassim region in KSA. *Life Science Journal, 10*(1): 1036–1044. http://www.lifesciencesite.com.

Al Kahtani, N. S., Nawab, A. K., & Allam, Z. (2016). Unfair HRM practices in the telecom sector in Saudi Arabia. An empirical investigation of selected public and private sector companies. *International Journal of Applied Business and Economic Research, 14*(10), 6377–6396.

Al Kuwaiti, A., & Subbarayalu, A. V. (2019). *Quality of work life of academicians in Saudi universities*. Mauritius: LAP Lambert Academic Publishing.

Al Mousa, H. A., Alzuwaed, J., & Binsaeed, R. H. (2020). Assessing work life balance among Saudi Arabian working women—A descriptive study on selected employees. *TEST Engineering & Management, 82*, 363–375.

Aldhobaib, M. A. (2017). *The relationship between organisational culture and individual behavior in Saudi Arabia* (Doctoral Thesis, Cardiff Business School, Cardiff University). Retrieved from https://orca.cf.ac.uk/107352/1/2017AldhobaibA%20phd.pdf.

Aldossary, A., While, A., & Barriball, L. (2008). Health care and nursing in Saudi Arabia. *International Nursing Review, 55*(1), 125–128. https://doi.org/10.1111/j.1466-7657.2007.00596.x.

Aldubai, S., Aljohani, A. M., Alghamdi, A. G., Alghamdi, K. S., Ganasegeran, K., & Yenbaawi, A. M. (2019). Prevalence and associated factors of burnout among family medicine residents in Al Madina, Saudi Arabia. *Journal of Family Medicine and Primary Care, 8*(2), 657–662. https://doi.org/10.4103/jfmpc.jfmpc_268_18.

Al-Ghalayini, B. M. K. (2018 October 14). Women's empowerment in the Saudi workplace. *Arab News*. Retrieved from https://www.arabnews.com/node/1387356.

AlGhamdi, T. A. (2014). Balance between career and family life among female doctors in King Abdul-Aziz Medical City, Riyadh, Saudi Arabia. *International Journal of Medical Science and Public Health, 3*(2), 203–211.

Al-Hanawi, M. K., Khan, S. A., & Al-Borie, H. M. (2019). Healthcare human resource development in Saudi Arabia: Emerging challenges and opportunities-A critical review. *Public Health Reviews, 40*, 1. https://doi.org/10.1186/s40985-019-0112-4.

Alharthi, R., & Damanhouri, A. M. S. (2018). Factors influencing Saudi nurses turnover empirical study in Ministry of Health Hospitals—Jeddah city. *International Journal of Engineering Research and Management (IJERM), 5*(2), 1–10.

Almahdi, H. K. (2019). Promotion and participation of Saudi universities towards the development of entrepreneurial leadership-An empirical study in Saudi Arabian context. *Journal of Entrepreneurship Education, 22*(6), Retrieved from https://www.abacademies.org/articles/Promotion-and-participation-of-saudi-universities-1528-2651-22-6-485.pdf.

Al-Mahmoud, S., Mullen, P., & Spurgeon, P. (2012). Saudization of the nursing workforce: Reality and myths about planning nurse training in Saudi Arabia. *Journal of American Science, 8*(4), 369–379.

Almalki, M. J., Fitzgerald, G., & Clark, M. (2012). Quality of work life among primary health care nurses in the Jazan region, Saudi Arabia: A cross sectional study. *Human Resources for Health 10*, 30. https://doi.org/10.1186/1478-4491-10-30.

Almazan, J. U., Albougami, A. S., & Alamri, M. S. (2019). Exploring nurses' work-related stress in an acute care hospital in KSA. *Journal of Taibah University Medical Sciences, 14*(4), 376–382.

Al-Munajjed, M., 2010. Women's employment in Saudi Arabia: A major challenge. Retrieved from http://www.saudigazette.com.sa/index.cfm?method=home.regcon&contentID=2010033067859.

Alosaimi, F. D., Alawad, H. S., Alamri, A. K., Saeed, A. I., Aljuaydi, K. A., Alotaibi, A. S., et al. (2018). Patterns and determinants of stress among consultant physicians working in Saudi Arabia. *Advances in Medical Education and Practice, 9,* 165–174. https://doi.org/10.2147/AMEP.S155113.

Alqahtani, A. M., Nabil J. Awadalla, N. J., Alsaleem, S. A., Alsamghan, A. S., & Alsaleem, M. A. (2019). Burnout syndrome among emergency physicians and nurses in Abha and Khamis Mushait Cities, Aseer Region, Southwestern Saudi Arabia. *The Scientific World Journal, 2019*(4515972), 1–14. https://doi.org/10.1155/2019/4515972.

Alsaqri, H. S. (2014). *A survey of intention to leave, job stress, burnout and job satisfaction among nurses employed in the Hail region's hospitals in Saudi Arabia* (Doctoral Dissertations). RMIT University Melbourne, Australia. Retrieved from https://researchbank.rmit.edu.au/eserv/rmit:160699/Alsaqri.pdf.

Alsayed, S., & West, S. (2019). Exploring acute care workplace experiences of Saudi female nurses: Creating career identity. *Saudi Critical Care Journal, 3*(2), 75–84.

Al-Shuhail, A. S., Al-Saleh, S., Al-saleh, S. S., Elhassan, I., & Wajid, S. (2017). Prevalence of burnout among national guard health affairs physicians in Dammam, Saudi Arabia—A crosssectional Study. *Asian Journal of Pharmaceutics, 11*(4), S924–S929.

Al-Smadi, M. S., & Qblan, Y. M. (2015). Assessment of Job Satisfaction among faculty members and its relationship with some variables in Najran University. *Journal of Education and Practice, 6*(35), 117–123.

Altaf, A., Attar, L., Marzouki, H. Z., Maghrabi, A. A., Tashkandi, H., Jamal, W., et al. (2019). Predictors of career satisfaction among physicians: Observations from a tertiary care center. *Saudi Surgical Journal, 7*(3), 87–94.

Altakroni, H., Mahmud, I., Elmossad, Y. M., Al-Akhfash, A., Al-Hindi, A., & Joshva, K. (2019). Healthcare productivity, and its sociodemographic determinants, of Saudi female nurses: A cross-sectional survey, Al-Qassim, Saudi Arabia. *International Journal of Health Sciences, 13*(6), 19–25.

Anderson, S. E., Coffey, B. S., & Byerly, R. T. (2002). Formal organisational initiatives and informal workplace practices: Links to work-family conflict and job-related outcomes. *Journal of Management, 28*(6), 787–810.

Arab News. (2014 March 16). Modern Saudi work force prefers 'flexible working'. *Arab News.* Retrieved from https://www.arabnews.com/news/514991.

Arif, B., & Farooqi, Y. A. (2014). Impact of work life balance on job satisfaction and organisational commitment among university teachers: A case study of University of Gujrat, Pakistan. *International Journal of Multidisciplinary Sciences and Engineering, 5*(9), 24–29.

Bahudhailah, M. O. (2019). Exploring the barriers to work-life balance for women in Saudi Arabia (Doctoral Thesis, University of Hull). Retrieved from https://ethos.bl.uk/OrderDetails.do?uin=uk.bl.ethos.788911.

Bakker, A. B., Demerouti, E., & Sanz-Vergel, A. I. (2014). Burnout and work engagement: The JD–R approach. *Annual Review of Organisational Psychology and Organisational Behavior, 1*(1), 389–411.

Baqi, S., Albalbeesi, A., Iftikhar, S., Baig-Ansari, N., Alanazi, M., & Alanazi, A. (2017). Perceptions of gender equality, work environment, support, and social issues for women doctors at a university hospital in Riyadh. *Kingdom of Saudi Arabia. PloS One, 12*(10), e0186896. https://doi.org/10.1371/journal.pone.0186896.

Batayneh, M. H., Ali, S., Nashwan, A. J. (2019). The Burnout among Multinational Nurses in Saudi Arabia. *Open Journal of Nursing, 9,* 603–619. http://www.scirp.org/journal/ojn.

Bell, J. (2018a, September 28). Saudi Arabia's growing health pains and how to cure them. *Arab News*. Retrieved from https://www.arabnews.com/node/1378431/saudi-arabia.

Bell, J. (2018b, June 10). Saudi Arabia will need an additional 10,000 doctors by 2020, say experts. *Arab News*. Retrieved from https://www.arabnews.com/node/1317151/saudi-arabia.

Brough, P., Timms, C., O'Driscoll, M. P., Kalliath, T., Siu, O. L., Sit, C., et al. (2014). Work-life balance: A longitudinal evaluation of a new measure across Australia and New Zealand workers. *International Journal of Human Resource Management, 25*(19), 2724–2744.

Chadda, R. K., & Deb, K. S. (2013). Indian family systems, collectivistic society, and psychotherapy. *Indian Journal of Psychiatry, 55*(Suppl 2), S299–S309. https://doi.org/10.4103/0019-5545.105555.

Chan, Z. C., Tam, W. S., Lung, M. K., Wong, W. Y., & Chau, C. W. (2013). A systematic literature review of nurse shortage and the intention to leave. *Journal of Nursing Management, 21*(4), 605–613. https://doi.org/10.1111/j.1365-2834.2012.01437.x.

Chen, P. Y., & Spector, P. E. (1992). Relationships of work stressors with aggression, withdrawal, theft, and substance use: An exploratory study. *Journal of Occupational and Organisational Psychology, 65*(3), 177–184.

Collier, R. (2016). Work-life balance. In C. Ashford & J. Guth (Eds.), *The legal academic's handbook* (pp. 31–33). London, England: Palgrave Macmillan.

Dhas, B. (2015). A report on the importance of work-life balance. *International Journal of Applied Engineering Research, 10*(9), 21659–21665.

Dhas, B., & Karthikeyan, P. (2015). Work-life balance challenges and solutions: Overview. *International Journal of Research in Humanities and Social Studies, 12*(12), 10–19.

General Authority for Statistics, KSA. (2019). Labour market third quarter of 2019. Retrieved from https://www.stats.gov.sa/en/34.

Global Media Insight. (2020 January 9). Saudi Arabia's population statistics of 2020. Retrieved from https://www.globalmediainsight.com/blog/saudi-arabia-population-statistics/.

Greenblatt, E. (2002). Work/life balance: Wisdom or whining. *Organisations Dynamics, 31*(2), 177–193.

Greenhaus, J., & Beutell, N. (1985). Sources of conflict between work and family roles. *Academy of Management Review, 10*(1), 76–88.

Groccia, J. E., Alsudairi, M. A. T., & Buskist, W. (2012). *Handbook of college and university teaching: A global perspective* (p. 80, 1st ed.). New York: Sage Publications. http://dx.doi.org/10.4135/9781412996891.

Groner, E. S. (2018). The effect of organisational culture on work-life balance. *Student Publications, 643*. Retrieved from https://cupola.gettysburg.edu/student_scholarship/643.

Hameed, T. K., Masuadi, E., Al Asmary, N. A., Al-Anzi, F. G., & Al Dubayee, M. S. (2018). A study of resident duty hours and burnout in a sample of Saudi residents. *BMC Medical Education, 18*, 180. https://doi.org/10.1186/s12909-018-1300-5.

Havergal, C. (2017). *Hiring foreign academics, a 'last resort', Saudi universities told. Saudization' drive sees public institutions urged to hire local staff*. Times University Ranking. Retrieved from https://www.timeshighereducation.com/news/hiring-foreign-academics-last-resort-saudi-universities-told.

Higher Education Council (HEC). (1998). *Draft copy of the university regulations for Saudi personnel including staff members and the like*. Majmaah University, Kingdom of Saudi Arabia. Retrieved from https://www.mu.edu.sa/sites/default/files/content/2016/01/Regulations%20for%20Saudi%20Universities%20Personnel.pdf.

Holland, P., Tham, T. L., Sheehan, C., & Cooper, B. (2019). The impact of perceived overload on nurse satisfaction with work-life balance and intention to leave the occupation. *Applied Nursing Research, 49*(2019), 70–76.

ICEF Monitor. (2018). Saudi Arabia's expanding higher education capacity. Retrieved from https://monitor.icef.com/2018/07/saudi-arabias-expanding-higher-education-capacity/.

Jansen, M. (2016). *The seven challenge areas for work-life balance*. Retrieved from https://www.lifecoach-directory.org.uk/memberarticles/the-7-challenge-areas-for-work-life-balance.

Kamal, S., Al-Dhshan, M., Abu-Salameh, K., Abuadas, F., & Hassan, M. (2012). The effect of nurses' perceived job-related stressors on job satisfaction in Taif governmental hospitals in Kingdom of Saudi Arabia. *Journal of American Science, 8*(3), 119–125.

Kamel, M. M. (2013). The mediating role of affective commitment in the relationship between quality of work life and intention to leave. *Life Science Journal, 10*(4), 1062–1067.

Khayati, A., Selim, M., & Sheng-Ju Chan, S.-J. (2019). The status of innovation in Saudi Universities. *Cogent Education, 6*(1), 1653635. https://doi.org/10.1080/2331186X.2019.1653635.

Kohll, A. (2018, March 27). *The evolving definition of work-life balance*. Retrieved from https://www.forbes.com/sites/alankohll/2018/03/27/the-evolving-definition-of-work-life-balance/#5572a6439ed3.

Kono, Y. (2013, July 1). *Globally mobile Saudi students: Agents of economic, social & cultural transformation?* Retrieved from https://wenr.wes.org/2013/07/globally-mobile-saudi-students-agents-of-economic-social-cultural-transformation.

Kuwaiti, A., Bicak, H., & Wahass, S. (2019). Factors predicting job satisfaction among faculty members of a Saudi higher education institution. *Journal of Applied Research in Higher Education*, Ahead-of-print. Published online: 18 July 2019. https://doi.org/10.1108/JARHE-07-2018-0128.

Lajtman, M. K. (2016). *Impact of personal factors on the work life conflict and its co-influence with organisational factors on employee commitment in Croatia* (Doctoral Dissertation no. 4529). University of St. Gallen, Switzerland. Retrieved from https://www1.unisg.ch/www/edis.nsf/SysLkpByIdentifier/4529/$FILE/dis4529.pdf.

Lapierre, L. M., Spector, P. E., Allen, T. D., Poelmans, S., Cooper, C. L., O'Driscoll, M. P., et al. (2008). Family-supportive organisation perceptions, multiple dimensions of work–family conflict, and employee satisfaction: A test of model across five samples. *Journal of Vocational Behavior, 73*(1), 92–106.

Lundberg, U. (2002). Psychophysiology of work: Stress, gender, endocrine response, and work-related upper extremity disorders. *American Journal of Industrial Medicine, 41*(5), 383–392.

Maben, J., Al-Thowini, K., West, E., & Rafferty, A.-M. (2010). Uneven development: Comparing the indigenous health care workforce in Saudi

Arabia, Bahrain, and Oman. *International Journal of Nursing Studies, 47*(3), 392–396.

Major, D. A. & Germano, L. M. (2006). The changing nature of work and its impact on the work-home interface. In F. Jones, R. J. Burke & M. Westman: *Work-life balance: A psychological perspective* (pp. 13–38). USA: Psychology Press.

Malik, M. I., Saif, M. I., Gomez, S. F., Khan, N., & Hussain, S. (2010). Balancing work and family through social support among working women in Pakistan. *African Journal of Business Management, 4*(13), 2864–2870.

Ministry of Health (MOH). (2017). *Annual statistical book*. Riyadh: Ministry of Health; 2017. Retrieved from https://www.moh.gov.sa/en/Ministry/Statistics/book/Documents/ANNUAL-STATISTICAL-BOOK-1438H.pdf.

Mone, F. H., Ashrafi, D. M., & Sarker, A. R. (2019). Work life balance of female doctors in Bangladesh: An overview. *Journal of Health and Medical Sciences, 2*(3), 410–421.

Mungania, A. K. (2016). Influence of family responsibilities on performance of the banking industry in Kenya. *International Journal of Advanced Multidisciplinary Research (IJAMR), 3*(8), 6–13.

Muramalla, V. S. S. R., & Alotaibi, K. A. (2019). Equitable workload and the perceptions of academic staff in universities. *The International Journal of Educational Organisation and Leadership, 26*(2), 1–19.

Nurumal, M. S., Makabe, S., Jamaludin, F. I, C., Yusof, H. F. M., Aung, K. T., & Kowitlawakul, Y. (2017). Work-life balance among teaching hospital nurses in Malaysia. *Global Journal of Health Science, 9*(8), 81–89.

Odle-dusseau, H. N., Britt, T. W., & Bobko, P. (2012). Work-family balance, wellbeing, and organisational outcomes: investigating actual versus desired work/family time discrepancies. *Journal of Business and Psychology, 27*(3), 331–343.

Padma, S., & Reddy, S. (2013). Role of family support in balancing personal and work life of women employees. *IJCEM International Journal of Computational Engineering & Management, 16*(3), 93–97.

Parveen, M. (2013). Faculty Stress in a Saudi government university. *International Journal of Humanities and Social Science, 3*(18), 180–192.

Patalong, F. (2016, August). *Vision 2030 and the transformation of education in Saudi Arabia*. Retrieved from https://www.tamimi.com/law-update-articles/vision-2030-and-the-transformation-of-education-in-saudi-arabia/.

Rajan, D. (2017). Negative impacts of long working hours: A comparative study among nurses. *MOJ Applied Bionics and Biomechanics, 1*(2), 60–67.

Ramady, M. (2013). Gulf unemployment and government policies: Prospects for the Saudi labour quota or Nitaqat system. *International Journal of Economics and Business Research, 5*(4), 476–498.

Roberts, K. (2007). Work-life balance-The sources of the contemporary problem and the probable outcomes: A review and interpretation of the evidence. *Employee Relations, 29*(4), 334–351.

Rodrigo. (2016). Occupational stress and work-life balance in the public sector in Saudi Arabia. *The WritePass Journal*. Retrieved from https://writepass.com/journal/2016/11/occupational-stress-and-work-life-balance-in-the-public-sector-in-saudi-arabia/.

Ross, M., Rideout, E., & Carson, M. (1993). Nurses' work: Balancing personal and professional caregiving careers. *The Canadian journal of nursing research = Revue canadienne de recherche en sciences infirmieres, 26*(4): 43–59.

Saquib, N., Zaghloul, M., Saquib, J., Alhomaidan, H., Al- Mohaimeed, A., & Al-Mazrou, A. (2019). Association of cumulative job dissatisfaction with depression, anxiety, and stress among expatriate nurses in Saudi Arabia. *Journal of Nursing Management, 27*(4), 740–748.

Satpathy, S., Patnaik, C. M., & Jena, S. (2014). A comparative study on work-life balance of nursing staff working in private and government hospitals. *International Journal of Innovative Research in Science, Engineering and Technology, 3*(1), 82654–88261.

Saudi Gazette. (2016, October 8). *The Saudization crisis in the education sector*. Retrieved from http://live.saudigazette.com.sa/article/164873/The-Saudization-crisis-in-the-education-sector.

Saudi Gazette Report. (2019, October 21). Employment gap between men and women in Government jobs drops to 37.8%. *Saudi Gazette*. Retrieved from http://saudigazette.com.sa/article/580440.

Schaufeli, W. B., & Bakker, A. B. (2004). Job demands, job resources, and their relationship with burnout and engagement: A multi-sample study. *Journal of Organisational Behavior, 25*(3), 293–315.

Schneider, B., Ehrhart, M. G., & Macey, W. H. (2013). Organisational climate and culture. *Annual Review of Psychology, 64,* 361–388. https://doi.org/10.1146/annurev-psych-113011-143809.

Shafai, A. A. (2018). *The perceptions of Saudi Arabia higher educational leaders on servant leadership: The use of authority and power* (Doctoral Dissertations, 461). Retrieved from https://repository.usfca.edu/diss/461.

Shahid, S. A. M., Amdan, S., Alwi, A., Syazreena, F., & Hassan, C. N. (2016). Social support, negative affectivity, and work personal life balance of academics. *International Journal of Social Science and Humanity, 6*(7), 500–504. https://doi.org/10.7763/IJSSH.2016.V6.699.

Shaikh, P., & Dange, U. (2017). Antecedents of work life balance: A study of healthcare sector. *IRA-International Journal of Management & Social Sciences, 8*(1), 1–7. http://dx.doi.org/10.21013/jmss.v8.n1.p1.

Shivakumar, K., & Pujar, V. (2016). Work life balance in the health care sector. *Amity Journal of Healthcare Management, 1*(2), 45–54.

Slimane, N. S. B. (2017). Motivation and job satisfaction of pharmacists in four hospitals in Saudi Arabia. *Journal of Health Management, 19*(1), 39–72. https://doi.org/10.1177/0972063416682559.

Staines, G. L. (1980). Spill-over versus compensation: A review of the literature on the literature on the relationship between work and non-work. *Human Relations, 33*(2), 111–129.

Subbarayalu, A. V., & Al Kuwaiti, A. (2019). Quality of Work life of teaching staff working at a higher education institution in Saudi Arabia: A cross-sectional study. *Journal of Social Service Research, 45*(4), 530–542.

Tabassum, A., Rahman, T., & Jahan, K. (2012). An evaluation of the quality of work life: A study of the faculty members of private universities in Bangladesh. *ABAC Journal, 32*(2), 36–57.

Taylor, C., & Albasri, W. (2014) The impact of Saudi Arabia king Abdullah's scholarship program in the U.S. *Open Journal of Social Sciences, 2*(10), 109–118. https://doi.org/10.4236/jss.2014.210013.

Thompson, C. A., Beauvais, L. L., & Lyness, K. S. (1999). When work–family benefits are not enough: The influence of work–family culture on benefit utilization, organisational attachment, and work–family conflict. *Journal of Vocational Behavior, 54*(3), 392–415.

Varma, M. M., Kelling, A. S., & Goswami, S. (2016). Enhancing health-care quality by promoting work-life balance among nursing staff. *Journal of Hospital Administration, 5*(6), 58–62.

Vogel, S. (2012). Overtime hours threaten work-life balance. *Global Business Knowledge*. Retrieved from http://globaledge.msu.edu/blog/post/1274/overtime-hours-threaten-work-life balance.

Walga, T. K. (2018). Job satisfaction and satisfaction with work-life balance across cultures. *Journal of Intercultural Management, 10*(2), 159–179.

Winefield, A. H. (2003). Stress in university academics. In D. Maureen, H. R. Winefield, & A. H. Winefield (Eds.), *Occupational stress in service professions* (pp. 237–260). New York: Taylor & Francis.

Part III

Asia

9

Work–Life Conflict in China: A Confucian Cultural Perspective

Sudong Shang, Xi Wen Chan, and Xuchu Liu

Introduction

The present chapter focuses on the factors influencing work–life conflict in China. We extend the concept of "work–family conflict" to "work–life conflict" which is a type of inter-role interference across work and non-work domains. Work domain refers to an individual's paid employment, while the non-work domain comprises all other components of life, including family, recreation, community activities, and personal life (Dewe, O'Driscoll, & Cooper, 2010). Although research on non-US populations has emerged in recent years, a considerable gap still

S. Shang
Griffith University, Gold Coast, QLD, Australia

X. W. Chan (✉)
Griffith University, Brisbane, QLD, Australia
e-mail: carys.chan@griffith.edu.au

X. Liu
Henan University of Chinese Medicine, Zhengzhou, China

T. A. Adisa and G. Gbadamosi (eds.), *Work-Life Interface*,
https://doi.org/10.1007/978-3-030-66648-4_9

exists in our knowledge of cross-cultural work–life issues (Foster & Ren, 2015). That is, the generalisability of work–life theories across different cultural contexts remains uncertain (Crawford, Thompson, & Ashforth, 2019; Powell, Greenhaus, Allen, & Johnson, 2019), and the extant cross-cultural work–life research has not explored the influence of specific cultural values in one nation beyond the prevailing macro-level cultural frameworks (i.e. Hofstede, 2010) on the mechanisms underlying work–life phenomena. To capture the influence of the aforementioned research limits, this chapter aims to discuss work–life conflict in the Confucian culture, which is a specific cultural context of China. This chapter focuses on how Confucian values embedded in Chinese society mould Chinese employees' work–life experiences. In doing so, we hope this chapter can pave the way for future work–life research conducted in China and contribute to the advancement of work–life theories.

Work–Life Conflict in Brief

The seminal paper of Greenhaus and Beutell (1985) defined work–family conflict as "a form of inter-role conflict in which the role pressures from the work and family domains are mutually incompatible in some respects" (p. 77). The notion of inter-role conflict has its roots in Goode's (1960) scarcity theory, which assumes that resources such as time, skills, and energy are fixed and limited and that resources expended in one role deplete those available for other roles. Therefore, individuals who participate in multiple life roles (e.g. work and family) are more likely to experience conflict between those roles due to the diminished quality of roles that received fewer resources (Kahn, Wolfe, Quinn, Snoek, & Rosenthal, 1964; Katz & Kahn, 1978). Greenhaus and Beutell (1985) also conceptualised work–family conflict to be bi-directional: work-to-family conflict occurs when the pressures from the work and family domains are mutually incompatible, and as a result, participation in the family role is made more difficult by participation in the work role; family-to-work conflict occurs when participation in the work role is made more difficult by participation in the family role.

In recent times, work–family scholars (e.g. Keeney, Boyd, Sinha, Westring, & Ryan, 2013; Siegel, Post, Brockner, Fishman, & Garden, 2005; Skinner & Pocock, 2008) have extended "work–family" conflict to "work–life" conflict, reflecting the other life domains and interests (e.g. friends, sports, community, education, volunteering, and so on) beyond the family domain. Life domains refer to the spheres of activity that make up an individual's identity (Keeney et al., 2013). Therefore, work–life conflict describes how work interferes with one's personal life in general, including but not limited to the family domain. Additionally, while national policies tend to focus on the work and family domains out of concern for the well-being of children and working parents, it should be recognised that all employees, regardless of their circumstances and living arrangements, should have a right to a balanced relationship between their paid employment and other life domains (Skinner & Pocock, 2008).

In a recent meta-analysis by Xu and Cao (2019) of the antecedents and outcomes of work–life conflict, it was found that social support (including supervisor support, co-worker support, organisational support, and family support) and positive and negative affect predicted both work-to-life conflict and life-to-work conflict. Further, in another meta-analysis by French, Dumani, Allen, and Shockley (2018), it was found that social support emanating from the work domain consistently reduced work-to-life conflict and life-to-work conflict. French et al. (2018) also found that the strength of the relationships between social support and work–life conflict varies as a function of social support domain, form, source, type, and national context. Also, Xu and Cao's (2019) meta-analysis revealed that work-related characteristics (e.g. work overload and job control) only predicted work-to-life conflict. Work–life conflict, in turn, was negatively related to positive work- (e.g. job satisfaction, organisational commitment, and job performance) and non-work-related (e.g. life satisfaction) outcomes, and positively related to negative work outcomes such as burnout and turnover intentions. In an earlier meta-analysis by Amstad, Meier, Fasel, Elfering, and Semmer (2011), it was also found that work-to-life conflict was more strongly associated with work-related than non-work-related outcomes, and life-to-work conflict was more strongly associated with non-work-related than work-related outcomes.

The Chinese Context

China, with the largest population (approximately 1.4 billion) in the world, is also the second-largest economy in the world after the United States. Since economic reforms began in 1978, China's economy has rapidly transformed from a centrally planned system to a more market-oriented economy, and the private sector has since blossomed. The fast growth of its private sector has led to long working hours and work intensification for many employees, including managers and professionals, in a broad range of industries (Xiao & Cooke, 2012). Additionally, with its socialist ideology which emphasises gender equality both at work and home, China has one of the highest percentages of female employees in the Asia Pacific region (61.5% in the Year 2017) (The World Bank, 2018). Uniquely, China's one-party political system has imposed tremendous influence on Chinese society, which has led to some unique Chinese characteristics across workplaces in China. For example, China's Communist Party has established a party branch each in most state-owned and private organisations in China. Also, China is a large country geographically, and each area has its unique features due to different combinations of Westernisation, market liberalisation, and central control (Xiao & Cooke, 2012). Given its economic forces, a high work participation rate of women, a unique political system, and geographical variations, employees in different areas tend to have different values, attitudes, and behaviours related to their work and life. Hence, it is necessary to contextualise work–life theories to a Chinese context. Before discussing work–life issues in China in detail, we first provide an overview of Confucian values which have underpinned the Chinese society.

Confucian Values

National contexts (e.g. institutions and economy), policies and cultures have been shown to influence individuals' work–life conflict experiences (Allen, French, Dumani, & Shockley, 2015; Xiao & Cooke, 2012). In China, individuals' work–life conflict experiences are influenced by the traditional Chinese culture, characterised by Confucianism, to a large extent (Choi, 2008; Hofstede, 2001, 2010; Ren & Caudle, 2016). Although work–life scholars had suggested that work–life theories are "culture-sensitive", and urged more researchers to investigate the influence of culture on work–life phenomena a decade ago (Powell et al., 2009), current work–life theories still need to be further strengthened from a culture perspective (Powell et al., 2019). Researchers (e.g. Haar, Russo, Suñe, & Ollier-Malaterre, 2014; Ollier-Malaterre, 2014) have broadly applied macro-level cultural perspectives, such as national cultures and cultural values, to work–life conflict research. Those research studies have paved the way to envision a general picture that differences of work–life experiences occur in different national cultures. However, a micro-level cultural perspective about a specific culture may be more helpful and beneficial, if we want to unveil the nuanced work–life experiences in a given culture, which would provide rich information for implementing specific interventions and coping strategies (Hammer, Kossek, Anger, Bodner, & Zimmerman, 2011). Therefore, it is crucial to explore the subtle and specific values of the Chinese culture.

Although Westernisation and modernisation have imposed considerable influence on China's contemporary culture, Confucian values are still the foundation of it (Warner, 2010). The core of Confucianism has been elaborated along with seven values by Redding (2002): **Societal order**: preservation of established order, maintenance of harmony; **Hierarchy**: legitimacy of paternalism in the domains of family and organisation; the individual occupying the higher position should have the power to make decisions; **Reciprocity**: emphasis on the limited but adequate trust to ensure social exchange; individuals with close relationships are expected to exchange favours beyond their job scopes; **Control**: allocation of resources at superiors' discretion; **Insecurity**: need to insure against downturns and build reserves; **Family-based collectivism**: care for extended family, the importance of filial piety and family prestige; and **Knowledge**: value learning, intelligence, education, and resourcefulness highly. All these values have permeated every corner of China's society and are shaping individuals' work and family ideologies, and, by extension, the work–life experiences of Chinese employees.

Individual-, Organisational-, and Societal-Level Factors

By reviewing previous work–life research in the context of culture, Powell et al. (2009) suggested a culture-sensitive theory of work–life phenomena and articulated that "values related to the cultural meaning and enactment of work and family may influence the nature and strength of the relationship between individuals' experiences in these two domains" (p. 598). That is, particular cultural values, on the one hand, may generate some unique factors influencing work–life conflict; on the other hand, may moderate the relationships between some universal factors and work–life conflict (Aycan, 2008; Eby, Caspar, Lockwood, Bordeaux, & Brinley, 2005; Powell et al., 2009). Drawing on the growing number of research studies conducted in the context of Confucianism, the objectives of this chapter are to identify unique factors existing in the Confucian culture, and to explore how Confucian values influence the relationship between universal factors and work–life conflict. We categorised those factors into three levels: individual, organisational, and societal. It should also be noted that this chapter does not aim to comprehensively introduce all factors influencing work–life conflict in China, but rather to illustrate the most salient factors, which we hope can shed light on future work–life conflict research on Chinese employees who are immersed in Confucianism. The factors we will be discussing are listed in Table 9.1.

Table 9.1 Factors influencing work–life conflict in China

	Factors
Individual level	• **Work-related factors**: workload and working hours; job insecurity; *yingchou* (after-work hours business entertainment); work prioritisation • **Family-related factors**: family demands (high family expectations, and the paradox of elder parents' support); harmonious family environment • **Social network-related factors**: leader-member exchange (LMX) and *guanxi* • **Personality-related factors**: neuroticism; internal locus of control; workaholism; face consciousness
Organisational level	• Family-friendly policies, practices, and culture • Supervisory support under paternalistic leadership • Communist Party of China unit
Societal level	• Constant work connectivity • Ramifications of the one-child-per-family policy • Gender role expectations • The policy of Protection of the Rights and Interests of Older Workers

Individual-Level Factors

Individual-level factors refer to employees' attributes, including attitudes, behaviours, demands, and beliefs, which can influence work–life conflict. Historically, work–life research has been primarily guided by role theory (Powell et al., 2019), aiming to investigate how individuals' behaviours led by their understanding of the roles of work and life can cause the interference between work and life domains. Therefore, it is not surprising that many previous work–life research studies have focused on individual-level factors of work–life conflict. In the following section, we categorise individual-level factors into four themes: work-related factors, family-related factors, social network-related factors, and personality-related factors and elaborate on a few salient variables under each theme based on a cultural perspective.

Work-Related Factors

Workload and Working Hours

Numerous studies have found that workload and work hours are associated with greater work–life conflict (e.g. Hill, Erickson, Holmes, & Ferris, 2010; Skinner & Pocock, 2008). For example, based on data collected in a national Australian study, Skinner and Pocock (2008) found that work overload was the strongest predictor of full-time employees' work–life conflict, and work hours demonstrated small to moderate associations with work–life conflict. Further, Ilies, Schwind, Wagner, Johnson, DeRue, and Ilgen (2007) found that employees' perceptions of workload predicted work-to-life conflict over time, even after controlling for the number of hours spent at work. More recently, China's technology (or "tech") industry has endorsed the "996" culture, which refers to Chinese tech employees' punishing work schedule of 9 a.m. to 9 p.m., six days a week, often with no extra pay (Gao, 2019). The rise of China's "996" culture mirrors the United States' Silicon Valley's "hustle" culture. As a result of the long intense work hours, many Chinese tech employees suffer from mental (e.g. stress) and physical health problems (e.g. poor sleep quality, fatigue, and spine and neck disorders) (Wang, 2019). They also barely have time for their families and personal life (Wang, 2019), sacrificing most of their non-work time for work. The combination of high workload and long working hours is not only for the pursuit of higher salaries, but it is also the result of the cultural value of insecurity. The insecurity aspect generally leads many Chinese to take on a long-term orientation and "prepare for rainy days" (*wei yu chou mou*) (Yao, Arrowsmith, & Thorn, 2016). Generally, Chinese employees value working hard because it is a reliable way to improve their quality of life, and prepares them for any uncertainties (e.g. financial hardship in a downturn) in the future (Hofstede, 2010).

Also, there is a greater emphasis on preserving harmony across all life domains among Chinese employees, as maintaining balance is regarded as one of the highest virtues by Confucius (Burke, Astakhova, & Hang, 2015). Therefore, Chinese employees generally seek harmonious passion, which is the autonomous internalisation of activity into one's identity (Vallerand & Houlfort, 2003). For the same reason, they are more likely to view their work and life domains as integrated than segmented and accommodate long working hours and intense job demands (Chen, Zhang, Sanders, & Xu, 2018; Yang & Poelmans, 2005). Chinese employees also perceive a greater need for integrating work and family roles because work is viewed as a key instrument to provide the family with financial support (Chen et al., 2018). However, as with millennial (1981–1996) and generation z (1997–present) employees in most developed economies, younger Chinese employees are becoming less tolerant of bad working conditions and long working hours (Wright, 2018) and more aware of the negative work-to-life spillover and personal consequences resulting from the intense workload and long working hours (Burke et al., 2015).

Job Insecurity

Job insecurity, or concern over losing one's job, has gained increased importance due to globalisation and its associated changes, such as major organisational restructuring and downsizing, as well as workplace automation enabled by technologies (Richter, Näswall, & Sverke, 2010). It is a strain-based demand that threatens the economic well-being necessary for the stability and quality of family life (Voydanoff, 2004). In fact, a number of scholars (e.g. Batt & Valcour, 2003; Richter et al., 2010; Westman, Etzion, & Danon, 2001) have found that high levels of job insecurity are associated with high levels of work–life conflict. As with many other developed economies, the concept of an "iron rice bowl" (i.e. an occupation with guaranteed job security, as well as steady income and benefits) in China has eroded since the late 1990s. Chinese employees are also no longer guaranteed lifetime employment, as advanced technologies, economic downturns, and global competition have led organisations to lay off employees to reduce costs and inefficiencies, and have collectively contributed to high levels of anxiety, distress, and fear of losing jobs among employees who remain in these organisations (Lam, Liang, Ashford, & Lee, 2015). As we have discussed earlier, insecurity is one aspect of the Chinese culture and it causes Chinese employees to constantly worry about uncertainties in the future (Hofstede, 2010). Therefore, it is anticipated that Chinese employees would be more sensitive to job insecurity, and the cultural aspect of insecurity is likely to intensify the positive relationship between job insecurity and work–life conflict.

Yingchou

Yingchou, which refers to after-work hours business entertainment involving activities such as banqueting, binge drinking, and Karaoke singing (Bedford, 2016), is a uniquely Chinese phenomenon. *Yingchou* is an integral component of working life in China, as it can facilitate business transactions through entertaining current and potential clients and promote individual career advancement through socialising with colleagues and supervisors after work (Bedford, 2016). It has been regarded as the most salient and common work-related stressor for Chinese employees across industries and occupations (Chang, Chen, & Chi, 2014). Within a culture emphasising social order and hierarchy, it is an implicit norm that Chinese employers or managers have the prerogative to summon their employees to attend to business matters after legal working hours, such as in the evening or over the weekend (Xiao & Cooke, 2012), and employees normally feel obliged to abide by such requirements. Therefore, individuals are connected to their work 24/7, and their actual number of working hours could be much more than the legal working hours (approximately 40 h per week). Accordingly, some research have empirically demonstrated that *yingchou* can severely intensify work–life conflict among Chinese employees as it significantly extends working hours (Chang et al., 2014).

Work Prioritisation

Prioritisation refers to individuals' preference for how they prioritise their life roles. In the last four decades, China's enormous economic achievement has encouraged a popular goal among many Chinese—to "get rich first, enjoy life later"—reflecting the value paid to work more than family and personal time in their lives (Hofstede, 2010; Xiao & Cooke, 2012). In one study, Shenkar and Ronen (1987) found that mainland Chinese managers rated lower importance on family and personal time than on paid work, similar to their counterparts in Hong Kong, Taiwan, and Singapore. Work prioritisation in China is also derived from the Confucian value of insecurity, as Chinese employees need to build up and accumulate resources for their future and are willing to constrain their short-term material or emotional gratification (Hofstede, 2010; Redding, 2002). Therefore, Chinese employees are more likely and willing to sacrifice non-work activities and personal time to progress at work.

Family-Related Factors

Family Demands

Stressors from the family are also a primary contributor to work–life conflict (Zhang & Liu, 2011). Spouse/partner's work, stress and work hours generally increase the difficulty of balancing work and non-work, leading to work–life conflict (Jacobs & Gerson, 2004; Westman & Etzion, 2005). Family demands, which refer to the time spent, level of commitment to, and responsibilities associated with fulfilling family-related obligations such as the tasks of housekeeping and childcare, are also another contributor to work–life conflict (Choi, 2008). In particular, dependent care (such as caring for children and elderly parents or other dependents) generates burden on the focal employee, increasing tensions between their work and non-work roles (Greenhaus & Beutell, 1985; Michel, Kotrba, Mitchelson, Clark, & Baltes, 2011), and leads them to experience work–life conflict (Dugan et al., 2016). Among various family demands, we will focus on two unique factors: high family expectations from children, and the paradox of elderly parents' support.

High Family Expectations from Children

Given the cultural value of knowledge, Chinese parents are extremely obsessed to give their offspring the best education to help them succeed in life, which can be represented by a prevalent idiom, hoping one's son/daughter to become a dragon/phoenix (in Chinese: *Wang Zi Cheng Long* or *Wang Nv Cheng Feng*). In other words, all Chinese parents want their children to achieve great success. Chinese parents' high expectations of their children have been heightened by the three-decade-long one-child-per-family policy, as parents pin high hopes on their only child, and channel their attention and emotional and instrumental support on their child's education (NPR, 2008). Therefore, "tiger parenting", which refers to the act of parents consistently pushing their child to achieve higher, has become a popular way to educate children in China (Shang, O'Driscoll, & Roche, 2018). However, being a tiger parent comes at a great cost. Parents need to spend more of their time studying the content their child is learning at school and take it upon themselves to guide and supervise their child's study daily (NPR, 2008). As such, having high educational expectations of their children is likely to lead to high levels of work–life conflict, especially for Chinese employees with children as they have to dedicate a large portion of their time to their children's study which may have negative spillover effects on their work and other life domains.

Paradox of Elderly Parents' Support

In China where people are influenced by the value of family-based collectivism, most tend to emphasise the integral benefit of their extended family (Hofstede, 2010). As such, parental support is more prevalent in China compared to Western societies (Strom, Strom, & Xie, 1996). Elderly parents in China are also willing to provide any necessary support to their adult children, and therefore adult children can access excessive support from their elderly parents, for instance, doing household chores and looking after grandchildren. Research has shown that support from family can attenuate the conflict between work and life (e.g. Dewe et al.,

2010). As opposed to their Western counterparts, Chinese employees are expected to be filial to their parents, which may be considered an additional role and responsibility of caring for their ageing parents. That is, they have to provide considerable instrumental and psychological support for their elderly parents (Ling & Powell, 2001), which may be regarded as a significant stressor contributing to their work–life conflict. Such detrimental effects can be intensified by the one-child-per-family policy (see details in the section of ramifications of the one-child-per-family policy). Therefore, adult children in China would very often face the paradox of receiving parental support, as they are also expected to care for their elderly parents alongside their full-time employment and caring for their spouse and children. When employees want to access parental support, they need to take into account the negative effects of parental demands on family-to-work conflict and weigh up the advantages and disadvantages between parental support and parental demands (Shang, O'Driscoll, & Roche, 2017).

Harmonious Family Environment

The Confucian value of order also requires the Chinese to devote themselves to maintain harmonious interpersonal relationships in their life domains. Previous cross-cultural research has consistently suggested that Chinese place greater importance on interpersonal harmony than their Western counterparts (e.g. Ling & Powell, 2001; Shang et al., 2017). In the family domain, members are interdependent and obligated to express concern for each other's instrumental and emotional demands to maintain a harmonious family environment (Ling & Powell, 2001). In particular, many Chinese prefer an extended family, and two or more generations to live together, which sometimes make maintenance of family harmony even harder, as worldview and personal values can be fairly disparate between generations. Failing to do so, family members are more likely to feel embarrassed, frustrated, or ashamed, and it is not easy for both sides to be freed from it (Ling & Powell, 2001). To remedy or restore the relationship, members will need to expend considerable energy and time, which are likely to spill over negatively to their work domain and social networks, increasing work–life conflict. Hence, the particularly strong emphasis on the maintenance of harmony could intensify the negative family-to-life conflict experience of Chinese employees.

Social Network-Related Factors

Leader-Member Exchange (LMX) and Guanxi

LMX refers to a relationship-based approach to leadership that focuses on the two-way or dyadic relationship between leaders and employees. A few studies have examined LMX in a work–life context and they have generally demonstrated that high LMX is associated with lower work-to-life conflict as it reduces employees' work pressure (Major, Fletcher, Davis, & Germano, 2008; Tummers & Bronkhorst, 2014). For example, in a high-quality LMX, subordinates may take on extra job tasks to assist their leaders, and in turn, their leaders may provide more resources and opportunities to support them, which reduces work–life conflict (Hsu, Chen, Wang, & Lin, 2010; Major & Morganson, 2011). On the contrary, a low-quality LMX is likely to result in leaders being less supportive, or in some cases, engage in leader incivility with their subordinates, leading to work–life conflict (Thompson, Buch, & Glasø, 2018). In China, the concept of *guanxi* is strongly associated with LMX (Hsu et al., 2010), and is highly related to the value of reciprocity. *Guanxi* between leaders and subordinates refers to a type of abstract, implicit understanding, commitment or obligation in interpersonal connections or relationships (Tsang, 1998). LMX in Western settings tends to focus only on the exchange of job-related resources (Graen & Uhl-Bien, 1995), while *guanxi* in China may involve the exchange of non-job resources, such as information about the well-being of families, giving colleagues souvenirs after returning from a vacation, and providing assistance with non-work-related tasks (Law, Wong, Wang, & Wang, 2000). Nevertheless, the principles are the same. Employees with high-quality *guanxi* with their leaders generally receive more recognition, interpersonal assistance, and emotional support, which helps to relieve their work-related stress and reduces the likelihood of work–life conflict (Wu, Yuan, Yen, & Xu, 2019). Conversely, employees who have low-quality *guanxi* with their leaders will face added work pressure as they are more likely to receive fewer resources, support, and recognition from their leaders (Wu et al., 2019).

Personality-Related Factors

Personality refers to the characteristic sets of behaviours, cognitions, and emotional patterns that evolve from biological and environmental factors (Corr & Matthews, 2009). General cognitive, affective, and behavioural propensities, such as internal locus of control and neuroticism, may influence employees' perceptions of their work–life conflict. Accordingly, individuals high in an internal locus of control generally feel greater control over their work and non-work responsibilities, while individuals high in neuroticism tend to feel high levels of psychological distress, anxiety, and dissatisfaction in any work–life conflict situations (Michel et al., 2011).

Neuroticism

Neuroticism is typically characterised by high levels of trait-based psychological distress, anxiety, and dissatisfaction (Watson, Clark, & Tellegen, 1988). Negative affect is also considered a component of neuroticism (Judge & Ilies, 2002), and both negative affect and neuroticism have been examined as antecedents of work–life conflict because they influence how individuals perceive both their work and life situations (Bouchard & Poirier, 2011; Rantanen, Pulkkinen, & Kinnunen, 2005). Neurotic individuals are more likely to experience negative affect in response to challenges and view themselves and their surrounding environment negatively (Rantanen et al., 2005). In particular, Bouchard and Poirier (2011) found that men high in neuroticism were more likely than women to feel that the role pressures from work and family were mutually incompatible leading them to experience work–family conflict.

A handful of studies on neuroticism and work–life conflict conducted in China (e.g. Cao, Yuan, Fine, Zhou, & Fang, 2019) also found that neuroticism is related to negative behaviours such as aggression, which subsequently have negative flow-on effects on other non-work domains (e.g. conflict with a spouse).

With the emphasis on societal order, Chinese individuals are expected to endure the unpleasant nature of interpersonal conflict to maintain a harmonious environment. With the emphasis of hierarchy, Chinese employees are sometimes expected to endure abusive supervision. With the value of reciprocity, Chinese are expected to engage in an excess of social exchange to maintain *guanxi*. Therefore, endurance (*ren*) is a praised virtue in Chinese culture (Xing, 1995). We expect that endurance may play a role in either escalating or mitigating the negative effects of neuroticism and negative affect on work–life conflict, depending on how the employee deals with the impacts of enduring.

Internal Locus of Control

Internal locus of control refers to the extent to which an individual feels outcomes are caused by the individual or self, as opposed to external variables such as chance (Rotter, 1966). A handful of studies (e.g. Andreassi & Thompson, 2007; Hsu, 2011) have been conducted on the relationship between locus of control and work–life conflict. For example, Andreassi and Thompson (2007) demonstrated that internal locus of control was negatively related to work–life conflict, while Hsu (2011) found that internal locus of control assisted Taiwanese correctional officers to gain greater control over their task requirements and moderate the negative effect of work–life conflict on job satisfaction. This is because employees with a high internal locus of control are more likely to be satisfied with their work and identify ways to overcome work and non-work demands, as compared to those with a low internal locus of control, leading to lower levels of work–life conflict (Hsu, 2011). From a cultural perspective, Chinese values such as social order, hierarchy, and reciprocity provide structural expectations of emphasising the interdependence of individuals within a larger group such as the family.

Guided by such values, Chinese are likely to attribute the success to people related to them, which is contrary to their Western counterparts who tend to attribute success to their efforts or competencies because of their emphasis on self-reliance (Hofstede, 2010; Hsu, 1981). Therefore, Chinese employees are expected to have lower levels of internal locus of control compared to their Western counterparts. Based on the above, we propose that Chinese values of social order, hierarchy, and reciprocity can indirectly influence work–life conflict through the internal locus of control.

Workaholism

Workaholism refers to an addiction to work where individuals work longer and harder than their job duties necessitate, often to the neglect of other non-work roles (e.g. family and friends), and they persistently and frequently think about work when they are not working (Scott, Moore, & Miceli, 1997). Ample evidence has shown that workaholism is related to negative non-work outcomes, such as lower family satisfaction (Shimazu & Schaufeli, 2009), greater marital dissatisfaction with one's spouse, as well as greater work–life conflict (Bakker, Demerouti, & Burke, 2009). Clark, Michel, Stevens, Howell, and Scruggs (2014) also found that workaholism exhibited a positive relationship with both work-to-family and family-to-work conflict. Clark et al. (2014) further explained that workaholics typically strive to reach some unattainable level of performance and, consequently, experience a high level of anxiety and disappointment. Specifically, they found that workaholism had a positive indirect effect on work-to-family conflict through work anxiety and disappointment, as well as a positive indirect effect on FWC through home anger and disappointment. In a comparative study by Hu et al. (2014), employees in China had the highest level of workaholism across countries such as Japan, the Netherlands, Spain, and Finland, and the authors attributed this to the Confucian values of hard work and valuing work as a familial responsibility.

Face Consciousness

Face consciousness refers to the extent to which individuals believe they can increase their social status by exhibiting flaunting behaviours (Zhang, Cao, & Grigoriou, 2011). Although concerns with status is a fundamental human concern, in the highly interdependent and hierarchical culture of China, such concerns are even more salient, as it can result in experiencing status anxiety, as people would worry about where they rank in society (De Botton, 2005; Tse, 1996). Immersed in a culture that emphasises face consciousness, many Chinese consume brand products not merely for material possessions but for social needs, such as a desire to have favourable social self-worth and to be respected about others and social activities (Liao & Wang, 2009). Such face consciousness-related behaviours can lead to increased stress for Chinese employees, both mentally and financially, as they often feel the need to "keep up with the Joneses". Considerable research has since demonstrated that mental stress consistently creates tension between work and non-work domains, as it is destructive to performance in all life domains (Dewe et al., 2010). Additionally, financial stress will push individuals to work even harder to earn monetary resources, which is certainly not constructive for obtaining work–life balance.

Organisational-Level Factors

Organisational-level factors refer to institutional conditions, including organisational structure, policies, culture, and supervision system, which can directly mould employees' work behaviours. Those working behaviours can be uplifting, enabling employees to approach the interface between their work and non-work domains positively. On the contrary, some working behaviours can be noxious for employees to achieve work–life balance. In the following section, we elaborate on the relationships of family-friendly policies and practices, culture, supervisor support, and the Communist Party of China Unit with work–life conflict.

Family-Friendly Policies, Practice, and Culture

Organisations can help employees cope with work–life conflict through a variety of mechanisms, including formal family-friendly policies and practices and informal family-friendly culture. Family-friendly policies and practices often aim to provide employees with increased flexibility, autonomy, and legal protections (Chou & Cheung, 2013). The range of policies typically adopted by organisations include paid sick leave and carers' leave, flexible work arrangements, and opportunities for telecommuting (Su, Li, & Curry, 2017; Wadsworth & Facer, 2016). However, it is unclear whether these family-friendly policies and practices are as accessible to employees in Asian countries as in western countries, especially since researchers have argued that their availability depends on both a government's approach to welfare and cultural values (Chou & Cheung, 2013; Gornick & Heron, 2006). Alongside formal policies and practices, organisations may foster a culture that supports the family, enabling employees to reduce work–life conflict (Beauregard, 2011; Chang, Chin, & Ye, 2014; Fiksenbaum, 2014).

As discussed earlier, influenced by the Chinese culture, working hard and prioritising work are ubiquitous norms among Chinese. Many managers work intelligently around family-friendly policies, while still abiding by the law. The most prominent example is the "996" culture. Although the "996" culture deviates from existing family-friendly policies and even violates the Labour Law in China, it is still the default working mode among many employees in the technology sector in China. Multiple studies have demonstrated that even when formal family-friendly policies are implemented, such policies tend to be underutilised (Feeney, Bernal, & Bowman, 2014) because there have been many accounts of a "*backlash*" effect when employees made use of the family-friendly practices but ended up working more after office hours (Field & Chan, 2018), leading to work-to-life conflict, or showed decreased work engagement and performance (Timms et al., 2015). Cech and Blair-Loy (2014) also observed that while organisations may attempt to help employees cope with work–life conflict, the focal employee's colleagues and supervisors may regard the need and use of flexible work arrangements as a sign of reduced commitment to the organisation, leading to a phenomenon known as the "*flexibility stigma*". Hence, formal family-friendly policies and practices have to be implemented with a supportive organisational culture for them to be effective in reducing employees' work–life conflict.

Supervisory Support Under Paternalistic Leadership

In most workplaces, supervisors are the most crucial link between management and employees as they deal with subordinates daily, at the same time representing them to upper management (Major & Morganson, 2011). Research has consistently suggested that supervisory support is an effective means to reduce employees' work–life conflict, as employees can access instrumental aid, emotional concern, informational, and/or appraisal functions from their immediate supervisor, which will, in turn, lead to a reduction of the time, attention, and energy required for work performance, thereby alleviating work–life conflict (Michel et al., 2011).

It should be noted that whether employees receive supervisory support and the type of support they obtain depends on their supervisor's leadership style. Therefore, in Chinese culture, it is necessary to discuss supervisory support under paternalistic leadership which is a widespread people management approach in Chinese organisations (Chen, Eberly, Chiang, Farh, & Cheng, 2014). Chinese paternalistic leadership is developed from a combination of the values of hierarchy and reciprocity (Chen et al., 2014), and is defined as "a style that combines strong discipline and authority with fatherly benevolence and moral integrity couched in a personalistic atmosphere" (Farh & Cheng, 2000, p. 91). Research shows that paternalistic leaders are usually aware of their subordinates' family lives and provide care and support for them when necessary, and in turn, these leaders expect to earn respect from their subordinates (Chen et al., 2014). Therefore, we propose that Chinese paternalistic leadership may enhance the positive aspects of supervisory support and reduce employees' work–life conflict.

Communist Party of China (CPC) Unit

The CPC unit is a unique Chinese feature present in organisations to maintain control in Chinese society. A CPC unit is set up in nearly every Chinese organisation, including governmental organisations, public institutions, state-owned enterprises, private enterprises, and even foreign enterprises. The purpose of the CPC unit is to convey the intentions and policies of the CPC to its party members and build close relationships among the CPC, party members, and non-partisan employees. All employees, especially party members, are expected to dedicate a portion of their time to learn and reflect on the CPC's recent policies, guidelines, activities, and events. As these are typically considered non-work-related activities and can be time- and energy-consuming, they are likely to aggravate work–life conflict.

Societal-Level Factors

Societal-level factors refer to the systems that enact rules or phenomena that produce norms, which are used to organise and constrain human interactions in their life domains. For example, labour laws as a system directly influence employees' rights and welfare, such as their working hours and leave entitlement, which are highly relevant to work–life conflict. Technological advancement as a social phenomenon has enhanced the possibility of working at home or on holiday, which has further weakened the boundaries between work and non-work domains (Field & Chan, 2018). In the following section, we explore four pertinent social trends that are affecting Chinese employees' work–life conflict experiences.

Constant Work Connectivity

Proliferating information and communication technologies (ICTs), often mobile, are connecting people, but also intensifying work beyond traditional offices and working hours (Ciolfi & Lockley, 2018). The boundaries of time and space that traditionally provided a clear distinction between work and non-work are vanishing (Field & Chan, 2018). Without clear boundaries, employees now remain connected to the workplace from any location, at any time. Therefore, "anytime, anyplace connectivity" has become "all the time, everywhere" connectivity (Richardson & Benbunan-Fich, 2011). Continuous or 24/7 connectivity makes employees feel as if they need to be constantly connected and constantly available (Field & Chan, 2018). In Field and Chan's (2018) study, it was revealed that constant availability for work has become a proxy for organisational commitment. Virtual displays of employee engagement through 24/7 work connectivity have also become the norm. Some employees in Field and Chan's (2018) study sample also worked during the holidays to avoid out-of-control work situations, leading to short-term work-to-life conflict, but potentially reducing their medium-to-long-term work–life conflict. In China, work is viewed as a family responsibility, thus working after hours can be viewed as a virtue and self-sacrifice made for the benefit of the family (Xie, Ma, Zhou, & Tang, 2018). Coupled with the pervasive use of mobile phones in both urban and rural parts of China, Chinese employees are more likely than employees in Western countries to send and receive work-related calls and text messages after office hours. Consequently, constant work connectivity and ICT use are likely to intensify job demands for Chinese employees and increase work–life conflict drastically.

Ramifications of One-Child-Per-Family Policy

The one-child-per-family policy was implemented nationwide in China in 1980 to limit most Chinese families to one child each to decrease the rapid growth of the country's population. The policy has significantly reduced the average family size and hence family demands related to childcare and household chores (Yang et al., 2000), which was beneficial for earlier generations of Chinese employees. However, the ramifications of such a policy for younger generations of Chinese employees are highly detrimental, as they are heavily burdened by not only their parents but also their parents-in-law, and they do not have siblings to share such family demands (Choi, 2008). These family demands typically lead to role overload and work–life conflict for Chinese employees. Further, as the elderly retirement and pension schemes are still not widely available to most Chinese retirees, elderly parents tend to rely heavily on their working adult children for support. Their adult children may also be publicly shamed if they do not take care of their parents as this violates the cultural values of family-based collectivism which emphasises filial piety (Hofstede, 2010).

Protection of the Rights and Interests of Elderly People

In 2013, China passed a law entitled "*Protection of the Rights and Interests of Elderly People*" to legally mandate that children should visit their parents in person and check in on them regularly. Also, companies are obliged to provide employees time off from work to look after the needs of their elderly parents. The fact that such a law was passed indicates that Chinese society values family-based collectivism to a large extent (Powell et al., 2017). This law elevates the duty of looking after elderly parents from an affectionate level to a legal level, which will likely increase some employees' family pressure, especially rural migrants who move to urban cities to work and are thus separated from their elderly parents.

Gender Role Expectations

In China, since Mao Zedong declared that "women hold up half the sky", female employment has increased drastically (Riley, 1996). However, the influx of female employees in the workplace has not reduced female workers' household responsibilities (Choi, 2008). Female employees continue to spend a large amount of their time at work and are also expected to perform domestic chores and childcare at home (Cooke 2007; Zuo & Bian, 2004). This can be attributed to the deeply held cultural convictions in China which view the family as a woman's domain and paid employment as a male domain (Foster & Ren, 2015). Therefore, Chinese employees—in particular, female employees—typically experience high levels of work and non-work demands, and by extension, work–life conflict (Xiao & Cooke, 2012). Further, the Chinese culture also scores high on masculinity which has led to a preference for achievement, assertiveness, and material rewards for success (Hofstede, 2001), reinforcing the notion of hierarchy (i.e. wives should obey their husbands). As a result of such cultural characteristics, the Chinese society thus holds the belief that men should be primarily responsible for their family's finances, whereas women are mainly responsible for matters about the family domain, such as housework and taking care of family members (Chen et al., 2018). Also, women in China are frequently frowned upon if their careers are more advanced than their husbands'. Even though more Chinese couples are now dual earners and career couples (Chen et al., 2018; Cooke 2007; Zuo & Bian, 2001), the conventional norm that the husband deals with external matters and the wife look after domestic chores remains highly pervasive in modern China, and that has led many female employees to experience role conflict.

Recommendations and Future Research Directions

Based on the individual-, organisational-, and societal-level factors we explored above, we carve out a future research agenda highlighting future areas of research on the issue of work–life conflict in the Chinese culture. First, future work–life research in China should further explore the role of specific Chinese cultural constructs about Chinese employees' work–life conflict. Identifying specific cultural constructs beyond Hofstede and GLOBE cultural dimensions is important for both work–family theory development and theory testing (Yang et al., 2000). Hofstede and GLOBE cultural dimensions are undeniably helpful for researchers to understand the role of culture in work–life conflict, especially on a national level. However, those universal approaches may limit our capability to understand specific aspects of the Chinese culture (e.g.

reciprocity is hardly discussed in the two cultural approaches), and to recognise the uniqueness of Chinese culture (e.g. it is hard to distinguish the nuanced differences between two cultures with similar scores on the metrics). Therefore, applying a specific Chinese cultural construct, like Reeding (2002), to work–life research in China may reveal more insights. On the one hand, it can help researchers to identify some unique factors influencing work–life conflict among Chinese, which has not been discussed under other cultural contexts. On the other hand, it can also assist scholars to obtain an in-depth understanding of the causes of work–life conflict. For example, some studies (e.g. Lu et al., 2010; Ollo-López & Goñi-Legaz, 2017) found a significant positive relationship between power distance and work–life conflict but did not probe further. By using specific Chinese cultural constructs, we would understand that the Confucian values of hierarchy and social orders jointly contribute to the perception of power distance. Once we understand the Chinese conceptualisation of power distance, it is a lot more helpful for us to comprehend this relationship and offer coping strategies to mitigate work–life conflict.

Second, work–life researchers should contextualise workplace policies and practices to work–life research in China. Chen et al. (2018) found that two types of flexible work arrangements—namely, flexible working time and compressed workweeks—were key drivers of positive work-to-family spillover for employees in China. In particular, their study showed that both types of flexible work arrangements led to increased job satisfaction and decreased turnover intention. Chen et al. (2018) also anticipate that more organisations in China will implement flexible work arrangements going forward, given that an increase in workplace flexibility (especially time flexibility) helped employees to reduce their perceived job stress and strain. Given that Chinese employees are influenced by a collectivistic culture, they are also more likely to integrate their work and family roles than separate them (Ashforth, Kreiner, & Fugate, 2000). However, research on work–life conflict and workplace policies and practices among Chinese employees remains scant (Foster & Ren, 2015). In general, the number of work-life studies conducted in a Chinese context is also much lower than the number of studies conducted in a Western context (Chen et al., 2018; Foster & Ren, 2015).

Work–life studies conducted in the West often assume that work–life conflict is gender-neutral and can be alleviated through policies that enhance flexibility and individual choice (Lewis, Gambles, & Rapoport, 2007), but in collectivist cultures such as China, the relationship is not as straightforward. Correspondingly, we recommend that future studies contextualise and explore more workplace policies and practices that may alleviate work–life conflict for Chinese employees, taking into consideration the traditional patriarchal Confucian values and gender role expectations prevalent in modern Chinese workplaces.

Third, future research should also consider societal-level factors in their theoretical models and discussions. The contextualisation of work–life research is hindered by the complexity of identifying country-level variables (Ollier-Malaterre & Foucreault, 2017). As suggested in the call for papers as well as in some other articles (e.g. Bear, Bear 2019; Crawford et al., 2019), more work–life theories are needed from a societal or national culture perspective. A societal cultural perspective is suggested by Leslie, King, and Clair (2019) who found that travel and immigration policies and social welfare systems shape work–life ideologies. Further, Bear (2019) also examined social policies that support caregiving as a moderator in her theoretical model, proposing that they influenced people's work–life experiences. Also, several articles (e.g. Allen et al., 2015; Ollo-López & Goñi-Legaz, 2017) have incorporated the influence of societal culture in their models by including gender roles and gender role socialisation and examining how they shape people's work–life experiences. However, dimensions of national culture that may influence linkages among work–life phenomena have seldom been explicitly incorporated into work–life theories to make them "culture-sensitive" (Powell et al., 2009). We thus recommend additional theory that examines the role of societal similarities and differences in the meaning of work and other life domains to explain how dimensions of national culture affect employees' work–life experiences.

Conclusion

For decades, work–life scholars have been constantly calling for the contextualisation of extant work–life theories to different cultures since such theories generally assume that work–life phenomena are similar across cultures and thus are not "culture-sensitive". In response to the call, this chapter holistically investigates the individual-, organisational-, and societal-level factors that may influence employees' work–life conflict in China from a Confucian cultural perspective. Simply put, we portrayed the potential impacts of the specific Confucian values on the individual-, organisational-, and societal-level factors, and provided recommendations for future areas of research that can help to contextualise work–life conflict research to the specific Chinese cultural context.

References

Allen, T. D., French, K. A., Dumani, S., & Shockley, K. M. (2015). Meta-analysis of work–family conflict mean differences: Does national context matter? *Journal of Vocational Behavior, 90,* 90–100.

Amstad, F. T., Meier, L. L., Fasel, U., Elfering, A., & Semmer, N. K. (2011). A meta-analysis of work–family conflict and various outcomes with a special emphasis on cross-domain versus matching-domain relations. *Journal of Occupational Health Psychology, 16*(2), 151–169.

Andreassi, J. K., & Thompson, C. A. (2007). Dispositional and situational sources of control. *Journal of Managerial Psychology, 22*(8), 722–740.

Ashforth, B. E., Kreiner, G. E., & Fugate, M. (2000). All in a day's work: Boundaries and micro role transitions. *Academy of Management Review, 25*(3), 472–491.

Aycan, Z. (2008). Cross-cultural approaches to work-family conflict. In K. Korabik, D. S. Lero, & D. L. Whitehead (Eds.), *Handbook of work-family integration* (pp. 353–370). Boston: Academic Press.

Bakker, A. B., Demerouti, E., & Burke, R. (2009). Workaholism and relationship quality: A spillover–crossover perspective. *Journal of Occupational Health Psychology, 14*(1), 23–33.

Batt, R., & Valcour, P. M. (2003). Human resources practices as predictors of work-family outcomes and employee turnover. *Industrial Relations: a Journal of Economy and Society, 42*(2), 189–220.

Bear, J. B. (2019). The caregiving ambition framework. *Academy of Management Review, 44*(1), 99–125.

Beauregard, T. A. (2011). Direct and indirect links between organizational work–home culture and employee well-being. *British Journal of Management, 22*(2), 218–237.

Bedford, O. (2016). Crossing boundaries: An exploration of business socializing (ying chou for guanxi) in a Chinese society. *Psychology of Women Quarterly, 40*(2), 290–306.

Bouchard, G., & Poirier, L. (2011). Neuroticism and well-being among employed new parents: The role of the work-family conflict. *Personality and Individual Differences, 50*(5), 657–661.

Burke, R. J., Astakhova, M. N., & Hang, H. (2015). Work passion through the lens of culture: Harmonious work passion, obsessive work passion, and work outcomes in Russia and China. *Journal of Business and Psychology, 30*(3), 457–471.

Cao, H., Yuan, X., Fine, M., Zhou, N., & Fang, X. (2019). Neuroticism and marital satisfaction during the early years of Chinese marriage: The mediating roles of marital attribution and aggression. *Family Process, 58*(2), 478–495.

Cech, E. A., & Blair-Loy, M. (2014). Consequences of flexibility stigma among academic scientists and engineers. *Work and Occupations, 41*(1), 86–110.

Chang, A., Chen, S. C., & Chi, S. C. S. (2014a). Role salience and support as moderators of demand/conflict relationships in China. *European Journal of Work and Organizational Psychology, 23*(6), 859–874.

Chang, E., Chin, H., & Ye, J. (2014b). Organizational work-family culture and working mothers' affective commitment: How career expectations matter. *Human Resource Management, 53*(5), 683–700.

Chen, X. P., Eberly, M. B., Chiang, T. J., Farh, J. L., & Cheng, B. S. (2014). Affective trust in Chinese leaders: Linking paternalistic leadership to employee performance. *Journal of Management, 40*(3), 796–819.

Chen, W., Zhang, Y., Sanders, K., & Xu, S. (2018). Family-friendly work practices and their outcomes in China: The mediating role of work-to-family enrichment and the moderating role of gender. *The International Journal of Human Resource Management, 29*(7), 1307–1329.

Choi, J. (2008). Work and family demands and life stress among Chinese employees: The mediating effect of work–family conflict. *The International Journal of Human Resource Management, 19*(5), 878–895.

Chou, K. L., & Cheung, K. C. K. (2013). Family-friendly policies in the workplace and their effect on work–life conflicts in Hong Kong. *The International Journal of Human Resource Management, 24*(20), 3872–3885.

Ciolfi, L., & Lockley, E. (2018). From Work to Life and back again: Examining the digitally-mediated work/life practices of a group of knowledge workers. *Computer Supported Cooperative Work (CSCW), 27*(3–6), 803–839.

Clark, M. A., Michel, J. S., Stevens, G. W., Howell, J. W., & Scruggs, R. S. (2014). Workaholism, work engagement and work–home outcomes: Exploring the mediating role of positive and negative emotions. *Stress and Health, 30*(4), 287–300.

Cooke, F. L. (2007). 'Husband's career first' renegotiating career and family commitment among migrant Chinese academic couples in Britain. *Work, Employment & Society, 21*(1), 47–65.

Corr, P. J., & Matthews, G. (Eds.). (2009). *The Cambridge handbook of personality psychology* (pp. 748–763). New York: Cambridge University Press.

Crawford, W. S., Thompson, M. J., & Ashforth, B. E. (2019). Work–life events theory: Making sense of shock events in dual-earner couples. *Academy of Management Review, 44*(1), 194–212.

De Botton, A. (2005). *Status anxiety*. New York: Vintage.

Dewe, P., O'Driscoll, M., & Cooper, C. (2010). *Coping with work stress: A review and critique*. Chichester: Wiley-Blackwell.

Dugan, A. G., Fortinsky, R. H., Barnes-Farrell, J. L., Kenny, A. M., Robison, J. T., Warren, N., et al. (2016). Associations of eldercare and competing demands with health and work outcomes among manufacturing workers. *Community, Work & Family, 19*(5), 569–587.

Eby, L. T., Casper, W. J., Lockwood, A., Bordeaux, C., & Brinley, A. (2005). Work and family research in IO/OB: Content analysis and review of the literature (1980–2002). *Journal of Vocational Behavior, 66*(1), 124–197.

Farh, J. L., & Cheng, B. S. (2000). A cultural analysis of paternalistic leadership in Chinese organizations. In J. T. Li, A. S. Tsui, & E. Weldon (Eds.), *Management and organizations in the Chinese context* (pp. 84–127). London, UK: Macmillan.

Feeney, M. K., Bernal, M., & Bowman, L. (2014). Enabling work? Family-friendly policies and academic productivity for men and women scientists. *Science and Public Policy, 41*(6), 750–764.

Field, J. C., & Chan, X. W. (2018). Contemporary knowledge workers and the boundaryless work-life interface: Implications for the human resource management of the knowledge workforce. *Frontiers in Psychology, 9,* 2414.

Fiksenbaum, L. M. (2014). Supportive work–family environments: Implications for work–family conflict and well-being. *The International Journal of Human Resource Management, 25*(5), 653–672.

Foster, D., & Ren, X. (2015). Work–family conflict and the commodification of women's employment in three Chinese airlines. *The International Journal of Human Resource Management, 26*(12), 1568–1585.

French, K. A., Dumani, S., Allen, T. D., & Shockley, K. M. (2018). A meta-analysis of work–family conflict and social support. *Psychological Bulletin, 144*(3), 284–314.

Gao, Y. (2019, May 12). In China Tech, '996' means work, work, and more work. *Bloomberg Businessweek.* Retrieved February 1, 2020, from https://www.bloomberg.com/news/articles/2019-05-11/in-china-tech-996-means-work-work-and-more-work-quicktake.

Goode, W. (1960). A theory of role strain. *American Sociological Review, 25*(4), 483–496.

Gornick, J. C., & Heron, A. (2006). The regulation of working time as work-family reconciliation policy: Comparing Europe, Japan, and the United States. *Journal of Comparative Policy Analysis, 8*(2), 149–166.

Graen, G. B., & Uhl-Bien, M. (1995). Relationship-based approach to leadership: Development of leader–Member exchange (LMX) theory of leadership over 25 years: Applying a multi-level multi-domain perspective. *Leadership Quarterly, 6*(2), 210–247.

Greenhaus, J., & Beutell, N. (1985). Sources of conflict between work and family roles. *Academy of Management Review, 10*(1), 76–88.

Haar, J. M., Russo, M., Suñe, A., & Ollier-Malaterre, A. (2014). Outcomes of work–life balance on job satisfaction, life satisfaction and mental health: A study across seven cultures. *Journal of Vocational Behavior, 85*(3), 361–373.

Hammer, L. B., Kossek, E. E., Anger, W. K., Bodner, T., & Zimmerman, K. L. (2011). Clarifying work–family intervention processes: The roles of work–family conflict and family-supportive supervisor behaviors. *Journal of Applied Psychology, 96*(1), 134–150.

Hill, E. J., Erickson, J. J., Holmes, E. K., & Ferris, M. (2010). Workplace flexibility, work hours, and work–life conflict: Finding an extra day or two. *Journal of Family Psychology, 24*(3), 349–358.

Hofstede, G. (2001). *Culture's consequences: Comparing values, behaviors, institutions and organizations across nations.* Thousand Oaks, CA: Sage.

Hofstede, G. (2010). The GLOBE debate: Back to relevance. *Journal of International Business Studies, 41*(8), 1339–1346.

Hsu, F. L. K. (1981). *Americans & Chinese: Passage to differences* (3rd ed.). Honolulu, HI: The University Press of Hawaii.

Hsu, Y. R. (2011). Work-family conflict and job satisfaction in stressful working environments. *International Journal of Manpower, 32*(2), 233–248.

Hsu, B. F., Chen, W. Y., Wang, M. L., & Lin, Y. Y. (2010). Explaining supervisory support to work-family conflict: The perspectives of guanxi, LMX, and emotional intelligence. *Journal of Technology Management in China, 5*(1), 40–54.

Hu, Q., Schaufeli, W., Taris, T., Hessen, D., Hakanen, J. J., Salanova, M., et al. (2014). East is east and west is west and never the twain shall meet: Work engagement and workaholism across eastern and western cultures. *Journal of Behavioral and Social Sciences, 1*(1), 6–24.

Ilies, R., Schwind, K. M., Wagner, D. T., Johnson, M. D., DeRue, D. S., & Ilgen, D. R. (2007). When can employees have a family life? The effects of daily workload and affect on work-family conflict and social behaviors at home. *Journal of Applied Psychology, 92*(5), 1368–1379.

Jacobs, J. A., & Gerson, K. (2004). Understanding changes in American working time: A synthesis. In C. F. Epstein & A. L. Kalleberg (Eds.), *Fighting for time: Shifting boundaries of work and social life* (pp. 25–45). New York, NY: Russell Sage.

Judge, T. A., & Ilies, R. (2002). Relationship of personality to performance motivation: A meta-analytic review. *Journal of Applied Psychology, 87*(4), 797–807.

Kahn, R. L., Wolfe, D. M., Quinn, R. P., Snoek, J. D., & Rosenthal, R. A. (1964). *Organizational stress: Studies in role conflict and ambiguity*. New York, NY: Wiley.

Katz, D., & Kahn, R. (1978). *The social psychology of organizations* (2nd ed.). New York: Wiley.

Keeney, J., Boyd, E. M., Sinha, R., Westring, A. F., & Ryan, A. M. (2013). From "work–family" to "work–life": Broadening our conceptualization and measurement. *Journal of Vocational Behavior, 82*(3), 221–237.

Lam, C. F., Liang, J., Ashford, S. J., & Lee, C. (2015). Job insecurity and organizational citizenship behavior: Exploring curvilinear and moderated relationships. *Journal of Applied Psychology, 100*(2), 499–510.

Law, K. S., Wong, C. S., Wang, D., & Wang, L. (2000). Effect of supervisor–subordinate guanxi on supervisory decisions in China: An empirical investigation. *International Journal of Human Resource Management, 11*(4), 751–765.

Leslie, L. M., King, E. B., & Clair, J. A. (2019). Work-life ideologies: The contextual basis and consequences of beliefs about work and life. *Academy of Management Review, 44*(1), 72–98.

Lewis, S., Gambles, R., & Rapoport, R. (2007). The constraints of a 'work–life balance approach: An international perspective. *International Journal of Human Resource Management, 18*(3), 360–373.

Liao, J., & Wang, L. (2009). Face as a mediator of the relationship between material value and brand consciousness. *Psychology & Marketing, 26*(11), 987–1001.

Ling, Y., & Powell, G. N. (2001). Work-family conflict in contemporary China: Beyond an American-based model. *International Journal of Cross Cultural Management, 1*(3), 357–373.

Liu, S., Zhang, Y., Chen, L., Guo, L., & Yu, D. (2015). Enterprise WeChat groups: Their effect on work–life conflict and life-work enhancement. *Frontiers of Business Research in China, 9*(4), 516–535.

Lu, L., Cooper, C. L., Kao, S.-F., Chang, T.-T., Allen, T. D., Lapierre, L. M., … Spector, P. E. (2010). Cross-cultural differences on work-to-family conflict and role satisfaction: A Taiwanese-British comparison. *Human Resource Management, 49,* 67–85.

Major, D. A., Fletcher, T. D., Davis, D. D., & Germano, L. M. (2008). The influence of work-family culture and workplace relationships on work interference with family: A multilevel model. *Journal of Organizational Behavior, 29*(7), 881–897.

Major, D. A., & Morganson, V. J. (2011). Coping with work-family conflict: A leader-member exchange perspective. *Journal of Occupational Health Psychology, 16*(1), 126–138.

Michel, J. S., Kotrba, L. M., Mitchelson, J. K., Clark, M. A., & Baltes, B. B. (2011). Antecedents of work–family conflict: A meta-analytic review. *Journal of Organizational Behavior, 32*(5), 689–725.

NPR. (2008). *China's only children face great expectations.* Retrieved from https://www.npr.org/templates/story/story.php?storyId=90722632 on 22 February 2020.

Ollier-Malaterre, A. (2014). Cross-national work-life research: A review at the individual level. In T. D. Allen & L. E. Eby (Eds.), *Oxford handbook of work and family* (pp. 315–330). Oxford, UK: Oxford University Press.

Ollier-Malaterre, A., & Foucreault, A. (2017). Cross-National work-life research: Cultural and structural impacts for individuals and organizations. *Journal of Management, 43*(1), 111–136.

Ollo-López, A., & Goñi-Legaz, S. (2017). Differences in work–family conflict: Which individual and national factors explain them? *The International Journal of Human Resource Management, 28*(3), 499–525.

Powell, G. N., Francesco, A. M., & Ling, Y. (2009). Toward culture-sensitive theories of the work–family interface. *Journal of Organizational Behavior, 30*(5), 597–616.

Powell, G. N., Greenhaus, J. H., Allen, T. D., & Johnson, R. E. (2019). Introduction to special topic forum: Advancing and expanding work-life theory from multiple perspectives. *Academy of Management Review, 44*(1), 54–71.

Powell, G. N., Greenhaus, J. H., Jaskiewicz, P., Combs, J. G., Balkin, D. B., & Shanine, K. K. (2017). Family science and the work-family interface: An interview with Gary Powell and Jeffrey Greenhaus. *Human Resource Management Review, 28*(1), 98–102.

Rantanen, J., Pulkkinen, L., & Kinnunen, U. (2005). The Big Five personality dimensions, work-family conflict, and psychological distress: A longitudinal view. *Journal of Individual Differences, 26*(3), 155–166.

Redding, G. (2002). The capitalist business system of China and its rationale. *Asia Pacific Journal of Management, 19*(2), 221–249.

Ren, X., & Caudle, D. (2016). Walking the tightrope between work and non-work life: Strategies employed by British and Chinese academics and their implications. *Studies in Higher Education, 41*(4), 599–618.

Richardson, K., & Benbunan-Fich, R. (2011). Examining the antecedents of work connectivity behavior during non-work time. *Information and Organization, 21*(3), 142–160.

Richter, A., Näswall, K., & Sverke, M. (2010). Job insecurity and its relation to work—Family conflict: Mediation with a longitudinal data set. *Economic and Industrial Democracy, 31*(2), 265–280.

Riley, N. E. (1996). Holding up half the economy. *China Business Review, 23*(1), 22–24.

Rotter, J. B. (1966). Generalized expectancies for internal versus external control of reinforcement. *Psychological Monographs, 80*(1), 1–28.

Scott, K. S., Moore, K. S., & Miceli, M. P. (1997). An exploration of the meaning and consequences of workaholism. *Human Relations, 50*(3), 287–314.

Shang, S., O'Driscoll, M. P., & Roche, M. (2018). Mechanisms linking acculturation, work–family conflict, and subjective well-being among Chinese immigrants in New Zealand. *Human Resource Management, 57*(5), 1097–1109.

Shang, S., O'Driscoll, M. P., & Roche, M. (2017). Moderating role of acculturation in a mediation model of work–family conflict among Chinese immigrants in New Zealand. *Stress and Health, 33*(1), 55–68.

Shenkar, O., & Ronen, S. (1987). Structure and importance of work goals among managers in the People's Republic of China. *Academy of Management Journal, 30*(3), 564–576.

Shimazu, A., & Schaufeli, W. B. (2009). Is workaholism good or bad for employee well-being? The distinctiveness of workaholism and work engagement among Japanese employees. *Industrial Health, 47*(5), 495–502.

Siegel, P. A., Post, C., Brockner, J., Fishman, A. Y., & Garden, C. (2005). The moderating influence of procedural fairness on the relationship between work–life conflict and organizational commitment. *Journal of Applied Psychology, 90*(1), 13–24.

Skinner, N., & Pocock, B. (2008). Work—life conflict: Is work time or work overload more important? *Asia Pacific Journal of Human Resources, 46*(3), 303–315.

Strom, R. D., Strom, S. K., & Xie, Q. (1996). Parent expectations in China. *International Journal of the Sociology of the Family, 26*(1), 37–49.

Su, X., Li, X., & Curry, E. (2017). Understanding workplace flexibility in state agencies: What facilitates employee access? *The American Review of Public Administration, 47*(8), 977–990.

The World Bank. (2018). *Labor force, female (% of total labor force), China, 2017*. The World Bank Databank. Retrieved from https://data.worldbank.org/indicator/SL.TLF.TOTL.FE.ZS?locations=CN.

Thompson, G., Buch, R., & Glasø, L. (2018). Low-quality LMX relationships, leader incivility, and follower responses. *Journal of General Management, 44*(1), 17–26.

Timms, C., Brough, P., O'Driscoll, M., Kalliath, T., Siu, O., Sit, C., & Lo, D. (2015). Flexible work arrangements, work engagement, turnover intentions, and psychological health. *Asia Pacific Journal of Human Resources, 53*(1), 83–103.

Tsang, E. W. (1998). Can guanxi be a source of sustained competitive advantage for doing business in China? *Academy of Management Perspectives, 12*(2), 64–73.

Tse, D. K. (1996). Understanding Chinese people as consumers: past findings and future propositions. In M. H. Bond (Ed.), *The handbook of Chinese psychology* (pp. 352–363). Hong Kong: Oxford University Press.

Tummers, L. G., & Bronkhorst, B. A. (2014). The impact of leader-member exchange (LMX) on work-family interference and work-family facilitation. *Personnel Review, 43*(4), 573–591.

Vallerand, R. J., & Houlfort, N. (2003). Passion at work: Toward a new conceptualization. In D. Skarlicki, S. Gilliland, & D. Steiner (Eds.), *Social issues in management* (Vol. 3, pp. 175–204). Greenwich, CT: Information Age Publishing.

Voydanoff, P. (2004). The effects of work demands and resources on work-to-family conflict and facilitation. *Journal of Marriage and Family, 66*(2), 398–412.

Wadsworth, L. L., & Facer, R. L. (2016). Work–family balance and alternative work schedules: Exploring the impact of 4-day workweeks on state employees. *Public Personnel Management, 45*(4), 382–404.

Wang, S. (2019, May 28). China's tech workers burn out in a rat race they call '996'. *CNN.* Retrieved February 1, 2020, from https://edition.cnn.com/2019/05/27/health/china-996-tech-workers-intl/index.html.

Warner, M. (2010). In search of Confucian HRM: Theory and practice in Greater China and beyond. *International Journal of Human Resource Management, 21*(12), 2053–2078.

Watson, D., Clark, L. A., & Tellegen, A. (1988). Development and validation of brief measures of positive and negative affect: the PANAS scales. *Journal of Personality and Social Psychology, 54*(6), 1063–1070.

Westman, M., & Etzion, D. L. (2005). The crossover of work-family conflict from one spouse to the other. *Journal of Applied Social Psychology, 35*(9), 1936–1957.

Westman, M., Etzion, D., & Danon, E. (2001). Job insecurity and crossover of burnout in married couples. *Journal of Organizational Behavior: The International Journal of Industrial, Occupational and Organizational Psychology and Behavior, 22*(5), 467–481.

Wright, T. (2018). Labour protest in China's private sector: responses to Chinese communism with capitalist characteristics. *Economy and Society, 47*(3), 382–402.

Wu, T. J., Yuan, K. S., Yen, D. C., & Xu, T. (2019). Building up resources in the relationship between work–family conflict and burnout among firefighters: Moderators of guanxi and emotion regulation strategies. *European Journal of Work and Organizational Psychology, 28*(3), 430–441.

Xiao, Y., & Cooke, F. L. (2012). Work–life balance in China? Social policy, employer strategy and individual coping mechanisms. *Asia Pacific Journal of Human Resources, 50*(1), 6–22.

Xie, J., Ma, H., Zhou, Z. E., & Tang, H. (2018). Work-related use of information and communication technologies after hours (W_ICTs) and emotional exhaustion: A mediated moderation model. *Computers in Human Behavior, 79,* 94–104.

Xing, F. (1995). The Chinese cultural system: Implications for cross-cultural management. *SAM Advanced Management Journal, 60*(1), 14–21.

Xu, S., & Cao, Z. C. (2019). Antecedents and outcomes of work–nonwork conflict in hospitality: A meta-analysis. *International Journal of Contemporary Hospitality Management, 31*(10), 3919–3942.

Yang, N., Chen, C. C., Choi, J., & Zou, Y. (2000). Sources of work-family conflict: A Sino-US comparison of the effects of work and family demands. *Academy of Management Journal, 43*(1), 113–123.

Yang, N., & Poelmans, S. A. Y. (Eds.). (2005). *Work and family an international research perspective.* Mahwah, NJ: Erlbaum.

Yao, C., Arrowsmith, J., & Thorn, K. (2016). Exploring motivations in Chinese corporate expatriation through the lens of Confucianism. *Asia Pacific Journal of Human Resources, 54*(3), 312–331.

Zhang, X. A., Cao, Q., & Grigoriou, N. (2011). Consciousness of social face: The development and validation of a scale measuring desire to gain face versus fear of losing face. *Journal of Social Psychology, 151,* 129–149.

Zhang, J., & Liu, Y. (2011). Antecedents of work-family conflict: Review and prospect. *International Journal of Business and Management, 6*(1), 89–103.

Zuo, J., & Bian, Y. (2001). Gendered resources, division of housework, and perceived fairness—A case in urban China. *Journal of Marriage and Family, 63*(4), 1122–1133.

Zuo, J., & Bian, Y. (2004). Gendered resources, division of housework, and perceived fairness—A case in urban China. *Journal of Marriage and Family, 63*(4), 1122–1133.

10

Work-Life Balance in India: Policy, Practices and the Road Ahead

V. Chandra

Introduction

The term work-life balance (WLB) entered corporate corridors some thirty years back (Singh, 2014) in the western world as more and more women entered workforce (Lambert, 2000). The term garnered immediate attention of behavioural scientists and WLB has now become an integral part of work systems. Supportive WLB policies and practices help employees manage multiple roles more efficiently in a stress-free manner. They also help organizations build and nurture a robust engaged workforce, thus contributing significantly to its productivity. Abundant literature on the positive relationship between work engagement and performance (Kim, Kolb, & Kim, 2012) is available. Studies reveal a positive influence on employee job satisfaction, turn over intentions, increases organizational loyalty and commitment, reduces absenteeism

V. Chandra (✉)
International Management Institute, New Delhi, India
e-mail: vchandra@imi.edu

T. A. Adisa and G. Gbadamosi (eds.), *Work-Life Interface*,
https://doi.org/10.1007/978-3-030-66648-4_10

(Bedeian, Burke, & Moffett, 1988; Dex & Scheibel, 1999; Duxbury & Higgins, 2001; Frone, Russel, & Cooper, 1992; Groover & Crooker, 1995; Kossek & Ozeki, 1998; Lobel & Kossek, 1996; Parasuraman & Greenhaus, 2002), increases individual and organizational performance (Osterman, 1995; Sand & Harper, 2007). Indian subcontinent is too large a country with varied and diverse practices that it is difficult to identify a single standard for WLB programmes. Most research on work and family in Indian context falls under two distinct domains. One domain centred round women subordination at work and home as an offshoot of patriarchal social context targeting the underprivileged sections of society. The other focusing on work family conflicts (Rajadhyaksha & Smita, 2004). However, unlike the western counterparts, not much evidence is available on impact of these practices from organizational perspective (Poster, 2005; Rajadhyaksha & Smita, 2004; Wang, Lawler, Shi, Walumbwa, & Piao, 2008).

Historical Development of Work-Life Balance Initiatives in India

India traditionally being an agrarian country, nature of work was primarily home based. Even after industrial revolution, though people started working in factories various sectors like agriculture, family businesses, retail, etc., continued to operate as home-based units. WLB was best handled at the family level where the husband went for paid employment and the wife took care of the household work. Technology brought a new impetus to the nature and meaning of work.

National Context and WLB

The services sector, comprising of both organized and unorganized sectors, contribute to a large chunk of Indian economy contributing significantly to the country's GDP. The last two decades have seen exponential growth in services sector especially in the information and communication technology space. While both organized and unorganized sectors contribute to the country's GDP, there was greater transparency and accountability in transactions of the organized sector.

Since independence public sector firms were at the forefront of Indian economy. They prospered as mini replicas of Indian national culture where employee development and talent retention are greatly valued. With the thrust area being nation development, institution building and welfare orientation formed the bedrock. Respect for age, seniority, authority is well documented. They are also significant factors in employee and organizational performance. Perceptions about organizational thinking and practices are deeply rooted and guided by cultural assumptions. High power distance (PD) is a characteristic feature of Indian culture suggesting a more centralized decision-making and hierarchical relationships (Sagie & Aycan, 2003). When power and authority rests only with few individuals, team participation is often assumed and taken for granted (Hofstede, 2001). Studies by Indian behavioural scientists in the early eighties suggest that unequal distribution of power is not only culturally and socially accepted but also encouraged (Thiagarajan & Deep, 1970). An ideal boss subordinate relationship is a nurturant task relationship (Sinha, 2004) where seniors have the responsibility to guide juniors and juniors are obligated to respect seniors and authority (Carl, Gupta, & Javidan, 2004) unquestioningly. Job security is a common denominator for all public sector organizations. Power of authority moderates the relationship between the behavioural and psychological constructs (Hauff & Richeter, 2015).

Another strong pillar for Indian economy since independence has been the contribution of the family owned businesses. Of the top 20 business houses in India today, 15 are family owned. 16 of the top business groups are a result of post-independence economic growth. While both private public sector firms had similar work ideologies during their initial years, the 1991 economic reforms opened new vistas for doing business (Sinha, 2004). Business groups that adapted to the changing business scenario survived and continue to grow while other fell off the race (Sarkar & Sarkar, 2012).

Twentieth century has witnessed major demographic shifts with a significant inflow of women entering paid workforce. There was a major move in women employment from agriculture to services sector changing the gender equilibrium both at workplace as well relationship within the family (Sun, 2008). Between 1971 and 1999, women employment figure in public sector has increased by 327% and private sector by 175%. In the past half century, the percentage of stay at home mums dropped from 76 to 28% (Mary, Cynthia, & Black, 2007). Multiple perspectives about work and work norms; life and life priorities have emerged. While there are studies that point towards the convergence of unpaid work, there are equal number of studies pointing to the perceived unequal distribution of household responsibilities (Barnett & Hyde, 2001; Sun, 2008). The late 1990s saw a trend towards family-friendly policies with management's main agenda to safeguard the interests of women employees specially working mothers (Lewis, Gambles, & Rapoport, 2007). The policies and regulations were more on healthcare, nutrition, townships and residential facilities for employees, schools, etc. Relationship focused education was not their prime focus area. Many first-generation urban youths found it difficult to strike a balance between work- and non-work-related roles (Gore, 1994). A need for reviewing management strategies and people practices was felt as more and more global firms started establishing their foothold on the Indian soils. This essentially entails not only skills and competencies matching global standards, but also changes in mindset, prevailing norms and values which fall under the domain of national socio-economic and political spheres (Budhwar & Sparrow, 1998; Hofstede, 2011).

Gender Egalitarianism

Work and life have varied definitions (Guest, 2002). Work refers to paid employment and every other activity of the individual beyond the realm of paid employment comes under the purview of 'Life'. Researchers associate this ambiguous definition of 'work' and 'life' to the societal gender division (Ransome, 2007). Several factors both at the individual level as well as national level are responsible for the gendered division of household responsibilities (Sun, 2008).

India has since ancient times held its women in high esteem. Hindus who constitute the majority community typically pray to goddess Saraswati for knowledge and learning, goddess Lakshmi for wealth and goddess Durga for strength to fight evil forces. Indian women have excelled various walks of life, including as saints (Meera Bai) and warriors (Rani Jhansi and Rani Rudrama Devi). Swami Vivekananda, one of the greatest exponents of Hindu Culture, exhorted that a civilization is known by the way it treats its women. India is a predominantly patriarchal society. Still, some states like Kerala in the southern India and several states in Northern India, which are advanced states in the country in terms of UNDP's Human Development, are matriarchal societies.

Constitutionally there is no discrimination against women. Rather Indian constitution has deliberately tried to force policies in favour of the 'fairer Sex' through its Fundamental Rights and Directive Principles. The various constitutional privileges include not only equal opportunity in employment, but also directs state to adopt various affirmative action plans in favour of women. Through various employment legislations it is aimed to build a secure and environment-friendly workplace for female work force where social, economic and political disparities are minimized.

Mythologically women enjoyed a special status in India. Yet demographic, social and economic indicators point out that women continue to be disadvantaged in terms of their access to education and employment. Attitudes about gender role, social belief systems, customs and physical infrastructure have perpetuated the relative conservativeness and vulnerability of women in society though this trend is slowly changing in the urban side.

In India as is with most Asian countries, WLB even today is seen as a gender issue pertaining to a women's struggle in an otherwise male-dominated world of work (Chandra, 2012). Studies have also revealed that family obligations are more demanding for women than men even when they are equal co-earners (Bharat, 2003; Gershuny, 2000; Pleck, 1997; Ramu, 1989). This gendered public psyche is so deeply rooted that many working women too view themselves first as home-makers. Compromising for less demanding job roles to manage dual responsibilities is common.

Technology and Employment Trends

Technology gave a new impetus to the nature and meaning of work. Traditional forms of nine to five, eight-hour permanent jobs are giving way to a variety of new work arrangements (Briscoe, Hall, & De Muth, 2006). Linear organizational structures and rigid views about jobs about careers (Greenhaus, Callanan, & Godshak, 2000) underwent swift transformation giving way to matrixed structures with multiple reporting systems. Work practices became more dynamic and less predictable. Though flexible working arrangements have been very well accepted in the west, it was somewhat a new trend for Indian community. With technology as a great enabler the possibility of managing work and family encouraged more and more women to look for corporate jobs and individuals started integrating multiple roles.

With the wave of information and communication technologies (ICTs) redefining the way work is done it has also interfered with the ideologies that prospered during the times of industrial modernization (Townsend & Batchelor, 2005). Agile technologies, pod structures, scrum tools have all rewritten the way work is being done. Work is now seen more as an activity than a place to go. As a transformational tool, technology has helped organizations and individuals to work more smartly and effectively, thus increasing productivity in a very cost-effective manner. Agile working is based on the complete flexibility of work drive long-term organization success. While it can unlock value for both employer and employee it will be driven by business needs (Employers Network for Equality & Inclusion, 2013).

Causes and Consequences

Though the boundaries between work and home are getting blurred, they still continue to remain as very distinct entities (Duxbury & Smart, 2011; Greenhaus & Powell, 2006). They are like two sides of the same coin. While family contributes significantly to individual's performance at workplace (Baral & Bhargava, 2009), employees who perform well in their jobs also contribute positively to family well-being. What causes work-life imbalance and how one perceives and reacts to it are very different (Muna & Mansour, 2009; Poelmans, Kalliath, & Brough, 2008). The spillover effects are very many both for the organizational performance as well as for individual well-being. Most research on WLB revolves round two closely linked and overlapping yet very distinct streams—one focusing at the individual level and the other measured at the business and organizational performance level. Both individual as well as organizational drivers are influenced by the socio-cultural context in which they operate. National culture of the land, individual's orientation towards self and market dynamics can be considered as some of the main reasons behind these variations (Delcampo & Hinrichs, 2006).

Individual Factors

Individual's life philosophy plays a major role in managing conflict. Where focus is on 'being' individuals tend to seek satisfaction in what one is and accept situation as it comes. On the other hand, where life philosophy is on 'becoming', achievement orientation becomes important. It is said that greater the conflict between being and becoming, lower is the WLB (Singh & Awasthy, 2009). Traditionally, issues related to WLB were viewed from worker and work perspective. So, individuals tend to achieve this balance through the personal choices they make. Individual personality type, personal values and attitude towards work and family are some of the key areas that this domain focusses. Even today for women family obligations take precedence over paid employment and often had to make career sacrifices for family needs. Going by Vineeta Chandra (2010), work family conflict affects men and women differently and McClelland's need hierarchy acts as an antecedent to work family conflict. Balancing work and personal life continues to be a challenge. The ride could be bumpy enough especially for dual career couple (Schulz & Schulz, 2005). The first-generation female working families find even more difficult as the values they grew up with are drastically different from the ones they currently face (Henry & Parasarathy, 2010).

Organizational Factors

Maintaining a healthy WLB is essential for the health of the individual as well as the organization, though it effects individuals and organizations very differently. Organizations are fast realizing that work and family issues are not separate entities and should be looked at as part of the whole continuum. Several studies have demonstrated the relationship between work-life conflict and job performance, job satisfaction, employee and organizational performance (Lyness & Judiesch, 2008). Workplace plays an important role in not only helping employees manage their workspace but also help coordinate and manage personal roles and responsibilities (Bowen, 1988; Kamerman & Kahn, 1987; Thomas & Ganster, 1995; Voydanoff, 1987; Warren & Johnson, 1995). An internal poll at Accenture as stated by Klun (2008), over 80 per cent of employees emphatically stated that their commitment to continue with the company is influenced by their ability to manage WLB. The poll also reveals that 32% of employees have turned down offers in the past two years because it would destabilize their WLB.

Research in this domain suggests that WLB initiatives and interventions are of utmost importance not just for people with family responsibilities but for all employees irrespective of their family commitments. WLB is a much broader concept and HR professionals are increasing using it as a strategic tool (Perry-Smith & Blum, 2000) in bringing about innovative employee-friendly practices and thereby help them take care of their personal needs. Glass and Beth (1997) classified these initiatives into three broad categories that aim at: policies that aim at reducing work hours, policies that allow flexibility in time and location, and policies that provide social support. By reducing the number of work hours per week, employees get to spend quality time with their families and shoulder caregiving responsibilities more effectively. Studies have demonstrated that work autonomy, work family responsibility are high in priority for employees. Employers too have acknowledged the positive effect of work-life balance on work engagement which in turn contributes to overall business performance (Meyer, Paunonen, Gellatly, Goffin, & Jackson, 1989). Organizations have faced setbacks due to absenteeism, reduced productivity, job satisfaction, turnover, which are all a result of poor attention to WLB policies (Batt & Valcour, 2003; Beauregard & Henry, 2009).

Flexible working hours have been very popular in the west. In the Indian context studies reveal that flexible work arrangements have positively impacted employee relations, enhanced commitment and loyalty towards organization, reduced attrition (Venkata Ratnam & Chandra, 2009). However, there is also indication of operational and administrative challenges. The legal and institutional framework for social support followed by Government of India is adopted from the several conventions framed by International Labour Organization (ILO) and enacted through legislative measures. Government, employers, trade unions and civil societies have together joined hands and took their first baby steps in the direction.

Consequences of Work-Life Imbalance

Work to family spillover retards the individual and his/her family functioning. Family to work spillover negatively effects not just individual performance but also hampers organizational productivity and turnover intentions (Glass & Beth, 1997). Over worked parents may not be able to give adequate attention to the much-needed sensitive care that is instrumental in developing cognitive and social skills. The flexibility that comes with the blurring of boundaries is viewed differently by different individuals. ICTs infiltration on WLB can be viewed both positively as well as negatively. While some embrace technological convenience more easily and manage professional and personal spillovers with greater ease, others take this infiltration as an interference and prefer strict boundarics between personal and professional life (Nam, 2014). There is however more research on the negative consequences. Opportunity of juggling multiple roles has created more work for employees which ultimately results in more private costs (Brett & Stroh, 2003; Clark 2001; Eikhof, Warhurst, & Haunschild, 2007; Pococock & Clarke, 2005; Walsh, 1999). Unpleasant consequences reported include overwork and workaholism (Olson & Primps, 1984) resulting in what Gore (1994) calls choice anxiety—anxiety stemming from increased autonomy and choice. Variable pay could often be lucrative monetarily but is negatively correlated WLB. On an average Indians spend around 1,437 hours yearly which is among the three highest scores globally (Thacker, 2018). 1980s and 1990s saw a rapid increase in issues related to both 'work-family' and 'family-work' conflict (Hewlett & Luce, 2006; Lewis et al., 2007). Disturbed personal life and broken relationships are also on the rise. Legal experts in Family Law see a steady increase in the number of divorce cases with many getting separated through mutual consent in less than a year of marriage (Henry & Parthasarathy, 2010).

Job-related stress, professional burnout, frequent headaches and depression have become today's workplace realities. This is seen to be more prevalent the Indian IT industry. Long working hours, graveyard shifts, workover weekends, project driven assignments cut across time and space could have all contributed to the existing scenario (Chiang, Birtch, & Kwan, 2010). With sedentary lifestyle, ailments like diabetes, hypertension and obesity are hitting employees much earlier than the earlier generations. While life expectancy for an average Indian has gone up, quality of life has deteriorated. Diabetes in urban India is growing at an alarming rate retaining the name of being the diabetic capital. One in three Indian adults above 25 has high blood pressure.

Coping Strategies

Social protocols and cultural norms are still largely gender specific. Structurally too within the household, care-giving responsibility is shouldered by the female members. With the breaking up of the joint and or extended family systems, nuclear family structures became dominant household forms following the patterns prevailing in most industrial nations (Coltrane, 2000). With the rise in working women population, there grew a need to look at alternate modes for childcare and household work. As work family conflict is seen as women's problem and a personal choice, coping strategies also tend to be individual driven (Chandra, 2012). Outsourcing domestic work is a common trend. As compared to the developed countries, reliable domestic help is more easily and economically available. However, quality day-care facilities in India especially in tier two cities are still at its nascent stage. Even in the bigger cities with larger number of dual earning couple's childcare and elderly care services does not sufficiently meet the growing demand (Rajadyaksha et al., 2020). Indian pre-school/childcare market is expected to grow at 19% during 2019–2024 (Government of India, 2013). Some take the help of parents and parents-in-law. While there isn't much empirical data available there is a trend towards young couples living closer to either the husband's parents or relatives (patrilocal residence) or the wife's parents or relatives (matrilocal residence). In fact, life course theorists see a global trend in intergenerational relationships (Dannefer, 2003; Putney & Bengtson, 2003).

Select Best Practices

As opportunities of globalization unfolded, India became a favoured destination for foreign investments (FDI, 2017). Table 10.1 shows the top ten companies across the globe in terms of work-life balance. Seven of these have their branches in India. Glassdoor.com which is globally one of the most widely used employment and review sites seeks to capture what the employees actually feel about their workstations.

Table 10.1 Top 10 companies for WLB

Sl. no.	Company name	WLB rating[b]
1	SAS	4.5
2	National Instruments	4.3
3	Slalom[a]	4.1
4	MITRE[a]	4.1
5	Orbitz Worldwide[a]	4.1
6	Mentor Graphics	4.1
7	FactSet	4.1
8	Agilent Technologies	4.1
9	Nokia	4.1
10	MathWorks	4.1

Source Glassdoor.com; [a]Companies that do not have offices in India; [b]Rating on a five-point scale

Flexible work environment is a common feature most appreciated by the employees of these companies. Lower salary and limited growth opportunities as compared to the head office emerged as a common concern.

Table 10.2 shows ten top companies to work for in India. The list consists of companies that have been consistently rated among the top ten within their industry by various rating agencies in the country during the past five years. What really makes a company an ideal place to work is its employee-friendly policies and not necessarily pay packages. Flexibility of time and location, caring and nurturing work environment, healthcare facilities seem to be common across the organizations. These companies look at WLB in a much broader perspective and are consciously adopting more inclusive strategies while care is taken to incorporate the special needs for women. The IT and IT-enabled services take a lead when it comes to innovative policies. Many tech companies are going the extra mile by ensuring not just the balance between work and life, but by bringing life into work through various engagement activities.

Techstop, an in-house one stop solution provider for all hardware and software issues, is one of the most favoured facilities provided by Google for its employees. Employees can also avail and experiment with beta-test products even before they hit the market. Resource groups like 'Businesswomen network' at SAP offer employees an opportunity for self-reflection as well as provides a platform for exchange of new ideas and experiences. Google's 'Women Techmakers' programme aimed at women empowerment regularly rolls out programmes helping them grow in leadership roles. 'People Leader Learning Path' (PLLP) initiative by American Express offers its employees a provision to look beyond their jobs and identify their long-term potential. American Express was also the first to join hands with other leading multinational companies and start a collaborative learning platform and regularly organizes workshops, focused learning circles across partnering organizations. Employees go through a continuous learning process so that work remains interesting and employees engaged. SAP Labs India offers 'Run Mummier' programme where a buddy is assigned to female employees going on maternity leave. This practice of assigning a buddy helps the employee

Table 10.2 Ten best companies to work for in India

Company Name	Employee-friendly practices	Practices for women empowerment
RMSI	Great work culture, flexible work environment, high level of empowerment and accountability, focus on employee well-being and overall health through regular health check-ups, stress management through yoga, meditation, pranic healing, etc.	Anti-sexual harassment policy, self-defence workshops like tai chi, etc. Extended maternity leave, part-time/flexi working/work from home options, options for short career breaks, etc.
Google India	Excellent work environment, colourful ambience to promote creative thinking, fun activities like TGIF(thank God it's Friday), access to best facilities like beta-test products, Techstop, a host of recreational facilities like table tennis, pool, air hockey, sleep pods, etc., world class gym with customized health plans, free cafeteria facilities, annual day celebrations where employees children are encouraged to participate	Supports employee resource groups Women @Google. Offers academic scholarships outstanding women achievers
Marriott Hotels India	Employees are referred to as associates, company's core value—taking care, friendly work environment and training facilities, great discount policies for employees, health insurance, etc.	Equal opportunity employer. Deliberate effort on recruitment of female employees at managerial levels. Mentorship programmes for high potential women employees for leadership roles

(continued)

Table 10.2 (continued)

Company Name	Employee-friendly practices	Practices for women empowerment
American Express India	Creating an inspiring work environment, offers programmes like 'People Leader Learning Path' and employee relation fundamentals programme for promoting talent growth, hosts fun activities like blue bucket challenge, Reach Out, smart savings for financial wellness	Focus on gender parity. Flexible work hours
Sap Labs India	'Care for life' fund, part-time work for new fathers, temporary part-time work, varied interest groups to encourage individual passion	Businesswomen network, extended maternity leave, options for part-time/leave without pay, crèche, Run Mummier programme, in-house crèche
Godrej Consumer products	Nurturing work environment. High emphasis on diversity and inclusiveness, employee referral policy, Godrej LOUD (live out your Dream), Godrej Fellows programme	'Godrej alliance for women', six-month maternity leave, work from home/part-time work options
Intuit Technology services	High priority on inclusiveness and diversity, adoption perks and leave, health check-ups, medical insurance, stock options, concept of unstructured time	Tech Women@ intuit dedicated parking spaces for pregnant women employees. transport facilities, day-care discounts at partnering creches

(continued)

stay connected as she juggles multiple parenting roles. The programme also acts as a retention tool. The Run Mummier programme and Mobile app helped lower attrition from 40% in 2010 to 6% within eight years (*Business Line*, 2018).

Table 10.2 (continued)

Company Name	Employee-friendly practices	Practices for women empowerment
Ernst and Young	Opportunity for collaborative learning, flexible work arrangements, inclusive work culture	Career watch, special programmes for high potential women employees into leadership roles, everywoman network, EY WIN learning hub, opportunities for career break and re-entry
Tech Mahindra	Friendly, transparent work environment. Bereavement leave, a 12-week paid adoption leave for same-sex couples, attractive employee social options (ESOPs). Volunteering programmes, school donation policy	All Women Tech Mahindra SMART Healthcare Academy, Digital key chains with GSM chips to women employees for safety
Lifestyle international	Openness, transparency, camaraderie and trust form core values, get connected, connect over coffee, flexible working hours, group term life insurance, whistle blower policy, etc.	Focus on caring and respectful work environment for female workforce

Source Author

Many Indian industrialists claim that progressive forward-looking Indian organizations have similar work values comparable to global standards. However, given the diversity in nature and scale of organizations, it would be unfair to generalize for the country as a whole. A study carried out by Great Place to Work and *The Economic Times* (*Economic Times*, 2018), whose sample cuts across 20 sectors and 700 companies, 1.8 lakh employees believe that WLB at MNCs is superior to Indian companies. Technology as a great enabler has helped employees manage and regulate the pace of their work thus striking a balance between professional and personal fronts (Hill, Hawkins, Ferris, & Weitzman,

2001; Middleton, 2008; Towers, Duxbury, Higgins, & Thomas, 2006). As more and more multinational companies started exploring Indian markets, workforce gradually got exposed to flexible working styles of the western world. Many forward-looking organizations proactively initiated several WLB practices along with flexitime and flexilocation policies like compulsory annual leave, creches at workplaces, compensatory leave, no incentives for overtime, no meetings to be scheduled after core working hours, etc. Developing innovative policies that cater to different generation is a challenge. 'Future leave' initiated by Accenture has been very popular across generations. Employees are entitled to take an unpaid sabbatical of one to three months without giving any specific reason.

The public sector firms have been in forefront for their welfare measures through statutory and non-statutory benefits while private sector has a very paternalistic approach in dealing with WLB issues. The Maternity Benefit Amendment Act which was passed in 2017 came as welcome relief as it increased the paid leave from 12 to 26 months for female workforce. With the financial burden falling directly on employers, not all employers find this a positive move. The provision for paternity leave was introduced for government employees in 1999 (Vazquez, 2020) where young dads of newborn can avail a 15-day paid leave. There is however no available information on how many are availing it. There is no law that mandates private sector though many bigger companies have been liberal with their paternity leave policies which range from five days to 17 weeks.

Generational Values and Career Attitudes

What constitutes WLB has always been a point for debate. Some consider the term itself to be misnomer (Guest, 2002). Societal perceptions about gendered distribution of work are slowly changing, though the role spillover for male employees is still very less (Bartnett & Hyde, 2001). Given that individual needs and personal responsibilities change with different stages in individual's life some have construed WLB as a phase in a continuum. Organizations have started looking at WLB with a broader perspective beyond the needs of working women, more specifically working mothers. Both men and women have work and non-work responsibilities (Kossek & Ozeki, 1998). Sturges (2008) looks at WLB as a stage in an individual's career. Developing innovative policies that cater to different generation is a challenge. As a whole it is said Gen Y prefers relaxed work atmosphere (Deal, Altman, & Rogelberg, 2010).

India is not only one of the fastest growing economies, it also has a very large population of young workforce. Its working population is predicted to reach 95 crores by 2026 (Nilekani, 2009) and currently almost 50% belongs to generation Y (Nayar, 2013) with average age being 29 years. This is considerably low when compared with many other countries, 37 in China and the USA, 45 years in Europe and 48 in Japan (India's New HR Challenge, 2014). The new demographic diversity posed both a challenge as well as opportunity for organizations. With millennials entering workforce intergenerational differences became glaringly visible. Accordingly, career preferences, attitude towards work and work engagement are fast changing and significantly different across generations. When it comes to reward preferences variations are not significant (Chawla, Dokadia, & Rai, 2017). Generation X and Y no longer believe it to be a personal issue to be handled at the individual level. They are demanding their right for a more balanced work-life and exerting pressure in bringing about more attractive options (Guest, 2002; Klun, 2008; Ng, Schweitzer, & Schweitzer, 2010; Sheahan, 2005). Vinita Chandra (2010) observes that the negative spillover is getting reduced with the millennials entering work stream.

Latent Challenges

While the intent behind WLB interventions is to bring about institutional transformation, at the implementation level these policies still operate in a very patriarchal setup with gender-biased norms of understanding (Chandra, 2010). In many cases, flexible work arrangements are handled on a one-to-one basis at an informal level based on the business and personal needs. This is more so in smaller businesses. The inability of workplace to accept and adapt to a condition where every adult family member is a working professional is the biggest challenge (Prasad, 2006). India is ranked 129th in Human Development Index out of 189 countries (UNDP Report, 2019). One of the main reasons for this low score is unemployment and underemployment which is reflected in quality of life. WLB scenario in the metropolitan cities in India is found to be extremely low (Thacker, 2018) as compared to their western counterparts. Pressure to perform becomes inevitable given the tough competition. With fluctuations in economy, job insecurity and fear of losing job remains lingering factors. There is also a general increase in contingent workforce including contractual, part-time and self-employed. When relationship between employer and employee is more transactional, there is little investment in employee development (Sharma, Budhwar, & Verma, 2008). As WLB practices reap long-term rewards benefits are often underestimated as compared to the immediate costs that occur. Motivating the employers to see the big picture is sometimes a challenge. Fear may not always be a great motivator, especially when employees are constantly on stretch targets (Kim et al., 2012).

Conclusion

Technological advancements, demographic shifts and changing business environment have together raised the level of awareness about WLB, from accepting the imbalance as part of life to demanding it as part of employee rights. It is an emergent issue and businesses big and small are offering a wide array of programmes. Employers have realized that WLB policies and practices are no longer choices to make, they are business imperatives. New age organizations are using WLB policies as strategic tools to attract and retain talent. Broadly two trends are visible. Welfare-oriented initiatives continue to be the hallmark of PSUs. Multinational and private sector firms are adopting practices which are more popular among the younger generations that can be compared with the global best practices. Cultural undercurrents seem to be closely interwoven with WLB practices and often interfere at the implementation level. Quite often, there is a gap between what is stated and what is practiced. There is also a general perception that these policies come with unquantifiable hidden costs suggesting a preference for not availing such benefits (Chandra, 2017). For more positive outcomes there is a need to look at the whole process in a more holistic manner. It is important to see the interdependency of these interventions and not as separate entities. People development teams in organizations can play a more proactive role in bringing this transformational change. It is time the HR gives a critical thought to the buzz about WLB, listen to the silent voices of its employees and collectively bridge the gap if any, for the benefit of the employees, the employers and the society at large. In the Indian context, WLB is still seen as a gender issue. Ninety per cent of working women earn their living in the unorganized sector, thus contributing to the unaccounted national income. The very many employee-friendly policies that the new age organizations proactively practice, especially in the white goods sector, are applicable to a very small educated elitist group. This chapter attempts to look at WLB for white collared professionals in organized sector. While it is beyond the scope of this chapter, equally pertinent and critical are the issues of the blue collared workers be it in organized or unorganized sectors.

All in all, the Indian subcontinent presents a wide spectrum of WLB initiatives sharing many similarities with both developed and developing countries. The gendered societal protocols at work and non-work are similar to those across other collectivistic countries. Stiff competition, pressure to perform to make ends meet without much thought on WLB is a common denominator that India shares with many developing countries. At the same time, corporate India takes pride in nurturing a wide basket of WLB initiatives that are at par with the global best. The mosaic of diverse practices thus created at times can lead to cross comparisons and conflicting interests.

References

Baral, R., & Bhargava, S. (2009). Work-life balance practices in Indian organizations: Challenges and prospects. *NHRD Network Journal, 7*(2), 53–58.

Barnett, R. C., & Hyde, J. (2001). Women, men, work and family. *American Psychologist, 56,* 786–796.

Batt, R., & Valcour, P. M. (2003). Human resource practices as predictors of work family outcomes and employee turnover. *Industrial Relations, 42*(2), 189–220.

Beauregard, T., & Henry, L. (2009). Making the link between work life balance practices and organizational performance. *Human Resource Management Review, 19*(1), 9–22.

Bedeian, A., Burke, B., & Moffett, R. (1988). Outcomes of work-family conflict among married male and female professionals. *Journal of Management, 14*(3), 475–491.

Bharat, S. (1995). Attitude and sex-role perceptions among working couples in India. *Journal of Comparative Studies, 26,* 371–388.

Bharat, S. (2003). Women work and family in urban India: Towards new families? In B. J. W, R. Mishra & R. Tripathi (Eds.), *Psychology in human and social development: Lessons from diverse cultures* (pp. 156–169). New Delhi: Sage.

Bowen, G. (1988). Corporate support for the family lives of employees: A conceptual model for program planning and evaluation. *Family Relations, 37,* 183–188.

Brett, J., & Stroh, L. (2003). Working 61 hours a week: Why do managers do it? *Journal of Applied Psychology, 88*(1), 76–78.

Briscoe, J., Hall, D., & DeMuth, R. (2006). Protean and boundaryless careers: An empirical exploration. *Journal of Vocational Behavior, 69*(1), 39–47. https://doi.org/10.1016/j.jvb.2005.09.003.

Budhwar, P., & Sparrow, P. (1998). National factors determining Indian and British HRM practices: An empirical study. *MIR: Management International Review, 38,* 105–121. https://doi.org/10.2307/40228485.

Business Line. (2018, January 23). *Tech firms turn mother hen to retain young moms*. Retrieved from Business Line: https://www.thehindubusinessline.com.

Carl, D., Gupta, V., & Javidan, M. (2004). Power distance. In R. J. House, P. Hanges, M. Javidan, P. Dorfman, & V. Gupta (Eds.), *Culture, leadership and organisations, the GLOBE study of 62 societies* (pp. 513–563). Thousand Oaks, CA: Sage.

Chandra, V. (2010). Women and work-family interface: Indian context. *Journal of Asia Pacific Studies, 1*(2), 235–252.

Chandra, V. (2012). Work-life balance: Eastern & western perspectives. *The International Journal of Human Resource Management, 23,* 5–6.

Chandra, V. (2017, April 3). *The economics of maternity leave.* Retrieved from *Financial Express*: https://www.financialexpress.com/industry/the-economics-of-maternity-leave/612432/.

Chawla, D., Dokadia, A., & Rai, S. (2017). Multi-generational difference in career preferences, reward preferences and work engagement among Indian employees. *Global Business Review, 18*(1), 181–197. https://doi.org/10.1177/0972150916666964.

Chiang, F., Birtch, T., & Kwan, H. (2010). The moderating roles of job control and work-life balance practices on employee stress in the hotel and catering Industry. *International Journal of Hospitality Management, 29*(1), 25–32.

Clarke, S. C. (2001). Work culture and work/family balance. *Journal of Vocational Behavior, 58*(3), 348–365.

Coltrane, S. (2000). Work, research on household labor: Modelling and measuring the social embeddedness of routine family. *Journal of Marriage and the Family, 62*(4), 1208–1233.

Daneffer, D. (2003). Towards a global geography of the life course: Challenges of late modernity for life course theory. In J. Mortimer & M. Shanahan (Eds.), *Handbook of the life course* (pp. 647–660). New York: Kluwer Academic/Penum.

Deal, J., Altman, D., & Rogelberg, S. (2010). Millennials at work: What we know and what we need to know (if anything). *Journal of Business Psychology, 25*(2), 191–199.

DelCampo, R., & Hinrichs, A. (2006). A touch of class: Work and family balance in professional and working-class Hispanics. *Journal of Business and Management, 12*(1), 71–81.

Dex, S., & Scheibl, F. (1999). Business performance and family -friendly policies. *Journal in General Management, 24,* 22–37.

Duxbury, L., & Higgins, C. (2001). Work life balance in the new millennium: Where are we? Where do we need to go?, Work Network. *Canadian Policy Research Networks, Inc.*

Duxbury, L., & Smart, R. (2011). The myth of separate worlds: An exploration of how mobile technology has redefined work-life balance. In S. Kaiser, M. J. Ringlstetter, D. R. Eikhof, & &. M. Cunha (Eds.), *Creating balance?*

International perspectives on work-life integration of professionals (pp. 269–284). Berlin and Heidelberg: Springer.

Economic Times. (2018). India's best companies to work for 2018. *Economic Times.*

Eikhof, D., Warhurst, C., & Haunschild, A. (2007). Introduction: What work? What life? What balance?: Critical reflections on work-life balance debate. *Employee Relations, 29*(4), 325–333.

Employers Network for Equality & Inclusion. (2013). *Agile working: A guide for employers.* London: Employers Network for Equality & Inclusion.

FDI. (2017, February 21). *Fact sheet on Foreign Direct Investment (FDI).* Retrieved from FDI: http://dipp.nic.in/sites/default/files/FDI_FactSheet_21February2018.pdf.

Frone, M., Russel, M., & Cooper, M. (1992). Antecedents and outcomes of work-family conflict: Testing a model of the work-family interface. *Journal of Applied Psychology, 77*(1), 65–78.

Gershuny, J. (2000). *Changing times: Work and leisure in post industrial society.* Oxford, UK: Oxford University Press.

Glass Jennifer, L., & Beth, E. S. (1997). The family responsive workplace. *Annual Review of Sociology, 23,* 289–313.

Glassdoor. (2013). *Top companies for work life balance.* Retrieved from Glassdoor: https://www.Glassdoor.com/list/Top-companies-for-Work-Life-Balance-LST_KQ0,35.htm.

Gore, M. (1994). Changing marital family systems-challenges to conventional models in mental health. In J. Henry & R. Parthasarathy (Eds.), *The family and work connect: A case of relationship-focused family life education* (pp. 13–16). *Indian Journal of Occupational & Environmental Medicine, 14*(1).

Government of India. (2013). *National early childhood care and education (ECCE) Policy.* New Delhi: Ministry of Women and Child Development.

Greenhaus, J. H., & Powell, G. N. (2006). When work and family are allies: A theory of work-family enrichment. *Academy of Management Review, 31,* 72–92.

Greenhaus, J. H., Callanan, G., & Godshalk, V. (2000). *Career Management* (3rd Ed). Fortworth, TX: Dryden Press.

Groover, S., & Crooker, K. (1995). Who appreciates family-responsive human resource policies, the impact of family friendly policies on the organizational attachment of parents and non-parents. *Personal Psychology, 48,* 271–288.

Guest, D. (2002). Perspectives on the study of work-life balance. *Social Science Information, 41*(2), 255–279.

Hauff, S., & Richter, N. (2015). Power Distance and its moderating role in the relationship between situational job characteristics and job satisfaction: An empirical analysis using different cultural measures. *Cross Cultural Management, 22*(1), 68–89. https://doi.org/10.1108/CCM-11-2013-0164.

Henry, J., & Parthasarathy, R. (2010, January–April). The family and work connect: A case of relationship-focussed family life education. *Indian Journal of Occupational Medicine, 14*(1), 13–16.

Hewlett, S. A., & Luce, C. (2006). Extreme jobs: The dangerous allure of 70-hour work week. *Harvard Business Review*, 49–59.

Hill, J., Hawkins, A. J., Ferris, M., & Weitzman, M. (2001). Finding an extra day a week: The positive influence of perceived job flexibility on work and family balance. *Family Relations, 50*(1), 49–58.

Hofstede, G. (2001). *Culture's consequences: Comparing values, behaviours, institutions and organizations across nations*. London: Sage.

Hofstede, G. (2011). Dimensionalising cultures: The Hofstede model in context. *Online Reading in Psychology and Culture, 2*(1). http://doi.org/10.9707/2307-0919.1014.

Kamerman, S., & Kahn, A. (1987). *The responsive workplace*. New York: Columbia University Press.

Kim, W., Kolb, J., & Kim, T. (2012). The relationship between work engagement and performance: A review of empirical literature and a proposed research agenda. *Human Resource Development Review*, 1–29.

Klun, S. (2008). Work-life balance is a cross generational concern—And a key to retaining high performers at accenture. *Global Business Excellence, 27*(6), 14 20.

Kossek, E., & Ozeki, C. (1998). Work-family conflict, policies, and the job-life satisfaction relationship, a review and directions for organizational behavior-human resource research. *Journal of Applied Psychology, 83,* 139–149. Retrieved from *Journal of Applied Psychology*.

Lambert, S. (2000). Added benefits, the link between work-life benefits and organizational citizenship behavior. *Academy of Management Journal, 43,* 801–815.

Lewis, S., Gambles, R., & Rapoport, R. (2007). The constraints of a work-life balance approach: An international perspective. *International Journal of Human Resource Management, 18*(3), 360–373.

Lobel, S., & Kossek, E. (1996). Human resource strategies to support diversity in work and personal lifestyles, beyond the family friendly organisation'. In E. Kossek & S. Lobel (Eds.), *Managing diversity, human resource strategies for transforming the workplace* (pp. 221–243). Cambridge, MA: Blackwell.

Lyness, K., & Judiesch, M. (2008). Can a manager have a life and a career? International and multisource perspective on work-life balance and career advancement potential. *Journal of Applied Psychology, 93*(4), 789.

Mary, Cynthia, & Black. (2007, January). Opting in versus opting out: Women using flexible work arrangements for career success. *CGO Insight*.

Meyer, J. P., Paunonen, S. V., Gellatly, I. R., Goffin, R. D., & Jackson, D. N. (1989). Organizational commitment and job performance: It's the nature of the commitment that counts. *Journal of Applied Psychology, 74*(1), 152–156. https://doi.org/10.1037/0021-9010.74.1.152.

Middleton, C. (2008). Do mobile technologies enable work-life balance? In D. Histop (Ed.), *Mobility and technology in the workplace*. Abingdon: Routledge.

Muna, F. A., & Mansour, N. (2009). Balancing work and personal life: The leader as acrobat. *Journal of Management Development, 28*(2), 121–133.

Nam, T. (2014). Technology use and work-life balance. *Applied Research Quality Life, 9,* 1017–1040. https://doi.org/10.1007/s11482-013-9283-1.

Nayar, V. (2013). *Handing the keys to gen Y*. Retrieved from *Harvard Business Review*: http://hbr.org/2013/05/handing/the-keys-to-gen-y/ar/1.

Ng, E. S., Schweitzer, L., & Lyons, S. (2010). New generation, great expectation: A field study of the millennial generation. *Journal of Business and Psychology, 25*(2), 281–292.

Nilekani, N. (2009). *India's demographic moment*. Retrieved from Strategy + Business, 56: https://www.strategy-business.com/article/09305/?pg=all.

Olson, M., & Primps, S. (1984). Working at home with computers: Work and non-work issues. *Journal of Social Issues, 40*(3), 97–112.

Osterman, P. (1995). Work/family programmes and the employment relationship. *Administrative Science Quarterly, 40,* 681–700.

Parusuraman, S., & Greenhaus, J. H. (2002). Towards reducing some critical gap in work-family research. *Human Resource Management Review, 12,* 299–312.

Perry-Smith, J., & Blum, T. (2000). Work-family human resource bundles and perceived organisational performance. *Academy of Management Journal, 43,* 1107–1117.

Pleck, J. (1997). The work-family role system. *Social Problems, 24,* 417–427.

Pocock, B., & Clarke, J. (2005). Time, money and job spill over: How parent's jobs affect young people. *Journal of Industrial Relations, 47*(1), 62–76.

Poelmans, S. A., Kalliath, T., & Brough, P. (2008). International expert commentary achieving work-life balance: Current theoretical and practical issues. *Journal of Management and Organisation, 14,* 227–238.

Poster, W. (2005). Three reasons for a transnational approach to work-life policy. In E. Kossek & S. Lambert (Eds.), *Work and life integration: Organisational, cultural, and individual perspectives* (pp. 375–400). London: Laurence Erlbaum Associates.

Prasad, G. (2006). *The great indian family: New roles, old responsibilities*. India: Penguin.

Putney, N. M., & Bengston, V. L. (2003). Intergenerational times. In J. Mortimer & M. Shanahan (Eds.), *Handbook of the life course* (pp. 647–660). New York: Kluwer Academic/Penum.

Rajadhyaksha, U., & Smita, S. (2004). Tracing a timeline for work and family research in India. *Economic and Political Weekly, 24*(2), 1674–1680.

Rajadhyaksha, U., Korabik, K., Lero, S. D., Jugec, L., Hammer, B., & Beham, B. (2020). Work family interface: Implications and recommendation for policy and practice. *Organizational Dynamics, 49,* 1–11. https://doi.org/10.1016/j.orgdyn.2019.01.001.

Ramu, G. (1989). Indian husband: Their role perceptions and performance in single and dual-earner households. *Journal of Marriage and Family, 49,* 903–915.

Ransome, P. (2007). Conceptualising boundaries between life and work. *International Journal of Human Resource Management, 18*(3), 374–386.

Sagie, A., & Aycan, Z. (2003). A cross-cultural analysis of participative decision-making in organizations. *Human Relations, 56*(4), 453–473. https://doi.org/10.1177/0018726703056004003.

Sands, J., & Harper, T. (2007). Family- friendly benefits and organisational performance. *Business Renaissance Quarterly, 2,* 107–126.

Sarkar, J., & Sarkar, S. (2012). *Corporate governance in India*. New Delhi: Sage.

Schulz, K. H., & Schulz, N. N. (2005). Work-life balance for dual career faculty couples. In *ASEE Annual conference & exposition: The changing landscape of engineering and technology education in a global world* (pp. 12–15). Portland, OR.

Sharma, T., Budhwar, P., & Verma, A. (2008). Performance management in India. In A. Verma, P. S. Budhwar, & D. Nisi (Eds.), *Performance management systems: A global perspective*. Oxon: Routledge.

Sheahan, P. (2005). Generation Y: Thriving and surviving with generation Y at work. *Prahran Hardie Grant Books*, 72–77.

Singh, A. K., & Awasthy, R. (2009). Work-life balance: Causes, consequences and interventions. *NHRD Network Journal, 7*(2), 59–67.

Singh, S. (2014). Measuring work-life balance in India. *International Journal of Advance Research in Computer Science and Management Studies, 2*(5).

Sinha Jai, B. (2004). *Multinationals in India: Managing the interface of cultures.* New Delhi: Sage.

Sturges, J. (2008). All in a day's Work? Career self-management and the management of the boundary between work and non-work. *Human Resource Management Journal, 18*(2), 118–134.

Sun, S. (2008). Housework and gender in nuclear versus extended Family households: Experiences of Taiwanese immigrants in Canada. *Journal of Comparative Family Studies, 39*(1), Intergenerational Relations: Evidence from East and West, 1–17.

Thacker, H. (2018). Work-life balance in India v/s the western countries. *The CSR Journal*. Retrieved from https://thecsrjournal.in/csr-work-life-balance-in-india-v-s-the-western-countries/.

Thiagarajan, K., & Deep, S. (1970). A study of supervisor-subordinate influence and satisfaction in four cultures. *Journal of Social Psychology, 82*(2), 173.

Thomas, L., & Ganster, D. (1995). Impact of family-supportive work variables on work-family conflict and strain: A control perspective. *Journal of Applied Psychology, 80,* 6–15.

Towers, I., Duxbury, L., Higgins, C., & Thomas, A. (2006). Time thieves and space invaders: Technology, work and the organisation. *Journal of Organizational Change Management, 19,* 593–618.

Townsend, K., & Batchelor, L. (2005). Managing mobile phones: A work/non-work collision in small business. *New Technology, Work and Employment, 20*(3), 259–267.

Vazquez, J. (2020, January 11). What is the state of paternity leave in India (2020). *Bel India.*

Venkata Ratnam, C., & Chandra, V. (2009). Work-life balance: Review of literature. *NHRD Network Journal., 7*(2), 89–97.

Voydanoff, P. (1987). *Work and family life.* Newbury Park, CA: Sage.

Walsh, J. (1999). Myths and counter-myth: An analysis of part-time female employees and their orientation to work and working hours. *Work, Employment & Society, 13*(2), 179–203.

Wang, P., Lawler, J., Shi. K, W. F., & Piao, M. (2008). Family-friendly employment practices: Importance and effects in India, Kenya, and China. *Advances in International Management, 21,* 235–265.

Warren, J., & Johnson, P. (1995). The impact of workplace support on work-family role strain. *Family Relations, 44*(2), 163–169.

Wharton, University of Pennsylvania. (2014, February 14). *India's new HR challenge: Managing a multigenerational workforce.* Retrieved February 7, 2015, from Wharton, University of Pennsylvania: http://knowledge.wharton.upenn.edu/article/indias-new-hr-challenge-managing-multigenerational-workforce/.

11

The Implicit and Explicit Influence on Work-Life Balance in Malaysia

Wee Chan Au

Introduction

Workers in Kuala Lumpur, the capital of Malaysia, have the worst work-life balance (WLB) (ranked 40 out of the 40 cities surveyed), with Helsinki, Munich, Singapore, Hong Kong and Tokyo ranked 1st, 2nd, 32nd, 35th and 39th, respectively (Tay, 2019). On average, people in Kuala Lumpur not only work 46 hours a week, with 22 per cent of people working for more than 48 hours per week, but also took the third lowest number of paid leave (12.3 days/year) (Wong, 2019). This made Kuala Lumpur the fourth most overworked city, behind Tokyo, Singapore and Washington. Accordingly, Malaysia is an interesting context to explore the implicit and explicit influencing factors that shape the Malaysian workers' WLB.

W. C. Au (✉)
School of Business, Monash University Malaysia, Bandar Sunway, Malaysia
e-mail: au.wee.chan@monash.edu

T. A. Adisa and G. Gbadamosi (eds.), *Work-Life Interface*,
https://doi.org/10.1007/978-3-030-66648-4_11

WLB refers to "issues relating to the integration of paid work and the rest of life" (Lewis, 2003, p. 343). As work and nonwork spheres are the two main aspects of a working adult's life, reconciliation between the two, in terms of WLB, is important to most if not all individuals. Although WLB is an individual experience, it reflects social, political, economic and organizational developments and concerns (Lewis, Gambles, & Rapoport, 2007). In other words, to fully understand an individual's experience of WLB, his or her broader environment should also be taken into account. Neglecting this aspect, as is common in many existing studies, omits a major influencing factor in WLB.

This chapter explores institutional factors at the national and organizational level shaping experience of WLB within Malaysia. WLB is a western-rooted concept and is largely unexplored in non-western settings. This makes the investigation of WLB in different contextual settings particularly important. Contextual influence in work-life practices has attracted considerable research interest in developed economies, especially European contexts (Hobson, 2011; Ollier-Malaterre, 2009; Poelmans et al., 2003). A few studies have been conducted in Asian settings, such as Hong Kong and Singapore (Lo, Stone, & Ng, 2003; Thein, Austen, Currie, & Lewin, 2010). However, little is known regarding the issue of WLB in Malaysia (e.g. Au & Ahmed, 2015, 2016)—a developing nation in Southeast Asia. Multi-level proponents highlight that there are limitations in conducting work-life research based on the assumption of homogeneity of legal and cultural characteristics in a particular region or sector (Poelmans & Sahibzada, 2004). Therefore, it is important to identify the specific attributes of Malaysia in terms of economy, culture, social and other contextual features that shape the distinctive work-life experience in Malaysia.

Literature Review

Multi-Level Contextual Framework of WLB

In work-life literature, there is an emerging recognition that an individual's broader context serves as an interactive backdrop influencing the reconciliation between work and nonwork domains (Lewis et al., 2007; Voydanoff, 2005). Most such studies focus on the influence of contextual features in the implementation and adoption of work-life practices (Bardoel & De Cieri, 2006; Lewis & Smithson, 2001; Ollier-Malaterre, 2009). In addition, a number of cross-national work-life studies identify the potential of contextual elements, culture in particular, in explaining the differences across nations (Hill, Yang, Hawkins, & Ferris, 2004; Lu et al., 2010; Spector et al., 2004).

Poelmans and Sahibzada (2004) proposed a multi-level framework that facilitates the systematic study of contextual features of WLB. This framework is aligned with the contextualist approach of HRM, which emphasizes the embeddedness of HR policies in a specific environment (Brewster, 1999). According to the multi-level framework, an individual's context is made up of macro-, meso- and micro-environments that determine an individual's WLB experience. Economic, social, technological, legal and the political system are typical macro-contextual features; meso-level variables consist of organizational culture, leadership style and human resource practices; and finally job autonomy, status, reputation, seniority and gender form the set of micro-level variables (Poelmans, 2003). A multi-level framework is important and useful in understanding the experience of WLB in a particular context. Researchers claim that a multi-level contextual approach is insightful for work-life research since it highlights the inter-linkages between social policies at the macro-level, corporate practices at the meso-level, and individual needs and expectations at the micro-level (Bardoel & De Cieri, 2006; Ollier-Malaterre, 2009). In other words, the multi-level approach is useful to study how public policies and cultural expectations frame employer practices and employees' experiences of managing work and nonwork roles (Klein & Kozlowski, 2000; Korabik, Lero, & Ayman, 2003).

Key to the multi-level approach is "the intrinsic coherence created and nurtured by interactions between the macro-, meso-, and micro-levels in each country" (Maurice, Sellier, & Silverstre, 1982 as cited in Ollier-Malaterre, 2009). According to Poelmans (2003), it is the accumulated misfits within and between different levels of context that brings about a dynamic environment which leads to conflict between work and nonwork roles. Therefore, in addition to analysing the various contextual elements in the respective context level, it is also important to study the interaction of contextual elements within each level, as well as the interaction between levels in shaping the experience of WLB in a particular country.

Sen's Capabilities Framework and WLB

In general, WLB refers to "issues relating to the integration of paid work and the rest of life" (Lewis, 2003, p. 343). WLB is deemed as a functioning (Sen, 1992), as it can affect one's health and well-being (Hobson, Fahlén, & Takács, 2011). Furthermore, it is a valuable functioning as it enhances capabilities and agency for attaining a better quality of life (Drobnič & Rodríguez, 2011; Hobson et al., 2011). The capabilities approach proposed by Sen (1999) provides a framework that captures multi-level processes that embed individual agency into specific institutional/normative settings. The key of relating capabilities approach to WLB is to assess people's capabilities to achieve functioning, namely a satisfactory balance between work and nonwork life. As an alternate to the multi-level framework (that consists of macro-, meso- and micro-level) proposed by Poelmans and Sahibzada (2004), a multi-layered conversion factors framework based on capabilities approach is proposed by Hobson et al. (2011). The conversion factors are categorized into (1) institutional factors (including both policy and firm level); (2) societal factors (such as societal and community norms); and (3) individual factors (such as network and partner's resources). Hobson et al. (2011) highlight that these resources may be converted into substantive freedoms to make choices and constraints that lead to work-life imbalance.

Using Sen's (1999) capability approach, a number of researchers have investigated the gap between availability of public policies and legislations that are WLB friendly and the agency of individuals to claim them within European contexts (i.e. the capabilities and agency freedom to actually use such arrangements) (den Dulk et al., 2011;

Hobson et al., 2011; Mrčela & Sadar, 2011). To assess a person's capability set in successfully attaining WLB, the broader environment and societal context have to be taken into account to understand which societal resources can be translated into agency and capability (Drobnič & Rodríguez, 2011). In specific, researchers suggest that reconciliation of paid work and nonwork commitment, especially parenthood, is embedded in multi-layered processes that involve individual, institutional and societal resources (Fagan & Walthery, 2011; Mrčela & Sadar, 2011). The evidence arising from these studies highlights that the capabilities framework of WLB is context specific.

A common feature of the multi-level contextual framework by Poelmans and Sahibzada (2004) and the multi-layered conversion factors by Hobson et al. (2011) is the emphasis on investigating the contextual influence of WLB in an integrated manner (den Dulk et al., 2011; Fagan & Walthery, 2011). Therefore, in addition to the specific influence of each contextual element, the interaction of contextual aspects within and between layers should also be taken into account in understanding the contextual influence on WLB.

Research Method

This chapter is based on an in-depth interview of 25 Malaysian working adults. The contextual contingencies of the study were also incorporated as part of the analysis. Semi-structured interviews, each lasted between 50 to 75 minutes, were conducted. All interviews were digitally recorded and transcribed verbatim. The interview guide was used flexibly to maintain consistency of the main agenda while allowing the researcher to probe the participants further with unscripted questions when new ideas emerged. The study employed a snowball sampling approach. The researcher first contacted participants from her personal network and invited them to participate. Individuals from her personal network were also asked to forward the email invitation within their own networks. All potential participants were provided with the study information sheet. Those who were interested in participating reached out to the author to schedule an interview. All interviews were held in-person.

Participants represented a variety of industries including education (20%), construction (24%), manufacturing (12%), engineering (16%) retail, etc., in the private and public sectors, and varying organizational levels, including non-supervisory (28%), professionals (48%), middle management (16%) and senior management (8%). Examples of positions held by participants include procurement manager, project executive, teacher, engineer, auditor and support staff. Fifteen participants (60%) were female, nineteen participants (76%) were married and the sample had an average age of 36 years, with an average of 2 children among the married participants.

Inductive thematic analysis was adopted to analyse the data. The inductive approach is a data-driven process (Braun & Clarke, 2006; Patton, 2002) in which the data coding is done "without trying to fit it into a pre-existing coding frame, or the researcher's analytic preconceptions" (Braun & Clarke 2006, p. 83). The analysis guide proposed by Braun and Clarke (2006) was followed closely. To become familiar with the interview data, the researcher read the full transcripts multiple times before starting the coding process. The researcher completed the coding procedure for the first transcript and then moved on to the next transcript. After coding the first three transcripts, the researcher started to search for themes based on all the codes. With the initial themes established, the researcher continued coding the rest of the transcripts. During the coding procedure, each code was assigned to a particular theme immediately. Existing themes were refined, and new themes were also developed as needed. This procedure of developing new themes, reviewing themes and naming themes continued until the last transcript was completely coded.

Presentation of the Findings

Multi-Level Contextual Analysis of WLB in Malaysia

In this section, contextual factors that frame the Malaysians' experience of reconciling work and nonwork life were described. Representative quotations from the interview transcripts were presented to support the findings. To ensure anonymity, all participants were given a pseudonym. The contextual contingencies were also incorporated as part of the analysis. To capture the macro (including economy, legislation and social) and meso (such as organizational practices and culture, supervisor) environmental aspects of the study, in the descriptions, (*macro*) and (*meso*) were added when referring to contextual contingencies.

WLB in Malaysia

Malaysia, a middle-income country, shifted from an agriculture and mining economy in the 1970s to an industrial economy in 1980s (*Macro-Economy*). As a developing country, the necessity to earn for survival remains high among most Malaysians, as their income levels are relatively low. With economic pressure for survival, the drive to work hard to ensure the sustainability of financial return and wealth accumulation outweighs the interest of WLB. In other words, Malaysians are willing to work excessively hard to earn more money, although doing so may jeopardize their WLB interest. Teoh and Rizal, single and married, respectively, shared similar sentiments:

> Honestly, at this moment, pay matters [more]. Because living expenses keep increasing. And I'm still young; this is the time to work harder and save more while I can, yup. (Teoh, Engineer)
>
> For now, it's a bit hard to achieve something like what we call – the WLB. In Malaysia, even working couples like us find it hard to go through the days, to survive. We have so many things to handle, house, transportation, and food. (Rizal, Draftsman)

The Group Interest (Economic Need of the Family) Is Emphasized

The urge to work for survival was also clearly featured among female participants. Married female participants shared that relying solely on their husband as breadwinner place the sustainability of household at high risk. According to Fatimah and Neelem, both are working as a teacher, are encouraged by their family members to continue working full-time. The bottom line is that their family commitments are well taken care of despite their employment:

> My husband will never let me stop working. He said if anything happens to him, how am I going to survive with my children? At least I'll have my own income and career. As long as I am able to balance my career and family, he doesn't mind. He wouldn't let me stop. (Fatimah, Teacher)
>
> My sister-in-law, my husband's brother's wife, she quits her job. My mother-in-law was not happy. Actually, she was very angry… I don't think she would be happy if I become a full-time mum… She wants her daughters-in-law to work and manage the family at the same time. (Neelem, Teacher)

Such a trend also partly attributed to the collectivist culture in Malaysia, where family welfare is given upmost importance (Triandis, 1995) (*Macro-Social*). Accordingly, being part of a strong collectivist society, Malaysians show a high level of tolerance and a greater willingness to deal with work-life imbalance given that the group interest (economic welfare of family) tends to outweigh individual interest (need for WLB).

Men's Obligation Towards Childcare Is Not Recognized in the Legislation

Looking at Malaysian policies and legislation closely, one notices the "one-sided" nature of this legislation. WLB is largely deemed to be a women's issue at the national level. Indeed, it was first brought onto the national platform as part of the agenda in The Women Summit (2008 and 2009), initiated by the Ministry of Women, Family and Community Development, Malaysia (*Macro-Policy*). Its intention was to boost women's participation in the labour force.

Compared to 60 days of mandatory maternity leave, Malaysian fathers' role and right in childbearing responsibility are not mandated formally (*Macro-Legislation*). Such a situation demonstrates that while the expectation of women's obligation in childcare is reflected liberally, Malaysian men's obligation for childcare continues to be neglected.

Malaysia's national policy and legislation, together with the deep-rooted traditional gender role, which places high social expectations on women for childcare and family responsibilities (*Macro-Social*), suggest that Malaysian women are expected to bear most, if not all, of the childcare and household responsibilities. As shown in the excerpt taken from Bathma, a highly educated woman, Malaysian women continue to be predominantly responsible for household matters despite being employed:

> They don't have [a] negative idea on me working, but they want me to still play the [domestic] roles... I cannot say I am earning and I can't ... the role is still there, the expectations are there, that sometimes might impose problems, it does... say you have to take care of your husband, to make sure his clothes are ready, his food is ready, the house is kept well, so he comes back, and he feels good. Well, not only your husband, you have your husband's side to come around, and you also need to keep them happy. I also have to teach the children, that responsibilities automatically come to me, my husband doesn't take those responsibilities... So, once you are married, women have more roles to play, as a daughter-in-law, as a mother, as a wife, as a housewife, as a housekeeper, it becomes more complicated. Men? They just earn money. (Bathma, Lecturer)

Traditional gender role expectations in Malaysian society remain a major obstacle in discouraging women from joining the formal workforce. In 2019, the labour force participation rate among Malaysian women was 56.1% (Department of Statistics Malaysia, 2019). According to the Statistics on Women Empowerment in Selected Domains, the labour force participation rate for Malaysian women (54.3%) was relatively low as compared to other countries: Malaysia stood lower than Singapore (66%), Thailand (70%), United Kingdom (71%) and Australia (71%) (Department of Statistics Malaysia, 2017) (*Macro-Economy*). In line with Malaysia's traditional gender role expectation, there is a high social expectation upon women in terms of childcare and family roles (*Macro-Social*). Given that childcare and domestic chore falls almost totally on women, married women who stay active in the workforce tend to experience great challenge in juggling work and family commitments. Even their male counterparts feel sympathetic towards the situation:

> Actually, I feel not quite fair for her (his wife). She has to work and has to take care of the family. But for me, easier, I just concentrate on work. But for her, work and the family, both together. (Wong, Quality assurance manager)
>
> In terms of children, spent time with them, helped them with studies... my wife did most of it... She works in the shop; she also has to do what mothers do, cooking and all that... Her resting time is very short because she has to work and cook. Usually, it's after 7 pm or 8 pm then she has her own space and time, doing her own stuff. (Tan, Businessman)

Materialistic Nature of Local Private Firms

Growth of the industrial economy does not only shape the employment pattern in Malaysia but also national policies and employment legislation. As a developing economy, Malaysia's national policy mainly focuses on how to maximize the productivity of its human capital to improve economic growth (*Macro-Policy*). Such national policy may further shape the materialistic practices among the employers (*Meso-Organisational Practices*). To strive for higher financial returns, employers tend to emphasize the cost and profits, which often undermines employees' WLB.

> When my children were young, one got sick, the other follows, oh goodness... I took leaves. They (supervisors) warned me, "you have to do something about it, either to get your husband to take care, or you get a maid". Of course, it is not fair to bring family [issues] to the company. Their mindset is "You come to here to work; you have to work. We pay you; you have to settle your family problem". This is normal; I think most companies are like this. (Lian, Project executive)
>
> If you talk about WLB, I don't think any company will take it seriously... Like when I was in XYZ (name of a local firm), they kept pushing the [factory] operators to work 12 hours [a day], sometimes 7 days continuously... That's not good, but no one aware that we need to do something about it. (Laila, Procurement manager)

Primacy of Paid Work Outweighs the Interest of WLB

The findings showed that Malaysian employees exhibit high tolerance of work-life imbalance, given their primary aim to provide income for survival. Accordingly, the potential of work overload is high in Malaysian work settings, which is detrimental to WLB significantly. The subservient and harmony seeking behaviour of Malaysian has important ramifications in the experience of WLB (Au & Ahmed, 2014) (*Macro-Social*). The prevalence of non-assertive behaviour provides considerable opportunity for employers to place higher demands on employees. The resulting increased work demand leads to overload and higher stress for employees in their efforts to integrate work and nonwork life. Long working hours, sometimes even up to 12 hours a day, was common among the participants. Hui and Mei, at their late 20s and late 30s, respectively, shared that overworked seems like a norm in their daily life:

> I spent more time at work than at home or for myself. I don't get enough personal time; I spend too much [time] on doing or finishing (work). It's kind of obvious, because like one week, [we are] supposed to work five days, and we (colleagues) see each other 6 days and is usually more than 8 hours a day.... (Hui, Assistant brand manager)
>
> I usually start around 8.45am and work till about 10 pm, every day, Monday to Friday, and certain weekends I work as well... if I could be home by 6 pm, that would be nice. Unfortunately, in my current career, I can't do so. (Mei, Marketing manager)

Likewise, Lian, who is a project executive in an engineering consultancy firm, shared the rigidity of higher management in allowing her time off to attend to family commitments. This is mainly owing to the heavy workload in the company. She accepted the pay-cut arrangement. However, many Malaysian workers, especially those from lower-income group, would have financial pressures to compromise with a pay cut for time off to attend family matters.

> Once, my mum was sick, I took a whole day leave, and he (the higher-level manager) wrote there [on the leave application form] "No, why didn't she come back? She can come back [for] half [a] day". So, they

> deducted my pay... I didn't argue, doesn't matter, that's the company policy. (Lian, Project executive)

Compounding this is that Malaysians do not use up their annual leave for vacation or other nonwork matters because they fear their boss would not be happy if they did. Wong, who works at the senior team of a factory, shared that although the senior team members are entitled to more paid annual leaves due to seniority, most of them only utilize less than half of their entitlement.

> Some of my colleagues, they have [paid] annual leave of about 40 days. Most of them would just spend less than 10 days, the balance of 30 days' annual leave, they will burn [it] off. They just spend as much time in the work environment. Because sometimes our management, they will judge which person is more hardworking, they will see... "ahhh, this person took quite many annual leaves." (Wong, Quality assurance manager)

Who Should Be Responsible for Workers' WLB?

Limited Legislation on WLB

Malaysia is weak in enacting legislation to protect employees' WLB. According to the Employment Act 1955, which is the primary encapsulation of employment legislature, employees are entitled to paid annual leave from 8 to 16 days, depending on the length of service within the organization (*Macro-Legislation*). In terms of maternity leave, working mothers in private sectors are entitled to sixty-day leave while their female counterparts at the public sector have additional thirty-days. Whereas working fathers in public sectors have three days of paternity leaves while those from the private sector does not have any mandatory provisions. In particular, participants stressed that most government-initiated policies are recommended but not enacted in the private sectors, which limited its effect on making a positive change on individuals' WLB.

> They [the government] may not be able to influence the private companies to follow. It's very difficult for them to do that… Like the recent [national] budget announcement, they are initiating something for the WLB, like flexi-hour in the government department, work-from-home for the government servants. They are encouraging the private companies to follow, but you know…. (Ravi, Group leader)

For example, in 2019, the Malaysian government has urged the private sector to match the maternity and paternity leaves with the public sector (Landau & Babulal, 2019; Lim, 2019) (*Macro-Legislation*). However, until such provisions are enacted, workers from the private sectors continue to struggle in juggling work and nonwork demands.

> Two months [paid maternity leave] is too short. I would like to still breastfeed my kid. When I started working, I can only breastfeed her at night. If I have three months, it is much better… I can monitor the day-care centre, to see if it is good or not. Now with two months, I had to send her there straight and keep worrying about her. Worrying if they take good care of my baby, whether they feed my baby or not (laugh). Thousands of questions in my head. (Aishah, Support staff)

Limited legal provisions that are favourable to employees' nonwork interest, together with the materialistic characteristics of some private organizations, bring about limited provisions from the organizations that support employees' WLB needs. To make the situation worse, participating in workers' union is not common in Malaysia. In 2017, only six per cent of the workers in Malaysia was union members (Hector, 2017; *Macro-Policy*). Hence, workers have restricted outlet to push for more legal provisions concerning their WLB and well-being.

> For [paid] annual leave, the government policy is only eight days or maybe 14 days… That's the minimum guideline. [If] companies wish to give more, it's up to them. And of course, they don't care, all they care is how to pay less tax every month, that's it… My ex-boss followed exactly what is stated in the rules and regulation. (Nazura, Secretary)
>
> The Labour Law said the minimum is eight days per year… To me, our Malaysian Labour Law is very weak. My company follows rigidly,

> just add [additional] two [days]. The work we do covers the whole Asia Pacific, and the workload is quite high. Ten days' annual leave is too low [little]… Our unions, the worker unions, are very weak. Well, they [the employer] don't encourage you to be in the union anyway. So, the rights of the workers are greatly oppressed. (Fadzli, Engineer)

Other than leave-related statutes, legislation over flexible work arrangements and childcare facilities that is directly relevant to WLB remains yet to be enacted in Malaysia. In 2019, the Malaysian government rolled out ten million Ringgit Malaysia (approximately 2.3 million in USD) to set up childcare facilities at the public sector's workplaces for the first time (Timbuong, 2019). The private sectors are encouraged to do the same (*Macro-Policy*). Despite the positive steps, the importance placed on WLB at the national and organizational level continues to remain low.

> WLB policies? There's not much, for career women in Malaysia, there is no [childcare] centre in our working place. We worry about our children… There is nothing like this with the current policy; we have been waiting for this for long. The recent [national] budget said they [the government] will try out in certain places, but only in a few places. (Wani, Teacher)

In all, WLB is not the key agenda at the national level despite government recognition of its importance. The Malaysian government has yet to implement any legal enforcement or policy to address citizens' WLB concerns specifically. Nevertheless, the Malaysian government has made gentle moves in urging and encouraging employers to adopt WLB initiatives.

WLB Provisions at Organizational Level

Building on the limited legal provisions at the macro-level, analysis at the meso-level (industry and organizational) was conducted to explore the lived experiences of Malaysians' WLB. The findings show that provisions available in the public sector are more favourable than the private sector. Other than additional provisions in terms of maternity and paternity leaves, civil servants in Malaysia also have more paid annual leaves (20 to 35 days), while those from the private sector only have eight to 16 days. These differences contribute to a varied experience of WLB among individuals from the public and private sectors.

The analysis also showed the individuals working in local firms and MNCs had varied WLB experiences. An increasing number of MNCs and joint ventures have set up their businesses in Malaysia, which has opened up alternate employment options. Some of the MNCs adopt home country's WLB practices and other organizational policies that are friendly to employees' nonwork commitment in their Malaysia operations (*Meso–Organisational practices*). Flexi-hours and work-from-home are the most commonly cited WLB-friendly practices by the participants from MNCs.

> If you come at 7 am, you can leave at 4.30 pm; and if you come at 9am then you leave at 6.30 pm. If you come [in] between that, you just adjust your time. Yup, that's the flexi hours... Everyone should be in between 9 am to 4.30 pm, it's just good enough time to do meeting, discussion. It's very flexible, even [if] you come in later, they don't mind as long as you finish your job... because this is a French company and they have this European mentality of not so calculative. (Rajesh, Engineer)
>
> My first company is an MNC; all the upper and middle management are from Europe. The Europeans, in general, have very strong [belief in] WLB. So, they sort of also incorporated that culture into the Malaysian environment... They have groomed me into this... As an employee, I would look for company that gives me this environment. (Sugu, Engineer)

In addition to the flexibility in terms of time and place to work in the MNCs, which is helpful for individuals' WLB, participants identify with the organizational culture in MNCs where individuals' nonwork interest is highly valued and respected. They have much less pressure to attend to work after working hours and during weekends.

> The culture in XYZ (name of the MNC), they are American [firm], they don't want you to work [on] Saturday, Sunday, which is good. And they

care about WLB. So, I can look after my family. (Laila, Procurement manager)

My company is a Belgian base, so they follow the European norms… They respect you if you don't answer your emails after office hours. I mean they appreciate if you do, but they won't judge you if you don't answer, respond to their emails… If I have a call from my colleague in Europe, and if I say I am on leave on that day, they'll immediately put down the phone. Ya, because they respect my off-work time. (Fadzli, Engineer)

Such positive and favourable experiences in MNCs are in contrast with the rigid and materialistic characteristics of some of the local firms. As shown in the quotes below, local firms were identified to be more calculative and inflexible, where employees' nonwork interests tend to give way to the force of higher financial return for the company. Individuals working in such firms face considerable challenges in dealing with WLB as compared to individuals working in MNCs.

They're very strict. [Latest] 8.30 am clock in, 5.30 pm earliest to clock out. So, you have to clock in and out, even for lunchtime. If you clock in late or you clock out early more than five times a month, warning letter. Warning letter, after that counselling, then they'll release you. I mean, if you repeat [the] offence then they'll release you. (Teoh, Engineer)

I've experienced working in three different companies. One is a Bumi (local indigenous) company, the other two are from overseas. I can see the difference…The first company, you have to be really punctual and there were lesser benefits. (Rizal, Draftsman)

However, some participants identify the invisible costs in WLB while working in MNCs, which should not be overlooked. To illustrate, working in MNCs means that one has to work together with American and European counterparts on a regular basis, which has eight to 12 hours' time difference with Malaysia. To suit the overseas counterparts' working schedule, one may be required to work at odd hours, which have a negative implication on their social and family life.

Most of my affiliates are from Europe. So, I need to work at nights sometimes, to attend [the] late meeting, the latest one that I have attended was till 12 am or 1 am... Because most of my teammates are from Europe, so I have to sacrifice. (Tham, System developer)

Starting this year, I have to keep constant contact with my European contacts, which is usually in the evening and at night. So that eats into a lot of my family time...The time difference is about seven to eight hours. So, at night, sometimes, I have to answer emails or calls from my colleagues from Europe, because they are working at that time. So, my WLB has actually deteriorated a lot...The family relationship, I mean sometimes when we go out for dinner, or somewhere else, I still have to answer emails. (Fadzli, Engineer)

Supervisors as the Key Determinant

Apart from organizational culture and norms, participants shared that their immediate supervisors are the key persons at the workplace that influence their WLB experience. Whether it is in MNCs or local firms, trust and close relationships with immediate supervisors have been identified as the key in making a difference in supporting their WLB needs. Given the rigidity in some of the local firms, informal arrangements with supervisors include swapping duties, flexibility in start and end time, unrecorded leave and other initiatives to help employees manage their WLB.

We don't really have [work-from-home], but some line managers trust some of their staff well enough, then those staffs have the privilege to work from home. (Sugu, Engineer)

I took leave, I tried to swap duties. But if they are very strict, then it's difficult... I sometimes negotiated with my supervisor, come in early, or go back late, informally, nothing formal. It was quite difficult because it's a fixed hour [work]. (Bathma, Lecturer)

The good thing here is, it's the discretion of the supervisor...My superior allows staff to take unrecorded leave. As long as the HR manager doesn't know about it...He gives me a lot of freedom. I'm in good relationship with my superior, he knows what I'm doing, my dedication etc. (Fadzli, Engineer)

Participants do not only show favourable attitude towards the MNCs workplace that tends to be WLB friendly, but they also identified Europeans to be the most WLB-friendly supervisor. Participants who are currently or had worked in MNCs before share the contrasting experiences with Asian supervisors (e.g. Malaysian, Japanese and Singaporean) and European supervisors. For example, Sugu who is an engineer stressed that Asian supervisors tend to embrace face time more.

> I function better if my immediate boss is a European, more specifically, a central European. I tend to have a lot of problems if my direct boss is an Asian (Laugh)... For the Asian, they themselves don't practice it, so when they don't practice it, they expect their staffs also not to practice it. In general, most of the European, especially Central European, they practice work-life [balance]. That's very important for them, that's how they have 35 hours per week, they'll disappear immediately after work. (Sugu, Engineer)

The expected paternalistic role of supervisors in collectivist society is not compatible with the materialistic characteristics of some local firms (Au & Ahmed, 2014) (*Macro-Social*). Even if the supervisors are sympathetic to the subordinates' nonwork commitments, they are powerless to change business practices. In other words, paternalism of middle-level managers loses out to singular money-making focus of leaders.

> In the middle management level, I have to report to my upper management. At the same time, I have to make sure my subordinates complete the tasks being assigned... I had been through that as well, so I understand what exactly the feeling... when they are under tremendous tight deadline to complete a task. Sometimes, I tried to explain to the upper management... But they will only give one advice, saying things like "this is very important for the company, so you must ensure that everybody delivers, ok?" With that, I have no choice but keep pushing my subordinates. (Hui, Assistant brand manager)

Low Sense of Entitlement of State and Employer WLB Provisions

Overall, the participants demonstrate a low sense of entitlement towards state and formal WLB provisions. Working within the developing country and emerging economy context, the participants show high tolerance and understanding towards the lack of provisions from the government and the employers. They understood that the priority of the government and the businesses is economic development.

> Of course, at the moment, whatever government policy is not enough... But I mean there are so many other things that they [the government] should focus on rather than focusing on this. (Ravi, Group leader)
>
> It's not really the government ['s obligation]...but there was good example [initiative], like abolishing of [working on] Saturday... So, we have extra time, that's quite good... [Paid annual] leaves as well... Of course, in terms of WLB, the more, the better. But from the economy point of view, I don't know how much more free time the company can afford to give their employees. (Sugu, Engineer)

While some participants expect the employers to play a more active role, most of them feel that it is the personal responsibilities of individuals to manage the incompatible demands between work and nonwork roles.

> No, I don't think [the] government could... I never considered [the] government to... Well, how could [the] government help? Because WLB is you, also depends on the organization that you are working. (Laila, Procurement manager)
>
> Eventually, it is [an] individual's responsibility. Boss too plays an important role. Not so much from the government. What can they give? If the boss doesn't understand, it'll make us woman very stressful, you know? (Wani, Teacher)

Family as the Main Source of Support

Among the married participants, as described earlier, traditional gender role still very much being practiced in most Malaysian households.

Women are expected to carry out family and childcare commitments, despite their full-time work commitment. The most common child-care/household chores shared by their husband are sending and picking up children to/from schools, childcare centre and parents/parents-in-law' house, before or after work.

Sixty per cent of the participants (n = 15) stay together with or close by with their parents or parents-in-law. Accordingly, they access to a generous amount of support from their family, including home-cook meals after work, less burden on house-chores and also aid in child-care for married participants. Relatives are their second-best option for childcare support when their immediate families are not available. This reflects the collective culture among Malaysian, where family welfare is given upmost importance (Triandis, 1995; *Macro-Social*).

> I'm staying with my parents; my mum is taking care of the kids. My husband's work is also about 1 hour ['s drive from home]. So, if any emergency, say my kids have [a] fever, my dad will bring them to [the] clinic and all… Even if we move out, my mum wants me to stay some-where near to them, so that I have time with them. (Laila, Procurement manager)
>
> My mother take care of them [the children], she will go and pick them up [from school] and take them to her house, feed them, their homework and all, take care of them basically. (Mei, Marketing manager)

For young parents moved from the rural area, their parents or parents-in-law move in with the family to take care of the grandchildren until they reach schooling-age is also not uncommon among Malaysian house-holds (*Macro-Social*). For young parents who do not have the access of such support, paid supports including domestic helper, day-care centre and kindergarten become the next best feasible alternative. It is esti-mated that there are approximately 300,000–400,000 migrant domestic helpers in Malaysia (ILO, 2018; *Macro-Social*). For a live-in domestic helper, one may expect to pay MYR900 to MYR1200 per month. Without family support, childcare responsibilities intensify the burden upon young parents both financially and mentally. Domestic helpers, whether in the form of full-time or part-time, play a huge role in reducing women's burden of household chores in Malaysia. Nine out of nineteen of married participants rely on paid support for their childcare responsibilities.

Discussion and Conclusion

Guided by the multi-level contextual framework by Poelmans and Sahibzada (2004) and the multi-layered conversion factors by Hobson et al. (2011), findings of the study are summarized in Fig. 11.1.

The legislation and practices relating to WLB in Malaysia (both at the national and organizational level) are at an infancy stage, as compared to developed economies. In addition to annual leave, public holidays and maternity leave, there is no other legislation or statute that covers the interest of WLB. The concepts of job sharing, work time flexibility, workplace flexibility (e.g. work-from-home) remain unfamiliar to most Malaysian employers.

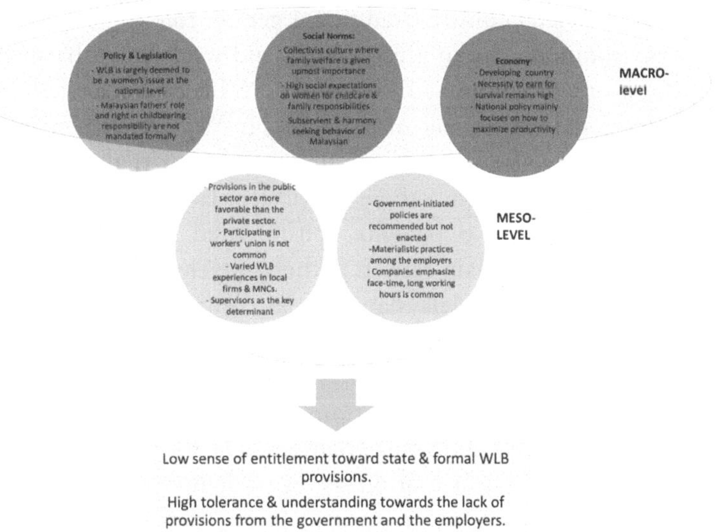

Fig. 11.1 Multi-level approach in understanding implicit and explicit influence on WLB in Malaysia

Given the strength and persistence of the traditional gender role assumption, the Malaysian government has adopted a cautionary position for taking the initiative to enact legislation enforcing businesses to account for work-life considerations. Here it is observed that societal norms strongly influence agency positions, even powerful ones such as government. In this case, strong social norms have allowed the Malaysian government to desist from introducing legislative change despite the emergence of conflict in women's WLB experience. The existence of deep-rooted traditional gender role has a major influence on the experience of WLB among Malaysians, especially women. On the one hand, the persistence of traditional gender role expectations of women is reflected within national policies; on the other hand, the government encourages Malaysian women to participate in the formal labour force. Such "clash" between two macro-environment features eventuates in difficulty for Malaysian women to attain WLB. This finding is in line with Joplin, Shaffer, Francesco, and Lau (2003) proposition, who in reference to Social Identity Theory (Burke, 1996; Thoits, 1991) notes that clashes between environmental changes (expectation to enter labour market) and societal culture (traditional gender role expectations) at the macro-environment lead to greater stress and work-life imbalance.

Furthermore, it is observed that lack of WLB practices at the organizational level and passive role of employers in WLB (meso-environment) is evidenced by the lack of policies and legislation at the national level (macro-environment). Since there are no legislated policies that enforce employers to offer WLB benefits, self-initiated WLB practices at the organizational level remain rare. It is therefore clear that lack of government legislation in the Malaysian context contributes to slow adoption of WLB facilities among Malaysian organizations. This is in line with past research which identifies the effectiveness of WLB practices depends not only on organizational conditions, but also legislative and cultural conditions of specific countries (Bardoel, De Cieri, & Santos, 2008; Lewis et al., 2007). This situation serves to demonstrate the interaction of contextual features between context layers (macro- and meso-levels) contributes to shaping Malaysians' experience of WLB.

A large number of Malaysian middle-class households depend on domestic help for household chores and childcare support. In addition to that, the collectivist nature of Malaysian society also facilitates support from immediate families. Domestic help and family members are observed to be the primary source of nonwork support. This situation suggests that Malaysia fits is a "conservative welfare regime" as classified by Esping-Andersen (1990, 1999), in which family is an essential provider of welfare, and there are very low provisions from state or employer. A strong male-breadwinner model which emphasizes traditional gender role ideology, where dependent care is presumed to be a woman's responsibility, is another key characteristic of a conservative welfare state (Esping-Andersen, 1990, 1999; Lewis & Smithson, 2001) which fits the Malaysian context. However, one should not assume that paid support and family members are the preferred source of support over employer and government support among Malaysians.

As stressed by one of the participants, "*[WLB friendly] policy? There's not much, for career women in Malaysia, there is no [childcare] centre in our working place. We worry about our children... There is nothing like this with the current policy; we have been waiting for this for long*". Given that there is a lack of supportive social policies and a near absence of support available from the organization, such "choice" seems to be the best choice out of no choice. This situation is similar to Fagan and Walthery (2011)'s findings that part-time arrangement may be a "choice" in liberal societies but a "constraint" in a context in which gender inequalities and low public provisions exist. In other words, Malaysians' reliance on domestic helpers and family members for nonwork responsibilities is confined within the limited freedom of an individual to choose between feasible alternative ways of doing things, i.e. constrained capability (Sen, 1999). Sociological Preference Theory postulates that women in modern liberal societies are able to choose between a family-oriented or career-oriented lifestyle (Hakim, 2000). Accordingly, it would suggest that Malaysia has not reached this stage but remains an entrenched conservative welfare state.

There is a growing gap between employees' increasing awareness of the importance of WLB and the availability of work-life support from employers and government in Malaysia. The constant mismatch between employers' attitude towards employees' WLB interest (meso-level) and employees' expectations (micro-level) reflects a misfit between context levels. Such misfit not only constrains individuals' capability to attain WLB, but also prompts individuals to look out for alternate employer that could meet their expectations. As one of the participants expressed "*Actually I was spoiled by my first company (chuckles). My first company is an MNC, all the upper and middle management are from Europe. The Europeans in general have very strong [belief in] work-life balance. So, they sort of also incorporated that culture into the Malaysian environment... They have groomed me into this... As an employee I would look for company that gives me this environment. If it doesn't, most likely I will leave (laugh). I have a very high expectation on this*". According to Poelmans (2003, p. 271), "when employees are aware of and start demanding family supportive policies, but companies are not aware of, refuse to implement, or are slow in implementing these policies, the experience of work–family conflict can be more severe".

In addition to the misfit between employees' growing expectation and employers' slow response, there is a gap in practices concerning employees' WLB between local firms and MNCs operating in Malaysia. MNCs often import WLB-friendly practices from their home country into Malaysian operations. Malaysian individuals working in MNCs generally enjoy more favourable conditions in dealing with work and nonwork demands. According to Poelmans (2003), perceived inequality between effort and reward leads to negative emotion and intensive conflict between work and family. This is in accordance to Equity theory (Greenberg, 1990) whereby inequality exists if an individual is aware that another person working in a different firm but in similar work and the same sector receives more rewards (wages plus work-life support) for the same effort. It is thus no surprise to observe that Malaysian employees perceive MNCs much more favourably than local companies when selecting an employer, especially if WLB is a priority for the individual.

Theoretical and Practical Implications

The capabilities framework (Sen, 1999) which has been used extensively in developed nations to determine the capability and agency freedom of individuals in utilizing wide availability of WLB practices helped to show that even when capability exists in the Malaysia setting, individuals lack freedom to take advantage of it, i.e. they are strongly constrained. The study also highlights the relevance and usefulness of the multi-level framework (Poelmans & Sahibzada, 2004) as a descriptive lens for the study of WLB of a particular society needs to be complemented with analytic frameworks such as the multi-layer conversion framework (Hobson et al., 2011) as a way to fully capture the unique unfolding of WLB experience in Malaysia. The importance of systems-level thinking (Carlson & Grzywacz, 2008; Lewis & den Dulk, 2010), which emphasizes the interaction between mutual and dynamic influences of multiple social systems, is supported in this study. In adopting an integrated multiple lenses to draw a rounded and fine-grained picture of the multiple social systems involved in WLB, this chapter serves as a starting point for an empirical study of the work-life reconciliation phenomena in Malaysia, and other developing neighbour countries, such as Indonesia and Thailand.

For policy implications, the findings of this study suggest that to facilitate Malaysian workforce's WLB, the Malaysian government may look beyond recommendations, to mandate certain legislation (e.g. mandated paternity leaves) and impose tax incentives to push employers to initiate more WLB-friendly provisions. Most importantly, the monitoring mechanism should be in place to ensure effective execution of the legislation and tax incentives. For practical implications, the findings suggest that Malaysian employers need to take active action in acknowledging and trying to address the issue of WLB. Without this, local enterprises will remain at a highly disadvantaged position in attracting and retaining talented human resources as compared to MNCs, who not only recognize but also offer a variety of WLB supports to their employees. Malaysian employers should take note of the long-term impact of employees' work-life (im)balance on their organization since there is considerable evidence that stress in WLB incurs significant additional costs for the business in terms of absenteeism, turnover, recruitment costs and lost productivity (Joplin et al., 2003). On the other hand, healthy and committed employees bring about significant positive gains in terms of organizational performance and competitiveness (Brough, Holt, Bauld, Biggs, & Ryan, 2008; Nishii, Lepak, & Schneider, 2008).

References

Au, W. C., & Ahmed, P. K. (2014). Sustainable people management through work-life balance: A study of the Malaysian Chinese context. *Asia-Pacific Journal of Business Administration, 6*(3), 262–280. https://doi.org/10.1108/APJBA-02-2014-0024.

Au, W. C., & Ahmed, P. K. (2015). Exploring the effects of workplace support on work-life experience: A study of Malaysia. *Human Resource Development International, 18*(4), 346–365. https://doi.org/10.1080/13678868.2015.1019816.

Au, W. C., & Ahmed, P. K. (2016). Relationships between superior support, work role stressors and work-life experience. *Personnel Review, 45*(4), 782–803. https://doi.org/10.1108/PR-08-2014-0175.

Bardoel, E. A., & De Cieri, H. (2006). Developing a work/life strategy in a multinational enterprise (MNE). In *Sloan work and family encyclopaedia.* http://wfnetwork.bc.edu/encyclopedia_entry.php?id=3814&area=All.

Bardoel, E. A., de Cieri, H., & Santos, C. (2008). A review of work-life research in Australia and New Zealand. *Asia Pacific Journal of Human Resources, 46*(3), 316–333. https://doi.org/10.1177/1038411108095762.

Braun, V., & Clarke, V. (2006). Using thematic analysis in psychology. *Qualitative Research in Psychology, 3*(2), 77–101. https://doi.org/10.1191/1478088706qp063oa.

Brewster, C. (1999). Different paradigms in strategic HRM: Questions raised by comparative research. In P. Wright, L. Dyer, J. Boudreau, & G. Milkovich (Eds.), *Research in personnel and HRM* (pp. 213–238). Greenwich, CT: JAI Press.

Brough, P., Holt, J., Bauld, R., Biggs, A., & Ryan, C. (2008). The ability of work-life balance policies to influence key social/organisational issues. *Asia Pacific Journal of Human Resources, 46*(3), 261–274. https://doi.org/10.1177/1038411108095758.

Burke. (1996). Social identities and psychosocial stress. In H. B. Kaplan (Ed.), *Psychosocial stress: Perspectives on structure, theory, life-course* (pp. 141–174). New York: Elsevier Science & Technology.
Carlson, D. S., & Grzywacz, J. G. (2008). Reflections and future directions on measurement in work-family research. In K. Korabik, D. S. Lero, & D. L. Whitehead (Eds.), *Handbook of work-family integration* (pp. 57–73). New York: Academic Press. http://www.sciencedirect.com/science/article/pii/B978012372574550007 7.
den Dulk, L., Peper, B., Sadar, N. Č., Lewis, S., Smithson, J., & van Doorne-Huiskes, A. (2011). Work, family, and managerial attitudes and practices in the European workplace: Comparing Dutch, British, and Slovenian financial sector managers. *Social Politics: International Studies in Gender, State and Society, 18*(2), 300–329.
Department of Statistics Malaysia. (2017). *Statistics on women empowerment in selected domains, Malaysia*. https://www.dosm.gov.my/v1/index.php?r=column/pdfPrev&id=dHNTVHV0My9QK1MxNHBtSnRucVJqZz09.
Department of Statistics Malaysia. (2019). *Principal statistics of labor force, Malaysia, fourth quater (Q4)*. https://www.dosm.gov.my/v1/index.php?r=column/cthemeByCat&cat=149&bul_id=Z1VDRGt3ZFluOVZLWjF3UnJaNHdPQT09&menu_id=U3VPMldoYUxzVzFaYmNkWXZteGduZz09.
Drobnič, S., & Rodríguez, A. M. G. (2011). Tensions between work and home: Job quality and working conditions in the institutional contexts of Germany and Spain. *Social Politics: International Studies in Gender, State and Society, 18*(2), 232–268.
Esping-Andersen, G. (1990). *The three worlds of welfare capitalism*. Cambridge: Polity Press.
Esping-Andersen, G. (1999). *Social foundations of postindustrial economies*. Oxford: Oxford University Press.
Fagan, C., & Walthery, P. (2011). Individual working-time adjustments between full-time and part-time working in European firms. *Social Politics: International Studies in Gender, State and Society, 18*(2), 269–299.
Greenberg, J. (1990). Organizational justice: Yesterday, today, and tomorrow. *Journal of Management, 16*(2), 399–432. https://doi.org/10.1177/014920639001600208.
Hakim, C. (2000). *Work-life style choices in the 21st century: Preference theory*. Oxford: Oxford University Press.
Hector, C. (2017, October 11). History of the labour movement in Malaysia. *Aliran*. https://aliran.com/aliran-csi/aliran-csi-2017/history-labour-movement-malaysia/.

Hill, E. J., Yang, C., Hawkins, A. J., & Ferris, M. (2004). A cross-cultural test of the work-family interface in 48 countries. *Journal of Marriage and Family, 66*(5), 1300–1316.

Hobson, B. (2011). The agency gap in work-life balance: Applying Sen's capabilities framework within European contexts. *Social Politics: International Studies in Gender, State and Society, 18*(2), 147–167.

Hobson, B., Fahlén, S., & Takács, J. (2011). Agency and capabilities to achieve a work-life balance: A comparison of Sweden and Hungary. *Social Politics: International Studies in Gender, State and Society, 18*(2), 169–198.

ILO. (2018). *TRIANGLE in ASEAN quarterly briefing note: Malaysia.* ILO. https://www.ilo.org/wcmsp5/groups/public/—asia/—ro-bangkok/documents/genericdocument/wcms_614381.pdf.

Joplin, J. R. W., Shaffer, M. A., Francesco, A. M., & Lau, T. (2003). The macro-environment and work-family conflict: Development of a cross cultural comparative framework. *International Journal of Cross Cultural Management, 3*(3), 305–328. https://doi.org/10.1177/1470595803003003004.

Klein, K. J., & Kozlowski, S. W. J. (2000). From micro to meso: Critical steps in conceptualizing and conducting multilevel research. *Organizational Research Methods, 3*(3), 211–236. https://doi.org/10.1177/109442810033001.

Korabik, K., Lero, D. S., & Ayman, R. (2003). A multi-level approach to cross cultural work-family research: A micro and macro perspective. *International Journal of Cross Cultural Management, 3*(3), 289–303. https://doi.org/10.1177/1470595803003003003.

Landau, E., & Babulal, V. (2019, November 13). *7 days paternity leave proposal to cabinet soon.* NST Online. https://www.nst.com.my/news/nation/2019/11/538281/7-days-paternity-leave-proposal-cabinet-soon.

Lewis, S. (2003). The integration of paid work and the rest of life. Is post-industrial work the new leisure? *Leisure Studies, 22*(4), 343–345. https://doi.org/10.1080/02614360310001594131.

Lewis, S., & den Dulk, L. (2010). Parents' experiences of flexible work arrangements in changing European workplaces. In K. Christensen, & B. Schneider (Eds.), *Workplace flexibility. Realigning 20th century jobs for a 21st century workforce*. Ithaca, NY: Cornell University Press.

Lewis, S., Gambles, R., & Rapoport, R. (2007). The constraints of a 'work–life balance' approach: An international perspective. *The International Journal of Human Resource Management, 18*(3), 360–373. https://doi.org/10.1080/09585190601165577.

Lewis, S., & Smithson, J. (2001). Sense of entitlement to support for the reconciliation of employment and family life. *Human Relations, 54*(11), 1455–1481. https://doi.org/10.1177/0018726701541 1003.

Lim, I. (2019, October 6). Ministry moots raising maternity leave to 98 days, introducing three-day paternity leave | Malay Mail. *The Malay Mail*. https://www.malaymail.com/news/malaysia/2019/10/06/ministry-moots-raising-maternity-leave-to-98-days-introducing-three-day-pat/1797622.

Lo, S., Stone, R., & Ng, C. W. (2003). Work-family conflict and coping strategies adopted by female married professionals in Hong Kong. *Women in Management Review, 18*(3/4), 182.

Lu, L., Cooper, C. L., Kao, S. F., Chang, T.-T., Allen, T. D., Lapierre, L. M., et al. (2010). Cross-cultural differences on work-to-family conflict and role satisfaction: A Taiwanese-British comparison. *Human Resource Management, 49*(1), 67–85. https://doi.org/10.1002/hrm.20334.

Mrčela, A. K., & Sadar, N. Č. (2011). Social policies related to parenthood and capabilities of Slovenian parents. *Social Politics: International Studies in Gender, State and Society, 18*(2), 199–231.

Nishii, L. H., Lepak, D. P., & Schneider, B. (2008). Employee attributions of the "why" of HR practices: Their effects on employee attitudes and behaviors, and customer satisfaction. *Personnel Psychology, 61*(3), 503–545. https://doi.org/10.1111/j.1744-6570.2008.00121.x.

Ollier-Malaterre, A. (2009). Organizational work–life initiatives: Context matters. *Community, Work & Family, 12*(2), 159–178. https://doi.org/10.1080/13668800902778942.

Patton, M. Q. (2002). Qualitative research & evaluation methods (3rd ed.). Thousand Oaks, CA: Sage.

Poelmans, S. (2003). The multi-level 'fit' model of work and family. *International Journal of Cross Cultural Management, 3*(3), 267–274. https://doi.org/10.1177/1470595803003003001.

Poelmans, S., & Sahibzada, K. (2004). A multi-level model for studying the context and impact of work–family policies and culture in organizations. *Human Resource Management Review, 14*(4), 409–431. https://doi.org/10.1016/j.hrmr.2004.10.003.

Poelmans, S., Spector, P. E., Cooper, C. L., Allen, T. D., O'Driscoll, M., & Sanchez, J. I. (2003). A cross-national comparative study of work/family demands and resources. *International Journal of Cross Cultural Management, 3*(3), 275–288. https://doi.org/10.1177/1470595803003003002.

Sen, A. (1992). *Inequality re-examined*. Oxford: Oxford University Press.

Sen, A. (1999). *Development as freedom*. Oxford: Oxford University Press.

Spector, P. E., Cooper, C. L., Poelmans, S., Allen, T. D., O'driscoll, M., Sanchez, J. I., Siu, O. L., Dewe, P., Hart, P., & Lu, L. (2004). A cross-national comparative study of work-family stressors, working hours, and well-being: China and Latin America vs. the Anglo world. *Personnel Psychology, 57*(1), 119–142. https://doi.org/10.1111/j.1744-6570.2004.tb02486.x.

Tay, R. (2019, August 8). Workers in Kuala Lumpur have the worst work-life balance in the world, and they're also one of the most overworked. *Business Insider Malaysia*. https://www.businessinsider.my/workers-in-kuala-lumpur-have-the-worst-work-life-balance-in-the-world-and-theyre-also-one-of-the-most-overworked.

Thein, H. H., Austen, S., Currie, J., & Lewin, E. (2010). The impact of cultural context on the perception of work/ family balance by professional women in Singapore and Hong Kong. *International Journal of Cross Cultural Management, 10*(3), 303–320. https://doi.org/10.1177/1470595810384585.

Thoits, P. A. (1991). On merging identity theory and stress research. *Social Psychology Quarterly, 54*(2), 101–112. https://doi.org/10.2307/2786929.

Timbuong, J. (2019, July 12). Childcare centres at workplace a good thing. *The Star Online*. https://www.thestar.com.my/news/nation/2019/07/12/childcare-centres-at-workplace-a-good-thing.

Triandis, H. C. (1995). *Individualism & collectivism*. Boulder, CO: Westview.

Voydanoff, P. (2005). Toward a conceptualization of perceived work-family fit and balance: A demands and resources approach. *Journal of Marriage and Family, 67*(4), 822–836.

Wong, L. Z. (2019, August 7). KL lowest among 40 cities in terms of work-life balance. *The Star Online*. https://www.thestar.com.my/lifestyle/living/2019/08/07/kl-ranks-lowest-among-40-cities-in-terms-of-work-life-balance/.

12

Pakistani Women and Traditional Values: The Role of Culture in Work-Life Balance

Ibrahim Noorani and Khurram Shakir

Introduction

Culture incorporates a variety of frameworks and social activities, ranging from education to economics, politics to creative arts, ethnic and racial mannerisms to religious ideologies, domestic lifestyles to travel and tourism, and technologies to artisanship and accommodates diversification. Mogherini (2016) defines culture as a social setting where individuals celebrate their differences as a collective unit and integrate societal behaviours and value systems existing in human communities. Culture emerges from human interactions, which Herskovits (1995) refers to as a man-made creation. The Pakistani culture comprises a variety of values and beliefs that are peculiar within and across diverse regions within the country (Abbas et al., 2019). Such cultural proclivities have both positive and negative impacts on the achievement of work-life balance (WLB), particularly among Pakistani women.

I. Noorani (✉) · K. Shakir
Benazir Bhutto Shaheed University, Karachi, Pakistan

T. A. Adisa and G. Gbadamosi (eds.), *Work-Life Interface*,
https://doi.org/10.1007/978-3-030-66648-4_12

Pakistan is located in the southern region of Asia, with a population of over 220 million people (fifth largest in the world) across six major ethnic groups (Central Intelligence World Factbook, 2019). Governed by a federal parliamentary republican government, the Pakistan economy thrives with a gross domestic product (GDP) of 1.061 USD as of 2017, with about 64 million people comprising its labour force (Central Intelligence World Factbook, 2019). The females constitute 49 per cent of the country's population, and the estimated female unemployment rate is 6.8 per cent as of 2018 (Pakistan Bureau of Statistics, 2020).

Islam is the dominant religion in Pakistan and contributes fairly towards its cultural formations. However, being part of the Indian subcontinent, the country still owes many of its cultural traditions to Hinduism and thus integrates a blend of both religions. Furthermore, the broader perspective of Pakistani culture cannot be divorced from its provincial history, caste, creed, tradition, hierarchical structures and tribal associations. Pakistan belongs to the geographical region which Caldwell (1982) describes as 'Patriarchal Belt' in which women generally have limited access to life's resources compared to men. In the Pakistani society, the decisions regarding economic well-being, education facilities, healthcare options, skill development and participation in politics and work settings primarily rest with men. Moghadam (1993), describes this kind of culture as, 'a culture against women'. Against this backdrop, this study examines the WLB of working women in Pakistan in the face of the Pakistani patriarchal regime. Further, we explore the family system and the nature of womanhood in Pakistan. After that, a review of the literature on the WLB of women in Pakistan was highlighted. The research methodology and findings were presented and followed by the discussion and conclusion.

Culture in WLB: An Overview

The role of culture in achieving WLB cannot be overemphasized, given that cultural values are different across societies (Ollier-Malaterre & Foucreault, 2017). Culture is based on implicit values and assumptions that guide people's behaviour (Hodgetts, 2005). Kassinis and Stavrou

(2013) argue that culture is an instrumental factor in an individual's work and life engagement because it shapes the mode of interaction between the two fundamental domains of human life. Although culture has been defined in several contexts, however, there is no precise definition of the concept (Glovan et al., 2010). Nevertheless, in his popular literature, Hofstede (1980) defines culture as the values, assumptions and individuals' shared beliefs based on common historical experiences. Ollier-Malaterre and Foucreault (2017) further explored Hofstede's cultural definition and the role of structural impacts (legal, economic and social institutions) as a primary predictor of several outcomes in the work-life interface.

Over the years, Hofstede's cultural dimensions have remained a blueprint for exploring the concept of culture in diverse perspectives. As such, in the WLB academia, researchers have revised the cultural framework within the work and life hemisphere to include components such as individualism and collectivism (Spector et al., 2004), institutional and humane orientation (Beham et al., 2014), gender egalitarianism (Allen, French, Dumani, & Shockley, 2015), masculinity and femininity (Joplin, Shaffer, Francesco, & Lau, 2003), power distance (Lu et al., 2010), horizontal and vertical (Mortazavi, Pedhiwala, Shafiro, & Hammer, 2009), uncertainty avoidance (Lucia-Casademunt, García-Cabrera, & Cuéllar-Molina, 2015), and survival and self-expression (Snir & Harpaz, 2009). Extrapolating from some of these dimensions, this chapter focuses on the national context of culture to explore its roles in shaping the work and life spheres of women in Pakistan.

Family System in the Pakistani Culture

The Pakistani culture evinces family as a crucial and functional component of the society based on collective and not individualistic behavioural patterns (Chattoo, Atkin, & McNeish, 2004). The collectivistic pattern arises mainly because 63% of the population still reside in the rural areas of the country, where tribal and feudal systems take precedence over all activities of life (National Institute of Population Studies—NIPS, 2019). A traditional Pakistani family is consanguineous and lives together in a joint family set-up, and each member contributes their quota to the overall socio-economic well-being within their family roles (Hussain, 1999). The Pakistani culture mirrors a patriarchal hegemonic system arising from the dominance of the male gender (grandfather, father, elder brother or husband) over the females within the family and the wider society (Chattoo et al., 2004). Like in many other less egalitarian communities, the Pakistani culture situates autonomous power in the hands of the dominant males (mostly, heads of the family) to make decisions regarding distribution of resource among the family (Nauman, 2015).

Prevailing family types consist of nuclear and semi-nuclear in the urban areas, while joint and extended families are existent in the rural areas of Pakistan (Chattoo et al., 2004). Nonetheless, joint and extended families also exist in the metropolitan cities, in which larger families consisting of several generations cohabit together (Chattoo et al., 2004). Sathar and Kazi (2000) claim that women in the urban areas of the country have relatively higher levels of freedom compared to their counterparts in rural areas. Besides, their studies found that women in nuclear and semi-nuclear family structures are more involved in the decision-making process and have comparatively better access to education, health care and work opportunities. However, women in rural areas, particularly those that are surrounded by larger groups of people are subject to increasing levels of control by the males in the family and have less autonomy and control over life's resources (Sathar & Kazi, 2000).

ul Haq, Akram, Ashiq, and Raza (2019) submit that the sexist ideology prevalent in Pakistan exposes a majority of the women to exploitations and remains a common phenomenon in most parts of the country. According to Hussain (2011), the patriarchal mindset regarding the division of work compels women to be solely responsible for the household work, while the responsibilities of the men are focused mainly on the external affairs (political and economic activities). Consequently, women have limited access to resources and are subjected to discrimination, physical and mental abuse and restricted movement in the public sphere (ul Haq et al., 2019). Nevertheless, women are expected to exercise exceptional time-management skills and undertake additional duties at home after work also referred to as 'a second shift', and as a result, they become less motivated to be engaged in the external societal affairs like their male counterparts (Cohen, 2002). Moreover, female members of the family and younger men as well define themselves by the value system created by the male family heads, and such system influences the living patterns within the family and the society at large (Nauman, 2015).

Womanhood in Pakistan

In many societies with a less egalitarian system, women societies are regarded as weak and vulnerable under the autonomous control of the males in the society (McGinn & Oh, 2017). In such cultural setting, women are regarded as primary caregivers and carriers of the family honour, and as a result, they are considered valuable, which compels men to act as a primary guardian of their vulnerabilities (Chattoo et al., 2004). Hence, only women that adhere to these cultural norms are considered respectable in the society. Hussain (2009) reports this phenomenon to have escalated even further in urban societies. As Pakistan progresses towards modernization, women dignification is evidently increasing due to their association (particularly in marriage) with the men and career progression, which enables them to earn a better livelihood (Nauman, 2015).

Tabassum (2016) foregrounds that the Baradari (or patrilineage), caste and tribal structures are predominant among Pakistani family organizations. Social, political and economic alliances are all interlinked within the Baradari system. This plays a vital role in shaping societal values, norms and beliefs (Tabassum, 2016). The prevailing hegemonic system makes distinct the division of work between males and females in the family. According to Qadir and Afzal (2019), within the patriarchal system, men are considered as the breadwinners and active participants within the political and economic domains of the society, while women are primarily confined to look after the family affairs as their core responsibilities including cleaning, cooking, child-rearing, stitching, forming strong familial relations by organizing family events and also helping out in some aspects of farming. Since women are unpaid workers, having comparatively less contribution to economic maintenance, they are considered insignificant to the decision-making process (Akhter & Akbar, 2016). Thus, women are left disadvantaged in the labour market.

Furthermore, Sayeed and Ansari (2019) aver that the required practice for most women in Pakistan to cover themselves with veils outside of their homes (including at work) contributes to their desires to remain housewives or domestic workers. This has been argued to cause further gender segregation in the society. Similarly, Shaikh, Shah, Katpar, and Shah (2019) attribute the segregation of women from men as a norm in Islam, which is predominant in Pakistan. The religious practice requires that females dress modestly following strict Islamic instructions—thus separating them from strangers and unrelated menfolk (Sayeed & Ansari, 2019). Although these practices are considered to preserve the female heritage, however, men in this society have overturned the practices as a means of restricting women activities outside of the homes (Zia, 2009).

Women and Work-Life Balance in Pakistan

The influx of women into the workforce became apparent in 1987 during the first government of Prime Minister Benazir Bhutto. Since then, over a span of three decades, women have formed almost 24 per cent of the total labour force in Pakistan (Amir, Kotikula, Pande, Bossavie, & Khadka, 2018). However, the present government led by Prime Minister Imran Khan claims to be taking measures to improve and modernize the country as a means of facilitating economic welfare and encouraging higher levels of female participation in the labour market (Sayeed & Ansari, 2019). The China–Pakistan Economic Corridor (CPEC) also motivates women to participate in the labour force to earn a living (Mukhtar & Ummar, 2016). Similarly, Saad et al. (2019) argued that the CPEC programme was initiated to enhance women participation in the labour force as well as alleviating the issues regarding work-life imbalance among them.

Women WLB remains a subject of interest as the increasing number of women participation in the labour force over the years has stimulated several debates regarding workforce planning (Duong, Hussain, & Subramaniam, 2020). This breeds issues of juggling work and family responsibilities simultaneously. The expectations of working women to assume dual responsibilities in the Eastern culture pose severe threats to their physical and mental well-being (Abbas et al., 2019). Shaikh et al. (2019) report that the number of Pakistani women in the workforce has increased phenomenally in recent years. In contrast, Sayeed and Ansari (2019) claim that such increases remain statistically insignificant, given that the Pakistani women remain the lowest in labour force participation in the region. Nevertheless, the female workforce comprises working mothers, single parents and unmarried women working in both public and private organizations. Multi-nationals, service industries, academics and government services are areas where women majorly work (Shaikh et al., 2019). This thus puts working women, especially mothers, under tremendous pressure to maintain role-balancing.

Akhter and Akbar (2016), in their study on working women in Punjab, reported that the majority of the working women were satisfied with the government's efforts towards women empowerment and improvement in their quality of life. In recent years, Pakistani women have benefited from compensations for their historical deprivation in the whole power structures (Abbas et al., 2019). They are provided jobs and political quotas, better education opportunities, property rights, healthcare facilities, equal employment opportunities and prospects for a positive self-image within their respective societies (Abbas et al., 2019). Generally, Pakistanis love female child and are often elated at their birth (Akhter & Akbar, 2016). Families ensure that their female children are well supported so that they excel in life. However, the scenario for many working women changes after marriage. Married women are consistently reminded of their initial responsibility as the primary care provider in the family and are discouraged to work outside of their homes after marriage (Khursheed, Mustafa, Arshad, & Gill, 2019).

Umer and Zia-ur-Rehman (2013) reinforced the presence of patriarchy within the Pakistani household and its adverse effect on women WLB. They argued that the involvement of Pakistani women in multiple roles often results in negative spillover from home to work and vice versa. Aside from engaging fully in domestic duties, working Pakistani women (mostly in the urban areas) also contribute financially to their households (Arif et al., 2017). However, juggling both roles simultaneously is a huge problem for them and often create imbalance and conflicts between their work and nonwork lives. This, according to Frone et al. (1996) negatively affects the well-being of women and results in poor health, mental stress, demotivation, reduced satisfaction, emotional exhaustion and increased anxiety and depression. Although both men and women face these consequences, women are generally more disadvantaged (Umer & Zia-ur-Rehman, 2013).

Malik (2011), in his study of working women in Baluchistan, found that socially weaker groups, particularly women, are employed within the hospitality sector primarily for reasons that they are unable to oppose tasks assigned to them. Women have considerably less knowledge of the local surroundings and are often victims of abuse by customers and co-workers, as they are deemed to be vulnerable, which often expose them to the dangers of continuous stress and mental illness (Abbas et al., 2019). Hisrich and Brush (1988) and Umer and Zia-ur-Rehman (2013) have consistently found that in South Asia, the decision to work outside of the home for married women is exclusively their husbands. Duong et al. (2020) aver that working women prefer to operate their businesses from home because they like to be in charge of their work and family lives. The Pakistani culture expects women to fully fulfil their primary responsibility of homemaker before thinking of engaging in paid employment (Abbas et al., 2019). This, therefore, makes achieving WLB difficult for women in Pakistan (Tabassum, 2016).

Similarly, women find it challenging to adjust to the patterns of work compared to their male counterparts. This is because they are subsumed into their multiple roles depriving them the time and space to learn new ways of coping with the enormous responsibilities (Duong et al., 2020). Contrastingly, Arif et al. (2017) argue that the requirements within the job roles of the female workforce compel women to dedicate more hours to their workplaces to the detriment of their familial roles; however, they sacrifice their weekends and holidays to reconcile the deficiencies in their home duties. Nevertheless, the main opposition for married working women does not necessarily emanate from their husbands, but rather the pressures from the non-working women within the household. This corroborates with the studies of Cartwright (1978) and Keith and Schafer (1980), which argue that women cohabiting in a large-sized family have increasing demands from their womenfolk compared to those in smaller family settings. Qadir and Afzal (2019) posit that an overwhelming number of household chores leave women in these families to experience more conflicts managing work and family lives. However, research has found this phenomenon to be more prevalent in the lower- and middle-class families, while working women in the upper-middle and elite classes that have better dignifying jobs are more likely to cope better since they can outsource some of their domestic responsibilities (Abbas et al., 2019; Duong et al., 2020). Many women in Pakistan have limited options available in terms of working outside of the home (Mehmood et al., 2018).

Furthermore, Ahmed (2018) reports that with a majority of the females working in the informal sector, they are persistently exposed to unsafe and life-threatening conditions without legal protection. Such females are predominantly working as domestic workers, housemaids and piece-rate workers for factory owners. Ahmed (2018) further argues that despite the passage of bills by the governments in Sindh and Punjab for the protection of domestic workers, law enforcement remains a challenge for these group of workers. This neglect on the part of the government has adverse effects on female participation in paid work because of the possibility for sexual harassment, gender discrimination and pay inequality which discourages families from allowing women to work.

Research Methodology

The study adopts qualitative research method with interpretative phenomenological approach. This allows researchers to capture and interpret the lived experiences of WLB among working women in Pakistan. This study adopts Hughes, Kinder and Cooper's (2019) multi-dimensional WLB matrix which covers eight areas of work-life: career and work, financial administration and management, partnership and romance, family and social life, health, fitness and recreation, and creativity and personal growth. Following the interpretative phenomenological approach, the study examines the implications of the Pakistani

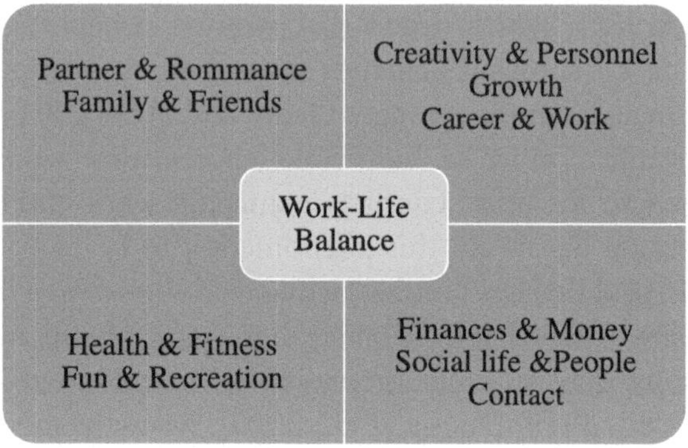

Fig. 12.1 Work-life matrix

culture on the WLB of working women in Pakistan through the lens of the identified work-life matrix (Fig. 12.1).

Hughes et al. (2019) proposed a matrix which consists of eight areas of work-life balance that may help to create a balance in one's life. A lack in level of satisfaction in any of the matrix engenders work-life imbalance. In this study, we have used this matrix to probe into interviewees' lived experiences about work-life balance.

Time and Locale for the Study

Data was collected over a period of six months (May–November 2019) in Karachi, Pakistan. Being one of the few mega cities in the country, Karachi is recognized as the economic hub of Pakistan (NIPS, 2019). The city is well known for its metropolis activities and gender diversity. With a population size of over 20 million people, Karachi remains one of the cities with the largest influx of migration from other parts of the country (NIPS, 2019).

Participant Selection

Fifty-five working women with varied backgrounds were interviewed for this study (see Table 12.1). The participants are women working in different sectors of the economy: banking, telecommunication, hospitality, multinational FMCGs, academia and household/domestic sectors. The participants' ages range between 18 and 41 years. 75% of the participants are working mothers, 65% are married, 10% are divorced, and 25% are single women. The participants ranged between high-income, moderate-income and low-income families. These were selected to gain a better insight into the WLB dynamics of high- and low-income working women. The table below provides a summary of the participants' profile.

Data Collection and Analysis

Date was collected through in-depth semi-structured interviews and participant observations with the consent of the participants. Participants shared their lived experiences along the lines of the work-life matrix. The study adopts the convenience and snowball sampling techniques. First, the researchers employed the convenience sampling technique by recruiting a small group of participants that were easy to reach in Karachi. Second, the snowball technique, which allows researchers to recruit other participants from existing participants (Saunders, Lewis, & Thornhill, 2016), was employed. Thus, participants from the convenience samples suggested friends and colleagues for the study. According to Creswell (2014), the non-probability sampling method is presumed to eliminate bias in the choice of participants, therefore giving every participant equal chances of selection. The interviews were tape recorded in order for the responses to be captured verbatim. The initial interviews lasted between 45 and 60 minutes; however, some of the participants were contacted a second time for further questionings based on their responses from the initial interviews. The interviews were conducted in Urdu and then translated into the English language by the researchers.

Table 12.1 Details of the respondents

Serial No.	Age	Occupation	Sector	Marital status	No. of children
1	36	Manager	Education	Married	2
2	40	General Manager	Health	Married	3
3	30	Marketing Manager	Telecom	Single	0
4	36	Engagement Manager	FMCG	Divorced	2
5	26	Digital Marketer	Hospitality	Single	0
6	33	Facility Manager	Hospitality	Married	2
7	41	Director	Health	Married	2
8	34	Accountant	Insurance	Married	2
9	28	Software Engineer	IT	Married	2
10	31	Domestic worker	Household	Married	3
11	23	Social Media Coordinator	Footwear	Single	0
12	41	Domestic worker	Household	Married	5
13	31	Domestic worker	Household	Married	3
14	30	Office Assistant	Automobile	Married	2
15	29	Receptionist	Oil & Gas	Married	2
16	34	Lecturer	Education	Single	0
17	27	Domestic worker	Household	Married	4
18	35	Guest Services Manager	Hospitality	Divorced	2
19	35	Entrepreneur	Fashion	Married	3
20	28	Operational Manager	Banking	Married	1
21	35	Fashion Designer	Textile	Married	3
22	36	Assistant Professor	Education	Single	0
23	42	Assistant Professor	Education	Married	3

(continued)

Table 12.1 (continued)

Serial No.	Age	Occupation	Sector	Marital status	No. of children
24	37	Entrepreneur	Commerce	Married	3
25	34	Accountant	Consultancy	Married	3
26	38	Gynaecologist	Health	Married	2
27	25	Retail Manager	Garments	Single	0
28	35	HR Officer	FMCG	Married	2
29	31	Sales Manager	Insurance	Married	2
30	37	Domestic worker	Household	Married	7
31	41	Domestic worker	Household	Married	3
32	28	HR Specialist	Banking	Single	0
33	33	Teller	Banking	Married	2
34	35	Sweeper	Education	Married	4
35	18	Domestic worker	Household	Single	0
36	32	Administrative Assistant	Oil & Gas	Married	3
37	35	Janitor	Education	Married	3
38	26	Digital Marketer	Media	Married	1
39	22	Research Assistant	Education	Single	0
40	34	Lecturer	Education	Married	2
41	21	Domestic worker	Household	Single	0
42	32	Microbiologist	Pharmaceutical	Married	1
43	35	Financial Advisor	Financial Services	Married	3
44	22	Echo Technician	Health	Single	0
45	26	Office Manager	Automobile	Single	0
46	33	Finance Manager	Financial	Married	2
47	40	General Manager	FMCG	Divorced	2
48	38	Civil Servant	Civil Services	Married	3
49	26	Service Quality Manager	Food & Beverage	Single	0
50	34	Marketing Manager	Hospitality	Divorced	1

(continued)

Table 12.1 (continued)

Serial No.	Age	Occupation	Sector	Marital status	No. of children
51	32	Customer Service	Banking	Divorced	1
52	28	Electrical Engineer	Energy	Single	0
53	30	PR Specialist	Hospitality	Married	2
54	28	Relationship Manager	Health & Beauty	Married	1
55	38	General Manager	Textile	Married	3

Field notes were also taken to provide the needed contextual information to gain better insight into the phenomenon. Pseudonyms are used to protect the participants' confidentiality.

Following the interviews and transcription, thematic analysis procedure (TAP), as suggested by Gibbs (2007), was used. The procedure required that codes were generated following the identified WLB matrix, which enabled the researchers to organize the codes under the identified themes carefully. Thorough processing of the recorded interviews was organized, arranged and interpreted in a structured manner, such as narrations, descriptions, definitions, classifications, comparisons, analogies and cause and effect dimensions.

Study Findings

Career and Work

Generally, our data evinces that female attitude and orientation towards career development and work management have progressively shifted over the years. Although it is evident that a majority of the participants were mainly motivated by the need to achieve financial liberty, it is believed that engaging in meaningful and dignifying jobs also promotes self-esteem among women. Many participants were driven by the need to prove their worth to family members and particularly the menfolk rather than being defined as mere wives or mothers. However, this perception differs across the social spectrums given that working women in the upper-income class with unlimited access to good education and social facilities take up paid employment as a way of boosting their self-esteem. In contrast, women in the middle- and low-income class were more concerned about the economic or financial benefit from working as a means of providing for their families. The following highlights some of the responses:

> I work because my financial independence is dear to me [...] it is not a luxury but rather a necessity [...] my economic survival depends upon it [...] to maintain a certain living standard, I have to work because my husband's income is not enough to fund my need – fashion, dressing, lifestyle etc. (Participant 40)
>
> My work is not just an escape from home responsibilities; it is a way of life. I cannot just be a depressing housewife, and child-rearing stops at a certain age [...] when they grow up they want to have their own way of life [...], so you have to have something other than children to look forward to. (Participant 6)
>
> I come from an educated family, and it helps a lot [...] my dad pushed me to go work outside because he didn't want me to waste my MBA by sitting at home [...] the constant sense of achievement I get from work gives me an essential sense of productivity and meaningfulness. (Participant 30)
>
> My working outside gives me a women's perspective of career development which men cannot contribute [...], I can now give a different take on what career my kids should choose since my husband has a different gathering of friends and I have a different set of friends which give me a different take on life. (Participant 42)

Family support has been identified by many participants as crucial for career progression and for achieving WLB. Participants, regardless of their marital status, found it challenging to cope with familial responsibilities, especially with little or no support from their spouses. For many married women, the multiple roles of working and undertaking the 'second shift' at home to attend to domestic chores and caregiving duties proved challenging and resulted in work-life conflict (WLC). The majority of the participants that were single and childless claimed that their employers were less considerate compared to their married and with children colleagues. These are the people who benefit from workplace flexibility and less workload. This corroborates Akanji et al.'s (2020) study that employers often think that single and childless professionals do not have WLB issues and problems because they have little or familial duties and more time to focus on their career. However, unknown to these employers, single and childless employees equally have familial roles such as caregiving to their dependents (e.g. parents, nieces, nephews and grandparents) and also the time to concentrate on finding a suitable partner or building the readily existing relationships. Some of the respondents commented:

> Family support is essential for career progression – since I don't have anyone at home to take care of my kids many a time I have to pass opportunities to take on challenging work that can be a real career booster because I have to head home as fast as I can – but women who have parents or in-laws to help out with their children don't feel that pressure and so can focus on career. (Participant 36)
>
> Marriage means the end – end of the career before it begins [...]. I will marry only when it feels right, but for now, I need to make a name for myself and prove my worth to my family. (Participant 26)
>
> It is quite difficult being single to achieve work-life balance [...]. Imagine that my employer thinks because I am single or childless, then I do not have the same or as much access to flexible working arrangements given to my colleagues that are married or have children [...], I always have to work more and sometimes take work home, and that gives me no time for myself nor my family. (Participant 27)

As Arif et al. (2017) have argued, when women are unable to find a balance between work and family, they find themselves in disillusionment from both work and marriage, which is likely to engender family crisis and increase divorce rates. Although gendered roles influenced by patriarchy in Pakistan contribute to the decline in female well-being, we found that the caste system, particularly in the cities (e.g. Karachi), was a major determinant to the achievement of WLB. While the women in the high-income class could reduce the role stress by outsourcing some of their familial duties by employing domestic workers, the women in the middle- and low-income classes may not be able to afford such a luxury; hence, many of them have no choice but to personally perform these duties. Interestingly, most of the women in the low-income class worked as domestic helpers in the homes of those in the upper caste system. For many, work is merely an activity for meeting their basic needs, particularly that of their children. The lack of spousal support or support from other members of the family engenders WLC for women since they have to engage in multiple jobs and even self-employment to cater for their family needs at the detriment of their personal well-being. The following comments highlight some of the responses:

> My husband doesn't work, he only orders, so I have to work to meet household expenses [...]. I can clean, cook, wash so I should do that [...] I want to give my children decent life resources even though I earn but money brings no respect for me at home. [...], where I come from, men don't view their wives with respect, our husbands do not care if the house is taken care of or children are fed properly, so I have to manage all. (Participant 41)
>
> I have no money left to spend on myself [...], household expenses take away everything. My husband is a rickshaw driver, and it's hard for us to save because everything is too costly [...] it is hard to manage within the income we make. (Participant 31)
>
> My Ladyship takes good care of me; they all treat me like one of their own [...]. Instead of cleaning five houses a day, I now have to take care of this one house the whole day. [...] I do this because I also want my children to go to English medium schools – it is important for me. (Participant 17)

These findings resonate with George (2007) and Rani and Saluja (2017) studies that women that engage in paid domestic work are unlikely to achieve WLB due to the unstructured nature of their work. The majority of the women in the upper caste system in Pakistan lack job security, healthcare facilities, reduced work-spans due to health issues and work only out of compulsion for economic survival. Similarly, Mustafa et al. (2019) explored the trend of micro-entrepreneurship among females in Pakistan. The report suggests that although the women lack adequate education and are subjected to overwhelming household responsibilities, they manage to run small enterprises successfully and learn to make the best use of the opportunities available to them. However, the level of autonomy in their personal and professional lives was severely limited. More so, these women were relegated continuously and forced to remember that work was merely a secondary activity which should not be taken as their 'first love', but rather, a sense of primacy is placed on familial responsibilities. One participant commented:

> I love my job, but the sad part is nobody understands the work I do. People around keep reminding me of my 'real responsibilities' [...]. My husband is supportive of my work [...], but that is only as long as I do my housework seamlessly [...] so even when I do have opportunity to succeed, I pass because I have to rush home. (Participant 28)

Financial Administration and Management

Financial planning and management can be gauged in terms of spending behaviours, savings and investment habits and contingency and risk management. Generally, men have been evidenced to be financially prudent compared to women and remain one of the reasons why in many less egalitarian societies, the males are the primary household finance decision-makers (Kim,Gutter, & Spangler, 2017). Similarly, Shaheen, Hussain, and Mujtaba (2018) argue that the influence of patriarchy in Pakistan stereotypes women as non-prudent financial advisors or counsellors. However, the study reports that there is an increasing trend among Pakistani women to become financially independent through gaining awareness from several knowledge sources such as the microfinance schemes. Our study found that some of the participants are able to manage their micro and small businesses successfully and use it to support their families financially. The following evinces some of the responses:

> My business affords me economic empowerment [...] I can support my husband; meet with family expenses and the best part I am no

> longer dependent on others for meeting my children's educational needs. (Participant 19)
>
> Whatever I earn, I save a substantial portion of it and buy gold items on instalments. I have seen my mother doing the same [...] it is an investment in the future of my daughters when they will get married. (21)

Our study also reveals that the majority (88 per cent) of the women, besides spending money on family needs, also saved a substantial proportion for buying gold. Investment in gold was deemed to be a culture among the women as they regarded it as a means of saving for the future. However, this culture was prevalent among the upper- and middle-income classes, while the majority of the low-income earners lacked the financial buffers for such luxury. Nevertheless, despite the increase in financial liberty among Pakistani women, an overwhelming number of them relied on their husbands, fathers or brothers to assist with financial planning. Some of the respondents commented that:

> I am not good with the whole banking stuff [...], it creeps me out [...] thank God my husband is very good with this kind of stuff, so that is taken care of. (Participant 38)
>
> My husband and I have invested in a plot [...]. Buying a property is a huge thing, and men are generally good at these things [...], this area is dominated by men and women aren't taken seriously, so it helps having my husband by my side while making such decisions. (Participant 38)

Although our findings reveal that the Pakistani women's quest for financial liberty has increased compared to previous findings (Hussain, 2011), the level of dependence on their male partners and relatives reveals that they still struggle to make effective financial decisions. This could be because throughout their upbringing, women are generally not involved in financial decision-making. As opined by Akhter and Akbar (2016), the ingrained patriarchal system dissuades women from partaking in decisions on economic and financial issues. Further, our findings reveal that women generally save either for their children's future, for dowry payments or for rainy days. Dowry payment is an important cultural rite for Pakistani women. Mustafa et al. (2019) opine that women are accustomed to taking out some portion of their earnings to purchase and store items needed to be presented as dowry for their wedding. However, they mostly save up such money without the knowledge of their husbands since the men are likely to invest the funds in properties or businesses. Some participants commented:

> [...] I do not inform my husband of my savings to purchase gold because generally, our men do not believe in such things. They would instead buy a plot of land or set up a new business if possible [...]. So, we do more work than usual just to enable us to save some extra money. (Participant 7)
>
> As a Pakistani woman, it is our culture to make sure that we save enough money to buy golds and jewellery for our daughters and also for the dowry rites. [...] my husband could not care less, he would persuade me to spend the entire money, so I rather hide it from him [...] but of course, they are aware that we are hiding some money. Kitties are very popular in this city, so it is a much-preferred way of saving even though I sometimes have to do some menial jobs to earn more money. (Participant 26)

It is evident that working beyond the usual working time is prevalent among the participants. This is done to raise extra savings for various reasons. However, it causes WLC for the majority of the women. We also found that working women of all classes tend to save through participating in kitties. The kitties is a voluntary financial contribution (or financial cooperatives) among 20 people predominantly in the Bachat Committee (BC), where low-income earners, rather than borrowing from a bank, form a group that periodically contribute and access funds. Generally, Pakistani women are more risk-averse, which reflects in their financial planning and contingency management as they would rather opt for safe and interest-free investments such as gold, foreign exchange and most commonly BCs.

Partnership and Romance

According to Abbas et al. (2019), strong relationships thrive upon the availability of self-disclosure, social support and physical intimacy among partners. These elements are paramount in the lives of women, especially working women. Rao (2017), in describing the situation of women in South Asian countries, propounded that generally in these societies, the reasons for getting married comprise social security, companionship, happiness, love, desire to breed their own families, sexual motivation and to a greater extent evade social isolation. Abbas et al. (2019) argue that social support is crucial for sustaining marriages and families because it plays a crucial role in the reduction of anxiety and stress for both working and non-working women in Pakistan. Some participants commented:

> Work is tough but having a supportive husband at home helps a lot [...], we share our day to day happenings, and honestly, it helps in reducing the stress I get from work. [...] to know that you have someone caring waiting for you at home is very refreshing. (Participant 31)

Although the participants were evasive about their intimate lives with their partners, we drew some assumptions from our observations. Women of all classes mirrored their sexual intimacy to be a revitalizing activity and a significant contributor to power, security, confidence and active participation at work. Women who were having satisfactory relationships were found to have reduced work and home conflicts. These findings resonate with the previous claims made by Rasool, Zubair, and Anwar (2020) that intimacy among spouses produced stress reliefs and fostered love and compassion, particularly in the interest of the women. However, women (predominantly in the lower caste system) with no physical and social intimacy were generally observed to display low self-esteem and increased anxiety due to work-family conflicts. Nevertheless, despite being sexually active, the majority of the women found it challenging to combine work with home duties. One participant stated:

> [...] I have six kids, and seventh is on the way [...] five minutes of my husband's pleasure, and I am stuck with this for another nine months. (Participant 30)

From our observations, we found that a limited number of the participants were satisfied with their romantic lives and more importantly, the level of support from their spouses. Resurfacing the outcomes in spousal support across the different social caste system was different but only marginally. The majority of the upper- and middle-income classes had more support because they could afford to hire domestic workers and have more time for intimate activities, while the reverse was the case for the low-income earners.

Family and Social Life

The communal-family setting in Pakistan fosters in-depth relationships among family members and friends. Our data evinces the significance of the family institution to the participants as they, regardless of their marital status, had several ties to families which they recognized as a fundamental part of their life. Family and friends' support comes in various ways such as helping each other with work, finances and providing social support. Our findings reveal that familial support is crucial for all working women. However, women in the low-income cadre often prioritize family over other things. The strong family culture among the Pakistanis often propels them to prioritize family and friends over their work engagements and at times are willing to quit their jobs just to attend to a family event. Some participants commented on the significance of family:

Family is family, even if I can't do much to help them. [...], I can at least wipe tears off the bereaved. (Participant 41)

As a woman, I am required to participate in all the family events [...], it doesn't matter how tired I am from work I am expected to get dressed and be present at all the family gatherings, otherwise women in the family take it as if I am too pompous or arrogant to participate with them which is not true. (Participant 33)

Rasool et al. (2020) suggest that one of the coping mechanisms for dealing with work-family conflict for the Pakistani women is family and friends' supports. We found that working women who receive support from family and friends find it easier to achieve career progression. In contrast, Sarwar and Imran (2019) found that many of these women are subjected to a glass ceiling and gender discrimination, which transcends into working overtime as a means to prove their worth to their male counterparts in particular, and achieve their career goals. One of the respondents mentioned:

> Ever since I started working, my family takes my opinions seriously [...], no one says the, 'how would you know' phrase anymore. [...], I am involved in the decision-making process, and now I do not have to have kids to feel important at home, work is good enough. (Participant 28)

However, due to increase in working time and workload in an attempt to gain self-esteem, these women are exposed to various health hazards, increasing family crisis and hysterics. Also, many participants alluded to the importance of having a social life or network consisting of close friends as a means of relieving work stress. Besides, our data reveals that women with limited familial support take advantage of social gatherings and friendships to reduce work stress. Some of the respondents commented:

> Hanging out with friends is better than any family gatherings [...], I can be my true self with them, and I don't have to pretend to be civil with friends as they don't judge me. [...] family events are usually about match-making, as older women in the family are usually looking for potential brides. (Participant 22)
>
> No matter how busy I get; I always try to assure that my presence is felt at all social gatherings I am invited to. [...] it is a huge motivating factor for me. (Participant 34)
>
> Being nice to others never goes unpaid. Just the other day I did an echo for a gentleman who happened to be the general manager of a big fashion outlet, he was so happy with my work that he sent me two new branded suits afterwards [...]. (Participant 33)

The above excerpts reveal that socialization forms a vital part in the lives of Pakistani women. However, we found that the high-income class represented the majority of the women that prioritized friends and non-family social gatherings over their family. This corroborates the findings of Zafar (2019) which posits that women of higher income and educational status in Pakistan value friendships over family through developing social network, whereas the low-income earning women with low educational backgrounds give primacy to their families.

Furthermore, our findings reveal that religion is recognized as an essential social institution for Pakistani women. Although all the participants were Muslims, only 82 per cent of them practise Islam. The practising women sought their religious activities as a form of socialization while adhering to the religious principles. The majority of Pakistani women are less interested in politics; however, they envision some aspects of politics to create platforms for networking and meeting new friends. Some of the participants mentioned:

> I do not know much about politics, but I am a huge fan of Imran Khan; I know he will do good for the country. [...] we are more interested in what Marium Nawaz (a politician) is wearing rather than what she is doing. (Participant 34)

Nevertheless, it is sometimes challenging for these women to keep up with their social life and work obligations simultaneously due to workload at work and familial responsibilities.

Health, Fitness and Recreation

The deplorable state of the healthcare system remains a common problem in Pakistan. However, women are vulnerable to the backlash effect due to the limited access to good healthcare facilities which exacerbate the resurgence of WLC (Hussain, 2011). According to the Pakistan Demographic and Health Survey (PDHS) conducted by the NIPS (2019), Pakistani women are predominantly oblivious to their health issues, which engenders further complications and results in the high mortality rate of women in both rural and urban areas. Our findings reveal that similar to other WLB matrix, the caste system in Pakistan favours the high- and middle-income classes given that they have access to and can afford good healthcare systems, while the low-income earners are subjected to a continuous health deterioration under the inexperienced hands of quack doctors and oftentimes self-medication. These findings reinforce the research of Tabassum (2016) which asserted that women's income and educational levels have a direct impact on their health conditions. Regardless of the social caste groups, our findings revealed that 87 per cent of the participants engaged in fitness activities as a means of keeping fit and healthy. Some participants commented:

> Looking good is an essential part of the job [...], I pay extra care to my physical grooming [...] I can't be fat or slobby at work because my job demands me to be always surrounded with people, so I have to look always good. (Participant 40)
>
> Dieting is my way of being fit, it is cheap, easy and workable [...], I have subscribed to some YouTube channels and get many hacks from there [...] it works for me. (Participant 26)

Our findings highlight that the women in the lower caste system consider the access to good health facilities as a luxury; as such, a majority within this group have resorted to a few activities to keep them fit and healthy. Despite such attempts, these women often find it challenging to cope with work, family and fitness activities. In contrast, participants in the upper- and middle-income cadre can afford to hire domestic workers to allow more time for health and fitness activities. Similar to our findings, Murtaza and Khan (2017) argue that the working conditions of women as it relates to the lack of adequate transport facilities, poor health care and fitness amenities at work, unavailability of day-care facilities and organizational inflexibility mirror the factors that engender WLC for a majority of the working women in Pakistan.

Additionally, our findings present mixed reactions in the reality of recreational activities for the participants. First, despite the limited availability of recreational centres in Pakistan, working women intermittently take time to visit common places like the beach and parks and sometimes dine out, watch movies or socialize through the social media platforms. These practices, however, are prevalent among low-income earners and less ambitious working women. Second, women in the middle- and high-income levels often tend to take less time for recreation, and such trends are consistent for those that are extremely ambitious, where work has become a form of recreation. Some of the respondents commented:

> I would go crazy if I do not work now [...]. If I had not tasted this lifestyle, I might be contended being a stay at home mom, but now it is difficult to imagine my life without the office [...] the office environment offers new experiences every other day. (Participant 7)
>
> When I am depressed, I do my shopping [...], men smoke to release stress, women shop. (Participant 30)
>
> Women in our neighbourhood have since come up with recreational activities [...]. Every month we do a little Hi-Tea or something at someone's house, we dress up and talk a lot [...], it is very refreshing. (Participant 48)

Consistent with Lenneis and Pfister (2017), women from under-developed societies are generally not accustomed to recreational and sporting prospects. This lends credence to our findings which suggest that the culture of the Pakistani women limits their experiences of exploring a variety of recreational activities compared to their male counterparts. Such outcomes emerge as a result of lack of time due to the multiple roles of working women. Also, Laar et al. (2019) suggest that religious and cultural obligations to wear hijabs, long dresses with full sleeves and veils, discourage many women to participate in physical activities.

Creativity and Personal Growth

Hughes et al. (2019) evince the importance of individual's ability to connect with personal imaginations and utilize varying creative expressions to develop and adapt to the conditions within the environment. Our findings reveal that working women utilize their work experiences and exhibit unusual levels of creativity in their routines both at work and at home. For the majority, juggling both work and home demands generates ideas and skills for managing both life domains. Some participants commented:

> I am so much into meeting deadlines at work that now I am conditioned to do the same at home [...], I carry out my home responsibilities in a very disciplined manner – laundry, cooking, cleaning, helping kids with their stuff [...] everything is chartered out. (Participant 3)

Our study corroborates with the findings of Ruhana (2020) that suggest that the quality of work-life heavily influences an individual's personal growth. Adequate pay, protective but challenging work environments and healthy physical conditions are factors that guarantee competency and development. Thus, working women are more likely to exhibit increased levels of creativity and personal growth. Similarly, Rashid and Ratten (2020) argue that the increasing number of women in developing countries investing in entrepreneurial ventures and assuming leadership roles transcends into creative and innovative mechanisms. Such mechanisms contribute to the maximization of business potentials as well as the creative capacity to handle the pressures at home.

Discussion and Conclusion

Significant assumptions can be drawn from the initial observation of this phenomenon. Post-modernism may be the dominant ideology within the discourse, but the corporate structure mirrors along the lines of modernism. Since Pakistani society is on the verge of transformation from traditional conventional structures to modernist market-oriented constructions, the role of the workforce is changing quite radically (Hussain, 2009). Growing capitalism has increased the demand for skilled workforce, and technology taking off the pressure from manual labour has allowed for female participation in the workforce to increase radically.

Mehmood, Chong and Hussain (2018) aver that the increasing literacy rate of Pakistani women has resulted in the cultural shift from a vastly conservative and religious country to a liberal and secular nation. Their investigation revealed that female's enrolment in higher education institutions has increased from 36.8 per cent to 47.2 per cent. Although gender inequality persists, primarily due to various socio-cultural factors such as poverty, unequal redistribution of economic resources and resistance to co-education, this gap is steadily reducing owing to the proliferation of women in paid employment.

Moreover, feminism is taking its toll upon traditional societal structures, particularly in the urban areas of the country. However, Jamal (2005) and Zia (2009) argue that such feminist movement engenders a form of antagonism towards Islamization in the country. Critelli (2010) advocated that gender equality in Pakistan can only be assured when the demands exceed beyond the sphere of political and civil rights towards social justice for women in the form of equal opportunities and rights to education, nutrition, health care and income. Also, this study evinces an increasing rate of WLC among Pakistani women due to their persistent desire to either engage in paid employment for economic reason, financial liberty and self-esteem. The feminist view as postulated by ul Haq et al. (2019) imperatively advocates for equality in power-sharing between both genders as a means to encourage the women's interest in workforce participation and to alleviate oppression. However, this approach unintentionally establishes a belief that the society created by men is absolutely perfect and deprives women of getting a fair share in the world created by men. Yet, such advocacies may also blur the individual roles of men and women in the society. However, the existing patriarchal system in Pakistan may be a huge barrier for good well-being and achieving WLB.

Additionally, our findings reveal that the social caste system strongly influences the reality of WLB among Pakistani women. Based on our six WLB matrix or framework adopted from Hughes et al. (2019), this study finds that the Pakistani caste system generates some contradictory outcomes among the working women across the three dominant social classes (upper, middle and lower). Although the experiences of the women generally appeared similar in some instances, but oftentimes, contrasting outcomes ensued in spite of the cultural similarities. Regarding career and work, consistent with the study of Duong et al.

(2020), women in the upper caste were primarily driven by the need for self-esteem, while those in the middle and lower caste focused mainly on the economic and financial benefits. Nevertheless, in both cases, an increase in WLC was evident as each category of need resulted in an increased workload. We also found that a majority of the women persistently depend on their male spouses or relatives concerning financial administration and management. However, corroborating with Mustafa et al. (2019), an overwhelming number of Pakistani women through extra hours of work perceived the purchase of gold and jewellery as a medium of savings, particularly for their unmarried daughters. Such extra hours of work interfered with the time allocated to familial responsibilities, further challenging their efforts to gain WLB.

Partnership and romance constitute another significant factor that Pakistani women considered important to achieving WLB. However, despite the marginal differences across the caste system, we maintain that working women in the middle and lower caste enjoyed better intimacy with their spouses given their financial capacity to employ domestic workers in exchange for intimate vacations. In contrast, women in the lower social system faced intimacy challenges due to their constant need to satisfy their work duties and home responsibilities (household chores and childcare). Pakistani women, however, found the family and social life aspect of the WLB matrix as a fundamental factor. The communal-family structure in this society presumes that family is an integral part of work and life; therefore, a majority of the women depended on close relatives and friends as a medium for relieving the stress that emerges from juggling both work and home duties. This is consistent with the study of Rasool et al. (2020), which suggests that family and friends form part of the coping mechanisms for working women. More so, despite the deplorable state of the health system in Pakistan, women alternatively find fitness and recreational activities as a means to sustain good health which is a requirement for successfully juggling work and home duties. Nevertheless, such practices remain low particularly among the low-income earners due to the need to do more work with little or no time for such activities and at the detriment of their health and well-being (Lenneis and Pfister, 2017). Finally, as reported by Rashid and

Ratten (2020), we also find that the inevitable need for women (particularly low-income earners) to combine work and home duties triggers a variety of coping skills and creativity which is sometimes found useful in the workplace.

Thus, work-life balance is a critical phenomenon for working women, where substantial policymaking is required to ensure women's professional and personal well-being in Pakistan. The provision and equal access to improved infrastructural facilities across the state would be beneficial to women in particular. Likewise, employers' roles in the implementation and employees' utilization of adequate flexible working arrangement would facilitate the achievement of WLB among women in Pakistan and worldwide. More so, regarding the roles of HRM, there are several implications for the future of work for Pakistani women as the country plies the route to modernism.

References

Abbas, J., Aqeel, M., Abbas, J., Shaher, B., Jaffar, A., Sundas, J., et al. (2019). The moderating role of social support for marital adjustment, depression, anxiety, and stress: Evidence from Pakistani working and nonworking women. *Journal of Affective Disorders, 244,* 231–238.

Ahmad, I. (2018, March 10). No country for working women. *The Express Tribune.* Retrieved from http://tribune.com.pk.

Akanji, B., Mordi, C., Simpson, R., Adisa, T. A., & Oruh, E. (2020). Time biases: Exploring the work–life balance of single Nigerian managers and professionals. *Journal of Managerial Psychology, 35*(2), 57–70.

Akhter, N., & Akbar, R. A. (2016). Critical analysis of life of Pakistani women: Views of educated women. *Journal of Elementary Education, 26*(1), 111–121.

Allen, T. D., French, K. A., Dumani, S., & Shockley, K. M. (2015). Meta-analysis of work–family conflict mean differences: Does national context matter? *Journal of Vocational Behavior, 90,* 90–100.

Amir, S., Kotikula, A., Pande, R. P., Bossavie, L. L. Y., & Khadka, U. (2018). *Female labor force participation in Pakistan: What do we know (English).* Washington, DC: World Bank Group. Retrieved

from http://documents.worldbank.org/curated/en/444061529681884900/ Female-labor-force-participation-in-Pakistan-what-do-we-know.
Arif, S., Ejaz, A., & Yousaf, N. (2017). Career aspirations and opportunity for FWAS: perceptions of Pakistani women. *Journal of Management and Research, 4*(1), 1–28.
Ayub, M., & Khan, R. A. (2019). Glass ceiling or personal barriers: A study of underrepresentation of women in senior management. *Global Social Sciences Review, 4*(4), 126–134.
Beham, B., Drobnič, S., Prag, P., Lewis, S., & Baierl, A. (2014). *Work-to-family enrichment across national cultures: A study among employees from seven European countries.* Paper presented at the 2014 Work and Family Researchers Network Conference, New York.
Caldwell, J. C. (1982). *Theory of fertility decline*. London, UK: Academic Press.
Cartwright, L. K. (1978). Career satisfaction and role harmony in a sample of young women physicians. *Journal of Vocational Behaviour, 12*(2), 184–196.
Central Intelligence World Factbook. (2019). *About Pakistan.* Retrieved from https://www.cia.gov/library/publications/the-world-factbook/geos/pk.html.
Chattoo, S., Atkin, K., & McNeish, D. (2004). *Young people of Pakistani origin and their families: Implications for providing support to young people and their families*. Leeds: Centre for Research in Primary Care, University of Leeds.
Cohen, S. (2002). The nation and the state of Pakistan. *The Washington Quarterly, 25*(3), 109–122.
Creswell, J. W. (2014). *Research design: Qualitative, quantitative and mixed methods approaches* (4th ed.). Thousand Oaks, CA: Sage.
Critelli, F. M. (2010). Beyond the veil in Pakistan. *Affilia, 25*(3), 236–249.
Duong, M. T., Hussain, I. A., & Subramaniam, A. (2020). Job Stress, co-worker support, role expectation conflict and work-life balance among working women: A quantitative study on multinational companies in Vietnam.
Fatima, N., & Sahibzada, S. A. (2012). An empirical analysis of factors affecting work life balance among university teachers: The case of Pakistan. *Journal of International Academic Research, 12*(1), 16–29.
Frone, M. R., Russel, M., & Barnes, G. M. (1996). Work-family conflict, gender, and health-related outcomes: A study of employed parents in two community samples. *Journal of Occupational Health Psychology, 1*(1), 57–69.
Glovan, A. M., Fackrell, T., Buswell, L., Jones, B. L., Hill, E. J., & Carroll, S. J. (2010). The work-family interface in the United States and Singapore: Conflict across cultures. *Journal of Family Psychology, 24,* 646–656.

George, T. (2007). Domestic workers and career women: The dilemma of family stability. *Gender and Behaviour, 5*(2), 1229–1239.
Gibbs, G. R. (2007). *Analyzing qualitative data.* London: Sage.
Herskovits, E. (1995). Struggling over subjectivity: Debates about the "self" and Alzheimer's disease. *Medical Anthropology Quarterly, 9*(2), 146–164.
Hisrich, R. D., & Brush, C. G. (1988). Women entrepreneurs: Problems and opportunities. In S. Rose and L. Larwood (Eds.), *Women's careers, pathways and pitfalls* (pp. 193–207). New York, NY: Greenwood Press.
Hodgetts, R. M., Luthans, F., & Doh, J. (2005). *International management: Culture strategy and behavior* (6th ed.). Irwin: McGraw Hill.
Hofstede, G. (1980). *Culture's consequences: International differences in work-related values.* Beverly Hills, CA: Sage.
Hughes, R., Kinder, A., & Cooper, C. L. (2019). Work-life balance. *The wellbeing workout* (pp. 249–253). Cham: Palgrave Macmillan.
Hussain, I. (2009). *Problems of working women in Karachi.* Pakistan: Cambridge Scholars Publishing.
Hussain, I. (2011). *An exploratory study of knowledge, attitudes, and perceptions of Pakistani Americans regarding what constitutes a healthy and happy family.* Sacramento: California State University.
Hussain, R. (1999). Community perceptions of reasons for the preference for consanguineous marriages in Pakistan. *Journal of Biosocial Science, 31*(4), 449–461.
Jamal, A. (2005). Transnational feminism as critical practice: A reading of feminist discourses in Pakistan. *Meridians: Feminism, Race, Transnationalism, 5*(2), 57–82.
Joplin, J. R. W., Shaffer, M. A., Francesco, A. M., & Lau, T. (2003). The macro-environment and work-family conflict: Development of a cross cultural comparative framework. *International Journal of Cross Cultural Management, 3,* 306–327.
Kassinis, G. I., & Stavrou, E. T. (2013). Non-standard work arrangements and national context. *European Management Journal, 31,* 464–477.
Keith, P., & Schafer, R. (1980). Role strain and depression in two-job families. *Family Relations, 29*(4), 483–488.
Khursheed, A., Mustafa, F., Arshad, I., & Gill, S. (2019). Work-family conflict among married female professionals in Pakistan. *Management Studies and Economic Systems, 4*(2), 123–130.
Kim, J., Gutter, M. S., & Spangler, T. (2017). Review of family financial decision making: Suggestions for future research and implications for financial education. *Journal of Financial Counseling and Planning, 28*(2), 253–267.

Laar, R., Zhang, J., Yu, T., Qi, H., & Ashraf, M. A. (2019). Constraints to women's participation in sports: A study of participation of Pakistani female students in physical activities. *International Journal of Sport Policy and Politics, 11*(3), 385–397.

Lenneis, V., & Pfister, G. (2017). When girls have no opportunities and women have neither time nor energy: The participation of Muslim female cleaners in recreational physical activity. *Sport in Society, 20*(9), 1203–1222.

Lu, L., Cooper, C. L., Kao, S.-F., Chang, T.-T., Allen, T. D., Lapierre, L. M., et al. (2010). Cross-cultural differences on work-to-family conflict and role satisfaction: A Taiwanese-British comparison. *Human Resource Management, 49,* 67–85.

Lucia-Casademunt, A. M., García-Cabrera, A., & Cuéllar-Molina, D. G. (2015a). National culture, work-life balance and employee well-being in European tourism firms: The moderating effect of uncertainty avoidance values. *Tourism & Management Studies, 11*(1), 62–69.

Lucia-Casademunt, A. M., Garcia-Cabrera, A. M., & Cuellar-Molina, D. G. (2015b). National culture, work-life balance and employee well-being in European tourism firms: The moderating effect of uncertainty avoidance values. *Tourism & Management Studies, 11*(1), 62–69.

Malik, N. (2011). A study on occupational stress experienced by private and public banks employees in Quetta City. *African Journal of Business Management, 5*(8), 3063.

McGinn, K. L., & Oh, E. (2017). Gender, social class, and women's employment. *Current Opinion in Psychology, 18,* 84–88.

Mehmood, S., Chong, L., & Hussain, M. (2018). Females higher education in Pakistan: An analysis of socio-economic and cultural challenges. *Advances in Social Sciences Research Journal, 5*(6), 379–397.

Moghadam, V. M. (1993). *Modernizing women: Gender and social change in the middle east*. Boulder, USA: Lynne Rienner.

Mogherini, F. (2016). Europe needs vision and realism. The Willy Brandt Lecture, 7.

Mortazavi, S., Pedhiwala, N., Shafiro, M., & Hammer, L. (2009). Work–family conflict related to culture and gender. *Community, Work & Family, 12,* 251–273.

Mukhtar, A., & Ummar, F. (2016, September 22). The China-Pakistan economic corridor—A possible 'game-changer' for empowering women. *United Nations Women*. Retrieved from https://asiapacific.unwomen.org/en/news-and-events/stories/2016/09/the-china-pakistan-economic-corridor.

Murtaza, A., & Khan, R. A. (2017). Impact of work life balance on job satisfaction of female faculty members of business school of Karachi. *Journal of Business Administration and Management Sciences, 1*(2), 65–83.

Mustafa, M., Mazhar, N., Asghar, A., Usmani, M. Z., Razaq, L., & Anderson, R. (2019, May). Digital financial needs of micro-entrepreneur women in Pakistan: Is mobile money the answer? In *Proceedings of the 2019 CHI Conference on Human Factors in Computing Systems*, pp. 1–12.

National Institute of Population Studies. (2019). *Pakistan demographic health survey (PDHS)2017–18*. Retrieved from https://dhsprogram.com/pubs/pdf/FR354/FR354.pdf.

Nauman, S. (2015). Investing in education: Pakistan as a traditional society in a modern world. *Journal of Education and Educational Development, 2*(1), 50–65.

Ollier-Malaterre, A., & Foucreault, A. (2017). Cross-National work-life research: Cultural and structural impacts for individuals and organizations. *Journal of Management, 43*(1), 111–136.

Pakistan Bureau of Statistics. (2020). *Labour force statistics*. Retrieved from http://www.pbs.gov.pk/content/labour-force-statistics.

Qadir, F., & Afzal, M. (2019). Impact of cultural factors on earnings of working women in Khyber Pakhtunkhwa, Pakistan. *European Online Journal of Natural and Social Sciences: Proceedings, 8*(1), 92.

Rani, E., & Saluja, R. (2017). An empirical study of working conditions and work life balance of domestic help workers in Punjab, India. *International Journal of Business Quantitative Economics and Applied Management Research, 4*(5), 39–49.

Rao, S. L. (2017). Marital adjustment and depression among couples. *The International Journal of Indian Psychology, 4*(87), 34–42.

Rashid, S., & Ratten, V. (2020). A systematic literature review on women entrepreneurship in emerging economies while reflecting specifically on SAARC countries. In *Entrepreneurship and Organisational Change* (pp. 37–88). Cham: Springer.

Rasool, I., Zubair, A., & Anwar, M. (2020). Role of perceived self-efficacy and spousal support in psychological well-being of female entrepreneurs. *Pakistan Journal of Psychological Research, 34*(4) https://doi.org/10.33824/pjpr.

Ruhana, I. (2020). The effect of quality of work life (QWL) on job satisfaction and organisation citizenship behavior (OCB) (A study of nurse at numerous hospitals in Malang, Indonesia). *Journal of Public Administration Studies, 4*(2), 51–58.

Saad, A., Xinping, G., & Ijaz, M. (2019). China-Pakistan economic corridor and its influence on perceived economic and social goals: Implications for social policy makers. *Sustainability, 11*, https://doi.org/10.3390/su11184949.

Sarwar, A., & Imran, M. K. (2019). Exploring women's multi-level career prospects in Pakistan: Barriers, interventions and outcomes. *Frontiers in Psychology, 10*, 1376.

Sathar, Z. A., & Kazi, S. (2000). Women's autonomy in the context of rural Pakistan. *The Pakistan Development Review*, 89–110.

Saunders, M., Lewis, P., & Thornhill, A. (2016). *Research methods for business students*. Harlow: Pearson Education Limited.

Sayeed, A., & Ansari, N. (2019). Women's mobility, agency, and labour force participation in the megacity of Karachi C-37429-PAK-1.

Shaheen, I., Hussain, I., & Mujtaba, G. (2018). Role of microfinance in economic empowerment of women in Lahore, Pakistan: A study of Akhuwat supported women clients. *International Journal of Economics and Financial Issues, 8*(2), 337.

Shaikh, S. S., Shah, S. A. S., Katpar, N. K., & Shah, S. K. B. (2019). Factors affecting work-life balance of women working in NGOs of Pakistan. *The Women-Annual Research Journal of Gender Studies, 11*(11).

Shujat, S., Cheema, F., & Bhutto, F. (2011). Impact of work life balance on employee job satisfaction in private banking sector of Karachi. *Journal of Management and Social Sciences, 7*(2), 8–15.

Snir, R., & Harpaz, I. (2009). Cross-cultural differences concerning heavy work investment. *Cross-Cultural Research, 43*, 309–319.

Spector, P. E., Cooper, C. L., Poelmans, S. A. Y., Allen, T. D., O'Driscoll, M. P., Sanchez, J. I., et al. (2004). A crossnational comparative study of work-family stressors, working hours and well-being: China and Latin America versus the Anglo world. *Personnel Psychology, 57*, 119–142.

Tabassum, N. (2016). *Women in Pakistan: Status in socio-cultural and politico legal domains*. Islamabad: Higher Education Commission, Pakistan.

ul Haq, M. A., Akram, F., Ashiq, U., & Raza, S. (2019). The employment paradox to improve women's empowerment in Pakistan.

Umer, R., & Zia-ur-Rehman, M. (2013). Impact of work life balance and work life conflict on the life satisfaction of working women: A case study of higher education sector of twin cities of Pakistan. *Academic Research International, 4*(5), 445.

Yadav, R. K., & Dabhade, N. (2014). Work life balance and job satisfaction among the working women of banking and education sector-A comparative study. *International Letters of Social and Humanistic Sciences, 21,* 181–201.
Zafar, R. (2019). Impact of income and education on socio-political values of women: An empirical study of Pakistani working women. *Journal of Asian and African Studies, 54*(5), 691–701.
Zia, A. S. (2009). The reinvention of feminism in Pakistan. *Feminist Review, 91*(1), 29–46.

Part IV

South America

13

Towards Achieving a Meaningful Balance Between Work and Private Life: Insights from Argentine Workers

Gisela Delfino and Camila Botero

Introduction

Current changes in the world of work are conditioned by economic and social situation. Data from Argentina social context reflect increased socio-occupational segmentation, with a high association between predominant labour scenario and poverty. This impacts on quality of life and households' conditions (Donza, 2019). In other words, there is a highly fragmented market that produces deprivation for many workers and, consequently, affects living conditions of family groups.

G. Delfino (✉) · C. Botero
Pontifical Catholic University of Argentina (UCA), National Scientific and Technical Research Council (CONICET), Buenos Aires, Argentina
e-mail: gisela_delfino@uca.edu.ar

G. Delfino
Doctorado en Edudacion y Sociedad, Universidad Andres Bello, Santiago, Chile

T. A. Adisa and G. Gbadamosi (eds.), *Work-Life Interface*,
https://doi.org/10.1007/978-3-030-66648-4_13

Another aggravated aspect in Argentina is the quality of employment. Labour informality is a recurrent aspect of job insecurity and represents the main job quality deficit in Argentina (Bertranou et al., 2014). "Latin America, and Argentina in particular, has been characterized throughout history by macroeconomic instability and its negative effects, both static and dynamic, on the labour market (on the level of employment, real wages, labour informality, among others)" (Bertranou & Casanova, 2015, p. 12). Therefore, the macroeconomic environment and growth strategies become a basic fundamental aspect to generate quality employment.

It is also important to address the new ways of structuring and organizing companies, which bring with them new changes, for example, the introduction of new technologies. The International Labour Organization has expressed that technological transformations society is currently forcing its way to reviewing skills and labour competences, making it possible to include what is expected in the near future. Therefore, in developing countries, like Argentina, it is essential to think new and better techno-productive systems since current processes of industrialization and modernization of the productive structure are insufficient and unfinished (Ernst & Robert, 2019).

Economic and social changes pose new challenges for workers' protection: for example, part-time employment and therefore reduced working hours; increased number of self-employed workers; increased number of subcontractors and officials with temporary contracts; increased work and service contracts and temporary employment; new forms of employment in the information and communication sectors (teleworking, virtual companies on the Internet, etc.); greater alternation between employed and self-employed jobs (Bullinger, 2000). In Argentina, between 2018 and 2019, there was a drop in salaried workers and an increase in self-employed workers (Indec, 2019).

Considering the labour situation in Argentina, new responses to it have arisen. Global fragmentation of value chains, the interconnection of productive capacities, and the blurring of the boundaries among producers, sellers, and consumers are other outstanding characteristics (Fisher & Fuchs, 2015). In Latin America, there is growing concern regarding new forms of work and the impact that new technologies will have on employment, its characteristics, and the uncertainty about the resulting labour relations. If regulations do not consider new work forms, job insecurity will grow. Training and organization alternatives are required to guarantee workers' protection from the mismatch between existing labour policies and regulations and new forms of employment (Bensusán, 2016).

Home delivery platforms are a pioneering experience in Latin America. They have been driven by workers engaged in goods (Rappi, Glovo) and people (Uber, Cabify, among others) transporting. The precariousness of delivery workers' conditions is evident in low wages, insecurity to which they are exposed, lack of social security, and long working hours. Complaints of disagreement have already started to arise. This type of work is in a labour market limbo. It is assumed that employment protection and regulation do not apply since it is proposed as an eventual virtual job—that is, an activity that allows the distribution of personal time between studies, work, or any other activity (del Bono, 2019). A large proportion of people who dedicate themselves to this type of work have university studies and are immigrants. In this context of high vulnerability and lack of regulation, relationship between new technologies and new forms of job insecurity deepens.

How new technology affects work, well-being, and individual and organizational performance depends not only on how advanced it is. Objectives of those who introduce it, procedures used to introduce it, and how well it adapts to the existing social system in the workplace are also relevant (Blackler & Brown, 1986; Burnes, 1989). As mentioned by Arnold and Randall (2012), it is clear that, in many countries, individuals are increasingly aware and therefore less satisfied with the imbalance that sometimes occurs between the amount of time they spend at work and the amount of time they spend outside of it. Hence, there is a new challenge for employers who want to attract the best workers; they must also ensure that their workforce is satisfied and engaged. This way, demands that workers face in daily life, trying to achive a balance between work and non-work activities, have become problematic. "Work-life integration" concept captures the dynamics of employees trying to balance a wide range of work and non-work activities (Lewis & Cooper, 2005).

Considering some society groups, such as low-income families, work-life balance often depends on the social support network, which is frequently essential for childcare (Kossek et al., 2008). It may even happen that what is stressful is not the time spent away from the family; for some women who work outside the home, returning home is what they find most stressful (Westman et al., 2008).

Lewis and Lewis (1997) have already mentioned the importance of job flexibility in terms of flexible and informal work arrangements. It has already been studied (Burke, 2001a) that there is a negative association between work addiction and organizational values that fosters the balance between personal and work life: work-addicted people obtain higher scores in organizational values that are negative in terms of balance between personal and work life.

Results obtained from the quarterly survey carried out by Randstad Human Resources Company (2019) show that new technologies create tensions between work and personal life: 59% of Argentinians consider that their employer expects them to be available even after working hours. Employees' perception shows, for example, that 61% do not mind having to look at work matters in their free time at a convenient time and 66% said they answer calls or e-mails immediately when they are outside of their regular working hours. About 49% of those surveyed considered their employer expects them to be available also during their vacations. According to Randstad (2019), in Argentina and Uruguay, organizations need to work more actively so that the concept of work-life balance is incorporated into the corporate culture.

Importance of Work in Adult Life

Well-being is closely related to living conditions and living standards (García-Viniegras & López González, 2003). Thus, satisfaction arises when a balance is achieved between future expectations and current achievements in different areas such as work, family, health, material conditions of life, interpersonal relationships, and couple's sexual and emotional relationships (García-Viniegras, 2005). Personal satisfaction is one of the fundamental components of well-being. It interacts between the person and his/her micro- and macro-social environment involving material and social objective conditions that offer different opportunities for personal fulfilment (García-Viniegras & González Benítez, 2000).

Researchers have pointed out the importance of work in adult life and its relationship with other aspects of life. Global satisfaction with life is necessary and is achieved when it is distributed within a set of different activities: family, work, social relationships, food, hobbies, sports, etc. Each one reaches a greater or lesser level of importance in the life of each person. Nevertheless, if the individual becomes frustrated in one or more of these facets, he/she can focus attention on one, neglecting the rest (Fernández-Montalvo & Echeburúa, 1998).

Work concept, its social assessment, and work motivation have undergone a great change throughout history. Work activity is a fundamental aspect of mental health (Fernández-Montalvo & Echeburúa, 1998). Nowadays, working requires great dedication of daily time. It is not only an activity aimed to making money; its importance transcends a person's identity. It allows inclusion into the sociocultural environment and the achievement of economic independence (Fernández-Montalvo, 1998). Work implies that the person can carry out his/her work activity freely; that is, when working, one can deploy his/her potential and develop it in a responsible way. In order to develop work in the best possible way, and to contribute to personal fulfilment, abilities and personality traits must be evaluated. Each worker has his/her style, which must be detected and improved (Griffa & Moreno, 2011).

Conditions in which a job is developed turn out to be important for the mental health of the worker. Aspects such as opportunity of control, adequacy between demands that the position requires and capabilities of the person who performs it, interpersonal relationships, and physical security intervene on psychological well-being (Arnold & Randall, 2012). It is important to observe the degree of influence that a person's behaviour, in their professional field, has on their behaviour outside of it, and how external aspects influence the well-being at work (Fernández-Montalvo & Echeburúa, 1998; Fernández-Montalvo, 2000).

Some authors have suggested that different organizations are responsible for attracting, selecting, and conserving different kinds of people (O'Reilly, 1991; Rousseau, 1995; Schneider, 1987). Those that prioritize work are attracted to companies that offer them challenges and risks and therefore a greater labour involvement compared to normal employment (Harpaz & Snir, 2003).

It is relevant to take into account the centrality of work, as the importance that fulfils the role of work in relation to other roles in the subject's life, such as family, community activities, and leisure (Alonso García, 2004). In 1987, the Meaning of Working (MOW) International Research Team had pointed out the importance of work at a general level and of work at any time in the life of a subject. They differentiated absolute centrality, where the role of work is extremely important, from relative centrality, where other facets, such as leisure, community, and religion, are taken into account. When work value is absolutized, work activity would hinder and be dysfunctional to the other areas of a person's life (Griffa & Moreno, 2011). According to Salanova et al. (1991), it is necessary to take into account the meaning of work and the associated values according to the cultural-historical context, since in each period work is conceptualized in different ways: as a punishment, as an obligation, as a possibility of self-realization, and even as an addiction.

During work activity, working conditions and the environment, that is, the environment in which this function is carried out, favour the life and health of the worker in some way. Work allows or contributes to personal fulfilment, to the development of the personality of those who execute it, and defines a crystallized social identity in the profession or trade (Neffa, 1999). While people work, some of the physical, biological, psychic, and mental capacities of the human being are constantly updated, conditioned by the feelings of belonging or inclusion in a group, category, or profession. At the same time, within social identity, something unique is displayed in each worker with respect to the other workers, where it creates strong feelings of belonging (Neffa, 2015).

As Dejours (1998) mentions, work demands a subjective mobilization at mental and psychic level of the worker. It will be necessary to compensate for the failures of the work prescribed by others and to deal with the random problems and incidents found in the reality of the labour process. The centrality of work can be both a health operator, insofar as it allows the construction of a balance with other areas of life, and it can also be presented as a limitation to personal development that may eventually cause pathological and destabilizing health effects (Alonso García, 2004; MOW International Research Team, 1987). In this sense, it has been argued that making work a number one priority over other aspects of life can be detrimental to physical, mental, and social health (Fernández-Montalvo, 1998).

Another interesting aspect to be analysed is what being employed can generate on a personal level, offering the possibility of building a sense of existence and finding meaning in what is being done. On the other hand, frustration can arise if the worker is prevented from building that sense of existence by a given organization or employer (Neffa, 1999). In some cases that feeling of frustration can find compensation in the possibility of having access to knowledge, improvement programs, continuous training, thus obtaining financial autonomy, establishing relationships, being part of a work group and building identity. We should highlight financial autonomy as a goal of utmost importance (Neffa, 2015).

From the perspective of mental health, work plays relevant roles: (a) it balances the level of activity, through physical and mental energy expenditure; (b) it structures daily routines, distinguishing periods dedicated to work and leisure; (c) it allows exchange of social roles: satisfying social bonds and complementing family emotional relationships; (d) it helps develop personal identity by granting social status (Fernández-Montalvo, 2000). The degree to which a job meets these requirements is strongly associated with job satisfaction and mental health.

Argentina: A Context with Structural Inequalities

It is important to give a context to the factors that articulate work. Various international organizations such as the World Health Organization (WHO), the International Labour Organization (ILO), the Pan American Health Organization (PAHO), and numerous national associations of professionals such as doctors, jurists, sociologists, psychologists, ergonomists, and labour economists agree that not only conditioning factors should be considered: economic and social determinants of health, such as the economic, technological, social, political context, and the labour market should be taken into account as well.

The United Nation Sustainable Development Goals mark a path to harmonize three basic elements: economic growth, social inclusion, and environmental protection. They are essential for the well-being of people and societies, and promote sustainable, inclusive, and equitable economic growth to create greater opportunities for all. On the other hand, studies show that social rights in force in Argentina demonstrate structural inequalities that are a real point of concern. Well-being, material conditions and social integration are necessary for full sustainable human development. Therefore, when analysing living conditions, a set of operations associated with sources of well-being is considered. This implies access to basic services and goods, protection of economic resources for life support, and decent habitat conditions. To achieve a definition of human and social development, beyond considering the indicators of income and monetary poverty, a set of aspects that allow for economic satisfaction and material achievements by households must be considered. The definition of well-being is much more complex since it covers not only economic indicators, but also social rights that imply a criterion of justice (Bonfiglio et al., 2019).

The Argentine Social Debt Observatory (ODSA) has been monitoring, since 2004, material and subjective deficiencies that have an impact on the essential capacities for personal and social development. Regarding the labour market, taking into account the last decades, after the 2001 crisis and until 2007–2008, there was a favourable socio-labourer progress—for example, investment growth, increased international competitiveness due to devaluation, taking advantage of significant idle capacity and policies aimed for domestic market expansion and extending to different countries. Therefore, adding to this, labour policies regained legal importance to protect work. As of 2009, the consumption-based model reached its limits due to lack of investment; additionally, changes in the international market did not favour Argentina; job creation decreased, and improvements in the labour market stagnated. As of 2016, the scenario has become even more negative as the adverse international context, the lack of private investment, and low public investment have continued. In addition, anti-inflationary policy has had a direct impact on the labour context. The following two years added the devaluation process with its recessive effects, so inflation increased, generating income and consumption capacity decrease. One of the most used alternatives to measure the well-being of a society is economic deficiencies through monetary income. This is a fundamental resource to obtain goods and services that are basic to achieve well-being (Donza, 2019).

As in other developing countries with emerging economies, salaried and registered work with social security organizations comprises less than half of the economically active population. This situation must be taken into account within the conditions and environment that a worker submits and how this affects psychically and socially since the objective of entrepreneurs is often to maximize their profit or that of the organization without taking into account the employees' well-being (Neffa, 2015).

On the labour scenario, a segmentation has been generated, known as the micro-informal sector, which has a typical feature that easily oscillates between periods of occupation and others of unemployment. This is reflected in the fact that the annual income decreases due to this permanent dynamic, lack of employment relationship consolidation, seniority loss, training interruption, and permanent discontinuity of contributions to the social security system. Donza (2019) shows that labour turnover has had a marked impact in this sector, with little specialization in labour, and vulnerable labour relations with greater exposure to unemployment since the cost of layoffs for the employer is minor or null.

Workers in the informal sector are approximately 49.3% of the country's economically active population (Donza, 2019). They tend to be young (aged between 18 and 34 years), and they spend, in general, their time in precarious or unstable activities, with poor working conditions, low income, lack of social protection, and limitations to exercise labour rights. According to statistics (Donza & Salvia, 2018), 74.5% of their income comes from their employment and the remaining 25.5% is shared by retirement and pension income, social assistance programmes, employment plans, and other non-labour income. There is a higher percentage of women who belong to this sector; the distribution of occupations is very different according to sex. The most frequent work in women is non-professional self-employment (45.4%) and 22.9% work as domestic workers in households. On the men side, 57.9% perform activities as non-professional self-employed. Women, compared to men, have 40% lower probability of working in full employment (Donza, 2019).

However, another point of view to take into account is not only how Argentina's situation affects its workers in the micro-informal segment, but those that overwork as well, regardless of socioeconomic status. It is important to consider the salary relationship, the social security system, the workers' access to education, housing, urban planning, and public services (Ramazzini, 2004). All these variables position salaried workers in a particular place of social stratification and insert them together with their family in social life, establishing relationships with others (Ansoleaga, 2013). Therefore, the relationship of these factors in each person will define the general conditions of life and the impact on health. In this sense, health can be seen as the result of a constant search for balance of human beings with their peers and with the environment, which depends on the resilience capacities of the subject to risk factors (Neffa, 2015).

Work-Private Life Balance

Dedicating long hours to work has been perceived as an appropriate behaviour, and it is socially accepted. It also responds to certain values of responsibility and a vision of progress in success and power (Fernández-Montalvo & Echeburúa, 1998). In Latin America, employees work long hours. The idea that free time is equivalent to lost time is imposed. There is an implicit idea in organizations to consider leisure time negatively and, with time, the worker internalizes this culture. Working hours in Argentina and Chile go from 40 and 45 hours per week, that is, 1,974 hours per year. However, other Latin American countries such as Colombia, Mexico, and Costa Rica stand out for higher number of working hours, with 2,496 hours per year according to the International Labour Organization (BAE Negocios, 2019). When Argentinians are consulted about the number of hours they work, 59% say they work

10 hours or more per day, 25% affirm they work 8 hours, and finally, 16% declare they work 9 hours (Universia Argentina, 2013).

Europe is usually taken as a reference to promote reduction of working hours. In countries such as Denmark, Norway, Holland, and Germany, workweek is between 25 to 40 hours (BAE Negocios, 2019). Nevertheless, of those who exceed in Argentina the typical 8-hour workday, 46% say that it is due to work volume while 39% referred financial need (Universia Argentina, 2013). Latin American countries have a number of factors such as high rates of independent workers, poorly paid jobs, job insecurity, and even cultural aspects that do not contribute to carry out this change (BAE Negocios, 2019). For example, in Argentina, of those working in the micro-informal sector, 75.9% do not have retirement contributions, 51.3% do not have health coverage, 30% were unemployed at least once in the last year, and 45.1% require more hours of work (Donza, 2019).

The main aim people try to achieve when planning to balance their work and personal life is well-being. Worker's subjective well-being is a fundamental social right that when absent confines equal opportunities (Salvia et al., 2016). A contrasted measure of well-being is psychological distress. It implies a deficit of emotional and cognitive resources, little capacity to respond to daily life's demands and difficulty in social relationships. Prevalence of employees' psychological distress varies according to working sector. In private or public sector, it is around 18% while in the micro-informal sector it rises up to 23%. People working in the last sector endure worse psychological conditions too: 24.1% have a negative approach to problems that arise, 16.6% said they feel nothing or little happy, and 14.1% have a belief of external control (Donza, 2019).

There are differences in the well-being reported by gender; women report greater psychological distress than men do. At non-professional status, 17% of women undergo psychological distress, while only 9.9% of men reports that. At working class level, the relation is 24.4% vs. 15.2%, and at marginal worker level, it is 49.9% vs. 24.3%. Regarding happiness, women at working class report a greater happiness deficit than men (19.9% vs. 10.4%) (Donza, 2019). Mismatches between the vital trajectory and the possibility of accompanying a professional career with economic solvency generate unconformity due to the lack of adaptation between working time and family life (Neffa, 2015). When comparing local workers with people working in Argentina but born and socialized in other regions, some differences related to work happiness arise. Foreign workers highlight the importance of teamwork, organizational culture, and sustainability, while Argentinians give high relevance to work environment, distance to work and recognition more important. In this way, Argentinians take more into account factors that affect their own happiness at work, while foreigners consider more factors that impact organizational happiness (Celada et al., 2016).

A study carried out in seven big cities of Argentina shows that almost half of Argentine workers are affected by mood and material deterioration. Millennials (Y generation) are the ones that display the highest rates of exhaustion and feeling that work is not returning the levels of satisfaction they expected to find. There is a lack of harmony between expectations and what persons receive (Observatorio de Tendencias Sociales y Empresariales, 2019). Y generation demands jobs that fit needs of workers who want to build careers and family at the same time. They want to sustain a quieter life compared to their parents (Holliday Wayne, 2009; Howe & Strauss, 2000). When needing to decide whether to take or change jobs, educated new generations of Argentinians especially value company aspects such as prioritizing the emotional well-being of its employees, open and transparent communication between managers and subordinates, wellness programmes, sports and health care, professional development and training, and the balance between personal and professional life (Cuesta et al., 2009). They privilege professional projects and think about them as a structuring factor of life.

Career development, learning opportunities, and interest in work are central for men and women, but they do not neglect the relevance of work-private life balance (Golik, 2013). They assign more importance to flexible hours and to possibilities of continuing training, than to remuneration. Argentine youths say they are happier when work centrality is relative. For them, friends, social networks, free time, sharing experiences, and travelling are considered the same or more important than work. Therefore, they are less concerned about losing a job (Hernández

& Serravalle, 2014). This could be interpreted as if they did not balance properly personal life with work and as if they lacked a true commitment to work.

Labour flexibility tends to be presented as opposed to traditional conception of work, exemplified by Taylorism and Fordism that seek quality and excellence at the lowest possible cost, making use of the latest technologies. Labour flexibility is currently one of the work's characteristics most valued by employees: 65% state that they would like to work less hours and explain they devote a large amount of time to routine tasks (Zodziejko, 2006). As reported by Celada et al. (2016), young Argentine employees explain that work flexibility allows them to improve the balance between work and personal life and organize better their schedules to establish family and social relationships on a regular basis. They also value the fact they can make better use of their free time to perform other activities and hobbies, and some have even reported that it allows them to free themselves of the stress generated by work.

Teleworking

Flexible schedules and remote work are valued as facilitators of balance between work and personal life (Hewlett et al., 2009). It is more and more frequent to find employees teleworking or doing home office and companies that are full home office. A classical definition explains that teleworking occurs when salaried workers perform all or part (regularly or occasionally) of their work, outside the usual place of their activity—normally from home, using information and communication technologies (ICT) (José Andrés et al., 2001). This modality allows employee to be connected and producing no matter where the individual is (Alonso-Fernández, 2003; Ballesteros et al., 2004). In this way and given people can do their work tasks at home, they may work non-working days, like weekends, or even when they are sick (Del Líbano et al., 2004). This can occur in a strongly competitive work environment, where incentives are offered for greater productivity (Quiceno & Venaccia Apli, 2007). Teleworking somehow becomes a form of work flexibility, which in many cases can denote a labour dependency, varying according to employers' regulations. For this reason, different European Union and Latin American countries and companies have decided to develop a regulatory framework related to health and safety when the employee carries out this work modality (Osio Havriluk, 2015).

Anderson et al. (2002) and Lapierre and Allen (2006) argue that organizations can implement policies such as time and space flexibility like home office because it makes it easier for employees to organize and assist their families. Without a doubt, teleworking can offer different benefits and can help reconciliation between work and private life. It also gives the opportunity to incorporate women and people with disabilities into the world of work (Osio Havriluk, 2015). In 2010, Telecom Argentina, based in Buenos Aires, decided to develop its own manual to regulate teleworking. It has had a positive impact on other service companies (Osio Havriluk, 2015). Argentina has achieved relevant results in the area of health and safety in teleworking.

Flexible schedules offered by teleworking can increase motivation levels and help achieve better performance and productivity. Nevertheless, it can generate negative consequences if not approached properly, especially with regard to separation between work and family life. It could also influence in terms of stress and productivity if it failed to define working hours. Therefore, it is necessary to establish a series of agreed common standards in relation to work uninterrupted concentration, as well as privacy and data protection issues (Escalante et al., 2006). Since 2007, Argentina has had a law related to hygiene and safety at work that incorporates the recommendations given by the International Labour Organization's Manual of Good Practices in Teleworking. It promotes the use of teleworking and allows inclusion of people with disabilities and those excluded from the current Argentine labour market. It also encourages youth employment, better working conditions through the use of ICT, and, above all, reconciling employees' family and working life. The Superintendence of Labour Risks is the state agency in charge of controlling work risk insurers and guaranteeing that medical assistance and monetary benefits are granted in case of work-related accidents or occupational diseases. In 2012, it defined teleworking and developed a Manual of Good Health and Safety Practices in Teleworking (Osio Havriluk, 2015).

Unemployment

In Argentina, the rate of unemployment is significantly high. According to Indec (2019), the rate of unemployment is 9.7%, but there is also a 24.7% that are beneficiaries of assistance programmes or employment plans. Thus unemployment rate rises up to 34.4%. There are some differences according to gender. Women report higher unemployment rates compared to men (12.8% vs. 7%). When considering the socio-occupational status, women's unemployment is more significant in the working class (18.8% vs. 3.8%). This situation is reversed as professional development increases, and at professional workers' level, unemployment of women is 2.1% while that of men is 4%. The possibility of working in the micro-informal sector increases 13.5 times when comparing workers in households of very low socioeconomic status with those of the medium high level. In low socioeconomic level, there are less possibilities of full employment. Workers in medium low-level households are 31% less likely to be in full employment. It decreases by 65% and 84% if they have low or very low socioeconomic status, always compared to the situation of workers of homes of medium high level (Donza & Salvia, 2018). The region where workers reside differentiates the probability of insertion in the productive structure too. People living in Buenos Aires suburbs are 1.8 times more likely to work in the informal sector than those who live in the City of Buenos Aires (Donza, 2019).

Given a labour market with oversupply of workers, employers intensify the use of informal recruitment channels and their discriminatory practices. Ethnographic studies show employers can use greater discretion in their recruitment and hiring practices. Being a man of 40 years old or a woman of 35 years old operates as a limitation to being able to obtain a job. Women explain that if they are married, mother of small children and around 35 years old, their chances of finding a job are very low. In other words, having those characteristics is a safe passport to unemployment (Cerruti, 2000)). Usually, there is no recognition of skills and abilities acquired over time (Neffa, 2015). As declared by individuals, experience, knowledge accumulated over the years, becomes their main handicap when looking for a job. Being unemployed at midlife can precipitate severe depression or psychosomatic disorders. High unemployment rates lead to an increase in poverty levels and social marginality (Beccaria & Lopez, 1996).

Moreover, in Argentina, some people do not work because they prefer not to. Between women, the rate is 36.3% while in men it is 10.3%. The biggest difference between genders is found at working class, where 47.3% of women reports it while in men it represents 13.1%. This asymmetry between men and women decreases as socio-occupational level increases, and at professional working level, 11.1% of women do not work because they do not want against 4.7% of men (Donza, 2019). Dominant cultural stream determines working and generating money as man's identity trait. In this way, loss of work implies, in many cases, a crisis of the masculine identity. To reconquer spaces and achieve an imaginary compensation, men (former) heads of family appeal with wild spontaneity to physical and/or verbal violence. Frequently, regressive behaviours of sullen resentment or resurgence of attention demands are directed to the wife (Beccaria & Lopez, 1996). Compared with the formal (14.4%) and public sector (10.8%), more micro-informal workers (30%) were unemployed at least once in the last year. Additionally, if they have not completed high school, they have a 11% less chance of having full employment. Finally, 45.1% of micro-informal workers explains they would like to work more hours inspite of having a full working day (8 or 9 h). In the formal sector, this willingness to increase working hours is about 21% (Donza, 2019). Exceeding 45 hours per week is considered an over-occupation. Most of the time, in the micro-informal sector, workers need to increase income. In the formal sector, generally, necessity of finishing the task, regardless of salary, is the main motivation (Donza & Salvia, 2018).

Women and Household Work

In Argentina, women have been incorporated into the labour field for several decades. However, there are still obstacles that make their labour insertion conflictive (Burin, 2008). Generally, women used to be associated with domestic space. This implied that women had to give up their aspirations to compete in the economic and political sphere because it was considered a man's function. The concept of domestic work hinders the construction of individuality and self-esteem (Vega Montiel, 2007). Many times, household work is still not recognized as work. It is non-remunerated, done after "paid" work without a schedule regulation, and tasks are performed inclusive during weekends, holidays, and vacations (Arnold & Randall, 2012). When entering the formal labour market, women's household work is not reduced. It increases the effort and obliges women to generate different strategies to avoid neglecting household chores. Since it is done privately, it tends to be seen as a woman's obligation and this leads to a clear inequality between genders (Vega Montiel, 2007). Sometimes this situation correlates with depression in middle-aged women that work in the formal labour market (Burin, 1993). Women who are doctors, psychologists, biologists, dentists, architects, entrepreneurs, and professors explain they tend to be overwhelmed and need to be very creative to deal with obligations: formal work and household work (Burin, 2008). Interestingly, women who consider themselves more traditional in the way they played both maternal and labour roles usually also found themselves in a "sticky floor" from which it was very difficult to separate. They encountered difficulties in being able to separate private life from public sphere, and many times this arises as a difficulty in accessing or maintaining their career development (Burin, 2008). Within the different effects, that household work has on women's lives is that it hinders their well-being. Depression is often found as a latent problem that generates feelings of monotony, isolation, and dissatisfaction (Oakley, 2018).

Psychosocial Disturbances at Work

Nowadays, there are psychosocial disturbances that befall at work, that been less visible than physical pathologies are seldom perceived directly. Occupational psychopathology studies the psychodynamic analysis of the intrapsychic and intersubjective processes that are manifested from the encounter with work (Sivadon & Fernandez-Zöila, 1983), trying to look at and treat the pathogenic effects of work on mental health.

In other words, it studies the psychological alterations derived from work activity, studying disorders that manifest themselves from the alterations that arise directly from work: work stress, negative consequences of working hours, interpersonal conflicts at work, and work addiction (Fernández-Montalvo, 2000).

In Argentina, absence from work has been on the increase due to problems related to work stress, panic attacks, and depression. These are psychological problems, and it has often been difficult to demonstrate that they are related to the workplace and need to be treated as medical conditions like physical illnesses (Neffa, 1999). Even employers often consider that the duration of a sick leave granted may be exaggerated or easily obtained. According to the legislation, all workers, if registered, are entitled to a maximum of three months of sick leave, without loss of salary or danger of dismissal for just cause. With more than five years of seniority or family charges, this figure doubles and the licence can go up to one year, during which the position and salary are retained. From a business perspective, the absence of an employee implies a high cost for the employers without major consequences for the employee (Neffa, 2015).

It is also common to encounter strikes that are protest mechanisms against some type of negative situation, such as low wages or poor working conditions. According to the Argentina's Ministry of Labour, in 2012, 8,333,295 individual days not worked were registered, almost double than in 2011, when the amount was 4,303,615. The public sector is where absenteeism occurs the most, which is where more sick leave is authorized too; nevertheless, absences have also increased in the private sphere (Neffa, 2015). In order to preserve health in the work environment, it is necessary to provide a means to quickly identify these risks. To be recognized by the social security system, it should be possible to verify the nature of occupational disease and the direct and essential relationship between habitual activity and the disease. However, the causal relationships of these pathologies, whose effects are diffused and deferred, are difficult to establish (Neffa, 1999). There must be a dynamic that is built collectively in a relationship with others, through communication, cooperation, exchange, recognition, and social support from peers. It is also important to get companies involved in social psychic risks at work since they directly affect motivation, generating little involvement in tasks, labour and interpersonal conflicts that influence costs, generating lack of attention in employees, reducing productivity, and causing greater risk in occupational accidents (Neffa, 2015).

Workaholism and Burnout

Family, social, and labour relations will determine the degree of interference that work addiction might have on the employee's life (Echeburúa & del Corral, 1994). This negative interference is related to physical health, personal happiness, and family and social relationships. It includes routine activities that could be carried out by other people, but the employee resist delegation to keep control over them (Fernández-Montalvo & Echeburúa, 1998). Initially, consequences begin to affect their health, presenting cardiovascular alterations related to stress; family relationships are impaired, with social isolation, sense of humour loss, disinterest in interpersonal relationships that do not turn out to be productive and do not involve labour issues, and non-spontaneous sexual relations (Botero & Delfino, 2019). In terms of health, deterioration is frequent, since these people neglect personal needs such as sleeping hours, regular rest, and periodic check-ups. It is also common to come across a wide variety of physical problems such as obesity, hypertension, and even psychoactive addiction such as excessive smoking and alcohol consumption (Fernández-Montalvo & Echeburúa, 1998). Álvarez (2011) adds to this list the generation of bone-muscle problems, dermatitis, headaches, dental problems, low back pain, among others.

Many organizations have become used to continuing working once the workday has been completed. It is even considered a trait of success to dedicate as much time as possible to work, not taking the lunch break, or not having time for leisure or social life. Holidays and free time are achieved only at the retirement stage. As a rule, they are not only required to work as much time as possible, but they even demanded of 24 hours availability, as well. Those who meet these expectations are considered outstanding employees (Castañeda Aguilera, 2010; Moreno et al., 2005). In both large and small companies, there is a phenomenon of social contagion, in which the labour involvement implicated in the excess of daily work hours is transmitted from employees who fulfil a greater hierarchical function or company managers to employees. Therefore, work addiction can also be due not only to a personal orientation with respect to such activity but it can be the result of a social interaction with others, as well (Moreno et al., 2005). In other cases, people who overwork, became happy shifters and enjoy working long hours (Novoa, 2011).

A study carried out by a recognized employment agency in Argentina reveals that 46% of Argentinians perceive themselves as having characteristics associated with work addiction, and 35% have reported that overwork has caused them health problems such as stress (18%), back, shoulder and neck pain (16%), headache (15%), gastric problems (12%), sleeping problems (11%), and depression (10%) (Adecco, 2019). In fact, working more than twelve hours a day increases the probability of suffering a disease by 37%. Only 3 out of 10 Argentinians, especially in the hierarchical positions, manage to take distance from their job responsibilities (Universia Argentina, 2013). Work recess is not synonymous of abandoning their tasks. However, when executives are consulted if given holidays by law are sufficient, 47% say they are not enough. On the same page, 35% say they keep an eye on the cell phone and e-mail just in case any labour issue shows up, and 32% claim to be available only for an emergency. Similarly, 24% of executives consider themselves essential and believe that their absence will negatively affect the operation of the company (Adecco, 2019). A great challenge for companies' top managers is to be able to reach balance between professional and personal life, to carry out activities that allow rest, distraction, and escape from work for a few hours, thus improving performance and health as well (Jaén, 2016).

Two realities may affect workaholism. On one hand, the organizational culture often encourages this type of behaviour because budget control causes some employees to accomplish the function of two working positions or more. On the other hand, the danger of unemployment makes people cling to their work and make it a fundamental aspect of their lives (Castañeda Aguilera, 2010). Burke (2001b) explains that people on higher organizational levels and those workers with less seniority tend to work longer hours. Similarly, companies struggle to continue in a highly competitive market and need workers who are ready to work longer hours too. Therefore, the profiles they usually look for include a high level of work commitment, responsibility, great dedication, thus promoting workaholism. Because of this, there has been a mark increase in people suffering from work addiction (Del Líbano et al., 2004). According to ODSA data (Donza, 2019), in Argentina, there has been an increase in work exhaustion between 2018 and 2019. The highest levels of burnout are found in individuals with low educational level and low income. Almost 10% of these workers show high values of both cynicism and exhaustion. Women are more likely to experience burnout than men (13% vs. 7%). This may be due to women's difficulty recovering emotionally after work because, in general, they continue to perform work tasks after hours. This is particularly interesting since although women are part of the labour market, they are also the main caretakers at home.

Conclusion

According to last data, in Argentina, half of employees work at the micro-informal sector. They undergo high difficulty accessing to basic services, such as good academic training. Most women become just housewives due to their low percentage of insertion in the workforce. Thus most of them depend on state subsidies. Given the economic situation the country is going through, balancing work and private life is a challenge of utmost importance. Almost half of Argentine workers are affected by mood and emotional disorders, and this is not always directly associated with salary. Argentine employees are dissatisfied with work; they feel overwhelmed and receive low salaries. Youths are especially affected. On the positive side, educated new generation employee are not only satisfied with getting a good salary; they value private life-work balance as well.

It is difficult to achieve balance, particularly for the lower socioeconomic level citizen in a high unemployment context. Young people are the most damaged. The challenge is then to be able to achieve significantly better working conditions, increasing youth insertion and balancing traditional forms of work. Work organisation methods should be able to provide more effectively this needs of both business and the workers, thus also helping significantly to increase new forms of mobility.

References

Adecco. (29/01/2019). *Sólo 3 de cada 10 ejecutivos logran desconectarse durante sus vacaciones [Only 3 out of 10 executives manage to disconnect during their vacations]*. https://www.adecco.com.ar/noticias/solo-3-de-cada-10-ejecutivos-logran-desconectarse-durante-sus-vacaciones/.

Alonso García, M. A. (2004). Centralidad del trabajo y metas en el trabajo: dos variables claves en orientación laboral [Centrality of work and goals at work: two key variables in employment guidance]. *Revista de Educación, 335*, 319–344.

Alonso-Fernández, F. (2003). *Las nuevas adicciones [New addictions]*. Madrid: TEA.

Álvarez, R. (2011). Adicción al trabajo como riesgo psicosocial [Workaholic addiction as psychosocial risk]. *Éxito Empresarial, 162*, 1–3.

Anderson, S. E., Coffey, B. S., & Byerly, R. T. (2002). Formal organizational initiatives and informal workplace practices: Links to work-family conflict and job-related outcomes. *Journal of Management, 28*(6), 787–810.

Ansoleaga, M. E. (2013). *Sintomatología depresiva y consumo riesgoso de alcohol en trabajadores expuestos a factores psicosociales laborales adversos: un asunto pendiente en salud pública [Depressive symptomatology and risky alcohol consumption in workers exposed to adverse labor psychosocial factors: A pending issue in public health]*. PhD thesis. Santiago de Chile: Universidad de Chile.

Arnold, J., & Randall, R. (2012). *Psicología del trabajo: comportamiento humano en el ámbito laboral [Work psychology: human behavior in the workplace]*. Mexico: Pearson Educación.

BAE Negocios (11/09/2019). Workaholics: Cuáles son los países en donde más se trabaja [Workaholics: What are the countries where you work most]. *BAE Negocios*. https://www.baenegocios.com/edicion-impresa/Workaholics-Cuales-son-los-paises-en-donde-mas-se-trabaja-20190910-0062.html.

Ballesteros, A., Mestre, H., Pechobierto, N., Puigdoménech, A., & Ramos, M. (2004). Influencia de las variables de personalidad en la adicción al trabajo en un estudio con profesores universitarios [Influence of personality variables in work addiction in a study with university professors]. *Fórum de Recerca, 9,* 1–11.

Beccaria, L., & López, N. (1996). *Sin trabajo. Las características del desempleo y sus efectos en la sociedad argentina [Jobless. The characteristics of unemployment and its effects on Argentine society].* Buenos Aires: UNICEF/Losada.

Bensusán, G. (2016). *Nuevas tendencias en el empleo: retos y opciones para las regulaciones y políticas del mercado de trabajo [New trends in employment: challenges and options for labor market regulations and policies].* Santiago de Chile: Comisión Económica para América Latina y el Caribe (CEPAL).

Bertranou, F., & Casanova, L. (2015). *Las instituciones laborales y el desempeño del mercado de trabajo en Argentina [Labor institutions and the performance of the labor market in Argentina].* Buenos Aires: International Labour Organization.

Bertranou, F., Casanova, L., Jiménez, M., & Jiménez, M. (2014). Empleo, calidad del empleo y segmentación laboral en Argentina [Empleo, calidad del empleo y segmentación laboral en Argentina]. *Revista de Economía Laboral, 11,* 24–64.

Blackler, F., & Brown, C. (1986). Alternative models to guide the design and introduction of the new information technologies into work organizations. *Journal of Occupational Psychology, 59*(4), 287–313. https://doi.org/10.1111/j.2044-8325.1986.tb00231.x.

Bonfiglio, J. I., Vera, J., & Salvia, A. (2019). *Pobreza monetaria y vulnerabilidad de derechos. Inequidades de las condiciones materiales de vida en los hogares de la argentina urbana (2010–2018) [Monetary poverty and vulnerability of rights. Inequities of material living conditions in the homes of urban Argentina (2010–2018)].* Buenos Aires, Argentina: Educa.

Botero, C., & Delfino, G. (2019). Adicciones al trabajo: factores psicológicos predisponentes, consecuencias de la adicción y tratamientos psicológicos [Work addictions: predisposing psychological factors, consequences of addiction and psychological treatments]. *Hologramática, 30*(1), 69–87.

Bullinger, H. (2000). The changing world of work: prospects and challenges for health and safety. *Magazine of the European Agency for Safety and Health at Work, 2,* 8–13.

Burin, M. (1993). *Mujeres y salud mental: un estudio acerca de los estados depresivos en mujeres de mediana edad [Women and mental health: a study about depressive states in middle-aged women].* PhD thesis, Universidad de Belgrano, Buenos Aires.

Burin, M. (2008). Las "fronteras de cristal" en la carrera laboral de las mujeres. Género, subjetividad y globalización [The "glass frontiers" in the women's career. Gender, subjectivity and globalization]. *Anuario de psicología/The UB Journal of Psychology, 39*(1), 75–86.

Burke, R. J. (2001a). Workaholism in organizations: The role of organizational values. *Personnel Review, 30*(6), 637–645. https://doi.org/10.1108/EUM0000000005977.

Burke, R. J. (2001b). Predictors of workaholism components and behaviors. *International Journal of Stress Management, 8*(2), 113–127.

Burnes, B. (1989). *New technology in context: The selection, introduction, and use of computer numerically controlled machine tools*. Aldershot: Avebury.

Castañeda Aguilera, E. (2010). Adicción al trabajo (Workaholism). Patología psicosocial del siglo XXI [Workaholism. Psychosocial pathology of the 21st century]. *Salud de los Trabajadores, 18(1)*, 57–66.

Celada, S., Gomes, F., & Varela, J. (2016). *Felicidad en el trabajo [Happiness at work]*. Bachelors thesis. Universidad Argentina de la Empresa, Buenos Aires.

Cerrutti, M. (2000). Intermittent employment among married women: A comparative study of Buenos Aires and Mexico City. *Journal of Comparative Family Studies, 31*(1), 19–43.

Cuesta, E. M., Ibáñez, M. E., Tagliabue, R., & Zangaro, M. (2009). La nueva generación y el trabajo [The new generation and work]. *Barbarói, 2*(31), 126–138.

Dejours, C. (1998). *Souffrance en France: La banalisation de l'injustice sociale [El sufrimiento en Francia: la trivialización de la injusticia social]*. París: Seuil.

Del Bono, A. (2019). Trabajadores de plataformas digitales: condiciones laborales en plataformas de reparto a domicilio en Argentina [Workers of digital platforms: Working conditions in on-demand delivery platforms in Argentina]. *Cuestiones de Sociología, 20*, 083. https://doi.org/10.24215/23468904e083.

Del Líbano, M., García, M., Llorens, S., & Salanova, M. (2004). ¿Existen relaciones significativas entre adicción al trabajo y satisfacción? *Fórum de Recerca, 9*, 1–9.

Donza, E., & Salvia, A. (2018). *Características de los trabajadores del sector micro-informal y efectos sobre el desarrollo humano: 2010–2017 [Characteristics of workers in the micro-informal sector and effects on human development: 2010–2017]*. Buenos Aires: Observatorio de la Deuda Social Argentina, Universidad Católica Argentina.

Donza, E. (2019). *Heterogeneidad y fragmentación del mercado de trabajo (2010–2018) [Heterogeneity and fragmentation of the labor market (2010–2018)]*. Buenos Aires: Educa.

Echeburúa, E., & del Corral, P. (1994). Adicciones psicológicas: Más allá de la metáfora [Psychological addictions: Beyond the metaphor]. *Clínica Y Salud, 5*(3), 251–258.

Ernst, C., & Robert, V. (2019). *Cambio tecnológico y futuro del trabajo. Competencias laborales y habilidades colectivas para una nueva matriz productiva en Argentina [Technological change and future of work. Labor competencies and collective skills for a new productive matrix in Argentina]*. Buenos Aires: International Labour Organization.

Escalante, Z., Cendrós, J., & Urdaneta, E. (2006). El teletrabajo y sus implicaciones legales en el estado Zulia [Teleworking and its legal implications in Zulia state]. *Revista Gaceta Laboral, 12*(2), 232–266.

Fernández-Montalvo, J. (1998). Los trastornos psicológicos derivados del trabajo: Hacia una psicopatología laboral [Psychological disorders arising from work: towards an occupational psychopathology]. *Clínica Y Salud, 9*(3), 607–620.

Fernández-Montalvo, J. (2000). La psicopatología laboral: una disciplina olvidada en las relaciones entre la salud y el trabajo [Occupational psychopathology: A forgotten discipline in the relationships between health and work]. *Huarte de San Juan. Psicología Y Pedagogía, 6–7,* 127–142.

Fernández-Montalvo, J., & Echeburúa, E. (1998). Laborodependencia: Cuando el trabajo se convierte en adicción [Labor dependency: When work becomes addiction]. *Revista de Psicopatología Y Psicología Clínica, 3*(2), 103–120.

Fisher, E., & Fuchs, C. (2015). *Reconsidering value and labour in the digital age*. Hampshire, UK: Palgrave Macmillan.

García-Viniegras, C. (2005). El bienestar psicológico: dimensión subjetiva de la calidad de vida [Psychological well-being: subjective dimension of quality of life]. *Revista Electrónica de Psicología Iztacala, 8*(2), 1–20.

García-Viniegras, C., & González Benítez, I. (2000). La categoría bienestar psicológico: Su relación con otras categorías sociales [The psychological well-being category: Its relationship with other social categories]. *Revista Cubana de Medicina General Integral, 16*(6), 586–592.

García-Viniegras, C., & López González, V. (2003). Consideraciones teóricas sobre el bienestar y la salud [Theoretical considerations on well-being and health]. *Revista Habanera de Ciencias Médicas, 2*(7), 1–21.

Golik, M. (2013). Las expectativas de equilibrio entre vida laboral y vida privada y las elecciones laborales de la nueva generación [The equilibrium expectations between work and private life and the new generation's labor choices]. *Cuadernos de Administración, 26*(46), 107–133.

Griffa, M. C. & Moreno, J. E. (2011). *Claves para una psicología del desarrollo. Adolescencia, adultez, vejez [Keys to a developmental psychology. Adolescence, adulthood, old age]*. Buenos Aires: Lugar.

Harpaz, I., & Snir, R. (2003). Workaholism: Its definition and nature. *Human Relations, 56*(3), 291–319.

Hernández, R. A., & Serravalle, C. D. (2014). *Felicidad en el trabajo [Happiness at work]*. Bachelor thesis. Universidad Argentina de la Empresa, Buenos Aires.

Hewlett, S. A., Sherbin, L., & Sumberg, K. (2009). How Gen Y and Boomers will reshape your agenda. *Harvard Business Review, 87*(7–8), 71–76.

Holliday Wayne, J. (2009). *Does reputation matter and if so, why? The effects of compensation, work-family, and managing diversity efforts on millenials' job pursuit intentions.* 24th Annual Conference of the Society of Industrial/Organizational Psychology. New Orleans.

Howe, N., & Strauss, W. (2000). *Millennials rising: the next great generations.* New York: Vintage.

Indec [Instituto Nacional de Estadística y Censos] (2019). *Mercado de trabajo. Tasas e indicadores socioeconómicos (EPH). Tercer trimestre de 2019 [Work market. Rates and socioeconomic indicators (PHS). Third quarter of 2019]*. Buenos Aires: Ministerio de Economía, Prisidencia de la Nación.

Jaén, C. (13/11/2016). Trabajo, trabajo, trabajo,...obligación vs adicción [Work, work, work,... obligation vs. addiction]. *Grandes Pymes,* https://www.grandespymes.com.ar/2016/11/13/trabajo-trabajo-trabajoobligacion-vs-adiccion/.

José Andrés, J., Olano Ocáriz, M., & Lete Murugarren, A. (2001). *Perspectiva internacional del trabajo: Nuevas formas de trabajo en la sociedad de la información [International work perspective: New ways of working in the information society]*. Madrid: Ministerio de Trabajo e Inmigración.

Kossek, E. E., Pichler, S. M., Meece, D., & Barratt, M. E. (2008). Family, friend, and neighbour child care providers and maternal well-being in low-income systems: An ecological social perspective. *Journal of Occupational and Organizational Psychology, 81*(3), 369–391. https://doi.org/10.1348/096317908X324387.

Lapierre, L. M., & Allen, T. D. (2006). Work-supportive family, family-supportive supervision, use of organizational benefits, and problem-focused coping: implications for work-family conflict and employee well-being. *Journal of Occupational Health Psychology, 11*(2), 169–181.

Lewis, S., & Cooper, C. (2005). *Work-life integration: Case studies of organisational change*. Cornwall: Wiley.

Lewis, S., & Lewis, J. (1997). *The work-family challenge: Rethinking employment*. London: Sage.

Moreno, B., Gálvez, M., Garrosa, E., & Rodríguez, R. (2005). La adicción al trabajo [Work addiction]. *Revista Psicología Conductual, 13*(3), 417–428.

MOW International Research Team. (1987). *The meaning of working*. London: Academic Press.

Neffa, J. C. (1999). Actividad, trabajo y empleo: Algunas reflexiones sobre un tema en debate [Activity, work and employment: Some reflections on a topic under debate]. *Orientación Y Sociedad, 1*, 127–162.

Neffa, J. C. (2015). *Los riesgos psicosociales en el trabajo: contribución a su estudio [Psychosocial risks at work: contribution to their study]*. Buenos Aires: Centro de Estudios e Investigaciones Laborales, CONICET.

Novoa, C. (08/11/2011). *¿Es feliz en su trabajo? Tal vez usted sea un "happyshifter" y todavía no lo sabe [Are you happy at your job? Maybe you are a "happyshifter" and you still don't know]*. https://www.iprofesional.com/notas/116972-Es-feliz-en-su-trabajo-Tal-vezusted-sea-un-happyshifter-y-todava-no-lo-sabe.

Oakley, A. (2018). *The Sociology of Housework*. Bristol, UK: Policy Press.

Observatorio de Tendencias Sociales y Empresariales (2019). *Índice de bienestar emocional y estres laboral 2019 [Emotional well-being and work stress index 2019]*. Cordoba: Universidad Siglo 21.

O'Reilly, C. A., Chatman, J., & Caldwell, D. F. (1991). People and organizational culture: A profile comparison approach to assessing person-organization fit. *Academy of Management Journal, 34*(3), 487–516.

Osio Havriluk, L. (2015). Salud y seguridad en el teletrabajo. Caso: Argentina [Health and safety in teleworking. Case: Argentina]. *Visión Gerencial, 2*(2), 410–426.

Quiceno, J., & Vinaccia Alpi, S. (2007). La adicción al trabajo "workaholism" [Work addiction "workaholism"]. *Revista Argentina de Clínica Psicológica, 16*(2), 135–142.

Ramazzini, B. (2004). *Disertación acerca de las enfermedades de los trabajadores [Dissertation about workers' diseases]*. La Plata: Sociedad de Medicina del Trabajo de la Provincia de Buenos Aires.

Randstad (2019). *Balance entre trabajo y vida personal en jaque [Balance between work and personal life in check]*. https://www.randstad.com.ar/tendencias-360/archivo/balance-entre-trabajo-y-vida-personal-en-jaque_452/.

Rousseau, D. (1995). *Psychological contracts in organizations: Understanding written and unwritten agreements*. London: Sage.

Salanova, M., Osca, A., Peiró, J. M., Prieto, F., & Sancerni, D. M. (1991). Significado del trabajo en los jóvenes en la transición e incorporación al mercado laboral [Meaning of work in young people in the transition and incorporation into the labor market]. *Revista de Psicología General Y Aplicada, 44*(1), 113–125.

Salvia, A., Bonfiglio, J. I., Donza, E., Hermida, J. C., Rodríguez Espínola, S., & Vera, J. (2016). *Tiempo de Balance: Deudas sociales pendientes al final del Bicentenario. Necesidad de atender a las demandas del desarrollo con mayor equidad e inclusión social [Balance Time: Social debts pending at the end of the Bicentennial. Need to meet the demands of development with greater equity and social inclusion]*. Buenos Aires: Educa.

Schneider, B. (1987). The people make the place. *Personnel Psychology, 40*(3), 437–453.

Sivadon, P. & Fernandez-Zöila, A. (1983). *Temps de travail, temps de vivre. Analyses pour une psychopathologie du temps [Work time, time to live. Analyzes for a psychopathology of time]*. Brussels: Pierre Mardaga.

Universia Argentina. (2013). *El 46% de los argentinos se considera adicto al trabajo [46% of Argentines consider themselves addicted to work]*. https://noticias.universia.com.ar/empleo/noticia/2013/11/20/1064599/46-argentinos-considera-adicto-trabajo.html.

Vega Montiel, A. (2007). Por la visibilidad de las amas de casa: rompiendo la invisibilidad del trabajo doméstico [For the visibility of housewives: breaking the invisibility of domestic work]. *Política Y Cultura, 28,* 181–200.

Westman, M., Etzion, D., & Gattenio, E. (2008). International business travels and the work-family interface: A longitudinal study. *Journal of Occupational and Organizational Psychology, 81*(3), 459–480. https://doi.org/10.1348/096317908X310265.

Zodziejko, M. (2006). *Análisis de los cambios en las expectativas socioculturales de la oferta laboral: La brecha entre propuestas de valor ofrecidas por las empresas y demandas por los jóvenes profesionales de la República Argentina [Analysis of the changes in the socio-cultural expectations of the labor supply: The gap between value propositions offered by companies and demands by the young professionals of the Argentine Republic]*. Masters thesis, Universidad Torcuato di Tella, Buenos Aires.

Index

T. A. Adisa and G. Gbadamosi (eds.), *Work-Life Interface*, https://doi.org/10.1007/978-3-030-66648-4

D

E

F

The manufacturer's authorised representative in the EU is Springer Nature Customer Service Centre GmbH, Europaplatz 3, 69115 Heidelberg, Germany. If you have any concerns regarding our products, please contact ProductSafety@springernature.com

Printed and bound by CPI Group (UK) Ltd, Croydon, CR0 4YY
30/09/2026
02225702-0019